HANDBOOK
OF
PRACTICAL
PROGRAM
EVALUATION

HANDBOOK
OF
PRACTICAL
PROGRAM
EVALUATION

JOSEPH S. WHOLEY
HARRY P. HATRY
KATHRYN E. NEWCOMER

EDITORS

Jossey-Bass Publishers • San Francisco

Substantial discounts on bulk quantities of Jossey-Bass books
are available to corporations, professional associations, and other
organizations. For details and discount information, contact the
special sales department at Jossey-Bass Inc., Publishers.
(415) 433-1740; Fax (415) 433-0499.

Jossey-Bass Web address: http://www.josseybass.com

Manufactured in the United States of America. Nearly all Jossey-Bass
books and jackets are printed on recycled paper that contains at least
50 percent recycled waste, including 10 percent postconsumer waste.
Many of our materials are also printed with vegetable-based ink; during
the printing process these inks emit fewer volatile organic compounds
(VOCs) than petroleum-based inks. VOCs contribute to the formation
of smog.

Library of Congress Cataloging-in-Publication Data

Wholey, Joseph S.
    Handbook of practical program evaluation / Joseph S. Wholey, Harry
P. Hatry, Kathryn E. Newcomer.
       p.   cm. — (A Joint publication in the Jossey-Bass public
administration series, the Jossey-Bass nonprofit sector series, and
the Jossey-Bass social and behavioral science series)
    Includes bibliographical references and index.
    ISBN 1-55542-657-3
    1. Policy sciences. 2. Political planning—Evaluation.
I. Hatry, Harry P. II. Newcomer, Kathryn E., date. III. Title.
IV. Series: Jossey-Bass public administration series. V. Series:
Jossey-Bass nonprofit sector series. VI. Series: Jossey-Bass social
and behavioral science series.
H97.W48 1994
    658.4—dc20   93–48623
                                                      CIP

FIRST EDITION
HB Printing   10 9 8 7   *Code 9460*

A joint publication in
The Jossey-Bass
Nonprofit and Public Management Series,
and The Jossey-Bass
Social and Behavioral Science Series

James L. Perry

Consulting Editor
Public Management and Administration

Contents

Preface   xiii

The Editors   xv

The Contributors   xvii

1. Meeting the Need for Practical Evaluation Approaches:
An Introduction   1
Kathryn E. Newcomer, Harry P. Hatry, and Joseph S. Wholey

**Part One:
Evaluation Design:
Qualitative and Quantitative Approaches**   **11**

2. Assessing the Feasibility and Likely Usefulness
of Evaluation   15
Joseph S. Wholey

3. Designing and Using Process Evaluation   40
Mary Ann Scheirer

4. Using Qualitative Approaches   69
Sharon L. Caudle

5. Outcome Monitoring   96
Dennis P. Affholter

6. Constructing Natural "Experiments"   119
Debra J. Rog

7. Convincing Quasi-Experiments: The Interrupted
    Time Series and Regression-Discontinuity Designs   133
    Richard J. Marcantonio and Thomas D. Cook

8. Ethical and Practical Randomized Field Experiments   155
    Michael L. Dennis

9. Synthesizing Evaluation Findings   198
    David S. Cordray and Robert L. Fischer

**Part Two:
Practical Data Collection Procedures   233**

10. Use of Ratings by Trained Observers   239
    John M. Greiner

11. Designing and Conducting Surveys   271
    Thomas I. Miller

12. The Systematic Use of Expert Judgment   293
    Harvey A. Averch

13. Acting for the Sake of Research:
    The Use of Role-Playing in Evaluation   310
    Margery Austin Turner and Wendy Zimmermann

14. How to Use Focus Groups   338
    Debra L. Dean

15. Managing Field Data Collection from Start to Finish   350
    Demetra Smith Nightingale and Shelli Balter Rossman

16. Collecting Data from Agency Records   374
    Harry P. Hatry

**Part Three:
Practical Data Analysis   387**

17. Using Statistics Appropriately   389
    Kathryn E. Newcomer

18. Using Regression Models to Estimate Program Effects   417
    Charles S. Reichardt and Carol A. Bormann

19. Benefit-Cost Analysis in Program Evaluation   456
    James Edwin Kee

Part Four:
Planning and Managing
Evaluation for Maximum Effectiveness   489

20. Making Evaluation Units Effective   493
     Eleanor Chelimsky

21. Managing Evaluation Projects Step by Step   510
     James B. Bell

22. Evaluators as Change Agents   534
     Richard C. Sonnichsen

23. Making a Splash: Reporting Evaluation Results Effectively   549
     Michael Hendricks

24. Maximizing the Use of Evaluation Results   576
     Reginald Carter

25. Conclusion: Improving Evaluation Activities and Results   590
     Harry P. Hatry, Kathryn E. Newcomer, and Joseph S. Wholey

     Name Index   603

     Subject Index   611

Preface

"Practical Program Evaluation." Sounds good, but what does it mean? The editors of this handbook are advocates of efforts to assess systematically the performance, and particularly the outcomes and impacts, of public and nonprofit programs and policies. This is not an easy task, however. Comprehensive, powerful evaluations often require random assignment or sophisticated data gathering and analysis techniques, sometimes involving the complex use of comparison groups. While ideally desirable, such methods often are not feasible for most programs for which evaluation information is needed. Such evaluation efforts usually demand extensive financial or staff resources. They can also require considerable time to complete—more time than may be available to policymakers and managers who need the information to help them make current decisions. And such sophisticated evaluations may require extensive data that are very difficult and costly to secure, if they can be secured at all. Thus, policymakers and managers usually have little information on program results when making the many program and policy decisions required of them each year.

This handbook, therefore, provides suggestions about evaluation that will enable policymakers and managers to obtain more information, more frequently, and on more programs than before, even though the evidence of program effectiveness will not be as strong as might be desirable. We asked our chapter authors to describe evaluation procedures that, although not ideal, nevertheless are likely to provide useful and reasonably reliable information at an affordable cost. At the same time, chapter authors have been given the latitude to suggest more sophisticated procedures that can be used in those instances when adequate resources are available to do more complex evaluations.

We believe that many public and private agencies have greatly underutilized program evaluation procedures, thus denying themselves valuable information that they could use to improve their services. A major obstacle to evaluation in the past has been the perception that it costs too much, is too hard to do, and takes too long. We hope that the variety of ideas presented in this book will encourage more use of systematic evaluation. We also hope that each reader of this handbook will come away with at least one important new idea that he or she can put into practice to make program evaluation more practical and more useful. Our philosophy in assembling this handbook is that "it's better to be roughly right than to be precisely ignorant."

Acknowledgments

We would like to thank the many good people who have assisted us in making this handbook a reality. We thank Alan Shrader of Jossey-Bass Publishers, who first approached Harry with the idea for the handbook; we thank James Perry of Indiana University who, with Alan, guided preparation of the handbook. We thank our chapter authors, who, with few complaints, produced draft after draft in response to the editors and other reviewers. We thank our three anonymous reviewers, whose suggestions significantly contributed to the quality of the book. We thank Patterson Lamb, the copyeditor of our book, and the Jossey-Bass team, Noelle Graney, Danny Gromfin, Efrat Lev, Alan Shrader, Frank Welsch, and Susan Williams, who turned the manuscript into a high-quality publication. Finally, we thank our cheerful, energetic, and capable support team, Gail Collins and Elizabeth Lee-Halverson of George Washington University and Susan Radville, executive assistant at the University of Southern California's Washington Public Affairs Center. Our thanks to all who contributed to the success of this enterprise.

Washington, D.C.   Joseph S. Wholey
June 1994   Harry P. Hatry
                                                 Kathryn E. Newcomer

*The Editors*_____

JOSEPH S. WHOLEY is a professor in the University of Southern California's School of Public Administration and is director of the university's Washington Public Affairs Center. He received his B.A. degree in mathematics from Catholic University, and an M.A. degree in mathematics and Ph.D. degree in philosophy from Harvard University. His research focuses on the use of performance monitoring and evaluation to improve government performance and credibility.

Before coming to the University of Southern California he served as director of evaluation in the Department of Health, Education, and Welfare in the Johnson administration, and as deputy assistant secretary of Health and Human Services in the Carter administration. He has chaired the Virginia Board of Social Services and the Washington Metropolitan Area Transit Authority as well as Hospice of Northern Virginia and the Arlington County Board.

Wholey is author, coauthor, or coeditor of many journal articles and seven books, including *Improving Government Performance* (1989, with K. E. Newcomer) and *Evaluation and Effective Public Management* (1983). He is a fellow of the National Academy of Public Administration, cochair of the Academy's Panel on Improving Government Performance, and a principal in the Council for Excellence in Government.

HARRY P. HATRY is a principal research associate and director of the State and Local Government Research Program for the Urban Institute in Washington, D.C. He received his B.S. degree in engineering from Yale University and an M.S. degree from Columbia University's Graduate School of Business. Before taking his current position he was with The George Washington University, the Department of Defense, and the General Electric Company. He is a principal author of *Practical Program Evaluation for State and Local Government Officials* (second edition, 1981), *Program Analysis for State and Local Governments* (1987), and *How Effective Are Your Community Services? Procedures for Measuring Their Quality* (second edition, 1992).

Hatry has been a national leader in developing performance measurement and evaluation procedures for public agencies since 1970. He has led a number of efforts by state and local agencies to develop outcome measurement procedures for such services as public safety, transportation, sanitation, parks and recreation, social services, mental health, environmental protection, and economic development. He was a principal participant in the undertaking of the Governmental Accounting Standards Board to improve service efforts and accomplishments reporting and was a member of the Association of Government Accountants Task Force on Performance Auditing.

He is a fellow at the National Academy of Public Administration, cochair of the Academy's Panel on Improving Government Performance, and a member of the U.S. Department of Education's Evaluation Review Panel. He received the 1985 Elmer B. Staats Award for Excellence in Program Evaluation and the 1984 American Society for Public Administration Award naming him Outstanding Contributor to the Literature of Management Science and Policy Science. In 1993 he was a recipient of a National Public Service Award, jointly awarded by the American Society for Public Administration and the National Academy of Public Administration.

KATHRYN E. NEWCOMER is a professor and department chair in the Department of Public Administration at The George Washington University, where she teaches courses on research design, statistics, and program evaluation. She received her B.S. degree in secondary education and M.A. degree in political science, both from the University of Kansas, and her Ph.D. degree in political science from the University of Iowa.

Newcomer has taught at the National Chengchi University, the University of Nebraska, the University of Denver, the University of Iowa, and Grinnell College. She has served as principal investigator for a number of evaluation projects, including studies related to teleconferencing administrative hearings, public policy implementation, federal regulation, and federal offices of the inspector general. She has evaluated programs within a number of national nonprofit organizations based in Washington, D.C. She has also worked as a consultant to the General Accounting Office, and the departments of Army, Interior, State, and Agriculture.

Newcomer was coeditor of *Improving Government Performance* (with J. S. Wholey, 1989). She has published articles in several journals and books including *Law and Policy Quarterly, The Journal of Public Management, Legislative Studies Quarterly, Women and Politics, Urban Affairs Quarterly, Evaluation Review, Information Management Review,* and *The Public Administration Review.*

The Contributors

DENNIS P. AFFHOLTER is the owner, president, and principal consultant of Affholter & Associates, building organizational capacity for outcome measurement and evaluation to systematically improve results. He has worked previously for the human service agencies of Florida and Maryland, the National Academy of Sciences' National Research Council, the Center for Policy Research of the National Governors Association, and Abt Associates, Inc. He received his B.G.S. degree (general studies) from the University of Michigan and his M.A. degree in political science from the University of Wisconsin, Madison, where he also completed an interdisciplinary doctoral minor in applied statistics.

HARVEY A. AVERCH is an economist, policy analyst, and expert on science and technology policy serving as director of the Department of Public Administration, Florida International University. From 1961 to 1971 he served as an economist at the RAND Corporation. From 1971 to 1989, he held posts at the National Science Foundation in Washington, D.C. At Florida International University, his research concerns science and technology policy and advice giving. He received his A.B. degree in economics, summa cum laude, from the University of Colorado and his Ph.D. degree in economics from the University of North Carolina.

JAMES B. BELL directs James Bell Associates, a firm specializing in health and human services program evaluation. From 1974 to 1979, Bell worked with Joseph Wholey and other members of the Urban Institute's Program Evaluation Group to develop evaluability assessment and other approaches to planning useful evaluations of federal programs. He received his B.A. degree in political science from the University of California, Los Angeles, and his M.A. degree in political science from California State University.

CAROL A. BORMANN is a graduate student in psychology at the University of Denver. She received her B.A. degree in psychology from the

University of Denver and her M.S. degree in psychology from Purdue University.

REGINALD CARTER operates MacGregor Management Consultants in Lansing, Michigan. He has been assistant vice-president for reimbursement for the Health Care Association of Michigan since 1984 and specializes in assisting private and public agencies to develop monitoring systems for measuring program effectiveness. He was director of planning and evaluation for the Michigan Department of Social Services from 1974 to 1984; his writing on evaluation topics includes *The Accountable Agency,* published in 1983. Carter received his B.A. degree in sociology from the University of Windsor (Ontario), his M.A. degree in sociology from Bowling Green State University, and his Ph.D. degree in industrial psychology from Michigan State University.

SHARON L. CAUDLE is a consultant with a special interest in information technology management and policies. She has worked in public agencies at the federal, state, and local levels of the U.S. government and has taught at Auburn and Syracuse Universities. She has published widely on information resource management. She received her B.A. degree in social services and corrections from the University of Nevada, Reno, and her M.P.A. and Ph.D. degrees in public administration from George Washington University.

ELEANOR CHELIMSKY is assistant comptroller general for program evaluation in the U.S. General Accounting Office (GAO). Since 1980, she has also been director of GAO's Program Evaluation and Methodology Division. Previously she was with the MITRE Corporation, where for ten years she directed the corporation's work in planning and policy analysis, criminal justice, program evaluation, and research management. From 1966 to 1970, Chelimsky was an economic analyst for the United States Mission to the North Atlantic Treaty Organization (NATO) and before that, a Fulbright Scholar in Paris. She is a past president of the Evaluation in Research Society and received the 1982 Myrdal Award for Government Service, GAO's Distinguished Service Award for 1985, and GAO's Meritorious Executive Award for 1987. In 1991, she was selected to receive GAO's top honor, the Comptroller General's Award. Chelimsky earned her B.A. degree in economics from the University of Maryland, pursued graduate study in political science at the University of Maryland, and received the *Diplôme Supérieur* from the University of Paris.

THOMAS D. COOK is professor of sociology, psychology, education and social policy at Northwestern University. He has received the Evaluation Research Society's Myrdal Prize for Science and the Donald T. Campbell Prize for Innovative Methodology, awarded by the Policy Sciences Organization. One of his major research interests is routes out of poverty, especially for racial minorities. A second interest is methodology, dealing with design and execution of social experiments, methods for promoting causal generalization, and theories of evaluation practice. Among the works he has written or edited are *"Sesame Street" Revisited* (1975, with others), *Annual Review of Evaluation Studies* (Vol. 3), *Quasi-Experimentation: Design and Analysis Issues for Social Research in Field Settings,* and *Qualitative and Quantitative Methods in Evaluation.* Cook received his B.A. degree in German and French from Oxford University and his Ph.D. degree in research communications from Stanford University.

DAVID S. CORDRAY is professor of public policy and psychology as well as chair of the Department of Human Resources at Vanderbilt University. He also is director of the Center for the Study of At-Risk Populations and Public Assistance Policy at the Vanderbilt Institute for Public Policy Studies. Prior to joining the faculty at Vanderbilt, he was associate professor in the Division of Methodology and Evaluation Research at Northwestern University and assistant director of federal welfare and statistical policy in the Program and Evaluation Methodology Division of the U.S. General Accounting Office. Among his publications are *Secondary Analysis of Program Evaluations* (1981, coedited with R. Boruch and P. Wortman), Volume Two of the *Evaluation Studies Review Annual* (1987, coedited with M. Lipsey), and *Meta-analysis for Explanation: A Casebook* (1992, with others). His current research areas include homelessness, data sharing and scientific integrity, and methods for improving the quality of meta-analytic studies.

DEBRA L. DEAN owns her own market research business in the Washington, D.C., area. She specializes in focus group moderating and survey analysis. Most of her experience is in communications research, including organizational communications audits, and technical publications. Dean is formerly a visiting professor of public administration at George Washington University where she taught research methods and statistics. She is also a former Associated Press reporter and a former assistant professor in the School of Management of the University of California, Irvine. She received her B.S. degree in journalism from the University of Maryland and her Ph.D. degree in American state and local public policy from Indiana University.

MICHAEL L. DENNIS is a senior research psychologist in the Center for Social Research and Policy Analysis at the Research Triangle Institute (RTI) where he serves as a methodologist and program evaluator. He received his B.A. degree in psychology and political science from Macalester College and his Ph.D. degree in psychology, methodology, and evaluation research from Northwestern University. Both during his graduate work and while at RTI, he has been actively involved in the design, management, and analysis of more than a dozen community-based trials in criminal justice, drug abuse treatment, and vocational rehabilitation.

ROBERT L. FISCHER is a Ph.D. candidate in policy development and program evaluation at Vanderbilt University. He is currently involved in research with the Center for the Study of At-Risk Populations and Public Assistance Policy at the Vanderbilt Institute for Public Policy Studies. The subject of his doctoral dissertation is a meta-analysis of U.S. job training interventions over the last twenty years. He received his A.B. degree in public policy studies from Duke University and his M.P.P. degree from Peabody College, Vanderbilt University.

JOHN M. GREINER is a management analyst with the Office of Management and Budget of Prince Georges County (Maryland). He has also been a private consultant and for twelve years a research associate at the Urban Institute. Greiner has directed and participated in numerous projects on the development, testing, and evaluation of service effectiveness measures, productivity innovations and incentives, and responses to fiscal stress. Among his publications are two coauthored books — *Productivity and Motivation* (1981) and *How Effective Are Your Community Services?* (second edition, 1992). Greiner holds B.A. and M.S. degrees from Yale University and an M.S. degree in operations research from the University of Pennsylvania.

MICHAEL HENDRICKS is an independent consultant specializing in program planning and evaluation, organizational development, and technical assistance and training. He has worked with all levels of government — in the United States and overseas — and with private and nonprofit organizations. He has taught graduate students at George Washington University and the University of Southern California. He received his B.S. degree in psychology from Michigan State University and his M.A. and Ph.D. degrees from Northwestern University in social psychology/methodology and evaluation research.

JAMES EDWIN KEE is senior associate dean in the school of business and public management, George Washington University. Before joining the university in 1985, Kee held a number of policy and administrative positions in Utah and New York, including the posts of counsel to the New York State Assembly and budget director and executive director of administrative services for the state of Utah. He was managing editor of *Public Budgeting & Finance* and is a frequent contributor to academic and practitioner journals. He is coauthor of *Out of Balance* (1986, with former Utah governor Scott M. Matheson) and of the forthcoming *Federalism's Unfinished Revolution* (with John Shannon). Kee received his B.A. degree in history, his masters degree in public administration, and his J.D. degree in law.

RICHARD J. MARCANTONIO is a postdoctoral visiting fellow at the Center for Urban Affairs and Policy Research at Northwestern University. He also serves as a research specialist in the health sciences at the medical campus of the University of Illinois, Chicago. He received a B.A. degree in psychology from Northeastern Illinois University and a Ph.D. degree in psychological methods and measurement from the University of Illinois, Chicago.

THOMAS I. MILLER is director of the Center for Policy and Program Analysis for Boulder, Colorado, and an adjunct associate professor at the University of Colorado. He is coauthor of *Citizen Surveys* (1991, with M. A. Miller) and has published articles on citizen surveys and local government policy-making, as well as on a variety of topics related to outcomes of social policies including those concerned with health care, growth management, social accounting, crime victim restitution, child care, transit, and drug therapy.

DEMETRA SMITH NIGHTINGALE is director of the Welfare and Training Research Program at the Urban Institute in Washington, D.C. Her research over the past seventeen years has concentrated on the implementation of social policies, particularly employment and training and welfare programs. She has been involved in developing and refining conceptual and theoretical models of implementation analysis and in the design and conduct of evaluations using multiple data collection and analytic methods. She received her B.A. degree in political science from George Washington University and is pursuing graduate work in public policy at the same institution.

CHARLES S. REICHARDT is professor of psychology at the University of Denver. His research focuses on the logic and practice of causal inference. He is coeditor of *Qualitative and Quantitative Methods in Evaluation Research* (with T. Cook) and *Evaluation Studies Review Annual,* Volume 12 (with W. Shadish). Currently, he is coresearcher (with N. Baucht and M. Kirby) on a three-year study of homeless individuals with alcohol or other substance abuse problems. He received his B.A., M.A., and Ph.D. degrees in psychology from Northwestern University.

DEBRA J. ROG directs the Washington office of the Vanderbilt University Center for Mental Health Policy and holds a research assistant professorship in the Department of Public Policy. She is currently evaluating the Robert Wood Johnson Foundation/Department of Housing and Urban Development Homeless Families Program, a nine-city demonstration focused on establishing comprehensive service systems for homeless families with multiple problems. Other ongoing areas of research involve services-enriched housing, children's mental health, and knowledge dissemination. Prior to joining Vanderbilt, Rog served as associate director in the National Institute of Mental Health Office of Programs for the Homeless Mentally Ill where she was responsible for developing and implementing research and evaluation activities. She is a recognized research methodologist, with publications in applied social research and program evaluation, and has served as coeditor of the *Applied Social Research Methods Series* since its inception. She received her B.S. degree in psychology from American International College, her M.A. degree in psychology from Kent State University, and her Ph.D. degree in social psychology from Vanderbilt University.

SHELLI BALTER ROSSMAN is a senior research associate for the State Policy Center of the Urban Institute. Her work has focused on program evaluation, policy analysis, and training and development for criminal justice, public health and safety, educational, and environmental projects. She is currently co-director of a two-year evaluation of a national dropout prevention program that promotes school-based case management and services integration approaches targeted at high-risk youth and their families. Concurrently, she is serving as the senior analyst for a longitudinal impact evaluation of the Strategic Interventions for High-Risk Youth (SIHRY) demonstration projects. She received her B.A. degree in sociology from the University of Pittsburgh and her M.A. degree in sociology from Temple University, and has pursued other graduate studies in sociology at Temple University.

MARY ANN SCHEIRER is an independent consultant in program evaluation working in Annandale, Virginia, after an extensive career in universities, private research firms, and the federal government. She is a sociologist with more than twenty years' experience and has emphasized the evaluation of health promotion, social services, and educational programs. Her work on the organizational aspects of program implementation has been widely published and cited. She received her B.A. degree in sociology and history from the College of Wooster, her M.P.I.A. degree from the University of Pittsburgh, her M.A. degree in sociology from the State University of New York, Binghamton, and her Ph.D. degree in sociology from Cornell University.

RICHARD C. SONNICHSEN, for twenty-eight years a special agent in the Federal Bureau of Investigation, is currently deputy assistant director in charge of the bureau's Office of Planning, Evaluation, and Audits. He is also a member of the adjunct faculty at the University of Southern California's Washington Public Affairs Center. An active member of the American Evaluation Association, he has published several pieces on advocacy evaluation. Sonnichsen received his B.S. degree in forestry from the University of Idaho and his M.P.A. and D.P.A. degrees in public administration from the University of Southern California.

MARGERY AUSTIN TURNER is deputy assistant secretary for research, evaluation, and monitoring in the U.S. Department of Housing and Urban Development. She served as deputy research director for the Urban Institute's national fair housing audit, the Housing Discrimination Study, and is conducting ongoing research on housing segregation and discrimination. In addition, she directed the Urban Institute's pioneering audit study of hiring discrimination against young black men applying for entry-level employment. The author of several articles and books on urban housing markets and programs, she previously analyzed rent control programs in Los Angeles and the District of Columbia, and coauthored a book about the impacts of Reagan administration policies on urban housing in the 1980s. Turner received her B.A. degree in government from Cornell University and her M.A. degree in urban and regional planning from George Washington University.

WENDY ZIMMERMANN is a research associate at the Urban Institute. Since joining the staff of the institute in 1989, she has focused her research on testing for discrimination in employment and on immigration and immigrant policy. Her recent publications include (both coauthored with M. Fix) a chapter on immigrant policy in *Immigration and Ethnicity: The Integration of America's Newest Immigrants* (1994) and an Urban Institute report *Educating Immigrant Children: Chapter 1 in the Changing City* (1993). Zimmermann received her B.A. degree in political science and French from Duke University and her M.A. degree in Latin American studies from Stanford University.

HANDBOOK
OF
PRACTICAL
PROGRAM
EVALUATION

1

Meeting the Need for Practical Evaluation Approaches: An Introduction

Kathryn E. Newcomer, Harry P. Hatry,
Joseph S. Wholey

We are in an age when elected officials, the media, and the public have become much more demanding about accountability and receiving quality services in return for tax dollars and donations to private foundations. Funding for both public and private services never seems adequate for the many, always increasing, demands for both old and new services.

Which of these services are producing adequate results? Which are not? Who are being helped by these services? Who are not? Which program variations are working? Which are not? Where are improvements needed? If improvements are attempted, do they achieve the desired results? Such questions are vital for all service programs. In the past, they have been addressed primarily by officials and program administrators drawing on their own personal experiences and on informal feedback from others—usually with little systematic, even roughly valid, evidence. Program evaluation attempts to provide processes that agencies of all kinds can apply to obtain better, more valid, answers to these questions.

Trade-offs are typically required as policymakers and managers try to obtain valid, timely, but not overly expensive evaluative information. "It is better to be roughly right than to be precisely ignorant." This paraphrase of an old saying is the theme of the handbook. Program evaluation is an increasingly sophisticated field, but sometimes attempts to increase rigor have discouraged smaller scale and less expensive efforts to evaluate programs—leading to major gaps in the information available to both the public and those responsible for the service programs.

The handbook editors believe that there is ample room for evaluations with both more and less rigor. The problem with rigor is that it can be costly to achieve. A demand for considerable precision in all cases would mean that our nation could afford to evaluate only very small numbers of public programs and only at very infrequent intervals; most private agencies would

1

not be able to afford these exercises at all. Governments and private agencies operate thousands of programs, however, and program officials have to make thousands of decisions every year. Most of these decisions are made with little, if any, information on program outcomes. Administrators, public officials, and the public need more frequent feedback on how programs are performing.

We use the term *practical program evaluation* because most of the procedures presented here are intended for application at reasonable cost and without extensive involvement of outside experts. For each chapter, the authors were asked to identify *practical program evaluation approaches:* approaches that are relatively low in cost, do not require highly specialized personnel, and will help program managers and staff members improve program performance. Some of our authors have provided more advanced and potentially more costly techniques for use in situations where they may be required. Qualitative as well as quantitative approaches are included. Some of the approaches described are just emerging; others are well established. We have included some material that has seldom been offered in works on program evaluation, such as material on data collection procedures and data analysis, as well as coverage of a wide variety of evaluation designs.

One of our major themes throughout this work is that evaluation, to be practical and worth its cost, should not only assess program results but also identify ways to improve the program evaluated. Although accountability will continue to be an important purpose for program evaluation, the major goal should be to improve program performance, thereby giving customers and funders better value for money. When program evaluation is used only for external accountability purposes and does not help managers improve their programs, the results are often not worth the cost of the evaluation.

Meeting the increasing demand for evaluation information to improve programs in a feasible and efficient manner is the objective of this handbook. This chapter identifies the intended audience for the guidance offered here, outlines the scope of the subject matter covered, discusses the need for and content of the handbook, and describes the contents and organization of the material provided.

Intended Audience

The intended audience for this handbook includes (1) managers, management analysts, policy analysts, and evaluators in federal agencies, state and local governments, and school districts; (2) managers and analysts in private nonprofit organizations; (3) independent auditors and management consultants; and (4) faculty members and students in professional schools, such as schools of public affairs and administration, business administration, education, public health, and social work.

The information presented here is intended to help those involved in program evaluation, those who fund programs, those who operate programs, staff members in the legislative and executive branches of government, those in universities, and those in the consulting world — both people new to evaluation and experienced evaluators who may find some new ideas to add to their current tool kit.

Scope and Treatment

Considerable diversity exists in the professional training of individuals charged with evaluating service programs; this handbook recognizes and explores the many approaches that fall under the rubric of program evaluation. As we use the term in this volume, a *program* is a set of resources and activities directed toward one or more common goals, typically under the direction of a single manager or management team. A program may consist of a very limited set of activities in one agency or may be a complex set of activities implemented at many sites or at two or more levels of government. In the public arena and in the private nonprofit sector, there is always a cacophony of unsystematic feedback on program performance. *Program evaluation* is the systematic assessment of program results and, to the extent feasible, systematic assessment of the extent to which the program caused those results. The handbook includes process evaluations, which assess the extent to which a program has been implemented as intended, even when such evaluation does not assess the longer-term results of program implementation. The handbook covers both ongoing monitoring of program performance and ad hoc studies of past and present programs. Except when evaluators develop recommendations for program improvement, our use of the term *program evaluation* excludes attempts to judge the worth of future programs.

Program evaluation may provide feedback on program expenditures, program operations, or program results. It can be useful in developing new legislative proposals and in reauthorizing existing programs; in developing, debating, and deciding among budget alternatives; in implementing, operating, and improving public programs and programs operated by private nonprofit organizations; and in managing, auditing, and reporting on the uses of public funds.

Background

The demand for program evaluation information is growing. The U.S. Congress, state legislatures, local legislative bodies, foundations, and other funding agencies are increasingly demanding information on how program funds were used and what those programs produced. Both program advocates and fiscal conservatives need information on program results. "Quality Management" approaches are involving increasing numbers of program managers and staff in specifying performance standards and using information on organizational performance to improve performance.

The U.S. Office of Management and Budget and the U.S. General Accounting Office are encouraging and assisting program performance measurement in a wide variety of federally funded programs. The Chief Financial Officers Act of 1990 requires federal agencies to provide "systematic measurement of performance" and to provide information on the "results of operations" in audited financial statements (U.S. Office of Management and Budget, 1993). The Government Performance and Results Act of 1993 requires federal agencies to establish annual quantitative performance targets and report annually on actual results. The contributing public is also becoming more demanding about how its donated dollars are used in the private sector.

The environment in which evaluators work has become more challenging as taxpayers, legislators, the media, and the general public have begun to insist on economy, efficiency, and return on investment. External entities are increasingly assessing the results of public programs. Auditing has evolved from concentration on financial issues toward performance auditing, a close relative of program evaluation. More and more audit organizations of government are being asked to undertake performance audits that explore both efficiency and effectiveness (Davis, 1990). National audit organizations in the United States, Australia, Canada, France, and the Scandinavian countries have developed experience with, and expertise in, program evaluation.

At the federal level in the United States, a variety of staff offices provide oversight over service delivery and results. These bodies include the Congressional Budget Office, the Congressional Research Service, the General Accounting Office, and the Office of Technology Assessment, all of which report to the Congress; the Office of Management and Budget, which reports to the president; offices of the inspector general, reporting to Congress as well as to their agency heads; and planning and evaluation offices at agency and bureau levels. Congress has increasingly mandated program evaluation in authorizing legislation.

Paralleling oversight at the federal level, a growing number of state and local audit offices are being required by legislatures, boards of supervisors, and city councils to undertake performance audits of program results. The Governmental Accounting Standards Board, the Association of Government Accountants, and the National Association of Local Government Auditors have all made significant efforts to encourage a focus on performance results. Interest in program performance has generated interest in evaluation among state and local officials. As of this writing, a number of state governments—including Oregon, Texas, Minnesota, North Carolina, and Virginia—are beginning to track the results of their programs. Requests for evaluative information from those outside government have grown over time, in part as a response to the antigovernment sentiment and taxpayer revolts of the past decade.

Accountability issues have been the major motivating factor in the pressures described above. However, other less dramatic movements also are increasing the demand for evaluation information. The Total Quality Management movement at all three levels of government and some private agencies encourages employees to assess service quality and customer satisfaction and to identify steps to obtain measurable improvements.

Various governments have in recent years initiated attempts to link rewards or sanctions to results. Sometimes the rewards or sanctions apply to organizations and sometimes to individual employees. Under the banner of educational reform, for example, some local school boards and state boards of education have reduced process requirements in return for improved school performance, with *school performance* defined in terms of agreed-on goals and performance indicators developed by school board members, principals, teachers, and parents. Similarly, the Government Performance and Results Act of 1993 authorizes experiments at the federal level in giving managers more flexibility in their use of funds, personnel, and procurement matters in exchange for more accountability focused on results. All these trends increase the demand for useful and usable evaluation information.

Meeting the Need for Evaluation

Selection among evaluation options is a challenge to both program personnel and evaluators interested in allocating resources efficiently and effectively. The value of program evaluation endeavors is likely to be enhanced when clients for the information know what they are looking for. Clients, program managers, and evaluators all face many choices.

Resources for evaluation and monitoring are typically constrained; prioritization among programs should therefore reflect the most urgent information needs of decision makers. As there may be many demands for information on program performance, not all of which can be met at reasonable cost, what criteria can guide choices?

Three basic questions should be asked about any program being considered for evaluation or monitoring: (1) Can the results of the evaluation influence decisions about the program? (2) Can the evaluation be done in time to be useful? (3) Is the program significant enough to merit evaluation? More specific criteria for setting an evaluation agenda are presented in Exhibit 1.1 (see Hatry, Winnie, and Fisk, 1981).

In recent years the watchword of the evaluation profession has been utilization-focused evaluation (see Patton, 1986). *Utilization-focused* means that an evaluation is designed to answer specific questions raised by those in charge of a program so that the information provided can affect decisions about the program's future. This test is the first criterion for an evaluation. Programs for which decisions must be made about continuation, modification, or termination are good candidates for evaluation — at least in terms of this first criterion. On the other hand, programs for which there is considerable support, such as the Head Start program, are less likely candidates under this criterion.

Exhibit 1.1. Criteria for Setting an Evaluation Agenda.

---

1. Can the results of the evaluation influence decisions about the program?
   a. Are decisions pending about continuation, modification, or termination?
   b. Is there considerable support for the program by influential interest groups that would make termination highly unlikely?
2. Can the evaluation be done in time to be useful?
   a. Are the data available now?
   b. How long will it take to collect the data needed to answer key evaluation questions?
3. Is the program significant enough to merit evaluation?
   a. Does the program consume a large amount of resources?
   b. Is program performance marginal?
   c. Are there problems with program delivery?
   d. Is program delivery highly inefficient?
   e. Is this a pilot program with presumed potential for expansion?

Timing is important in evaluation. If an evaluation cannot be completed in time to affect decisions to be made about the program, the second criterion, evaluation will not be useful. Some questions about a program may be unanswerable because the data are not currently available and cannot be collected in a reasonable time period.

The last criterion deals with significance, which can be defined in many ways. Programs that consume a large amount of resources or are perceived to be marginal in performance are likely candidates for evaluation using this third test—assuming that evaluation results can be useful and the evaluation can be done in a reasonable amount of time. New programs, and in particular pilot programs for which costs and benefits are unknown, are also good candidates.

Even with the explosion of quantitative and qualitative evaluation methodologies over the last thirty years, evaluation remains more an art than a science. The planning of each evaluation effort requires difficult trade-off decisions as the evaluator attempts to balance the feasibility and cost of alternative evaluation designs against the likely benefits of the resulting evaluation work in improving program performance or communicating the value of program activities.

Wherever possible, evaluation planning should commence before the program does. The most desirable window of opportunity for evaluation planning opens when new programs are being designed. Desired data can be more readily obtained if provision is made for data collection from the start of the program, particularly for such information as clients' preprogram attitudes. Data of this type would be very difficult, if not impossible, to obtain later.

Designing an evaluation project requires selecting methods of data collection and data analysis that will best meet information needs. Evaluators must be able to anticipate how the assessment results might be used and how decision making might be shaped by the availability of the performance data collected. Exhibit 1.2 presents the key questions that should be answered in designing an evaluation project.

Exhibit 1.2. Choices Facing Evaluators.

Evaluation Design (see chapters in Part One)

What are the evaluation questions?
What comparisons are needed?
What measurements are needed?
How will be resulting information be used?
What "breakouts" (disaggregations of data) are needed, such as by facility or type of client?

Data Collection (see chapters in Part Two)

What are the primary data sources?
How should data be collected?
Is sampling required? Where and how?
How large a sample is needed?
How will data quality be ensured?

Data Analysis (see chapters in Part Three)

What analytical techniques are available (given the data)?
Which analytical tools will be most appropriate?
In what format will the data be most useful?

Getting Evaluation Information Used (see chapters in Part Four)

How should evaluation findings be packaged for different audiences?
Should specific recommendations accompany evaluation reports to encourage action?
What mechanisms can be used to check on implementation of recommendations?

Selecting an Evaluation Design

Identification of the key evaluation questions is the first and a frequently quite challenging task faced during the design phase. Anticipating what clients need to know is essential to effective evaluation planning. For example, the U.S. General Accounting Office (GAO) conducts many program evaluations in response to legislative requests. These requests, however, are frequently fairly broad in their identification of the issues to be addressed. The first task of GAO evaluators is to identify what the committees or members of Congress want to know, and then to explore what information the legislative requesters really need to answer the questions they have loosely defined.

Matching evaluation questions to a client's information needs can be a tricky task. When there is more than one client, as is frequently the case, there may be multiple information needs, and one evaluation project may not be able to answer all the questions raised. Evaluators may also have to convince clients that likely answers to the original questions will not be useful to them.

Identifying clear, useful, and answerable evaluation questions is probably the most difficult conceptual task in all of evaluation work. Setting goals for information gathering can be like aiming at a moving target, for information needs change as programs and environmental conditions change. Negotiating researchable questions with clients can be fraught with difficulties for evaluators as well as for managers who may be affected by the findings.

Anticipating clients' information needs affects selection of an evaluation design as well as specific strategies for data collection and analysis. Selecting a design requires the evaluator to anticipate the amount of rigor that will be required to produce convincing answers to the client's questions. Evaluators must specify the comparisons that will be needed to demonstrate whether a program has had the intended effects.

Cost issues will almost always constrain design choices; staff costs, travel costs, data collection burdens on program staffs, and political and bureaucratic expenses may limit design options. Evaluation design decisions, in turn, affect where and how data will be collected. To help evaluators and program personnel make the best design decisions, a pilot test of proposed data collection procedures should be considered. *Pilot tests* may be valuable in refining evaluation designs; pilot efforts can clarify the feasibility and costs of data collection as well as the likely utility of different data analysis strategies.

Data Collection

Data collection choices may be politically as well as bureaucratically tricky. Exploring the use of existing data involves identifying potential political barriers as well as more mundane constraints such as incompatibility of computer systems. Planning for data collection in the field should be quite extensive to help evaluators obtain the most relevant data in the most efficient manner.

Data Analysis

Deciding how the data will be analyzed affects data collection for it forces evaluators to clarify how each data element will be used. Collecting too much data is an error frequently committed by evaluators. Developing a detailed analysis plan as part of the evaluation design can help evaluators decide which data elements are necessary and sufficient, thus avoiding the expense of gathering unneeded information.

An analysis plan helps evaluators structure the layout of a report for it identifies the graphic presentations and tables through which the findings will be presented. Anticipating how the findings might be used forces evaluators to think carefully about presentations that will address the original evaluation questions in a clear and logical manner.

Getting Evaluation Results Used

Identifying relevant questions and answering them with data that have been analyzed and presented in a user-oriented format should help ensure that evaluation results will be used. However, communicating evaluation results entails more than simply drafting attractive reports. If the findings are indeed used to improve program performance, the evaluators must understand the bureaucratic and political context of the program and craft their findings and recommendations in such a way as to highlight their usefulness.

Program improvement is the ultimate goal for most evaluators. Consequently, they should use their skills to produce useful, convincing evidence to support their recommendations for program change.

The most effective evaluators are those who plan, design, and implement evaluations that are sufficiently relevant and credible to stimulate program improvement. In evaluation, effectiveness often goes hand in hand with efficiency, and use of practical, low-cost evaluation approaches will generally encourage the evaluation clients — the management and staff of the program — to accept the findings and use them to improve their services.

Handbook Organization

This handbook is divided into four parts: evaluation design, data collection, data analysis, and a final section that offers guidance on evaluation planning, management, and utilization issues. In Part One, chapter authors explore different approaches to evaluation design, the comparisons to be made in judging program performance. Evaluation design should ensure that the benefits of the evaluation outweigh its costs. The chapters in Part One cover nonexperimental, quasi-experimental, and experimental designs. First, several important nonexperimental evaluation designs, including evaluability assessment, process evaluation, and outcome monitoring, are discussed. Then designs are presented that provide increasingly stronger evidence of the extent to which program activities caused program results. Each of the authors in this part of the handbook offers advice on the design of useful evaluations. The authors discuss the purpose of each of the evaluation designs examined, the types of questions that can be answered with these designs, and requirements that must be met to use them properly. The authors illustrate the use of alternative designs in evaluating public programs and programs operated by nonprofit agencies.

In Part Two, the chapter authors describe practical data collection procedures: methods for collecting data on program performance within tight time and resource constraints. The authors describe both well-established and newer procedures for collecting information on program performance, including ratings by trained observers, surveys, use of expert judgment, role-playing, use of focus groups, fieldwork based on semistructured interviews, and use of agency records. They identify the uses of those data collection procedures in program evaluation and indicate the types of quality control needed to ensure that the resulting data are valid.

Because evaluation designs and data collection methods often include procedures for data analysis, some of the authors in Parts One and Two also discuss ways to analyze evaluation data. In Part Three, the chapter authors provide further advice on important methods for analysis: use of appropriate statistics and statistical tests, regression models, and cost-effectiveness and cost-benefit analysis. The authors also discuss requirements that must be met to use these data analysis techniques and present examples illustrating their application to the analysis of evaluation data.

In Part Four, the chapter authors describe methods for planning and managing evaluation units and projects as well as procedures for getting the results used. They offer advice on how evaluators can plan for the success of their evaluation units, manage evaluations that enhance the performance of the program being assessed, develop effective recommendations, and report their results more persuasively.

The final handbook chapter examines several additional evaluation topics, including the selection and training of evaluators, quality control of the evaluation enterprise, standards and ethics in evaluation work, and the creation of incentives for undertaking program evaluation and using its findings. The chapter and the handbook close with the editors' discussion of current and future trends in program evaluation.

References

Davis, D. F. "Do You Want a Performance Audit or an Evaluation?" *Public Administration Review,* 1990, *50, 35–41.*

Hatry, H. P., Winnie, R. E., and Fisk, D. M. *Practical Program Evaluation for State and Local Governments.* Washington, D.C.: The Urban Institute Press, 1981.

Patton, M. Q. *Utilization-Focused Evaluation.* Newbury Park, Calif.: Sage, 1986.

U.S. Office of Management and Budget. "Budget Baselines, Historical Data, and Alternatives for the Future." Washington, D.C.: Executive Office of the President, January 1993.

Part One

Evaluative Design: Qualitative and Quantitative Approaches

The *design* for an evaluation effort includes (1) a set of quantitative or qualitative measurements of program performance and (2) a set of analyses that use those measurements to answer key questions about program performance. Evaluation designs include ways to *describe* program resources, program activities, and program outcomes as well as methods for estimating the *net impacts of program activities,* that is, the difference between program outcomes and the outcomes that would have occurred without the program.

In designing evaluation efforts, evaluators first compare the probable costs and the probable value of different ways of measuring program performance; then they examine various methods of comparing actual program performance to some standard of expected performance. *Evaluation costs* include calendar time; the time of policymakers, program managers, program staff, clients, and others affected by the evaluation process; political and bureaucratic costs including perceived disruptions and increased work load that may occur as a result of the evaluation process as well as possible loss of goodwill among program staff who are affected by the procedure; and the financial costs of data collection and analysis. The *value* of evaluation is measured in the strength of the evidence produced; the credibility of the evaluation to policymakers, managers, and other intended users of the results; and use of the derived information in influencing public policies, program activities, or program results. Data collection and data analysis tend to be costly, and the credibility and usefulness of evaluation are less than certain; therefore, evaluators should explore a range of more and less costly designs and consider pilot testing the proposed ones, that is, collect and analyze small samples of data on program performance and present preliminary findings to intended users.

The chapters in this part of the handbook discuss alternative evaluation designs. The authors discuss both qualitative and quantitative approaches

11

(Chapters Two through Four and Chapters Five through Nine, respectively), designs for descriptive studies, and increasingly powerful designs for impact evaluation. The chapters cover the following:

- Evaluability assessment
- Various forms of process evaluation
- Qualitative evaluation
- Systems for monitoring program outcomes
- Natural experiments, which attempt, without intruding on program activities, to estimate the extent to which these activities cause program outcomes
- Quasi-experimental designs: interrupted time series and regression-discontinuity designs, which provide more convincing evidence on the extent to which program activities cause program outcomes
- Randomized experiments, which provide the strongest evidence of program impact
- Evaluation syntheses, which estimate program impacts using as data the results of past evaluations

Each design illuminates an important aspect of program reality. Evaluability assessment explores the information needs of policymakers and managers, the feasibility and cost of answering alternative evaluative questions, and the likely use of subsequent findings—for example, use of the evaluation information to improve program performance or to communicate the value of program activities to higher levels. Process evaluation, qualitative evaluation, and outcome monitoring are typically used to answer questions that ask for description: "What's happening?" Qualitative evaluation, natural experiments, quasi-experiments, and randomized experiments provide increasingly stronger evidence to answer questions that ask for explanation: "What difference does the program make?" Many evaluations use a combination of these approaches to answer questions about program performance.

Joseph S. Wholey, in Chapter Two, discusses *evaluability assessment,* a process developed to help plan evaluations that would actually be used to improve the performance of the programs evaluated. Evaluability assessment is a process that can be used to evaluate program designs, explore program reality, and help ensure that programs and program evaluations meet three criteria: (1) program goals, objectives, important side effects, and priority information uses are well defined, (2) program goals and objectives are plausible, (3) evaluators and clients agree on intended uses of evaluation information. The chapter describes the evaluability assessment process and illustrates how the process helps in planning useful program evaluation efforts in complex political and bureaucratic environments. The chapter also examines problems that arise in evaluability assessment and outlines workable solutions.

Mary Ann Scheirer, in Chapter Three, presents procedures for *process evaluation,* which documents what a program is intended to be, what the program is in reality, and whether and to what extent the intended services are being delivered to intended recipients. The chapter describes the use of process evaluation to help design effective program interventions, to monitor program implementation, to understand the processes underlying service delivery, and to help managers improve program designs prior to evaluation of program effectiveness.

Sharon L. Caudle, in Chapter Four, discusses *qualitative data collection and analysis.* The chapter presents several qualitative data collection strategies including observation, examination of documents, and unstructured interviewing. Data analysis activities discussed include content analysis, abstracting and transforming raw data during the data collection process, developing data displays organizing the data, and drawing and verifying conclusions during and after data collection. The chapter explains how to accomplish each of these qualitative data collection and analysis activities and lists references that provide further guidance. The chapter suggests several approaches that evaluators can use to enhance the credibility, generalizability, and objectivity of qualitative evaluation efforts — for example, triangulation, peer debriefing, informant feedback, and the use of "auditors" to assess the evaluation process and product.

Dennis P. Affholter, in Chapter Five, discusses *outcome monitoring:* the regular measurement and reporting of program results. Outcome monitoring is increasingly being used to assess the performance and results of federal, state, and local programs as well as programs operated by nonprofit organizations.

The chapter discusses the purposes of outcome monitoring, presents examples that illustrate the value of such systems in improving program performance and credibility, shows how evaluators can design and implement useful outcome monitoring systems, and examines pitfalls in their use.

Debra J. Rog, in Chapter Six, discusses natural *"experiments,"* which use data from naturally occurring comparison groups to rule out plausible rival explanations for observed results and to estimate the impacts of program activities. The chapter presents two of the more common evaluation designs used in natural experiments, the *pretest-posttest design* and the *comparison group design,* as well as the less commonly used *multiple case study design* and *differential dose design,* showing how appropriate measurement systems and data analysis strategies can help evaluators produce valid conclusions on program effectiveness.

Richard J. Marcantonio and Thomas D. Cook, in Chapter Seven, discuss stronger designs that evaluators can use to estimate program impacts: *interrupted time series designs* and *regression-discontinuity designs.* The chapter shows how these designs can provide convincing evidence of program impacts and how evaluators can overcome problems that arise in using these strategies.

Michael L. Dennis, in Chapter Eight, discusses and illustrates the use of *randomized experiments* to determine the impacts of programs implemented in community settings — with typical types of clients, typical resource levels, and typical types of program staff. The chapter explores the times when it is appropriate to conduct a randomized experiment in a community setting, shows how to determine adequate sample size and resolve other design issues, and provides further references on the more technical issues that arise. Dennis explains how to implement and manage a controlled experiment, with discussions of gaining and maintaining staff and client cooperation, monitoring program implementation, and minimizing attrition. Finally, the chapter shows how evaluators can analyze the data from experiments to estimate program impacts overall and for relevant client subgroups.

David S. Cordray and Robert L. Fischer, in Chapter Nine, show how evaluators can *synthesize the results of prior evaluations* to estimate program effectiveness. The chapter discusses meta-evaluation and other quantitative techniques for summarizing prior studies and explores key issues at each stage in evaluation synthesis: formulating the problem, collecting relevant studies, assessing the quality of each of the studies, extracting pertinent data, comparing and attempting to account for differences in study results, and presenting the results of the synthesis. To the extent possible, given the present stage in the development of evaluation synthesis methodology, the chapter shows how these issues can be resolved.

All the authors discuss evaluation design issues, provide advice on the planning and design of useful evaluations, and illustrate that advice in specific program evaluation efforts. Because topics in the handbook necessarily overlap, most of the chapters in Part One also provide advice on relevant data collection and data analysis strategies.

2

Assessing the Feasibility and Likely Usefulness of Evaluation

Joseph S. Wholey

Program evaluation includes the measurement of program performance—resource expenditures, program activities, and program outcomes—and the testing of causal assumptions linking these three elements. One important potential contribution of program evaluation is its use by policymakers, managers, and staff to change program resources, activities, or objectives to improve program performance. Evaluation remains more an art than a science, however. The planning of each evaluation effort requires difficult trade-off decisions as the evaluator attempts to identify the questions to be answered. He or she must balance the feasibility and cost of possible designs against the likely benefits of the evaluation results in improving program performance or communicating the value of program activities to policymakers or to the public.

In planning evaluations intended to improve program performance, evaluators begin by identifying the program goals, objectives, and performance indicators (types of evidence) by which the program will be evaluated and by identifying the data sources to be used for the measurements, comparisons, and analyses that will be required. At this point, four problems typically emerge: (1) evaluators and intended users fail to agree on the goals, objectives, side effects, and performance criteria to be used in evaluating the program; (2) program goals and objectives are found to be unrealistic given the resources that have been committed to them and the program activities that are under way; (3) relevant information on program performance is often not available; and (4) administrators on the policy or operating level are unable or unwilling to change the program on the basis of evaluation information (see Horst, Nay, Scanlon, and Wholey, 1974;

Portions of this chapter are adapted from Wholey (1983, 1987).

15

Wholey, 1983). To the extent that these problems exist, investments in evaluation are unlikely to result in program improvement.

If evaluators and intended users fail to agree on program goals, objectives, information priorities, and intended uses of program performance information, those designing evaluations may focus on answering questions that are not relevant to policy and management decisions. If program goals and objectives are unrealistic because insufficient resources have been applied to critical program activities, the program has been poorly implemented, or administrators lack knowledge of how to achieve program goals and objectives, the more fruitful course may be for those in charge of the program to change program resources, activities, or objectives before formal evaluation efforts are undertaken. If relevant data are unavailable and cannot be obtained at reasonable cost, subsequent evaluation work is likely to be inconclusive. If policymakers or managers are unable or unwilling to use the evaluation information to change the program, even the most conclusive evaluations are likely to produce "information in search of a user." Unless these problems can be overcome, the evaluation will probably not contribute to improved program performance.

These four problems, which characterize many public and private programs, can be reduced and often overcome by a qualitative evaluation process, *evaluability assessment,* that documents the breadth of the four problems and helps programs—and subsequent program evaluation work—to meet the following criteria:

1. *Program goals, objectives, important side effects, and priority information needs are well defined.* There is at least implicit agreement on a set of program goals, objectives, and performance indicators that will be used to manage and evaluate the program. In particular, there is agreement on questions to be answered by program evaluation efforts.
2. *Program goals and objectives are plausible.* There is some likelihood that the program goals and objectives will be achieved.
3. *Relevant performance data can be obtained:* There are feasible measures of program performance. Relevant program performance data can be gathered at reasonable cost.
4. *The intended users of the evaluation results have agreed on how they will use the information*—for example, to improve program performance or to communicate the value of program activities to higher policy levels.

Evaluability assessment is a process for clarifying program designs, exploring program reality, and—if necessary—helping redesign programs to ensure that they meet these four criteria. Evaluability assessment not only shows whether a program can be *meaningfully* evaluated (any program can be evaluated) but also whether evaluation is likely to contribute to improved program performance. The original purpose of evaluability assessment was to determine whether evaluation was likely to help managers improve the performance of their programs and to get management agreement on specific evaluations to be undertaken and specific uses that would be made of the resulting information. As in the examples presented below, evaluability assessment can also be used in planning evaluations to meet policymakers' needs for information about the impacts of programs.

Evaluability assessment is appropriate under these conditions: there is policy- or management-level interest in improving program performance and a willingness to invest in evaluation, but administrators have not yet defined program performance in terms of realistic, measurable objectives or decided on their intended uses of specific evaluation information. Evaluability assessment is most useful in large, decentralized programs in which policy-making and management responsibilities are dispersed, evaluation criteria are unclear, and program results are not readily apparent. Evaluability assessment may be a separate process or the initial step in a larger evaluation effort. When a reasonable set of evaluation criteria have already been specified or the purpose of evaluation is accountability rather than program improvement, evaluability assessment may not be appropriate.

Rather than having the evaluator construct an evaluation design that may prove to be irrelevant, infeasible, inconclusive, untimely, or otherwise useless to those who wish to improve program performance, evaluability assessment begins the evaluation planning process by carrying out a preliminary assessment of the program design. This phase addresses the following: (1) comparing and contrasting the expectations and assumptions of those who have the most important influence over the program, (2) comparing those expectations with the reality of program activities underway and program outcomes that are occurring or are likely to occur, (3) determining whether relevant program performance information will be obtainable at reasonable cost, and (4) exploring which of the evaluations that could be conducted would be most useful. The commitment that may be required to plan relevant, feasible evaluation work is likely to repay itself in averting the greater costs of irrelevant, inconclusive evaluations that contribute little to improved program performance. The most time-consuming step that may occur in evaluability assessment—helping managers and policymakers redesign their program prior to further evaluation work—is likely to be appropriate only when evaluability assessment reveals that (1) specific program objectives are unrealistic given the resources that have been allocated and the program activities that are underway, and (2) intended evaluation users believe that the program should be redesigned before further evaluation is done.

This chapter describes the evaluability assessment process, presents examples of evaluability assessment, and suggests solutions to problems that arise in the evaluability assessment process. The chapter draws on and reflects developments in evaluability assessment over the past twenty years (Horst, Nay, Scanlon, and Wholey, 1974; Schmidt, Scanlon, and Bell, 1979; Rutman, 1980; Nay and Kay, 1982; Strosberg and Wholey, 1983; Wholey, 1983; Wholey, 1987).

Key Steps in Evaluability Assessment

Exhibit 2.1 outlines the key steps in evaluability assessment, each of which is discussed below. Though every step is important, it is essential not to bog down in any one of them. Evaluability assessment can take days, weeks, or even months depending on the time available and the magnitude of the likely evaluation efforts. To keep the project moving, the key steps should be touched but not lingered on.

Exhibit 2.1. Evaluability Assessment: Key Steps.

1. Involve intended users of evaluation information.
2. Clarify the intended program from the perspectives of policymakers, managers, staff, and other key stakeholders.
3. Explore program reality, including the plausibility and measurability of program goals and objectives.
4. Reach agreement on any needed changes in program activities or objectives.
5. Explore alternative evaluation designs.
6. Agree on evaluation priorities and intended uses of information on program performance.

Involve Intended Users

Evaluators often operate in isolation from policymakers and program staff. Evaluability assessment, however, encourages interactions with key policymakers, managers, and staff. These interactions help ensure that the program designs developed by evaluators conform to the expectations of those who have the greatest influence over and involvement in the program. Evaluability assessment also helps shape those expectations by informing key policymakers and managers of the expectations of others, by confronting them with the reality of the program as it is currently operating, and in some cases by helping them explore the implications of possible changes in program activities or objectives.

In recent years, many evaluability assessments have used *policy groups* and *work groups* to facilitate policymaker, manager, and staff participation in evaluation. Work groups generally involve managers, program staff, and evaluators (Rog, 1985). Policy groups tend to involve higher-level managers and policymakers, who are briefed periodically on findings and options as the evaluability assessment and subsequent evaluation work proceed (Wholey, 1983).

Clarify Program Intent

For many programs, the existing design is vague or implausible. This vagueness may have been a deliberate strategy of the initial planners, as too much precision about intended program activities or objectives might have inhibited the political compromises needed to initiate the program and gain the resources needed for its maintenance and expansion. Thus, an important first task in evaluability assessment is to clarify the assumed relationships among program resources, program activities, and expected program outcomes from the perspectives of key policymakers, managers and staff, and interest groups. Here the evaluator documents program goals and objectives, expectations, causal assumptions, and the information needs and priorities of key stakeholders, clarifying the performance indicators, or types of evidence, by which the program will be assessed. The evaluators use two sources of information on program intent. The first is program documentation, including the program's authorizing legislation, if it is in the public sector, and a grant or contract if it is private; they will also examine, where appropriate, legislative history, regulations and guidelines, budget justifications, grant applications, monitoring and audit reports, research and evaluation studies, and other reports of program accomplishments. The second source is interviews with policymakers, managers, and interest group representatives. The interviews focus on program priorities, expected program accomplishments, problems facing the program, and information needs. Exhibit 2.2 presents the questions that evaluators should explore in their review of relevant program documentation and in interviews and meetings with key stakeholders.

**Exhibit 2.2. Guide for Interviews with Key Policymakers,
Managers, and Interest Group Representatives.**

---

1. From your perspective, what is the program trying to accomplish and what resources does it have?
2. What results have been produced to date?
3. What accomplishments are likely in the next year or two?
4. Why would the program produce those results?
5. What are the program's main problems?
6. How long will it take to solve those problems?
7. What kinds of information do you get on the program's performance and results? What kinds of information do you need?
8. How do you (how would you) use this information?
9. What kinds of information are requested by the Office of Management and Budget and the Legislature (for public programs), by the board of directors (for private programs)?

On the basis of information from these sources, the evaluators should now develop two sets of products that promote fruitful dialogue between evaluators and intended users of evaluation information: program design models and lists of currently agreed-on program performance indicators. These products document the extent of agreement on program goals and objectives among policymakers, managers, and interest groups, and the types of information that could be developed in terms of agreed-on performance indicators.

Program design models identify the resources allocated to the program, intended program activities, expected program outcomes, and assumed causal linkages, as seen by managers, policymakers, and key interest groups. An important part of developing program design models is identification of intermediate outcome objectives that connect program activities to program goals. Program design models focus the attention of managers and evaluators on the kinds of assessments that might be useful: occurrence of expected program results can be tracked in a performance monitoring system or management information system (see Affholter, Chapter Five, this volume); assumed causal connections can be tested through the use of one of the impact evaluation designs discussed below (see Rog, Chapter Six; Marcantonio and Cook, Chapter Seven; and Dennis, Chapter Eight, this volume).

In evaluability assessment, evaluators do not hypothesize the program design. Instead, they extract the program design—in particular, the intermediate outcomes expected to connect program activities to intended impacts—from relevant documentation and key actors in and around the program. The evaluators ensure that the program design is acceptable to the primary intended information users before a full-scale evaluation is undertaken. Management's program design, which may evolve during the course of an evaluability assessment, is the framework for decisions on the collection and analysis of program performance data.

In many programs, managers and policymakers agree on the intended program in all important respects. In other instances, however, there will be conflict among managers and policymakers over the program objectives. As long as some of those in charge are interested in a particular objective, it is likely to be included in management's program design and in subsequent monitoring and evaluation activities.

In meetings with program managers and policymakers, evaluators should use models of program resources, activities, intended outcomes, and assumed causal linkages to highlight differences in expectations and to facilitate agreement on the "intended program" between themselves and the primary intended users of evaluation information. Those meetings should also review possible measures of program performance to ensure that there is a common understanding of the goals, objectives, and performance indicators to be used in subsequent evaluation activities.

Explore Program Reality

The second focus of evaluability assessment is on program reality. Here the evaluator documents the feasibility of measuring program performance and estimates the likelihood that program objectives will be achieved. Believing that evaluators too often attempt measurements and comparisons that later prove to be unrealistic or too costly, Nay and his colleagues recommended that those planning and designing evaluations spend some time documenting program reality (Nay and others, 1977; Comptroller General, 1977). Examination of program operations and results may reveal that program reality is far from the program design envisioned by those at higher management and policy levels.

Using existing documentation—output of program data systems, monitoring reports, project reports of accomplishments, research and evaluation studies, and audit reports—and site visits to a small number of projects, the evaluators should compare the intended program with actual program resources, activities, and outcomes; identify problems inhibiting effective program performance; and identify feasible measures of program performance. Exhibit 2.3 presents issues that evaluators should explore through review of relevant documents and discussions with those involved in service delivery.

Exhibit 2.3. Guide for Interviews with Operating-Level Managers and Staff.

---

1. What are *your* objectives for the project or program?
2. What are the major project activities?
3. Why will those activities achieve those objectives?
4. What resources are available to the project?
   - Number of staff
   - Total budget
   - Sources of funds
5. What evidence is necessary to determine whether objectives are met?
6. What happens if objectives are met? Not met?
7. How is the project related to local priorities?
8. What data or records are maintained?
   - Costs?
   - Services delivered?
   - Service quality?
   - Outcomes?
   - Other?
9. How often are these data collected?
10. How is this information used? Does anything change based on these data or records?
11. What major problems are you experiencing?
12. What results have been produced to date?
13. What accomplishments are likely in the next two to three years?

Reach Agreement on Any Needed Changes in the Program Design

The first focus of evaluability assessment was on program intent; the second, on program reality. In some cases, a third focus will be on management's use of evaluability assessment information to improve program design and program performance. This focus suggests that evaluability assessment, in addition to its role in evaluation planning, is itself a qualitative evaluation process (see Caudle, Chapter Four, this volume), one that is closely related to some of the forms of process evaluation discussed by Scheirer (Chapter Three, this volume). Evaluability assessment goes beyond process evaluation by using site visits, the program's data system, prior audits and evaluations, and interviews with knowledgeable observers to produce preliminary estimates of the program's likely success in producing intended outcomes. As such, evaluability assessment may lead to changes in program design or improvements in program implementation before more formal efforts to evaluate the program occur.

Using the information gathered and analyzed in the first two evaluability assessment steps, the evaluators now work with management to examine the implications of what has been learned and, if necessary, explore options for program change and program improvement. Comparing the intended program with program reality may indicate that changes should be made in the program prior to further investments in evaluation. In some cases, for example, the evaluability assessment reveals that program objectives are implausible given the manner in which the program is currently being operated. Insufficient resources may have been allocated for effective program performance, the intended program may have been poorly implemented in the field, or available technology may be insufficient to achieve program goals and objectives. In other cases, higher-level managers and policymakers may find that the program's actual accomplishments suggest the desirability of adding program goals that capture some of those accomplishments. At this point, the evaluator may suggest changes in the program design that appear likely to improve program performance. Such changes might include either the addition of new program activities or the deletion of "rhetorical" program goals and objectives that seem unattainable at current or probable resource levels.

Explore Alternative Evaluation Designs

Although reality is complex, the portion of reality that can usefully be evaluated is relatively simple, especially when time and other resources are limited. The next seven chapters describe specific evaluation design options; succeeding chapters discuss data collection procedures, data analysis techniques, and ways to ensure that evaluation efforts are useful. The decision to proceed with an evaluation usually focuses on specific portions of the intended program: measuring specific variables or testing specific causal assumptions to provide information that policymakers or managers intend to use in specific ways. At this point the evaluator should outline a set of *evaluation design options:* measurements that could be taken, comparisons that could be made, likely costs of those measurements and comparisons (dollar costs; costs in the time of evaluation staff, program staff, and clients; calendar time; important political and bureaucratic costs), and uses that would be made of the resulting information.

Agree on Evaluation Priorities and
Intended Uses of Evaluation Information

When policymakers or managers select an evaluation design of the form just suggested, they will at least tentatively be agreeing on how the resulting information will be used. By explaining the implications of the status quo option (no further evaluation) and the costs and potential uses of various evaluation options, the evaluator encourages policymakers and managers to commit themselves to using the evaluation information at the same time they decide to collect and analyze specific information on program performance.

Example: Tennessee's Prenatal Program

The assessment of Tennessee's prenatal program provides an example of how a successful evaluation is designed.

In July 1981 the Tennessee Department of Public Health began the last year of a five-year, federally funded, $400,000-per-year project, "Toward Improving the Outcome of Pregnancy" (TIOP). The federal project grant provided funds for prenatal and infant care for low-income patients in nineteen rural counties. Pilot projects in local health departments provided community outreach, screening and diagnostic services, treatment, education, and referral and follow-up of women with high-risk pregnancies and high-risk infants. The department of public health faced the end of the federal project grant and likely constraints on state funding for prenatal care. An evaluation of the program was funded as provided for under the terms of the federal grant. Evaluability assessment was used to clarify the design of the department's prenatal care program and to determine the evaluation activities that would be most useful as federal project grant funding came to an end (see Smith, 1986; Wholey, 1987).

In a total of forty-eight staff days of effort over a five-week period in June and July 1981, two evaluation consultants worked with department of public health staff to plan an evaluation of the prenatal program and to establish a decision process that would use the evaluation findings. During this time, the evaluators held a series of working meetings with managers and staff, reviewed documents describing the TIOP project and related prenatal services, and visited one of the six regional projects that then made up the program. (Originally there had been seven regional projects but one had closed, reducing the number of counties served from nineteen to eighteen.) These activities helped the evalutors to (1) identify likely users of the planned evaluation; (2) clarify the program design; (3) compare the intended prenatal program with actual program resources, activities, and outcomes; (4) determine the likely availability of relevant data; and (5) determine which of the feasible evaluation options would be most relevant and useful.

Involving Intended Users

To facilitate the evaluation and use of its findings, the department established a work group and a policy group that would provide ongoing input to the evaluation. The work group included key central office maternal and child health staff, personnel from three of the regional prenatal TIOP projects, and the evaluation consultants. The policy group included executive and management staff from region, section, and bureau levels; the deputy commissioner of health; and key budget staff from the department of public health and the department of finance and administration.

Documenting the Intended Program

The evaluators identified prenatal program resources, activities, intended outcomes, and assumed causal linkages by analyzing program documentation and holding interviews and working meetings with managers and staff. From the perspective of policymakers and managers in the department of public health, TIOP and related prenatal care program activities were intended to achieve the objectives displayed in Figure 2.1 (the program design model presented to the department). Based on feedback from the work group and policy group, the evaluation team revised the program design model slightly; this version guided subsequent evaluation work but was never formally presented to the department.

Through implementation of model projects in selected high-risk areas across the state, Tennessee's prenatal program sought to bring together state, regional, and local agencies and private providers to develop comprehensive systems for the delivery of prenatal care to low-income patients. Central office staff were expected to provide planning, guidelines and standards, training, monitoring and evaluation, and technical assistance. Regional office staff were expected to assist in project development, hiring and training of staff, and coordination with local health departments and private providers. Local health departments were expected to provide community outreach, screening and diagnostic services, comprehensive prenatal services, and referral and follow-up of women with high-risk pregnancies and high-risk infants. Private providers were asked to provide cooperation and support, including consultation and backup, staffing of clinics, management of high-risk cases, and delivery (with or without partial payment from project budgets). The program was expected to (1) increase the numbers of low-income women entering prenatal care in their first trimester of pregnancy; (2) reduce the numbers of low-birthweight infants (infants weighing less than 5.5 pounds at birth); and (3) reduce infant morbidity, infant mortality, and mental retardation.

Through review of department of public health documents and interaction with staff in the central, regional, and local health department offices, the evaluation team found broad agreement on the types of evidence that could be used to assess the performance of TIOP and related prenatal care activities. The team identified approximately sixty possible indicators of program performance (inputs, activities, and outcomes). Quantitative performance measures were available for most of the indicators in the department's prenatal care program design (Figure 2.1); for example, trimester of pregnancy in which prenatal care was initiated and infant birthweight. Qualitative performance information could be obtained for other important events, such as descriptions of the support provided by the local medical community. Agreed-on performance indicators were lacking, however, for some of the project objectives, such as provision of prenatal services to high-risk patients.

Exploring Program Reality

The evaluators interviewed department of public health staff and reviewed annual reports from regional health offices and prenatal projects, project budgets and expenditure reports, data from the prenatal program's quarterly reporting system, and annual monitoring reports by central office staff; they also made a site visit to one of the regional projects. From this data collection the evaluators made preliminary assessments of fiscal flows, services being delivered, outcomes of services, and flows of information on the prenatal program. They concluded that Tennessee's actual prenatal program closely resembled the intended program but had a number of problems that could have threatened effective performance. Based on the information available, none of the program objectives appeared to be unrealistic. No changes in program activities or objectives were suggested at that time.

Development of Evaluation Options

Next, the evaluation team developed a set of evaluation options for consideration by the work group and the policy group. Members of these groups were asked to review a list of sixty possible indicators of program performance and to select the specific types of quantitative and qualitative data that would be of greatest use for policy-making or management. Using these indicators, the evaluation team outlined several sets of comparisons that could be made: (1) TIOP success in meeting statewide standards; (2) intra-program comparisons among TIOP projects or counties; (3) before-and-after comparisons and interrupted time series analyses using data on all births in the counties served by TIOP; (4) before-and-after and interrupted time series comparisons using data on all births in counties served by TIOP and data on all births in other counties in the same region not served by TIOP; and (5) before-and-after and interrupted time series comparisons among TIOP projects offering different services at different costs.

When the evaluation team identified especially effective projects or types of projects, the design provided for the team to make site visits to document project resources, services, and service outcomes. To the extent that time and funds permitted, the evaluation team was also to examine the existing service delivery system and make recommendations on maintenance and expansion of prenatal services after TIOP funding was to end in fiscal year 1982.

Decisions on Evaluation Priorities

In early July 1981, the work group and the policy group met separately to react to the evaluability assessment. Prebriefings and individual meetings were held with key members of both groups. The evaluability assessment resulted in (1) agreement among evaluators and key policymakers, man-

Figure 2.1. Tennessee's Prenatal Program:
Resources, Activities, Intended Outcomes.

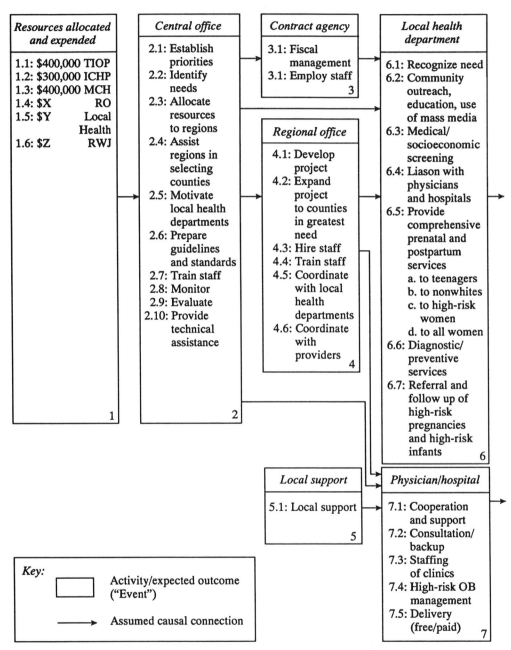

Resources allocated and expended

1.1: $400,000 TIOP
1.2: $300,000 ICHP
1.3: $400,000 MCH
1.4: $X   RO
1.5: $Y   Local
              Health
1.6: $Z   RWJ

1

Central office

2.1: Establish priorities
2.2: Identify needs
2.3: Allocate resources to regions
2.4: Assist regions in selecting counties
2.5: Motivate local health departments
2.6: Prepare guidelines and standards
2.7: Train staff
2.8: Monitor
2.9: Evaluate
2.10: Provide technical assistance

2

Contract agency

3.1: Fiscal management
3.1: Employ staff

3

Regional office

4.1: Develop project
4.2: Expand project to counties in greatest need
4.3: Hire staff
4.4: Train staff
4.5: Coordinate with local health departments
4.6: Coordinate with providers

4

Local health department

6.1: Recognize need
6.2: Community outreach, education, use of mass media
6.3: Medical/ socioeconomic screening
6.4: Liason with physicians and hospitals
6.5: Provide comprehensive prenatal and postpartum services
  a. to teenagers
  b. to nonwhites
  c. to high-risk women
  d. to all women
6.6: Diagnostic/ preventive services
6.7: Referral and follow up of high-risk pregnancies and high-risk infants

6

Local support

5.1: Local support

5

Physician/hospital

7.1: Cooperation and support
7.2: Consultation/ backup
7.3: Staffing of clinics
7.4: High-risk OB management
7.5: Delivery (free/paid)

7

Key:

[ ] Activity/expected outcome ("Event")

——→ Assumed causal connection

Figure 2.1. Tennessee's Prenatal Program:
Resources, Activities, Intended Outcomes, Cont'd.

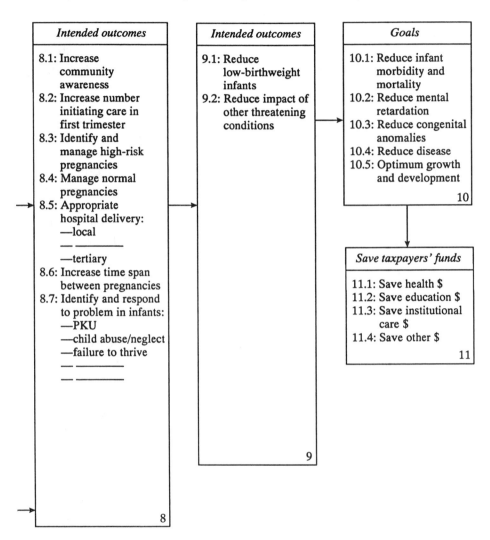

Intended outcomes	*Intended outcomes*	*Goals*
8.1: Increase community awareness	9.1: Reduce low-birthweight infants	10.1: Reduce infant morbidity and mortality
8.2: Increase number initiating care in first trimester	9.2: Reduce impact of other threatening conditions	10.2: Reduce mental retardation
8.3: Identify and manage high-risk pregnancies		10.3: Reduce congenital anomalies
8.4: Manage normal pregnancies		10.4: Reduce disease
8.5: Appropriate hospital delivery: —local		10.5: Optimum growth and development
—tertiary		
8.6: Increase time span between pregnancies		
8.7: Identify and respond to problem in infants: —PKU —child abuse/neglect —failure to thrive		

Save taxpayers' funds

11.1: Save health $
11.2: Save education $
11.3: Save institutional care $
11.4: Save other $

Source: Wholey and Wholey, 1981a, pp. 111-3a, 111-3b. Reprinted by permission of the publisher.

agers, and staff on the design of Tennessee's prenatal care program (intended program inputs, activities, and outcomes, and assumed causal linkages among these) and (2) agreement on the objectives and performance indicators that would be the major focus of the evaluation. The evaluation would focus particular attention on whether the prenatal care program was effective in achieving an intermediate outcome objective: reducing numbers of low-birthweight infants. Low birthweight was known to be closely associated with infant morbidity and mortality and with mental retardation; reduction of the incidence of low birthweight was an outcome objective that program managers considered realistic and one for which they believed they could fairly be held accountable. Though program managers did not believe that they could demonstrate significant impact on infant mortality rates, reduction of infant mortality was retained as an objective because the deputy commissioner of health believed that questions would be asked on that subject.

After reviewing the information on the intended program and on program reality, the department agreed to focus the evaluation on a subset of the intended program that included resources expended, numbers of patients served, types of services delivered, trimester in which prenatal care was initiated, incidence of low birthweight, and infant mortality rates (see Table 2.1). It was agreed that the evaluation would be used in making budget decisions for fiscal year 1983, in planning for the prenatal care to be provided in fiscal year 1983 and beyond, in developing formulas for allocating funds to maintain or expand prenatal services, in reexamining the guidelines and standards for prenatal care, and in making regional and local decisions on the types of prenatal care to be provided.

The evaluation contract had included a planned evaluation of the prenatal program in terms of the input and process objectives stated in the

Table 2.1. Tennessee's Prenatal Program: Key Performance Indicators.

Event	Performance Indicator	Data Source
1. Patients served	1. Number of new admissions	1. Quarterly reports
2. Costs	2a. Staff time	2a. Project records
	2b. Funds expended	2b. Annual reports
	2c. Cost per patient	1,2b
3. Physician support	3. Staffing of clinics	3. Survey of project staff
4. Early initiation of care	4. Trimester in which care was initiated	4. Quarterly reports
5. Morbidity	5. Birthweight	5. Quarterly reports
6. Infant mortality	6a. Neonatal mortality	6a. _____*
	6b. Postneonatal mortality	6b. _____*

*Data source not yet identified.

original grant application. The decision was made, however, not to focus on them because the annual project reports to the federal government had monitored progress in terms of those objectives, and interviews with department of public health staff had revealed relatively little demand for additional information on progress toward those objectives.

Results

The evaluability assessment resulted in the decision to add to the evaluation an interim report that would be available by November 1981, for use in the state's budget process for fiscal year 1983. The interim evaluation (Wholey and Wholey, 1981b) showed that the prenatal program had reduced the incidence of low birthweight: Information compiled by the evaluators from project reports and other available data indicated that the number of low-birthweight infants born to prenatal program patients was well below the rate of low-birthweight babies in appropriate comparison groups.

Smith (1986) notes that the interim evaluation was used in preparing the department's plan to extend prenatal care throughout Tennessee and also in budget deliberations over the proposed statewide program. Additionally, the interim evaluation was used in establishing realistic objectives for improved prenatal care throughout Tennessee: securing the cooperation of private physicians; maximizing Medicaid reimbursement to local health departments for prenatal care; ensuring early initiation of prenatal care; and reducing the incidence of low birthweight, neonatal mortality, and infant mortality.

Although the politically powerful Governor's Task Force on Mental Retardation had already called for improvements in prenatal care and the department of public health and the department of finance and administration had reached agreement that the governor would request a $500,000 appropriation to continue the pilot projects, it appears that the interim evaluation was a factor in the executive branch decision to propose $2 million in state appropriations for initiation of a statewide prenatal program. The positive evaluation findings were used in successful advocacy within the executive branch for inclusion of the $2 million request in the governor's fiscal-year 1983 budget at what otherwise was a time of budget retrenchment in Tennessee.

Example: Family Preservation Programs

As illustrated in the following example, evaluability assessment does not depend on production of elaborate program design models. The key is to involve intended users in clarifying and if necessary refining the program design, defining the criteria to be used in evaluating the program, and specifying evaluation work that is likely to be useful to program managers and policymakers.

In 1992, in the context of rising foster care caseloads and increasing federal and state foster care costs, both the states and the federal government were interested in time-limited, very intensive home-based services to families in crisis. The aim was to improve family functioning when children were at risk and to prevent their placement in foster care. Given the likelihood of major federal investments in such "family preservation" programs and the lack of prior authoritative research, a definitive evaluation was needed. In response to a request for proposals from the U.S. Department of Health and Human Services, evaluators used evaluability assessment to develop a design for evaluating family preservation programs (see James Bell Associates, 1992; Kaye and Bell, 1993).

The evaluators formed an intergovernmental work group and a technical advisory panel to provide input into the evaluability assessment. (The two groups were later merged into a single technical advisory committee that consisted of twenty-five policymakers, managers, and evaluators.) The evaluators held discussions with federal agency staff and national private sector organizations to learn the views of national policymakers on the definition of family preservation programs, services provided, target populations, and expected program outcomes (James Bell Associates, 1992). The evaluators reviewed thirty-one documents—literature on family preservation programs and earlier evaluations—to identify variations in family preservation efforts, the findings of past evaluations, and the methodologies used. They talked by telephone with state and local representatives of family preservation programs (ten states, five counties, five cities) to get descriptions of their programs and to identify relevant unpublished research and evaluation studies. The evaluators made site visits to four family preservation programs to develop models of program operations, obtain input from state and local policymakers on expected program outcomes, and explore the feasibility of implementing alternative evaluative designs. They held meetings with members of the technical advisory committee to discuss key issues, implications for evaluation design, and evaluation design alternatives (Kaye and Bell, 1993).

The evaluability assessment compared and contrasted the views of policymakers (federal administrators, congressional staff, and state legislative staff), program managers, and operating-level staff (child protective services and foster care workers, family preservation program staff, and other child-welfare services personnel on four key dimensions: (1) the goals of family preservation programs and related outcome measures; (2) aspects of the child welfare systems that affect family preservation programs; (3) the target population for family preservation programs ("imminent risk" criteria); and (4) the characteristics that distinguish family preservation programs from other home-based services. The evaluability assessment concluded that current family preservation programs were not consistently targeted at families with children who were at imminent risk of foster care placement and that, as a result, the primary goal of policymakers could not be achieved as these programs were currently operated (Kaye and Bell, 1993).

The evaluability assessment then explored three other issues that affected the feasibility of useful evaluation: (5) whether existing program operations could be modified to achieve the consistency needed for a useful impact evaluation; (6) whether program sites would be willing to employ a design that called for random assignment of families to treatment and control groups; and (7) whether the data needed to describe the services, costs, and outcomes associated with family preservation programs and other parts of the child welfare system were available and accessible. To measure the impact of family preservation programs on foster care placements and related costs, the evaluators recommended a design based on random assignment of cases in which children were at risk of imminent placement, as determined by a judge, a child welfare agency attorney, or senior program managers. The recommended evaluation design would "establish . . . a set of procedures for determining that cases referred for family preservation are those that would otherwise be placed in foster care. . . . Cases in which there was a determination that it was unsafe or not feasible to avoid placement would be excluded from the evaluation and presumably placed in foster care" (James Bell Associates, 1992).

Issues, Problems, and Solutions

This section examines issues and problems that arise in doing evaluability assessments and suggests solutions based on past experience. Exhibit 2.4 summarizes the suggestions presented in this and earlier sections.

Gaining and Holding the Support of Managers

Evaluators often take a long time to do their work while the time scales of their intended audiences tend to be highly compressed. Moreover, it takes time to gain managers' confidence and to produce program change. Evaluators need mechanisms that will convince managers it is worth their while to become and to stay engaged in the evaluation process.

Getting off to a good start can be a problem. At a minimum, evaluators should begin an evaluability assessment by clarifying the types of products and results expected from evaluability assessment and from subsequent evaluation work.

By quickly providing objective, credible information relevant to problems that managers face, the evaluability assessment process tends to overcome managers' skepticism. The steps in an evaluability assessment facilitate the briefings and discussions needed to keep evaluators' work relevant to management needs. Each such briefing can be used to present a preliminary evaluability assessment product (for example, expectations of policymakers and managers, findings from site visits, or options for changes in program activities or the collection and use of information on program performance) and to elicit the feedback needed to reach agreement on a revised product or identify the need for collecting additional data. These meetings

Exhibit 2.4. Practical Suggestions for the Evaluability Assessment Process.

Gaining and Holding the Support of Managers

1. Form a policy group and a work group to involve policymakers, managers, and key staff in evaluation.
2. Clarify the types of products and results expected.
3. Use briefings to present the perspectives of policymakers and managers, the reality of program operations, and options for changes in program activities or the collection and use of information on program performance.

Clarifying Program Intent

4. Develop program design models documenting program resources, program activities, important intended program outcomes, and assumed causal linkages from the perspectives of key policymakers, managers, and interest groups.
5. Develop program design models at varying levels of detail.
6. Use more detailed program design models to ensure that evaluators and managers have a common understanding of the intended program, including important negative side effects to be minimized.
7. Use less detailed program design models to focus briefings and discussions on key issues.
8. Develop lists of currently agreed-on performance indicators and possible new performance indicators to ensure that there is a common understanding of the goals, objectives, important side effects, and performance indicators to be used in subsequent evaluation work.

Exploring Program Reality

9. Focus on descriptions of actual program activities and outcomes, reviews of performance measurement systems currently in use, and descriptions of especially strong project performance and of problems inhibiting effective program performance.
10. Use site visits and prior reports to make preliminary estimates of the likelihood that program objectives will be achieved.
11. Identify feasible measures of program performance.

Reaching Agreement on Any Needed Changes in Program Design

12. If appropriate, suggest changes in program design that appear likely to improve program performance.
13. Proceed by successive iterations, spelling out the likely costs and likely consequences of the program change options of greatest interest to program managers.

Exploring Alternative Evaluation Designs

14. Spell out the costs and intended uses of evaluation options: measurements of specific variables or tests of specific causal assumptions.
15. Present examples of the types of data that would be produced.
16. Interact with intended evaluation users at frequent intervals.
17. Hold managers' interest by providing early evaluability assessment products.
18. Brief key managers and policymakers on evaluability assessment findings and options.
19. Explain the implications of the "status quo option" (no further evaluation) and the costs and potential uses of various evaluation options.
20. Ensure that a mechanism is available for speedy initiation of follow-on evaluation efforts.

Documenting Policy and Management Decisions

21. Conclude each phase of an evaluability assessment with a brief memorandum documenting significant decisions made in meetings with managers and policymakers.

Proceeding by Successive Iterations

22. Do the entire evaluability assessment once early in the assessment; obtain tentative management decisions on program objectives, important side effects, evaluation criteria, and intended uses of evaluation information; and redo portions of the evaluability assessment as often as necessary to obtain informed management decisions.

Reducing Evaluability Assessment Costs

23. Minimize production of intermediate written products.
24. Use briefings that present the information required for management decisions.

---

allow the evaluator to determine which policymakers and managers want and need evaluation information.

Clarifying Program Intent

Program design models can be developed at varying levels of detail. These models help build a common understanding between managers and evaluators on program resources, intended program activities, intended program outcomes, and assumed causal linkages. Such agreement is a prerequisite for evaluation work that is likely to be useful to management. The program design models display, in shorthand form, the relevant evaluations that could be conducted, since they display the key events (inputs, activities, outcomes) that could be monitored and the assumed causal linkages that could be tested in evaluations of the program.

The question here is one of the appropriate level of detail in the program design model. More detailed program design models, like that shown in Figure 2.1, are useful in ensuring that the evaluator has a clear understanding of the program and that evaluators and managers have a common understanding of the way the program is intended to achieve its results. These models are best communicated in papers that managers and staff can study before meeting with the evaluator.

For briefings and discussions with higher management and policy levels, evaluation should use less detailed program design models (see, for example, Figure 2.2). Simpler program design models allow the evaluator to focus briefings and discussions on key issues. They also facilitate clear distinctions between those program objectives for which management will take responsibility and those for which managers believe they cannot fairly be held accountable.

Exploring Program Reality

The second phase of the evaluability assessment is carried out to document program reality. In some evaluability assessments, however, efforts to document the actual program have resulted only in additional, more detailed models of intended program activities and outcomes; in other cases, site visit reports have required a long preparation time but have yielded little useful information. In this phase, the evaluators' activities should focus on descriptions of program activities actually occurring and program outcomes actually being achieved; reviews of the program and project measurement systems

Figure 2.2. Tennessee's Prenatal Program: Resources, Activities, Important Outcomes.

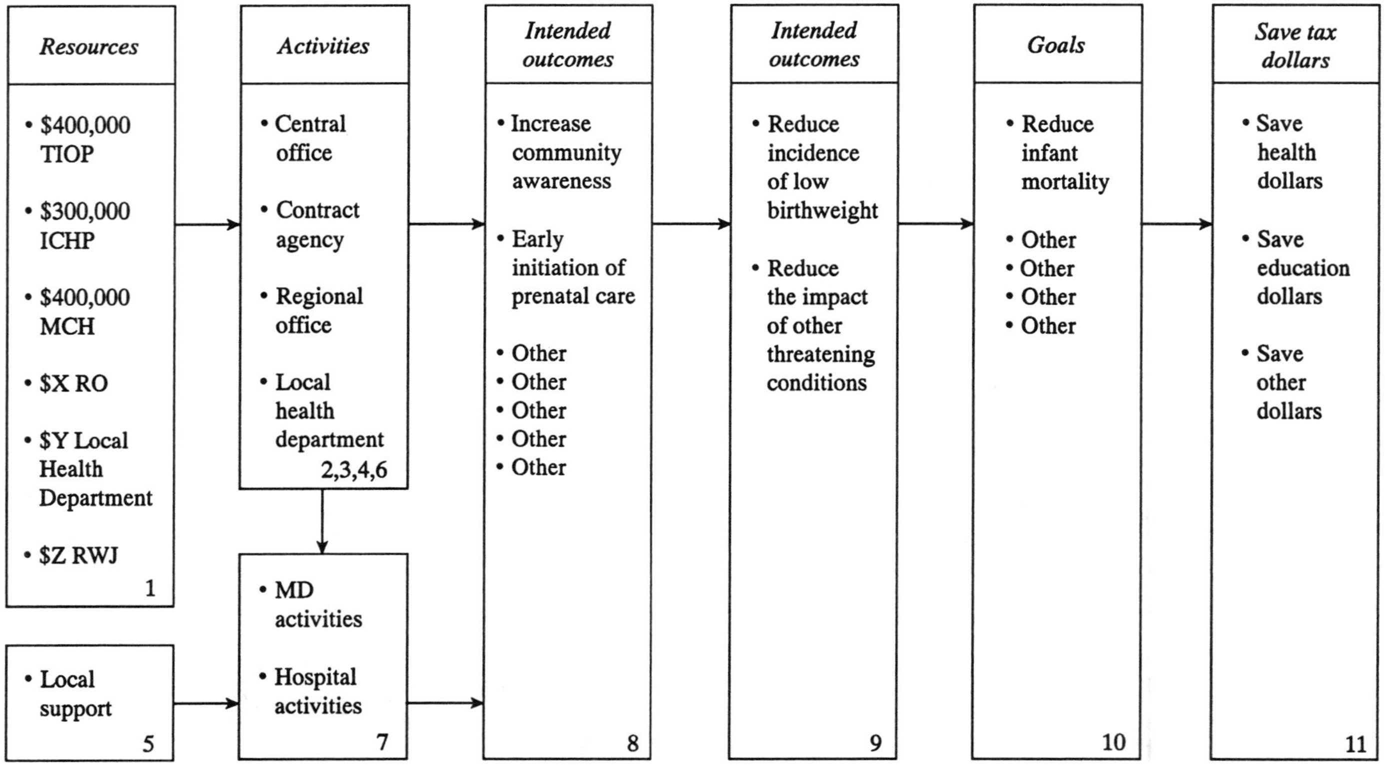

currently in use; descriptions of especially strong project performance and of problems inhibiting effective program performance; and collection of project estimates of likely accomplishments over the new few years.

A key evaluability assessment product is the evaluator's preliminary assessment of the likelihood that program objectives will be achieved. Successful completion of this product requires firsthand contact with program reality, through relatively small numbers of site visits, and secondhand contact, through analyses of program expenditures, project reports, monitoring reports, audits, past research and evaluation studies, and information from knowledgeable observers of the program.

Reviews of successful and unsuccessful evaluability assessments strongly suggest that a small number of site visits are needed early in the assessment. Guided by a preliminary version of the program design model, the evaluators can gather needed information about actual levels of resources, program activities actually under way, program outcomes actually occurring, and trouble spots that seem to be emerging. The evaluators can then make preliminary judgments of the likelihood that program objectives will be achieved. New information from the field gives the evaluability assessment credibility. The early warning nature of the plausibility analysis allows the evaluators to raise problems in the program design or in program reality while there is still time for management to act.

Reaching Agreement on Any Needed Changes in Program Design

Reviews of successful and unsuccessful evaluability assessments suggest the advisability of successive iterations in getting management agreement on any needed changes in the program design. After identifying problems inhibiting effective performance, the evaluators should get preliminary management reactions as to the program changes that are worth pursuing. The evaluators can then spell out the preferred options in more detail to allow more informed management commitment to specific changes in the program and effective implementation of any program change options finally selected. An important part of the job of spelling out options for changes in the program design is that of clarifying the likely costs of such changes in terms of dollars, staff time, management time, and other resources.

In a number of the more successful evaluability assessment efforts, continual interaction between evaluators and managers has led to agreement on implementation work needed to improve program performance. These implementation activities were either incorporated as additional tasks in the evaluability assessment or, as in Tennessee's prenatal care program, commissioned as specific follow-on activities by the evaluation team.

Exploring Alternative Evaluation Designs

The exploration of evaluation design options should include estimates of the costs of the various options. These include the expense of collecting, analyzing, and using specific types of program performance data. Also included should be hypothetical or real examples of the types of data that would be produced and specific indications of how that information would be used.

Agreeing on Evaluation Priorities and Intended Uses of Evaluation Information

The most important step in evaluability assessment is getting decisions from intended evaluation users on the program objectives and performance indicators that will be used to evaluate the program and how the resulting information will be used. The keys to securing the necessary decisions appear to be (1) holding the interest of those in charge of the program through provision of early evaluability assessment products; (2) continuing interaction with intended evaluation users; (3) briefing key managers and policymakers on evaluability assessment findings and options to clarify the findings and get their positions on the options; and (4) providing the additional information needed to clarify the findings and prepare for implementation of the highest-priority options. When the evaluability assessment is the initial phase of a larger evaluation effort or another mechanism is available for speedy initiation of follow-on evaluation work, implementation of useful evaluation work is more likely.

Documenting Policy and Management Decisions

Some evaluability assessments have failed to document policy and management decisions on the objectives and performance indicators in terms of which the program is to be evaluated. This is an omission that can lead to later misunderstanding. Evaluators should conclude each phase of an evaluability assessment with a brief memorandum documenting significant decisions made in meetings with managers and policymakers.

Proceeding by Successive Iterations

Evaluators have sometimes exhausted the resources available for evaluability assessment without achieving management decisions on the objectives on which the program is to be held accountable, the types of information to be used to assess progress toward those objectives, or the intended uses of program performance information.

Evaluability assessment is often more successful when it proceeds by successive iterations. With this strategy, the evaluators do all the steps of the evaluability assessment once early in the process; they obtain tentative management decisions on program objectives, evaluation criteria, and intended uses of evaluation information; then they redo portions of the evaluability assessment as often as necessary to achieve informed management decisions and, if necessary, a better-designed program. Each iteration of the evaluability assessment allows the evaluator to provide new information and get a better sense of management's positions on which options appear most useful.

Reducing Evaluability Assessment Costs

Some evaluability assessments have been heavily procedural, requiring many intermediate written products. In more effective evaluability assessment efforts, evaluators have emphasized the spirit of the evaluability assessment approach, communicating the information required for management decisions to program managers and staff through briefings rather than written reports. Focusing on essentials makes the evaluability assessment process more efficient and thus reduces its costs.

Conclusion

Useful program evaluation is inhibited by four problems: (1) lack of agreement on the goals, objectives, side effects, and performance criteria to be used in evaluating the program; (2) program goals and objectives that are unrealistic given the resources that have been committed to the program and the program activities that are under way; (3) unavailability of relevant information on program performance; (4) inability of policymakers or managers to act on the basis of evaluation information. When evaluation has been requested in terms of appropriate, clearly specified evaluation criteria or the purpose of evaluation is not performance improvement, evaluability assessment may not be needed. When appropriate evaluation criteria have not been identified or the intended uses of evaluation are unclear, however, evaluability assessment will often be an important initial step.

In evaluability assessment, evaluators do not develop the assessment criteria by relying only on their own knowledge and expertise. Instead, as in the prenatal program and family preservation program examples, evaluators involve key policymakers, managers, and staff members in activities that clarify program intent and program reality, including the criteria to be used in evaluating the program. They collect data on the expectations of key actors and on the reality of program operations as part of the evaluation planning process. When a program has been designed on a sound theoretical base, evaluability assessment makes the program design explicit before choices are made concerning evaluation measures, sample sizes, and tests of specific causal assumptions. When a program lacks a sound theoretical base, evaluability assessment makes policymakers and managers aware of this lack and helps to supply that base for subsequent evaluation work.

Evaluability assessment helps evaluators and program managers understand, and in some cases modify, the expectations of those who have the most important influence over the program. Evaluability assessment clarifies differences among the assumptions and expectations of key policymakers, managers, and relevant interest groups, and documents differences between intended and actual program inputs, activities, and outcomes. Evaluability assessment helps policymakers and managers agree on the program activities and outcomes that will be monitored and the causal assumptions that will be tested in subsequent evaluation work. Evaluability assessment helps policymakers, managers, and evaluators to explore the probable costs, feasibility, and likely usefulness of alternative evaluation designs and to select measurements and comparisons that will produce useful information on program performance. As in Tennessee's prenatal program, evaluability assessment tends to focus evaluation resources on intermediate outcomes that are subject to the influence of, but not completely under the control of, program managers.

Finally, evaluability assessment encourages policymakers and managers to act on the basis of evaluation results. Evaluability assessment is often useful in planning evaluations that will be used to stimulate improved program performance. On occasion, evaluability assessment can also be valuable in planning evaluations that executives and managers will be able to use to convince others of the worth of the program.

References

Comptroller General of the United States. *Finding Out How Programs Are Working: Some Suggestions for Congressional Oversight.* Washington, D.C.: U.S. General Accounting Office, 1977.

Horst, P., Nay, J. N., Scanlon, J. W., and Wholey, J. S. "Program Management and the Federal Evaluator." *Public Administration Review,* 1974, *34*(4), 300–308.

James Bell Associates. *Evaluation Design: Evaluability Assessment of Family Preservation Programs.* Arlington, Va.: James Bell Associates, 1992.

Kaye, E., and Bell, J. *Final Report: Evaluability Assessment of Family Preservation Programs.* Arlington, Va.: James Bell Associates, 1993.

Nay, J., and Kay, P. *Government Oversight and Evaluability Assessment.* Lexington, Mass.: Heath, 1982.

Nay, J. N., and others. *The National Institute's Information Machine: A Case Study of the National Evaluation Program.* Washington, D.C.: The Urban Institute, 1977.

Rog, D. J. "A Methodological Analysis of Evaluability Assessment." Unpublished doctoral dissertation, Vanderbilt University, 1985.

Rutman, L. *Planning Useful Evaluations: Evaluability Assessment.* Newbury Park, Calif.: Sage, 1980.

Schmidt, R. E., Scanlon, J. W., and Bell, J. B. *Evaluability Assessment: Making Public Programs Work Better.* Rockville, Md.: Project Share, U.S. Department of Health and Human Services, 1979.

Smith, J. D. "Communicating the Value of Tennessee's Prenatal Program." In J. S. Wholey, M. A. Abramson, and C. Bellavita (eds.), *Performance and Credibility: Developing Excellence in Public and Nonprofit Organizations.* Lexington, Mass.: Heath, 1986.

Strosberg, M. A., and Wholey, J. S. "Evaluability Assessment: From Theory to Practice in the Department of Health and Human Services." *Public Administration Review,* 1983, *43*(1), 66–71.

Wholey, J. S. *Evaluation and Effective Public Management.* Boston: Little, Brown, 1983.

Wholey, J. S. "Evaluability Assessment: Developing Program Theory." In L. Bickman (ed.), *Using Program Theory in Evaluation.* New Directions for Program Evaluation, no. 33. San Francisco: Jossey-Bass, 1987.

Wholey, J. S., and Wholey, M. S. *Evaluation of TIOP and Related Prenatal Care Programs: Proposed Approach to Parts A, B, and C of the Evaluation.* Arlington, Va.: Wholey Associates, 1981a.

Wholey, J. S., and Wholey, M. S. *Evaluation of TIOP and Related Prenatal Care Programs: Interim Report.* Arlington, Va.: Wholey Associates, 1981b.

3

Designing and Using
Process Evaluation

Mary Ann Scheirer

Process evaluation is the use of empirical data to assess the delivery of programs. It is a natural complement to impact evaluation, which focuses on inferring what outcomes (intended or unintended) resulted from a program, particularly by using experimental and quasi-experimental designs. In contrast, process evaluation verifies what the program *is,* and whether or not it is delivered as intended to the targeted recipients and in the intended "dosage." In order to undertake process measurement, the program itself must be specified in detail. For this reason, process evaluation forces clear thinking and planning during program development—about what the program is, why it is expected to produce its results, for what types of people it may be effective, and in what circumstances. In short, process evaluation opens up the "black box" behind a program label to reveal the realities of its day-to-day program delivery.

Background

This chapter discusses why process evaluation is important, defines several purposes for process evaluation in relation to stages of program development, explores types of data useful for these purposes, and provides guidance on how to accomplish each purpose. After introductory material, the chapter is divided into three sections, corresponding to three major questions addressed by process evaluation: (1) what is the program *intended* to be? (methods to develop and specify program components); (2) what is *delivered,* in reality? (methods for measuring program implementation); and (3) why are there *gaps* between program plans and program delivery? (assessing influences on the variability of implementation).

Discussion of process evaluation in textbooks and other references for evaluators has been limited in scope and inconsistent in approach (see, for example, Judd, 1987; King, Morris, and Fitz-Gibbon, 1987; Rossi and Freeman, 1989; Windsor, Baranowski, Clark, and Cutter, 1984). Consequently, dialogues among program managers and evaluators often are ambiguous about what the term *process evaluation* means and what data should be collected for it. Sometimes the term refers to formative evaluation to help design the components of a program. Other sources equate process evaluation with monitoring the implementation of ongoing programs. Still others use the term to refer to the processes underlying the treatment, similar to the uses for theory discussed below. This chapter discusses and illustrates each of these uses for process evaluation, to clarify each use and to guide appropriate applications.

Definition of a Program

A program is defined in Chapter One as "a set of resources and activities directed toward one or more common goals." The inclusion of both resources and activities in this definition focuses attention on the intended behaviors of program staff and on other resources needed to deliver program services. In practice, "programs" are of two quite different types, with different implications for process evaluation: aggregate or multisite programs and well-specified "targeted" programs. Aggregate programs often occur within federal and state agencies when the term "program" is a funding classification for activities oriented around a global objective. The specific activities undertaken locally tend to be quite diverse among sites. Program evaluation for aggregate programs often focuses on monitoring participants and activities, then measuring outcomes, with little emphasis on methods for inferring whether the program caused the outcomes.

In contrast, "targeted" programs develop a detailed specification of activities designed to achieve one or more measurable outcomes, usually based on an underlying theory. For example, behaviorally developed programs to help people stop smoking are likely to specify steps for local delivery, with directions for the activities needed in each of several stages of ending smoking. Evaluations of targeted programs are similar in logic to other research on the effectiveness of interventions, using experimental and quasi-experimental designs. In general, one needs to match the specificity of the process evaluation with the degree of specificity in the program.

Why Is Process Evaluation Necessary?

The measures and methods for process evaluation are necessary to cope with the fact of variations in program delivery. These variations derive from differences among program deliverers and recipients, from differences among sites, from changes in delivery and recipients across time, and often from "breakdowns" between what was intended and what was delivered. Unless the program is described and its delivery measured with process evaluation, impact evaluations risk assessing non-events or activities very different from those intended by program developers. This has been termed the "Type III" error in evaluation, adding to the statistical Type I error of incorrectly inferring program effectiveness, and the Type II error of inferring that the program was ineffective when it was in fact effective (Basch and others, 1985; Dobson and Cook, 1980).

Variability and change in program delivery complicates the use of an experimental research model for program evaluation. Within the classical experimental model, one assumes that the so-called "treatment" is controlled by the researcher, or is strictly controlled during manufacturing, as when testing a new medication. This assumption cannot be made for program evaluation: program delivery must be measured and monitored. This requirement is strongly supported by evaluation methodologists (for example, Lipsey and others, 1985; Patton, 1979; Rossi and Freeman, 1989; Sechrest and others, 1979) but is frequently violated in practice. Because the extent of program delivery cannot be assumed, an impact evaluation that does *not* include a process evaluation component will seldom provide information in which decision makers can have confidence.

Several other reasons underscore the importance of process evaluation. First, process measures provide feedback on the quality of ongoing intervention delivery, information that can stimulate greater efforts to make delivery congruent with an intended program. Second, process data indicate who is receiving program services and to what extent, allowing program managers to assess whether the program is reaching its intended recipients. Third, process evaluation increases knowledge of what program components contribute to outcomes achieved, enabling program managers to design more effective future programs. Finally, process evaluation aids in understanding how programs can be successfully implemented within complex human organizations and communities. Each of these functions is amplified in the sections below.

Process data may be more useful than comparative experimental or quasi-experimental designs for evaluating programs in complex human systems, particularly when aggregate programs have different program components in multiple sites. These programs frequently do not have a single end point for measuring "impacts" but have multiple outcomes occurring at different times. If management decisions do not require precise causal inferences, process data can indicate what is happening in the field, who is participating, and what outcomes are occurring, without attempting a comparative design.

Chains of Events

Appropriate roles for process evaluation can be identified by examining the chain of events surrounding an intended program and its recipients, shown in Figure 3.1 as two interacting levels for analysis. This figure also provides

Figure 3.1. Chain of Events Logic for Process and Impact Evaluation.

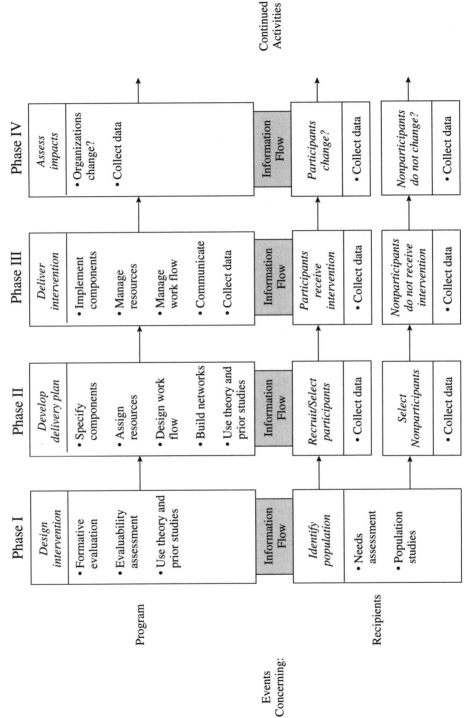

an overview of important stages in program development and delivery that can be used as a template by both program managers and evaluators. Although Figure 3.1 groups events into categories labeled "phases" for clarity of discussion, in reality the activities in each phase are likely to overlap, to occur out of sequence, or to require recycling back to an earlier phase during implementation. These concepts are amplified in the remainder of the chapter.

The chain of events begins with program design in Phase I. Several types of process evaluation — formative evaluation, evaluability assessment, and using theory — help to specify what interventions are most likely to lead to program goals. Needs assessment and population studies should also be used at this stage to identify potential recipients and their characteristics, but they are not usually part of process evaluation.

Developing the service delivery plan in Phase II requires a management plan for assigning resources, devising how the necessary work will be organized, and building communication networks. This stage is likely to benefit from theory and prior studies on how to manage implementation processes, discussed in the third major section of this chapter. A plan for recruiting, selecting, and sustaining the involvement of intended participants is often needed as well as parallel plans for any comparison groups to be included in the evaluation.

The chain of events then moves to delivering the intervention in Phase III, using the management plans already developed. Process evaluation should measure the extent of delivery and the interventions received by participants; it should also confirm that comparison or control groups did not receive similar interventions from other sources.

If the intervention design was sound and the delivery was of adequate scope and accuracy, the treatment should produce the impacts intended, shown as Phase IV. Impact measures may include changes in the delivery organizations as well as participant change. In comparative designs, data from participants will be compared with data from nonparticipants to confirm that nonparticipants do not show equivalent changes even without the intervention. Apart from assessing impacts, process evaluation is the generic term for using empirical data to document or measure many aspects of this complex chain of events, as will be amplified in the remainder of this chapter.

Process Evaluation to Develop and Specify Program Components

A major function for process evaluation is using data to help design interventions in order to clarify and obtain agreement on what *is* the intended program. Program managers and evaluators should spell out the components (strategies, activities, processes, and technologies) that make up the intended program and specify the characteristics of the intended recipients. While this design step is quite properly the responsibility of content specialists, program evaluators can often help in the process, using tools described in this section — formative evaluation, evaluability assessment, and application of program theory. A synthesis of available data about the problem and prior intervention evaluations is also an important tool for program design but is not part of process evaluation (see discussion of meta-analysis by Cordray and Fischer, Chapter Nine in this volume). This section first discusses the nature of program components, then provides guidance about several tools for developing and specifying them.

Ideally, program development takes place prior to full-scale operation, but the same methods can be used to specify the intended components for an ongoing program. When the intended program, that is, the activities that should be delivered, is not specified, all too often the program goals are agreed on within political processes, then resources are allocated, but the actions necessary to achieve the intended impacts are not identified and measured. In this situation, impact evaluation usually leads to inconclusive results because data about outcomes are not linked to information about activities that produced those outcomes.

Program Components

A full description of program components is the foundation for assessing program delivery. Components are the strategies, activities, behaviors, media products, and technologies needed to deliver the program, along with a specification of the intended recipients and delivery situations. Table 3.1 lists major categories of program components for typical service delivery programs and examples for each category. It is not an exhaustive list. For example, components describing intended delivery are likely to require detailed description if the same activities are to be provided by many staffers in separate locations. If program delivery is intended to vary among localities, based on the judgments of individual staff members, at least key components should be specified.

The number of components in a program is one indicator of the complexity of the program. For example, evaluation of the implementation of a cavities-prevention program for school children (the fluoride mouth-rinse program) revealed it to be quite simple, having just seven major components (Scheirer and Griffith, 1990):

1. Within classrooms, children use a 0.2 percent solution of sodium fluoride to rinse their mouths once per week.
2. They rinse for sixty seconds each week.
3. The rinsing is timed by the teacher or supervisor to obtain the correct "dosage."
4. The children wait for thirty minutes after rinsing before eating or drinking.
5. The fluoride mouth rinse is administered in classrooms every week for at least eight months of a school year.
6. All classrooms in an elementary school participate, with a target of 80 percent or more of a school's classrooms used to designate high implementation.

7. All children within a classroom receive parental permission to participate, with a target of 80 percent or more of the children in each classroom, on the average, used to show high implementation for a school.

To collect data about the extent of local implementation, interviewers asked questions about this list of components in telephone interviews with the principals of a national sample of schools believed to be using the program. Only 23 percent of the principals reported doing all seven correctly; 20 percent of the supposed "users" reported implementing *fewer* than five of the seven components. This self-report data may have even overestimated actual use.

Table 3.1. Types of Components for Service Delivery Programs.

Types of Components	*Examples*
Intended Recipients	
Background characteristics appropriate for program	Age range; intended ethnicities; income level; health status; gender
Eligibility requirements	Only minorities; only those unemployed for six months or more; only those eligible for Medicaid or Medicare
Recruitment mechanisms	Through existing organizations; via mass media ads; via word of mouth
Selection process	Self-selected; first-come, first-served; competitive application or examination
Intended Context	
Types of agencies that will deliver program, and their characteristics	Local welfare offices; state educational agencies and local public schools
Community context	Business collaboration with public schools; community locations for Head Start centers
Intended Delivery	
Activities: Who does what? With whom?	Staff member gives information to client; students use small groups for classroom learning; physician guides smoker through dialogue on quitting
Staffing: What types, backgrounds, and skills will be used?	Physician or health educator for health program; state employment service staff with skills in behavioral counseling
Materials needed for delivery	Educational pamphlets in clients' languages; instructional manuals for science teachers
Information and information systems	Access to computerized records of eligible recipients; production records for a quality control system
Intended Scope of Program	Number of agencies in program; expected number of recipients

Examples of component specification for more complex programs were provided by an implementation study of eight education or criminal justice programs within 129 local sites (Emshoff and others, 1987). For example, Experience-Based Career Education (EBCE) was analyzed as having 61 components, including numerous specifics for each of the following actions: developing individualized academic plans; enabling students to attend example career sites; career exploration; staff functions; physical facilities needed; and parental involvement. With such complex programs being implemented in multiple sites, it is not surprising that program impacts will vary.

Developing an explicit listing of program components is essential for later measurement of implementation. This can be a time-intensive task, as program managers and evaluators realize that details of the intended program have been left unspecified. This list will also contribute to program management by clarifying needed activities and the persons responsible for each, and by uncovering any differences of opinion among staff members about what should be done. Often considerable discussion and work are required to develop the intervention into agreed-on and measurable components. For multisite programs with local autonomy, the listing of program components usually should be undertaken locally. Comparison across projects can be facilitated by having the central government office (or a support contractor) work with local projects to develop a common vocabulary, foster the use of the same measuring tools, and summarize similarities and differences among the projects.

When specifying program components, evaluators and program managers should use the following *criteria* for measurable program components (Leithwood and Montgomery, 1980; Sechrest and others, 1979; Yeaton, 1985).

1. Specify activities as behaviors that can be observed rather than as goals or objectives.
2. Ensure that each component is separate and distinguishable from other components so that each one can be separately measured.
3. Explicitly link each component to its underlying theoretical rationale (see section on "Use of Theory to Aid Program Specification" below).
4. Include all activities and materials intended for use in the intervention. Even if not all components will be measured, listing them will permit a clear picture of the aspects that will be measured and those that are intended to be delivered but not measured.
5. Identify the aspects of the intervention that are intended to be adapted to the setting, and those that are intended to be delivered as designed.

If local adaptations are intended, it is wise to specify a range of behaviors for delivery components—from the ideal for each part of the intervention through acceptable delivery to unacceptable but "tempting" deviations (Hall and Loucks, 1978). For example, in a science education curriculum using "hands-on" materials for students, the ideal might be to have small groups of three or four students work cooperatively with the materials; an acceptable alternative might be to have students work alone or in pairs, but an unacceptable variation would be to have the teacher demonstrate the materials without allowing students to handle the items themselves. Indicating ideal, acceptable, and unacceptable modes of delivery provides a basis for examining the *quality* of program delivery. Specifying the behaviors that would constitute "pro forma" delivery may also help to avoid program dilution, to increase the strength and integrity of delivery, and thus to increase the likelihood of achieving the intended outcomes.

Techniques for Program Specification

The three techniques discussed below—formative evaluation, evaluability assessment, and use of theory—all provide further guidance on how to specify the intended program.

      Formative Evaluation. As the term is used in this chapter, *formative evaluation* focuses on data collected from pilot situations and recipients while developing an intervention to obtain feedback about the feasibility of proposed activities and their fit with the intended settings and recipients. Although the term is sometimes used synonymously with "process evaluation," we advocate using the term "formative evaluation" only in the context of program development, in order to clarify other functions for process evaluation. The term was initially used in reference to educational curricula, as it is desirable to try out each sequence of content and each activity for students (Scriven, 1967). Formative evaluation questions for a new curriculum would include the following: Do the pilot students understand it? Can teachers use the activity in a normal classroom? How well does the new curriculum fit with the remaining parts of the older procedures?

      The logic of formative evaluation should also be incorporated into the development of large-scale governmental programs. For example, if the program will supply funding to state and local governments, important formative evaluation questions are these: What activities are these governmental levels likely to deliver with the funding? Would the proposed regulations and guidelines operate as intended, or would they inhibit creative local approaches to making the program work? Does the program design include all the components needed to be effective?

      Systematic data collection to address formative questions should use pilot recipients or demonstration projects; example methods are outlined in Table 3.2. These methods often focus on how the pilot recipients interpret the intended program and whether it fits within their cultures and subcultures. Frequently, qualitative methods are used, with a small but intensive scope of data collection. Using several methods will solicit different types of information, such as observation of trial service delivery along with focus groups of pilot recipients, or on-site testing of the technical aspects of equip-

Table 3.2. Data Collection Methods for Formative Evaluation.

Method	Description	Examples
Focus Groups	Small group discussion is held among program delivery staff or recipients, focused on their reactions to a proposed intervention or their experiences during pilot delivery.	Conduct focus groups of teachers who tried out a new curriculum module. Use focus groups of local public housing officials to predict the workability and likely impact of a proposed new program regulation.
Observation	Evaluator observes actual pilot delivery or video recordings of initial delivery.	Observe teacher delivery and student classroom reactions during pilot delivery of a new curriculum module. Observe videos of physicians trying out a counseling intervention to stop patient smoking.
Open-ended Interviews	Evaluator asks probing questions of prototypical recipients or deliverers, using an interview protocol without preset response categories.	Briefly interview shoppers after their taste tests of new foods for a low-cholesterol diet. Interview Head Start directors by telephone to assess their reactions to a new programmatic use for Head Start funds.
Ethnographic Analysis	Evaluator uses methods from anthropology (including observation and interviews) to obtain in-depth understanding of recipients' cultures.	Observe the study habits and strategies for learning calculus of students of various ethnicities, by having evaluators live in college dormitories. Attend meetings of local hospital officials to learn how they make decisions to purchase new medical technologies.
Message or Forms Analysis	Evaluator probes pilot recipients for their understanding of and reactions to specified aspects of a written or media communication.	Interview taxpayers after their first exposure to proposed new IRS forms and instructions. Talk to example recipients about the meaning, acceptability, and likely response to an AIDS-prevention pamphlet.
Expert Judgment	Panel of individuals with extensive prior experience in the content area is convened to offer opinions on proposed program components.	Convene panels of scientists for opinions on the appropriateness of a new strategic plan for the research grant program of the National Institutes of Health.
Equipment Trial	Equipment to be used in intervention is tried out to check its feasibility in intended situation.	For a computerized job search program for unemployed teenagers, try out the pilot version of hardware and software in a video arcade or shopping mall.

ment along with interviews with pilot users. Guidelines for many of these data collection methods appear elsewhere in this volume (see Dean, Chapter Fourteen, on focus groups; Turner and Zimmermann, Chapter Thirteen, on observation; Nightingale and Rossman, Chapter Fifteen, on interviews; and Averch, Chapter Twelve, on expert judgment).

Evaluability Assessment. Many governmental programs have not been well specified during their infancy and no fully articulated program description exists from which to develop measures of processes or outcomes. Facing this dilemma, Wholey and others developed the technique called *evaluability assessment* (Nay and Kay, 1982; Wholey, 1979, 1987). Evaluability assessment is a set of systematic processes for developing the underlying program theory and clarifying intended uses of data before initiating a full-scale evaluation. Its major steps include the following:

- Involving key policymakers, managers, and staff in a series of meetings to clarify their expectations for the program and for its evaluation
- Using flow diagrams called program models to detail the expected causal links among three aspects: provision of program resources, delivery of local level program activities, and expected outcomes
- Refining the underlying program theory, using brief site visits and available information (from program documents, monitoring systems, and prior evaluations) to examine the reality of field operations and the plausibility of the theory
- Clarifying intended uses of evaluative information, in discussions with policymakers and program managers, including links with potential changes in the program itself

Evaluability assessment was originally presented as a technique for planning full-scale evaluations, but recent users report that it frequently does not lead to later impact evaluation (Smith, 1989, 1990). Instead, detailing the objectives, activities, and intended outcomes in flow diagrams is helpful to program staff for their development and specification of the program; the flow charts provide a good vehicle for communication among program administrators, staff members, and evaluators. Thus, evaluability assessment can be viewed as a form of process evaluation to help decide what the program is intended to be as well as a technique for planning useful impact evaluations.

Use of Theory to Aid Program Specification. Another tool for designing program strategies is applying theories relevant to the content area and using data to elucidate the underlying processes. The term "process evaluation" in this case refers to analyzing the assumptions underlying the program, especially processes the program uses or stimulates to produce the intended changes (Judd, 1987). This type of process evaluation not only helps to specify the intended program but also links descriptors of program activities with outcome measures in later impact evaluation.

The term "theory" refers to a set of interrelated principles that explain and predict the behavior of a person, group, or organization (Chen, 1990; Rimer, 1991). Chen's important work (1990) distinguishes two major types of theory: "normative" and "causal" theory. "Normative theory" is a framework for defining what the program *should be*—for example, from the perspectives of program managers and other stakeholders, as examined in evaluability assessment. "Causal theory" empirically describes the *causal links* between treatments and outcomes, including intervening or mediating factors, derived from the scientific literature on the problem being addressed. Ideally, the normative theories on which program administrators base their actions should be congruent with relevant causal theories; however, there is often divergence between them. This discrepancy can be assessed by process evaluation.

Examples of the illuminating roles of theory for specifying the intended program occur for many health promotion interventions intended to stimulate processes of change within individuals. For example, the Midwestern Prevention Project (MPP) provided a school-based program for sixth and seventh graders to reduce the rates at which adolescents start using cigarettes, alcohol, and other drugs (Pentz and others, 1990). This ten-lesson program was based on well-researched social learning theories of behavioral change, including modeling, role-playing, group discussion, peer feedback, and home practice, which were used as components of the educational lessons. The study collected extensive measures of implementation as well as impacts and will be described further in later sections.

Other programs use quite different assumptions about behavior change. For example, microeconomic theory emphasizes the influence of monetary incentives on behavior and often underlies the design of work and welfare interventions. Federal programs that fund multiple local projects are likely to embody diverse implicit theories at the local level; this is one reason programs that work in one site may have no effect in another site, if quite different activities are delivered in the diverse sites. Further, program delivery involving multiple organizational levels is likely to encounter implementation problems; assessment of implementation has its own body of theory and empirical findings, discussed below.

Making explicit the theory underlying a program has several benefits for evaluators and program administrators (Chen, 1989; Lipsey and others, 1985; Sechrest, 1991). First, a clear statement of theory *illuminates the assumptions* about human behavior that underlie the interventions. Having such a statement encourages evaluators and program managers to examine the empirical support for the assumptions in the current research literature as a "preview" of likely program impacts. It can also stimulate them to search for alternative sets of assumptions (theories) that predict other outcomes or suggest different program designs. Second, articulating the underlying theory *clarifies what measures are needed* to analyze program delivery and what outcomes to look for at what time points, so that information about outcomes will be linked to data about actions that produced the outcomes. Third, articulating the theory *contributes to developing understanding* useful for designing more effective future programs in an iterative cycle of development, testing, and redesign. Theory should not be opposed to "practice" for, as Kurt Lewin (1935) stated more than fifty years ago, "There is nothing so useful as a good theory."

The same methods of data collection listed in Table 3.2 for formative evaluation can be used to examine the theories underlying programs and should be a part of the overall evaluation design. Constructing a chain-of-events diagram of expected causal linkages will help to clarify key points for measurement. With qualitative data, evaluators can examine recipients' self-perceptions about their own change processes and compare these perceptions with the program designers' assumptions. If the program is to intervene with intact social units, such as peers in adolescent groups or work groups in organizations, it is important to assess group as well as individual behaviors. The type of measures will differ with the nature of the underlying theory; the important point is to articulate assumptions underlying the program, use them to specify the program components, and include measurement of key changes predicted by relevant theories within the overall data collection design. Analysis of the validity or "truth" of the underlying theory is addressed below, in the section on linking process and outcome evaluation.

Summary

This section has described three techniques for process evaluation to improve program design and specification: formative evaluation, evaluability assessment, and the use of theory. Along with the results from prior program evaluations and research, these techniques should be used to develop a listing of the program components that constitute the intended intervention. For human service programs, this recommendation puts more emphasis on "up front" program design activity than traditionally takes place. Yet spending this time and effort at the beginning of a program is likely to facilitate the design of program evaluations that contribute to the knowledge needed to design more effective future programs.

Process Evaluation Methods
for Measuring Program Implementation

The program components are the basis for selecting or developing instruments to measure two key aspects of program delivery: the extent of implementation, in terms of the number and quality of program components actually delivered, and the scope of implementation, in terms of the number of recipients reached and their characteristics. Were the "right" program elements delivered to the "right" people? Given the complexity of many human service programs and the costs of data collection, often it is not feasible to measure all aspects of program implementation. The designer of process evaluations must suggest methods and data that will provide the most "bang" for the data collection "buck."

　　This section provides guidance for this type of process evaluation. First, the reasons for collecting data on implementation are discussed. Then methods for collecting such data are described and data analysis procedures are explored. Finally, suggestions are offered for linking process data with impact data.

Uses for Implementation Data

Data measuring program implementation are needed for three important purposes. The first is to monitor current activities in order to identify problems in program implementation, then improve service delivery. Feedback from comparisons of data among sites or program staff can stimulate improved delivery in locations where it is deficient. Program monitoring and feedback can be as simple as periodic telephone interviews to learn how a program is faring at diverse sites, or as elaborate as a full observation system to record the behaviors of those delivering services.

The second major purpose for implementation data is to measure variability in program delivery for later statistical analyses of program impacts. Although evaluators and program administrators have long recognized the need to include measures of treatment delivery/implementation when analyzing outcomes, reviewers of program evaluations report that only a minority of impact evaluations have used this advice. (Light, 1983; Lipsey and others, 1985). With measures of program delivery linked to impact analyses, conclusions about program impacts can be related to program inputs and activities. If outcome goals are not reached, implementation analysis shows whether to focus future efforts on different program designs or on improved implementation strategies, with specific recommendations to foster cumulative solutions in each problem area.

A third major purpose for program implementation data is for use as dependent variables in assessing why delivery is or is not carried out as intended. The chain-of-events model for examining program effects is thus extended to include individual and organizational aspects that *explain* the extent of program implementation. This function is further discussed below, after an examination of what implementation data to collect and how to do it.

What to Measure: Participants and Activities

One major type of implementation data is the number of participants reached and their characteristics; this information tells whether the program is reaching its intended target population. Further, an intervention may have different effectiveness among recipients in different categories of eligibility or with different reasons for participation. Rossi and Freeman (1989) point out that voluntary participation may yield recipients who are considerably different from the intended recipients for many reasons. The targeted group members may not be motivated to attend, they may lack resources for transportation or child care, or they may find one treatment more attractive than another, resulting in differential dropout rates. Treatment staff may inappropriately select only those most likely to benefit ("creaming") or inflate the numbers of actual or potential participants (those "in need of" the program) in order to maximize their program resources. Government programs often have detailed regulations regarding participants and these need to be tracked in the evaluation: for example, provisions about recruitment, instructions for selecting those eligible or most likely to benefit, and directions for avoiding discrimination among eligibles.

The selection process for participants in an experimental evaluation must avoid excluding major segments of the target population for the program. For example, a review of patients entering into experimental evaluations (clinical trials) of cancer therapies found that only about one-third of patients who were appropriate for the treatments in the experimental sites actually participated. This limitation in participation severely limited the generalizability of the resulting data because those who participated in the evaluations were not representative of the intended populations (Hunter and others, 1987).

Measurement of activity components similarly entails a number of complexities. Most interventions have some components that can readily be observed; for example, it is easy to see that students use the program's "hands-on" materials for science classes. Many also have components that are harder to verify, such as determining whether teachers use "guiding questions" to lead students toward critical thinking. For programs with many components, the evaluation team will need to decide which ones to measure explicitly and which to assess by proxy, or not at all. Programs involving multiple organizations or multiple governmental levels are likely to need measures of the organizational or community context as well as records of specific activities. Further, program delivery is likely to change over time; assessing implementation should extend at least throughout the time period that will be covered by impact evaluation.

How to Measure Program Implementation

Data collection methods for assessing program delivery can include nearly any method in the entire social science repertoire. Several useful strategies are listed in Table 3.3, along with a description and examples of each. Methodological guidance for many data collection plans appears in other chapters of this handbook. In some evaluations, the same method may be used for collecting data about both program delivery and impacts — such as a questionnaire or interviews. Methods for measuring delivery are not necessarily different from those for formative evaluation, but the *number of respondents* is usually larger in the assessment of ongoing delivery, and the *representativeness* of the data should be ensured in this type of evaluation. The amount of detailed data collected for each respondent is likely to be smaller, however, in measuring ongoing delivery than in assessing program development.

Each type of data collection method has its advantages and disadvantages. Methods listed near the top of Table 3.3 tend to require less human interpretation and thus are less prone to problems of observer bias than are

Table 3.3. Data Collection Methods for Measuring Extent of Implementation.

Method	Description	Examples
Use of Technical Equipment	Data collected directly from a physical device or piece of technical equipment.	A computer that automatically records the number of users of a computerized intervention; readings from medical instruments, such as a blood pressure cuff or breath analyzer.
Indirect Unobtrusive Measures	Indicators obtained from records kept for other purposes, or from physical traces left by normal activities.	Amount of fluoride mouth-rinse solution used by individual schools; sales records of "heart healthy" foods sold in cafeterias; column inches of newspaper coverage of a media campaign.
Direct Observation	Use by trained observer of prespecified formats and codes for recording in-person or videotaped observations.	Observations of teachers' behaviors in using hands-on science modules; street corner observations of number of drivers wearing seat belts; observations of interactions between job counselors and welfare mothers in job search program.
Activity or Participation Log	Brief record completed on site at frequent intervals by participant or deliverer, using format designed by evaluator.	Participants' sign-in log; daily record of foods eaten; welfare mother's log of attempted and completed job interviews.
Organizational Records	Data collection forms routinely kept by an organization for purposes other than for the evaluation.	Patient medical records; time sheets of staff members who record amount of time spent on different activities.
Written Questionnaires	Written survey, usually with prestructured questions, to obtain data by mail or in-person from providers or recipients.	Number of different activities each participant engaged in during an intervention; providers' assessment of amount of time they spent on each activity; characteristics of participants.
Telephone or In-Person Interviews	Procedure in which interviewer asks questions directly to providers or recipients, using either prestructured or open-ended questions.	Interviews with participants in a work-training program concerning actual training activities and their relevance to job aspirations; telephone interviews with program administrators about extent of delivery in their location.
Case Studies	Collection of multiple types of data about a site or example entity, usually by an observer who is on site and uses informal observations and interviews, combined with available data and document review.	Case studies of states in their process of implementing a program of systemic change in mathematics education; case studies of federal, state, and local legal systems implementing new regulations for overseeing savings and loan finances.

the more subjective methods near the bottom of the list. However, the methods listed near the bottom put the evaluator in touch with the respondents — the intended beneficiaries, front-line program deliverers, or agency administrators — to capture their interpretations of the situations surrounding a program. Some methods, particularly direct observation and multiple case studies, tend to be more expensive than others and may be infeasible for large-scale projects. Collecting data directly from program deliverers or recipients, such as by direct observation, activity logs, or written questionnaires, may influence their behavior as well as measure it if the collection procedure makes them more self-reflective than usual. This self-monitoring may improve program implementation, but such data collection then becomes a part of the program components that should be included in its description. If feasible, include several ways for measuring major components in order to balance their strengths and weaknesses. The potentially higher reliability of a standard technical instrument can be balanced with an open-ended procedure for increasing the depth of interpretation, perhaps with a smaller sample of respondents.

An example of using multiple measures to assess the extent of implementation is the Midwestern Prevention Project (discussed above) on school-based drug prevention strategies. The overall extent of classroom delivery of ten program modules was measured within questionnaires for teachers, which asked about the number of modules covered and the average length of each session. These data were later multiplied to yield estimates of program delivery hours, with scores that varied from 2.7 to 9.2 classroom hours per school for the twenty-seven schools in the experimental group (Pentz and others, 1990). These data were then cross-checked against ratings made by project staff members' observations of each classroom and by periodic phone calls to teachers and administrators.

Attention to the reliability and validity of implementation measures is also critical for the resulting data to have credibility. Scheirer and Rezmovic (1983) reviewed seventy-four studies that had measured the degree of implementation and found serious flaws in measurement quality. Reliability and validity were not even addressed in a majority of the studies and were judged to be adequately established in fewer than 20 percent. The representativeness of the data collected about implementation (sampling strategy) was described in only 27 percent of these studies. The studies had more favorable ratings on two other criteria: using multiple measures (74 percent) and providing an explicit operational definition of "implementation" (64 percent). The results of the review indicate that many evaluations that attempted to measure implementation, as of the early 1980s, did not provide readers with important evidence regarding measurement quality.

The use of computerized management information systems (MISs) can facilitate collecting, maintaining, and reporting data for program monitoring. Rossi and Freeman (1989) point out, however, that quality control is essential for an MIS, including proper planning for data elements that will be needed; explicit definitions and coding rules for each data element; training of those who collect and enter data locally; and continued communication to generate cooperation among collectors, evaluators, and users of data.

Availability of Standard Measures of Implementation

The effort of developing measuring tools for each program would be reduced if a standard measuring instrument or scale were available for this concept. Gene Hall and his colleagues developed a standardized procedure, the Level of Use (LoU) scale, for measuring the implementation of educational interventions (Hall and Loucks, 1977; Loucks, Newlove, and Hall, 1975). Although it can be commended as a pioneering work, the LoU scale is not recommended as a measure of implementation for widespread use, for several reasons. The procedures for the LoU are quite complex, calling for extensive training of both telephone interviewers and data coders. Conceptual problems with the scale are more serious, for in the LoU scaling procedures, adaptation of an intervention is coded as a higher "level" (better) implementation than fidelity to an a priori design. If the evaluator or data coder does not consider carefully the specific aspects that are "adapted" by the user, a measuring scale that favors adaptation over adherence to an original design may undermine well-developed interventions. Further, the LoU procedure incorporates many processes of implementation (discussed below) rather than focusing more narrowly on measuring the extent of delivery per se. We are left with the conclusion that instruments to measure the extent of implmentation must be designed for each particular program, if its specific components are to be assessed accurately.

Analysis of Implementation Data

Data from measuring the extent and scope of implementation and the types of recipients should be analyzed both quantitatively and descriptively. Qualitative analysis with rich description of typical program operation is often useful to communicate the essence of a program. Simple tallies of the number of program components delivered at each location over a specific time period provide useful monitoring and feedback data. Program delivery should not be viewed as a "yes-no" question (for example, that participants got the treatment, and control subjects did not) but analyzed as continuous data on several variables.

More detailed analyses and combined indexes are often needed to link data about the extent of implementation with measures of outcomes achieved. For example, the following steps can be used to create a percentage-based index of the extent of participation for each recipient:

1. Determine the program components in "ideal" program delivery, as discussed within the section on program specification.

2. Collect data about each component for each participant during a relevant time period, using one or more of the methods in Table 3.3, such as participant logs, questionnaires, or organizational records; sampling of participants may be needed.
3. Count the number of components received by each participant.
4. Divide that count by the number of components in the "ideal" program, and multiply by 100 to yield a percentage score (Scheirer and Griffith, 1990).

Each individual then has an extent of participation score, ranging from 0 for those who received no components (including comparison subjects, if they did not receive similar components from other sources), to perhaps 30 percent for those who participated only slightly (received 3 of 10 components), through 100 percent for full participation.

The same procedures can be followed for assessing a provider's delivery components or for a site as a whole, if the site is the unit of data collection and analysis. The time period when extent of implementation was measured should always be specified; data over time may be needed to show changes in the extent of implementation across time periods.

Many methods for constructing indexes of implementation are possible. A more precise procedure than the simple count of components described above would be to weight the program components differentially rather than count each component equally. Weighting would be appropriate if program developers or administrators hypothesize that some components are more essential than others. If quality or fidelity of program delivery has been measured, each component could be multiplied by its corresponding quality score rather than to count each component equally.

Data about the scope or penetration of a program across many organizations should be examined for the percentage of the target *population of organizations* (or other unit, such as communities or neighborhoods) delivering the program, *and* the percentage of individuals within each organization who participate. For example, for a health education program intended to be used in all the first grades in a state, data were collected about the scope of use at the school district, school, and classroom teacher levels (Brink, Levenson-Gingass, and Gottlieb, 1991). Telephone interviews with regional staff who distributed the materials reported that 89 percent of the districts had received them. However, questionnaires revealed that only about 45 percent of teachers in these districts reported receiving the materials, only 29 percent reported using them during the first school year, and only 17 percent reported delivering the intended amounts of classroom time. The full extent of implementation is likely to be affected by activities at each level involved in the delivery of a program.

Linking Process and Outcome Data

Methods for analyzing implementation data will differ among various types of impact evaluation designs. Within a monitoring approach, measures of the extent of implementation should be examined for changes over time, among the various delivery sites, and in relation to the extent of outcomes achieved, using cross-tabulations or correlations. One would expect outcome scores to be higher when implementation scores are high, with lower outcome levels in other places or times when delivery was only partial or nonexistent. Graphs are useful for showing these relationships visually. Another useful way to present monitoring data is to show the *numbers of people* affected by high versus low implementation. For example, one might find that 60 percent of welfare mothers who attended well-implemented job search training programs later found jobs, while only 30 percent of those attending poorly implemented programs were successful in finding employment.

Although program monitoring by itself does not provide the evidence necessary to rule out other explanations for observed relationships between extent of implementation and outcomes, supporting evidence about underlying causes may be available from other, more rigorous studies. If a relationship is found between strength of delivery and desired outcomes but the extent of delivery is low in some sites, the next step in achieving program goals may be to examine the causes of poor implementation and to design strategies for improving delivery. Alternatively, the monitoring data may show that the intervention works well for some types of recipients but not for all of them, a finding that would suggest analyzing delivery components to see whether modifications are needed for some types of recipients. Finally, if the intervention was well implemented in accordance with the intended design but still did not produce the outcomes intended, the program design or program theory is likely to be faulty. A "return to the drawing board" may be needed to design new approaches using other theories.

When an impact evaluation design is intended to examine whether an intervention *caused* the outcomes, statistical analyses should include data about variability in the extent of implementation within the analysis procedure used. Rather than simply analyzing whether there are differences in outcomes between treatment and control groups, data concerning delivery should be presented to confirm that the program was well implemented in the treatment group and was absent in the control group. An alternative statistical approach to using analysis of variance for groups is to analyze results in terms of an underlying causal model, especially if implementation scores vary considerably across delivery sites (Cohen, 1975; Judd, 1987). A causal model could be derived from a chain-of-events diagram linking variability in program interventions to variability in intended outcomes. Such analyses should also include statistical controls for other characteristics that are likely to affect the outcome or which may be correlated with the extent-of-implementation scores. Within regression-type models, the problem of "contamination" of control subjects who receive similar program components from another source can be handled readily by using their measured extent-of-implementation scores as variables in the model rather than assuming no treatment.

In the Midwestern Prevention Project (MMP), described above, an experimental design was used to assess the impacts of this classroom program on young adolescents' self-reports of cigarette, alcohol, and marijuana use (Pentz and others, 1990). Evaluators found that the extent of classroom implementation varied considerably among the teachers who were supposed to be delivering the intervention. The evaluators then used multiple regression analyses to examine differences in the impacts on students that related to high versus low implementation, and in comparison to the control group students, who received their usual health education. For all measures of impact (student use of each substance, either within the last week or within the last month), the increase in student use during one year was significantly lower within the MPP schools, but the differences between low and high extent of implementation were even greater than differences between experimental and control groups. For example, the percentage of students who stated they had smoked within the past month *increased* from 13 percent to 24 percent for the control group, *increased* from 13 percent to 20 percent in schools with low implementation, but *decreased* from 15 percent to 14 percent in schools with high implementation. Measurement of the extent of implementation thus uncovered strong impacts from the intended program that were obscured in the experimental analysis alone.

Summary

This section on measuring program implementation emphasizes the usefulness of a range of measures and procedures. Full-scale process evaluation is not a simple matter. It requires careful attention to the conceptual design of measurements, the creation of measuring tools, and the collection of quality data in order to fulfill its potential roles within program evaluation. After thoughtful data design and collection, quantitative data analysis methods can create indexes of the extent of implementation and link process evaluation with impact data.

Assessing Influences on the Variability of Implementation

The preceding sections have emphasized that the implemented program is likely to differ from original intentions, with variations among sites, deliverers, participants, and other program units, and across time. This divergence raises questions concerning why such variation occurs, how it affects program effectiveness, and what might be done to increase the extent of full implementation. Some variation may be desirable as adaptations to local conditions, but other variability may reflect real gaps between the intended program and the implemented program. These concerns are the domain of another type of process evaluation, in which reasons for variability in implementation are systematically assessed to provide recommendations for changes needed to achieve full implementation. This section discusses several types of implementation process evaluation, including an overview of variables likely to be influential on the extent of implementation achieved and suggestions for data collection and analysis.

These issues are examined in a considerable and growing body of literature, but no single framework has emerged to provide guidance for evaluators across disciplines and contexts (Basch, Eveland, and Portnoy, 1986; Palumbo and Calista, 1990; Roberts-Gray and Scheirer, 1988; Scheirer, 1981; Tornatzky and Fleischer, 1990). Studies relevant to understanding implementation processes are scattered across numerous content areas; researchers have thus far not used them to develop cross-disciplinary theories or comparative summaries of empirical findings. Reports often discuss perceived "barriers to" or "facilitators of" implementation, but do not examine the underlying organizational structures and processes that normally influence the extent of service delivery. Thus, it is difficult to know whether *post hoc* explanations (such as "the chief administrator did not support the program" or "the staff members' attitudes undermined the program") would be supported by more systematic studies of implementation. If evaluators and program managers wait for the results of an impact evaluation or wait to see whether there are implementation problems, it is often too late to collect reliable, "real-time" data about the organizational processes that affect implementation. Some evaluation studies should be specifically planned to focus on implementation processes, in order to build a body of systematic knowledge that will provide empirically based guidance for program managers.

In such studies, the extent of implementation of the program components in local sites is the dependent variable, and factors hypothesized to be influences on the variability in implementation are predictor (independent) variables. Are the same factors that are influential in one site, or for one type of program, also influential for other locations, at other times or in other programs? In addition, when evaluators do engage in *post hoc* explorations for sources of implementation difficulty, such investigations should be based on a systematic framework of possible influences. Data collection and analyses should include both successful and unsuccessful implementation sites, to confirm that the explanatory factors do differ with the extent of implementation success. Reports of findings should present information on *all* influences that were investigated as possible sources of implementation problems, in order to build an empirically based body of findings, including aspects that were examined but do not help to explain variability in implementation.

Types of Implementation Process Analysis

When variation in implementation is examined, a major distinction is necessary between macro-implementation and micro-implementation perspectives (Berman, 1978). The macro-implementation approach is most often used for studies of large-scale government programs, in which the focus is on the connecting links between the government agency or other umbrella organization and multiple layers of lower-level organizations, such as state and local governments, or school districts, schools, and individual classrooms. Explanatory influences identified by prior studies include the many decision points involved in multi-layered implementation, the competing priorities of those participating, the interests and resources of the various actors, and the diverse strategies used to obtain the desired changes in the system (Palumbo and Calista, 1990; Pressman and Wildavsky, 1984).

For example, Palumbo, Maynard-Moody, and Wright (1984) conducted a policy-oriented implementation study of a new state law in Oregon that fostered community-level correctional services for certain types of felons rather than imprisonment in the state's overcrowded prisons. Using data collected from open-ended and structured interviews, mail questionnaires, and state and local records, the researchers found wide variation among Oregon's counties in the extent and methods for implementing these policies. The more successful counties were more likely to have an active "fixer" to advocate the policies locally, to have both upper-level administrative support and high levels of commitment from the frontline parole officers, and to have modified the program only slightly to fit local needs. In jurisdictions where parole officers were employees of the state rather than of the county, some officers felt their job security was threatened by the new provisions and tended to undermine local-level implementation.

In contrast to this example of state-to-local macro-implementation, a micro-implementation perspective focuses on activities within one or more organizations to examine the types of individual and organizational change needed to achieve full implementation. A key perspective at the micro level is to examine the extent of compatibility between the pre-existing organization and the new program requirements. Programs requiring extensive change in the operating culture and procedures of local organizations are likely to be much more difficult to implement than programs that are compatible with existing structures and processes. For example, educational programs calling for peer teaching among students or cooperative work within small groups of students will be much easier to implement if teachers are already using such techniques than they will be in classrooms strictly organized around individually based learning. Specifying program components, as described above, provides guidance by suggesting which aspects of local systems will be affected, whose activities will change, and which parts of an organization will be involved in implementing each component. The ease of implementing a specific new program may differ even among organizations of the same type, since each is likely to have developed its own culture.

Many organizational processes influence the extent of micro-implementation but can be summarized only briefly here. They are amplified in the referenced literature (see particularly, Elmore, 1978; Goodman and Steckler, 1990; Roberts-Gray and Scheirer, 1988; Scheirer, 1981). The following listing should also be useful to program managers when planning implementation strategies as well as to evaluators studying these processes. Some influences derive from the organization as a whole, such as the following:

- The types of decision-making processes used — centralized or participatory
- Procedures and priorities for allocating resources
- The supportiveness of an organization's overall culture toward programs of the type being implemented
- The types of pressures emanating from the organization's environment of beneficiaries, supporters, competitors, and regulators

A second set of influences comes from the structures and processes in an organization's work units, such as wards within a hospital or departments within a governmental agency. In some contexts, several organizational layers or types of groups may be influential. At this level, evaluators and program managers should consider the following:

- Expectations and performance feedback from the supervisors in each unit
- Technologies in use and their fit with the new program
- Standard operating routines used to simplify and regularize the work flow
- Use of time and availability of time to learn activities for the new program
- Social norms governing ways of working that have developed within a unit
- Communication processes both within and between units

The individual program deliverers ("street-level workers") in the organization should not be ignored (Weatherley and Lipsky, 1977). Their individual actions are likely to be influenced by the following, as well as by the processes in their work units:

- Their own capabilities or skills in using the innovation
- Extent and types of training they are given for delivering the new program
- Their concerns about how it affects them personally, such as its possible effects on their future employment or job advancement
- External incentives and internal motivations to learn and to deliver the new program

Although this is a long list of potential influences on implementation, all have been identified in one or more studies as key causes for implementation success or failure (Scheirer, 1981; McDonald, 1991). Little systematic guidance is yet available to know *which* aspects will be most influential in specific circumstances. Implementation success is likely to be influenced by multiple factors, in which the lack of positive influence from any one of a fairly large number of organization factors can itself undermine the change processes necessary for successful implementation. The same program may fail to be well implemented in one location because supervisors did not provide supportive feedback to "street-level" workers, while in another location supervisors were supportive but work group norms fostered fears about long-term job security.

Methods for Data Collection and Analysis

Examination of implementation processes is often done with case study methods to compile data on the events, interests, actions, and reactions that accompanied an attempted change. (For more guidance on conducting case studies, see Caudle, Chapter Four of this volume; Miles and Huberman, 1984; Yin, 1984). Data collection for a case study usually includes review of program documents to trace the formal channels of information and open-ended interviews with a variety of organizational and external informants to explore their roles and reactions to the program. Sometimes direct observation of decision-making meetings, worker activities, or staff member contacts with external groups is possible. Although case studies use primarily qualitative information, the data collection should be structured by a well-developed framework detailing the organizational aspects to be examined. If possible, a priori hypotheses should be stated and tested so that empirical evidence can accumulate across studies concerning which aspects most often influence the variability in implementation. Yet, the evaluator collecting qualitative data should remain open to new possibilities suggested by organizational informants or emerging from the data.

Systematic surveys of organizational members can also be used to collect implementation process data. Interviews with representative samples of organizational members from multiple levels and units can provide data about most of the organizational influences introduced above. A mail questionnaire can elicit information about the extent of participation or delivery of a program, along with respondents' perceptions concerning relevant organizational factors. The same questionnaire might also contain items about program effectiveness, when the desired program outcomes are behaviors that are easily and validly self-reported. If feasible, self-report measures should be cross-validated with other data sources, perhaps collected only for a sample.

This methodology can economically provide data on at least three "links" in a chain-of-events evaluation model: hypothesized influences on the extent of implementation, measures of the variation in program implementation, and measures of the desired outcomes. Analyses of these data would apply normal methods for survey data analysis, but with special attention to its hierarchical structure, with individuals clustered within work groups and work groups within organizations.

When using data about implementation from individuals, the evaluator should guard against the tendency to view individuals' attitudes as the "cause" of their behavior. Social psychological findings reveal many examples in which the attitudes of people are not even predictive of their behavior, let alone the cause of it. In many instances, both attitudes and behaviors are strongly influenced by their organizational context. Further, individuals may not be aware of some factors affecting them, so the evaluator must be wary of accepting on face value the explanations of organizational informants concerning reasons for high or low implementation. Variability in the extent and scope of implementation should be further examined within systematic evaluation, just as program content and effectiveness have been systematically evaluated over several decades.

Conclusions

This chapter examines three major uses of process evaluation: identifying program components using formative evaluation, evaluability assessment, and theory; measuring the extent and scope of actual implementation by collecting data about program components and recipients; and assessing influences on the variability of implementation. The chain-of-events approach to thinking about program operations and effects suggests using multiple sources of data to link process and impact evaluations. Some basic themes emerge about suggested roles for process evaluation:

- The usefulness of evaluation for improving program management and delivery will be substantially increased by *more* emphasis on data about program processes.
- Evaluations of the impacts of program interventions should *always* include measures of the extent of program delivery.
- Understanding of program impacts, whether or not the desired change occurred, will be greatly strengthened by process evaluation data.
- The more that variation in program delivery is expected among multiple sites, the greater the need for process evaluation.
- The larger the scale of an evaluation study in number of sites and participants, the greater the need to measure the extent and processes of intervention delivery.

Process evaluation can serve a variety of purposes that require a variety of types of data. Simply collecting brief indicators of program delivery can be useful for program monitoring, but process evaluation may also encompass complex data collection and very sophisticated data analysis techniques. Evaluators and program managers should systematically consider which methods and functions are most applicable to their programmatic needs and their evaluation budgets.

References

Basch, C. E., Eveland, J. D., and Portnoy, B. "Diffusion Systems for Education and Learning About Health." *Family and Community Health,* 1986, *9,* 1–26.

Basch, C. E., and others. "Avoiding Type III Errors in Health Education

Program Evaluations: A Case Study." *Health Education Quarterly,* 1985, *12,* 315–331.

Berman, P. "The Study of Macro- and Micro-Implementation." *Public Policy,* 1978, *26,* 157–184.

Brink, S. G., Levenson-Gingass, P., and Gottlieb, N. H. "An Evaluation of the Effectiveness of a Planned Diffusion Process: The Smoke-Free Class of 2000 in Texas." *Health Education Research,* 1991, *6,* 353–362.

Chen, H. T. "Special Issue: The Theory-Driven Perspective." *Evaluation and Program Planning,* 1989, *12,* 297–398.

Chen, H. T. *Theory-Driven Evaluations.* Newbury Park, Calif.: Sage, 1990.

Cohen, J. "Multiple Regression as a General Data-Analytic System." In M. Guttentag and E. L. Struening (eds.), *Handbook of Evaluation Research.* Vol. 1. Newbury Park, Calif.: Sage, 1975.

Dobson, L. D., and Cook, T. J. "Avoiding Type III Error in Program Evaluation: Results from a Field Experiment." *Evaluation and Program Planning,* 1980, *3,* 269–276.

Elmore, R. F. "Organizational Models of Social Program Implementation." *Public Policy,* 1978, *26,* 185–228.

Emshoff, J., and others. "Innovation in Education and Criminal Justice: Measuring Fidelity of Implementation and Program Effectiveness." *Educational Evaluation and Policy Analysis,* 1987, *9,* 300–311.

Goodman, R. M., and Steckler, A. B. "Mobilizing Organizations for Health Enhancement: Theories of Organizational Change." In K. Glanz, F. M. Lewis, and B. K. Rimer (eds.), *Health Behavior and Health Education: Theory, Research and Practice.* San Francisco: Jossey-Bass, 1990.

Hall, G. E., and Loucks, S. F. "A Developmental Model for Determining Whether the Treatment Is Actually Implemented." *American Educational Research Journal,* 1977, *14,* 263–276.

Hall, G. E., and Loucks, S. F. *Innovation Configurations: Analyzing the Adaptations of Innovations.* Austin: Research and Development Center for Teacher Education, University of Texas at Austin, 1978.

Hunter, C. P., and others. "Selection Factors in Clinical Trials: Results from the Community Clinical Oncology Program Physician's Patient Log." *Cancer Treatment Reports,* 1987, *71,* 559–565.

Judd, C. M. "Combining Process and Outcome Evaluation." In M. M. Mark and R. L. Shotland (eds.), *Multiple Methods in Program Evaluation.* New Directions for Program Evaluation, no. 35. San Francisco: Jossey-Bass, 1987.

King, J. A., Morris, L. L., and Fitz-Gibbon, C. T. *How to Assess Program Implementation.* Newbury Park, Calif.: Sage, 1987.

Leithwood, K. A., and Montgomery, D. A. "Evaluating Program Implementation." *Evaluation Review,* 1980, *4,* 193–214.

Lewin, K. *A Dynamic Theory of Personality.* New York: McGraw-Hill, 1935.

Light, R. J., "Introduction to Research Reviews." In R. J. Light (ed.), *Evaluation Studies Review Annual.* Vol. 8. Newbury Park, Calif.: Sage, 1983.

Lipsey, M. W., and others. "Evaluation: The State of the Art and the Sorry State of the Science." In D. S. Cordray (ed.), *Utilizing Prior Research in Evaluation Planning*. New Directions for Program Evaluation, no. 27. San Francisco: Jossey-Bass, 1985.

Loucks, S. F., Newlove, B. W., and Hall, G. E. *Measuring Levels of Use of the Innovation: A Manual for Trainers, Interviewers and Raters*. Austin, Tex.: Southwest Educational Development Laboratory, 1975.

McDonald, R. M. "Assessment of Organizational Context: A Missing Component in Evaluation of Training Programs." *Evaluation and Program Planning*, 1991, *14*, 273–279.

Miles, M. B., and Huberman, A. M. *Analyzing Qualitative Data: A Source Book for New Methods*. Newbury Park, Calif.: Sage, 1984.

Nay, J., and Kay, P. *Government Oversight and Evaluability Assessment*. Lexington, Mass.: Heath, 1982.

Palumbo, D. J., and Calista, D. J. (eds.). *Implementation and the Policy Process: Opening Up the Black Box*. New York: Greenwood Press, 1990.

Palumbo, D. J., Maynard-Moody, S., and Wright, P. "Measuring Degrees of Successful Implementation: Achieving Policy Versus Statutory Goals." *Evaluation Review*, 1984, *8*, 45–74.

Patton, M. Q. "Evaluation of Program Implementation." In L. Sechrest (ed.), *Evaluation Studies Review Annual*. Vol. 4. Newbury Park, Calif.: Sage, 1979.

Pentz, M. A., and others. "Effects of Program Implementation on Adolescent Drug Use Behavior: The Midwestern Prevention Project (MPP)." *Evaluation Review*, 1990, *14*, 264–289.

Pressman, J. L., and Wildavsky, A. B. *Implementation*. (2nd ed.) Berkeley: University of California Press, 1984.

Rimer, B. K. "The Role of Theory in Improving Primary Care Practice." In H. Hibbard, P. A. Nutting, and M. L. Grady (eds.), *Primary Care Research: Theory and Methods*. Agency for Health Care Policy and Research Publication No. 91-0011. Rockville, Md.: Department of Health and Human Services, Public Health Service/Agency for Health Care Policy and Research, 1991.

Roberts-Gray, C., and Scheirer, M. A. "Checking the Congruence Between a Program and Its Organizational Environment." In K. J. Conrad and C. Roberts-Gray (eds.), *Evaluating Program Environments*. New Directions for Program Evaluation, no. 40. San Francisco: Jossey-Bass, Winter, 1988.

Rossi, P. H., and Freeman, H. E. *Evaluation: A Systematic Approach*. (4th ed.) Newbury Park, Calif.: Sage, 1989.

Scheirer, M. A. *Program Implementation: The Organizational Context*. Newbury Park, Calif.: Sage, 1981.

Scheirer, M. A., and Griffith, J. "Studying Micro-Implementation Empirically: Lessons and Dilemmas." In D. J. Palumbo, and D. J. Calista (eds.), *Implementation and the Policy Process: Opening Up the Black Box*. New York: Greenwood Press, 1990.

Scheirer, M. A., and Rezmovic, E. L. "Measuring the Degree of Program

Implementation: A Methodological Review." *Evaluation Review,* 1983, *7,* 599–633.

Scriven, M. "The Methodology of Evaluation." In R. W. Tyler, R. M. Gagne, and M. Scriven (eds.), *Perspectives on Curriculum Evaluation.* American Educational Research Association Monograph Series on Curriculum Evaluation, no. 1. Chicago: Rand McNally, 1967.

Sechrest, L. "Prevention in Primary Care: Several Perspectives." In H. Hibbard, P. A. Nutting, and M. L. Grady (eds.), *Primary Care Research: Theory and Methods.* Agency for Health Care Policy and Research Publication No. 91-0011. Rockville, Md.: Department of Health and Human Services, Public Health Service/Agency for Health Care Policy and Research, 1991.

Sechrest, L., and others. "Some Neglected Problems in Evaluation Research: Strength and Integrity of Treatments." In L. Sechrest and others (eds.), *Evaluation Studies Review Annual.* Vol. 4. Newbury Park, Calif.: Sage, 1979.

Smith, M. F. *Evaluability Assessment: A Practical Approach.* Boston: Kluwer Academic Publishers, 1989.

Smith, M. F. "Evaluability Assessment: Reflections on the Process." *Evaluation and Program Planning,* 1990, *13,* 539–564.

Tornatzky, L. G., and Fleischer, M. *The Process of Technological Innovation.* Lexington, Mass.: Lexington Books, 1990.

Weatherley, R., and Lipsky, M. "Street-Level Bureaucrats and Institutional Innovation: Implementing Special Education Reform." *Harvard Education Review,* 1977, *47,* 171–197.

Wholey, J. S. *Evaluation: Promise and Performance.* Washington, D.C.: Urban Institute, 1979.

Wholey, J. S. "Evaluability Assessment: Developing Program Theory." In L. Bickman (ed.), *Using Program Theory in Evaluation.* New Directions for Program Evaluation, no. 33. San Francisco: Jossey-Bass, 1987.

Windsor, R. A., Baranowski, T., Clark, N., and Cutter, G. *Evaluation of Health Promotion and Education Programs.* Mountain View, Calif.: Mayfield, 1984.

Yeaton, W. H. "Using Measures of Treatment Strength and Integrity in Planning Research." In D. S. Cordray (ed.), *Utilizing Prior Research in Evaluation Planning.* New Directions for Program Evaluation, no. 27. San Francisco: Jossey-Bass, 1985.

Yin, R. K. *Case Study Research: Design and Methods.* Newbury Park, Calif.: 1984.

4

Using Qualitative Approaches

Sharon L. Caudle

Complexity characterizes many service programs. When asked to evaluate a program with multiple purposes and implemented at many sites, evaluators must deal with multiple sources of data. Much of the data they need must be gathered from on-site observations, or from documents, or from program participants. Dealing with such complexities can be a formidable challenge to even the most experienced of evaluators. This chapter gives the reader ideas in how to deal with the challenge of qualitative data collection and analysis. It also discusses data collection activities and how they intertwine with data analysis. Last, the chapter discusses data analysis and ways to improve the credibility of the findings.

Underlying Assumptions of Qualitative Evaluation

As might be expected from its name, qualitative evaluation searches for "qualities" in inputs, processes, and outcomes, capturing the wide, diverse, mundane, and rich details of everyday life (Lofland and Lofland, 1984). "Natural" settings are the arena for its questions and its search for patterns to answer those questions (Patton, 1987). Qualitative evaluation is frequently called "naturalistic" evaluation as it does not attempt to manipulate these settings for study purposes. An intense investigative process of contrasting, comparing, replicating, cataloguing, and classifying what is under study is the trademark of qualitative methods (Miles and Huberman, 1984; Patton, 1980, 1987).

The Investigative Process

Quantitative methods also use an investigative process. The contrast between qualitative methods and quantitative approaches is most strongly seen in how the investigative process is conducted. First, in qualitative evaluation, the evaluator literally becomes the primary measurement instrument in the investigative process, in contrast to quantitative research where the researcher tries to stay removed from the process (Kidder and Fine, 1987; Tesch, 1990). Second, qualitative data collection and data analysis are mutually interdependent, interacting with one another as the investigation proceeds, unlike the distinct phases that characterize collection and analysis in quantitative research.

The evaluator collecting qualitative data looks for similarities and dissimilarities, inconsistencies in data, and the like. He or she asks why there are similarities and why there are differences. As data collection proceeds, the evaluator continually formulates propositions about findings tied to what is observed during data collection. Tentative conclusions lead to further data collection, perhaps even changes in the type of data that is collected, which leads to more findings. Data collection and data analysis are inextricably linked under qualitative evaluation approaches. Key conceptual and pragmatic issues can help the evaluator who is using these approaches.

Points in Using Qualitative Methods

If an evaluator is to use qualitative methods successfully, he or she should understand underlying conceptual beliefs about qualitative approaches, be open to a flexible design, have appropriate skills, and prepare for the evaluation.

Conceptual Beliefs

A good starting point for the qualitative evaluator is to examine the beliefs or principles that underlie qualitative methods. As Van Maanen (1982) describes it, a key belief is that qualitative work starts with close-up, detailed observation where patterns may or may not occur. The evaluator uses these initial close-up observations to interpret meanings, develop tentative general conclusions, and identify new variables and questions for further data collection. Subsequent data gathering builds on the ongoing analysis of the data gathered earlier. The evaluator makes additional observations, reviews the conclusions, and does it all again in an analytic induction process (Agar, 1986; Babbie, 1989; Lincoln and Guba, 1985; Lofland and Lofland, 1984; Posavac and Carey, 1989; Tesch, 1990).

Another primary belief is that the evaluator must observe concrete occurrences and occasions firsthand. He or she is directly in contact with what is under study. The evaluator observes the physical program setting, patterns of interaction in the human and social environment, program activities and participant behaviors, informal interactions and activities, the language of program participants, nonverbal communications, physical clues, program documents, and what does not happen (Patton, 1987).

Another belief described by Van Maanen (1982) is that qualitative evaluation focuses on a natural world. The evaluator looks at normal routines and tries to make sense of that activity. It is the study of ordinary behavior that is central to qualitative evaluation.

Additionally, the normal routines found in a natural world are believed to be the result of custom, present circumstance, and ongoing interaction. It is looking at customs, interactions, and other contextual factors that gives qualitative evaluation much of its power.

A final important belief is that qualitative evaluation has a highly descriptive focus, generally searching for descriptions of what occurs at a given place and time. Revelation and disclosure normally take precedence over explanation and prediction. However, that is not to say that qualitative analysis cannot attempt to explain or to explore possible hypotheses.

Flexible Design

Given these five beliefs, an evaluator cannot design a qualitative study in a very structured, definitive way before the study begins (Lincoln and Guba, 1985). A qualitative evaluation design takes shape in the field as the study progresses through early examination of the evaluation purpose, a literature search, sampling of subjects, inductive analysis of the data, development of grounded theory from the inductive analysis, and then projection of the next evaluation research steps. The process of data collection, analysis, and development of findings continues until the findings are fully explained (Babbie, 1989; Fielding and Fielding, 1986; Kidder and Fine, 1987).

For example, in a study of strategic information resources management in which the author participated, the initial aim of the study was to describe "best practices" for federal managers, using a case study approach. *Case studies* are a popular form of qualitative research, involving in-depth examinations of individuals, programs, or processes. A literature search defined certain areas of possible coverage, such as organizational structure, top management involvement and commitment, the development of a strategic management framework, and information resources management capabilities, such as a strong organizational structure and services. Organizations were selected for case studies on the basis of their reputation among the information resources management community and other research on them done in the past. Case study questions were formulated from the literature review and tested in two pilot organizations. After the pilots, the questions were further refined on the basis of the data that were collected. An early outline of findings was created, added to, and reorganized as other case studies were completed.

What the evaluator learns and presents depends on how well he or she understands and collects data at the field site, such as during a case study. The data must be collected and analyzed within their context, and understanding the context is an important evaluation process. For example, the study of best practices in strategic information resources management involved federal and state government organizations and private sector companies. Without asking about and understanding what was happening in the organizations that could affect strategic information resources practices, the investigators might have interpreted the data incorrectly, or perhaps failed to ask the right questions.

Design of the evaluation methodology, data collection, and analysis activities all come together in one process, shepherded by the evaluator, a very subjective instrument. As interviews were held in the best practices study and the data examined, the questions were revised to collect comparable data and also to provide a rich description of the context of each case study.

Evaluator Skills

Skills are another important aspect in qualitative evaluation. Several skills bolster what the human evaluation instrument can effectively achieve in qualitative data collection and analysis. First, a good qualitative evaluator asks questions that will not bias answers (Babbie, 1989). An interview question should not attempt to make a judgment or solicit a certain type of response by the way it is phrased. Nor should the evaluator slant the answer by the tone or emphasis with which he or she asks the question.

A good qualitative evaluator should be able to ask a question, listen to the answer, interpret its meaning in the context of the evaluation, and frame another question either to respond to the earlier answer or to redirect the respondent. This requires concentrating on what is being said, remembering what has been said earlier by the informant or other informants, and keeping the field research from straying away from the overall purpose of the evaluation. The evaluator also should be a good time manager, efficiently using his or her field time and the time of the informant.

The evaluator also needs to be a skilled observer to see indirect clues from indicators such as physical program settings and nonverbal communication. The absence or presence of equipment, support personnel, or windows may say more about the importance of a function in the organization than what an informant says in an unstructured interview. The evaluator also requires strong skills in writing descriptively, recording field notes in a disciplined way, separating detail from trivia, and using rigorous methods to validate observations (Patton, 1987). An example of lack of needed data collection skills is an evaluator who conducts a very perceptive in-depth interview but cannot carry that interview away in detailed, accurate field notes for subsequent data analysis and data collection. While the evaluator might have the information in his or her head and refer to the interview often in evaluation team discussions, there is no way for others to use that information effectively in data analysis.

Finally, the evaluator should not be trapped by personal ideologies or preconceptions before, during, or after the actual fieldwork. He or she should be sensitive and responsive to contradictory evidence (Yin, 1984).

Qualitative evaluators may lock on a particular pattern or give too much credence to one particular data source, unwilling to keep an open mind to other alternatives. And a good evaluator should accept a multidisciplinary approach, not limiting himself or herself to data collection or analysis activities that most closely match his or her discipline (Miles and Huberman, 1984).

Preparation

Strong qualitative evaluation skills in and of themselves are not enough, however. A firm grasp of the issues under study can come only from preparation (Yin, 1984). Gummesson (1991) calls this "preunderstanding"—the evaluator's insights into the problem and its context before the evaluation begins. The evaluator should gather basic information and become familiar with the natural setting so that he or she is then better able to understand significant processes such as decision making, implementation, and the management of change. Preunderstanding is influenced by factors such as the knowledge of theories, concepts, models, and approaches for identifying, diagnosing, defining, and analyzing major factors and relationships.

In the study of best practices in strategic information resources management, the author was guided by two other studies she had done in federal and state government on the same topic. Several of the case study organizations were ones she had visited in these earlier studies, and she used information from the prior research in framing questions, examining documents, and selecting individuals to interview in the best practices study. She had also done extensive reading about strategic management and had taught a course on strategic planning for information resources management, all of which added to her knowledge of theories and concepts that might be applicable to the best practices study.

Knowledge of organizational characteristics, such as standard operating procedures, decision-making structures, and coordination mechanisms specific to a certain industry, market, or service, is another example of preunderstanding. Public sector evaluators have to understand basic differences in culture between defense organizations and environmental protection agencies, or between a cabinet-level office and an operating program agency office. Private sector evaluators must understand the basic differences between public and private sector organizations and cultures. Frequently, major components of a qualitative study are assigned to evaluators who have special training and experience relevant to the component.

Costs

Costs will also affect qualitative evaluation design. Qualitative evaluation normally entails extensive, on-site evaluator observation that consumes considerable time and resources. Qualitative evaluation can be relatively inexpensive: one evaluator and a notebook. On the other end, however, it can involve a trained evaluation team with sophisticated recording equipment undertaking extensive travel (Babbie, 1989). Some argue that it is hard to conduct a cost-effective evaluation using qualitative methods (Posavac and Carey, 1989).

A good framework for estimating evaluation costs is found in Miller's text (1991). The framework specifies activities such as planning the study, conducting pilot studies and pretests, sampling, preparing observational materials, selecting and training evaluators, collecting and processing data, and preparing the final report. In comparison to quantitative methods, such as mail-out surveys, qualitative fieldwork often generates significantly more costs for field staff salaries, central office support, travel, and communication. Training multiple evaluators also is a cost factor, as are activities such as debriefings that characterize the progression of a qualitative study.

Primary Data Collection and Analysis Activities

Beliefs, design, skills, and preparation provide a sweeping context for considering qualitative evaluation. Yet, they only set the stage for the main activities of data collection and data analysis. Data collection is at its best when the evaluation questions clearly define the objectives of the study and lead to defensible sampling strategies.

Data Collection Strategies

Generally there are several qualitative data collection strategies that an evaluator can consider (Posavac and Carey, 1989). One is observation, which can take several forms. Direct or unrestricted observation is best done where the presence of an observer will not affect the data collection, where it is "natural" for the observer to take note of surroundings. For example, in studying best practices in strategic information resources management, the author observed settings. Elements such as the way offices were set up, what services were available, and how people interacted with one another were assessed through direct observation. In cases like these, the observer can simply record what he or she observes in considerable detail. If there are particular indicators important to the study that must be observed, such as people's interaction, the evaluator could use a specific data collection guide for that purpose. At the other end of the observation strategy spectrum is participant observation, where an evaluator actually is a full-fledged participant of the situation under study, such as a program client or staff member.

The second qualitative data collection strategy commonly used is document examination. Documents can be quite varied in coverage, detail, reliability, and consistency with other documents. In the best practices study, the author was interested in the type of policies and guidelines issued by the organizations under study. In doing analysis, she considered whether they supported one another. For example, if an organization had issued a strategic planning guidebook, did it support formal policy instructions for submitting a strategic plan and supporting budget? Did the organization have published criteria on how those plans and budgets would be evaluated for approval, and if so, how did they link back to the strategic planning guidebook? These types of comparisons provided information on how planning is actually implemented.

A third qualitative data collection tool is interviews. Qualitative interviewing generally is not highly structured. Data collection and analysis come together at virtually the same time. The interviewer follows leads in the interviews to new topics or tries to build fuller understanding by asking clarifying questions. In qualitative studies that the author has done, the ability to listen and explore actively frequently makes the difference between the success and failure of an interview. In scheduling interviews, the author generally provides the person to be interviewed a listing of "areas of coverage"—the possible areas and questions that might come up during the interview. The list is based on the research questions, literature search, discussions with advisory groups, and pilot tests. The list provided to interviewees in the best practices study covered the information resources management program and its organization, strategic information resources management activities, key organizational actors, planning methodologies and outcomes, performance expectations and evaluation activities, and key characteristics for building successful strategic information resources management processes.

The author always tells interviewees that the interviews will not be structured and that they will be tailored to their situation and expertise important to the study. For example, the area of emphasis of a budget official will be quite different from that of the top executive in an agency; the interview questions must be tailored accordingly. In addition, the first interviews at a site generally provide background information for the evaluator and suggestions for questions for later interviews. Some of the first interviews should be with the key official responsible for the area under study. In the best practices study, the author requested that the first interview be with the person responsible for strategic information resources management planning. He or she generally could provide the context of the existing process, including current strategic thrusts and problem areas, which could be explored in later interviews.

More structured questions may come toward the end of the study's interviews as tentative interpretations and findings are tested. In the best practices studies, early pilot case studies indicated that one area of special interest was the defining of champions or advocates for strategic information resources management, so a question generally was asked in the later studies about the presence and characteristics of champions. The author used examples from earlier case studies to learn whether similar champion activities were important.

Fieldwork generally combines all three data collection strategies, with field notes prepared on data sources in the form of transcribed interviews, observations, and document reviews. While one form of data may predominate, the evaluator should take advantage of all sources of information in building the qualitative database.

Analysis Preparation

Planning for the analysis activities in an evaluation should precede actual data collection, although the analysis strategies can change as data collection proceeds. In fact, Miles and Huberman (1984) note that the word *analysis* can be very broad in the qualitative approach, with analysis construed as three concurrent flows of activity. One activity flow is data reduction that narrows the collected data to be dealt with. A second is data display that is intended to organize the data better for analysis. The third is conclusion drawing and verification.

Data reduction really starts in the actual data collection stage. Data reduction is the process of selecting, focusing, simplifying, abstracting, and transforming raw data from field notes and other sources. The reduction of data occurs from the very beginning of the evaluation as the evaluator decides on questions, selects sites to sample, firms up data collection approaches, decides on possible ways to code and categorize data, and works with what has been selected as the unit of analysis.

Normally, a qualitative evaluator will rapidly accumulate a great deal of information in a short period of time. The evaluator's critical task by the end of the study is not to accumulate all the data possible but to get rid of most of the data which are accumulated (Wolcott, 1986). The data reduction goal is to provide sufficient context for the evaluation findings and to focus on the topic under study. In other words, the data that are collected should fit what is under study. Frequently, evaluators collect data almost haphazardly without keeping the collection within the framework of the study's coverage.

Structuring Collection

Data collection and preliminary analysis should be organized to capture the most relevant data. As was shown in the example of areas of coverage for an interview, the original evaluation questions should provide the overall framework for the analysis (Patton, 1987; Yin, 1984). It is helpful to prepare the major evaluation questions, derive subquestions, then formulate questions or areas of coverage for actual data collection. Before in-depth fieldwork, the evaluator might consider pilot testing these preliminary questions. In the best practices study, an overall evaluation question asked, "What are the key determinants for successful management of information technology in a public organization?" Subquestions covered organizational structures, policy initiatives, planning strategies, existing information technology applications, and upcoming legislative changes or executive decisions that might affect those applications. Questions in these areas can be tested in a pilot effort and revised before large-scale in-depth evaluation efforts proceed.

Converting Field Notes

As discussed under evaluator skills, asking the right questions will not ensure that the most relevant data are captured. An evaluator conducting interviews and observations should write up full field notes immediately or at least within twelve hours. The contents should be a complete description of context and activities that include people, events, what is heard, conversations, and physical settings. Field notes should be readable and placed in chronological order. They must include all the relevant details, since they will produce what the evaluator believes are patterns of what is happening.

Preliminary analysis starts to define these patterns. Verbatim accounts should be distinguished from those that are paraphrased or based on recall. Evaluators who "process" data into categories while writing field notes can make subsequent analysis difficult. Lost in this approach are the words of the interviewee in all their detail. Later on, if analysis indicates that one area—perhaps the role of a champion—is emerging as an important finding, there may be no way to capture similar indications in earlier interviews if categories are preset or what appear to be irrelevant notes are not transcribed into usable field notes.

The raw data, in either verbatim or paraphrased form, or in notes from the evaluator's memory, should be captured in an initial effort; then they should be analyzed for data categorization and classification. As collection and analysis proceed, categories and interpretations may change as the evaluator becomes more informed about what is happening. Preprocessed data cannot easily be used in the iterative process of categorizing and then adjusting later on.

Analysis: Filling in the Holes

The comprehensiveness of the data is important. The evaluator should ensure that all the necessary data are there and that any gaps in the data are identified. Case analyses should follow the preparation of a record that pulls data into a primary resource package for each case. Content analysis of the field notes, described in more detail below, should identify coherent and important examples, themes, and patterns. The evaluator should go through the field notes, such as interview transcripts and case records, and start labeling the data and formulating a data index.

In the field notes, the evaluator should include initial impressions, feelings, and analytic thoughts at the time the notes are formalized. When they are transcribed, the evaluator can place observations within the text in brackets. Thus, field notes include both empirical observations and the evaluator's interpretations of those observations (Babbie, 1989). Later, marginal notes can be added as the transcripts are examined again. In some cases, follow-up interviews or document reviews can provide missing information, particularly for data collection done in the early stages of the evaluation.

Table 4.1 shows what comments an evaluator might embed in the transcription text of an interview. Normally, the evaluator's comments would be placed in brackets in the text after or during the preparation of the transcript, or written in the margin.

Table 4.1. Evaluator Comments for Text.

Transcription Text	Evaluator Comments
We try to use a structured planning methodology here to come up with our goals for managing information technology, but that doesn't mean the agency has a clue as to how they fit in with the overall mission. Top management could care less, I mean, they are here a short time and just want to get some short-term results for the folks back home. We have problems getting anyone to care, I mean, information technology management is for the long haul because these databases and networks aren't built in a day. Everyone out there has his own solution and equipment. They don't think much of us, we have never been responsive, but we have new leadership here.	Need to find out which one and who uses it. Does the agency have an overall strategic management process? If so, how does information technology strategic planning fit in? Need to schedule interviews with top management political types to get perspectives: short term, lack of understanding of IRM[a] initiatives, delegation to IRM managers, some other reason? To what extent will planning for the long haul run up against an embedded base, inertia, and a poor reputation of the IRM people?

[a]information resources management

In the example in Table 4.1, the observations of the evaluator indicate areas that need further exploration in later interviews and some interpretations of barriers for a strategic information resources management process.

Content Analysis

As the interview sample shows in Table 4.1, qualitative evaluation analysis normally requires sorting through an immense amount of textual data (Pfaffenberger, 1988). Content analysis is an analytic method that investigates the meaning of data (Krippendorff, 1980). It is primarily a coding operation where any form of communication is coded or classified in line with some conceptual framework (Babbie, 1989). Communications can include written material, paintings, video material, and songs. Krippendorff (1980) provides a description of content analysis methodology and the need to distinguish relevant from irrelevant material, ferreting out the most accurate meaning of the material. Important considerations are dealing with interpretation of meanings, the unit of analysis, coding categories, and the actual coding techniques.

Communications do not necessarily have singular meanings and can be looked at from numerous perspectives. The context of the communications can clarify meanings as well. The evaluator who plans to do content analysis would have to decide what question is to be answered by a content analysis approach, select the communication form that is to be analyzed, set up a coding scheme, and decide how to sample the communications for data collection and analysis.

In content analysis, coding is the primary activity. Processing data involves the tasks of unitizing and categorizing (Lincoln and Guba, 1985). Unitizing means identifying the smallest piece of information about something that can stand by itself—literally units or chunks of information in a communication. The evaluator should be clear about what constitutes the unit of analysis for coding, like a sentence or multisentence chunk (Miles and Huberman, 1984). Categorization through coding brings those units or chunks together in some type of relationship where the codes serve as retrieval and organizing devices (Miles and Huberman, 1984). With them, the evaluator can spot patterns and manipulate the data through clustering and other analytical approaches.

Coding categories must be flexible enough to meet the evolving nature of the data collection and analysis methodology. As mentioned above, the practical difficulties involved in coding normally revolve around meanings of the chunks of data chosen as the unit of analysis. Also, an evaluator normally cannot anticipate which categories will be too small to stand alone and will be integrated into a larger category. Starting off with categories that are too broad will cause important analytical distinctions to be lost.

Coding in content analysis or other forms of qualitative research requires attaching category names to the basic units of field research data. Codes can be acts, activities, meanings, peoples' participation, relationships, settings, perspectives, processes, events, strategies, relationships, and social structures. Normally, a code is an abbreviation or symbol applied to a segment of words in field notes, interview transcriptions, and other documents to classify the words in some way. Coding can help identify inputs, processes, and outcomes.

There are two strategies for using categories, patterns, or themes to analyze the data (Patton, 1987). The evaluator may use the categories that people under study tend to articulate. Program staff and other participants frequently use special terms to describe differences in program activities, types of participants, and other characteristics in the setting. Another strategy is for the evaluator to select categories or patterns that are not articulated by program staff and other participants but which the evaluator identifies. In either case, the evaluator is looking for patterns that will suggest category systems. In the best practices study, *strategic planning decision making* was one category that was articulated by those who were interviewed. *User empowerment and control* was another category the evaluator identified.

Codes should be distinctive from other codes in significant ways. Codes that identify emerging themes, patterns, or categories are generally called inferential or pattern codes. Codes can even be used to categorize the reflective or analytical remarks an evaluator inserts into the text as he or she prepares field notes and interview transcriptions. Not all parts of the available text should be coded—only those directly related to the evaluation questions. The coding can be manual, done on index cards, or computerized, entered directly into a computer program.

Using the same interview sample from above, Table 4.2 shows how codes can be inserted in the text as part of content analysis. The codes that are initially used should be as detailed as possible. Later, they can be collapsed into larger categories if the data analysis leads that way.

Table 4.2. Coding Data.

Transcription Text	Coding Categories
We try to use a structured planning methodology here to come up with our goals for managing information technology, but that doesn't mean the agency has a clue as to how they fit in with the overall mission. Top management could care less, I mean, they are here a short time and just want to get some short-term results for the folks back home. We have problems getting anyone to care, I mean, information technology management is for the long haul because these databases and networks aren't built in a day. Everyone out there has his own solution and equipment. They don't think much of us, we have never been responsive, but we have new leadership here.	FORMAL IRM[a]-PLANNING METHODOLOGIES ESTABLISHMENT OF OVERALL IRM GOALS/FRAMEWORK MANAGEMENT ATTENTION REPUTATION OF IRM FUNCTION

[a]information resources management

Computerized Tools

Computerized tools can be quite helpful in coding activities for qualitative research (Tesch, 1990). Most software packages that are well developed to this point are mainly descriptive/interpretive analysis programs for narrative text, although some are beginning to facilitate theory building. Narrative text can include all types of input—field notes, interview transcriptions, questionnaire open-ended responses, diaries, administrative documents, and other narrative text. Two programs for mainframe computers, QUALOG and NUDIST, have been created for theory building.

Analysis programs for descriptive/interpretive analysis perform two basic functions: they allow the evaluator to attach codes to segments of text, and they will search through the data for the segments that were coded in a certain way and assemble them. Data can easily be recoded as the analysis proceeds.

General software packages for personal computers have been developed for coding and sorting qualitative data. Among the most widely used are ETHNO, Text Analysis Package (TAP), QUALPRO, TEXTBASE ALPHA, THE ETHNOGRAPH, and HYPERQUAL. With the exception of TAP and ETHNO, this software can be purchased from Qualitative Research Management, 73-425 Hilltop Road, Desert Hot Springs, California 92240. ETHNO is distributed by National Collegiate Software of Duke University Press, 6697 College Station, Durham, North Carolina 27708. TAP is available through the Department of Sociology, Southern Methodist University, Dallas, Texas 75275. QUALOG, a mainframe program, is available from the School of Computer and Information Science, Syracuse University, 4-116 Center for Science and Technology, Syracuse, New York 13244. Another mainframe system, NUDIST, is available from ACRI, La Trobe University, Bondoora, VIC 3083, Australia.

Other Tools

A contact summary form can be helpful as the evaluator begins analyzing the raw field notes. The form is a single sheet that contains a series of focusing or summarizing questions about a field contact (Miles and Huberman, 1984). To use it, an evaluator examines his or her field notes to see if there is anything of significance that should be briefly noted under each question on the summary form. The form identifies people, events, or situations; the main themes or issues in the contact; central evaluation questions addressed by the contact; new hypotheses or speculations suggested by the contact; and how the data collection should be tailored during the next contact.

Instead of using questions, the evaluator could design the contact summary form with main headers of important areas for the overall study. The form could then be used for interviews, direct observations, and document reviews. In the best practices study, field notes for each interview and collected documents were summarized in a contact summary form, using the categories shown in Exhibit 4.1.

Exhibit 4.1 shows a contact summary form with Document Summary as a final category. The evaluator can use this space or a separate document abstract for any document that looks significant to the evaluation (Miles and Huberman, 1984). Preparing an abstract increases the evaluator's awareness of the document's significance during analysis stages, especially when the amount of collected material might become overwhelming. A sample document abstract is shown in Exhibit 4.2, taken from the best practices study.

Planning ahead for handling the data is important; the evaluator should have tools such as formats and abstract forms designed before collecting any data. If interview transcript formats or document abstracts are to be used, they should be consistent across all sites and evaluators. If summaries are to be prepared or referenced, they should be consistent as well. A formal indexing and labeling system for all data might be developed, with data kept in separate files by topic or unit of analysis to serve as resource packages.

Exhibit 4.1. Contact Summary Form.

1. Strategic IRM[a] Performance Expectations
    Organizational outcome measures
    Information system input/output measures

2. Strategic IRM Determinants/Characteristics
    Environment/history of conditions
    Management attention
    IRM program placement and roles
    User empowerment and control
    Technical infrastructure and development
    Establishment of overall goals/framework for IRM
    Reputation of IRM function
    Champions
    Formal IRM planning methodologies
    Linkage other management control/incentive processes

3. Oversight Policies and Practices
    Legislative changes
    Central management agencies

4. Other Comments

5. Document Summary

[a]information resources management

Exhibit 4.2. Document Abstract.

Document: Computer Services Strategic Planning Structure, 8/21/92
Source: Computer Services Manager

Content: The document is a single-sheet model of the planning structure, including a vision statement, business philosophy, and business direction. Each area is defined, with actual language provided. The business direction includes objectives, goals, and tactics. The vision includes a one-sentence statement for Computer Services as well as the use of critical success factors. The business philosophy includes mission, policies, and principles. According to those interviewed, this framework has been very useful in guiding decision making and explicitly defines the components for strategic planning that organizational officials feel is important. This might be a good example to use as a model for the study.

The labels for the files might match the data categories that are being developed as the analysis proceeds. Using the contact summary form in Exhibit 4.1 as an example, a category, called Planning Methodologies might be added. Critical documents can be photocopied and kept with the resource package. If a key focus of the evaluation is a topic such as information technology planning instructions, any instructions should be pulled or copied and kept with the resource packages that will be used for analysis stages.

While narrative text is most often used in analysis, matrices, graphs, networks, and charts are also useful. Such graphic illustrations can supplement text, condensing and expediting the presentation of supporting detail (Wolcott, 1986). Creating and using data displays are also a part of data analysis in that their creation and interpretation involve analysis choices.

Data displays can be initially designed based on interview questions or the data categories coded into field notes or used in summaries. Frequently the evaluator prepares table shells for specific arrays of data (Yin, 1984). Table shells force the evaluator to identify explicitly the data collection boundaries; they can ensure that the same information is collected at different sites by different evaluators. Done correctly, they also assist in data analysis as the evaluator should choose categories for the shell that are important for the overall evaluation.

In the best practices study, the environment for strategic information resources management was an area the evaluator would emphasize in the final report. A data display table for one set of interviews in an organization could highlight which organizational actors mentioned which environmental factors, as shown in Table 4.3.

Table 4.3. Format Example.

Organization: Agency A	Level of Managers Mentioning the Factor		
Environmental Factor	Top	Mid-Level	IRM[a]
Funding limitations	X	X	X
IT[b] to replace personnel	X	X	
Key managers push IT solutions		X	X
Legislative push for better IT management	X		X
Crises regarding IT use or lack of use	X		
Staff computer literacy		X	
New agency leadership		X	X
Strong central management agency push	X		

[a]information resources management
[b]information technology

In interpreting the data array shown in Table 4.3, the evaluator should be able to identify the environmental factors that appear to affect all three types of managers as well as those that have a less consistent effect. Subsequent analysis may attempt to discover which environmental factors appear to be more important than others.

Comparing Across Cases

For the most part, the examples discussed to this point have not dealt with comparisons across cases. Yin (1984) describes case studies as being either explanatory, descriptive, or exploratory. With an explanatory purpose, a case study is designed to test and explain causal links in real-life programs whose complexity cannot be captured by a survey or experimental approach. For descriptive purposes, a case study can be used to describe the real-life context where a program takes place. It can also illustrate or describe the program itself. Finally, a case study can also be exploratory. A program may have no clear set of outcomes, and a case study approach can help identify performance measures or pose hypotheses for further evaluative work.

In many qualitative studies, individual case studies form the basis for an overall explanation, description, or exploration of what is under study. In the best practices study, information was drawn from eighteen case studies to illustrate best practices in the overall report. Integrating the data across the case studies is often the hardest part of the analysis. To make this task easier, care study summaries should use exactly the same categories across all cases. With uniform organization, these summaries of all data sources— interviews, observations, and documents—present the data so patterns can be spotted and differences examined.

Agranoff and Radin (1991) stressed the importance of such uniformity in their discussion of comparative case research methodology in public administration. They emphasized "formulating" the cases as an important step, involving the development of a preliminary case study and cross-case analysis outlines. Certain information must be gathered from all case study sites, reflected in a discussion guide. This technique is similar to the "areas of coverage" method discussed in the best practices example above. Each case is written in a common format, corresponding to the outline. Then each outline issue area can be analyzed across the sites.

In the best practices study, the headers for organizing the field notes into categories, shown in an earlier section, were used for developing case study outlines and the overall case study analysis framework. Document abstract information, evaluator field observations, and the interview field notes were inserted into the subcategories under the major categories of strategic IRM performance expectations, strategic IRM determinants and characteristics, oversight policies and practices, and miscellaneous. Information for each case study was placed in the same format. Then, the analysis across the cases used the subcategories as topic areas. For analysis of this type, tables and matrices showing cross-site data can be very effective.

Drawing and Verifying Conclusions

From the start of data collection, the evaluator interprets the data and formulates patterns and themes to summarize the information. Conclusions are verified, revised, or discarded as data collection, analysis, and interpretation proceed. As with quantitative evaluation, qualitative evaluators must describe the checks and balances, decision rules, and other design and implementation features of their work to bolster the consumer's confidence in the findings.

Problems That Impact Confidence

While "being there" is a very powerful technique for enhancing the credibility of evaluation findings (Babbie, 1989), qualitative evaluation measurements generally are very personal and reflect the evaluator's perceptions, values, and professional training. A human instrument is prone to errors such as inaccurate observation, believing a few similar events show evidence of a general pattern, and selectively observing behaviors and interactions that correspond to a pattern the evaluator believes exists. Generalizability is a problem as other evaluators may not replicate the first investigator's results. There is also the potential for biased sampling.

Quantitative evaluation has prescriptions for validity, reliability, generalizability, and objectivity; similar constraints are applied to qualitative evaluation. The most-cited work regarding qualitative data reliability and validity is that of Lincoln and Guba (1985), who state that qualitative evaluation criteria should speak to the trustworthiness of the evaluation findings. Their evaluation criteria are "truth value" (similar to internal validity), applicability (external validity and generalizability), consistency (reliability), and neutrality (objectivity). Lincoln and Guba (1985) explain each criterion in terms of what it emphasizes.

Internal Validity. Truth value or internal validity emphasizes credibility. It asks evaluators to establish confidence in the "truth" of the evaluation findings, as viewed through the eyes of those being observed or interviewed, and the context in which the evaluation was carried out.

Applicability. Applicability — or generalizability or external validity — emphasizes transferability. Evaluators look at how well their findings can be transferred to similar situations. The central notion is that for findings to be transferred, the contexts must be similar. Evaluators should help the reader fully understand the context in which the findings occurred and determine the extent to which the evaluation findings are applicable to other contexts or with other subjects.

Consistency. Consistency or reliability emphasizes dependability. The evaluator needs to take into account any factors that may affect the replicability of the evaluation, that is, having the same evaluation findings if the evaluation were done again with the same (or similar) subjects. Thus, the evaluation should dependably produce similar findings with similar cases.

Neutrality. Last, neutrality or objectivity emphasizes confirmability. Evaluators need to provide evidence that corroborates the data. The evidence should come from the subjects and the evaluation conditions, not from the biases, motivations, interests, or perspectives of the evaluator.

Strategies to Improve the Credibility of Findings

Following are suggestions for improving the credibility of evaluation findings. These include documentation of sampling decisions, evaluation team selection, interview strategies, site effects, triangulation efforts, data collection organization and analysis, evidence weighting, rival explanation efforts, replication activities, debriefings, documentation plans, external audits, and conclusion drawing efforts.

Sampling Strategies. First, the evaluation design should ensure that the sampling strategies are appropriate for the evaluation questions. Sampling involves decisions about which people to observe or interview and what settings, events, and social processes to investigate (Miles and Huberman, 1984). Sampling procedures should be specified clearly at the time of the preliminary evaluation research design. However, the sampling strategy can be changed in the course of the study if that is appropriate.

Whether changed from the initial sample plan or not, the purpose of the sample should always be kept in mind when the sampling strategy is selected. Several strategies are possible—convenience, purposeful, and probability sampling (Patton, 1987; U.S. General Accounting Office, 1987).

In *convenience sampling,* ease of data collection and the minimal use of resources are most important. For example, an evaluator may choose field sites to study that are geographically close to his or her office. Using this strategy, the evaluator's findings can speak only to the sites selected and are severely limited in applicability to other sites. It is the least desirable way to sample.

Purposeful sampling is a second major sampling strategy. The basis for sample selection is the search for settings, events, and processes directly derived from the evaluation questions. There is a "purpose" for selecting the cases, which can be of several types. One is selecting on the basis of extreme or deviant cases. This sampling selects extreme instances that are unusual or special. For example, the purposeful sampling strategy might bracket cases at the extremes and see what the differences are between the extremes. Or it might select the best cases or the worst cases using some relevant criterion for ranking the cases. The purpose of an evaluation of best cases might be to find out what might account for an effective program. A sample of worst cases might ask why a program is not effective in those instances.

Cluster selections are a second type of purposeful sampling that allows comparison of different types of programs. Samples of particular subgroups representing different program operations are selected for comparison, such as a sample of programs administered by contractors and a sample run by government employees.

Maximum variation purposeful sampling selects instances that represent a wide variation in setting, event, and process. The evaluator looks for common patterns that describe central themes or outcomes. The significance of the evaluation findings comes from the variation of what is under study. An evaluator interested in program operations according to size might select a sample of program sites with maximum variation in the number of participants served.

Typical case sampling, another type of purposeful sampling, examines instances that appear to be the norm. The evaluator might choose to study a number of program sites where funding levels, staffing patterns, and program participant profile are considered typical of a specific program.

Snowball or chain sampling is an additional way to do purposeful sampling. The evaluator relies on informants who point out cases that are central to what is under study. For example, an advisory group might initially be asked to provide names of individuals who should be interviewed regarding a policy issue. Those individuals in turn might provide references to others very knowledgeable about the issue.

Last, purposeful sampling can involve selecting cases that meet a special interest criterion or that are politically important. For example, any study of major federal information systems might have to include the Social Security Administration or the Internal Revenue Service given the scale of their information systems and their impact on huge federal programs. Other special interest selections might come after a study is under way and patterns are starting to emerge. The evaluator might consciously select cases that either do or do not fit the emerging patterns, trying to test preliminary findings. Here the evaluator might be looking for confirmatory cases that more fully describe or enrich initial patterns. Or he or she looks for cases that do not appear to fit the pattern and likely are the sources of alternative explanations or provide boundaries to what the evaluator can claim.

The final sampling strategy is *probability* or *random sampling,* where all members of the population under study have an opportunity to be selected as a case. The evaluator would select cases by techniques such as the use of a random number table.

Regardless of the sampling strategies used, the evaluator should be alert for overreliance on accessible and elite informants who might not be representative of events or activities and consequently would not be a good sample of respondents for data collection and analysis purposes. Knowledgeable leaders and experts may be reluctant to express to relative strangers views that could be taken as critical (Van Sant, 1989). They may not represent more isolated informants or they may overrepresent certain elite interests. The evaluator should also not overly weigh dramatic events, because the events may not be typical. The evaluator should always take great care when drawing inferences from the interactions, behaviors, and processes that they observe (Miles and Huberman, 1984).

The evaluator can try to overcome these overreliance problems by increasing the number of cases sampled, sorting the cases by key criteria to learn whether sampling is weak, and adopting probability or random sampling strategies. Evaluators should identify the most appropriate informants by consulting key participants, reviewing relevant documents, and asking for suggestions from other observers (Silverman, Ricci, and Gunter, 1990). Multisite sampling will ensure that several settings are examined and can provide enough variability to increase the explanatory power of a study if the purpose is explanation (Miles and Huberman, 1984). Using multiple-site samples, of course, can give evaluators more confidence in describing events within a particular program operated across sites. Moreover, such data collection and analysis can speak to programs operating in different regions and settings and at different points in their life cycles.

Selecting an Evaluation Team. Evaluator bias and interpretation can be troublesome during analysis of ongoing data collection (Babbie, 1989). Interpreting data according to an evaluator's own point of view, drawing hasty conclusions, coming up with questionable causes, suppressing the evidence, and picking out one position that may rule out another are dangers. These bias and interpretation errors can occur at an early stage just as easily as at later more intensive data analysis stages. For example, a well-stated, "juicy" quote the evaluator wants to use may not reflect overall themes in the data, or may be relevant to only a minor issue. An evaluator should make sure that quotes come from a wide range of informant sources, not only from those informants who state the issues particularly well. Using a well-selected evaluation team can help to reduce these errors and is the second strategy suggested for improving credibility.

If an evaluation team is used, the planner and administrator should look at the team's composition, characteristics, and training (Silverman, Ricci, and Gunter, 1990). If a single evaluator or evaluation team shares a common discipline, then there is no internal control for possible bias. Multidisciplinary teams can bring different perspectives. The process of reconciling those perspectives can strengthen the completeness and accuracy of the findings.

Field debriefings among the team are also helpful. Here, evaluators review interviews and examine other data to identify different perceptions and develop themes from the data as they reconcile the differences. In addition, interview content is shared so that the team has holistic knowledge of all data collection at one time and keeps the larger picture in mind. In the best practices study, the development of an initial "findings" outline with examples from the first pilot studies was especially helpful. As other case studies were completed, the outline was revisited and revised, with new examples added or categories of analysis changed. This dynamic outline helped all team members to know the status of data collection at any given time and allowed for a testing of preliminary findings as the research proceeded.

Taking efforts to have raw data recoded and reanalyzed is another helpful technique to combat evaluator bias. Evaluators coding the same data set can discuss their differences and difficulties, ultimately producing sharper coding definitions (Miles and Huberman, 1984). Having the same evaluator recode material and another evaluator independently code the same material can increase the accuracy of the coding. In the best practices study, two-person teams conducted all interviews. The person responsible for the transcription of the interviews sent the transcription to the other team member for collaboration and verification. Categorization of field notes into the case study outline was also verified.

Interview Strategies. Careful interview strategies are a third way to improve the trustworthiness of the evaluation findings. First, the interview format should be flexible (Lofland and Lofland, 1984). The evaluator should have a list of mandatory questions but must recognize they may not come in the order listed nor be asked in exactly the same way as originally phrased.

The evaluator should not ask leading questions that will give the respondent clues to a preferable answer. Whether taping, writing notes, or both, the evaluator must be alert to what the respondent is saying, and think about probes necessary for further explication or clarification. The interview probes must link the current discussion to what has already been said. Moreover, the evaluator has to think about what new questions should be posed given the current data collection effort. The interviewer must constantly ask about his or her own perceptions: Am I hearing this accurately? Is the respondent providing an accurate account? Is it internally consistent? Does it fit in with what other respondents have said? (Lofland and Lofland, 1984).

The use of multiple interviewers either in tandem or singly in questioning key informants is one strategy to increase the likelihood of obtaining more comprehensive and accurate information. It also increases the possibility of obtaining varying perspectives for data collection and analysis (Silverman, Ricci, and Gunter, 1990). Since key informant data are critical, using more than one interviewer allows the comparison of the perceptions and interpretations of several members of the evaluation team. Key informants can be reinterviewed to cross-check other sources, ensure full coverage of topics, or prioritize or emphasize specific issues.

Site Effects. The evaluator can affect the site and the site can affect the evaluator, both cause for concern in producing accurate findings. Evaluator and site effects can be combatted in various ways, which constitute the fourth strategy for improving the trustworthiness of the evaluation. These include having low-key prolonged observation, using unobtrusive measures, and ensuring that informants know clearly the reasons for the evaluation and how data will be used. An informant can be used to reflect on the evaluator's influence on the site. The evaluator can get away from the site by conducting interviews and reviewing documents off-site.

Triangulation. The evaluator can build in triangulation techniques as a fifth strategy for increasing credibility. Triangulation is the combining of methods, data sources, and other factors in examining what is under study. Triangulation of multiple and different sources of information, methods, and theories is used to strengthen data collection and analysis and is normally categorized in three different ways (Kidder and Fine, 1987). One is triangulation of measurement, when evaluators use more than one method (qualitative or quantitative) to describe the unit of analysis. For example, structured questionnaires can probe for responses to match against the results of unstructured interviews or participant observation. Content analysis of documents can be compared with information from other sources. Triangulation also can be used in examining conclusions within a study, when different measurements produce the same results or patterns or different informants give the same account. Triangulation of conclusions across studies that used different methods can also be done.

Congruence and/or complementarity of results from each method is the goal of triangulation. Congruence is defined as similarity, consistency, or convergence of results, while complementarity refers to one set of results expanding upon, clarifying, or illustrating the other. If done properly, triangulation should rely on independent assessments with offsetting kinds of bias and measurement error. Using multiple sources of evidence is one of Yin's (1984) principles of data collection.

However, there are some cautions on various types of data gathering and their analysis that speak to multiple sources of information (Van Sant, 1989). Mentioned earlier was the problem of overrelying on key informants. The review of documentation, such as written records or reports, can greatly facilitate communications between the evaluator and local informants. However, the documents generally do not provide much information on priorities or actual behavior. They also can be incomplete or inaccurate, or be a biased recording of behavior. Observation is also subject to considerable risk of misinterpretation and may be most useful as a supplement to other methods of data gathering.

Organized Data Collection and Consistent Analysis. A sixth way to improve evaluation credibility is to ensure rigor in data collection organization and consistent analysis. The completeness and accuracy of field notes and consistency in coding cannot be overemphasized. The use of similar research protocols is recommended, especially when multiple evaluators are used in multiple sites (Silverman, Ricci, and Gunter, 1990). For example, each case study should follow the same topical outline. Field notes should be organized into consistent categories.

Evidence Weighting. The seventh strategy is for the evaluator to consider weighting the evidence, that is, to give stronger data more weight in the findings or discard or downplay weak data (Miles and Huberman, 1984). Stronger data are those that come from knowledgeable informants, are collected later or after repeated contact, are seen or reported firsthand, are observed behavior or activities, are collected where the field worker is trusted, are collected in official or informal settings, are volunteered to the evaluator, or are collected when a respondent is alone with the evaluator. Stronger data also can be validated by other sources for accuracy or quality.

Rival Explanations. The evaluation research design should ensure considerable rigor in drawing contrasts and comparisons, the eighth way to improve the trustworthiness of the evaluation. The evaluator might look for rival or competing themes or explanations. Negative case analysis is the active search for and examination of cases that do not fit the pattern that appears to be emerging in the evaluation. Negative case analysis looks specifically for data that will not confirm whatever the evaluator has put forth as tentative findings (Popper, 1959). Negative instances force the qualitative evaluator to revise the findings to account for negative cases, thus clarifying the boundaries and meanings of the primary pattern emerging in the evaluation findings.

Using extreme cases may also help to verify and confirm conclusions and may serve as a way to explore key factors and variables. The evaluator might also look for other ways to organize the data or raise new questions that might result in different conclusions (Patton, 1987). He or she should look for other logical possibilities and data that might support alternative explanations.

Replication. Ninth, the evaluator should build in replication, if at all possible, to improve the trustworthiness of the evaluation findings. Replication means considering multiple cases as one would consider multiple experiments. Each case must be selected so that it either predicts similar results, called a literal replication, or produces contrary results but for predictable reasons, a theoretical replication (Yin, 1984). The evaluator should develop a theoretical framework that states the conditions under which a particular phenomenon might be found (a literal replication) and the conditions when it likely would not be found (a theoretical replication). The framework becomes the vehicle for generalizing to new cases, similar to cross-experimental designs.

There should be no random error discrepancies or variance (Fielding and Fielding, 1986). Hypotheses are revised until all the data fit. Where information is available from a number of independent cases, each extra case provides another observation to probe the hypotheses. In single case studies, each additional bit of information provides another instance to probe the hypotheses. There should be multiple instances of a particular construct that address validity and reliability, akin to repeated quantitative measurements. The evaluator should provide a very rich description or database if someone wants to look at the applicability or transfer of the findings to another setting (Yin, 1984; Lincoln and Guba, 1985).

Debriefings and Feedback. Tenth, any qualitative evaluation should use peer debriefing and informant feedback for corroboration of the findings, another way to improve the trustworthiness of the evaluation. Evaluators recommend having a reputable person or persons examine the evaluation findings in a devil's advocate mode (Lincoln and Guba, 1985; Miles and Huberman, 1984). The peer debriefer should be knowledgeable about what is being evaluated and the methods being used. Using a peer debriefer during the data collection and analysis can introduce rival explanations and help narrow the findings to the explanation that is most compelling. Informant feedback is also valuable (Miles and Huberman, 1984; Wolcott, 1986; Lincoln and Guba, 1985; Silverman, Ricci, and Gunter, 1990; Yin, 1984). This method should be used carefully during data collection so that bias is not introduced among informants.

A better way may be to wait until the findings are more complete and supported and then ask for feedback, which can be pursued more systematically at that time. Reviewers to provide feedback should be selected from stakeholder groups and from local settings, and should represent different perspectives. A common approach is to use an advisory committee that can review draft material and provide comments.

Documentation. An eleventh way to increase the trustworthiness of the evaluation findings is to document fully the evaluation process, analytical methods, and findings as if an auditor or other evaluator will review them. Documentation becomes one way to judge the rigor of the evaluation steps and subsequent findings.

The creation of a case study database of notes, documents, tabular materials, and well-cited narratives that other evaluators can access directly is one strong documentation approach (Yin, 1984). The database assists in maintaining a chain of evidence that allows an external observer to follow the data collection, analysis, and interpretation from the initial evaluation questions to the final conclusions and back again. Important reference materials should be archived for later review (Miles and Huberman, 1984).

Field notes become important as a reliability check (Kirk and Miller, 1986). Normally the same evaluator collects the data and prepares the analysis, but often he or she does not explain the field methodologies used in the collecting. Field notes that fail to describe the context of the data collection may not be intelligible to others. Evaluators should provide extensive, explicit, and perceptive field notes and self-analytical reporting of evaluation procedures and contexts. Sources should be documented, as should the bases for inferences and the evaluator's theories.

Systematic bias in data collection can be combatted by making methods accessible to ongoing critique and using sources of the most varied quality (Fielding and Fielding, 1986). The trustworthiness of field workers rests on the clarity and persuasiveness of the instances used to support their conclusions, and how well those conclusions coincide with other knowledge they and the evaluation's audience possess (Kidder and Fine, 1987).

External Evaluation Audit. Twelfth, the actual use of an auditor to examine the evaluation process and the product is proposed by Lincoln and Guba (1985) to increase the trustworthiness of the evaluation findings. An external evaluation audit reviews the methodological steps and substantive and analytic decisions made during the evaluation. The auditor looks for adherence to professional standards, soundness of logic and judgment, and defensibility (Greene and others, 1988; Whitmore and Ray, 1989).

The person auditing would examine data logs, the category system for analyzing and synthesizing the data, and the findings and the conclusions. The audit attempts to determine whether the findings and conclusions are grounded in the data, the inferences are logical, the rules put forth for categorizing were followed, and the category system has general utility. The auditor would require a complete audit trail of documentation, methods used, and analytic decisions.

Audit guidelines should be prepared as part of the evaluation strategy. When an audit is planned, the evaluator should maintain, organize, and review the audit trail materials during the evaluation rather than at the end. Such steps help identify methodological shortcomings and information gaps that can be corrected during the study, strengthening the audit's internal quality control. The auditor should examine all evaluation components to assess overall methods and procedures, and to obtain a more holistic understanding of the entire study.

Conclusion Drawing. The last way suggested to increase credibility of an evaluation is for the evaluator to be careful in the final interpretation and description of the data. The end result of data collection and analysis is drawing conclusions. In his or her interpretation, the evaluator considers causes, consequences, and relationships (Patton, 1987). While qualitative evaluation typically does not test causal linkages, the evaluator does talk about effects and outcomes as part of data-based speculation, conjecture, and hypothesizing.

Conclusion

Qualitative evaluation can have many applications (Guba, 1987). The evaluation can be exploratory when one is reviewing areas that are hard to conceptualize and attempting to establish foundations for more rigorous examination. The evaluation can be descriptive in providing "thick descriptions" of contextual information to support quantitative findings. It can be illustrative in providing examples for findings at a general level or providing anecdotal, real information. Qualitative evaluation can also be testing in that it tests possible hypotheses that an evaluator would pose ahead of the investigation.

Regardless of the application, description and interpretation in qualitative evaluation have to match (Wolcott, 1986). If the descriptive account is thin because the data are thin, that limitation has to be acknowledged. Extensive field notes and fieldwork experience can provide concrete illustrations and examples to reach the reader and support the evaluator's interpretations. Illustrations in figures, tables, and quotations should be purposefully used to support interpretation. However, too many illustrations and examples can bury the reader in detail, obscuring the overall pattern the evaluator wants to highlight.

Qualitative evaluators should report "what is," but they are vulnerable to making pronouncements of what ought to be (Wolcott, 1986). The difficulty is that judgment is imposed when the evaluators describe what they see. Inferences that are grounded in the data require knowledge and arguments based on past successes, contextual experiences, established theories, and representative interpreters (Krippendorff, 1980).

Perhaps the best advice for drawing conclusions comes from Lofland and Lofland (1984). They say that reflection may be the best tactic. Here, the evaluator draws back from the evaluation project and reflects on the total process. Analysis and description should be in balance, with analysis not leaving out the rich description that provides the concrete reality of "being there." Conducting qualitative evaluations requires considerable expertise and insight to match the evaluation purpose to evaluation methods that will tease out trustworthy interpretations and conclusions. In the end, it is the human instrument element that remains in play, as the evaluator decides how the details of everyday life can be described and interpreted in ways that are credible to the audience.

References

Agar, M. H. *Speaking of Ethnography.* Qualitative Research Methods Series, no. 2. Newbury Park, Calif.: Sage, 1986.

Agranoff, R., and Radin, B. A. "The Comparative Case Study Approach in Public Administration." In J. L. Perry (ed.), *Research in Public Administration: A Research Annual.* Vol. 1. Greenwich, Conn.: JAI Press, 1991.

Babbie, E. *The Practice of Social Research.* (5th ed.) Belmont, Calif.: Wadsworth, 1989.

Fielding, N. G., and Fielding, J. L. *Linking Data.* Qualitative Research Methods Series, no. 4. Newbury Park, Calif.: Sage, 1986.

Greene, J. C., and others. "Qualitative Evaluation Audits in Practice." *Evaluation Review,* 1988, *12*(4), 352–375.

Guba, E. G. "Naturalistic Evaluation." In D. S. Cordray, H. S. Bloom, and R. J. Light (eds.), *Evaluation Practice in Review.* New Directions for Program Evaluation, no. 34. San Francisco: Jossey-Bass, 1987.

Gummesson, E. *Qualitative Methods in Management Research.* Newbury Park, Calif.: Sage, 1991.

Kidder, L. H., and Fine, M. "Qualitative and Quantitative Methods: When Stories Converge." In M. M. Mark and R. L. Shotland (eds.), *Multiple Methods in Program Evaluation.* New Directions for Program Evaluation, no. 35. San Francisco: Jossey-Bass, 1987.

Kirk, J., and Miller, M. L. *Reliability and Validity in Qualitative Research.* Qualitative Research Methods Series, no. 1. Newbury Park, Calif.: Sage, 1986.

Krippendorff, K. *Content Analysis: An Introduction to Its Methodology.* The Sage CommText Series, no. 5. Newbury Park, Calif.: Sage, 1980.

Lincoln, Y. S., and Guba, E. G. *Naturalistic Inquiry.* Newbury Park, Calif.: Sage, 1985.

Lofland, J., and Lofland, L. H. *Analyzing Social Settings: A Guide to Qualitative Observation and Analysis.* (2nd ed.) Belmont, Calif.: Wadsworth, 1984.

Miles, M. B., and Huberman, A. M. *Qualitative Data Analysis: A Sourcebook of New Methods.* Newbury Park, Calif.: Sage, 1984.

Miller, D. C. *Handbook of Research Design and Social Measurement.* (5th ed.) Newbury Park, Calif.: Sage, 1991.

Patton, M. Q. *Qualitative Evaluation Methods.* Newbury Park, Calif.: Sage, 1980.

Patton, M. Q. *How to Use Qualitative Methods in Evaluation.* Newbury Park, Calif.: Sage, 1987.

Pfaffenberger, B. *Microcomputer Applications in Qualitative Research.* Qualitative Research Methods Series, no. 14. Newbury Park, Calif.: Sage, 1988.

Popper, K. R. *The Logic of Scientific Discovery.* London: Hutchinson, 1959.

Posavac, E. J., and Carey, R. G. *Program Evaluation: Methods and Case Studies.* (3rd ed.) Englewood Cliffs, N.J.: Prentice-Hall, 1989.

Silverman, M., Ricci, E. M., and Gunter, M. J. "Strategies for Increasing the Rigor of Qualitative Methods in Evaluation of Health Care Programs." *Evaluation Review,* 1990, *14*(1), 57–74.

Tesch, R. *Qualitative Research: Analysis Types and Software Tools.* New York: Falmer Press, 1990.

U.S. General Accounting Office, Program Evaluation and Methodology Division. *Case Study Evaluations.* Transfer Paper no. 9. Washington, D.C.: U.S. General Accounting Office, 1987.

Van Maanen, J. "Introduction." In J. Van Maanen, J. M. Dabbs, Jr., and R. R. Faulkner (eds.), *Varieties of Qualitative Research.* Studying Organizations: Innovations in Methodology, no. 5. Newbury Park, Calif.: Sage, 1982.

Van Sant, J. "Qualitative Analysis in Development Evaluations." *Evaluation Review,* 1989, *13*(3), 257–272.

Whitmore, E., and Ray, M. L. "Qualitative Evaluation Audits: Continuation of the Discussion." *Evaluation Review,* 1989, *13*(1), 78–90.

Wolcott, H. F. *Writing Up Qualitative Research.* Qualitative Research Methods Series, no. 20. Newbury Park, Calif.: Sage, 1986.

Yin, R. K. *Case Study Research: Design and Methods.* Applied Social Research Methods Series. Vol. 5. Newbury Park, Calif.: Sage, 1984.

5

Outcome Monitoring

Dennis P. Affholter

The routine and periodic monitoring of outcomes is an important development in the evolution of performance monitoring systems. Outcome monitoring requires the *routine* measurement and reporting of *important indicators of* (or related to) *outcome-oriented results.* It grows out of the continuing quest for accountability from governments (Carter, 1983; Fitz-Gibbon, 1990; Brizius and Campbell, 1991; U.S. General Accounting Office, 1992), an ancestry shared with public-management initiatives such as Total Quality Management (Sensenbrenner, 1991; Appenzeller, 1992). Outcome monitoring draws from work in public administration and management as well as program evaluation.

Many evaluation classics contain little or no reference to monitoring, and when they do, it is to something other than outome monitoring. For example, in *Creative Evaluation* Patton makes no reference to monitoring, but he notes that program staff are "often overlooked" as a "resource for data collection" (1987, p. 210). Cronbach's and colleagues' *Toward Reform of Program Evaluation* also is silent on monitoring in program evaluation, despite the observation that "evaluation ought to inform and improve the operations of the social system" (1980, p. 66). Rossi and Freeman, in *Evaluation: A Systematic Approach,* devote an entire chapter to program monitoring, but their treatment excludes the monitoring of outcomes: "monitoring [focuses on whether] (1) . . . the program [reaches] the . . . target population, and (2) . . . the delivery of services [complies] with program design" (1982, p. 123). Carter, in contrast, devotes the penultimate chapter in *The Accountable Agency* (1983) to this topic, entitling it "How to Develop an Outcome Monitoring System."

Outcome monitoring is a useful and important tool for stakeholders, including program managers and evaluators. Wholey and Hatry (1992, p. 604) argue that we need "performance-oriented program management" with

96

"[r]egular monitoring of service quality and program outcomes." The National Academy of Public Administration (1991, p. 2) notes that "government at all levels should . . . encourage agency heads . . . to monitor program quality and outcomes," recommending that public officials build and use outcome monitoring systems.

This chapter begins with a closer look at what outcome monitoring is, in contrast to other forms of monitoring. It goes on to the question of why outcome monitoring should be done, including examples of the benefits or potential that can be realized from the use of outcome monitoring systems. Design issues for outcome monitoring are taken up next. The chapter ends with pitfalls to be expected.

What Is Outcome Monitoring?

Outcome monitoring is the regular (periodic, frequent) reporting of program results in ways that stakeholders can use to understand and judge those results. The indicators measured should have some validity, some meaning that is closely tied to performance expectations. The ways in which they are reported should also have utility, that is, they must be easily interpreted and focus attention on the key points.

Other Forms of Monitoring

Monitoring often means site visits by experts (auditors, evaluators, program specialists, or analysts) for compliance-focused reviews of program operations. Such monitoring relies heavily on reviews of records and interviews with staff, supervisors, and sometimes clients. This kind of monitoring typically produces an evaluative report, often with action plans intended to remedy procedure deficiencies that are found. *Outcome monitoring should not be viewed as "monitoring" in this sense.* Outcome monitoring is outcome-focused or results-oriented; it is built into the routines of data reporting within program operations; it provides frequent and public feedback on performance; and it is not explanatory in itself, nor does it produce corrective action plans.

Other forms of monitoring measure important facets of program operations, especially when a new program or a demonstration project is being implemented. These may be reports, for instance, on inputs (the numbers of clients served, contracts let, or staff hired), on process (the number of police cars on patrol), or on outputs (the numbers of classes completed, miles of highway paved, or numbers of cases closed). Such performance monitoring often is essential, but without measures of outcome-oriented results, it is *not* outcome monitoring.

These more typical forms of program monitoring lack an outcome focus. They do not measure and report the results of the work performed. Examples of outcome-oriented performance measures, expressed as percentages or in some other standard or comparable form, are shown in Exhibit 5.1.

Exhibit 5.1. Examples of Outcome Measures.

The percentage of students who obtain a high school diploma or General Educational Development (GED) diploma; graduation rates.

The percentage of those served who achieve a certain level of skills, attitudes, or knowledge; the average change observed in those measures.

The percentage of those served who demonstrate specified, intended behavioral results (frequency, duration, and/or intensity) at a program's conclusion; the percentage who maintain those behaviors for some specified time after completing the program.

The average travel time and frequency or severity of accidents on an improved or newly constructed road.

The average lengths of stay in out-of-home placements; the percentage of those placed whose lengths of stay exceed policy standards.

Recidivism and suppression rates for criminal rehabilitation programs; re-abuse or re-neglect rates within a specified time after completing remedial service interventions.

Disruption rates within a specified follow-up period for families reunified after a child or children were removed because of abuse or neglect; adoption disruption rates within a specified period of time following adoption placement; proportions of foster care cases closed as adoption placements and those closed as reunifications.

The percentage of job training clients who are placed at or above specified wage levels or in jobs for which they were trained; the average or median wage at placement; the percentage who maintain employment at or above their placement wages for a specified period of time following placement.

Payment error rates in cash assistance, reimbursement, or insurance programs; rates of recovery of payments made in error.

Infant mortality and morbidity rates; age-adjusted death rates from specific causes (for programs designed to avoid, reduce, or ameliorate those causes).

Average birth weights or indicators of developmental risk at and shortly after birth, such as Apgar scores.

Outcome monitoring should not be confused, however, with program or outcome evaluation. Like program evaluation, outcome monitoring focuses on outcomes or results, and many of the skills that evaluators bring to their work are highly relevant to the design and use of outcome monitoring systems. Further, program evaluations often use outcome monitoring and other program monitoring data. Program evaluation, however, extends beyond the tracking and reporting of program outcomes into examination of the extent to which and the ways in which outcomes are caused by the program. Outcome monitoring is not explanatory. It cannot replace program evaluations.

Outcome monitoring should help key stakeholders better understand a program's outcomes and, therefore, help to target the use of resources for further evaluation work. Alone, the results of outcome monitoring can direct managers' attention to particular performance problems (something or somewhere not working as it should) as well as to specific performance opportunities (something or somewhere working more effectively than expected).

Outcome monitoring can direct other stakeholders' attention to specific areas (program as well as geographic targets) for their analysis and advocacy work.

An Analogy: Monitoring Personal Health Risk

Blood pressure and cholesterol readings cannot tell us everything we need to know about our risk of heart disease or how we should act to change that risk. When our blood pressure or cholesterol readings sound the alert, however, they focus our attention and energy on additional diagnostic steps needed to determine whether (or what) corrective actions may be required. Even without an alert, our attention to blood pressure and cholesterol levels often prompts behavioral changes: we may quit smoking, develop an exercise regimen, choose more carefully the foods we eat and how we prepare them. And so it is with outcome monitoring. When necessary, the measures or indicators reported may sound an alert, calling for further diagnosis and possible action. Even without an alert, though, outcome monitoring often induces improvements to agency performance.

The next section takes up the imperative for and the organizational benefits of outcome monitoring.

Why Do Outcome Monitoring?

To the question of why outcome monitoring should be done, the answer to some is self-evident: outcome monitoring keeps those who are responsible (and others who are interested) apprised of performance. Growing demands for results-oriented accountability require that program managers and policymakers develop and use outcome monitoring systems. Beyond this accountability mandate, however, managers and other stakeholders see other benefits from outcome monitoring. These include the following:

- The early detection and correction of performance problems as well as detection of opportunities for performance improvement
- The mobilization of widespread commitment to continuous improvement in performance
- More efficient uses of other organizational support resources
- Gains in confidence in the organization's ability to perform

After a look at the mandate for accountability, these other benefits of outcome monitoring are examined.

The Accountability Mandate

According to Brizius and Campbell (1991, p. 1), "what sets today's emphasis on public accountability apart is the part of the message involving *proof.*" Local, state, and national legislatures increasingly demand accountability for results, in response to widespread skepticism concerning governmental effectiveness.

For the past decade, American politicians at all levels have taken aim at poor performance in our public schools, giving birth to many different schemes for educational accountability. This focus on educational performance is not limited to the American political landscape; Fitz-Gibbon (1990) brings together a wide variety of perspectives on "performance indicators" for local educational agencies in Great Britain. And the educational performance initiatives in the United States are not limited to the kindergarten through twelfth grade (K–12) public school system.

The North Carolina community college system identifies and reports on "critical success factors," which helps the state board to set priorities for program improvements (North Carolina, 1991). The state's General Assembly adopted this approach to monitoring performance (including outcomes) in 1989, linked to certain decentralizing initiatives, as a way to maintain state-level accountability for results. The community college system's business plan for the 1991–1993 biennium includes measures and targets linked to those critical success factors. A sound outcome monitoring system is required to satisfy the demand for accountability for results.

Demands for results-oriented accountability extend beyond public education. In 1991, after five years of experience in one program area, the Florida Legislature required that its human services umbrella agency, the Department of Health and Rehabilitative Services, establish outcome monitoring systems (Florida Statutes, 20.19(18); Florida, 1991a). The Florida law speaks to "outcome evaluation," with an emphasis on annual reporting of outcomes for clients in most of the department's programs. The legislation calls for "the continuous flow of client-outcome information," and requires that "client-outcome measures [be included in] all contracts entered into by the department [for] the provision of services." Specific types of performance measures are required as well, including measures of successful program completion and recidivism-like measures of longer-term results. Many other states report growing demands for outcome-oriented accountability in their human services agencies and programs (Florida, 1989).

The U.S. Congress also wants greater accountability for results from investments of federal funds. The Chief Financial Officers Act of 1990 (P.L. 101-576) gives certain performance measurement responsibilities to the Office of Management and Budget (OMB); this act also creates the position of chief financial officer in twenty-three large agencies, and it requires (among other things) that each develop systematic measures of agency performance. The proposed "Government Performance and Results Act" (S. 20, sponsored by Senators John Glenn and William Roth) would, if enacted, require that federal programs establish within the budget itself outcome-oriented performance goals and annually report on program performance. Senator Glenn, chairman of the U.S. Senate Governmental Affairs Committee, requested of the U.S. General Accounting Office (GAO) an assessment of the current state of program performance measurement in federal agencies. The U.S. GAO report (1992, p. 11) concluded that although many agencies use a wide variety of measures to manage operations, few use such measures to manage for results: "most of the agencies . . . used measures to provide internal information relating to their past activities or present operations" instead of results or outcomes.

The Governmental Accounting Standards Board (GASB) also is promoting the measurement and reporting of outcomes, which along with outputs GASB considers to be "accomplishment" indicators. According to Hatry and Fountain (1990, p. 44), "The project team believes *it is now important for governmental entities to experiment widely with external reporting of [service effort and accomplishment] indicators*" (emphasis in original). This GASB project team proposed outcome measures in twelve service areas, from which to begin experimentation and further development.

Directed Performance Improvements

Outcome monitoring gives program managers a tool for making more efficient use of their resources. The essence of continuous quality improvement is the focused diagnosis of barriers to better performance, followed by the design of alternatives to remove or circumvent those barriers, the implementation of trials to test those alternatives, and finally the expansion of successful efforts to raise performance levels while shrinking variability in performance. Effective outcome monitoring focuses attention on higher payoff efforts for quality improvement.

When particular programs, contractors, or work units consistently show either better-than-typical or poorer-than-typical performance, public officials can focus on identifying explanations for those specific findings. Outcome monitoring tells them where to begin to look. When warranted, remedial action can improve the outcomes. More successful operations can provide a basis—grounded in operational reality—for expansion or for systemwide improvements. Recommendations, that is, need not come from outside experts or headquarters, who may be viewed as detached from reality and therefore dismissed by those in the field.

Example: Crisis Intervention Services

Many states buy crisis intervention services. The concept is to identify and help families where child abuse or neglect has occurred as a result of a temporary crisis. Florida began an Intensive Crisis Counseling Program (ICCP) as a demonstration in one site more than ten years ago. Under contract, professional counselors enter the home and work intensively with the family for relatively short periods to resolve the crisis, to remove the risk of subsequent or continued abuse or neglect, and thereby avert a placement in emergency shelter and, quite likely, in foster care. ICCP interventions are less expensive and less damaging to children's continued development than placement of the child or children outside the home (Florida, 1991a, p. 300).

Florida has used a simple outcome monitoring system for ICCP since its inception, collecting counts of families that remained intact at case closures and of families that were disrupted (children removed and placed in shelter or foster care). Based on good overall success rates (80 percent or more of the families served remained intact at case closure), Florida gradually expanded ICCP. Success rates continue to document sufficiently the value of this program. Continued demand—families eligible for this program but turned away because caseloads are full—supports continued recommendations for program expansion (Florida, 1991a, p. 301). The ICCP outcome monitoring system recently began to report data by individual contract provider, finding much variation in performance: from 70 percent to 93 percent of families remained intact at case closure, with even wider variation found within three months after cases were closed (Florida, 1991a, pp. 559–560).

Staff decided to look deeper into some providers with lower performance. Staff (personal communication) uncovered a critical problem for one of the poorest performers: over the years, the program had evolved into a service where the provider, although available twenty-four hours via a telephone hotline, no longer provided any but the initial assessments in the families' homes. The intensive, in-home nature of the intended service had been lost. State and local staff then worked to remedy this flaw in the program's implementation. Similarly, the outcome monitoring system's identification of highly successful performers helped this contract provider and state staff to find alternatives that might be adapted to improve this provider's performance.

Commitment to Continuous Performance Improvement

Outcome monitoring creates scorecard-like summaries of performance at all levels, from a facility or work unit or region (such as a county or service delivery district) all the way up to an aggregate for the whole organization. Such summaries offer a comparative snapshot of performance to all those who are responsible for outcomes. The simple act of measuring and reporting on results will itself promote improvements. People and organizations *do* respond to those aspects of performance on which they are measured.

Outcome monitoring also stimulates competition and unleashes creativity in making improvements. Outcome monitoring describes outcomes for managers, facilities, contractors, or programs. When performance measures are taken seriously, those who are responsible will generally wish to improve their own performance. The human desire to be on a winning team and to be recognized as winners can unleash potent forces for performance improvement even without other work to improve capacity and performance. Good managers often look for ways in which to motivate strong individual commitment to the organization's mission, and outcome monitoring puts another arrow in that quiver.

More Efficient Use of Support Resources

The ICCP problem identified above could have gone undetected for many more years. Traditional program audits and other controls had not uncovered it. By directing the attention of state specialists to specific providers, the payoff from the time invested by those state specialists is substantial: performance was improved in the field. This targeting is the key to more efficient uses of those staff support resources.

This idea is not new. Internal auditors in most large organizations routinely assess the risks of financial loss associated with different programs or cost centers. The auditors then target their internal audits to provide the greatest benefit (in loss-avoidance or risk-exposure terms). The identification of outliers for site-specific review is the most obvious efficiency promoted by outcome monitoring, as shown in the ICCP example described earlier.

Outcome monitoring also makes possible efficiencies in the conduct of program evaluations. These evaluations generally provide program managers with more in-depth analyses of program operations and effects than is possible through outcome monitoring alone. Despite growing demands for results-oriented accountability, the resources with which to conduct program evaluations continue to be scarce, and those resources (like all others at a manager's disposal) require sound stewardship.

Outcome monitoring can help in at least two ways. First, it provides raw data for evaluation efforts, data that otherwise would require additional investment in data collection. It makes possible small, focused evaluations that might not have been done or conceived.

Second, outcome monitoring can focus evaluators' attention on programs or questions more likely to be relevant to program managers and policymakers, making evaluation more useful to agencies. Outcome monitoring can help set agendas for more valuable investment of scarce evaluation resources.

Example: Recidivism and "Suppression" Effects

The outcome monitoring system that evolved over five years in Florida routinely produced estimates of recidivism (into the juvenile system only, an important limitation) following youths' releases from juvenile justice programs. Juvenile justice staff in Florida argued that the frequency and severity of subsequent offenses, when compared to prior offenses, offered a more realistic assessment of program effects than does recidivism. Studies done elsewhere support this idea (Florida, 1991a, p. 509).

The outcome monitoring system in Florida made it possible to design and conduct a special study of "suppression" effects and to test the feasibility of building "suppression" estimates into the ongoing outcome monitoring system (Florida, 1991a, pp. 509–526). They will be incorporated into routine reports from the monitoring system in the future. Without the outcome monitoring system, however, such a study would have been much more expensive to do and may not have been done. Florida's outcome monitoring system triggered the inclusion of a study of suppression effects on the evaluation agenda and also made such a study possible within existing resources.

Growing Confidence in Organizational Performance

Even when well designed and used effectively, outcome monitoring will not create for an agency a public relations nirvana. The media, government critics, dissatisfied customers, and disaffected workers will always find ammunition for attacks on government operations. A sound outcome monitoring system can help to limit the damage that such critics can do, however, by providing the evidence for continuing effort to improve and by offering a more comprehensive and balanced view of total performance. Sometimes, the bad-performance news can come from the agency itself (one result of an outcome monitoring system), and can be turned into a confidence-building tool for public managers. As Chase and Reveal (1983, p. 164) recommend, "anticipate the bad news, and beat the media to the punch when possible. . . . Nothing takes the wind out of the sails of aggressive investigative reporters like getting scooped by the responsible agency."

Good-news reports of performance success or continued incremental improvements will never compete for the media's (or the public's) attention with scandal, with malfeasance in the conduct of the public's business, or with the tragic failure to prevent a child's death while under state supervision. But the existence and use of outcome monitoring invites critical stakeholders into the process of defining and measuring organizational performance. When those stakeholders are invested in the performance measures and the monitoring system, it becomes more difficult for them to create and sustain a global us-versus-them posture. It becomes more difficult to paint an agency with the brush of gross incompetence based on selected, highly visible, and troublesome anecdotes.

Another confidence-building benefit arises from internal rather than external uses of outcome monitoring. Many, from the front lines to upper management, tend to lose sight of successes because they focus on failures and problems. The proverbial forest may be lost for all the problem trees that seem to come crashing down overnight, and perspective can be lost because of the immediacy of day-to-day crises. Outcome monitoring shows everyone the overall results achieved and the improvements that occur. These can help to restore a balanced perspective. Perspective and the self-confidence that it creates can make the difference between mediocre and excellent performance or deterioration and improvement throughout an agency. When managers and staff know the value of their efforts, they do more, take more risks, try more innovations — and show greater success.

Design Issues for Outcome Monitoring

Issues in the design of outcome monitoring systems include what to measure, how many measures to use, how (and how often) to measure and report, and how to present the information. Trade-offs between costs and utility will structure these design decisions. The decisions made will depend on context-specific factors and considerations, priorities, opportunities, and constraints. There are no magic wands, no silver bullets, no neat (cheap, easy, quick) answers.

What to Measure?

An outcome monitoring system must report indicators that either measure desired outcomes or are clearly relevant and linked to the achievement of those outcomes. Examples of outcome measures were presented in Exhibit 5.1, earlier in this chapter.

Because people and organizations respond to the indicators on which they are measured, a heavy responsibility ensues: to make sure that the measures are appropriate and that they sufficiently cover the range of intended outcomes. If one outcome is measured and reported to the neglect of other important outcomes, then measured performance will improve, but it may come at the expense of undetected and unexpected deterioration in performance on other dimensions. Brizius and Campbell note the possibility of perverse incentives when the measures do not sufficiently cover the outcomes intended (1991, pp. 26–27). Fitz-Gibbon (1990, pp. 1–2) notes that among possible misuses of educational performance indicators we must guard against both "punitive, heavy handed surveillance" and "choosing the wrong indicators," either of which may promote unbalanced or misguided, yet measured, improvements.

One state, for instance, persisted in using the number of new foster homes licensed as a key performance indicator for the goal of getting more appropriate placements for children with specialized and multiple problems. Workers responded; new homes continued to be recruited and licensed, and the measured performance expectations were met. But homes where parents had the required specialized skills were not easily recruited or licensed, and those who were recruited and licensed were not retained at the levels needed to meet service demand. Field staff persistently noted that the indicator missed the mark (personal communication). Placement performance did not improve; some reported that it got worse. Many newly licensed foster homes were underutilized because they were not appropriate for those children who were difficult to place and who continued to suffer a shortage of appropriate placement options.

Stakeholders — including field staff and contract providers, clients, advocates, and upper management — should be involved in identifying appropriate measures and the design of needed reporting mechanisms, if outcome monitoring is to cover the ground required for effective outcome-oriented measurement. The performance measures and standards used in the Job Training Partnership Act (JTPA) offer a useful example. Stakeholders were used to help the Department of Labor develop performance measures and models that established expected levels of performance. Six percent of the total JTPA funds may be used as incentives tied to local service delivery area performance that exceeds those expectations.

In its early years, the JTPA system appeared to encourage "creaming" (the deliberate selection of clients for whom positive outcomes were likely). The Department of Labor worked with various stakeholders to "adjust" the performance standards for client characteristics, to make the provision of service to those most in need a more attractive and rewarding option. Most states now use the adjustment models to encourage service delivery areas within the state to serve those who are more difficult to serve (see Wholey, 1991, p. 2). The U.S. Department of Labor built a decentralized system of service delivery, from federal to state to local programs, but tied all levels to nationally developed measures and standards while allowing states to adjust performance standards to reflect local conditions. According to "a senior labor official . . . this method of providing incentives had improved performance" (U.S. General Accounting Office, 1992, p. 9).

How Many Measures?

In some ways, determining the number of measures to use is the easiest topic to address; in others, the most difficult. The short answer is however many are required to do the job. Some argue forcefully for articulating and tracking only a small number of highly relevant outcome measures (Appenzeller, 1992; Florida, 1991b). Too much data actually hide pertinent information: they may not be easily understood, used, or acted upon. Early in the 1980s, for example, one field welfare office in New York City posted the "error rates" in case eligibility and payment on office walls for each work unit; the single measure provided the work standard. On the other hand, some proponents of Total Quality Management and customer-responsive performance argue the substantial need for fact-based analysis and decision making at all levels in the organization, which requires extensive data collection and reporting (see, for example, Peters, 1987, and Whiteley, 1991). Measure everything and improve what you can seems to be the hallmark of this perspective.

The opposition of these views is more apparent than real. The need for a clear focus and easy comprehension requires that top-level reports contain a limited number of carefully developed, clearly relevant, and easily used and understood indicators of performance. Of equal importance, however, is the need for careful analysis and continuous performance improvement at all levels. This requires more extensive performance measures to supplement the indicators needed by upper levels. The more extensive the performance reporting system, the more likely that other specialists — program monitors, policy analysts, program evaluators — can make use of the data reported from the monitoring system.

Peters and Waterman note that even for the famously successful one-page memorandum at a company like Procter & Gamble, "they have plenty of back-up analysis available, just like everyone else" (1982, p. 152). The key point here is not that "less is more" but that, to be effective, less must rest on more. The discipline of forcing top-level reporting into a very limited number of measures requires substantial analysis, reporting, and stakeholder-based agreements on the core elements of mission or purpose. It also forces managers down the line to be in command of their responsibilities, their resources, and their outcomes — and it provides the basic road map or compass points to show the direction. Outcome monitoring systems that work well in reporting, tracking, and using a small number of outcome-oriented measures *must* ride on substantial data collection and reporting systems that are quite extensive.

How (and How Often) Should Performance Be Measured?

It will always seem to be easier and cheaper to collect and report outcome-oriented data from automated information systems than it will be to design and operate ancillary, labor-intensive data collection and reporting systems. Automated systems also will more likely be able to report performance more frequently, and frequent feeedback is needed by program managers. Some stakeholders may need outcome information only annually; some outcomes may be so expensive or difficult to measure that measurements annually are all that can be afforded.

A good example concerns recidivism-type measures in human services programs. If service history is kept in the information system, then the work required to identify and report subsequent reentry into the services systems can be done by analysts and clerical staff rather than those who are doing the direct service delivery. Field staff will not need to follow up all clients (or a sample of clients) over some period of time after cases are closed because the computer system can be used to detect reentry into the services systems. Many reasons other than recidivism measurement might prompt follow-up studies, whether or not done by field staff, and recidivism may not be a good outcome measure for many programs. The point is that when an automated system keeps service history and when recidivism measures have value for outcome monitoring, then the system itself can be used to obtain those measures.

Similarly, most human service programs require that reasons for case closure (or status at case closure) be documented in the record. If those reasons are well defined, and if the information is captured in automated records, then the automated system can be programmed to calculate and report the appropriate measures at whatever level and frequency is required. Ancillary, labor-intensive reporting of reasons for case closure will not be needed.

Often, though, outcomes to be monitored cannot be obtained from existing information systems. Procedures must be designed to capture, calculate, and report such measures above and beyond the requirements of everyday operations. Unless an entirely separate staff unit can be dedicated to the measurement and reporting task, the tasks will have to be built into the routines of program operations. Care should be taken to keep such reporting burdens to a minimum, since every minute taken from the main activities of the program for record keeping or paper pushing will be seen to detract from the major purposes of the field staff's work. Again, decisions about what to capture (and how often) will be more relevant and more likely to be implemented if the field staff help to make those decisions.

Outcome monitoring systems should report measures at differing levels of aggregation or measurement. Individual managers, down the line, should be able to see and use their own performance data; a much higher level of aggregation is less likely to stimulate continuous improvement in performance. The linkage or connection between performance in discrete units and overall agency performance should also be clear. Recall the example discussed earlier of the ICCP program in Florida. The outcome monitoring system devised and used for about ten years rested on reports from providers of the numbers of families that remained intact at case closure, but these were not tallied and reported by contractor (even though they were received from contractors). Only when the results were tallied and presented for each contractor did staff discover the problem cited in the example.

In newer automated systems, user-friendly query and reporting capabilities may put the frequency and format of reporting decisions into the hands of managers themselves — potentially at the cost, however, of public scrutiny. Advocates, auditors, and legislators and their staffs often will not have daily or routine access to an agency's automated system, with its query capabilities. Although it is quite important to provide managers up the line with such access to performance data, public reporting of key results should be done on a known cycle.

Much creativity can be brought to the task of measuring and reporting outcome-relevant measures of performance. When not included easily in automated systems that support program operations, one alternative is to attach an outcome measurement form to the paperwork required for documentation at case closure, for payments made, or of work events started or completed. It is easy, then, to separate that section of the form and send it to a staff member whose job it is to tally and report on the performance measures so described. It will be all too easy to expect line workers to keep and tally outcome measures — and all too easy for those workers to resist the intrusion of burdensome paperwork into their "real" jobs. Minimize the reporting that must be done by line workers (whether agency or contractor staff) and design procedures where others (supervisors or clerical staff) take the basic information and do the tallies and reports required.

In certain instances, sampling may be done periodically, with measurements taken and tallied for carefully chosen samples. One drawback to samples, however, concerns the level at which estimates may be useful or valid: the smaller the sample, the less precise the estimates. Samples designed only to produce statewide or programwide estimates of performance may not generate useful estimates for lower levels (such as facility or district). And when those lower-level managers and their staffs cannot get useful feedback from an outcome monitoring system, their commitment to it is not likely to be high. So, for purposes of sampling designs, either make the results useful for those staff who must do the sampling, or use a separate staff (agency or contract support staff) to get the information. Telephone surveys may also be used. (See Chapter Eleven in this book, "Designing and Conducting Surveys.")

When public programs are implemented through contracts, the requirements for performance measurement and reporting should be included in the contract itself. Although this requirement may add to contract costs, contractors very often are quite receptive to collecting and using performance information. Good performance data can provide a competitive edge for many who must bid for these contracts or for those who wish to expand their operations, whether geographically or programmatically. Contractors often have business-based incentives to participate in outcome monitoring systems.

When performance is at the heart of particular, outside groups' interests, then they may be mobilized to collect and report outcome-relevant performance data. Chase and Reveal (1983, pp. 141–144) report using just such a mechanism in New York City when certain health care services were expanded in the city's public hospitals. When those services were to be made available to the poor, in public hospitals, these advocates devised their own monitoring system. It reported the availability of those services for the poor and the degree of accessibility of those services in the public hospitals.

Some risks accompany strategies along these lines. Initially, the New York City results were discounted by program managers and staff and the credibility of the measures reported by the interest groups were suspect. At the agency head's insistence, however, the reported results were verified and subsequent reports from the interest group were used to improve program performance, hospital by hospital. Outsiders' contributions to outcome monitoring systems should not be overlooked, but an organization's leadership should first verify the reports and ensure that the group's special-interest agenda does not affect sound, objective, and credible performance measurement.

There is no rule of thumb that will give an ideal frequency of reporting from an outcome monitoring system — except to note that many will want data more frequently than any such system can provide it. The Florida Legislature intends a "continuous flow" of data from the outcome monitoring system for its human services agency, an ideal far from realized. Annual reports often are the mechanism used for reporting, but annual data simply cannot keep pace with program managers' and policymakers' actions: data may be two or more years old, and much will have changed in law, policy, procedures, or clients over that period of time. To the extent possible, monthly or quarterly reports would seem to be ideal, and such frequent reporting may be possible from automated systems or from well-designed routine measurement procedures.

The lesson here is that "how many, how often" *is* whatever it takes. Too much, especially in early stages of outcome monitoring, can cripple an outcome monitoring effort; too little, and its value can be lost. As managers begin to focus their attention on explanations for the performance levels measured and on the design or discovery of options for improving performance, the measures must report at a level of operational reality. Statewide, program-wide aggregates obscure much variation that will be useful for making program improvements. Outcome monitoring systems, then, must be started and expected to grow, change, and improve themselves. They are neither panaceas nor quick fixes for accountability problems in large organizations.

Many information resources are available to the public official who would begin to build an outcome monitoring system. For child welfare services and for juvenile justice programs, see Florida (1987, 1988, 1989, 1990 and 1991a). Periodic literature reviews and surveys of other states are reported in those documents, especially the report for 1989, with selective follow-up in other states in the subsequent years. Carter (1983) remains a valuable reference.

The Governmental Accounting Standards Board also sponsors and publishes reports on outcome measures and studies concerning their inclusion in accounting standards for public agencies (see Hatry and Fountain, 1990, for an example). The Urban Institute has a long, respected history of studies of outcome measures and their uses in and for evaluations in public programs at all levels of government; for a small sampling, see Hatry (1985, 1989) and Hatry and others (1981, 1989, and 1992). The U.S. General Accounting Office is another valuable resource for outcome measurement information (see U.S. General Accounting Office, 1992, for example). Discipline-specific journals and measurement handbooks can be located through most any university library. Agency-based evaluators or monitors can often get useful information about outcomes to be measured and monitored from their legislative audit agencies, whether through state-specific or agency-specific program audit reports or from auditors who are familiar with GASB and/or GAO reports.

How to Present the Results from Outcome Monitoring

Results do not appear as if by magic from outcome monitoring systems. The presentation of results deserves a prominent place in the design of outcome monitoring systems. (See Chapter Twenty-Three in this book, "Making a Splash: Reporting Evaluation Results Effectively"). Unless results are used, outcome monitoring becomes another waste of scarce resources.

The keys to effective communication vary according to the message, the sender, and the receiver. Those who would promote outcome monitoring would do well to experiment with different uses of narrative, tables, and graphics at different levels of aggregation and with different emphases. Graphics probably offer the best tools for quick and effective communication of sometimes complex data (see Tufte, 1983, for an excellent discussion of this subject). Try reproducing your color-coded schemes on a black-and-white copier: some will copy just fine, with little loss of meaning, but other color schemes or compositions will lose all contrast (hence, meaning and value). Keep color schemes simple and effective enough to withstand black-and-white copying—or else prepare black-and-white versions for distribution, using color copies for special purposes and briefings. As with the identification of what to measure, stakeholders should help to determine how to present the results from outcome monitoring.

Remember that (as with most evaluations) outcome data must be comparative if they are to be useful. They may compare performance over time (trend), among similar reporting units (different contractors or facilities providing a like service), or against a performance standard (which may be set in law or in contractual performance requirements). To the extent that your graphics illustrate the appropriate or needed comparisons, they will be more useful. The comparative base may be shown separately (a line on a graph showing the standard as well as actual performance) or built into the measure itself (a deviation from average or from last month's or last year's performance, for instance). A single piece of data, absent any comparative reference, is not likely to tell anyone anything of interest or importance.

Periodically review and assess the effectiveness of the means by which results are presented. Over time, most of the key stakeholders will become comfortable with particular formats or charts or graphs and will come to assume that the outcome monitoring system reports what it should. Over time, however, priorities may change and different issues arise that demand changes in the performance reporting system. Such developments present opportunities to test and to improve reporting formats as well.

Pitfalls in Outcome Monitoring

Many pitfalls, however, await those who design outcome monitoring systems. Most are predictable, and they include unrealistic expectations, failing to focus on outcomes, irrelevance, and unwarranted conclusions.

Unrealistic Expectations

Unrealistic expectations can derail any worthwhile project and the development of useful outcome monitoring systems is not exempt. The first set of unrealistic expectations to be faced concerns the benefits or potential of out-come monitoring: outcome monitoring is not a panacea, a one-shot solu-tion to problems of accountability in agency performance. Outcome mon-itoring is but one very important item in an agency's accountability tool kit. It cannot and will not replace other forms of monitoring or reporting; it cannot replace program evaluations; it will not, on its own, create performance im-provements; nor will it alone create public and legislative confidence in the agency's management. Any tool must be used appropriately to realize its benefits: a screwdriver makes a lousy wrench.

A sound outcome monitoring system, once tested, may help to cut back on other forms of monitoring or reporting, but it cannot eliminate the need for on-site reviews or compliance-focused audits, for instance. Effec-tive outcome monitoring cannot replace program evaluation, either, because outcome monitoring systems alone cannot explain variations in performance. Similarly, outcome monitoring cannot replace sound judgment in making management decisions — from allocating resources to creating new programs, policies, or procedures. But sound outcome monitoring can help to focus that management attention on areas most in need of (or most opportune for) program or policy improvement.

Another unrealistic expectation is that the identification and collec-tion of outcome data will come easily. Some will assume that program or agency intent, as expressed in law or administrative rule, will sufficiently identify the outcomes to be measured. Disillusionment is inevitable; sub-stantial work is required to gain consensus among major stakeholders on a program's intent and on definitions of suitable outcome measures. Often, public programs embody multiple intents and the definition of measures that capture those intents is not a simple task.

Consider subsidized child day care, for example. Child day care, in most states, helps parents to obtain training or employment and gain finan-cial self-sufficiency. Child care also provides developmentally appropriate services to the children, making them more ready for school than they other-wise are expected to be. Some states use subsidized child care for families in which abuse or neglect has occurred and is still a risk. Child care serves both children (keeps them safe) and their parents (provides relief from the day-to-day demands of raising children while affording parents an opportu-nity to learn more effective ways of coping with those child-rearing stresses). Multiple measures may be identified for each kind of intent or purpose, and getting consensus on which measures to use (for any one purpose, let alone all of them) will require much time and effort. Florida's outcome monitor-ing system as yet produces no child care performance measure of readiness for school, only one limited measure of support for economic self-sufficiency, and only two measures of child safety (abuse or neglect while in care, and abuse or neglect within one year after leaving care).

Another unrealistic expectation concerns the size or scope of what will be required to make an outcome monitoring system useful. Upper-level managers and some key stakeholders outside of an agency will continue to beat the drum of collecting only a few, highly relevant performance measures. They often will assume that substantial data collection will not be required. This rarely is true.

Consider, for instance, a family preservation program, in which the aim is to keep a family intact and functioning well following an episode of child abuse or a history of documented neglect. For some families, the risk of further abuse or neglect may be removed or alleviated, the children can remain with their families, the children do not suffer the ills of foster care, and the public will save money by avoiding costs of emergency shelter and foster care, and in the longer run, through improved school performance, lowered risk of delinquency, and greater likelihood that the children will become productive citizens. Depending on which of these outcomes are to be measured and in what ways, the data collection required for an otherwise simple set of indicators can become quite extensive.

One program administrator (personal communication) specifically wants to know only one performance measure: how many shelter placements are avoided, that is, the number of children at imminent risk of placement but kept safely nonetheless with their families. The potential for unrealistic expectation arises, however, when that administrator or his staff assume that this measure is all that is required, that only appropriate families are served in fact, and that when an episode of family preservation service is concluded successfully, the family will not subsequently fall back into abusive or neglectful behavior that will then require a shelter placement (the performance measure is placements avoided, not delayed). Variations in the needs of families served by different service teams, and in the specific nature and duration of services provided, will suggest further analysis which in turn will require more data collection if the outcomes monitored are to prove useful for improving program performance.

Avoiding a Clear Focus on Outcomes

It is usually easier to measure program inputs, processes, and outputs than to measure program outcomes. Program managers may be tempted to leave the measurement and analysis of outcomes to program evaluators. After all, if managers design and implement programs properly, they expect positive outcomes. They may believe that they need not "waste" resources in measuring those outcomes. This attitude seems to underlie much of the development and expansion of public programs during the twentieth century, but it cannot be sustained. Legislatures increasingly demand proof of results, not simply of activities done in compliance with procedural requirements or evidence of competent design and implementation.

Some outcomes may be difficult or impossible to measure directly. In the search for more immediate and measurable results, it is easy to get backed into measuring outputs, procedures, or activities, or even program inputs. While it may be important to measure, analyze, and report more than only outcomes, an outcome monitoring system will fail to realize the benefits suggested earlier when it fails to measure and report key outcomes or results.

Persistence, good communications, and group facilitation skills will be required to overcome these kinds of objections and to keep the key stakeholders focused on results. In some cases, the law may help (as with Florida's outcome evaluation statute); in others, exposure to questioning from key legislators on appropriations or budget committees may also help. A clear focus on results and support from the agency head may be required to turn staff toward the measurement and improvement of performance. Witness the practice reported by Chase: "[W]hen I first became administrator . . . I would call in my commissioners and senior managers and ask them what they'd been doing. . . . Some . . . would [tell] me how many meetings . . . how many memos . . . how many staff . . . I'd look at them and say: 'But whom did you make healthy today (or last week, or last year) . . . and how do you know?'" (Chase and Reveal, 1983, p. 177).

Irrelevance

Another pitfall is irrelevance. If the outcomes measured and reported are far removed from operational reality and hence not subject to focused efforts to improve performance, then outcome monitoring might as well not be done. If stakeholders are involved in the identification of performance measures and in subsequent reviews and assessments of the outcome monitoring system, then this pitfall can be avoided.

The family preservation example cited earlier contains an instructive example: the administrator wanted to know placements avoided, whereas the evaluator reported a measure of successful program completion. The evaluator's credibility and his work's utility suffered. The definition and measurement of successful program completion was, in fact, the number of placements avoided, so the measurement was just what the administrator wanted. But the evaluator made it irrelevant by failing to recognize and use a label appropriate for the administrator's frame of reference.

Over time, policy priorities may change in any program, and performance measures must keep up with those changes to assure continued policy relevance. To the degree that performance measures are not relevant to the policy issues of the day, the outcome monitoring system will risk failure. Stakeholders' periodic reviews of outcome monitoring systems can help to assure their continued relevance to emerging policy concerns. For example, cocaine babies and infants born HIV-positive pose new and difficult challenges for hospitals, for child welfare services systems, and for schools as these children reach school age. New, more appropriate performance measures may be needed for service systems in response to these (and other) emerging problems and priorities.

Outcome monitoring systems should be audited periodically. It is all too easy to become complacent in the familiar routines of reporting what come to be standard performance measures. An audit of the outcome monitoring system may be required, as it is in Florida. The state's auditor general is charged with assessing the progress and performance of the outcome evaluation systems of the Department of Health and Rehabilitative Services and reporting to the legislature every five years. Even if it is not required, a periodic, outside review of the outcome monitoring system can be quite useful. It can promote continued stakeholder involvement, it can identify areas for improvement in the outcome monitoring system, and it can lend additional credibility to the products from the system.

Unwarranted Conclusions

An important pitfall is the probability of drawing unwarranted conclusions from outcome monitoring data. Certain key stakeholders will jump to conclusions based on outcome monitoring reports, conclusions that may be wrong or unfair. When they use these conclusions inappropriately, managers and policymakers undermine the credibility and value of the outcome monitoring system itself. Tipple (1990) describes well the dilemma felt by a school principal who requires adjusted student achievement scores, if the school's (and teachers') performance is to be fairly judged, while parents rightly are concerned about their children's achievement levels, not explanations for adjusting those achievement scores.

Programs, facilities, or contractors performing well or poorly will be identified from an outcome monitoring system — but it is wrong to conclude that these represent good and poor practices, absent further examination. If agency managers or administrators, or legislators, or other funders take precipitous action based solely on the outcome monitoring results, then agencywide performance may suffer, directly contrary to the intent of outcome monitoring.

This is perhaps the greatest pitfall for outcome monitoring. Legislators and some agency heads will want to know, simply and solely, what programs or contractors should be cut or ended because money spent on them is money wasted. Outcome monitoring systems can tell those key stakeholders where to begin more in-depth examinations, not which conclusions will be justified. Furthermore, eliminating a program or its funding source does not eliminate the needs of those who were served, however ineffective that service seems to be.

Good performance may be reported in one area, for example, because the problems to be addressed are not as serious in that area as they are in other areas. Schools that serve predominantly poor students, for instance, are not likely to appear as successful as those that serve predominantly well-to-do students. Hospitals that treat more seriously ill people may show greater mortality rates than other hospitals. Welfare-to-work programs that target those with long-term welfare dependency may not appear as successful as those programs that serve new welfare recipients who already have job skills and experience. Outcome monitoring systems should document actual results, which may be in accord with such expectations. Yet, what conclusions should be drawn, and what consequences should ensue? These are not easy questions to answer; the answers should not be expected to flow directly from the outcome monitoring system.

This pitfall, in some form or another, awaits everyone who would measure and report performance routinely. The most appropriate way to deal with it is to go slowly at first with any consequences planned as a result of measured performance. Those who would design outcome monitoring systems should think through the questions to be expected from initial performance reports and be ready with responses to those questions. Some questions will require additional analyses (perhaps appendices or special reports); others may suggest program evaluation, on-site monitoring, or special studies aimed at further diagnosis of potential problems. Another response may be to collect and report additional data through the outcome monitoring system, data with which to adjust the outcomes measured.

As Oscar Wilde reportedly said: "The truth is rarely pure and never simple." Outcome monitoring is less about truth and more the beginning of understanding. Outcome monitoring will not be pure—but it can be very useful.

A Postscript

The Florida Department of Health and Rehabilitative Services experienced a major reorganization during 1993. As part of that reorganization, its evaluation units were disbanded. Those positions (with many others) were reallocated, primarily to the field. This reflects the decentralizing focus of that reorganization.

Some evaluation functions were reassigned, with two staff, to the department's Office of Internal Audit. Responsibility for the department's performance measurement system, including outcome monitoring, was reassigned to its administrative services division, consolidating performance measurement with planning and budgeting functions. Different operational units now are expected to support those evaluation activities that each deems required.

The reorganization legislation kept the program-specific evaluation mandate that was referenced earlier in this chapter, but its citation is slightly different. That mandate now is found in Chapter 20.19(19), Florida Statutes.

References

Appenzeller, G. W. "Quality Assurance: You Know Quality When You See It, but Who Else Does?" Paper presented for a teleconference on quality assurance, hosted by the National Child Welfare Research Center, University of Southern Maine, July 24, 1992.

Brizius, J. A., and Campbell, M. D. *Getting Results: A Guide for Government Accountability.* Washington, D.C.: Council of Governors Policy Advisors, 1991.

Carter, R. K. *The Accountable Agency.* Newbury Park, Calif.: Sage, 1983.

Chase, G., and Reveal, E. C. *How to Manage in the Public Sector.* New York: Random House, 1983.

Cronbach, L. J., and others. *Toward Reform of Program Evaluation: Aims, Methods and Institutional Arrangements.* San Francisco: Jossey-Bass, 1980.

Fitz-Gibbon, C. T. (ed.). *Performance Indicators.* Clevedon, England: Multilingual Matters, 1990.

Florida. *Children, Youth and Family Services Outcome Evaluation Report: A First Step Toward Accountability.* Tallahassee, Fla.: Department of Health and Rehabilitative Services, Dec. 31, 1987.

Florida. *Children, Youth and Family Services Outcome Evaluation Report: A First Step Toward Accountability.* Tallahassee, Fla.: Department of Health and Rehabilitative Services, Dec. 31, 1988.

Florida. *Children, Youth and Family Services Outcome Evaluation Report: A First Step Toward Accountability.* Tallahassee, Fla.: Department of Health and Rehabilitative Services, Dec. 31, 1989.

Florida. *Children, Youth and Family Services Outcome Evaluation Report: A Further Step Toward Accountability.* Tallahassee, Fla.: Department of Health and Rehabilitative Services, Dec. 31, 1990.

Florida. *Children, Youth and Family Services Outcome Evaluation Report: A Further Step Toward Accountability.* Tallahassee, Fla.: Department of Health and Rehabilitative Services, Dec. 31, 1991a.

Florida. *Strategic Plan for Results in the 1990s.* Tallahassee, Fla.: Department of Health and Rehabilitative Services, Oct. 1991b.

Hatry, H. "State and Local Productivity and Performance Measurement." In J. Rabin and D. Dodd (eds.), *State and Local Government Administration.* New York: Marcel Dekker, 1985.

Hatry, H. "Determining the Effectiveness of Government Services." In J. Perry (ed.), *Handbook of Public Administration.* San Francisco: Jossey-Bass, 1989.

Hatry, H., and Fountain, J. R. *Service Efforts and Accomplishments Information: Its Time Has Come.* Norwalk, Conn.: Governmental Accounting Standards Board, 1990.

Hatry, H., and others. *Practical Program Evaluation for State and Local Government.* (2nd ed.) Washington, D.C.: The Urban Institute, 1981.

Hatry, H., and others. *Monitoring the Outcomes of Economic Development Programs: A Manual.* Washington, D.C.: The Urban Institute Press, 1989.

Hatry, H., and others. *How Effective Are Your Community Services? Procedures for Monitoring the Effectiveness of Municipal Services.* (2nd ed.) Washington, D.C.: International City/County Management Association and The Urban Institute, 1992.

National Academy of Public Administration. "Resolution on Performance Monitoring and Reporting by Public Organizations." Washington, D.C.: National Academy of Public Administration, Oct. 1991.

North Carolina. *1991 Critical Success Factors for the North Carolina Community College System: Second Annual Report.* Raleigh, N.C.: Department of Community Colleges, Apr. 1991.

Patton, M. Q. *Creative Evaluation.* (2nd ed.) Newbury Park, Calif.: Sage, 1987.

Peters, T. *Thriving on Chaos.* New York: HarperCollins, 1987.

Peters, T. J., and Waterman, R. H. *In Search of Excellence: Lessons from America's Best-Run Companies.* New York: HarperCollins, 1982.

Rossi, P. H., and Freeman, H. E. *Evaluation: A Systematic Approach.* (2nd ed.) Newbury Park, Calif.: Sage, 1982.

Sensenbrenner, J. "Quality Comes to City Hall." *Harvard Business Review,* Mar./Apr. 1991, pp. 64–75.

Tipple, C. "Reactions from a CEO." In C. T. Fitz-Gibbon (ed.), *Performance Indicators.* Clevedon, England: Multilingual Matters, Ltd., 1990.

Tufte, E. R. *The Visual Display of Quantitative Information.* Cheshire, Conn.: Graphics Press, 1983.

U.S. General Accounting Office. *Program Performance Measures: Federal Agency Collection and Use of Performance Data.* Washington, D.C.: General Accounting Office, May 4, 1992.

Whiteley, R. C. *The Customer-Driven Company.* Reading, Mass.: Addison-Wesley, 1991.

Wholey, J. S. Testimony Before the U.S. Senate Committee on Governmental Affairs' Hearing on S. 20, the Federal Program Performance Standards and Goals Act of 1991. May 23, 1991.

Wholey, J. S., and Hatry, H. P. "The Case for Performance Monitoring." *Public Administration Review,* Nov./Dec. 1992, pp. 604–610.

6

Constructing
Natural "Experiments"

Debra J. Rog

This chapter introduces the reader to the concept of natural experimentation. Natural experiments are intended to be alternatives to randomized evaluation studies and to the more rigorous quasi-experiments. They range in design from those commonly called preexperimental or nonexperimental to those classified as quasi-experimental, intended for evaluations in which the evaluator does not have control of the manipulation and administration of the intervention nor the assignment of units to treatment and control groups. In natural experiments, the evaluator maximizes naturally occurring bases of comparison within a program setting to control confounding influences that could cloud the outcomes. This chapter also explores how the evaluator can enhance the explanatory power of the natural experiment by collecting and analyzing additional information on the influence of other confounding factors that cannot be controlled.

The first section outlines and defines the various evaluation approaches that can be used to address questions of outcome and impact, with an expanded definition of natural experiments. In the second section of the chapter, several strategies for developing natural experiments are presented. The final section identifies the conditions that generally warrant natural experimentation.

Addressing Questions of Outcome, Effectiveness, and Impact

The span of evaluation has broadened over the years to answer descriptive and process questions such as "How does the program operate?" (see Scheirer, Chapter Three of this volume); yet evaluation still is most often commissioned to respond to the questions, "Did the program make a difference? Did it achieve its goals?" Policymakers may want to know whether a new gun control law has reduced the crime rate; school officials may be interested

119

in learning whether an after-school mathematics program has improved children's mathematical abilities above and beyond the standard school-day curriculum; a federal agency may need to know how well a new job training program creates meaningful job skills that lead to employment for program participants.

Questions of effectiveness and impact are causal questions, exploring the extent to which an intervention has brought about an outcome, such as the extent to which a gun control law has lowered the crime rate. The *true experiment* is generally considered the strongest and most appropriate design to address questions of effectiveness and impact (see, for example, Berk and others, 1985; Campbell and Stanley, 1966). The overwhelming strength of a true experiment is its ability to enhance the internal validity of a study by ruling out potential alternative explanations for the outcomes that result. The internal validity of a study refers to the extent to which the outcomes can be correctly attributed to the intervention (Cook and Campbell, 1979).

Threats to validity, also referred to as confounding conditions and rival explanations, are changes, situations, or phenomena operating in and around the intervention that could account for the outcomes. Cook and Campbell (1979) and Campbell and Stanley (1966) before them described a number of threats to validity that occur in studies. Two of the most common are *history* and *selection*. History is a threat when the outcomes may be caused by extraneous events that take place during the same time period as the intervention. Suppose a city that just enforced a gun control ordinance also recently put police on the beat in several of its prime business districts. To determine how much the new ordinance affected crime, regardless of the enhanced police presence, the evaluation design would have to be constructed to isolate the effects of the ordinance; that is, to control the effects that this confounding condition, police on the beat, might have on lowering the crime rate.

Selection is a potential threat to validity when there are differences in the types of units in the treatment group and in the comparison group, and when these differences could account for differences in the outcomes of the groups. For example, if students elected to take the after-school math program and were compared to students who did not choose the program, differences in the outcomes between the two groups could be due to self-selection factors; that is, the students who chose the program may have been mathematically gifted and may have scored higher than the comparison students because of this initial difference, not because of the program.

True experiments provide the most control over threats to internal validity through the use of random assignment. Through random assignment, all eligible units have an equal likelihood of being assigned to either the treatment condition or a control condition. The resulting groups are considered equivalent and differ only with respect to the intervention. In the example of the after-school mathematics program, randomly assigning all second graders to the program and control conditions would produce two equivalent groups for whom the only know difference would be receipt of the program. Dennis in Chapter Eight of this handbook describes the design, implementation, and analysis of controlled experiments in a variety of community settings.

There are a number of situations, however, in which randomized studies cannot be implemented. Such studies often are difficult to implement well, and at times, are not possible because of a variety of situational constraints. In the gun control ordinance example, it would be difficult to assign communities randomly to enact the ordinance. However, it still may be possible to study the effects of the ordinance on target communities. When random assignment is not possible, the evaluator should select a design that either attempts to control for extraneous variables or, at a minimum, provides enough information to demonstrate whether rival explanations are plausible. In addition, the design should not only allow the evaluator to *rule out* other explanations but should provide evidence to *rule in* the program or intervention as the cause (Cordray, 1986).

Quasi-experiments are designed to substitute for the true experiment in situations in which randomization is not possible or practical. The key driving force in a quasi-experiment is a basis of comparison for a treatment group that approximates the equivalence in the treatment and control groups brought about by random assignment. Marcantonio and Cook in Chapter Seven of this book describe two useful quasi-experimental designs: regression-discontinuity and time series. These designs are generally stronger than the designs discussed in this chapter; however, because the requirements for both designs can be difficult to meet, natural experiments often serve as fall-back designs to these two types of quasi-experiments. The chapter focuses on the *design* of natural experiments; the analysis of quasi-experiments and natural experiments is discussed by Reichardt and Bormann in Chapter Eighteen of this book.

Natural experiments as defined in this chapter can be quasi-experimental, preexperimental, or nonexperimental designs. They are not a distinct group or classification of designs but rather a set of design strategies for situations in which the evaluator has little control over the intervention. The term *natural experiment* is used therefore to refer to designs that utilize naturally occurring bases of comparison to control for plausible confounding factors or designs in which existing information is used to rule in or rule out these factors as rival explanations for the results.

The distinguishing feature of the natural experiment is that the evaluator lacks any control over the intervention and over who does and does not receive it. Thus, the design strives to utilize any control that may be inherent in the situation and maximizes it through patching up the design with additional information.

The term *natural experiment* has been used sparingly and yet in various ways in the evaluation literature. In some cases, the term has been used exclusively for those situations in which natural randomization occurs (Rossi and Freeman, 1989). Natural randomization occurs most often with natural or unplanned phenomena, such as disasters, in which a number of areas are equally vulnerable, but some are randomly spared while others are randomly struck. In these situations, the effects of a disaster, such as a tornado, on a variety of outcome measures can be studied between the different geographic areas. As Rossi and Freeman (1989) note, the disaster is the result of a known set of natural processes, but the selection of communities or areas that are struck is considered random.

For others such as Mohr (1992), natural experiments include those in which intervention and nonrandom comparison groups naturally occur. Under this definition, communities that have enacted a gun control ordinance could be compared on various outcome measures with communities that do not have a gun control ordinance. However, unlike the instance of natural randomization, it is likely that a community's decision to enact the ordinance was influenced by factors other than random events (such as an increased crime rate, more gun-related deaths than in other communities). Similarly, communities that have fluoridated water can be compared with communities that do not have fluoridated water on the basis of dental caries in its citizens. Although it is unlikely that individuals choose to live in a community specifically because it has fluoridated water, it is likely that there are known factors that determined whether one community has its water fluoridated and another has not.

In addition, there are hybrid designs, referred to as patched up designs (Campbell and Stanley, 1966), that use a variety of approaches to determine whether there may be explanations for the outcomes other than the intervention. As Weiss (1972) suggests, the patched up design may not be "neat or elegant" but it does provide clarity on the role of plausible confounding conditions.

Natural experiments can vary in how well they approximate the control brought about by the random assignment to groups. Comparison groups that provide accurate estimates of what would have happened *but for* the intervention provide the greatest explanatory power. Rossi's definition of natural experiment, involving natural randomization, provides the closest approximation to the true experiment. However, situations in which natural randomization occurs are rare, especially in program and policy situations that are typically the focus of our evaluations. Thus, in this chapter, although a broad definition of natural experiments will be used, the focus is on designing studies that maximize the naturally occurring bases of comparison within a program as well as a variety of sources that provide information on plausible confounding factors.

Designing Natural Experiments

A variety of strategies can be used to develop natural experiments, varying in the level of control they provide over plausible confounding factors. The ideal is for comparison between groups to provide an accurate estimate of what the situation would have been like without the intervention. The more accurate this estimate, the more control the experiment provides and the stronger the conclusions can be regarding whether the intervention did indeed *cause* the outcomes or *effects*.

In this section, four broad strategies for developing natural experiments are reviewed, ranging from stronger to weaker designs. The first three strategies involve identifying a basis of comparison. The fourth strategy, using information alone, is for situations in which it is not possible to identify comparison groups.

To illustrate some of the designs in the following sections, the notational system developed by Campbell and Stanley (1966) is used. In this system, X stands for receipt of the treatment or intervention, and O stands for an observation or measurement of the outcomes.

Pretest-Posttest (Reflexive Control) Designs

Sometimes the only available basis of comparison in an evaluation is the intervention group itself prior to its involvement in the program. In this instance, the basis of comparison is two sets of data from the same group, one set collected and analyzed before and one set after the group members receive an intervention. The strategy is referred to as the one-group pretest-posttest design (Cook and Campbell, 1979) and the reflexive control design (Rossi and Freeman, 1989). It is often considered a nonexperimental or preexperimental design because of the difficulty in drawing strong causal inferences from the results obtained. The design is presented in Table 6.1 in the notation style of Campbell and Stanley (1966).

Table 6.1. Pretest-Posttest Design.

Group 1	O	X	O
	Pretest Observation	Intervention	Posttest Observation

Using reflexive controls to evaluate a management training program, one might collect data from the participating managers before they enter and when they finish the training program. Measures could include the level of knowledge of management techniques, attitudes toward management principles, and intentions to change behavior to incorporate specific management principles.

This design has been criticized as being open to a number of threats to validity. For example, changes in subjects' knowledge could be a reflection of knowledge acquired through familiarity with the test itself after the pretest (testing). Changes in attitudes and behaviors could be attributed in part to the perceived social desirability pressures to report more positive attitudes and *correct* behavioral intentions. Or, changes might be due to the inordinate motivation and interest of this self-selected group (selection).

A partial design solution to the measurement problems would be to use standardized instruments that are less susceptible to testing effects and to pressures of social desirability. Although these threats and others may not be fully controlled by the design, additional data could be collected to determine the extent to which they may be valid rival explanations for the results. For example, information could be gathered on the motivation of participants.

History is a typical threat to validity that this design does not control. That is, the study does not control for other changes in the context that could account for increases in knowledge of management principles, changes in behavioral intentions, and the like. However, this threat is not plausible in this situation because of the short time period between measures. With each situation, therefore, the evaluator needs to assess the threats that are plausible and focus the design and data collection on these threats.

In social intervention programs, another threat arises because often the implementation of the treatment condition is variable — the *dose* of the intervention may vary for a number of reasons (such as provider accessibility, client interest and motivation, client needs, resource availability). For example, in a mental health program, the amount of time a client sees a case manager can vary because of the client's interests and/or needs, the case manager's work load, and/or demands in the program site.

Measuring the amount of intervention received and controlling the reasons for the differences (for example, client need) may allow the evaluator to detect differential outcomes related to differential treatment levels. Using regression, we might examine whether job readiness can be predicted by program dose (that is, the level of participation in a job training program).

This pretest-posttest design is open to several validity threats (such as self-selection and selection biases). Individuals who have a greater need for the treatment, for example, may have received disproportionately more treatment; however, those in greater need for treatment (such as individuals in need of alcohol treatment) may be in denial and thus may reject larger amounts of treatment or any treatment. Collecting additional data on the needs of these individuals and their attitudes toward treatment, however, and using these data as statistical controls in a multiple regression may aid in determining the biases that correlate with different treatment dosage levels. Clearly, if there is a consistent pattern of differences in program dose by program site, biases due to self-selection would be less relevant. Although other differences may account for the variation in program dose across sites (such as level of resources, program philosophy, different types of clients served across sites), it is likely that these differences can be taken into account and may allow for a stronger test of the outcomes of the intervention. To the extent that the differences are attributable more to site than client differences, tests of client outcomes based on dose may be stronger and provide more valid conclusions about the effectiveness of different levels of treatment.

Pretest-Posttest Nonequivalent Comparison Group Design

Nonequivalent group designs are typically considered a major type of quasi-experimental design involving data collection from two or more nonequivalent groups. A nonequivalent design involves the use of specific selection criteria rather than random assignment to create the comparison groups. In situations where the evaluator has little opportunity to create comparison groups, readily available groups may be found.

The most common quasi-experimental nonequivalent group design is the pretest-posttest nonequivalent comparison group design, denoted in Table 6.2.

Table 6.2. Pretest-Posttest Nonequivalent Comparison Group Design A.

Group 1	O	X	O
	Pretest Observation	Intervention	Posttest Observation
Group 2	O		O
	Pretest Observation		Posttest Observation

Using the management training example, various types of nonequivalent comparison groups are possible, such as the following:

- Managers who did not volunteer for the training program but met the program's eligibility criteria
- Managers who are slated to participate in the next scheduled training program
- Managers who met the eligibility criteria and were interested in participating in the program but could not participate because of space limitations, time constraints, or other seemingly arbitrary reasons
- Managers in another agency who are similar to those in the program
- Managers within the same agency or in another agency who are matched with program participants on individual characteristics that are believed to influence the results of the training program (such as matching on age, sex, and work experience)

Rog and Bickman (1984) describe the use of the nonequivalent groups design in an evaluation of a multiphase health improvement/stress management program for managers and their spouses in a Fortune 500 company. The design used for this study is stronger than those of most natural experiments. However, the example illustrates the importance of analyzing additional information that can help rule in possible alternative explanations for the outcomes.

In this evaluation, the participant group were managers and their spouses who volunteered for the program workshops. The comparison group included other managers who were selected from management divisions similar to those of the managers who participated in the program. One month prior to and six months following the workshops, both program and comparison group participants received questionnaires that measured attitudes, behaviors, and beliefs concerning stress, health, and general well-being. The design for this study is presented in Table 6.3.

Table 6.3. Pretest-Posttest Nonequivalent Comparison Group Design B.

Group 1				
	O	X	O	O
	Pretest Observation	Intervention	Immediate Posttest	Six-Month Posttest

Group 2				
	O		O	O
	Pretest Observation		Immediate Posttest	Six-Month Posttest

Overall, program participation was found to have no effects on the subjects. Inadequate measurement was ruled out as a plausible rival explanation for the results. Selection differences also were not viewed as a likely threat; pretest results did not indicate any major differences between the two groups on a number of key dimensions. In fact, the analysis of the pretest indicated that the lack of positive results very possibly reflected the mistargeting of the program to individuals who did not need this specific type of stress management program.

A review of the pretest results indicated a relatively low frequency of stressful events experienced and low levels of stress reported by participants and controls. Further examination of the pretest data across both groups (dropping the group distinction) led to a greater understanding of the type of stress experienced by these individuals and a realization that it was probably different from the type of stress the program was designed to reduce.

The use of statistical techniques such as regression can help to clarify and strengthen the findings in a study such as this one. Statistically controlling a variety of other factors such as initial stress level, the evaluator could determine whether program participation has any additional ability to predict level of stress at the posttest.

Posttest Only Design with Nonequivalent Groups

A weaker nonequivalent group design but one that is often needed when pretest measurement is not possible is the posttest only design with nonequivalent groups (Cook and Campbell, 1979). It is shown in Table 6.4.

Table 6.4. Posttest Only Comparison Group Design.

Group 1	X	O
	Intervention	Posttest Observation
Group 2		O
		Posttest Observation

This design is illustrated in the following example.

A national nonprofit association is interested in learning the effectiveness of its housing rehabilitation program, already in operation. The outcomes of interest include the extent to which the rehabilitation program leads to homeowners' increased ability to rent or sell their homes, more satisfaction among homeowners with their homes and neighborhoods, and higher resale values of the homes. Random assignment of possible housing units to the program is not possible as the houses are already selected prior to the start of the evaluation. Possible design alternatives include selecting comparison neighborhoods that are similar in housing costs, population composition, proportion of homeowners versus renters, and so on. Because the program is already in progress, collecting valid data about the neighborhoods prior to the program is unlikely. Therefore, the design is likely to involve comparing the neighborhoods following the program.

Patched-Up No Comparison Group Design

There are instances in which the evaluator cannot identify or utilize comparison groups but may be able to collect additional data to determine the plausibility of certain threats to validity. For example, in an evaluation of a job training program that has recently ended, the evaluation sponsor is interested in knowing how effective the program was in increasing employment. The desired measure of effectiveness is the number of individuals who were employed as a result of their participation in the program. Because the program has already occurred, there is no way to construct a randomized control group or another type of comparison group that could be tracked over the course of the program. There is no easy way to know what would have happened without the program. Is it possible that the individuals who participated were motivated to get jobs anyway? Was it this motivation that led them to participate in the program initially? Were there other changes in the job market that aided people in getting jobs?

Although establishing comparison groups may not be feasible, it may be possible to conduct interviews with the participants (through a sample survey [see Miller, Chapter Eleven] or focus groups [see Dean, Chapter Fourteen] to obtain a sense of their level of motivation for participating in the program initially and how they were selected for it (that is, did they volunteer or were they required to participate for some other reason?). The evaluator also could examine different levels of participation in the program and the relationship between participation level and obtaining a job. If the training program had specific skill tracks, the evaluator could get more detailed information on the type of training received and relate this to the type of employment obtained. Were individuals who participated in secretarial classes more likely to be employed in secretarial or office positions than in other types of positions? Were those who achieved the most knowledge gain in these areas most successful in obtaining relevant employment? It is possible that the motivation level of successful individuals increased their ability to obtain a job, but establishing a relationship between type of training and type of position increases the evaluator's confidence that the program may have had some effect on the type of employment received. What cannot be answered is more an external validity issue: Would the program work for individuals who were not self-motivated?

With respect to the history factors, the evaluator might identify other secondary sources on the nature and shifts of the job market that may help to determine the likelihood that the job market itself could have created the changes in employment. Outside influences can mask real program effects as well as create changes that are inappropriately attributed to the program. For example, negative changes in the job market could operate to depress the success of a program. A 5 percent change in employment of the participants may not be viewed positively until it is compared with employment figures of the overall population, which show a rise in unemployment. It is likely that with a more positive job market the gains of the program could be even stronger.

Conditions When a Natural Experiment Is Warranted

Given the variety of alternative designs that are possible, how does the evaluator determine the most appropriate one? How does the evaluator decide that other designs are not possible and that a natural experiment is warranted?

Selecting a design involves activities aimed at understanding the program and its context and the role an evaluation could play. This includes talking with key program contacts and other stakeholders, reviewing program documentation, and collecting information on the nature and quality of existing data. Armed with this information, the evaluator then should determine what is *necessary* to address the evaluation questions, what is *feasible* given resource constraints and other constraints in the program and the greater context, and what will provide the most *useful* information to the decision makers and other stakeholders. (Carter in Chapter Twenty-four of this handbook discusses strategies for maximizing the use and usefulness of evaluations.) In selecting a design, the evaluator therefore is simultaneously choosing data collection approaches, inventorying the resources that are available, assessing the feasibility of implementing the proposed design, and determining trade-offs with the choices that are selected (Hedrick, Bickman, and Rog, 1993). The next section reviews several of the program conditions that lead to using a natural experiment.

Limited Resources and Time

The amount and nature of the financial and other resources available to conduct an evaluation inevitably shape the type of study that can be conducted. Identifying and tracking comparison groups can be more costly than studying the intervention group itself. The ability to develop adequately and to maintain one or more comparison groups may depend on the funds available to reimburse participants for their time involved in data collection activities and to pay data collectors for maintaining contact with participants and conducting what could be extensive tracking. Lack of sufficient funds for these activities may result in loss of participants from the comparison group. When funds are not sufficient to construct a comparison group that can be maintained with integrity, the evaluator may need to look for other bases of comparison.

In an evaluation of a multiyear program for homeless individuals designed to increase their use of routine health services, including a comparison group of homeless individuals in the evaluation could be prohibitively expensive and resource intensive. Identifying a comparable group of homeless individuals is no easy task; enlisting their participation in the comparison group and maintaining it throughout the duration of the program would require a considerable amount of resources. Often, conventional methods of maintaining contact with homeless individuals cannot be used because they have no permanent addresses or telephones. Routine in-person contact with the participants and with other individuals and organizations who may be in touch with comparison group members is often needed to ensure that the comparison group does not lose participants. With a limited budget, resources may not be adequate to permit this level of contact. Therefore, in this situation, alternative bases of comparison could be explored; these might include data from existing studies of homeless individuals that provide some indication of their use of health services, or data from studies of non-homeless but low-income individuals that provide some indication of their use of services. Another alternative might be to incorporate ongoing, longitudinal measurement of the service utilization of the program participants themselves over the course of the program. Although none of the identified comparisons is perfect, each can help to strengthen the conclusions that can be drawn from the study; using multiple comparison sources can provide a stronger set of conclusions.

When do the resource constraints lead the evaluator to a natural experiment? Typically, natural experiments are indicated when limitation of resources precludes developing comparable comparison groups or collecting sufficient data both before and following an intervention to construct a time series design. For example, time frames of less than a year, particularly for complex initiatives, restrict the number and timing of observations that can be made. In addition, in a short-term study, it is often not possible to implement fully a complicated randomized procedure or even to collect primary data from participants in a program and those in a control condition unless data collection instruments are readily available.

Program Stage

Whether the program has begun, is about to begin, or has already finished is extremely important to the design of an evaluation. The greatest flexibility is realized when the evaluator can design the evaluation prior to the beginning of an intervention. Before a program begins, the evaluator can discuss the possibility of random assignment of eligible individuals to the program and to a control condition. If random assignment is not possible, the evaluator is still afforded the opportunity to identify other comparison groups (such as individuals from the program's waiting list), to collect data during the course of the intervention, and to have some data collection activities incorporated as part of the intervention rather than as an add-on or as a perceived extra burden.

It is impossible to assign individuals randomly to participate in a program that is no longer in operation. In addition, the types of data that can be collected may be much more limited after a program has already begun and especially if it has been completed. When the program is completed or near completion, the evaluator typically is restricted to using existing data. After the program is completed, it is particularly difficult to identify a comparison group for whom comparable data have been or could be collected. Thus, the evaluator's only option may be to develop a natural experiment that either uses a reflexive control group (the intervention group itself) if pretest data were already collected, or a comparison with existing data on another group. In either case, the evaluator would want to bolster the design with other information.

Possible Confounding Elements

Designing an evaluation involves determining the confounding variables that need to be controlled or at least explained. Certain program situations, however, are more vulnerable to specific threats and less vulnerable to others. It is important for the evaluator to identify these vulnerabilities when selecting a design, especially when a randomized study cannot be used. It is important to maximize the efficiency of the evaluation design by including comparison groups that focus on the most plausible confounding elements; controlling for threats that are highly unlikely is an inefficient use of resources.

In the job training example cited earlier, selection and history were the most probable threats. In some program evaluations, it is impossible to control for every plausible confounding variable and threat through the design. However, at a minimum, as the job training evaluation illustrates, the evaluation can include data that describe the extent to which job market shifts could be affecting the outcomes.

Constraints

Almost all program settings are subject to constraints that can influence the type of design that is possible. For example, a state legislative body may ask for an evaluation of the effects of a newly implemented statewide program for increasing voter registration. Political pressures might demand that the program be instituted in all counties in the same time period, thus precluding the ability to randomly assign the program to local governments. Various natural experimental alternatives could be considered. If data are available on past voter registration, it would be possible to look at trends in voter registration both before and following the implementation of the program. This alternative is dependent on the availability of reliable, valid, complete, and comparable information on voter registration historically and following the program. Other possibilities include inter-county comparisons if different variants of the program are instituted among the counties, comparison with voter registration in counties outside the state that appear to be comparable at least to a sample of the program counties, and comparison with selected national data. Each of these alternatives can help to clarify the extent of the program's effect on voter registration; however, choosing among the possible alternatives involves a variety of trade-offs and design considerations. Moreover, the different alternatives provide answers to different research questions. For example, comparison with past registration information answers the question, "How much has the program improved voter registration from past years?" Using national data, the evaluation would be focused on the question, "How much better or worse is voter registration in the area that has the program compared with voter registration nationally?"

As shown, political and situational constraints can block the ability to employ randomization procedures and limit the types of design that are possible. In other instances, ethical constraints operate and are particularly pertinent when the intervention is targeted at vulnerable populations who traditionally have gone unserved. For some interventions, withholding treatment from individuals who would otherwise be eligible is considered unethical, even though the treatment has not been proven effective. Although research has indicated that random assignment is perceived as the fairest strategy for allocating scarce resources (Wortman and Rabinowitz, 1980), program officials often believe that they will be politically safer if they use a first-come, first-served strategy or a needs-based strategy for selecting clients. Withholding treatment may be even more difficult to accomplish in programs that are longitudinal in nature and would therefore require that the control clients not receive treatment for the duration of the program (or at least for the data collection phase).

Finally, when the population of interest is too small to be divided randomly into equivalent groups, size constraints may lead one to choose a natural experiment. In a study of local counties, only four counties were eligible for the program and resources were available to collect data from only four control counties. Given the small number of counties, the evaluators purposefully selected the treatment and control counties to be as similar as possible on a few key criteria. In addition, with only eight counties, it would not be possible to set up an experimental design and examine the statistical differences between the treatment and control counties on county-level measures such as extent of coordination among county agencies. Thus, a natural experiment, including multiple case studies, might be a reasonable alternative design in this situation.

Conclusion

This chapter has presented strategies for designing natural experiments based on key features of the program to be evaluated and the context of the assessment. Several natural experiments were described. The emphasis has been on developing tailored designs that take advantage of the bases for comparison that occur naturally. A major theme of the chapter was designing studies that can discount rival explanations either by controlling for conditions that could confound the results or by providing enough information to determine whether rival explanations are plausible.

References

Berk, R. A., and others. "Social Policy Experimentation: A Position Paper." *Evaluation Review,* 1985, *9*(4), 387–429.

Campbell, D. T., and Stanley, J. C. *Experimental and Quasi-Experimental Designs for Research.* Chicago: Rand McNally, 1966.

Cook, T. D., and Campbell, D. T. *Quasi-Experimentation: Design and Analysis Issues for Field Settings.* Chicago: Rand McNally, 1979.

Cordray, D. S. "Quasi-Experimental Analysis: A Mixture of Methods and Judgment." In W. M. K. Trochim (ed.), *Advances in Quasi-Experimental Design and Analysis.* New Directions for Program Evaluation, no. 31. San Francisco: Jossey-Bass, 1986.

Hedrick, T. E., Bickman, L., and Rog, D. J. *Applied Research Design: A Practical Guide.* Newbury Park, Calif.: Sage, 1993.

Mohr, L. B. *Impact Analysis for Program Evaluation.* Newbury Park, Calif.: Sage, 1992.

Rog, D. J., and Bickman, L. "The Feedback Research Approach to Evaluation: A Method to Increase Evaluation Utility." *Evaluation and Program Planning,* 1984, *7,* 169–175.

Rossi, P. H., and Freeman, H. E. *Evaluation: A Systematic Approach.* Newbury Park, Calif.: Sage, 1989.

Weiss, C. H. *Evaluation Research.* Englewood Cliffs, N.J.: Prentice-Hall, 1972.

Wortman, C. B., and Rabinowitz, O. "Randomization: The Fairest of Them All." In L. Sechrest (ed.), *Evaluation Studies Review Annual,* vol. 4. Newbury Park, Calif.: Sage, 1980.

7

Convincing Quasi-Experiments: The Interrupted Time Series and Regression-Discontinuity Designs

Richard J. Marcantonio, Thomas D. Cook

An important goal of many evaluations is to demonstrate a clear causal relationship between an intervention that is designed to help people and an outcome that measures the intervention's success. It is not enough to show a *relationship* between the intervention and the outcome. We must attempt to show that the relationship is *causal* by ruling out other forces that would have brought about the same outcomes in the absence of the intervention under evaluation.

Drawing inferences of this type is easier as more control is exercised over the research setting and the forces that impinge on it. There are many ways to achieve such control, the best known being random assignment (see Dennis, Chapter Eight, this volume). When individuals or other units are randomly assigned either to an intervention group or to a comparison group that does not receive the intervention, we can assume that the groups being compared were identical before the intervention began. Thus, any group differences in the postintervention outcome cannot be explained by differences in the kinds of people in one group versus another.

Unfortunately, true experiments with random assignment are not always feasible. Sometimes there are political and ethical objections to delaying implementation of a program so that random assignment can be achieved, as when a program arises in response to a crisis such as an unusually high number of alcohol-related fatalities on public highways (Ross and Campbell, 1968; Ross, Campbell, and Glass, 1970). The program must then be evaluated after it has already begun. At other times, a new law or regulation has to apply to everyone so no comparison group can be formed. For example, an evaluation of cotton dust regulation in the textile industry had to work around the reality that the regulation was binding for all textile plants without exception (Viscusi, 1985).

Even when initially achieved, random assignment can break down during the course of a study. In an evaluation of the first year of *Sesame Street,* Ball and Bogatz (1970) discovered that some teachers of children who had been randomly assigned to a control condition demanded and achieved access to the program for their children during school hours. Reclassifying these children as *Sesame Street* viewers meant that the viewing and nonviewing groups were not equivalent on the average, though the data might also have been analyzed in a conservative fashion that preserved the original, planned assignment to groups.

For all these reasons, control through random assignment is not always possible and alternatives are required (Cook, 1990; Cook, 1991). One class of alternatives is called *quasi-experiments.* These are like true experiments in form and function. Functionally, they are designed to probe causal hypotheses about the effects of a presumed causal agent. In form, they entail an intervention, one or more comparison groups, outcome measures, assessments of the relationship between the intervention and outcome, and construction of the case that any demonstrated impact is due not to other factors but to the intervention. However, by definition, quasi-experiments do not have random assignment and must struggle to differentiate effects of the intervention from effects associated with the different kinds of people in each of the groups being contrasted.

Although many kinds of quasi-experiments exist (Cook and Campbell, 1979; Cook, Campbell, and Peracchio, 1990), two stand out because of the high quality of causal inference they often engender: interrupted time series designs and regression-discontinuity designs. *Interrupted time series designs* require a long series of observations on the outcome variables before and after an intervention. In this way, we can test whether the trend of the time series after the intervention differs from what it was before. Additionally, we can rule out alternative interpretations of why such changes at the point of intervention might have come about.

Regression-discontinuity designs require that we specify a point along some continuum on which treatment eligibility depends—for example, the annual income at which Medicaid eligibility is set for a family of a given size. Then the analysis probes whether the relationship between family income and an outcome (such as the number of physician visits) is the same on each side of the cutoff point (such as income level) that determines program eligibility. If there is a discontinuity in the relationship at that point, we conclude that the potential cause (income level) is differently related to the outcome (number of physician visits) on each side of the cutoff point, and that the treatment is responsible for the difference.

In a general sense, the two designs are alike since they both postulate a specific point on a continuum at which a relationship is supposed to change if an intervention is effective. In the interrupted time series case, the continuum is temporal; in the regression-discontinuity case, the continuum relates to the program eligibility criterion. The interrupted time series is particularly useful where an intervention or program is introduced at a specific moment in time and is expected to have a rapid effect (or an effect with known delay, as with the nine months between conception and birth among humans). The regression-discontinuity design, on the other hand, is particularly useful for programs targeted at the most needy or meritorious, provided that program eligibility depends on a score such as family income, grade point average, or weight.

Interrupted Time Series in Evaluation

Several variations of the time series design are discussed in this section. Also examined are practical considerations that must be addressed before a time series evaluation is undertaken.

Simple Interrupted Time Series

The basic structure of the interrupted time series design entails (1) a series of preintervention observations taken on the target population to establish a baseline trend, (2) an intervention at a known point in this sequence, and (3) a series of postintervention observations from which to infer change from before to after. The purpose of the analysis is to see whether the pre- and posttreatment series differ. This difference can appear in three major ways. The most common way is a change in the slope, or the rate of change, of the observation line from before to after the intervention. For example, before an intervention, an observation line may appear quite flat, indicating that the amount of change in the outcome variable per unit of time is very small. After the intervention, however, the line may become quite steep, indicating that large changes are taking place per unit of time. Another common type of change in the observations is a difference in their overall level. Such a difference indicates that a change has occurred in the mean of the posttreatment observations relative to its pretreatment value. Finally, the observations can differ in the amount of variation they show around the mean of the series. This kind of change indicates that the observations have become more or less variable after an intervention or that a seasonal trend has changed its form.

A simple but effective application of the basic interrupted time series design appears in a study by McSweeny (1978). The population in the greater Cincinnati metropolitan area had steadily grown during the 1960s, resulting in an increase in the volume of operator-assisted local telephone calls. The Cincinnati Bell Telephone company could not afford to continue operator-assisted calls as a free service. In March 1974, they initiated a fee-for-service plan designed to reduce the number of unnecessary local directory assistance calls. All telephone customers were allowed three free calls per month to local directory assistance, but each call over this limit would incur a 20-cent charge. An interrupted time series design was used to evaluate the effectiveness of the fee-for-service plan. Figure 7.1 depicts the results.

Figure 7.1. Single Group Interrupted Time Series Data:
Volume of Calls Received by Cincinnati Bell's Local Directory Assistance: 1968–1976.

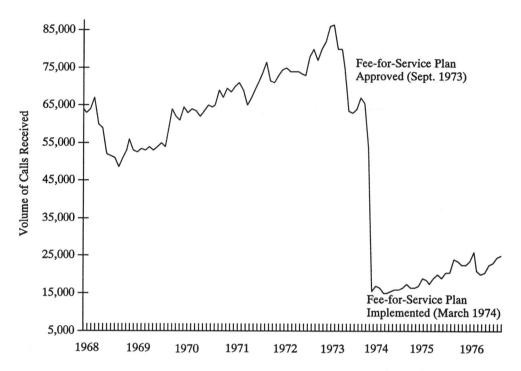

Source: Adapted from McSweeny, 1978, from data provided by John McSweeny.

The horizontal axis represents time while the vertical axis represents the number of calls placed each month to Cincinnati Bell's local directory assistance, as automatically recorded in a computerized database. Visual inspection suggests three changes worth discussion.

First, we see a gradual increase in the number of calls for assistance up to 1973. This is probably due to population growth and might well disappear if the data were plotted on a per capita basis. Second, we note a decrease in calls to the operator in the half-year before the new program came into effect. Assuming this is not due to chance—which could be tested statistically—it may well be due to publicity about the impending rate change. Of greatest interest to us, though, is the third relationship—the precipitous drop in calls after the new policy was initiated. Statistical analysis indicated that this drop was quite unlikely to have been due to chance.

Nor is the steep decline in calls likely to be due to *statistical regression to the mean,* which we define as the natural tendency of any probabilistic series to return to a more central level after an extremely high or extremely low observation. This conclusion is plausible because the preintervention time series showed a steady growth over the years and the one surge in the year prior to the intervention is not of a magnitude to account for the large effect observed. The drop shown in Figure 7.1 is to a level far below the true mean of the immediately preceding series.

The most viable alternative interpretation is that something else happened at the same time Bell introduced its charges and this something caused the observed decrease in use of operator-assisted calls. We call explanations of this type "history." But what could a specific alternative interpretation be? It would take mammoth, simultaneous population loss or a complete breakdown in equipment at the time to account for such a large drop in calls, and the alternative event would have to be one that occurred at exactly the same time the charge for directory services began. Unfortunately, a natural disaster did strike southern Ohio at the end of March 1974, in the form of a tornado. However, if the tornado caused the drop in the volume of calls, we would expect a large increase after March, perhaps to a higher level than before. Instead, the postintervention observations show the same steady increase that the early years showed, only at a substantially lower level. In light of this we are inclined to believe that the new charges caused the decrease in use of operator assistance to find local telephone numbers.

Note some of the other factors that contribute to this causal inference. If the time intervals were broader — perhaps years instead of months — it would not be so easy to link the exact point of the intervention with the time the response changed. If the effect were not an instantaneous one, it would not be as easy to rule out the possibility that other contemporaneous factors were responsible for the effect. If, for instance, a year was needed before an effect could be observed, all historical events occurring in this year would be potential alternative interpretations, and not just those that occurred in the one month after the change in payment plan was made. In this respect, it is likely that publicity about the new program led to citywide knowledge of the intervention and thereby facilitated an instantaneous response. Where an intervention diffuses slowly through a community — as is often the case with new laws or regulations — abrupt changes at the intervention point will be harder to detect. Finally, the importance of exact knowledge of the intervention point is worth noting. If such knowledge did not exist, it would be impossible to link the change in response to the exact point when the intervention was introduced, and many more alternative interpretations would become plausible.

We can see, then, that interrupted time series designs become less interpretable as the intervention point is less clear, when knowledge of an intervention or the intervention itself diffuses slowly through a community, when effects are delayed rather than instantaneous, when substantive theories do not predict the delay interval, and when the time intervals used in the analysis are longer rather than shorter.

Adding a Comparison Series: The British Breathalyzer Crackdown

The local directory-assistance data in Figure 7.1 are compelling because no alternative interpretations can be invoked that predict an effect at the exact point the new plan was introduced. However, we cannot know in advance that the data will be quite so specific. Given this, interrupted time series designs are strengthened by the addition of comparison series that suggest what would probably have happened in the intervention group had the treatment not been received.

A classic case in point is the British breathalyzer crackdown, discussed in Ross, Campbell, and Glass (1970). An increase in traffic fatalities in Britain prompted the government to enact legislation to crack down on people who were driving under the influence of alcohol. This legislation, effective October 1967, empowered the police to administer an on-the-spot breath test to determine the percentage of alcohol in the blood with a known amount of error. If motorists failed this "breathalyzer" test, they were then taken to the police station where more extensive blood and urine tests were performed. An intensive media campaign was launched before the effective date of the crackdown.

Figure 7.2 depicts the number of fatalities and serious casualties combined for the calendar years 1966, 1967, and 1968. The top line, marked "All Hours and Days," shows the total number of these events each month. A decrease can be seen at the intervention point, suggesting a treatment effect. But this possible effect might also be due to any number of historical factors that happened at the same time the breathalyzer rule went into

Figure 7.2. British Motor Vehicle Fatalities for the Years 1966, 1967, and 1968: Crackdown Effective Date: October 9, 1967.

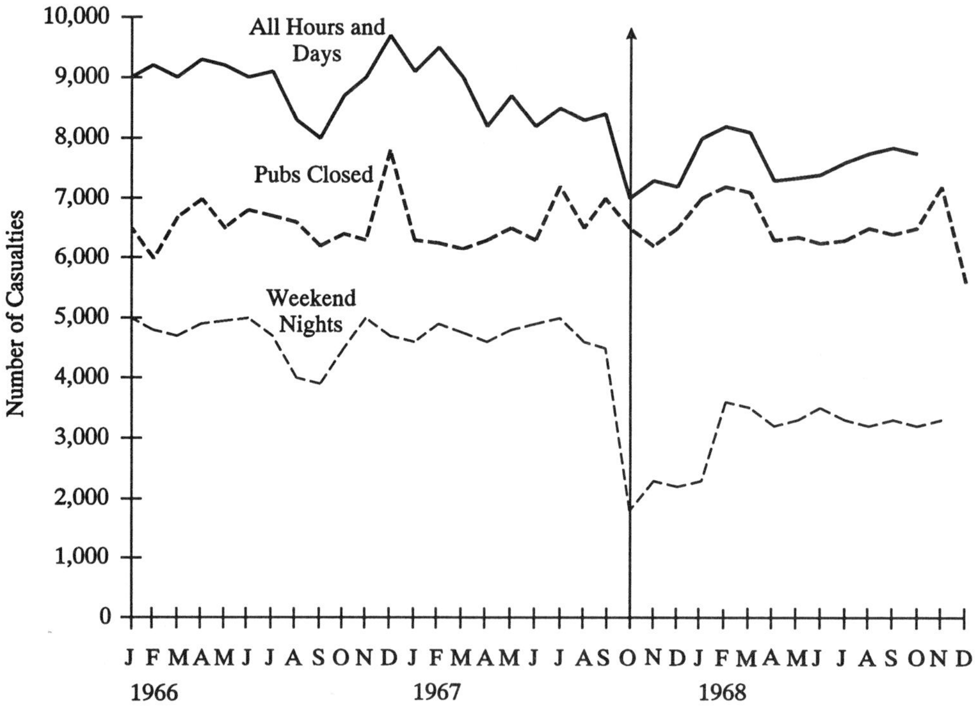

Source: Adapted from Ross, Campbell, and Glass, 1970.

effect — perhaps safer cars were introduced or the weather improved. To rule out these possibilities the data were disaggregated.

The middle line in Figure 7.2, marked "Pubs Closed," depicts the combined number of fatalities and serious casualties that occurred during hours when pubs were closed and little drinking presumably took place. The bottom time series, marked "Weekend Nights," depicts the number of fatalities and serious casualties during these times of the week, which are the hours when pubs are open and drinking alcohol is most prevalent. Since the breathalyzer rule had to apply to all drivers in Britain, ruling out random assignment, Ross and his colleagues treated the "Pubs Closed" data as a comparison series and assumed that the breathalyzer would have little or no impact during these hours of the week. Indeed, no effect can be observed in the "Pubs Closed" time series. But a large effect is evident in the "Weekend Nights" series when drinking is heavier.

The presence of the comparison series adds to the causal interpretation of the data, since it is not plausible to assume that this differential pattern of results at the very time the breathalyzer was introduced can be due to newer, safer cars or to better weather. There is no reason to believe that these forces operate some hours of the day and some days of the week, but not others. The causal interpretation depends on other factors, too, especially the crucial assumption that drinking in Britain is primarily a social event taking place in pubs and so is much heavier during the hours when pubs are open. If much drinking were private and done at all hours of the day, it would not have been sensible to predict the differential pattern of fatalities and serious casualties that was in fact obtained.

Interrupted Time Series with Switching Replications

Imagine a design with two independent samples: one group receives the intervention and the other serves as its control; then, at some later point, these roles are switched so that the treatment group becomes the control group and the controls become the treatment group. This variant of the interrupted time series is known as a *switching replications* design, and an example of its use can be found in a study by Hennigan and others (1982). Its inferential strengths are considerable.

The authors wished to test whether the introduction of television into the United States increased certain types of crimes. A time series with a single group of communities that received television in a particular year could not easily be used, for even if an increase in crime were detected, it would not be clear whether it was due to the introduction of television, to economic shifts, to an increase in the population of teenage boys, or to some other factor.

Television was not introduced uniformly throughout the United States. It came to larger and more affluent markets first. However, the process was not orderly, and the Federal Communications Commission imposed a freeze on issuing new broadcasting licenses that lasted from late 1949 until mid-1952. This broke the pattern of market-driven implementation and led to the situation where more and more communities were impatiently waiting to get television but were blocked from it. This circumstance permitted the construction of two groups of cities — those that received television signals before the freeze (the *prefreeze* group) and those that did not (the *postfreeze* group). The prefreeze communities would obviously be the treatment group before the freeze was lifted, while the postfreeze communities would be the controls. After the freeze, however, the roles of the two groups could be reversed. Then, television signals would be new to the postfreeze cities while the prefreeze cities would no longer be influenced by the introduction of television. They would have television, of course, but it would not be new.

The authors focused on two major types of crimes. *Violent crimes* were defined as murder and aggravated assault; *instrumental crimes* were defined as burglary, larceny theft, and auto theft. Yearly data were gathered for extended periods of time, from 1936 through 1976 for cities (matched on region of the country) that quickly became saturated with television sets. Because the number of larceny thefts differed so widely between regions, the authors found that using the original measuring scale (a simple count of the number of larceny thefts) was influenced by factors that were not of interest, such as the population density of the area. Therefore, the data were transformed by taking logarithms of the counts and in turn converting these to standardized scores (so that the mean was equal to zero and the standard deviation equal to one).

Figure 7.3 shows the results for larceny thefts. The solid vertical line indicates the beginning of the FCC freeze, the dashed vertical line, the end of it. The area between these two lines, the years 1949 to 1954, is the period when postfreeze cities served as controls for the prefreeze cities. During this time, we can see that the prefreeze cities did show an increase in the number of larceny thefts relative to the postfreeze cities. The area after the second vertical line is the area where the roles of the two groups reversed and where we would expect the postfreeze cities to "catch up" to the prefreeze cities. This is what happens, and there is very little variation between the two groups from then on.

Statistical analysis showed that the obtained pattern of results is not likely to be due to chance. Few other alternative explanations are viable. The effect cannot be explained by the presence of more television sets to steal; such thefts are burglaries, not larcenies. Perhaps readers more ingenious than we are can come up with alternatives that are plausible, for the process of finding and ruling out alternative interpretations is a social process dependent on critical commentary from a wide range of persons interested in the phenomenon under analysis.

Single Interrupted Time Series with Multiple Interventions

So far, we have noted several ways to strengthen the basic interrupted time series design. One of the most valuable has been the use of the comparison

Figure 7.3. Larceny Thefts for Selected Cities, 1936–1976.

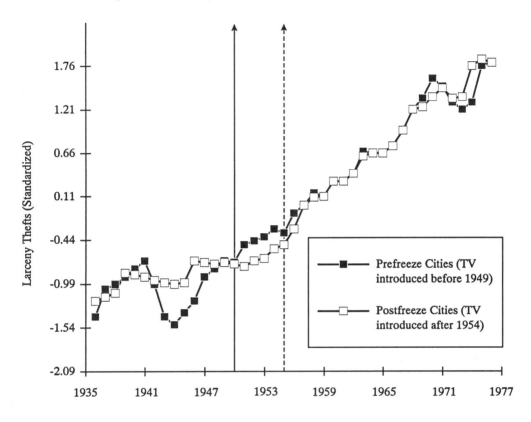

Note: The solid vertical arrow indicates the beginning of the freeze; the dashed arrow indicates the end of it.

Source: Adapted from Hennigan and others, 1982.

series. However, some interventions do not lend themselves to data disaggregation, as in the British breathalyzer example, or to the use of two independent groups, as in Hennigan and others (1982). What should we do, then, if a separate series is not possible? Occasionally, a comparison series can be approximated in the form of a *single group reversal* design where the same respondents are measured a number of times, sometimes when the intervention is present and sometimes when it is not. If the dependent variable varies systematically with the presence and absence of the intervention, this can indicate that the relationship between the intervention and the dependent variable is causal. An example will illustrate the basic idea.

Davis and Luthans (1984) examined the production problems of a small printing firm that silk-screened shirts. The primary difficulty revolved around the highly centralized process for scheduling the work. The production manager realized this and redesigned the work schedule to smooth out the process. The time series data are shown in Figure 7.4.

Figure 7.4. Single Group, Multiple Interventions.

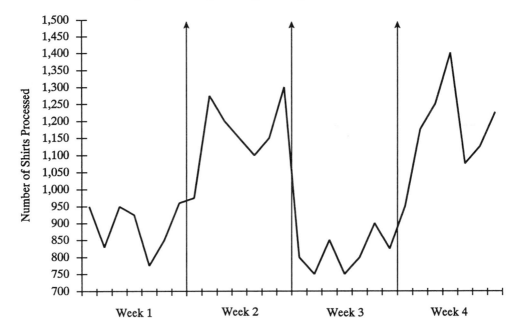

Note: Weeks 1 and 3 depict the number of shirts produced under the old work schedule; weeks 2 and 4 depict the number produced under the new schedule.
Source: Adapted from Davis and Luthans, 1984.

A quick examination of Figure 7.4 shows a clear difference between the weeks when the work was scheduled using the old system (weeks 1 and 3) and the weeks when the work was scheduled under the production manager's new system (weeks 2 and 4). The second replication of the effect, week 4, rules out many alternative explanations for the effect in week 2. For instance, the type of work that the silk-screeners were doing in week 2 could have been much simpler and high volumes of output not unexpected. It is highly implausible that a separate factor, acting independently of the new schedule, produced the same gains at the same time as the new schedule. In addition, if there had been changes in the ability level of the workers over this time period (a confounding effect known as *maturation*), it is more probable that the production level would steadily increase or decrease rather than fluctuate wildly on a biweekly basis.

Some Practical Considerations with Interrupted Time Series Designs

The four examples described above have shown that adding comparison series and repeating the same intervention make interrupted time series designs more complex but also promote even more convincing causal inference than is usually possible with a single time series. However, an important practical question remains: How feasible are interrupted time series designs of any kind, let alone the more complex designs advocated here?

Feasibility often depends on the cost of data collection. Interrupted time series designs are not suited to circumstances in which the evaluator has to go out and collect primary data from respondents. This is because of the long time periods and multiple measurement waves typically involved. In the social sciences, archives are therefore the major source of data for interrupted time series. Fortunately, archival data have become more abundant and accessible over the last several years. Kiecolt and Nathan (1990) have described some of the many sophisticated archive services that have been established across the United States, both academic and nonacademic. Such services function as data libraries, with most providing technical assistance and also referring interested individuals to other data archives if they do not have the data requested.

Although archival data have tremendous potential, they are not problem free. First, record-keeping methods change periodically, and these changes sometimes masquerade as treatment effects. This is especially likely when record keeping changes *because* of an intervention, as when Police Chief Orlando Wilson's reorganization of the Chicago police system included a reorganization of the way serious crimes were reported (Cook and Campbell, 1979). To deal with record-keeping changes requires identifying them and, preferably, collecting data over a limited time period with both the old and new measures so as to understand the relationship between them. A second problem with archival data is that, since they were not collected with any particular intervention in mind, they may not represent as valid a measure of outcomes as one would like. For example, the use of Uniform Crime Reports as an indicator of burglary might be criticized because many burglaries go unreported or are misclassified by the police (McCleary, Nienstedt, and Erven, 1982). Finally, archival data may not faithfully reflect quite the same target populations or geographic areas as are called for in the research question. For instance, if an intervention is targeted at Native Americans living in Chicago, then archival data on all minorities in Chicago would be problematic, as would national data on Native Americans living in major urban areas. There is overlap in all these cases, but not perfect overlap. We strongly urge all those planning to use interrupted time series designs to become intimately familiar with the archival data they propose to use.

Interrupted time series data are more difficult to interpret causally when an intervention is slowly diffused throughout the population. In the British breathalyzer example presented earlier, the intervention began at a known time point and was quickly diffused throughout the target population. In contrast, in the study by Hennigan and others (1982) of how the introduction of television influenced larcenies, the diffusion of television throughout the target communities was much more gradual, and the maximal point of effect due to television was indeterminate. If an intervention is gradual by nature, we strongly advise collecting data to describe the diffusion process so that you can analyze the dynamic relationship between the treatment, as it gradually builds up, and the outcome, as it gradually changes.

The most appropriate type of interrupted time series design for a particular evaluation depends on the nature of the effect being measured. In some cases, we expect swift-acting effects, such as the relatively abrupt changes observed in the Cincinnati directory-assistance study and the British breathalyzer crackdown. In other cases, we expect a long-term, gradual trend to emerge over time, as with certain communitywide health education programs (see Farquhar and others, 1990). Gradual effects do not lend themselves well to interrupted time series work unless a substantive theory clearly predicts the delay interval, or a switching replications design is used to probe whether similar trends occur in separate populations at approximately the same (unpredictable) time after an intervention. Switching replications is often a good idea, for neither of the groups is required to forego a potentially beneficial treatment. Adding another intervention does increase financial and logistical costs, however, and this must be considered in light of the increased explanatory power.

A final word regarding interrupted time series concerns the analysis of programs that are undertaken in response to an unexpectedly bad state of affairs. Many times, government agencies or institutions are pressured to respond immediately to a crisis, such as the one Connecticut faced in 1955 when motor vehicle fatalities reached a record high (Ross and Campbell, 1968). A tough new antispeeding law was quickly enacted, and, in the next year, the number of fatalities decreased by 12 percent. Was this decrease solely due to the crackdown? Alas, we cannot ignore the possibility that the number of fatalities was likely to decrease anyway. Statistical regression often occurs after unexpected extreme observations occur: the next observations tend to revert toward the mean of a series. Thus, when a program has arisen because of an unexpected steep rise in some social problem, we advise collecting an *extended* series of preintervention data to probe the suspicion that any observed change might be due to an extreme observation prior to the intervention. An extended time series has another advantage when the extension follows the intervention, for assessment can then be made of the long-term nature of any treatment impact.

Regression-Discontinuity in Evaluation

Interventions are often designed so that individuals with specific needs can receive special services, or so that those with special merit can receive extra resources. Although many individuals might benefit from these resources, we cannot afford to include everyone. In such cases, we are forced to admit only a select few, and a sense of fairness compels us to choose only those who are the neediest, for example. The regression-discontinuity design is appropriate for assessing the consequences of this decision. Its efficacy depends primarily on the assignment of individuals to groups based on a fully known quantitative score that defines program eligibility.

Since the regression-discontinuity design is not well known, its basic features are best explained in the context of a simple, hypothetical example. Assume that we can measure the severity of an illness and that lower scores mean greater severity. Assume further that a quantitative cutoff point has been established; patients scoring below it receive a novel medical treatment while the patients scoring above it receive the standard treatment. All patients are then retested to assess their condition. The question is, Has the new treatment made a difference?

We describe two separate scenarios. In the first, we assume that the treatment has no effect. Figure 7.5 shows a plot of the posttreatment scores as a function of the initial severity of the illness for 200 patients. We have assumed a very high correlation between the two scores; patients who were seriously ill at time 1 had almost certainly worsened at time 2. The vertical line at the score of 50 defines the cutoff, at or below which patients are assigned to the new treatment. Although it looks as though we have drawn only one regression line, two lines have actually been computed: one for the patients at or below the cutoff, who received the new treatment, and one for patients above the cutoff, who did not receive the new treatment.

Figure 7.5. Regression-Discontinuity Plot for Postintervention Symptoms as a Function of Initial Severity of an Illness: An Example of No Treatment Effect.

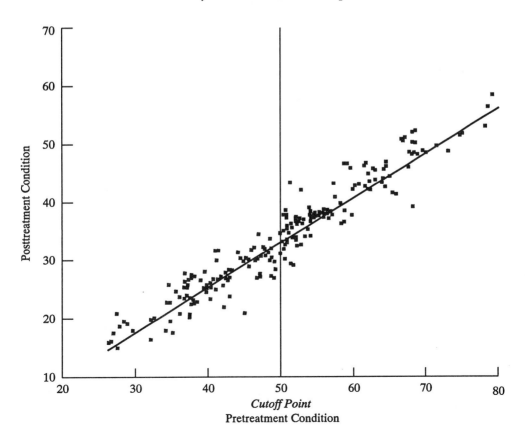

In Figure 7.5, the two lines seamlessly meet at the cutoff score, which means that a patient's condition at time 2 is not affected by whether he or she received the new treatment.

Now, let us take the second scenario and assume that the alternative hypothesis is that there is a treatment effect. Regression lines are again calculated for each group and appear in Figure 7.6. The group to the right of the cutoff is the control group, and their scores are exactly the same as in Figure 7.5. However, contrast the change in the treatment group with what happened in Figure 7.5. There is now a discontinuity between the two regression lines at the cutoff point, suggesting that the intervention increased the scores of the "new treatment" patients by about 15 points. The slopes of the regression lines are the same for both groups, which means that this 15-point gain is constant for all members of the "new treatment" group, no matter how ill they were at time 1. The slopes would be unequal if the new treatment had helped the most seriously ill patients (those below a score of 30, for example) more than it had helped patients nearer to the cutoff. Such slope differences would imply an interaction between group membership and the treatment.

Figure 7.6. Regression-Discontinuity Plot for Postintervention Symptoms as a Function of Initial Severity of an Illness: Example of a Treatment Main Effect.

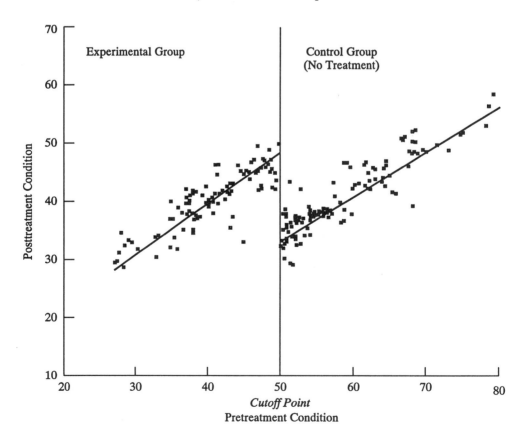

The strength of the regression-discontinuity design can be understood in two ways. The first depends on recognizing that usually, few alternative interpretations will exist for a change in regression lines occurring at the exact point on the assignment variable that determines program eligibility. Such point specificity of prediction is also what makes the interrupted time series design so interpretable, though there the specificity involves a time point rather than a specific assignment score. A second way of understanding the inferential power of regression-discontinuity is to realize that, like random assignment, the mechanism for assigning individuals to conditions is fully known.

Since governments and other institutions often seek to provide services to those in special need or with special merit, the regression-discontinuity design would seem to be especially useful in evaluation whenever compensatory services or merit-based awards are at issue. But several other assumptions must be made when using the design, and some of these are best understood in the context of specific examples.

A Regression-Discontinuity Analysis of Medicaid

Lohr (1972) was interested in exploring the effects of Medicaid, which was designed to make medical care more available to those with very low family incomes (under $3,000 per year, for example). The question was whether eligibility for the Medicaid program actually caused an increase in the average number of visits to the doctor by the poor. The relationship between these two variables is plotted in Figure 7.7. Notice the strong linear relationship

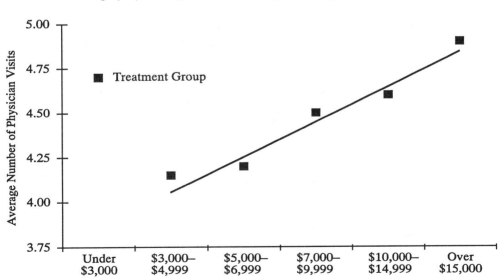

Figure 7.7. Regression-Discontinuity Plot:
Income Category by Average Number of Trips to a Physician for the Year 1967.

Source: Adapted from Cook and Campbell, 1979.

between income category and average number of physician visits for the five income categories over the $3,000 cutoff. The only discontinuity from this trend is for the treatment group, or those eligible to receive Medicaid. From the graph, we might draw the conclusion that Medicaid availability increased the number of trips to physicians by those who are eligible for it. However, are there any plausible alternative explanations for this trend?

The observed discontinuity could possibly be tied to several factors other than the availability of Medicaid. Among the aged, physician visits per year are probably high, and income low. While there is no compelling reason to believe that the aged are in fact so heavily concentrated in this category, the relationship can be empirically determined with archival data. A more reasonable possibility related to age is that those over age sixty-five are eligible to receive Medicare as well as Medicaid and probably take advantage of both programs. A fairer evaluation of Medicaid might control for this by doing two analyses—one with those over age sixty-five, and one without them. A second reason for the discontinuity might be that the lowest income category consists of a disproportionate number of women of child-bearing age and their children. If so, they may have had a high number of trips to physicians before the availability of Medicaid, perhaps on a non-payment basis. Again, such important demographic effects must be checked by separate subgroup analysis.

As informative as these subanalyses are, they do not provide information about the underlying relationship between income and the number of physician visits in the absence of the intervention. This is important because regression-discontinuity analysis assumes that the form of this relationship is known. For the Lohr example, a control group with the same income could not be used, since Medicaid applied to all families without exception. The alternative in this case would be to use archival data on income and physician visits for some time prior to the establishment of the Medicaid program. Lohr obtained such data for 1964, and they are plotted in Figure 7.8 along with the 1967 data, which had appeared alone in Figure 7.7.

From Figure 7.8 we can easily see that the form of the relationship between physician visits and income in the year prior to Medicaid was essentially linear. Of interest to us is that the pre-Medicaid (1964) data show no discontinuity, while a large discontinuity exists in the same data for 1967, long after Medicaid was in place. Thus, the pretreatment data have enabled us to describe the underlying relationship between the classification variable (income) and the outcome (number of physician visits), and ruled out the alternative intepretation that the two were related in some complex non-linear way that required no need to invoke Medicaid as a causal agent.

The regression-discontinuity design requires the assumption that the model chosen to analyze the data be functionally correct for a very important reason. We base our conclusions on the difference between the treatment and control groups at the cutoff point. However, remember that *there*

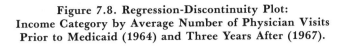

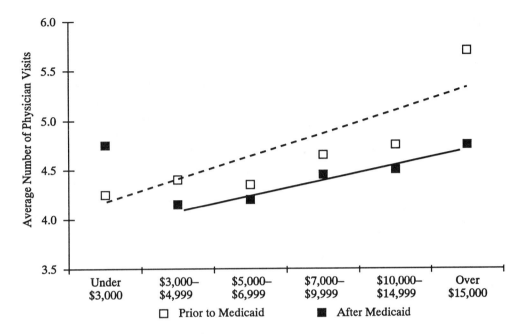

Figure 7.8. Regression-Discontinuity Plot:
Income Category by Average Number of Physician Visits
Prior to Medicaid (1964) and Three Years After (1967).

Source: Adapted from Cook and Campbell, 1979.

is no overlap between the treatment and control groups at the cutoff point. Hence, for one group (usually the controls), the regression line has to be extended beyond the range of the available data. Recall that this was the case for our medical example at the beginning of this section. All patients *above* the cutoff received the standard treatment, while those *at* or *below* the cutoff received the new treatment. This means that there is no overlap between the groups in terms of the qualifying score. Since we are in essence adding predicted values where there are no data to predict, we need to be able to assume that the relationship between the two variables in the range beyond the data is the same as it was in the area where there were data. The difficulty is that this assumption is not directly testable (Rubin, 1977). Indeed, we cannot know what the distribution would have been at any part of the initial classification score beyond the cutoff point.

Another issue in regression-discontinuity analysis is whether more complex forms of regression fit the data just as well or better than the linear regression models typically used on each side of the cutoff point and illustrated in the preceding graphs. When the underlying form of the relationship is curvilinear, linear fits on each side of the cutoff can give spurious discontinuities. Cook and Campbell (1979) discuss this in the context of a regression-discontinuity analysis of whether being put on the dean's list because of grades in one quarter caused an increase in a student's undergraduate grades the next quarter (Seaver and Quarton, 1976). The original analysis using linear regression concluded that being put on the dean's list improved later grades, but closer analysis suggested that the underlying relationship between grades in one quarter and the next is curvilinear (that is, a curved line rather than a straight line), and that such a curve fit the data without any need to invoke a causal effect of being on the dean's list.

Another assumption of regression-discontinuity analysis is that assignment to treatment conditions is perfect—that is, everyone who received the intervention was qualified for it while everyone who did not receive the intervention was not qualified for it. In reality, assignment errors—accidental or intentional—sometimes blur the distinction between treatment and control groups, creating a selection problem. For example, social workers have been known to modify income eligibility statements to make individuals close to the cutoff eligible for welfare services, and welfare applicants know what income they should report in order to receive services. Knowledge of cutoff points—and of the opportunities that go with them—can lead to classification errors that place individuals on the wrong side of the cutoff point. It is clearly advisable for any evaluator to know the assignment process intimately and to exclude all known misclassified cases.

Even so, some respondents may be tied at the cutoff score, forcing some extra assignment rule. The best way to handle this is to randomly assign the tied cases to the conditions under analysis. If sample size permits, these data can then be separately analyzed as a true experiment that complements the regression-discontinuity analysis. This creates a "tie-breaking experiment"; a good discussion of this situation can be found in the foreword by Campbell to Trochim's book on regression-discontinuity (1984).

The final major assumption made in regression-discontinuity designs is that we have included in the model all alternative causal interpretations. This assumption is not as problematic as it may seem at first, given that a conclusion about effectiveness depends on obtaining a discontinuity *at the cutoff point,* and nowhere else. Hence, any alternative interpretation has to predict the same discontinuity at exactly the same cutoff point. For the Lohr example, this would mean that if family size were an important causal variable, then its causal impact on the number of physician visits would have to occur at the $3,000 income cutoff, and not elsewhere.

Practical Considerations

Few examples of the regression-discontinuity design exist (see Berk and Rauma, 1983; Luft, 1990). This should embolden us to ask why this is the case and what should be done to stimulate greater use. One difficulty with this design is its potential for selection bias. That is, it is well known that the neediest individuals eligible for compensatory services often fail to hear about a program. Thus, the rate at which those who are eligible agree to participate may fall below 100 percent. When the participation rate falls far below 100 percent, an unrestricted analysis of the full sample may be vulnerable to selection bias. One might restrict the analysis to those subgroups of the population where participation rates are higher. Unfortunately, breaking a larger group into subgroups reduces the number of cases available for analysis, thus making it more difficult to detect a difference between groups. On the other hand, restricting analysis to certain subgroups minimizes selection bias. Even better, though, is making sure that the opportunity to participate in the program is well publicized, so that all individuals for whom the treatment is potentially applicable have a fair chance of participating.

If the cutoff score is a quantity that the potential applicant must supply, such as information about age or income, applicants can dissemble with an eye toward receiving the treatment (Campbell and others, 1974; Jencks and Edin, 1990). Also, scores can be altered by those seeking to "help" borderline cases (Trochim, 1990). When one knows for certain which cases are misclassified, they can either be eliminated from the analysis or can remain part of the data for subanalyses designed to probe the extent of any bias (Campbell and others, 1974). More commonly, misclassified cases will remain unknown. If so, a confidence interval might be constructed around the cutoff, and regression lines fit only to the cases that fall above and below this interval. Such range restriction creates its own difficulties, especially some loss of statistical power and the possibility of additional alternative interpretations. Still, the procedure is worth serious consideration.

In many administrative contexts, quantitative measures are not trusted enough to serve as the sole criterion for treatment assignment. They are often supplemented by other materials, such as the letters of recommendation that accompany Graduate Record Examination scores among applications to graduate schools. The regression discontinuity design is viable only where such qualitative sources can be made quantitative, as they sometimes can be. In any case, this design needs full quantification of the assignment criteria.

Conclusion

The interrupted time series and regression-discontinuity designs are similar in two major ways that are relevant for program evaluation. First, each tests a hypothesis that is causal, and each is capable of a strong test. They have this inferential power because each of them can show whether the relationship between an independent and a dependent variable changes at a specific, predetermined point on a time or program eligibility continuum. Such specificity enables us to rule out many plausible alternative explanations for the change in the relationship between the independent and a dependent variable, since few alternatives specify a precise change point identical with the one implied in a causal hypothesis about program effectiveness. Because one important goal of program evaluation is to establish a clear causal connection between a specific intervention and the behavior it was supposed to affect, the interrupted time series and regression-discontinuity designs are particularly relevant to program evaluation. Second, neither of these designs uses random assignment. Though random assignment is highly desirable in program evaluation, it is not always feasible. This is especially true with evaluations that are retrospective, where programs apply to an entire population, or where resources have to be allocated by need or merit. The examples in this chapter have shown that in situations where random assignment is not possible, interrupted time series and regression-discontinuity designs provide effective and efficient design alternatives.

Archives provide the data source for most interrupted time series analyses. Archival data are often inflexible, being collected for purposes other than evaluating the program on hand. Their strengths and weaknesses always depend on the context in which they are being used, and in most circumstances they will only approximate the desired variables. Several examples in this chapter have demonstrated the utility of archival data, however.

It is somewhat surprising to see the two designs described here used so infrequently in program evaluation, given the high degree of correspondence between their explanatory power and the need to establish program effectiveness. As many examples and references in this chapter show, the designs have been around for twenty or more years. Many researchers may see them as too complex to be practical, and they are indeed more complex than some of the weaker evaluation designs (see Rog, Chapter Six, this volume). This increased complexity does not necessarily mean they are totally impractical, however. If you go to the trouble to obtain archival data for two points in time, for example, you might with little more trouble obtain data for several points in time. The challenge before you, when seeking the clearest causal inference possible, is to know what data are available, how to obtain them, and how to use the available evaluation designs. In many program areas, an interrupted time series or regression-discontinuity design will provide the strongest evaluation design available.

References

Ball, S., and Bogatz, G. A. *The First Year of Sesame Street: An Evaluation.* Princeton, N.J.: Educational Testing Service, 1970.

Berk, R. A., and Rauma, D. "Capitalizing on Nonrandom Assignment to Treatments: A Regression-Discontinuity Evaluation of a Crime-Control Program." *Journal of the American Statistical Association,* 1983, *78,* 21–27.

Campbell, D. T., and others. "Quasi-Experimental Designs." In H. W. Riecken and R. F. Boruch (eds.), *Social Experimentation: A Method for Planning and Evaluating Social Intervention.* New York: Academic Press, 1974.

Cook, T. D. "The Generalization of Causal Connections: Multiple Theories in Search of Clear Practice." In L. Sechrest, E. Perrin, and J. Bunker (eds.), *Research Methodology: Strengthening Causal Interpretations of Nonexperimen-*

tal Data. Washington, D.C.: U.S. Department of Health and Human Services, May 1990.

Cook, T. D. "Clarifying the Warrant for Generalized Causal Inferences in Quasi-Experimentation." In M. W. McLaughlin and D. Phillips (eds.), *Evaluation and Education: At Quarter Century.* 1991 Yearbook, National Society for the Study of Education. Chicago: National Society for the Study of Education, 1991.

Cook, T. D., and Campbell, D. T. *Quasi-Experimentation: Design and Analysis Issues for Field Settings.* Boston: Houghton Mifflin, 1979.

Cook, T. D., Campbell, D. T., and Peracchio, L. "Quasi-Experimentation." In M. D. Dunnette and L. M. Hough (eds.), *Handbook of Industrial and Organizational Psychology.* (2nd ed.) Palo Alto, Calif.: Consulting Psychologists Press, 1990.

Davis, T.R.V., and Luthans, F. "Defining and Researching Leadership as a Behavioral Construct: An Idiographic Approach." *Journal of Applied Behavioral Science,* 1984, *20,* 237–251.

Farquhar, J. W., and others. "Effects of Communitywide Education on Cardiovascular Disease Risk Factors: The Stanford Five-City Project." *Journal of the American Medical Association,* 1990, *264,* 359–365.

Hennigan, K. M., and others. "Impact of the Introduction of Television on Crime in the United States: Empirical Findings and Theoretical Implications." *Journal of Personality and Social Psychology,* 1982, *42,* 461–477.

Jencks, C., and Edin, K. "The Real Welfare Problem." *The American Prospect,* 1990, *1,* 31–50.

Kiecolt, K. J., and Nathan, L. E. *Secondary Analysis of Survey Data.* Sage University Paper series on Quantitative Applications in the Social Sciences, series no. 07-001. Newbury Park, Calif.: Sage, 1990.

Lohr, B. W. *An Historical View of the Research on the Factors Related to the Utilization of Health Services.* Mimeographed research report. Rockville, Md.: Bureau for Health Services Research and Evaluation, Social and Economics Analysis Division, 1972.

Luft, H. S. "The Applicability of the Regression-Discontinuity Design in Health Services Research." In L. Sechrest, E. Perrin, and J. Bunker (eds.), *Research Methodology: Strengthening Causal Interpretations of Nonexperimental Data.* Washington, D.C.: U.S. Department of Health and Human Services, May 1990.

McCleary, R., Nienstedt, B. C., and Erven, J. M. "Uniform Crime Reports as Organizational Outcomes: Three Time Series Experiments." *Social Problems,* 1982, *29,* 361–371.

McSweeny, A. J. "Effects of Response Cost on the Behavior of a Million Persons: Charging for Directory Assistance in Cincinnati." *Journal of Applied Behavior Analysis,* 1978, *11,* 47–51.

Ross, H. L., and Campbell, D. T. "The Connecticut Crackdown on Speeding: Time-Series Data in Quasi-Experimental Analysis." *Law and Society Review,* 1968, *3,* 33–53.

Ross, H. L., Campbell, D. T., and Glass, G. "Determining the Social Effects of Legal Reform: The British 'Breathalyser' Crackdown of 1967." *American Behavioral Scientist,* 1970, *13,* 493–509.

Rubin, D. B. "Assignment to Treatment Group on the Basis of a Covariate." *Journal of Educational Statistics,* 1977, *2,* 1–26.

Seaver, W. B., and Quarton, R. J. "Regression-Discontinuity Analysis of Dean's List Effects." *Journal of Educational Psychology,* 1976, *68,* 459–465.

Trochim, W.M.K. *Research Design for Program Evaluation: The Regression-Discontinuity Approach.* Newbury Park, Calif.: Sage, 1984.

Trochim, W.M.K. "The Regression-Discontinuity Design." In L. Sechrest, E. Perrin, and J. Bunker (eds.), *Research Methodology: Strengthening Causal Interpretations of Nonexperimental Data.* Washington, D.C.: U.S. Department of Health and Human Services, May 1990.

Viscusi, W. K. "Cotton Dust Regulation: An OSHA Success Story?" *Journal of Policy Analysis and Management,* 1985, *4,* 325–343.

8

Ethical and Practical Randomized Field Experiments

Michael L. Dennis

The randomized field experiment is the most convincing design for determining the relative effectiveness of two or more interventions or control conditions and is being increasingly used to evaluate new social policies, programs, and interventions (Berk and others, 1985; Cook and Campbell, 1979; Fairweather and Tornatzky, 1977; Fisher, 1960). Well-implemented experiments have been demonstrated to be both highly influential (Lamas and others, 1992) and cost-effective investments (Detsky, 1989). Randomized field experiments, however, often fail. Foremost among the variety of logistical and design reasons for failure are (1) weak research designs that have insufficient statistical power, ill-defined experimental contrasts, insensitive instruments, and/or use of inappropriate analytic models and (2) insufficient control of the actual treatment that is received by clients both within and between treatment conditions (Ashery and McAuliffe, 1992; Cohen, 1990; Dennis, 1988, 1990; Farrington, Ohlin, and Wilson, 1986; Hall, 1984; Lipsey, 1990; Riecken and others, 1974; Sechrest and others, 1979).

Although such problems can often be reduced by limiting experiments to controlled research settings with highly qualified staff and resources, doing so limits them to tests of relative efficacy; such studies ask, "How well *can* the intervention work?" Unfortunately, such trials are not always replicated when they are tried with the more diverse staff and complicated clients encountered in community-based settings (Boruch and Gomez, 1979; Dennis,

The work for this chapter was partially supported by National Institute on Drug Abuse (NIDA) Grants No. 1-R18-DA7262-01 and I-P50-DA06990-01A1. The author thanks Robert Boruch for introducing him to randomized field experiments and challenging him to find better ways to conduct them. The author would also like to acknowledge assistance received in preparing the manuscripts, tables, and graphs from Jill Anderson, Linda B. Barker, Laurie B. Godwin, Richard S. Straw, Elizabeth D. MacDonald, and Anne C. Theisen, as well as comments on early drafts from J. Valley Rachal, the anonymous reviewers, and the editors.

1990; Riecken and others, 1974). To answer the applied question—"Does it work in practice?"—it is often desirable to conduct randomized field experiments with the actual types of clients, programs, and resource levels to test simultaneously feasibility, acceptability, and effectiveness.

The methodology of randomized field experiments is far less developed than traditional clinical trials; however, several reviews have demonstrated that they are feasible. These reviews have documented successful randomized field experiments in more than twenty industrialized and developing areas or countries, including Barbados, China, Colombia, Great Britain, Hong Kong, India, the Netherlands, Nicaragua, Peru, Sweden, Taiwan, and the United States. The same reviews have also cited successful experiments in such diverse subject areas as civil justice, criminal justice, communications, drug abuse treatment, education, employment, family planning, medicine, mental health, nutrition, postpartum care, prevention, and vocational training (Dennis, 1988, 1990; Dennis and Boruch, 1989; Riecken and others, 1974).

The goals of this chapter are to help the reader do the following:

1. Design a randomized field experiment of two or more interventions or control conditions that offer ethical, practical, and salient experimental contrasts
2. Implement and manage the experiment in a way that avoids common problems or at least allows them to be addressed in the analysis
3. Estimate the relative effectiveness of the interventions or control conditions overall and for relevant subgroups

The next section provides background on what a randomized field experiment is, when conducting one is appropriate, and how to recognize some of the common implementation problems that occur. The rest of the chapter then focuses on the design, management, and analysis of randomized field experiments.

Background

In order to understand, design, and conduct randomized field experiments, you must know the terms specific to these evaluations. The next section defines and discusses the most important of these.

Some Brief Definitions

Randomized field experiment refers to the random allocation of some kind of unit among two or more interventions or control conditions. The purpose of random allocation is to create groups of approximately equal composition so that the relative effectiveness of the interventions can be fairly assessed. The units can be people, counselors, street blocks, clinics, schools, days, or something else, but it is preferable that they be the primary units of the analysis. Furthermore, there can be multiple stages of random assignment (to a school, to a teacher within a school) and/or multiple dimensions of random assignment (counselors to a training program, clients to counselors). Note that this definition does not rule out other design options such as *blocking* assignments to ensure that key subgroups are evenly assigned, pairing units before assignment to reduce several dimensions of variability, making unequal assignment to groups to meet logistical constraints, or even combining with other designs such as regression-discontinuity or interrupted time series (see Chapter Seven by Marcantonio and Cook in this book) to address broader questions. In addition, there are many different names for this technique, including *randomly controlled trial* or *community-based experiment,* and *social policy experiments.*

The *interventions* or *control conditions* can differ by type, amount, provider, or even timing (that is, immediate versus delayed intervention). Although one group is often designated a *control* group, this does not necessarily imply the absence of an intervention. The control group in randomized field experiments often receives the services that were provided before the experiment began or may receive fewer services if the members of the control group are not permitted to work with a particular agency during the experiment. Throughout this chapter, the differences between interventions are referred to as the *experimental contrast.*

The commonly used term, *significant difference,* refers to a reliably measured difference between two or more groups. It is commonly reported as the probability of making a type I error, or *incorrectly* claiming there is a difference when there is not. This probability is typically set at a level of less than .05 (5 percent), .01, .001, or .0001. Thus, it is not a measure of practical significance but, rather, indicates how reliably the difference was measured.

The related term, *statistical power,* refers to the probability of reliably measuring the difference between two or more groups, given that a difference really exists. Going from 0 percent to 100 percent, the higher the statistical power of a given design, the more likely the evaluator is to *correctly* claim that a difference does exist. Assuming that the average evaluator believes in the experimental intervention, statistical power is the probability of finding what he or she is looking for. For a given level of type I error, statistical power can be increased by including more subjects, using more sensitive designs, or using more sensitive measures. As we will demonstrate, insufficient power has been a major problem in both general research and applied evaluation. A simplified approach to power analysis and recommendations for increasing design sensitivity to help avoid the problem of insufficient power are presented later in this chapter.

An *effect* of the *experimental contrast* is the difference between the experimental group and a comparison group on some outcome measure. The impact of the contrast on the outcome measure could be a difference between two means, two percentages, two pretest-to-posttest change scores,

two slopes in a regression equation, or even the cumulative difference between two sets of production functions, discriminant functions, or structural
equations. Since the groups were the same except for random assignment,
we expect their performance on the outcome measures to vary only by chance.
Statistical tests are used to determine whether the observed difference is larger
than one likely to have occurred simply by chance for a given level of type
I error. To calculate power across several measures or to combine results
across several studies in a meta-analysis, each effect is commonly converted
into an *effect size* (δ). For an interval measure (such as number of crimes,
income, or weeks of work), this is done by taking the difference between
the two means and dividing them by their standard deviation. The effect
size is analogous to a *t*-score for testing the difference between two independent groups (which is the difference between the means divided by their standard error). Other types of measures require different formulas but give a
similar effect size that can be interpreted like a *t*-score and combined with
the other effects.

A *critical effect size* is a substantive measure of how big a change an
evaluator wants to detect or the size of the smallest difference that can be
detected. Unlike Glass's effect size, the *critical effect size* (Δ) also incorporates
the effect of other design features that might affect sensitivity. These include
things such as unequal sample sizes, repeated measures, blocking, and type
of measurement.

When Is It Appropriate to Conduct a Randomized Field Experiment?

Many evaluations address the questions of whether a program or intervention is needed, whether it is being provided to the neediest group, and what
services are provided (Boruch and Cordray, 1980). The purpose of a randomized field experiment, however, is to assess the effectiveness of one or
more interventions relative to a control or standard practice group (Dennis,
1990; Fisher, 1960). Even when an evaluation does focus on the question
of relative effectiveness, several other threshold conditions should be met
before a randomized field experiment is contemplated. Expanding on earlier
works concerning general policy toward social experiments (Berk and others,
1985; Campbell, 1969; Federal Judicial Center, 1981; Riecken and Boruch,
1978; Riecken and others, 1974), Dennis and Boruch (1989) identified five
recurring threshold conditions that should be met before a randomized field
experiment is even considered.

- The present practice must be perceived as needing improvement.
- The efficacy of the proposed intervention must be uncertain under field
  conditions.
- There should be no simpler alternative for evaluating the intervention.
- The results must be potentially important for policy.
- The design must be able to meet the ethical standards of both the re-
  searchers and the service providers.

Underlying these conditions is the notion that randomized field experiments are difficult to implement, expensive, and time-consuming for both the subjects and the researchers. They should therefore be reserved for applied studies of significance to social policy and not be used solely to expand general knowledge. In an interview, Donald Campbell (an early advocate of social experimentation) argued that randomized field experiments are worthwhile only when a clearly defined program or intervention is being considered for widespread dissemination (Watson, 1986).

One of the most difficult aspects of deciding whether to conduct a randomized field experiment is to find two or more regimens that differ in significant ways (for example, arrest versus counseling for people who commit domestic violence), yet represent real and ethical options. To avoid trivial experiments (and findings), it is essential that the experimenter work closely with the relevant practitioners to identify the meaningful comparisons. Freedman (1987) calls this the search for a state of "equipoise" or balance where, based on the available data, either alternative is acceptable to a community of competent experts in the field.

Because randomized field experiments involve a wider variety of people and less control over treatment than traditional controlled trials, it is essential that they be monitored closely. Although the threshold conditions may have been met at the beginning of the experiment, the state of equipoise between the interventions and/or control conditions may be quickly lost in practice. In a debate on the ethics of randomized experiments to evaluate new medical procedures, Passamani (1991) suggested that data need to be carefully monitored during the experiment to determine when and if this state of equipoise is lost (that is, one or more interventions is shown to be more effective or ineffective), at which point the experiment should be stopped. Such a decision would be by definition a highly substantive one; determining how to make such a choice goes beyond the scope of this chapter.

Common Implementation Problems

Based on an extensive review of social policy experiments, the author and others (Ashery and McAuliffe, 1992; Berk and others, 1985; Dennis, 1990; Riecken and others, 1974) have identified six common problems that occur during the implementation of randomized field experiments and that can jeopardize their validity:

- *Treatment variation,* that is, the amount of each treatment component that was actually received affects the strength of the experimental contrast. Statistically uncontrolled variation in actual treatment levels leads to reduced statistical power.
- *Treatment contamination,* that is, the passing of knowledge or resources from the experimental group to the comparison group reduces the differences between the interventions and the likelihood that different outcomes will be observed.

- *Inadequate numbers of cases,* resulting from case-flow estimates that were higher than those actually experienced, often lead to early depletion of project resources and result in inadequate statistical power, cost over-runs, or extended field time.
- *Failure to follow the random assignment process* occurs both overtly (someone refuses the experimental intervention but stays in treatment) and covertly (an intake worker manipulates assignment to move a "needy" or "worthy" person into the experimental group). Both jeopardize the trial's valid-ity, although overt overrides can at least be controlled statistically.
- *Changes in the environment* include such elements as the availability of new resources or changes in federal regulations. Environmental changes create additional variation in the context in which treatment is delivered and may affect statistical power.
- *Planned changes in an experimental intervention over time* directly affect the treat-ment that is received. Although such changes are typically undesirable from a statistical viewpoint, they are often necessary for logistical rea-sons, such as changes in staff, or for ethical reasons, such as a change in the law or an advance in treatment.

One or more of these problems can result in a trial that is imprecise about what has been tested, unclear about the populations to whom the results can be generalized, or both. Appendix 8.A provides an example of treat-ment contamination from one of the very first randomized field experiments, the *Lanarkshire Milk Experiment* (Fisher and Bartlett, 1931; Leighton and McKinlay, 1930).

Weak Research Designs

Even in the absence of implementation problems, many of the studies in the published academic literature have (1) sample sizes that are too small to detect important differences between experimental and comparison groups overall or within important subgroups and (2) analyses that do not match their intervention. In one of the first meta-analyses, for instance, Cohen (1962) found that the median statistical power of studies published in the 1960 volume of the *Journal of Abnormal and Social Psychology* was only 46 per-cent. This finding means that if an intervention did work, the researchers would have been more accurate in determining this if they had flipped a coin (50 percent) rather than using the traditional nondirectional test with a type I error rate of .05 or less.

Over twenty-five years later, Lipsey (1988, 1990) found that the aver-age rate of statistical power was still only 45 percent in 1,859 statistical tests compiled from thirty-nine meta-analyses in several fields. This finding trans-lates into a 55 percent rate of making type II errors, or incorrectly rejecting the treatment's effectiveness when a meta-analysis suggested it worked. The chief culprit appears to be the lack of sufficient statistical power. On average, the studies produced a relatively moderate effect size ($\delta = .45$) but were capable of reliably (90 percent power) detecting only a relatively large effect size ($\delta = .74$). The major reason for this gap was that the sample size per condition averaged only about forty people. It is therefore clear that although numerous handbooks have been published showing how to do power analysis (Cohen, 1977; Kraemer and Thiemann, 1987; Lipsey, 1990), few investigators are doing them; as a result, it is very difficult for a subsequent reviewer of these studies to know reliably that the intervention or program worked.

Lipsey and colleagues (1985) also conducted a meta-analysis on the quality and appropriateness of research designs; they used a random sample of 168 evaluation research studies they identified during a three-year period in *Psychological Abstracts, Sociological Abstracts,* and the *Current Index to Journals in Education.* While over 70 percent of these used experimental or quasi-experimental designs to evaluate the intervention or program, the investigators found that most studies had several moderate-to-fundamental flaws.

- *Many use inappropriate analysis models:* while 77 percent of the evaluations involved multidimensional and multiexposure interventions, more than 84 percent analyzed the independent variable as a categorical dichotomy or black box only (for example, by using chi-square or analysis of variance).
- *Most studies are nontheoretical:* despite the complexity of the proposed interventions, 69 percent of the studies lack any theory or even hypotheses about why they might work; instead, they offer only labels, strategies, or process objectives.
- *Few measure the actual intervention that was provided:* fewer than 30 percent of the studies measured whether subjects had actually received the intervention, and even fewer measured its amount or duration.
- *Few consider the quality of the outcome measures they are using:* less than 30 percent even mentioned, let alone tested, the reliability, validity, or sensitivity of the outcome measures they were using.

In light of such practices, practitioner skepticism about the results of individual studies and evaluations has become not only common but, perhaps, warranted.

Designing a Randomized Field Experiment

To avoid the inadequacies just cited, evaluations must be clearly thought out and must incorporate sufficient statistical rigor to produce reliable results. The parts of this section discuss the various elements of a design and what each should include.

Defining the Experimental Contrast

Inadequately defined interventions and experimental contrasts have led to the equally absurd findings that "nothing works" (Martinson, 1974) or that everything works "equally well" (Luborsky, Singer, and Luborsky, 1975).

To avoid this pitfall, it is useful to state explicitly and measure carefully the actual intervention received by each participant in terms of timing, duration, intensity, content, and context (Dennis, 1990; Fairweather and Tornatzky, 1977; Sechrest, White, and Brown, 1979). Experimental contrasts are more likely to produce an effect when the intervention and comparison groups vary on one or more of these dimensions and when they represent real and meaningful alternatives to the relevant providers or clinicians. Because randomized field experiments involve real and often disadvantaged people, it is particularly important that the time, hopes, and even lives of these individuals not be wasted on poorly defined interventions or trivial comparisons. Appendix 8.B provides an example from the Methadone-Enhanced Treatment (MET) Study and illustrates the benefit of using actual measures over mere labels. We will also return to it to show how measuring the intervention received can help in managing and analyzing the experiment.

An important consideration in designing experiments is the occasional misapplication to other areas of medical standards for conducting experiments on individuals. In a medical experiment, it is the individual who has discretion and must decide whether to participate. In many legal and administrative experiments, however, it is an official (such as a police officer, judge, or case manager) who, acting within the legal and ethical limits of his or her own discretion, must decide whether the individual will participate (Boruch and Cecil, 1979; Federal Judicial Center, 1981). Examples of this situation include the *Minneapolis Domestic Violence Experiment* (Sherman and Berk, 1984), *Nebraska Prehearing Conference Program* (Rohman, 1987), and the *Philadelphia Bail Guidelines Experiment* (Goldkamp and Gottfredson, 1985). Of course, it is still critical that such studies be conducted under the supervision and protection of an institutional review board's (IRB's) human subjects panel.

Drawing Out the Design Implications

To translate the proposed experimental contrast into a research design for a randomly controlled trial, it is also important to look at its implications for other aspects of the study. Some specific considerations include these:

- *Who is the target population, and are they different from the program's regular clients?* How can these people and their needs be identified? What barriers currently prevent them from fully using the intervention or using it more effectively?
- *How can the proposed changes in the intervention address the needs of this group?* What new components are needed? Does everyone need every component or service to the same extent or level?
- *How can the intervention be designed to accommodate the needs and desires of both the targeted clients and the practitioners?* How will the intervention be integrated into the existing service system? What resource gaps must be filled to make the intervention work in the existing system?

- *What changes is the intervention expected to produce?* How soon will they occur? How large will they be? What secondary effects might they have?
- *Is the intervention or level of competing services likely to change during the experiment?* Will more services be added? What is the expected rate of staff turnover? Are there major programs starting up or ending in the community that may affect the main outcome measures?
- *What are the likely threats to the experiment's validity?* Are clients or practitioners likely to refuse participation or resist some components? Are any of the components likely to produce experimental contamination or compensatory rivalry?

In a field- or community-based setting, compensatory rivalry can take on many forms. On the one hand, an administrator may allocate more discretionary funds or services to the control group or program. On the other hand, an administrator may actively oppose the experiment. In a randomized field experiment of a community penalties program, for instance, Wallace (1987) found that lawyers in a district attorney's office thought that an experimental program was too prodefense and refused to plea bargain with defendants in the experimental groups.

Because most randomized field experiments require organizational changes, staff behavioral changes, and diffusion of innovations (whether devices or procedures), they must be designed in thoughtful ways to encourage both their implementation and management. In the Methadone-Enhanced Treatment Study (Dennis, Fairbank, and Rachal, 1992), for instance, our first three-day round of counselor training led to few changes in the counselors' actual behaviors. In the second round, we followed training with audiotape reviews of the first few client sessions, the creation of on-site treatment teams to talk through problem cases, and follow-up training back in the program. Supplemented by feedback and more local support, the second round of training led to widespread changes in counselor behaviors.

Improving Generalizability

The more similar target clients are to clients in a program or type of program, the more comfortable the evaluator will be in generalizing his or her results to these larger groups. Attrition at any stage of the research limits generalizability. Howard and colleagues (1986, 1990) described the many points at which attrition may occur and demonstrated its deleterious effects on the external validity of controlled trials. These points can be broadly classified into two main types:

- *Preinclusion attrition* occurs before clients enter the study—during intake or as a result of screening.
- *Postinclusion attrition* occurs after assignment, whether during treatment or follow-up, and will be addressed in a subsequent section.

Here we will talk about preinclusion attrition and its implications for generalizability. We will return to postinclusion attrition later. The *Disulfiram Experiment* for the treatment of alcoholism (Fuller and others, 1986) in Appendix 8.C is an excellent example of preinclusion attrition. In this experiment over 76 percent of the clients were screened out, and then nearly two-thirds of the remaining clients refused to participate. Such large-scale preinclusion attrition makes generalization to the original population almost impossible because analyses of randomized experiments in various substantive areas have demonstrated that interventions are not equally effective for all subgroups (Berk and others, 1985; Dennis, 1988; Riecken and others, 1974).

As the evaluation focus shifts from "can it work?" to "how well does it work in the real world?" it also becomes increasingly more important to examine the generalizability or representativeness of the program, staff, resource levels, and clients. Although conducting research in community-based settings increases generalizability, it can also worsen problems such as control of the intervention, variability in the quality and quantity of what people get, and postinclusion attrition. These problems can be overcome, at best, and measured, at least.

Some important steps can be taken to reduce or at least measure the extent of pre- and postinclusion problems:

- Clearly identify the target population of programs, staffing levels, and clients to which the results should be generalized.
- Carefully document who was screened out or refused and why. If possible, collect some information on them directly or from records to allow comparisons of participants and nonparticipants.
- Focus on interventions that represent feasible options and the reasons programs, staff, and clients would want them. Develop a specific protocol for "selling" the project — be careful to make only realistic promises or claims.
- Collect information from programs, staff, and clients that allows comparisons with larger groups.

The last point is perhaps one of the most important strategies and yet is often overlooked. Data can be collected using an existing instrument with known norms or by asking questions that allow comparison to larger epidemiological studies or program surveys. In drug abuse treatment, for instance, the *D.C. Initiative* (Appendix 8.E) incorporated a clinical battery of existing instruments and used core patient- and program-level instruments adapted from several large studies (Flynn and others, 1992).

Determining the Sample Size and Statistical Power

The next, and perhaps most overlooked, step of planning is determining the sample size requirements and other characteristics of the design that can affect its statistical power and sensitivity. Such words need not strike terror in the hearts of would-be experimenters because they essentially mean figuring out the probability of finding what you are looking for.

The best approach to power analysis is to review the literature or conduct preliminary analyses to determine the likely value of an outcome measure and the amount it is expected to change. To determine the power, we would calculate an effect size (δ) by taking the difference between the two group means and dividing them by either their pooled standard deviation or the control group standard deviation. The latter formulation is often referred to as "Glass's effect size" after Eugene Glass. When the pooled standard deviation is used, one assumes that the variances or distributions are the same in each group except for a change in the means. This is analogous to a regular t-test on the difference between two independent groups. In many randomized field experiments, however, the intervention involves multiple components, multiple exposures, or client decisions after random assignment about whether to continue participating. In such cases it is necessary to test for differences in both the mean and variance between the experimental and standard groups. Alternatively, we can replace the pooled standard deviation with the control group standard deviation and test for differences in the distributions of the outcome measures.

To understand the implications of this difference for planning, imagine that we are designing an experimental training program to make counselors address more employment issues in drug abuse treatment. We could use preliminary data from the Methadone-Enhanced Treatment Study to show that the number of employment-related counseling sessions increased from an average of 2.54 times per client in the first six months for standard counselors to 3.63 per client for the experimentally trained counselors. The standard deviation also increased from 3.41 to 4.42, suggesting that some clients took greater advantage of the opportunity than others. Equation (1) shows the resulting effect size using the pooled standard error and Equation (2) shows the resulting effect size using the control group standard error that also takes into account the intervention's effect on the distribution.

(1) Effect Size = $(\text{MEAN}_{\text{Experimental}} - \text{MEAN}_{\text{Control}})/\text{STANDARD DEVIATION}_{\text{Pooled}}$

$\delta \quad = (\bar{x}_e - \bar{x}_c)/\text{SD}_p$

$.26 = (3.63 - 2.54)/4.19 = 1.09/4.19$

(2) Effect Size = $(\text{MEAN}_{\text{Experimental}} - \text{MEAN}_{\text{Control}})/\text{STANDARD DEVIATION}_{\text{Control}}$

$\delta \quad = (\bar{x}_e - \bar{x}_c)/\text{SD}_c$

$.40 = (3.63 - 2.54)/3.41 = 1.09/3.41$

In this example, use of the control group standard deviation increased the effect size 1.54 times (.40/.26) and required only 43 percent (108/251.5) of sample size per group for the same level of statistical power (80 percent). Thus it is very important to consider carefully whether the intervention is likely also to affect the distribution.

The required sample size for an expected effect size can be estimated from power tables in numerous books. Lipsey (1990) offers a relatively straightforward approach for calculating effect sizes and offers several tables for converting a variety of other measures (such as percentage differences for discrete measures and correlation coefficients). His book also presents simple formulas for calculating the impact of several other design features on power (discussed further below) and power graphs to estimate the necessary sample sizes. Kraemer and Thiemann (1987) provide an alternative and slightly more sophisticated approach that introduces an intermediary parameter called the *critical effect size* (Δ) to facilitate the comparison of alternative evaluation designs. This parameter starts with the effect size (δ) and then incorporates the design effect due to unequal sample sizes, repeated measures, and planned method of analysis (we will return to this in a moment). Cohen (1977) provides the most detailed and sophisticated formulas for directly calculating sample sizes for a given level of statistical power by using one of numerous formulas for different designs.

Simplified Power Analysis

Unfortunately, there are several problems with the traditional approach to power analysis for evaluation research. First, there is often little or no explicit information about community-based interventions and, consequently, no basis upon which to estimate the sample size requirements. Second, when such information does exist, few investigators know how to calculate the power analysis. Third, other factors such as the budget, a limited number of available cases, or the need to have multiple groups (such as sites or types of clients) may be what is actually determining the sample size.

To address this problem, let us turn power analysis on its side and say, given a specific sample size, what can I do with it? Though far from ideal, this approach is certainly better than blindly starting an analysis or study that is destined to fail. Note that in many randomized field experiments, multiple comparisons are being made — each with different numbers of observations (n). This kind of analysis can help to focus the evaluator on those things that can be addressed well and to reduce the laundry list of other things that cannot.

Table 8.1 presents a simplified form of power analysis for comparing two groups assuming that the units are divided equally between each of two conditions. The user starts by identifying the row that corresponds to number of units per group (n/grp) for a particular comparison in the design. For a given number per group, 80 percent power, and a type I error rate of

.05 or less ($\alpha < .05$), the next four columns identify the smallest detectable effect (δ), t-score, percentage change (P_2-P_1), and correlation coefficient (R, r). Notice how the effect size parallels the t-scores between the group means on interval or ratio outcome measures (such as counts, measurements, or money). More specifically, formula (3) shows the exact relationship between the effect size (δ) and the t-score for a given number of units in the experimental (n_e) and standard (n_s) groups.

$$(3)\ t = \frac{\delta}{\sqrt{\dfrac{1}{n_{\text{Experimental}}} + \dfrac{1}{n_{\text{Standard}}}}}$$

The percentage point changes for discrete variables are given in ranges because a specific change, such as 10 percent, has an increasingly larger effect size as P_2 approaches 0 percent or 100 percent. The tabled values are meant only as approximations and refer to the change in discrete variables (for example, recidivism dropping from 35 percent to 20 percent would be a change of 15 percent) where P_2 is between 10 percent and 90 percent. The correlation (r) and percentage of variance explained (PVE or r^2) can be used for simple regression or multiple regression, as long as there are enough observations or units to equal the minimum within-group degrees of freedom plus two (for the two groups) plus the number of independent variables.

Note that the evaluator will have to use his or her own substantive knowledge or consult with other experts to determine whether it is reasonable to expect the proposed clinical contrast to produce these outcomes. Specific analytic models may also introduce additional constraints. It is generally recommended, for instance, that chi-square tests not be done unless at least five people are expected in every cell, and that multiple regression equations should be based on ten to thirty times more observations than the number of variables in the equation (Pedhazur, 1982; Winer, 1971).

Table 8.1 can also be used to provide conservative estimates of the power for subgroup comparisons, and pairwise comparisons when there are more than two groups or unequally sized groups (using the smaller sample size). For unequally sized groups, however, Table 8.1 becomes very conservative as the assignment ratio starts exceeding 2 to 1.

Below is an example of how the text for such a power analysis actually looked in a recent proposal the author submitted to conduct a controlled trial of outreach to victims of autoimmune deficiency syndrome (AIDS) using three sites and with planned subgroup analyses for women and African Americans.

> The target outcome measures include both continuous (frequency of injection, frequency of condom use) and discrete (entered treatment, HIV seropositive) variables. With 630 people per condition, the design should be able to detect an effect size

Table 8.1. Smallest Detectable Outcome for Various Sample Sizes, Assuming Two Groups, 80 Percent Power, and 5 Percent Type I Error Rate.

Minimum Number per Group (n/grp)	Smallest Detectable Outcomes			
	Effect Size (δ)	t-Score (t)	Percentage (%) Point Differences ($P_2 - P_2$)	Correlation Coefficient (ϱ,R,r)
39243	0.02	2.8	1–5	0.01
9810	0.04	2.8	1–5	0.02
4359	0.06	2.8	1–5	0.03
2452	0.08	2.8	1–5	0.04
1569	0.10	2.8	5	0.05
1089	0.12	2.8	5–10	0.06
800	0.14	2.8	5–10	0.07
612	0.16	2.8	5–10	0.08
484	0.18	2.8	10	0.09
392	0.21	2.9	10–15	0.10
324	0.23	2.9	10–15	0.11
272	0.25	2.9	10–15	0.12
232	0.27	2.9	10–15	0.13
200	0.29	2.9	15	0.14
174	0.31	2.9	15–20	0.15
152	0.33	2.9	15–20	0.16
135	0.36	2.9	15–20	0.18
120	0.38	2.9	15–20	0.19
108	0.40	2.9	20	0.20
97	0.42	2.9	20–25	0.21
80	0.47	3.0	20–25	0.23
68	0.51	3.0	25	0.25
57	0.56	3.0	25–30	0.27
49	0.60	3.0	30	0.29
42	0.65	3.0	30–35	0.31
38	0.69	3.0	35	0.33
33	0.74	3.0	35–40	0.35
30	0.79	3.1	40	0.37
26	0.84	3.1	40–45	0.39
24	0.89	3.1	45	0.41
18	1.01	3.1	50	0.45
14	1.13	3.1	GT 50	0.49
12	1.26	3.1	GT 50	0.53
10	1.39	3.1	GT 50	0.57
8	1.53	3.1	GT 50	0.61
7	1.67	3.1	GT 50	0.64
6	1.81	3.1	GT 50	0.67

of .16 or larger with 80% power and a significance level of .05 or less. This is the equivalent of a 2.8 t-score difference between the group means, a 5% to 10% point difference on discrete variables, or a multiple correlation of .08.

We also propose to conduct both within site analyses and demographic subgroup analyses (on the combined data set). Here we will need to examine the power of the site or subgroup size. With 210 people per condition within each of the three sites, the design should be able to detect an effect size of .29 or more, a t-score of 2.9 or more, a change of 15% or more, and a correlation of .14 or more. The key analyses will also be replicated within a subgroup of approximately 220 women and a subgroup of approximately 400 African American men. Assuming an equal split between conditions due to blocking (110 and 200, respectively), the design should be able to respectively detect minimum effect sizes of .40 and .29, t-scores of 2.97 and 2.90, percentage changes of 20% and 15%, and correlations of .20 and .14.

It is clearly better to use an exact power test, but this simplified form of power analysis is intended as an easier tool for initial planning and an alternative to no power analysis at all.

Balancing Logistical Constraints and Design Sensitivity

The results of a simple power analysis usually suggest that the evaluator does not have enough observations to evaluate the program using conventional posttest-only comparisons between two groups. The two obvious solutions are either to increase the sample size or to improve the design sensitivity. Although increasing the sample size seems easier, financial resources, number of units available, or the length of time often preclude this option. It is therefore useful to explore the potentially large impact of the experimental design on the sample size requirements.

To incorporate the effect of the design, we will use Kraemer and Thiemann's (1987) critical effect size (Δ). The values of Δ will range from 0 to 1.00 and are a measure of "practical" significance rather than statistical significance. A value of 0 (or less) implies that a researcher's theory is false, while a value of 1.00 implies it is true. Like the regular effect size, the larger the expected critical effect size, the easier it is to detect and the smaller the number of subjects the study will require. Since randomized field experiments often involve multiple comparisons, our discussion will be generic enough to encompass the major experimental and quasi-experimental designs.

Although there are many types of research designs, there are only three primary ways to estimate treatment effectiveness: (1) comparing client/unit outcomes to their own baseline or historical control, which includes interrupted time series designs, functional analyses, and simple pre-post designs; (2) comparing client outcomes with those of another group at a single point in time, which includes posttest-only randomized trials, case control studies, and studies that use population parameters or a standard to evaluate the treatment; and (3) defining outcomes as change or improvement in scores and comparing them with another group, which includes randomized trials with pre-post measures, nonequivalent comparison group designs, time series designs with control groups, and prospective cohort designs. Baseline controls are typically the most efficient in terms of the required number of subjects, but they are vulnerable to many threats to validity (maturation, selection, mortality; see Cook and Campbell, 1979). Posttest-only controls work well when repeated measures on the same client (drug use at time one and at time two) are correlated at less than 0.5 ($r < 0.5$). However, they can suffer from several threats to internal validity (discussed later) unless random assignment is used or the research has a specific standard against which to compare the treatment's effectiveness (Cook and Campbell, 1979). The change-score control group works best when repeated measures on the same client explain 25 percent or more of the variance, or $r > .5$. Note that, although a randomized experiment is less efficient in terms of how many subjects it uses, such an experiment is presumed to produce better evidence (Fisher, 1960).

Table 8.2 shows the required sample sizes per group (n/grp) for each of these designs to detect the critical effect size (δ) with 80 percent power, given a type I error (α) of .05 or less and a two-tailed test of significance. The critical effect sizes (Δ) and minimum sample size requirements are given for five possible effect sizes ($\delta = .10, .25, .50, .75,$ and 1.00), by five possible correlations (ϱ) between repeated measures ($\varrho = .01, .25, .50, .75,$ and $.90$), by the three types of analysis (baseline, posttest only, and change score). Note that, like Table 8.1, this table assumes that there are two groups with equal allocation to groups. Unequal allocation to groups has only a small effect on the total sample size for a seventy–thirty split but can more than double the required total sample size when it is a ninety to ten split.

The sample size requirements would be more than 20 percent lower if the power was reduced to 70 percent, a one-tailed test was used, the type I error (α) was increased to .10, or if more than two observations were collected for each unit. Also note that these sizes would be the final sample sizes per group (or subgroup) for the core analysis. To the extent that attrition or nonresponse is expected, the sample sizes would need to be further inflated by dividing them by the expected completion rate [(desired "n")/(1-attrition rate)]. Thus if a sample of 272 is desired and an attrition rate of 15 percent is expected, the evaluator would need to start out with $272/(.85) = 320$ clients per group.

Implementing and Managing an Experiment

No matter how well an experiment is designed, if it is not implemented carefully it can fail. This section points out the elements that are critical if the experiment is to be successful.

Gaining and Maintaining Cooperation

Because an experiment typically represents a change in the status quo, it requires that existing staff modify their current behavior. Moreover, it typi-

Table 8.2. Critical Effect Sizes (Δ) and Sample Size Requirements (n/grp) for Baseline, Posttest-Only, and Change Score Control Group Designs ($\alpha = .05$, $\beta = .20$).

Expected		Baseline Control		Posttest-only Control		Change-score Control	
δ	ϱ	Δ_1	n_1/grp	Δ_2	n_2/grp	Δ_3	n_3/grp
0.10	0.10	0.07	800	0.05	1,569	0.04	2,452
0.10	0.25	0.08	612	0.05	1,569	0.04	2,452
0.10	0.50	0.10	391	0.05	1,569	0.05	1,569
0.10	0.75	0.14	199	0.05	1,569	0.07	800
0.10	0.90	0.22	80	0.05	1,569	0.11	323
0.25	0.10	0.18	120	0.12	272	0.09	483
0.25	0.25	0.20	97	0.12	272	0.10	391
0.25	0.50	0.24	67	0.12	272	0.12	271
0.25	0.75	0.33	35	0.12	272	0.17	135
0.25	0.90	0.49	15	0.12	272	0.27	53
0.50	0.10	0.35	31	0.24	68	0.18	120
0.50	0.25	0.38	26	0.24	68	0.20	97
0.50	0.50	0.45	18	0.24	68	0.24	67
0.50	0.75	0.58	10	0.24	68	0.33	35
0.50	0.90	0.75	6	0.24	68	0.49	15
0.75	0.10	0.49	15	0.35	31	0.27	53
0.75	0.25	0.52	13	0.35	31	0.29	45
0.75	0.50	0.60	10	0.35	31	0.35	31
0.75	0.75	0.73	6	0.35	31	0.47	16
0.75	0.90	0.86	6	0.35	31	0.64	8
1.00	0.10	0.60	10	0.45	19	0.35	31
1.00	0.25	0.63	9	0.45	19	0.38	26
1.00	0.50	0.71	6	0.45	19	0.45	18
1.00	0.75	0.82	6	0.45	19	0.58	10
1.00	0.90	0.91	6	0.45	19	0.75	6

Note: Where δ is Glass's effect size, ϱ is the correlation between repeated measures, and critical effect sizes (Δ) and number of people per group (n/grp) is calculated for a two-tailed test comparison of two conditions with 80% power and 5% type I error rate. The estimates are based on Kraemer and Thiemann (1987, pp. 46–47, 109–110).

cally requires practitioners to learn new material and to do additional paperwork. Gaining and maintaining cooperation is absolutely essential for a randomized field experiment to succeed. The researchers and providers must practically form a marriage — seeking their mutual benefit and being prepared to compromise. One of the great mistakes of early experiments was to assume that just because the head of an agency agreed, the organization and clients would follow. In introducing an experiment, it is important to develop, test, and implement a protocol for gaining the cooperation of everyone — from the chief administrators to the staff to the clients.

Note that cooperation must be more than nominal. Staff will often agree to a change and then simply not do it. Worse yet, if they are not persuaded of the clinical equipoise of the interventions (and hence the need for the experiment), they may actively subvert the experiment because of ethical concerns. Appendix 8.D provides an example from the *Oxygen Experiment* in which nurses actively subverted an experimental treatment for premature babies because they thought it was life threatening (Silverman, 1977).

Several strategies, listed below, are available to researchers for gaining and maintaining staff cooperation. (Strategies for clients are discussed later in this section.)

- *Explain to the staff why the study is being done and how the information is being used.* They need to be persuaded just like everyone else.
- *Present the draft instruments and procedures to the staff for critique and input.* They may not be able to tell you what to do, but they will almost always be right in what they tell you will cause a problem.
- *Be responsive to staff concerns and make some accommodations.* Even if you cannot eliminate every problem raised by the staff (for instance, more paperwork), accommodating the staff on some issues will make them more likely to go along in other areas.
- *Give the staff feedback on the study's progress and findings.* Many experiments take several years. As in any endeavor, staff should be given pep talks. Letting them know that you are actually using all of that extra paperwork is the best way to get it done and done well.
- *Be sensitive to internal time horizons and deadlines.* Minimize the extent to which your procedures and reporting guidelines conflict with the program's operations. Much of the information you will collect may have alternative uses by the program staff and should be shared where feasible.

A final strategy is to stay in touch with the program after the experiment. It is all too common that after using staff members in a study for several years, an investigator simply leaves—never sending copies of the findings or even telling the program staff what was discovered. Remaining in touch with the program may not benefit your study, but it may make the program staff more likely to participate in future studies.

Assignment Mechanism

It is a common misconception that all experiments ignore preexisting differences and that units must be allocated evenly (Boruch, 1976). In fact, statistical precision can often be greatly improved (and sample size requirements reduced) by either pairing or blocking units into groups prior to randomization (Fisher, 1960; Winer, 1971). Groupings can be done on the basis of ability, similar needs, subject characteristics, or provider, or even by site. Because many randomized field experiments take in clients over time, it is also often desirable to block assignments over time (so that each condition gets three out of every six clients) or sometimes to allocate clients (or units) unevenly to accommodate logistical constraints or programmatic concerns. Examples of such accommodations include avoiding so many consecutive admissions to one group that the program's intake procedures are overloaded, being aware of differences in the expected length of stay between conditions, and keeping track of costs to serve difficult types of clients (Boruch, Dennis, and Greer, 1988).

Blocking subjects can also be used as a form of damage control. In evaluating a program that allowed women to have their children with them at a therapeutic community during drug treatment, for instance, Renner and Sechrest (1992) found that some women did not want their children present, and that still others also had to contend with the wishes of the local child welfare agency. It might have been possible to identify and take into consideration whether women wanted their children with them and/or whether their children were under the supervision of the child welfare agency. By randomly assigning women within each block or stratum, the evaluators would have had four small experiments that could be combined or legitimately analyzed separately if the experiment failed to be successfully implemented for one or more types of women. Thus, to the extent that likely dimensions of motivation or barriers to implementation can be identified in advance, it may be helpful to use them as a guide for creating blocks of subjects as a form of analytic insurance.

When the intervention requires the saturation of an area, such as a prevention or public education program, it may be necessary to assign clusters of units randomly. For example, in evaluating the Drug Abuse Resistance Education (DARE) program, an intervention that called for the saturation of the school and community with DARE-related materials, Curtin, Ringwalt, and Rosenbaum (1992) had to make random assignments by schools/communities rather than individuals or classrooms. It is important to note that in such experiments the most appropriate unit of analysis would be the community, not the individual.

Unlike their application in classical experiments, assignment ratios in randomized field experiments are often set to match the logistical flow of the interventions (a twenty-eight-day intervention will take in five to six times more clients per year than a six-month intervention with the same number of slots). Assignment ratios and options can also be varied for different population subgroups (minorities, adolescents, heavy drug users). Single women might be randomly assigned to a women's program or a co-ed program, while single mothers might be randomly assigned to a women's program, a co-ed program, or a family program. Such multiple assignment patterns are statistically less efficient, but they allow more people to be included in the study. Appendix 8.E contains an illustration of such a scheme from the *D.C. Initiative*.

Numerous mechanisms can be used for actually implementing random assignment. The author found four major methods in a 1988 review of forty experiments in criminal and civil justice.

- *Envelopes with randomly ordered assignments.* Typically, a statistician or the researcher used a set of random numbers blocked in groups of six to sixteen to determine assignments; these were put into sealed, sequentially numbered envelopes — with a master list kept to detect violations of order.
- *Client logs with assignments.* The researcher or statistician used a set of random numbers to order the assignments on a blank log, often covering them with tape. Client information was written in as clients entered the program, and the tape was removed. The list was often maintained by a third party or kept at another location to avoid cheating.
- *Computerized assignment.* This system either was based on the tick of a computer clock (1/100 of a second) or used a random number generator, often incorporating some level of blocking on offense, subject characteristics, or time.
- *Systematic random assignment from a roster.* For studies in which all the clients could start at once and were already listed on some form of roster, the researcher would use a coin or random number to assign the first person, then assign every other person (or every third or fourth person, depending on the number of conditions) to that same condition.

Where prior information allows a criterion or scale to be used to make assignments, an experimenter can also explore the feasibility of other assignment mechanisms that can be used in field experiments. Two useful alternatives are regression-discontinuity (Trochim, 1990) and/or a randomly controlled cutoff trial (Trochim and Cappelleri, 1990). These designs may allow more people to be included than would a randomized field experiment in which exclusion criteria limit the population (Trochim, Cappelleri, and Reichardt, 1991). They are also ethically desirable when the equipoise is shifting in one direction because those who are most likely to benefit from treatment are assigned to treatment. In regression-discontinuity or cutoff designs, one group of people are automatically put in intervention A and another group in intervention B, based on a criterion involving some common dimension such as income, performance, or need. In a randomly controlled cutoff trial, one or more middle groups are defined and group assignments are made to them randomly. For example, suppose the common dimension is income and the treatment contrast is whether someone gets child care assistance. It may be essential that families who are indigent always receive child care, but people who are wealthy may never need it. Criteria could be set to define these two automatic assignment groups (below $10,000 per year family income, above $100,000 family income). Everyone between the two criteria ($10,001 to $99,999 family income) would then be randomly assigned as to whether they would receive child care assistance. Although recent advances have been made with randomly controlled cutoff trial and regression-discontinuity designs, they are still only about 85 percent to 95 percent as statistically efficient (in terms of sample size requirements) as simple randomized trials (Trochim, Cappelleri, and Reichardt, 1991) and are not without their own critics (Stanley, 1991).

Attrition Prevention

Attrition is the Achilles' heel of both traditional controlled trials and randomized field experiments. Few experiments reach the ideal of no attrition, and many have some degree of differential attrition by group. Even if the nominal level of attrition is the same in every group, we have no way of knowing whether the people in each group left for the same types of reasons (one group may have left an experimental training program because it was too strict while the other group left the control condition because it had nothing to offer). The best course, then, is to prevent attrition from happening in the first place.

Much of the work in this area is in technical documents and methodological reports of limited distribution (Gilbert and Maxwell, 1987; Howard, Cox, and Saunders, 1990; Purcell, Anderson, Cavanaugh, and Hubbard, 1983; Sobell, 1978). Some of the key approaches that have been used by the author and others to reduce attrition include these:

- *Explaining the study thoroughly to the client and eliciting a commitment.* This may sound obvious, but many clients do not realize what commitment they are making. For some clients, information about how the information will be used may also affect their commitment to the study—particularly if it can be related to something in which they have a vested interest (parents of a child with cystic fibrosis [CF] are more likely to keep their child in a trial of a new CF medicine than of a cold medicine).
- *Providing incentives for cooperation.* Besides telling the client how the information will be used, it is often useful to offer monetary or token (food, toiletries) incentives for completing an interview and to even offer a separate incentive for scheduling and completing the interview on time.
- *Collecting locator information.* One of the most basic techniques is to collect information about the client and about other people who would know where to contact the client at the time of follow-up.
- *Staying in contact.* Researchers are learning to stay in contact with clients, either indirectly through program staff or directly with telephone calls or even postcards. Some studies provide incentives to clients for staying in touch with the researcher by stopping in, calling, or returning a postcard.
- *Using official records.* Some of the more sophisticated techniques include tracking people through the Social Security Administration, state driver's license bureau, the National Death Registry, crime reports, and even credit agencies.
- *Employing outreach workers.* For hard-to-reach populations such as injection drug users or homeless people, many studies employ indigenous

workers familiar with the client's community to help locate people who cannot otherwise be found for follow-up.

- *Giving it time.* With enough money and time, it seems that field staff can always find "one more" case. Although there is clearly a point of diminishing returns, the locating process should actively begin several weeks in advance of the target date and continue as long as it is still cost effective. Note that it is better to have an interview three weeks late than have no data at all.

Another strategy, which is discussed later in the analysis section, is to plan at least some measures for which there will be no attrition. The most common of these involve measures based on observations or program records. Examples of this strategy include retention in drug abuse treatment research or recidivism in criminal justice research.

Implementing and Monitoring the Intervention

In implementing an intervention, it is important not to underemphasize the need to train people in how to make even simple changes. Consider, for example, the first randomized field experiment of social worker caseloads in the 1940s. Simon and Devine (1985) found that counselors who had their caseloads raised from thirty to forty-five clients continued to provide the same level of services as before, became stressed out, and either quit or burned out. Counselors who had their caseloads reduced from thirty to fifteen clients also continued to provide the same level of services and did not use the saved time to provide more services. In both cases, the experimenter had failed to address how the experimental manipulation of caseloads fit into the work that was being done or to suggest new strategies for addressing the changes.

Although evaluators can attempt to anticipate some of these problems through training, it is also useful to consider some general techniques for improving training effectiveness. In their book on workplace supervision and training, Dennis and Onion (1990) recommended that training be followed up with debriefings, field visits, refresher courses, and as much feedback as possible. The training procedures used in the Methadone-Enhanced Treatment Study to increase counselor effectiveness (Fairbank, Dennis, Bonito, and Rachal, 1991; also see Appendix 8.B) included the following:

- Three days of training using a manual, lectures, role-playing, and demonstrations
- Audiotaping initial sessions that were critiqued by the trainers and followed up with a teleconference to provide feedback
- Two days of follow-up training on site that included a review, individual debriefing, group discussion, and review of treatment plans
- Continuation of weekly staff meetings for the experimentally trained counselors to have them provide each other with feedback

The fact that a client (or practitioner) is assigned at random to receive (or provide) a specific level of treatment does not necessarily mean that he or she actually receives (or provides) that level of treatment. Problems may arise both from client noncompliance or from failure of treatment personnel to follow the intervention. Further, if the application of treatment is not measured in some way, the analyst has no way of knowing whether a lack of difference in outcome between treatment and control groups is due to a lack of efficacy of the experimental treatment or a failure to actually apply the treatment. Dennis, Fairbank, Bonito, and Rachal (1990) developed and tested (Dennis and others, 1991b; Dennis, Rachal, and Bohlig, 1990) a methodology for addressing these problems. Briefly, the strategy entails measuring the amount of treatment received by each client, collecting information to test constructs or theories about what is happening in treatment (that is, identifying the active ingredient), and answering three basic questions:

1.   To what extent have the experimental and/or control interventions been implemented as planned?
2.   To what extent do the experimental and/or control interventions differ from each other, even in unplanned ways?
3.   To what extent does the experiment represent a *fair* or valid test of any observed differences?

Conceptually, the first two questions may be considered a form of treatment validation analysis for the main study. Even if one or more interventions are not what was expected, important information about effectiveness can still be learned. The last question is traditionally addressed in the context of Cook and Campbell's (1979) threats to internal validity (such as contamination, history, maturation, measurement bias, selectivity). It is important to note that even when randomization is successfully implemented, some threats to internal validity may still exist—in particular, differential attrition and compensatory rivalry.

Analyzing the Experiment

As demonstrated throughout this chapter, conducting randomized field experiments can be complex. To the extent that problems are not avoided, it is necessary to address them during the analysis. This section discusses the elements that should be given attention in analyzing a field experiment.

Assessing the Quality of the Experiment

Because a randomized field experiment is often subject to more problems than a traditional controlled trial, it is essential to assess the quality of its research design, as it was *actually* implemented, in terms of internal validity, external validity, and the control of treatment factors (Dennis, 1990).

Internal validity refers to the extent to which factors such as attrition, selectivity, maturation, confounding variables, contamination, compensatory rivalry, Hawthorne/placebo effects, and instrument error can be ruled out (see Campbell and Stanley, 1963, or Cook and Campbell, 1979, for a detailed description of these threats). An experimenter should *not* assume that random assignment necessarily removes these threats. Rather, he or she should treat a randomized field experiment as a very good quasi-experiment until its integrity has been demonstrated relative to the most likely threats. External validity means the extent to which the results for each study will be generalizable to other treatment programs and clients (see Cook and Campbell, 1979, or Cronbach, 1983). Control of treatment factors refers to the extent to which differences in the services received by different clients can be measurably and intentionally changed (see Dennis, 1990). In a randomized field experiment, control of treatment factors also refers to the extent that the intervention was delivered as planned.

A key strategy in this approach is to collect multiple measures of treatment (service logs, client records, laboratory test results, and client interviews) that can be used in a multimethod/multimeasure matrix (Campbell and Fiske, 1959) for treatment validation and to develop measures of dosage (Dennis and others, 1991b). The records data can also be used to assess the extent of preinclusion attrition or selectivity (Howard, Krause, and Orlinsky, 1986; Howard, Cox, and Saunders, 1990) as well as the potential bias of any subsequent attrition (Ellickson and Bell, 1992). Analyses of data from the period just before the experiment was implemented can be used as a quasi-experimental baseline group to determine the extent of any treatment contamination during the main study or to evaluate the effectiveness of the current interventions relevant to an earlier intervention or pilot program (see, for instance, Bertrand and colleagues' 1986 study of postpartum care in Barbados).

The quality of randomized field experiments can be assessed with methods outlined by Dennis (1990) to understand their limitations and to support future research. These methods include the following:

- Measuring the actual amount and quality of treatment received by each client
- Comparing treatment levels before and after the implementation of the randomized experiment in an interrupted time series design to assess potential treatment contamination or compensatory rivalry
- Comparing the treatment received with the proposed level of treatment to measure compliance
- Carefully monitoring random assignments to detect violations
- Monitoring and incorporating into the analysis environmental changes that might affect both groups
- Incorporating planned intervention changes into the analysis

These analyses should look at the implementation problems, treatment compliance, and validity of each study and develop recommendations for addressing the problems both logistically and analytically. Wherever possible, they should also compare the clients and programs in each trial to larger epidemiological databases to examine their external validity.

Relative Effectiveness

Typically, hypotheses are addressed by using standard statistical tests fitted to a specific sample distribution. Discrete variables such as current employment status are typically evaluated through nonparametric tests such as chi-square, Wilcoxon-Mann, Whitney-U, survival analysis, or logistic regression. Logistic regression and/or analysis of survival curves are particularly important if repeated exposures to the intervention are required or the outcome is expected to follow a normal *s-curve* instead of a straight line. Continuous and normally distributed variables, such as thirty-day drug use, are typically analyzed with parametric models such as *t*-tests, analysis of variance, or multiple regression. If they are asymmetrical or have multiple modes, the main effects analysis can be done with equivalent tests on their *rank order*. Such tests make no assumptions about normality but have 95 percent of a *t*-test's statistical power (Siegel and Castellan, 1988).

Recall from the earlier example with data from the Methadone-Enhanced Treatment Study that we must be careful to test the impact of an intervention on both the mean and variance. The impact of the intervention on the variance or distribution should be calculated before you use the pooled standard error or traditional tests that might be overly conservative if the variances are significantly different. The simplest test is to divide the larger of the variance estimates for the two groups by the smaller to get an F statistic, where the degrees of freedom are equal to the number of people in each group minus one. In one MET site, for example, we increased the variance of the "days retained" in treatment from 1592.00 to 5451.67. With 47 standard clients and 44 enhanced clients, F would be calculated as

$$F_{(46,43)} = 5451.67/1592.00 = 3.65, p < .0001$$

A simple regression-discontinuity or randomly controlled cutoff design (see Chapter Seven by Marcantonio and Cook, or Chapter Eighteen by Reichardt and Bormann, this volume) can also be analyzed by using the actual change score or through multiple regression.

Incorporating Implementation and Treatment Data

Because randomized field experiments are more likely to vary in the extent to which they are implemented and to have more intervention variability in general, it is important to measure and incorporate dosage information — particularly for interventions involving multiple exposures or testing over multiple sites. As these problems have become more widely recognized (for example, Sechrest and Redner, 1979; Scott and Sechrest, 1989; Sechrest,

White, and Brown, 1979), investigators conducting randomized field experiments have begun to focus more attention on treatment integrity and dosage (compare Cook and Poole, 1982; Dennis, 1988). These developments are consistent with the movement in the larger evaluation research arena toward greater emphasis on implementation evaluation—ensuring that the intervention being studied was in fact implemented, and implemented as intended (Brekke, 1987; Palumbo and Oliverio, 1989; Rezmovic, 1984; Sechrest and Redner, 1979; Wholey, 1983).

Contrary to common expectations, analyzing units as they were randomized (regardless of actual treatment) does not always provide the most conservative estimate of impact or even go in a consistent direction across measures within a single study. Continuing our example from the Methadone-Enhanced Treatment Study, Table 8.3 compares analyses based on the assigned counselor versus analyses based on the counselor actually making the most comments in the client's records. It uses two measures: the days retained in treatment during the first six months and the six-month retention rate. Note that although analysis of the outcomes according to the treatment "received" is more sensitive for the interval measure, it is less sensitive for the percentage variable. Thus, failure to examine even the most rudimentary treatment data may have led to misinterpretation of the impact.

Table 8.3. Impact of Methadone-Enhanced Treatment (MET) on Retention by Treatment Condition Assigned and Received in Pittsburgh.

| Treatment Condition | Days Retained | | | Six-Month Retention | | |
	Mean	(SE)[a]	t	Percent	Odds Ratio	χ^2
As Assigned						
Standard (n = 47)	145.7	(10.7)		65.95		
MET (n = 44)	169.2	(5.8)*	2.18**	86.36	3.27	4.87**
As Received						
Standard (n = 43)	141.7	(11.6)		67.44		
MET (n = 47)	174.2	(4.3)*	2.80**	85.11	2.76	3.76**

*Probability that the within-group variances are equal is less than .0001.
**Probability that the distributions are equal (using the standard group SE) is less than .05.
[a]Standard error.

A parallel problem is noncompliance with the intervention assignment, which can be in the form of an outright refusal to participate, early dropout, or failure to follow instructions closely. It is the clinical equivalent to attrition and leaves the researcher wondering what the effect would have been had everyone received the assigned treatment. Below are some of the specific approaches that can be taken to address this problem:

- *Assessing the intervention's effect both as assigned and as delivered.* Berk (1990; Berk and Sherman, 1988) and Dennis (1990) argued for calculating the effect both ways to create an upper and lower bound of sorts.

- *Making a participation effect adjustment to inflate the treatment effect.* Like a survey's nonresponse rate adjustment, the observed effect is divided by the fraction of people who participated. Bloom (1984) argued that this would represent the expected effect if everyone had participated.
- *Stratifying conditions on the basis of the treatment received.* Cook and Poole (1982) found that even crude measures of the treatment received (none/any) were capable of increasing the statistical power by more than 10 percent. Cook and Campbell (1979) recommended looking at the pre-post effect of groups with different dosages of treatment — expecting to see a fan-spread pattern if dosage is important.
- *Constructing a discriminant function to predict treatment use among the experimental group, then subsetting both groups on the basis of the equation (regardless of actual treatment use).* Vinokur, Price, and Caplan (1991) found that this approach could be used to construct a matched control group and estimate the effect of likely service users.

Each of these is a second best approach compared to controlling the intervention dosage. Furthermore, each raises potential alternative hypotheses that must be ruled out through other means (to the extent possible).

Overall, the best approach seems to be to present a conservative analysis (analyze them as you randomized them), followed by the experimenter's recommended adjustments (and rationale for making them). This approach satisfies the methodologists by creating a benchmark and the practitioners by focusing on the intervention's potential effect.

Our ability to interpret these problems and differences has improved recently through new models to measure what is actually being provided (Dennis, Fairbank, Bonito, and Rachal, 1990; Efron and Feldman, 1991; Fairbank, Dennis, Bonito, and Rachal, 1991) and for incorporating this information into the main analyses (Bentler, 1986, 1991; Blalock, 1985; Dennis and others, 1991a; Ellickson and Bell, 1992; Hawkins, Catalano, and Wells, 1986). Biomedical Data Processing, Inc. (BMDP) has recently introduced a new structural equations software package, EQS (Bentler, 1989) that can be used to predict outcome variables as a function of preexisting differences, intervention implementation, and experimental groups. Although it was developed primarily for analyzing nonexperimental data, it provides one of the few unified frameworks for combining implementation, treatment dosage, and outcome data. A marked improvement over earlier software, EQS can read in a variety of statistical files, includes a disturbance term (equivalent of an error term for a latent variable), and has its own graphics package.

Analysis of Subpopulations and Subgroups

Because many randomized field experiments involve multifaceted treatments and diverse clients, they are more likely to face Bernard's dilemma (1865; as translated in Yusaf, Wittes, Probstfield, and Tyroler, 1991, p. 93) that "the response of the 'average' patient to therapy is not necessarily the response of the patient being treated." For interventions of individualized treatment, the concept of an *average* treatment designed for an *average* patient may not even be meaningful. In the Methadone-Enhanced Treatment Study (Appendix 8.B), for instance, the treatment protocol called for a standardized needs assessment followed by individualized counseling on the main problem area. Although significant differences were in the top quartile, fewer than half the clients talked about ten out of the twelve topic areas (Fairbank, Dennis, Bonito, and Rachal, 1991). It is therefore important to explore the pattern of actual services received and to consider subgroup analysis (including its implications for planning the sample size). Note that subgroups can be formed on several bases, including demographic characteristics, need, prior patterns of behavior, and actual treatment received.

When analyses are planned for specific subgroups or when a group characteristic explains much of the variability of the dependent measure, then it is often useful to divide or *block* clients into these groups prior to randomization. In the Training and Employment Program (TEP), for instance, the author blocked clients by gender (male/female), vocational engagement (in school or work/wanting to be in school or work/other) and sample type (volunteer/random sample). Twelve randomization lists were created, one of each of the 12 blocks formed by crossing the three types of groups. This brings the distribution as close to equal as possible and ensures the most statistical power for a given number of people or units. It does come at the cost of reduced degrees of freedom and so is typically only done on one to three variables.

Increasingly more common to health research, some of the other reasons for blocking include: to consider subgroup analyses as semi-independent experiments, to control for the loss of one or more particularly problematic subgroup groups, and to avoid logistical problems. Two of the simplest and most common forms of blocking are to randomly assign people within site and balancing assignments within groups of four, six, or eight. The former helps balance assignments logistically across sites and within site analyses. The latter helps to avoid long strings of assignments to one group or the other and allows analyses of trends over time.

Coping with Attrition and Noncompliance

As previously noted, the ideal is to prevent attrition. Should that fail, explanations might be found using multiple outcome measures (with at least some from records affected by attrition). Nonetheless, most analysts find themselves trying either to explain away the attrition and noncompliance that has occurred or to adjust for it statistically. One of the most common approaches to assessing the probable damage from attrition (which is by definition unknown) is to compare the characteristics of the people who were retained and those who dropped out of the research. Unfortunately, investigators too often limit this approach to demographic characteristics only instead of including more substantive variables such as drug use patterns, criminal activity, treatment exposure, or other intermediate outcomes.

Statistically, the main reason that people try to adjust for attrition is that incomplete data can severely limit the use of multivariate and logistic regression analyses. Researchers who have at least partial data often attempt to replace missing information with either a mean or a regression equation, or a thorough hot-deck imputation. Mean substitution is the most straightforward and provides markedly better estimates than does list-wise deletion (Jones, 1991). Means can be calculated for the group overall or for mutually exclusive subgroups. A regression equation simply factors in several items rather than creating several subgroups. Hot-deck imputation consists of sorting the data on a core set of variables and then randomly selecting the value from either the prior or following record. It has less effect on the variance, which is often slightly reduced by mean substitution.

Many evaluators have been tempted to "define away" attrition after the fact. Doing this typically involves the reapplication of exclusionary criteria after randomization and raises the possibility that group assignment will interact with what is known about the client. The topic was hotly debated in the quarterly cross-site meetings of the Spousal Assault Replication Project from 1987 to 1988. The basic concern was that the police were more likely to find out about outstanding warrants (an exclusionary criterion) for people assigned to an "arrest" condition than for those assigned to a "separation" condition. Although numerous alternatives involving use of data obtained after randomization were proposed, the committee repeatedly rejected each as having real potential biases.

Conclusion

The goals set forth at the beginning of this chapter were to help the reader (1) design a randomized field experiment of an ethical, practical, and salient experimental contrast; (2) implement and manage the experiment in a way that avoids common problems or allows them to be addressed in analysis; and (3) estimate the relative effectiveness of the intervention overall and for relevant subgroups. Some of the key problems that have been learned from early randomized field experiments are reprised below.

- *Prior to implementing a randomized experiment in a community setting, five threshold conditions should be met:* the present practice must need improvement, the efficacy of the proposed intervention must be uncertain, no simpler alternatives should exist for evaluating the intervention, the results should be potentially important for policy or program development, and the design must be able to meet the ethical standards of both the researchers and service providers.
- *Randomized field experiments are susceptible to several implementation problems:* variability in the actual treatment that was delivered, treatment contami-

nation or compensatory rivalry, inadequate numbers of cases or case flow, failure to follow the random assignment process, changes in the environment, and planned changes that occur in the experimental intervention over time.

- *Over half the studies in the published literature have weak research designs:* insufficient statistical power to detect the effect they are looking for, use of overly simplistic statistical models, failure to measure the actual intervention provided, and/or failure to consider the quality of the outcome measures being used.

Fortunately, each of these problems can be and has been addressed in some studies. Some of the helpful approaches that were identified and recommended are these:

- *Defining a relevant experimental contrast and asking questions to draw out its implications:* What is the target population? How can the proposed changes in the intervention address the needs of this group? How can the intervention be designed to accommodate the needs and desires of both the targeted clients and practitioners? What changes is the intervention expected to produce?
- *Minimizing the preinclusion attrition to improve generalizability:* clearly identifying the target population to which the study will be generalized; carefully documenting who is screened out of the study and why; focusing the intervention on feasible options and selling them to staff and clients; collecting information on programs, staff, and clients that will allow comparisons with larger groups.
- *Conducting statistical power analyses to identify the questions that can be reasonably addressed:* trying to do a traditional power analysis; at least doing a simplified power analysis; and considering possible design changes, such as blocking and repeated measures, to improve the power without increasing the sample size.
- *Gaining and maintaining staff and client cooperation:* explaining why a study is being done and how the information will be used; having staff and clients critique the draft instruments, procedures, and interventions; being responsive to staff concerns and sensitive to their internal time horizons; and giving the staff feedback on the study's progress and findings as soon as possible.
- *Using assignment mechanisms that are under the control of the evaluator or a third party and that incorporate logistical and analytic concerns:* blocking to make it possible to analyze subgroups and to ensure against partial failures, using uneven assignment to accommodate case flow or capacity, and assigning unit clusters where the experiment involves a systems-level intervention or contamination is likely.
- *Minimizing attrition to maximize the degree of internal validity:* explaining the study thoroughly to participate and eliciting a commitment, providing

incentives for cooperation, collecting detailed locator information, staying in regular contact, using official records, employing outreach workers, and giving the process time to succeed.

- *Implementing the intervention so that it will become an intrinsic part of the provider's daily operations:* training that anticipates barriers; immediate follow-up to make sure it is initially implemented; longer-term follow-up training and feedback; and creation of systems, such as treatment teams, that create intrinsic support.

- *Assessing the quality and validity of an experiment:* assuming that a randomized field experiment is a very good quasi-experiment and carefully testing potential threats to its validity, measuring the actual intervention received, comparing levels of intervention with targeted levels and/or baseline levels, carefully monitoring random assignment, and incorporating changes in the intervention or overall environment into the analysis.

- *Analyzing effectiveness in terms of the total distribution and multiple measures:* testing for effects on the mean and the variance, testing for intervention effects as assigned and as delivered, and looking at the pattern of effects over multiple measures.

In this context, previous debates between quantitative and qualitative research — in which experiments are often viewed as one extreme — can be seen as trivial. No randomized field experiment is likely to succeed or be useful without a lot of good qualitative work including working with practitioners and clients to define the questions and develop meaningful interventions, explaining the intervention to the participants in a way that makes them willing to participate, carefully monitoring the actual implementation to detect unexpected problems or the need to refine the experiment, working with practitioners and staff to identify and interpret key phenomena. Though there is not a comprehensive work currently available on the role of qualitative evaluation in the management of randomized field experiments, there are models such as "Ethnographic Auditing" that could be readily adapted for monitoring organizations in general (for a brief review, see Fetterman, 1990).

Thus the use of randomized experiments to evaluate real programs is feasible, but not without a wide range of methodological, logistical, managerial, and analytical challenges. This chapter has demonstrated that many early efforts failed because they were ill conceived, poorly designed, and/or poorly executed. In randomized field experiments, programmatic expertise on needs, management, and organizational changes can be just as important as methodological expertise about research design or analysis. Given the intensive level of human and organizational resources involved, it also becomes an ethical imperative that randomized field experiments be designed to serve multiple audiences and involve multiple levels of research design. This breadth merely recognizes that in the real world, program managers and policymakers are rarely interested in answering just a single question or serving only the "average" or "model" client.

References

Ashery, R. S., and McAuliffe, W. E. "Implementation Issues and Techniques in Randomized Trials of Outpatient Psychosocial Treatment for Drug Abusers: Recruitment of Subjects." *American Journal of Drug and Alcohol Abuse,* 1992, *18*(3), 305–329.

Bentler, P. M. *Theory and Implementation of EQS: A Structural Equations Program.* Los Angeles: BMDP Statistical Hardware, 1986.

Bentler, P. M. *EQS Structural Equations Program Manual.* Los Angeles: BMDP Statistical Software, 1989.

Bentler, P. M. "Modeling of Intervention Effects." In C. G. Leukefeld and W. J. Bukoski (eds.), *Drug Abuse Prevention Intervention Research: Methodological Issues* (National Institute on Drug Abuse Research Monograph 107, pp. 150–182). Rockville, Md.: National Institute on Drug Abuse, 1991.

Berk, R. A. *What Your Mother Never Told You About Randomly Controlled Trials* (No. 44 in the University of California, Los Angeles Statistic Series). Unpublished report available from the author. Los Angeles: Department of Sociology and Program in Social Statistics, University of California, Los Angeles, 1990.

Berk, R. A., and Sherman, L. W. "Police Response to Family Violence Incidents: An Analysis of an Experimental Design with Incomplete Randomization." *Journal of the American Statistical Association,* 1988, *83*(401), 70–76.

Berk, R. A., and others. "Social Policy Experimentation: A Position Paper." *Evaluation Review,* 1985, *9,* 387–429.

Bertrand, J. T., and others. *A Test of Two Strategies for Delaying a Second Pregnancy in Teenage Mothers in Barbados: Final Report* (Contract AID/DPE-0632-c-00-2007-00). Report prepared for the Agency for International Development, Department of Program Evaluation. New Orleans: Tulane University Medical Center, School of Public Health and Tropical Medicine, Applied Health Sciences Department, 1986.

Blalock, H. M. (ed.). *Causal Models in Panel and Experimental Designs.* New York: Aldine, 1985.

Bloom, H. S. "Accounting for No-Shows in Experimental Evaluation Designs." *Evaluation Review,* 1984, *8,* 225–246.

Boruch, R. F. "On Common Contentions About Randomized Field Experiments." In G. V. Glass (ed.), *Evaluation Studies Review Annual* (pp. 158–194). Newbury Park, Calif.: Sage, 1976.

Boruch, R. F., and Cecil, J. S. *Assuring Confidentiality of Social Research Data.* Philadelphia: University of Pennsylvania Press, 1979.

Boruch, R. F., and Cordray, D. S. *An Appraisal of Educational Program Evaluations: Federal, State, and Local Agencies.* Evanston, Ill.: Northwestern University, 1980.

Boruch, R. F., Dennis, M. L., and Greer, K. C. "Lessons from the Rockefeller Foundation's Experiments on the Minority Female Single Parent Program." *Evaluation Review,* 1988, *12,* 396–426.

Boruch, R. F., and Gomez, H. "Power Theory in Impact Evaluations." In

L. E. Datta and R. Perloff (eds.), *Improving Evaluations* (pp. 139–176). Newbury Park, Calif.: Sage, 1979.

Brekke, J. S. "The Model-Guided Method of Monitoring Program Implementation." *Evaluation Review,* 1987, *11,* 281–300.

Campbell, D. T. "Reforms as Experiments." *American Psychologist,* 1969, *24,* 409–429.

Campbell, D. T., and Fiske, D. W. "Convergent and Discriminant Validation by the Multitrait-Multimethod Matrix." *Psychological Bulletin,* 1959, *56,* 81–105.

Campbell, D. T., and Stanley, J. S. "Experimental and Quasi-Experimental Designs for Research on Teaching." In N. L. Gage (ed.), *Handbook of Research on Teaching.* Chicago: Rand McNally, 1963.

Cohen, J. "The Statistical Power of Abnormal-Social Psychological Research: A Review." *Journal of Abnormal and Social Psychology,* 1962, *65,* 145–153.

Cohen, J. *Statistical Power Analysis for the Behavioral Sciences.* New York: Academic Press, 1977.

Cohen, J. "What I Have Learned (So Far)." *American Psychologist,* 1990, *45,* 1304–1312.

Cook, T. D., and Campbell, D. *Quasi-Experimentation: Design and Analysis Issues for Field Settings.* Boston: Houghton Mifflin, 1979.

Cook, T. J., and Poole, W. K. "Treatment Implementation and Statistical Power: A Research Note." *Evaluation Review,* 1982, *6,* 425–430.

Cronbach, L. J. *Designing Evaluations of Educational and Social Programs.* San Francisco: Jossey-Bass, 1983.

Curtin, T. R., Ringwalt, C. L., and Rosenbaum, D. "Methodological Findings from the Drug Abuse Resistance Education Program (DARE) Evaluation." Paper presented at the American Evaluation Association Annual Conference, Seattle, November 1992.

Dennis, L. E., and Onion, M. L. *Out in Front: Effective Supervision in the Workplace.* Chicago: National Safety Council, 1990.

Dennis, M. L. "Implementing Randomly Controlled Trials: An Analysis of Criminal and Civil Justice Research." Unpublished doctoral dissertation, Division of Methodology and Evaluation Research, Psychology Department, Northwestern University, 1988.

Dennis, M. L. "Assessing the Validity of Randomly Controlled Trials: An Example from Drug Abuse Treatment Research." *Evaluation Review,* 1990, *14,* 347–373.

Dennis, M. L., and Boruch, R. F. "Randomized Experiments for Planning and Testing Projects in Developing Countries: Threshold Conditions." *Evaluation Review,* 1989, *13,* 292–309.

Dennis, M. L., Fairbank, J. A., Bonito, A., and Rachal, J. V. *Treatment Process Study Design* (Technical Document No. 7, National Institute on Drug Abuse Contract No. 271-88-8230). Research Triangle Park, N.C.: Research Triangle Institute, 1990.

Dennis, M. L., Fairbank, J. A., and Rachal, J. V. "Measuring Substance

Abuse Counseling." Paper presented at the 100th Annual Conference of the American Psychological Association, Washington, D.C., August 1992.

Dennis, M. L., Rachal, J. V., and Bohlig, E. M. "Measuring Substance Abuse Counseling: The Methadone Enhanced Treatment (MET) Trials Approach." Paper presented at the American Evaluation Association Meeting (J. Valley Rachal, Chair), Washington, D.C., 1990.

Dennis, M. L., and others. *Developing Training and Employment Programs to Meet the Needs of Methadone Treatment Clients* (Technical Report Under National Institute on Drug Abuse Grant #1R18 DA06383-02). Research Triangle Park, N.C.: Research Triangle Institute, 1991a.

Dennis, M. L., and others. "Reducing Injection Drug Use Through Methadone-Assisted Rehabilitation: Factors Other Than Methadone Dosage. In *Proceedings of the National AIDS Demonstration Research Conference, Washington D.C., October 31 to November 2.* Rockville, Md.: National Institute on Drug Abuse, 1991b.

Dennis, M. L., and others. *Individualized Substance Abuse Counseling (ISAC) Manual* (NIDA grant no. 1-R18-DA-7262 and R01-DA-07864). Research Triangle Park, N.C.: Research Triangle Institute, 1993.

Detsky, A. S. "Are Clinical Trials a Cost-Effective Investment?" *Journal of the American Medical Association,* 1989, *262,* 1795–1800.

Efron, B., and Feldman, D. "Compliance as an Explanatory Variable in Clinical Trials." *Journal of the American Statistical Association,* 1991, *86*(413), 9–17.

Ellickson, P. L., and Bell, R. M. "Challenges to Social Experiments: A Drug Prevention Example." *Journal of Research in Crime and Delinquency,* 1992, *29,* 79–101.

Fairbank, J. A., Dennis, M. L., Bonito, A. J., and Rachal, J. V. "Training Counselors to Provide Comprehensive Drug Abuse Counseling." Paper presented at the Third Annual National AIDS Demonstration Research (NADR) Meeting, Washington, D.C., 1991.

Fairweather, G. W., and Tornatzky, L. G. *Experimental Methods for Social Policy Research.* New York: Pergamon Press, 1977.

Farrington, D. P., Ohlin, L. E., and Wilson, J. Q. *Understanding and Controlling Crime: Toward a New Research Strategy.* New York: Springer-Verlag, 1986.

Federal Judicial Center. *Experimentation in the Law: Report of the Federal Judicial Center Advisory Committee on Experimentation in the Law.* Washington, D.C.: Federal Judicial Center, 1981.

Fetterman, D. M. "Ethnographic Auditing: A New Approach to Evaluating Management." In W. G. Tierney (ed.), *New Directions for Institutional Research,* 1990, *68,* 19–34.

Fisher, R. A. *The Design of Experiments.* (7th ed.) New York: Hafner, 1960.

Fisher, R. A., and Bartlett, S. "Pasteurized and Raw Milk." *Nature,* Apr. 18, 1931.

Flynn, P. M., and Clayton, A. C. *Random Assignment: Washington, D.C., Ini-*

tiative Controlled Study of Drug Abuse Treatment Approaches. Research Triangle Park, N.C.: Research Triangle Institute, 1992.

Flynn, P. M., and others. "Individual Assessment Profile (IAP): Standardizing the Assessment of Substance Abusers." Paper presented at the 100th Annual Meeting of the American Psychological Association, Washington, D.C., August 15, 1992.

Freedman, B. "Equipoise and the Ethics of Clinical Research." *New England Journal of Medicine,* 1987, *317,* 141–145.

Fuller, R. K., and others. "Disulfiram Treatment of Alcoholism." *Journal of the American Medical Association,* 1986, *245,* 1449–1455.

Gilbert, F. S., and Maxwell, P. J. "Predicting Attendance at Follow-Up Evaluations in Alcohol Treatment Outcome Research." *Journal of Studies on Alcohol,* 1987, *48,* 569–573.

Goldkamp, J. S., and Gottfredson, M. R. *Policy Guidelines for Bail: An Experiment in Court Reform.* Philadelphia: Temple University Press, 1985.

Hall, S. M. "Clinical Trials in Drug Treatment: Methodology." In F. M. Tims and J. P. Ludford (eds.), *Drug Abuse Treatment Evaluation: Strategies, Progress, and Prospects* (Research Monograph 51, pp. 88–105). Rockville, Md.: National Institute on Drug Abuse, 1984.

Hawkins, J. D., Catalano, R. F., and Wells, E. A. "Measuring Effects of a Skills Training Intervention for Drug Abusers." *Journal of Consulting and Clinical Psychology,* 1986, *54,* 661–664.

Howard, K. I., Cox, W. M., and Saunders, S. M. "Attrition in Substance Abuse Comparative Treatment Research: The Illusion of Randomization." In L. S. Onken and J. D. Blaine (eds.), *Psychotherapy and Counseling in the Treatment of Drug Abuse* (National Institute on Drug Abuse Research Monograph 104, pp. 66–79). Rockville, Md.: National Institute on Drug Abuse, 1990.

Howard, K. I., Krause, M. S., and Orlinsky, D. E. "The Attrition Dilemma: Towards a New Strategy for Psychotherapy Research." *Journal of Consulting and Clinical Psychology,* 1986, *54,* 106–110.

Jones, P. "Missing Data Options: What Difference Does It Make?" Paper presented at the American Evaluation Association Annual Conference, Chicago, November, 1991.

Kraemer, H. C., and Thiemann, S. *How Many Subjects? Statistical Power Analysis in Research.* Newbury Park, Calif.: Sage, 1987.

Kulka, R. A., and others. *Trauma and the Vietnam War Generation.* New York: Brunner/Mazel, 1990.

Lamas, G. A., and others. "Do the Results of Randomized Clinical Trials of Cardiovascular Drugs Influence Medical Practice?" *New England Journal of Medicine,* 1992, *327,* 241–247.

Leighton, G., and McKinlay, P. D. *Milk Consumption and the Growth of School Children* (Department of Health for Scotland). Edinburgh and London: Her Majesty's Stationery Office, 1930.

Lipsey, M. W. "Practice and Malpractice in Evaluation Research." *Evaluation Practice,* 1988, *9*(4), 5–24.

Lipsey, M. W. *Design Sensitivity: Statistical Power for Experimental Research.* Newbury Park, Calif.: Sage, 1990.

Lipsey, M. W., and others. "Evaluation: The State of the Art and the Sorry State of the Science." *New Directions for Program Evaluation,* 1985, *27,* 7–28.

Luborsky, L., Singer, B., and Luborsky, L. "Comparative Studies of Psychotherapies: Is It True That 'Everyone Has Won and All Must Have Prizes'?" *Archives of General Psychiatry,* 1975, *32,* 995–1008.

Martinson, R. M. "What Works? Questions and Answers About Prison Reform." *Public Interest,* 1974, *35,* 22–54.

Palumbo, D. J., and Oliverio, A. "Implementation Theory and the Theory-Driven Approach to Validity." *Evaluation and Program Planning,* 1989, *12*(4), 337–344.

Passamani, E. "Clinical Trials—Are They Ethical?" *New England Journal of Medicine,* 1991, *324*(22), 1589–1592.

Pedhazur, E. J. *Multiple Regression in Behavioral Research: Explanation and Prediction.* (2nd ed.) Chicago: Holt, Rinehart & Winston, 1982.

Purcell, A. T., Anderson, J., Cavanaugh, E. R., and Hubbard, R. L. *Followup Field and Methodology Report: 1979 and 1980 TOPS Admission Cohorts* (Technical report under National Institute on Drug Abuse Contract No. 271-79-3600). Research Triangle Park, N.C.: Research Triangle Institute, 1983.

Renner, B., and Sechrest, L. "Experimental Research in Therapeutic Communities." Paper presented at the American Evaluation Association, November 5–7, Seattle, 1992.

Rezmovic, E. L. "Assessing Treatment Implementation amid the Slings and Arrows of Reality." *Evaluation Review,* 1984, *8,* 187–204.

Riecken, H. W., and Boruch, R. F. "Social Experiments." *Annual Review of Sociology,* 1978, *4,* 511–532.

Riecken, H. W., and others. *Social Experimentation: A Method for Planning and Evaluating Social Programs.* San Diego: Academic Press, 1974.

Rohman, L. W. "The Nebraska Prehearing Settlement Conference Program: An Experimental Evaluation." Unpublished doctoral dissertation, University of Nebraska, Lincoln, 1987. (Available through Dr. John Berman, Psychology Department.)

Scott, A. G., and Sechrest, L. "Strength of Theory and Theory of Strength." *Evaluation and Program Planning,* 1989, *12,* 329–336.

Sechrest, L., and Redner, R. *Strength and Integrity of Treatments in Evaluation Studies: How Well Does It Work?* Washington, D.C.: National Institute of Law Enforcement and Criminal Justice, 1979.

Sechrest, L., White, S. O., and Brown, E. D. (eds.). *The Rehabilitation of Criminal Offenders: Problems and Prospects.* Washington, D.C.: National Academy of Sciences, 1979.

Sechrest, L., and others. "Introduction. Some Neglected Problems in Evaluation Research: Strength and Integrity of Treatments." *Evaluation Studies Review Annual,* 1979, *4,* 15–38.

Sherman, L. W., and Berk, R. A. *The Minneapolis Domestic Violence Experiment.* Washington, D.C.: Police Foundation, 1984.

Siegel, S., and Castellan, N. J. *Nonparametric Statistics for the Behavioral Sciences.* (2nd ed.) New York: McGraw-Hill, 1988.

Silverman, W. A. "The Lessons of Retrolental Fibroplasia." *Scientific American,* 1977, *236*(6), 100–107.

Simon, H. A., and Devine, W. R. "Controlling Human Factors in an Administrative Experiment." Reprinted in E. Chelimsky (ed.), *Program Evaluation: Patterns and Directions* (pp. 85–94). Washington, D.C.: American Society for Public Administration, 1985.

Sobell, L. C. "Critique of Alcoholism Treatment Evaluation." In G. A. Marlatt and P. E. Nathan (eds.), *Behavioral Approaches to Alcoholism* (pp. 166–182). New Brunswick, N.J.: Rutgers Center of Alcohol Studies, 1978.

Stanley, T. D. "Regression Discontinuity Design by Any Other Name Might Be Less Problematic." *Evaluation Review,* 1991, *15,* 605–624.

Student [a pseudonym for Gossett, W. S.]. "The Lanarkshire Milk Experiment." *Biometrika,* 1931, *23,* 398–406.

Trochim, W.M.K. "The Regression Discontinuity Design." In *AHCPR Conference Proceedings: Research Methodology: Strengthening Causal Interpretations of Nonexperimental Data* (Department of Health and Human Services Publication No. PHS 90-3454, pp. 119–140). Rockville, Md.: U.S. Department of Health and Human Services, 1990.

Trochim, W.M.K., and Cappelleri, J. "Cutoff Assignment Strategies for Enhancing Randomized Clinical Trials." Paper presented at the Annual Conference of the American Evaluation Association, Washington, D.C., 1990.

Trochim, W.M.K., Cappelleri, J. C., and Reichardt, C. S. "Random Measurement Error Does Not Bias the Treatment Effect Estimate in Regression Discontinuity." *Evaluation Review,* 1991, *15,* 555–570.

Vinokur, A. D., Price, R. H., and Caplan, R. D. "From Field Experiments to Program Implementation: Assessing the Potential Outcomes of an Experimental Intervention Program for Unemployed Persons." *American Journal of Community Psychology,* 1991, *19,* 543–562.

Wallace, L. W. "The Community Penalties Act of 1983: An Evaluation of the Law, Its Implementation, and Its Impact in North Carolina." Unpublished doctoral dissertation. University of Nebraska, Lincoln, 1987. (Available through Dr. John Berman, Psychology Department.)

Watson, K. F. "Programs, Experiments, and Other Evaluation: An Interview with Donald Campbell." *Canadian Journal of Program Evaluation,* 1986, *1*(1), 83–86.

Wholey, J. S. *Evaluation and Effective Public Management.* Boston: Little, Brown, 1983.

Winer, B. J. *Statistical Principles in Experimental Design.* (2nd ed.) New York: McGraw-Hill, 1971.

Yusaf, S., Wittes, J., Probstfield, J., and Tyroler, H. A. "Analysis and Interpretation of Treatment Effects in Subgroups of Patients in Randomized Clinical Trials." *Journal of the American Medical Association,* 1991, *266,* 93–98.

Appendix 8.A. The Lanarkshire Milk Experiment: Lessons About Treatment Contamination

Leighton and McKinlay (1930) conducted an early nutritional experiment for four months during the spring of 1930 in the schools of Lanarkshire, England. The purpose of the trials was to determine the effect on the pupils' weight and height of receiving daily either no milk (20,000 children), raw milk (10,000 children), or pasteurized milk (10,000 children). The 20,000 children who received milk were chosen from sixty-seven schools, with half the schools randomly assigned to receive raw milk and half to receive pasteurized milk. Within each school, 200 to 400 students were selected by the head teacher to represent the average children between the ages of five and twelve and then randomly assigned to be given either the local type of milk or no milk at all to drink. Assignment was made on the basis of either a blind ballot or systematically from an alphabetical list of names.

Although it was one of the first community-based studies ever conducted, the Lanarkshire Milk Trials illustrate the need to balance any attempts to accommodate local concerns with concerns about contamination. Student's (1931, p. 398) critique, which he labeled "ungraciously wise after the event," still offers insights into the conduct of such experiments today. The basic points related to treatment contamination include the following:

- Although the assignment of schools to milk conditions may have been administratively necessary to ensure that each child received the right type of milk, it changed the study from an experiment with 20,000 children to one with sixty-seven schools—a sample too small to guarantee that the groups (schools varying considerably in socioeconomic status) would necessarily be equivalent as a result of randomization. At a minimum, the schools should have been either paired or blocked prior to assignment.

- Even within schools, the investigators first invoked the "goddess of chance . . . [but] wavered . . . [and allowed] any group to which these methods had given an undue proportion of well fed or ill nourished children . . . [to] substitute [other children] in order to obtain a more level selection" (Student, p. 399). Having opened up the opportunity for reassignment, teachers (who were presumably swayed by their very human feelings for the poorer children who needed milk) systematically oversubstituted ill-nourished students into the milk conditions and undersubstituted them into the control condition. This concern could have been better addressed simply by pairing or blocking children prior to selection.

- No systematic procedure was implemented for measuring height and weight, resulting in a downward bias on weight (relative to height) in the spring when winter coats were no longer worn and a downward bias in poorer neighborhoods where less bulky clothes were worn (or could be afforded). These biases were then compounded by combining the control groups, which were from the full range of schools, for comparison with each of the experimental groups, which were each drawn from only a subset of schools.

Student (1931) argued that although many of the logistical concerns about facilitating milk distribution, balancing the sample of pupils, and weighing the pupils could have been appropriately incorporated at the design stage, failure to do so essentially threw the entire experiment into disrepute (also see Fisher and Bartlett, 1931).

Appendix 8.B. Methadone-Enhanced Treatment Study: The Advantage of Measuring Treatment

The Methadone-Enhanced Treatment Study was conducted from 1988 to 1991 with thirty-four counselors and 661 clients from four communities (Buffalo, New York; Camden, New Jersey; New Orleans, Louisiana; and Pittsburgh, Pennsylvania). The purpose of the experiment was to determine the effect on retention, drug use, employment, and criminality of both structural and therapeutic enhancements to counseling and access to ancillary services. These enhancements included counselor training, the addition of a community services coordinator, increased urine monitoring, more frequent counseling visits, standardized needs assessments, short-term behaviorally oriented treatment planning, problem-solving individual counseling, relapse prevention group counseling, and contingency management (Fairbank, Dennis, Bonito, and Rachal, 1991). Counselors were randomly assigned to receive or not receive training, and clients were then randomly assigned to counselors. Making assignments in this way permitted the independent evaluation of both the counselor training program and the client-level intervention.

Analyses of the amount, context, and topic of treatment revealed several important points about measuring treatment (Dennis, Fairbank, Bonito, and Rachal, 1990; Dennis, Rachal, and Bohlig, 1990; Fairbank, Dennis, Bonito, and Rachal, 1991). Some of these problems are listed below and are illustrated in Figure 8.1 using the number of individual counseling sessions during the first group.

- Initial levels of counseling received varied by more than fourfold among sites. The most services were provided by the two sites with medium counselor caseloads (28 to 37 clients per counselor), followed by the site with the lowest caseload (11 to 1) and the site with the highest caseload (50–80 to 1).
- The extent to which the targeted levels of counseling services in the experimental regimen were reached varied by site. Although the overall level of services received in the experimental regimen was related to the standard level of services, the magnitude of increased services within a

site was not. Moreover, although the site with the largest caseloads showed statistically significant increases, the site with the smallest caseloads did not.

- The effect of the experimental condition was evident on both the mean level of services received and the variance in the level of services received. Thus, the experimental regimen was not accepted by and/or equally implemented for every client — some rejected the increased level of control, others embraced the increased level of services.
- The effectiveness of training increased as the amount of follow-up training was increased in each subsequent site.

It is almost an axiom in social experimentation that if you conduct a multisite experiment, the results will vary by site. The preceding findings help to demonstrate that just like individuals, real site differences will affect outcomes and receptivity to the experimental intervention. Measuring them will aid in the analysis of treatment implementation and outcomes.

Figure 8.1. Number of Individual Sessions per Client During the First Six Months of Treatment, by Condition, Site, and Order of Training Session.

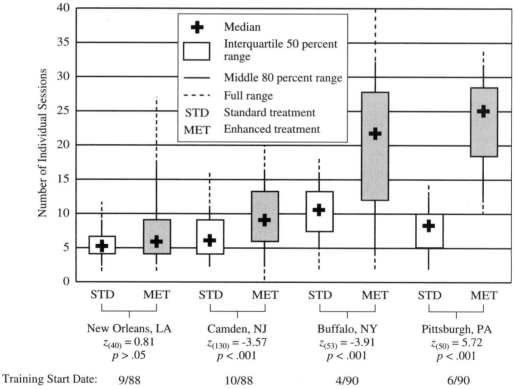

Source: Dennis and others, 1993.

Appendix 8.C. Disulfiram Experiment:
The Impact of Preinclusion Attrition on External Validity

Fuller and colleagues (1986) conducted a randomized field experiment in nine Veterans Administration (VA) medical centers with 612 male veterans to determine the efficacy of disulfiram for treatment of alcoholism. A variety of selection factors operated within the eligible population that may have influenced this experiment. A total of 6,629 clients who presented themselves for alcoholism treatment at the participating VA medical centers were screened for the study, but only 612 were enrolled and randomized. Of the total number of clients screened, 5,011 (76 percent) were deemed ineligible for the study (were ruled out on the basis of the study's exclusion criteria). The most frequent reasons for exclusion were that the client (1) lived alone (2,143 clients—32 percent of those screened), (2) had a contraindicating medical condition (1,103 clients—17 percent of those screened), or (3) lived more than eighty kilometers (approximately fifty miles) from the hospital (1,028 clients—16 percent of those screened). Additionally, of the 1,618 clients who were found to be eligible, nearly two-thirds (1,006 clients—62 percent of those eligible) refused to participate. Thus, only one in four clients presenting themselves for treatment was deemed eligible to receive the treatment, and nearly two-thirds of those eligible declined to participate. As a result, fewer than 10 percent of those who presented themselves for treatment at the participating centers, an already highly selected alcoholism treatment population, were actually enrolled in the study. Howard and colleagues (1990) suggested that this level of preinclusion attrition raises fundamental questions about the ultimate generalizability of the findings, even to the subpopulation of men who are veterans and seek treatment at VA medical centers. Moreover, the high level raises doubts about the potential utility of the treatment in real-world settings.

Additionally, findings from the National Vietnam Veterans Readjustment Study (Kulka and others, 1990) demonstrate that only a small and sociodemographically select subset of veterans who are eligible and in need of health or mental health treatment actually seek treatment at VA facilities. Thus, the treatment sites in which the study was conducted necessarily resulted in a highly selected subset of potential subjects, raising questions about the extent to which the findings would apply to the treatment of alcoholics in general.

Appendix 8.D. Oxygen Experiment:
The Importance of Staff Cooperation

The Oxygen Experiment was conducted in 1953 and 1954 using nearly 800 infants who weighed 1.5 kilograms (3 ⅓ pounds) or less and were born prematurely in one of eighteen hospitals throughout the United States (Silverman,

1977). The study was designed to determine the relationship between a then-emerging practice of putting premature babies in almost pure oxygen environments to reduce mortality and a corresponding ninefold rise in rates of retrolental fibroplasia (a form of blindness). Infants were randomly assigned to either the standard treatment of 50 percent to 100 percent pure oxygen or the minimal necessary (0 percent to 50 percent) oxygen environment. It is important to note that many doctors at the time strongly opposed the experiment as unethical because they trusted the results of observational studies, which suggested that an environment of pure oxygen decreased the mortality rate of premature babies. In fact, use of pure oxygen was later shown to be the primary cause of retrolental fibroplasia and to have no effect on the survival rate.

Unfortunately, the initial experiment was subverted by nurses who switched babies during the night shift so that each baby received at least half a day of full oxygen therapy (Silverman, 1977). In an attempt to appease their concerns, the trial was later delayed until after each infant had received at least forty-eight hours of oxygen therapy first — and the damage to the retina had been done. Although later analysis and studies clearly demonstrated the harm that was being done, the failure to persuade the nursing staff of the need for and ethicality of the study unnecessarily prolonged a sad chapter in perinatal medicine.

Appendix 8.E. D.C. Initiative: A Logistically Sensitive Assignment Plan

The D.C. Initiative is a cooperative agreement between the Washington, D.C., Alcohol and Drug Abuse Services Administration (ADASA); Genesis House; the Institute for Behavioral Resources (IBR); Koba Associates, Inc.; the National Institute on Drug Abuse (NIDA); the Office for Treatment Improvement (OTI); the Research Triangle Institute (RTI); and various local providers. It was designed to test and evaluate the effectiveness of several approaches to enhance drug abuse treatment through controlled trials. Started in 1991, the study involves the bulk of the public and non-profit drug abuse treatment system in Washington, D.C. When the appropriate treatment modality (drug-free outpatient, outpatient methadone, and residential) has been determined by a physician at either a program or central intake unit, clients are randomly assigned to either the enhanced or standard intervention within that modality. Within the paired treatment modality conditions, assignments are also blocked over time to help providers avoid unnecessary slot/bed vacancies, refrain from keeping lengthy waiting lists, and avoid bias that may be associated with time (Flynn and Clayton, 1992).

The procedures involve generating random numbers in blocks of eight to use in assigning clients to either the enhanced or standard treatment program. Each row of the list gives the block number, a research identification number, and a random code number between 1 and 8. Each number between 1 and 8 is used only one time within each block, and a separate random assignment list is generated for each of the three treatment modalities.

A rule is then established for translating the random number into an assignment in proportion to the number of available treatment slots in each condition. Thus, if both conditions have the same number of slots and a 50–50 split is desired, the rule would be to assign codes 1 to 4 to the enhanced intervention and 5 to 8 to the standard intervention. If the enhanced intervention has three times as many slots as the standard intervention and a 75–25 split is desired, the rule would be to assign codes 1 to 6 to the enhanced intervention and 7 to 8 to the standard intervention. To maintain balance over time, the rule is revised (and recorded) prior to the use of each new block of numbers.

9

Synthesizing
Evaluation Findings

David S. Cordray, Robert L. Fischer

Individual evaluation studies can serve many purposes. One purpose is to provide timely answers to questions raised by decision makers. A program manager, for example, may want to know the prevalence of mental health problems among homeless individuals in her city. The immediate, practical purpose of such a study is to inform decisions on program planning (such as the amount and types of services that might be needed). Another program manager might commission a study of the effectiveness of case management services in increasing the self-sufficiency of homeless individuals. The reason for this study is to justify next year's funding to the city comptroller. One could easily imagine similar studies being instigated in a variety of cities throughout the world. As the number of these studies has grown, a natural question that arises is, "Can we obtain a better understanding of how interventions work by looking across independent studies?"

This chapter describes a host of methods for addressing this type of evaluative question. It presumes that individual studies are the building blocks for our knowledge base about various aspects of social interventions. It also acknowledges that in their usual form, that is, written reports, the collection of local studies is, at best, the raw material for knowledge development. Often technical quality is uneven across studies, study results are not consistently nor completely reported and, in many cases, they do not even enter the public domain (they remain unpublished). To bring their collective messages into sharper relief, a technology for organizing this body of evidence is needed. The technology discussed in this chapter, variously known as *evaluation synthesis* (U.S. General Accounting Office, 1983) and *meta-analysis* (Hedges and Olkin, 1985), entails the use of a collection of methods to systematically assemble evidence derived from multiple evaluation studies. These methods

This chapter was supported in part by a grant from the Russell Sage Foundation.

share some features with meta-evaluation (Cook and Gruder, 1978) and secondary analysis (Boruch, Wortman, and Cordray, 1981). Notably they all involve judging the quality of evidence underlying a study or set of studies and some quantitative manipulation of prior data, but synthesis methods are sufficiently different from these other methods to warrant separate discussion (Cordray and Orwin, 1983).

The chapter is divided into two parts. Attention is first directed at the various types of synthesis techniques that have been developed to answer numerous types of policy or program evaluation questions. There had been a growing interest in synthesis methods over the past few years, and as practitioners have attempted to apply early techniques to their specific situations, synthesis methods have been adapted and expanded. There are now numerous forms of synthesis that can be applied to a variety of program evaluation and policy-oriented questions. As with all program evaluation studies, the questions that are to be answered and the time frame within which answers are needed play a large role in determining the specific types of techniques that are most appropriate.

After a review of the major methodological distinctions and commonalities among synthesis techniques, the second part of the chapter is directed at issues and practices associated with conducting various forms of synthesis. Synthesis methods are still being developed, technical refinements are still being made, and difficulties in conducting such studies are still being identified. As such, this chapter reviews some of the difficulties that emerge and some of the options for overcoming these difficulties that are available. Although there is no template for conducting a synthesis that is applicable across different types of questions, we offer general guidelines. To do this, we have broken the major synthesis processes into their component parts, identified technical issues, and offered practical solutions or tactics. Special attention is directed at avoiding or minimizing possible distortion in synthesis results due to "judgment calls."

Evaluation Synthesis and Its Variations

The past fifteen years have produced a proliferation of *quantitative* techniques for summarizing prior studies that go beyond traditional, narrative literature review procedures (see Bangert-Drowns, 1986, for a history of these methods). The basic idea behind these synthesis methods is that through the use of systematic and comprehensive retrieval practices (accumulation of prior studies), quantification of results using a common metric such as effect size, and statistical aggregation of the collection of results, it is possible to derive a more accurate and useful portrayal of what is known and not known about a given topic. Unlike secondary analysis or meta-evaluation, which examines and reanalyzes raw data from prior studies, synthesis techniques rely on reported results as the basis for analyzing findings. Generally, these results are intermediate statistics like means, standard deviations, proportions, and correlations. Because of the reliance on reported results, special statistical and nonstatistical considerations must be taken into account that differ from meta-evaluation or secondary analytic techniques.

Although new to behavioral and social sciences, synthesis practices have a rich history. Stigler (1986) traces the use of quantitative aggregation of results in statistics back to the early 1800s (see Cook and others, 1992, p. 6). And, after a great deal of debate about the applicability of these procedures to social science data, it is safe to say that quantitative forms of synthesis have become generally accepted and widely used. As evidence of this acceptance, Durlak and Lipsey (1991) estimate that over 600 meta-analyses of various types have been conducted since Glass (1976) introduced the technique to the behavioral and social sciences. To enhance the utility of these methods, it is useful to look at the differences in practices that have emerged. As we will see, some variations are more appropriate for specific types of program evaluation questions.

Variations in Practices and Perspectives

Lumping various forms of synthesis into a common nomenclature, such as meta-analysis or evaluation synthesis, is fairly common. Closer examination of the procedures that have been advocated under various labels, however, reveals substantial variation in actual practices, purposes, and perspectives. This variability has also led to different conceptions of what does and does not count within each type of synthesis. Therefore, it is useful to characterize some of the common and unique aspects of these methods.

Types of Syntheses

Table 9.1 provides a rough comparison of five synthesis methods on eight stereotypical dimensions of these methods. Of course, there is a great deal of variation in syntheses that purport to derive from a common perspective. With the table we offer this caveat: Table 9.1 is presented for heuristic purposes; it is not intended to capture all variations in practices. Shared features, across methods, are designated with an "X." So as not to overlook the obvious and to provide a benchmark for comparison, we have included the traditional literature review as one of the forms of synthesis.

Narrative Review. The *traditional, narrative literature review* is the cornerstone summary technique in most, if not all, disciplines. For generations it has served as a basis for accumulating what is known and not known on a given topic. In spirit, then, it is not inherently different from its quantitative counterparts (Cook and Leviton, 1980). In practice, it involves "judgment calls" similar to those found in quantitative procedures (see Guzzo, Jackson, and Katzell, 1987; Matt, 1989; Nurius and Yeaton, 1987; Wanous, Sullivan, and Malinak, 1989); but the traditional review does not fare as well as quantitative procedures with respect to documentation of these decision

Table 9.1. Comparison of Synthesis Tactics
on Key Features: Unique and Common Elements.

Feature of the Method	Type of Synthesis				
	Traditional Literature Review	Meta-Analysis	Explanatory Meta-Analysis	Evaluation Synthesis	Prospective Evaluation Synthesis
Multiple studies are located, reviewed, and summarized	X	X	X	X	X
Study data are processed		X	X	X	X
Study data are combined; magnitude estimate is derived		X	X	X	X
Results are tested for statistical significance		X	X	X	X
Method is policy or model driven			X	X	X
Method involves multiple lines of evidence/questions				X	X
Method specifies alternative methods for combining evidence	X			X	X
Method involves projections					X

rules (Beaman, 1991). As for its commonality with other methods, it shares one important feature with all other forms of synthesis: all methods involve locating, reviewing, and summarizing the results of *multiple* studies. What distinguishes the narrative review from the other forms is its limited use of quantitative procedures to synthesize the results. In turn, the statistical features of the more quantitative methods provide a foundation for assessing the influence of problems (for example, publication bias, uneven study quality, judgment calls) inherent in reviews that are not easily handled by narrative reviews.

On the other hand, traditional reviews should not be abandoned entirely. For example, theoretical integrations, as seen in more academic journals, might be better served by traditional methods than through quantification of empirical results because they tend to focus on hypothesized or demonstrated interconnections among hypothetical constructs. For example, Einhorn and Hogarth (1986) provide a thoughtful review of the results of numerous studies on naive causal reasoning, yielding a theoretical framework describing the processes by which causal inferences are formed. In all likelihood, their review would not have been enhanced by the use of quantitative synthesis methods. Furthermore, as practicing evaluators have gained experience in the "art and science" of reviewing literature, it is clear that using a combination of narrative and quantitative procedures is superior to using either alone (see Light and Pillemer, 1984; Slavin, 1986).

Meta-Analysis. Meta-analysis refers to the systematic location, retrieval, review, and summarization of prior studies. In its simplest form, it provides a quantitative *description* of the direction and magnitude of results appearing in a body of literature. As might be expected, meta-analysis comes in a variety of forms. Durlak and Lipsey (1991) stipulate four classes of meta-analytic procedures. These include methods directed at estimating *treatment effectiveness, group differences, test validity,* and *relationships among conceptual variables.* As implied by these labels, a main reason for conducting evaluation syntheses is to learn something about interventions or conditions, for example, the prevalence of mental health disorders, effects of interventions, or robustness of effects. The synthesis process has another side as well. By virtue of its attention to the methodological details underlying prior studies (see "Data Evaluation" in the second part of this chapter), the process amasses a great deal of technical information about evaluation methods. Therefore, we can add to Durlak and Lipsey's listing an additional class of meta-analysis, namely a *methodological synthesis* (see Cordray and Orwin, 1983; Cordray and Sonnefeld, 1985). Here, the methodological by-products of syntheses—design, measurement, and analysis characteristics—can be used to improve the technical quality of subsequent primary evaluations. Despite the variation in labels and purpose, these forms of synthesis share enough in common to be treated as a single set.

Using Beaman's (1991) explicit definition of what counts as meta-analysis, Table 9.1 shows that these procedures involve three features that focus on methods for reviewing and summarizing study results. Rather than simply relying on the results reported in prior studies, the meta-analytic process involves some form of data processing, including the use of statistical adjustments to enhance between-study comparability or acceptability for further statistical manipulation. An example of such an adjustment is correcting a preliminary effect size estimate for small sample bias. When the interest is in treatment effectiveness or group differences, *data processing* involves the transformation of study results into a metric known as *effect size.* An effect size is generally, but not exclusively, derived by dividing the difference between treatment or group means by the pooled, within-group standard deviation. As such, study results are expressed in standard deviation units.

To make this technique concrete, consider the following. If an experimental condition showed an increase in performance from pre- to posttest of 10 units, the control condition revealed change of 5 units, and the pooled standard deviation for the within-group difference (posttest minus pretest) was 15, the effect size would be .33 or $(10 - 5)/15$. That is, the magnitude of the between-group differences is one-third of a standard deviation.

Applying similar calculations for all study results forms the statistical basis for analyzing results across studies, even if they differ in designs, measures, intervention protocols, and populations served. Thoughtful coding of between-study differences (see part two of this chapter) avoids the image that meta-analysis is mixing "apples and oranges."

The second distinctive feature of meta-analysis is its reliance on statistical procedures for combining the common index that has been derived. In his original formulation, Glass (1976) relied on a simple averaging of the effect size estimates across all studies. Unlike simply counting, known as "vote-counting," (see Hedges and Olkin, 1985) to learn how many studies revealed positive, neutral, or negative results based on reported statistical analyses, these types of aggregation processes, by virtue of the common metric derived for each study, provide an estimate of the *magnitude* of the combined treatment effect, correlation, or group differences.

This simple aggregation rule has been refined by a variety of weighting schemes that are based on conventional statistical principles (see Hedges and Olkin, 1985; Hunter and Schmidt, 1990; Bryk and Raudenbush, 1988). For example, giving greater weight to studies that involve more precise estimates by virtue of their larger sample sizes is one basis for weighting the contribution of studies.

The third distinguishing marker for meta-analysis is the use of statistical procedures to assess whether the combined magnitude estimate is statistically meaningful. For example, the combined estimate of the treatment effect might be .20 standard deviation units. But the individual estimates (effect sizes from each study) will generally deviate by chance around this aggregate value. As with all inferential statistics, it is important to know whether the combined estimate of .20 is statistically different from zero. This hypothesis can be tested using a simple z test. The error of estimate for the combined magnitude estimate (here .20) is simply the inverse of the sum of weights applied to each study (see Hedges and Olkin, 1985).

One of the main criticisms of meta-analysis is that substantial between-study differences in designs, measures, interventions, and populations make it difficult to interpret the meaning behind aggregate results. Slavin (1984, p. 8) argues that meta-analysis represents a step backward because it introduces bias by the inclusion of poor studies or "senseless distillation of markedly different studies." In the early years of meta-analysis, this may have been a legitimate concern, but statistical procedures have been developed to test whether all studies share a common effect size. Suppose the combined effect size for twelve studies was .40. Suppose that further examination of the distribution of these twelve effect sizes suggested (1) considerable variation in individual estimates (ranging from .00 to .80) and two distinct clusters of studies (the distribution appeared to be bimodal, at .20 and .60). If this were the case, the average effect of .40 would be misleading. The statistical tests that have been developed provide a basis for examining the extent to which individual effect sizes come from the same population (here

.40). When these tests reveal between-study differences, as reflected by a statistically significant chi-square statistic, it is customary to search for factors that might account for differences and produce the bimodal distribution (see Cook and others, 1992; Hedges and Olkin, 1985; Hunter and Schmidt, 1990). As the pattern of Xs in Table 9.1 shows, each of the other synthesis methods can incorporate these meta-analytic features. They generally entail other considerations, however.

Explanatory Meta-Analysis

When factors like study quality, publication date, and gender differences are identified, the analyst has several options. All these options share the common goal of "explaining" differences in effects. First, results can be reported for distinct clusters or subgroups separately. Second, when multiple, interrelated factors are identified, multiple regression techniques can be used to adjust statistically or control for between-study factors. These techniques are generally employed to sharpen answers to substantive questions by controlling the influence of factors like study quality, program implementation level, and differences in clients, settings, and treatments.

As the name implies, explanatory meta-analysis moves beyond simpleminded adjusting and accounting for between-study differences by trying to explain relationships among variables or by explicitly testing broader theories or models using prior results. The Russell Sage Foundation (Cook and others, 1992) has been prominent in the development of this version of synthesis. Under its auspices, Becker (1992) used correlation coefficients derived from prior studies to test models of science and mathematics achievement. Devine (1992) used effect sizes from prior studies to probe the mediational processes underlying positive effects of psycho-educational interventions on medical outcomes. Using study characteristics and reviewer-generated ratings of key variables, such as experimenters' allegiance to the intervention, Shadish (1992) developed and tested multiple models of the process by which family therapies might work, and Lipsey (1992) used a series of hierarchical regression models to control for irrelevant methodological variation in juvenile delinquency studies to ascertain what types of programs are most effective. The explanatory meta-analysis perspective shows that careful consideration of important between-study differences can lessen many of the initial concerns that meta-analysis was camouflaging a "garbage in–garbage out" process.

Evaluation Synthesis. Evaluation synthesis represents a broader set of methods than does meta-analysis. Evaluation synthesis is akin to information synthesis (Goldschmidt, 1984; Mullen and Ramirez, 1987), integrative research reviews (Cooper, 1989), or, as Light and Pillemer (1984) put it, "summing up." These types of syntheses cast a broader informational net than the previous methods by virtue of their focus on additional policy-relevant questions.

Unlike traditional meta-analytic studies—which are generally instigated by a researcher or analyst—evaluation synthesis was originally developed by the U.S. General Accounting Office (GAO) (1983) to quickly answer questions posed by congressional committees. As such, the chief differences between meta-analysis and explanatory meta-analysis and evaluation synthesis are in who formulates the questions to be addressed. Given the nature of policy debates, questions of interest often involve opposing positions, different evaluative criteria, and different conceptions about what constitutes effectiveness. Cordray (1990) identifies several categories of policy questions that *could* be addressed using synthesis tactics. These include *deriving estimates of relative effectiveness and cost-effectiveness, identifying exemplary programs, and analyzing active ingredients within programs.*

For example, in response to a series of questions posed by Senator Jesse Helms (R-NC) about the Special Supplemental Food Program for Women, Infants, and Children (known as WIC), GAO (1984) conducted an evaluation synthesis. Congressional hearings on the effectiveness of WIC revealed conflicting testimony about what is actually known about the program's effectiveness. Proponents of WIC had cited evidence of the positive effects of WIC on a variety of outcomes; others criticized the studies on methodological grounds, saying they were not credible, nor representative.

Congress was not simply curious about "what the literature says" but had a quite specific list of effects they wanted examined. These included the overall effects of WIC, differential effects on prescribed at-risk groups, effects of differential exposure to WIC, and the relative effects of WIC components. GAO concluded that there was insufficient information to answer most of these questions, but there appeared to be a modest positive effect on birthweight of infants born to women in the program. In a more recent report, GAO (U.S. General Accounting Office, 1992) updated and extended the birth-outcomes analysis, showing substantial reductions in the percentage of very low birthweight infants. By combining estimates of the cost of caring for low birthweight (LBW) and very low birthweight (VLBW) babies with their estimate of the number of averted instances of dangerously small newborns, GAO projected that the preventive effects of WIC could result in large cost savings for other federal/state programs such as Medicaid and special education. GAO has also conducted evaluation syntheses to assess the effects of housing allowances (U.S. General Accounting Office, 1986a), the effects of drinking-age laws (U.S. General Accounting Office, 1987), and the relationship between capacity and volume of health services (U.S. General Accounting Office, 1991). These are useful resources for readers interested in the extent to which synthesis practices must be tailored to policy-oriented questions.

Prospective Evaluation Synthesis. Policy questions like "How well has WIC worked?" involve assessments of prior policies or programs. That is, most evaluation syntheses focus on summarizing what is known about the effectiveness of existing programs. However, there is another class of questions that are also important to policymakers; these involve future conditions and include questions like "Will a newly proposed policy or program attain its goals?" or "How fast will a problem grow if no ameliorative action is taken?" To answer these types of questions, GAO fashioned a method known as the Prospective Evaluation Synthesis (PES) (U.S. General Accounting Office, 1990). It is similar in spirit to the evaluation synthesis in that it is policy focused, but the PES is forward looking. GAO (U.S. General Accounting Office, 1986b) applied this method in its review of legislative proposals regarding teenage pregnancy.

Unique Features

Table 9.1 and the preceding discussion suggest several points of departure among types of syntheses. Chief among these distinctions is the notion that relative to strict meta-analytic procedures, the other synthesis methods generally are policy or model driven. That is, questions are derived from policymakers or the attributes of the theoretical models that are to be tested. The evaluation synthesis and PES share some of the model-driven features of explanatory meta-analysis but tend to focus on less formal theories. In particular, the PES was explicitly developed as a method of determining whether the conceptual and operational models underlying legislative proposals would perform as proposed, if enacted. As stated above, the evaluation synthesis is guided by questions developed by policymakers, some of which are motivated by conceptions of how programs ought to work. Therefore, we classify it as policy-model driven. Each of these methods goes beyond descriptive summaries of the evidence appearing in the literature, a feature that provides a logical framework for answering questions about what is and is not known about a given topic.

The evaluation synthesis and the PES methods are somewhat unique in the sense that they generally entail multiple questions (for example, about effects *and* costs, problem size, effects, *and* implementation issues); the answers to these must rely on multiple sources of evidence. Further, given the need to combine different types of information across policy questions, the policy-oriented syntheses make provisions for alternative methods of combining studies. These include the use of experts, case study methods, and cluster techniques (see U.S. General Accounting Office, 1983). Because it does not rely exclusively on quantitative procedures for deriving answers to questions, policy-oriented synthesis has a somewhat closer alignment to the traditional review process, involving greater dependence on the reviewer's judgment.

The PES involves an additional set of activities that distinguishes it from evaluation synthesis and meta-analysis. The PES does not end with an aggregation of prior results. Rather, within the PES framework, the analyst is required to make a judgment about the likely success of the proposed intervention. This projection is a form of generalization that must take into account the circumstances that will probably materialize in the future. As such, the projection task requires estimating what effects might be expected in other settings. This, in turn, requires gathering additional information from sources other than the reports that provide estimates of treatment effects. The GAO (U.S. General Accounting Office, 1992) evaluation synthesis of WIC relied on additional evidence on participation rates in all states, and medical and educational costs of caring for low birthweight infants. The prospective evaluation synthesis on teen pregnancy programs required examining population trends and projections, geographic distribution of teen pregnancies, and the likely availability of proposed program components in cities across the country. In deriving a summary conclusion about the feasibility of the proposals, a logical argument had to be made to integrate the various facts derived from the multiple sources of information that were reviewed.

If we look at the types of questions policymakers have asked, we find numerous opportunities to apply synthesis methods to answer a variety of program-related questions. In this way, individual studies can be used to achieve better program planning and to determine which programs should be given priority because the empirical evidence suggests that they are wise investments.

Conducting a Synthesis

The preceding review of the types of synthesis methods at our disposal should make several issues clear: (1) synthesis methods differ depending upon the questions that are to be addressed; (2) these methods have been refined, over time, through the development of statistical techniques that can be quite complex to execute; and (3) numerous steps are involved. The advances in statistical and nonstatistical aspects of synthesis have been dramatic over the past few years. Taking the lead in cataloguing the state of the art in this form of inquiry, under the sponsorship of the Russell Sage Foundation, Cooper and Hedges (forthcoming) have recently edited a thirty-two-chapter volume entitled *The Handbook of Research Synthesis*. This book covers a variety of topics ranging from the search and retrieval process to complex discussions of various forms of statistical methods for aggregating and testing results. Given the breadth and depth of information about synthesis practices contained in the Cooper and Hedges volume, it is impossible to summarize it adequately here. Rather, attention is directed at some of the major issues the authors address in undertaking these forms of inquiry. In this section, basic and essential procedural steps are discussed.

Essential Issues

In practice, synthesis probably is superior to traditional reviews because it is more explicit (Beaman, 1991), but comparison of the results from "replicate syntheses" (multiple syntheses on the same topic by different analysts) reveals several sources of concern. Replicate syntheses do not always yield the same results. Even when statistical results are roughly comparable, synthesizers do not always arrive at the same conclusions. Recent evaluations of multiple syntheses suggest that these differences are attributable to numerous "judgment calls" that must be made at each step within the synthesis process.

This section stresses two key issues we identified in reviewing replicate syntheses. First, it is essential to be clear about the goals of the synthesis. As the previous discussion demonstrates, different questions — prospective versus retrospective questions — imply the need to use different methods. In turn, different decision rules are likely to be operative. The second key issue is the need to *test* the influence of these decisions on the results. Synthesis is a relatively new enterprise. Although it has attracted a great deal of attention, there are no normative standards for what constitutes acceptable practice. Some analysts have used highly selective criteria for including studies. Others use broad inclusion rules. Some analysts operate under intense time pressures, particularly those conducting policy-driven syntheses; others have the luxury of unlimited time to do a comprehensive search of *all* potentially relevant studies. No approach is necessarily superior, however. The important point is to realize that differences in practices, such as decision making rules at each phase of the synthesis, can influence and potentially distort results. Logical and statistical means of testing the influence of these decisions are currently available and should be used in all synthesis efforts.

Procedural Steps: An Overview

As with any systematic form of inquiry, synthesis entails a sequence of steps that are *roughly* ordered. Although authors differ on the exact number of steps or substeps that are involved (Abrami, Cohen, and d'Apollonia, 1988; Cook and others, 1992; U.S. General Accounting Office, 1983; Wanous, Sullivan, and Malinak, 1989), there appears to be a consensus that at least five core steps are essential.

Step 1: Problem Formulation. The synthesis must begin with a clear statement of the problem or topic to be addressed. Syntheses differ with respect to how the initial agenda is developed. But, once the agenda is established, parameters for other steps are largely prescribed. The process is somewhat more dynamic than implied here, however. As the plan unfolds, modifications to the synthesis agenda are likely to result from a variety of factors.

Step 2: Data Collection. With the problem statement established, at least in a preliminary way, the activities in step 2 are directed at data collection. There are two important tasks within this step. Unlike most primary research or evaluation, prior studies are the "subjects" of the investigation.

The relevant universe must be enumerated and contacted. This step will be familiar to anyone who has conducted a census or survey, the major difference being that sampling and interview skills are replaced by bibliographic skills, such as locating and accessing reports. The second aspect of this step is data extraction. Using the survey analog, this phase is akin to asking questions. Here, however, the answers to the questions must be extracted or deduced from written documents. Just like survey responses, the information that is derived may be ambiguous. It is important that the search and retrieval process be as complete as possible.

Step 3: Data Evaluation. Data evaluation is the third step in synthesis. Several forms of data evaluation and judgments are involved. Before a great deal of time is invested in extracting information from the study, the relevance of a particular document must be assessed. This judgment has to be made on a case-by-case basis. Each document must be examined in light of the purposes of the synthesis, that is, the questions to be addressed.

Once *topical* relevance is established for a study, the technical adequacy of methods underlying the study results must be assessed. An evaluation of the data extraction process needs to be undertaken to assure that the judgments you make at each step do not introduce unwarranted bias. For example, a rater may unintentionally bias his or her rating of the quality of a study's design *if* the rater knows the results of the study. In particular, suppose an analyst who is predisposed toward a particular type of intervention strategy learns that a study reveals positive effects about this intervention. The study design used to produce this positive finding might not be as closely scrutinized as the methods in another research effort that shows no effect of the favored intervention. To avoid contamination of the study-quality ratings, a blinding procedure can be used wherein the analyst records results and rates methodological quality independently. Other elaborate procedures have been developed to minimize bias at this and earlier stages (see Cook and others, 1992; Cooper, 1989). In general, developing a detailed coding protocol, training assistants in the use of the protocol, continuously monitoring coding practices, and retraining periodically are steps used to minimize the potential for bias.

Step 4: Analysis and Interpretation. Analysis and interpretation constitute the fourth stage of the synthesis process. Here the objective is to organize and interpret the patterns of information extracted or derived from studies. As described earlier, study results are converted into a common metric, generally an effect size; this becomes the unit of analysis for the synthesis. The analysis usually proceeds in a series of iterative steps. Statistical procedures are used to test for publication bias and to detect outliers; then, results are combined to form a preliminary estimate of the combined magnitude of the effect. Additional statistical tests are conducted to determine whether the individual studies were derived from a common population. If study results are not similar, a search for variables that account for between-study differences is instigated. Finally, a series of reanalyses known as sensitivity analyses are usually conducted to examine the robustness of results in relation to alternative assumptions, calculational decisions, outliers, or differences in the specification of the statistical model (for example, ordinary least squares, weighted least squares, and structural modeling). Data evaluation, statistical analysis, and interpretation are conducted as a continuous and iterative process throughout the course of the synthesis.

Step 5: Presenting the Results. The final step in the synthesis process involves presentation of the results. The goal of this stage, especially in the policy arena, is to make the results as meaningful as possible. In practice, presenting the results of a synthesis is not inherently different from presenting the results of any type of study. The analyst must be clear about (1) the purpose(s) of the study, (2) how data were gathered, (3) the methods used to extract and analyze the data, and (4) the conclusions that can be drawn from the study. Limitations of the synthesis should also be acknowledged.

In policy arenas, the presentation of results needs to be carefully considered. For example, rather than providing Senator Helms with a great deal of technical information about the effects of the WIC program, GAO (U.S. General Accounting Office, 1983) prepared simple tables to highlight the results. Technical material should be available (it was placed in an appendix) as backup support for the simpler, more meaningful information that is presented. When multiple analyses are used in a synthesis to test the robustness of findings to different decision rules, such as decisions on liberal versus constricted inclusion rules, it is often necessary to provide a range of effects rather than a single point estimate (see Lehman and Cordray, 1992; U.S. General Accounting Office, 1988, 1989). Although providing ranges of estimates makes the presentation somewhat more complex, the guiding principle in disclosing the results of a synthesis is to provide sufficient information for the reader to understand the level of confidence that can be placed in the findings.

The Role of Judgment Calls

As noted earlier, quantitative forms of synthesis have become increasingly popular in recent years. In part, the popularity of these methods stems from the perception of many analysts that syntheses involve a relatively straightforward set of steps. A closer look at how syntheses have been conducted suggests some important factors that can influence the results and credibility of them as a program evaluation tool. In this section, findings from direct comparisons of meta-analyses conducted by different analysts are reviewed to show where major pitfalls can occur. In subsequent sections, procedures and practices designed to minimize these problems are discussed.

Results of Replicate Syntheses. In a number of substantive areas several syntheses have been conducted on the same topic. These replicate syntheses provide a unique opportunity to assess the robustness of the synthesis process, that is, the extent to which different analysts or groups report the same results and conclusions. Several of these assessments have been formally conducted and reported, providing some disturbing news about the potential frailty of these methods.

Wanous, Sullivan, and Malinak (1989) examined four pairs of independently conducted meta-analyses. Across pairs, they closely examined results and decisions that were made at each step of the process. Differences in results (across pairs) were ascribed to (1) differences in criteria for including studies, (2) statistical decisions to adjust or not adjust correlations, (3) inclusion of moderator variables, and (4) the treatment of outliers, studies that exhibited unusual results. Similarly, in a very thorough review of meta-analyses on research on the validity of student ratings of instructional effectiveness. Abrami, Cohen, and d'Apollonia (1988) traced differences in outcomes to differences in (1) criteria for including studies, (2) success in locating all seemingly relevant studies, (3) the extensiveness of coding study characteristics, (4) the accuracy of calculations, and (5) the appropriateness of statistical procedures that were employed.

Small but important differences in practices and results were also observed in a set of syntheses on the effects of desegregation on achievement (see Cordray, 1990). On the other hand, differences in results across studies are not always easy to understand. Chalmers and others (1987) found substantial disagreement across multiple syntheses on the same topic but could not trace them, using univariate analyses, to specific features of the synthesis processes that were employed.

Each of these meta-evaluations suggests that the synthesis process is vulnerable to the influence of judgment calls. Does this mean that the value of syntheses is diminished? We think not. Rather, these assessments suggest that steps must be taken to minimize unwanted bias and to assess empirically the consequences of the choices that are made at each step in the process. Providing ranges of estimates to account for uncertainty associated with different operational procedures is probably the safest way to enhance the usefulness of a synthesis.

Problem Formulation

Problem formulation involves several steps that rely on judgment calls to varying degrees. To some extent, the role of judgment calls is lessened by the type of synthesis that is being undertaken. For example, in policy-driven syntheses, collaborative relations between the requestor and the analyst help guard against the danger that the analyst's preconceptions will play a sole role in specifying the issues to be examined. If multiple constituencies are consulted in the problem formulation phase as recommended by GAO (U.S. General Accounting Office, 1983), the chance of overlooking alternative means of asking questions, defining the problem and terms, and setting the scope of the synthesis can be greatly reduced.

Investigator-Initiated Syntheses. In meta-analyses that are conducted by a single researcher or group, one obvious step where the decisions can influence the specification of the problem domain is in the problem formulation stage. Cooper (1989, p. 19) notes that in choosing research questions, primary analysts are "limited only by their imaginations." Synthesizers are, on the other hand, limited by the "state of the literature" (Cook and others, 1992; Cooper, 1989). At least two constraints define what is meant by the state of the literature. First, for synthesis purposes, a topical area *must* have been investigated in the past. Second, even if an area has been investigated, there must be a sufficient degree of quality evidence contained in prior studies to warrant conducting a synthesis.

Several judgment calls come into play. For example, we may be interested in the effects of various forms of surgery in relieving lower back pain. Depending upon what is meant by the phrase "quality evidence" (see below), the analyst who holds a relatively high standard of quality may be unable to conduct any substantive analysis because the low quality of evidence available on the topic will not support further synthesis. For investigator-initiated syntheses, several options are possible: the topic can be put on hold until more primary research is accumulated, the questions can be reformulated to better fit the nature of the available evidence, or primary research could be instigated. Another option is to summarize what is not known; here, the analyst could provide a summary of the extent to which information is missing. This is precisely what GAO (U.S. General Accounting Office, 1986b) did in its prospective evaluation synthesis of Senator Chafee's proposed legislation that would authorize programs for teenagers at risk of pregnancy.

If there is enough quality evidence, the analyst has a number of further choices. For example, in developing the data extraction protocol (see Cook and others, 1992), the analyst must specify variables representing key features of the methods, treatments, populations, and outcomes. Abrami, Cohen, and d'Apollonia show substantial differences across synthesizers on specification of such variables. In some of these cases conceptually important variables have not been empirically investigated or our understanding of what constitutes important between-study variables is poorly specified. To avoid idiosyncratic specification of variables to account for between-study differences, collaboration among experts in a given field may be useful as a means of developing a framework for understanding differences across primary studies.

Policy-Driven Syntheses. In policy-driven syntheses, the role of judgment calls within the problem formulation phase is lessened somewhat because the analyst has fewer degrees of freedom in defining, dropping, or redefining the problem. In the WIC evaluation synthesis (U.S. General Accounting Office, 1983), it was clear that part of Congress's concern revolved around the quality of the evidence. Regardless of the analysts' predispositions toward quality, to be responsive to Congress's request, they had to address this domain. Congress also expressed concerns about numerous outcomes, some of which had not been thoroughly investigated. As the case study reveals, GAO analysts reported not only on the synthesized results but also on the state of the literature. The same situation occurred in the Prospective Evaluation Synthesis for Senator Chafee on teenage pregnancy. Because analysts could not reformulate the questions, they had to find the empirical evidence that could support some aspects of the debate, even though it was silent on other aspects. It is important to stress that in order to make claims about what is not known, the search of the literature must be comprehensive. The domains to be searched must be clearly articulated through consultation with experts, constituencies, prior literature reviews, and, where possible, a review of applicable laws.

Policy-Oriented Syntheses. Policy debates can play a key role in the problem formulation stage. Policy-oriented syntheses are not always reactive to the demands of specific constituencies, however. For example, the welfare debate continues despite the numerous federal and state programs that have been implemented and tested. The policy debates, therefore, can guide proactive syntheses, that is, those that anticipate policy questions rather than react to questions formulated by policymakers. Consideration of current policies (laws, regulations, and rules), debates on these policies, expert opinions, and prior reviews often help establish the breadth and depth of an evaluation synthesis in quite specific ways. For example, within welfare reform, questions have been raised about the importance of work requirements, or "workfare," the effects of sanctioning clients for noncompliance, and the nature of training—quick placement versus basic skills development.

Under the auspices of the Russell Sage Foundation, an evaluation synthesis is currently underway by David S. Cordray and Robert L. Fischer. This effort is directed at deciphering the questions, "What type of job training works well, for whom, and under what conditions?" To answer this multidimensional question, current federal rules and regulations concerning eligibility for education and training and the types of services that are permitted have been used to structure the search for relevant studies and subsequent analytic tasks. For this study, a first step is to identify variations in training options that are allowed under federal law; these range from low to high intensity of training, low to high cost per client. These options are then cross-classified with client characteristics, such as four levels of attachment to the workforce ranging from no prior experience to recent labor force participation. The result is a matrix of possible client by intervention-type pairings. If, for example, there are ten levels of program intensity that are allowable and four categories of eligible clients, the resulting matrix would contain forty cells (10 by 4). Because this matrix is based on past and current available policy options in terms of *both* interventions and eligibility requirements, it could be viewed as a "policy space." Formulating a synthesis in this fashion provides a means of specifying which options have and have not been implemented and tested. The search process is thereby focused on studies that can be classified into each of the forty cells.

This method provides policymakers with a description of which options have been tested — what is known — and which have not been tested — what is not known. Other analytical questions can be addressed that can be very useful in policy and program development in the area of job training. In particular, the pattern of occupied and empty cells holds some interesting analytical promise. Using hierarchical regression analysis, a variant of Rubin's (1990) notion of response surface estimation, involving client, intervention (cost estimates) and study characteristics, it is possible to determine the following: (1) whether a relationship exists between the costs of training and outcomes, (2) whether changes in resources influence outcomes, and (3) whether altering eligibility criteria can lead to cost savings. In other words, this synthesis could be used as a policy/program planning device to test whether alterations are likely to yield greater effiency or effectiveness. Furthermore, it will allow analysts to examine the overall effects of intervention (across client groups), the differential effects associated with varying levels of intervention intensity such as cost per client, participation rates, hours of exposure, and type of training, and the interaction of intervention intensity with target-population characteristics, or level of attachment to the work force.

In the three policy-oriented cases described here, decisions or judgment calls regarding which studies to include are guided more by the policy questions of interest and less by the predispositions of the analyst. Choices about analytic plans are derived from the nature of the problem as it has been formulated. Although prior replicate syntheses suggest that judgment calls may distort findings, the use of policy debates to derive policy spaces that are based on external criteria — laws, rules, and regulations — helps to enhance the integrity of the problem formulation phase.

Other Constraints. The policy context introduces other constraints that influence decisions within the problem formulation phase. Specifically, the policy process is ongoing, and timing is important. To be useful, the synthesis must be completed in a timely fashion. Meeting timelines often requires adjustments in subsequent steps of the synthesis process. For example, because of the reporting schedule of a group of policy advisers (the Interagency Council on Homelessness), a meta-analysis of prior estimates of the prevalence of alcohol, drug, and mental health disorders among the homeless had to be completed within four months (Lehman and Cordray, 1992). Although it would have been desirable to include *all* studies, time did not permit such an inclusive review.

In delimiting the scope of the synthesis, other constraints include the time period covered by the review. An evaluation synthesis of training programs is restricted to studies conducted from 1973 to the present. This decision was made because current federal job training was markedly different prior to the advent of the Comprehensive Employment and Training Act of 1973 (CETA). In addition, attention to U.S. domestic policy generally restricts attention to studies that were conducted within the United States.

Consequences of Constraints. In an effort to be user oriented, the synthesis process is often constrained. This observation should not be seen as a criticism. Rather, in examining subsequent steps of the process and in judging the quality of a synthesis, it is necessary to keep in mind the original intent for the study and the constraints that are imposed. Within the policy context there are no absolute standards for what constitutes a quality synthesis. The quality and appropriateness of practices must be regarded as relative to the initial questions that were posed.

Data Collection and Literature Search

Practices associated with locating and accessing prior studies on a given topic involve numerous judgment calls. These include decisions about where to look for potentially relevant studies, whether to include published *and* unpublished work, what variables to use in the coding protocol to characterize studies, and so on. Substantial procedural guidance has been provided on this topic (see Cook and others, 1992; Cooper, 1989). State-of-the-art practices in literature searching specify a sequence of *multimethod* and *multimedia* strategies for avoiding publication bias, structuring the search process for published and unpublished studies, and winnowing the results of the search.

Structuring and Conducting the Search. In structuring the search, Cooper (1989) identifies three sources to investigate: *informal, primary,* and *secondary.* Although going directly to bibliographic databases (a primary channel) seems like a sensible plan, in practice it is useful to back up one step. As Cooper (1989) notes, searches generally begin more informally. Reading a narrative review, engaging colleagues, and reviewing one's own general knowledge of the field can help identify important concepts from which to begin electronic searches. These preliminary steps help the analyst focus the synthesis more clearly and avoid making judgments that prematurely constrain the search process.

There are several different types of resources that can be exploited for electronic searches of the literature. These include specific databases like the *Social Science Citation Index, Dissertation Abstracts International, Educational Resources Information Center (ERIC), Psychological Abstracts, Medlars, Medline, multiple database services (such as Dialog),* and *specialty databases (such as The National Center for Family Research).* In his synthesis of juvenile justice research, Lipsey (1992) utilized twenty-four separate databases that yielded 8,000 citations.

The search process is rarely completed in one session. It is usually iterative and can be quite time-consuming. In the job training search, Cordray and R. Fischer (forthcoming) started with five keyword combinations suggested by a review of key works in the literature (Gueron, 1988). Using seven databases and these keywords, the procedure generated over 6,000 citations. After reviewing the results of this search, nine additional keywords were identified and the search was repeated. Of the eighty-three studies that have been judged relevant to the synthesis, only twenty-two percent were directly identified through these sources. A large portion of studies (about one-third) were identified by careful review of the bibliography, footnotes, and references contained in each document. This is known as the ancestry method. Low technology procedures for locating studies should not be overlooked. These include searching the contents of recent issues of key journals by hand; this avoids the publication lag inherent in the preparation of electronic databases, CD-ROM issuances, and other forms of noncoverage. Contacts with experts in state and federal government offices, industry centers (or think tanks), and universities often turn out to be rich sources of reports that do not routinely appear in libraries, archives, or the literature; thirty-three (about 40 percent) studies in the job training synthesis were obtained through these informal channels.

Once the formal and informal sources are thoroughly examined, the preliminary bibliography should be circulated to experts in the field for a collegial review. These should include authors of reports, government officials who fund evaluations, and substantive experts in the area under investigation. The objective of such a review is to solicit any known studies that somehow escaped being captured by the other procedures. Chalmers and others (1989), in developing the Oxford Database on Perinatal Trials, took this notion quite seriously. In an effort to identify unpublished trials, they surveyed over 40,000 obstetricians and pediatricians in eighteen countries.

Publication Bias Should Be Avoided. In the introduction to this chapter, it was noted that some evaluation studies are conducted but do not appear in the public domain through conventional outlets or in bibliographic databases. Unless a concerted effort is undertaken to locate these studies through a variety of strategies, they are likely to be overlooked. Many unpublished studies remain in a file drawer (Rosenthal, 1978). To avoid publication bias, Cooper (1989) emphasizes the need for a broad search to ensure the retrieval of all potentially relevant studies.

Searching *Dissertation Abstracts International* provides a partial means of identifying unpublished work; there are likely to be other file drawers, however, that would not be represented in this database. At issue is the extent to which published literature is likely to present a biased or skewed picture of the effectiveness of an intervention. The logic is relatively simple. Because a premium is placed on rejecting the null hypothesis, only those studies that show effects tend to be published. Therefore some unknown number of null results may be lying around in file drawers.

The Potential Effects of Publication Bias Should Be Assessed. Several procedures have been developed to assess the potential effects of publication bias on the results of a synthesis that relies on more readily accessible documents. Three prominent methods have been used. Rosenthal (1978) and Orwin (1983) proposed a set of calculations, resulting in a fail-safe n, as a means of assessing the *potential* influence of overlooking unpublished studies. Their calculations assume that the unpublished findings are nonsignificant. The calculations that are used tell the analyst how many nonsignificant results would be necessary to overturn a significant aggregated effect size (Orwin) or combined probability (Rosenthal). If the calculations reveal that there would have to be a large number of unpublished studies to overturn the result, the analyst should be more confident that publication bias is not a major threat; a small number should raise concerns.

Shadish, Doherty, and Montgomery (1989) used a more empirical approach. They conducted a sample survey of members of a professional association to estimate how many studies might be locked away in file drawers. Although the confidence bands on their estimates were quite broad, they found that there may be as many unpublished as published studies. This does not tell whether the results would be different if these studies had been included, however. In a more direct assessment of publication bias, Dickersin, Min, and Meinert (1992) examined 737 studies that had been approved by two institutional review boards at a major university. In studies approved by the two review boards, 81 percent and 66 percent had been published. Dickersin and colleagues (1992) found a sizable association (adjusted odds-ratio of 2.85) between results reported to be significant and publication. In pursuing reasons for not submitting the study for publication, over 60 percent of their respondents indicated either that they experienced design or operational problems or that "the results were not interesting." This study suggests that excluding unpublished work is likely to lead to aggregated results that make interventions look more promising than they would be if all data were considered.

Within policy-driven syntheses, reliance on published *and* unpublished (or at least not published in a conventional manner) studies is highly variable. This means that for policy-oriented syntheses, it is important to conduct as broad a search as possible to locate all relevant studies, regardless of whether they have been published or not. In the synthesis of the WIC program (U.S. General Accounting Office, 1992) and the teen pregnancy problem (U.S. General Accounting Office, 1986b), more than two-thirds of the studies had appeared in journals. A similar fraction of studies in the synthesis of alcohol, drug, and mental health disorders among homeless persons (Lehman and Cordray, 1992) were found in journals. In many GAO evaluation syntheses, between 10 percent and 30 percent of the studies were obtained from journals. The remainder came from sources that required a great deal of digging. To overlook these would substantially reduce the utility of the resultant synthesis. As a general rule, it is not safe to assume that there will be few relevant unpublished studies lying around in file drawers.

Winnowing the Results of the Search. In some cases, there is a functionally infinite number of prior studies that *might* have some bearing on the questions specified in the problem formulation phase. In some areas, the opposite problem occurs. For example, GAO's review of prior estimates of the number of homeless individuals involved only eighty-three studies; Lehman and Cordray's (1992) synthesis of alcohol, drug, and mental health disorders among the homeless uncovered twenty-nine studies; and GAO's (1989) AIDS Forecasting study involved only thirteen studies reporting national estimates. At some point, there is insufficient information to perform any meaningful form of synthesis.

On the other hand, some areas have been studied for decades. A comprehensive search easily becomes overwhelming. Recall that Lipsey (1992) found over 8,000 citations to potentially relevant studies in the juvenile justice arena. Within the teenage pregnancy PES (U.S. General Accounting Office, 1986b), analysts uncovered about 1,100 potentially relevant studies. Regardless of the number of studies or estimates that are uncovered, the key issue at this phase of the synthesis process is that the search be as comprehensive as possible. Narrowing the field of study is part of the data evaluation process.

Once the search process is completed, the relevant studies must be identified. To do this systematically, it is important to have clearly specified criteria for judging relevance. These criteria are generally determined on a synthesis-by-synthesis basis. For example, if only high-quality studies are to be examined, inclusion rules would need to be established for determining whether a study meets the stated criteria. If the study focuses on a theoretical model, as in the case of Becker's (1992) assessment of science education, only studies that include relevant correlations were included in the final sample.

Data Evaluation

In introducing the data evaluation phase of the synthesis process, Cook and others (1992) make the following observation: "Meta-analysis is not simply a mechanical exercise. Research findings are not simply transcribed onto coding sheets, entered into a database and subjected to statistical evaluation. Rather, several forms of data evaluation must be undertaken prior to statistical analysis. These entail judgments and decisions on the relevance and technical adequacy of information from primary studies" (p. 295). There is *only one* hard and fast rule for these judgments: the analyst must tailor these criteria and rules to fit the specific needs of the synthesis.

Inclusion Rules. Decisions to include or exclude a particular study depend, in large measure, on the parameters specified in the problem formulation stage of the synthesis. A clear specification of the problem enables the analyst to filter studies on the basis of their *substantive* and methodological relevance. Bryant and Wortman (1984) argue that judgments about relevance can be cast in terms of construct validity and generalizability. As Cook and others (1992) note, the former refers to the "correspondence between operationalization of the treatments or outcomes with conceptual variables implied by the meta-analytic question" (p. 299). In practice, the complexity of these decisions varies. For example, in the AIDS Forecasting synthesis (U.S. General Accounting Office, 1989), studies were deemed relevant if they presented national projections of the cumulative number of AIDS cases by the end of 1991, or provided information from which this could be derived. No other restrictions applied; thirteen studies were located and all were found to be relevant.

Relevance of a study is not limited to the substance of a report. The inclusion rules for studies in the alcohol, drug, and mental health disorder (ADM) synthesis (Lehman and Cordray, 1992) were twofold: (1) the study had to have used formal methods (well-established diagnostic tests) to assess alcohol, drug, and mental health disorders, and (2) the technical quality of the research methods underlying the prevalence estimate had to be trustworthy. Specifically, studies had to have used sampling techniques that resulted in a reasonably representative sample of the target population (eliciting moderate to high response rates); the coverage of settings where homeless are known to "reside" had to be sufficiently broad to provide reasonable assurances of the generalizability of the results. This conjoint rule resulted in highly restrictive inclusion criteria. Ninety-two studies or reports were found to be relevant on substantive grounds, twenty-nine passed the first simple methodological review (used formal ascertainment methods), and twenty-four passed a more stringent methodological review (had an adequate sample). Further inspection of the individual studies showed that some study reports involved subgroups reported in other studies; eighteen independent samples from sixteen studies were ultimately retained for the synthesis.

This stringent inclusion rule had been negotiated with the policymakers prior to conducting the synthesis. For policy-driven syntheses, such negotiations are often necessary. The client, in this case federal officials at the National Institute of Mental Health (NIMH) and the National Institute on Alcohol Abuse and Alcoholism (NIAAA), wanted to know, based on best practices (Slavin, 1986), the prevalence of disorders among homeless individuals. Although it would have been interesting to examine the influence of "poor" practices on prevalence estimates, time did not afford that luxury.

Without time constraints, inclusion criteria can be more liberal. In general, evaluation syntheses are limited to studies that involve (1) experimentally or quasi-experimentally configured comparison groups, (2) quantitative measurement of outcomes, and (3) sufficient reporting of the nature of the intervention conditions and composition of the groups. Lipsey (1992) represents a clear example of the use of this type of decision rule. Analysts vary a great deal on the exact criteria that are used to operationalize these general concerns, however. Shadish (1992) limited his selection of studies to those using randomized designs. Chalmers and others (1989) in selecting studies for inclusion in the Oxford Database on Perinatal Trials used similar inclusion rules. At this point in the development of synthesis tactics, there does not appear to be a consensus on what constitutes acceptable practices for judging whether a study is of sufficient technical merit to be included in the database. Although there is considerable debate surrounding the inclusion of only the best studies *and* debate about the value of "throwing all studies into the mix," resolution of these issues is not evident. Many of the differences across syntheses can be attributed to this judgment call (for a complete example, see Wachter and Straf, 1990). Although these differences have been treated *as if* they represent errors or bias, they are clearly judgment calls, the influence of which can be assessed only if the analyst incorporates all studies into the analysis and *tests,* empirically, the consequences of differential quality (see Cordray, 1990).

Quality Assessments. Determining whether a study should be included based on its technical merits represents one step in data evaluation. Another aspect of data evaluation involves more fine-grained assessment of studies that are included. Although specific details for judging research quality are not easy to articulate, some general guidelines have been developed. As noted, judgments of a study's technical merit can be based on a variety of methods. Schemes for judging the quality of studies that are included in syntheses range from simple to complex. The GAO (U.S. General Accounting Office, 1990) summarizes four general tactics. These include the use of (1) single criteria, (2) multiple attributes with equal weight, (3) the fatal flaw procedure, and (4) multiple attributes with differential weights.

1.   Single Criteria. Sometimes there is a single feature that distinguishes acceptable from unacceptable studies. Sorting acceptable from unacceptable studies can be based on simple criteria like the use of a comparison group or the size of the samples employed (implying that larger samples yield more precise estimates). Because the components that determine the technical quality of a study are generally more complex than can be captured by a single criterion, this tactic has limited applicability.

2.   Equally Weighted, Multiple Criteria. There are several dimensions on which study quality can be assessed. The number of criteria that might be used in practice vary a great deal. Cook and Campbell (1979) list thirty-three "threats to validity," clustered around issues of statistical conclusion, internal, construct and external validity. Although these clusters can be ordered in terms of priority, there is no real consensus as to which threats should be given more or less weight. As such, the threat to validity framework, by itself, implies equal weighting across the multiple criteria within the Cook and Campbell conceptualization. Prior syntheses have tended to use a subset of the full listing of threats to validity. Chalmers and others (1989) relied on three criteria: selection bias, completeness of analysis, and the extent to which outcome assessment was conducted without knowledge of the condition a patient was assigned. In applying this scheme, each criterion was given a rating of 1 (low) to 3 (full credit) stars. Using this type of scheme, equal weighting across the criteria, a total quality score can be derived (ranging from 3 to 9). Similar schemes can be developed using other subsets of the Cook and Campbell criteria.

3.   Multiple Criteria, Fatal Error Method. Although multiple criteria can be specified for characterizing study or design quality, in some instances

priority factors can be established. A "fatal error" assessment is perhaps the most extreme form of such a prioritization. For example, suppose a study employed exceptional assignment techniques, the intervention was well implemented, the sample size was sufficient, but the measurement of outcomes was biased by knowledge of assignment to conditions. In this case, the synthesizer might be well justified in giving a low rating to the whole study simply because adequacy in the other domains cannot make up for the fatal design flaw (biased outcome assessment). This approach was used in rating methods underlying estimates of the prevalence of homelessness (U.S. General Accounting Office, 1988).

4. Differentially Weighted, Multiple Criteria. Cooper (1989) recommends a "mixed criteria" approach to rating study quality. The reviewer first codes multiple, objective features of the study design (e.g., randomized design, attrition levels, type of measurement, reliability of measures). These features can be quantified categorically (such as experiment = 1; other = 0) or rated on an interval or ordinal scale (such as level of attrition). With the objective features of the design described, a second judgment can be rendered that focuses on the presence or absence of common threats to validity in the design. For example, a poorly executed experiment might be rated low on internal validity because of excessive pretreatment nonequivalence between groups *and* differential attrition from conditions.

Using this mixed approach, the analyst can determine the "weight," through statistical analyses such as regression analysis assigned to design features or ratings on threats to validity. In essence, this form of weighting considers the relationship between design features or threats to validity and effect sizes. Using both types of information together is also possible. That is, by adding to the analysis the second judgment on the presence or absence of threats to validity, the analyst can obtain a weighting of the importance of variations in design features, relative to the clarity of the cause-effect relationship. Good illustrations of this mixed-method technique for rating quality can be found in Cook and others (1992). As an alternative to empirically deriving the weights to be assigned to study features, T. Chalmers and others (1981) have developed a quantitative scale for judging the merits of randomized trials. Unlike the work of I. Chalmers and others (1989), in this scheme, weights (points) are assigned for different criteria.

The applicability of any one scheme is dependent on factors like the nature of the designs that are being judged, whether surveys, experiments, or quasi-experiments, and the degree to which it is necessary to characterize all dimensions of quality. For some syntheses, a simple scheme that yields a rough quality sort is all that is required or feasible due to time or resource limitations.

Integrity of the Coding Process. Anyone who has read an evaluation report will note that the written descriptions of treatments, research methods, and results are sometimes clear and sometimes ambiguous (Orwin and

Cordray, 1985). Often, it is difficult to tell how groups were composed, how clients were selected, what conditions they experienced, and so on. This obscurity makes data extraction much more difficult, adding "noise" or bias to the synthesis process. On the other hand, most evaluation research has to contend with uncertainty associated with noise and bias; so, ambiguity is not unique to the synthesis process. Borrowing extensively from survey, observational, and case study methods, evaluation synthesis practices have evolved to take these problems into account. State-of-the-art prescriptions for conducting high-quality syntheses include a variety of quality control procedures. Chief among them is the use of a data extraction coding protocol, accompanied by detailed definitions concerning coding categories, decision rules, and provisions for exceptions. Naturally, the extensiveness of the protocol is highly dependent on how the problem was set up initially. The development of the protocol and documentation is also an iterative process, however. Fortunately, unlike survey research where recontacting the respondent is expensive or impossible, reliance on written records allows the analyst to revisit reports when he or she makes important changes to the coding protocol.

Having a protocol is necessary but not sufficient to ensure maximum quality of the synthesis. Preliminary training is essential, along with continuous monitoring to avoid the possibility of coder drift, fatigue, and inconsistent application of the coding scheme. The inevitability of having to make judgment calls as part of the coding process suggests the need for multiple independent coders and assessments of intercoder agreement levels. Several options exist. All reports can be coded independently by two or more individuals or a sample of studies can be coded twice (see Rosenthal, 1984). Further, multiple indices of agreement can be used (Orwin and Cordray, 1985). When all reports are multiply reviewed, a consensus or conference process can be used to iron out discrepancies.

Many of the discrepancies that are found among coders can be attributed to deficient reporting in the primary study. Orwin and Cordray (1985) suggest the use of confidence ratings as a means of keeping track of coding decisions that represent varying levels of certainty. Some important design variables, such as assignment rules, are not clearly described. Yet, the coder will be required to make a judgment: the assignment was or was not random. To capture the level of confidence a coder has in his or her decision, Orwin and Cordray (1985) suggest rating the decision that was made on a three-point scale ranging from 1 (this rating is a guess as to whether assignment was random) to 3 (a high degree of certainty).

Chalmers and others (1987) argue that bias in the coding of study characteristics can creep into the synthesis process if the study outcomes are known. To avoid this, they recommend rating the quality of methods independent of any knowledge of the study results (through a blind coding process in which a study's method section is separated from its findings section). As should be evident, there are numerous ways in which judgment calls can influence the evaluation synthesis process, producing results that are different across syntheses or biased in favor of a particular hypothesis. On the other hand, the quality control practices that have emerged can greatly reduce their influence, if properly executed.

Data Analysis and Interpretation

The discussion of types of syntheses implies that data analysis within various forms of synthesis involves three steps: (1) preaggregation manipulation of primary study results, (2) the application of statistical rules to develop an aggregate estimate, and (3) postaggregation probing of results to assess robustness of findings (a disaggregation phase). A great deal of attention has been given to the technical or statistical features of synthesis. The statistical aspects of these methods have become quite complex. In fact, half the Cooper and Hedges (forthcoming) *Handbook on Research Synthesis* is devoted to advances in statistical techniques. Although synthesis methods can be very useful in answering practical evaluation questions, they are not necessarily simple to use. Technical resources for computational aspects of synthesis are readily available, however (see Cook and others, 1992; Hedges and Olkin, 1985; Hunter and Schmidt, 1990).

Despite the technical complexities associated with aggregating results, the basic issues are relatively easy to articulate. Quantitative synthesis of prior evaluation results is possible because a common metric is derived for each outcome of interest. As mentioned earlier in this chapter, the most prevalent way to convert study results is to calculate an effect size. In the most straightforward case, the effect size is the difference between group means (such as treatment versus control) divided by a pooled within-group standard deviation.

In practice, preaggregation activities associated with deriving effect sizes is complicated by reporting problems and some additional technical considerations. Adjustments are often necessary to improve the between-study comparability of effect size estimates or to meet statistical rules. For example, because estimates derived from small samples are biased, it is necessary to correct this prior to deriving an effect size for each study. Hedges and Olkin (1985) provide a statistical rationale for other calculations that are needed to adjust for small sample biases, unreliability of measures, and so on. Lipsey (1990) shows how effect sizes can be derived for categorical data. In the case of meta-analyses that involve correlations, the common metric is the correlation coefficient. Hunter and Schmidt (1990) argue that technical issues like unreliability and other between-study differences (range restrictions) need to be accounted for prior to statistical aggregation. To deal with inconsistencies across studies in how results are reported, Lipsey (1990) also provides a highly readable discussion of the relationships among various effect size indicators such as correlations and regular effect size estimates. Glass, McGaw, and Smith (1981) provide a useful guide on how to derive approximate effect sizes when statistical tests (for example, t or F statistics) are reported, without means and standard deviations.

In the policy arena, answering specific questions posed by decision makers often requires the development of new means of deriving a common metric. In GAO's synthesis of the housing allowance studies, it was important to transform data on participation rates to derive a ratio that could index the degree to which subgroups were treated fairly. The AIDS Forecasting synthesis (U.S. General Accounting Office, 1989) had to rely on adjusted ranges of estimates within studies as a means of deriving a plausible range of estimates. GAO's analysis of the estimates of homelessness required the development of rates per 10,000 to allow comparisons between strong and weak methods of estimation. These alternative means of inducing comparability between studies have not had the same level of statistical scrutiny that more commonplace effect size indicators have undergone. As such, they should be used in connection with more standard procedures (see U.S. General Accounting Office, 1984). This combination provides a way to determine whether new, uncharted practices yield consistent results.

In describing meta-analysis methods earlier in this chapter, we noted that simply deriving a combined estimate across effect sizes was only part of the statistical process. Once a combined estimate is derived, it needs to be assessed to assure that differences across studies are not obscured. In essence, this phase of the synthesis process involves a form of *disaggregation*. The disaggregation process is particularly interesting because it represents a retreat from efforts to distill all prior studies into a simple summary, thereby avoiding some of the early criticisms of these methods (e.g., Slavin, 1984). The analytical backbone of the disaggregation process is testing for homogeneity through various tests developed by Hedges and Olkin (1985). If the individual study effect sizes are similar, within sampling error, to the aggregate effect size, they are said to be homogeneous. Aggregated results are meaningful to the extent that the results are not accounted for by important between-study or moderator variables. Rarely are results homogeneous— that is, they share a common population estimate. Efforts need to be directed at exploring the sources of these differences.

Extending this notion to testing, empirically, the influence of judgment calls provides a mechanism for resolving some of the conflicting results that might appear across syntheses. In the synthesis of prevalence estimates of alcohol, drug, and mental health disorders among the homeless, Lehman and Cordray (1992) recognized that decisions to include or exclude a study could have influenced their aggregate results. To estimate the likely influence of inclusion rules, they *re-estimated* their weighted estimates by systematically excluding one of the known studies as if it had been overlooked. The resulting set of estimates provided a range of estimates that would have been provided from each of the groups of N-1 studies. This form of assessment is known as *sensitivity analysis*. It tests the influence of methodological decisions by creating a bounded range of estimates. Similar procedures could be used to assess the consequence of different statistical aggregation rules.

Because it is not always clear what the most appropriate aggregation procedure might be, different estimation procedures can be employed on the same data. If the results are the same, regardless of the procedure used, we could conclude that the differences in assumptions underlying each procedure do not matter. When differences do emerge across procedures, highlighting the range of estimates derived from each of the series of sensitivity analyses provides the reader with a better understanding of the range within which the true effects, independent of decision rules, are likely to reside. The logic of conducting sensitivity analyses is similar to the logic of reporting confidence intervals rather than point estimates.

Generalization. One concern that has not been handled well within the synthesis literature is the extent to which findings from controlled studies represent the real situations where services are likely to be provided (Cordray, 1990). In interpreting the results of a collection of studies, it is often difficult to know how extensively the findings can be generalized. To make this point concrete, consider the following situation. Suppose a series of randomized experiments or controlled clinical trials were conducted in various university laboratories. The treatment protocol involved the delivery, at each site, of a precise "dosage" of the intervention by a highly trained staff member. Further, the treatment protocol stipulated careful monitoring of patients for compliance with the experimental conditions. These types of studies will appear to be internally valid but they lack generalizability. In contrast, studies performed in normal care settings generally involve less control and the internal validity of findings will be lower; potential generalization is far higher, however. To examine results from both types of studies can be very enlightening because they optimize information about efficacy — Does an intervention work under ideal conditions? — and effectiveness — Does it work in routine-care settings? At present, there is a great deal of interest among policymakers about the generalization of findings from highly controlled studies.

GAO (U.S. General Accounting Office, 1992) has developed the cross-design synthesis as a technique to address this type of question. The cross-design synthesis has as its goal developing estimates of the effects of interventions that have been assessed through very different means. Here the idea is to capitalize on data that are generalizable to actual intervention settings, although weak with respect to confident causal attribution, by synthesizing them with less general but more valid estimates derived from clinical trials or social experiments. This method draws heavily on meta-analysis, secondary analysis, and complex modeling tactics for deriving its integrative summary. Though the cross-design synthesis has not been applied to any particular problem area, it holds considerable promise for the future.

Presenting the Findings

Syntheses that rely on complex statistical modeling might seem too complicated to be of any value in the policy process, where a premium is placed on straightforward answers. Although the analytical process that is used to derive synthesis results is often quite complex, the analyst can deliver meaningful summaries of the results in nontechnical language. The WIC synthesis (U.S. General Accounting Office, 1992) converted the synthesis results into policy-meaningful terms by estimating the number of very low birthweight babies that might have been born without the program, as implied by effect sizes based on differences in the percentages reported in each study. Chalmers and others (1989) report the results of each study, ordered according to their methodological quality, *and* the aggregate results as a means of allowing practitioners to see the overall effects and variation in results across trials. Presumably this mix of synthesis and disaggregation—or listing, in this case—enhances the utility of the findings. GAO (U.S. General Accounting Office, 1989) followed the same practices in reporting its synthesis of corrected forecasts of the cumulative number of AIDS cases. By converting the results of local studies into estimates of homelessness per 10,000 *and* displaying the resulting range of estimates according to categories of methodological quality, GAO (U.S. General Accounting Office, 1988) also provided results that were easily understandable in policy-relevant terms. In short, we should not ignore the technical details associated with good synthesis practice out of fear that the results will be too complex for policymakers to use. Rather, we should recognize the value of complex analyses, report ranges of estimates when needed, and communicate in language and graphics that are meaningful and clear.

Summary Observations

A basic message of this chapter is that through the use of quantitative and qualitative means of summarizing prior studies, the longer-term value of conducting all types of evaluation studies can be optimized. At the simplest level, evaluation syntheses can allow us to answer policymakers' questions in a timely fashion, thereby enhancing the utility of the findings in the policymaking process where timing is everything (Chelimsky, 1988). A broader view of utility emerges within a knowledge development framework (Cordray and Lipsey, 1987). For example, Light (1984) argues that syntheses can answer important questions that are not well addressed by single studies. These include questions about the generalization of findings for specific types of interventions, such as across multiple implementations, client-treatment interactions, intervention processes, and ways to optimize the effects of social change efforts. Further, synthesis activities can help to improve the quality of subsequent primary evaluation studies.

　　Over the past fifteen years a great deal has been learned about using quantitative techniques to summarize the results of prior research and evaluation studies. Efforts to adapt these methods to a variety of policy and nonpolicy-oriented domains have produced a rich array of tools that have practical and conceptual appeal. On the practical side, synthesis tactics can help answer a variety of questions that are of interest to policymakers, program managers, and the public. On the conceptual side, these methods provide a powerful means of answering a broader set of evaluative questions about how and why programs fail or succeed. In the long run, the conceptual aspect will likely be the most enduring contribution of these methods.

Despite these advances, more work needs to be done if evaluation synthesis and its variations are to be optimally useful. An examination of actual practices reveals substantial room for error, bias, and other forms of distortion. On the bright side, a great deal of attention has been directed at improving practices. Methods have been developed to assess the influence of judgment calls, and best practices seem to suggest that synthesizers should devote more attention to the presentation of ranges of values rather than point estimates. In this way, battles about who is right, when differences are small, will not distract policymakers from the issues. In turn, attention can be directed at the important issues—namely, building better policies to address critical social ills.

References

Abrami, P. C., Cohen, P. A., and d'Apollonia, S. "Implementation Problems in Meta-Analysis." *Review of Educational Research,* 1988, *58*(2), 151–179.

Bangert-Drowns, R. L. "Review of Developments in Meta-Analytic Method." *Psychological Bulletin,* 1986, *99,* 388–399.

Beaman, A. L. "An Empirical Comparison of Meta-Analytic and Traditional Reviews." *Personality and Social Psychology Bulletin,* 1991, *17*(3), 252–257.

Becker, B. J. "Models of Science Achievement: Forces Affecting Male and Female Performance in School Science." In T. D. Cook and others (eds.), *Meta-Analysis for Explanation: A Casebook.* New York: Russell Sage Foundation, 1992.

Boruch, R. F., Wortman, P. M., and Cordray, D. S. *Reanalyzing Program Evaluations: Policies and Practices for Secondary Analysis of Educational and Social Programs.* San Francisco: Jossey-Bass, 1981.

Bryant, F. B., and Wortman, P. M. "Methodological Issues in Meta-Analysis of Quasi-Experiments." In W. H. Yeaton and P. M. Wortman (eds.), *Issues in Data Synthesis.* New Directions for Program Evaluation, no. 24. San Francisco: Jossey-Bass, 1984.

Bryk, A. S., and Raudenbush, S. W. "Heterogeneity of Variance in Experimental Studies: A Challenge to Conventional Interpretations." *Psychological Bulletin,* 1988, *104,* 396–404.

Chalmers, I., and others. "Materials and Methods Used in Synthesizing Evidence to Evaluate the Effects of Care During Pregnancy and Childbirth." In I. Chalmers, M. Enkin, and M. Keirse (eds.), *Effective Care in Pregnancy and Childbirth.* Oxford, England: Oxford University Press, 1989.

Chalmers, T. C., and others. "A Methodology for Assessing the Quality of Randomized Control Trials." *Controlled Clinical Trials,* 1981, *2,* 31–49.

Chalmers, T. C., and others. "Meta-Analysis of Clinical Trials as a Scientific Discipline II: Replicate Variability and Comparison of Studies That Agree and Disagree." *Statistics in Medicine,* 1987, *6,* 733–744.

Chelimsky, E. "Federal Evaluation in a Legislative Environment: Producing on a Faster Track." In C. G. Wye and H. P. Hatry (eds.), *Timely, Low-Cost Evaluation in the Public Sector.* New Directions for Program Evaluation, no. 38. San Francisco: Jossey-Bass, 1988.

Cook, T. D., and Campbell, D. T. *Quasi-Experimentation: Design and Analysis Issues for Field Settings.* Chicago, Ill.: Rand McNally, 1979.

Cook, T. D., and Gruder, C. "Meta-Evaluation." *Evaluation Review,* 1978, *2*(1), 3–50.

Cook, T. D., and Leviton, L. C. "Reviewing the Literature: A Comparison of Traditional Methods with Meta-Analysis." *Journal of Personality,* 1980, *48,* 449–472.

Cook, T. D., and others. *Meta-Analysis for Explanation: A Casebook.* New York: Russell Sage Foundation, 1992.

Cooper, H. M. *Integrating Research: A Guide for Literature Reviews.* (2nd ed.) Newbury Park, Calif.: Sage, 1989.

Cooper, H. M., and Hedges, L. V. (eds.). *The Handbook of Research Synthesis.* New York: Russell Sage Foundation, forthcoming.

Cordray, D. S. "Meta-Analysis: An Assessment from the Policy Perspective." In K. Wachter and M. Straf (eds.), *The Future of Meta-Analysis.* New York: Russell Sage Foundation, 1990.

Cordray, D. S., and Lipsey, M. W. (eds.). *Evaluation Studies Review Annual,* Vol. 11. Newbury Park, Calif.: Sage, 1987.

Cordray, D. S., and Orwin, R. G. "Improving the Quality of Evidence: Interconnections Among Primary Evaluations, Secondary Analysis, and Quantitative Syntheses." In R. J. Light (ed.), *Evaluation Studies Review Annual,* Vol. 8. Newbury Park, Calif.: Sage, 1983.

Cordray, D. S., and Sonnefeld, L. J. "Quantitative Synthesis: An Actuarial Base for Planning Impact Evaluations." In D. S. Cordray (ed.), *Utilizing Prior Research in Evaluation Planning.* New Directions for Program Evaluation, no. 27. San Francisco: Jossey-Bass, 1985.

Devine, E. C. "Effects of Psychoeducational Care with Adult Surgical Patients: A Theory-Probing Meta-Analysis of Intervention Studies." In T. D. Cook and others (eds.), *Meta-Analysis for Explanation: A Casebook.* New York: Russell Sage Foundation, 1992.

Dickersin, K., Min, Y., and Meinert, C. L. "Factors Influencing Publication of Research Results." *Journal of the American Medical Association,* 1992, *267*(3), 374–378.

Durlak, J. A., and Lipsey, M. W. "A Practitioner's Guide to Meta-Analysis." *American Journal of Community Psychology,* 1991, *19*(3), 291–332.

Einhorn, H. I., and Hogarth, R. M. "Judging Probable Cause." *Psychological Bulletin,* 1986, *99*(1), 3–19.

Glass, G. V. "Primary, Secondary and Meta-Analysis of Research." *Educational Researcher,* 1976, *5,* 3–8.

Glass, G. V., McGaw, B., and Smith, M. L. *Meta-Analysis in Social Research.* Newbury Park, Calif.: Sage, 1981.

Goldschmidt, P. *Information Synthesis: A Practical Guide.* HSR&D Document RES #29-07-110. Washington, D.C.: Veterans Administration, 1984.

Gueron, J. M. "Work-Welfare Programs." In H. S. Bloom, D. S. Cordray, and R. J. Light (eds.), *Lessons from Selected Program and Policy Areas.* New Directions for Program Evaluation, no. 37. San Francisco: Jossey-Bass, 1988.

Guzzo, R. A., Jackson, S. E., and Katzell, R. A. "Meta-Analysis." In L. L. Cummings and B. M. Staw (eds.), *Research in Organizational Behavior.* Greenwich, Conn.: JAI Press, 1987.

Hedges, L. V., and Olkin, I. *Statistical Methods for Meta-Analysis.* New York: Academic Press, 1985.

Hunter, J. E., and Schmidt, F. L. "Dichotomization of Continuous Variables: The Implications for Meta-Analysis." *Journal of Applied Psychology,* 1990, *75*(3), 334–349.

Lehman, A. F., and Cordray, D. S. "Prevalence of Alcohol, Drug, and Mental Disorders Among the Homeless: One More Time." Unpublished paper, 1992.

Light, R. J. "Six Evaluation Issues That Synthesis Can Resolve Better Than Single Studies." In W. H. Yeaton and P. M. Wortman (eds.), *Issues in Data Synthesis.* New Directions for Program Evaluation, no. 24. San Francisco: Jossey-Bass, 1984.

Light, R. J., and Pillemer, D. B. *Summing Up: The Science of Reviewing Research.* Cambridge, Mass.: Harvard University Press, 1984.

Lipsey, M. W. *Design Sensitivity: Statistical Power for Experimental Research.* Newbury Park, Calif.: Sage, 1990.

Lipsey, M. W. "Juvenile Delinquency Treatment: A Meta-Analytic Inquiry into the Variability of Effects." In T. D. Cook and others (eds.), *Meta-Analysis for Explanation: A Casebook.* New York: Russell Sage Foundation, 1992.

Matt, G. E. "Decision Rules for Selecting Effect Sizes in Meta-Analysis: A Review and Reanalysis of Psychotherapy Outcome Studies." *Psychological Bulletin,* 1989, *105*(1), 106–115.

Mullen, P. D., and Ramirez, G. "Information Synthesis and Meta-Analysis." *Advances in Health Education Promotion,* 1987, *2,* 201–239.

Nurius, P. S., and Yeaton, W. H. "Research Synthesis Reviews: An Illustrated Critique of 'Hidden' Judgements, Choices, and Compromises." *Clinical Psychology Review,* 1987, *7,* 695–714.

Orwin, R. G. "A Fail-Safe n for Effect Sizes." *Journal of Educational Statistics,* 1983, *8,* 157–159.

Orwin, R. G., and Cordray, D. S. "Effects of Deficient Reporting on Meta-Analysis: A Conceptual Framework and Reanalysis." *Psychological Bulletin,* 1985, *97*(1), 134–147.

Rosenthal, R. "The 'File-Drawer Problem' and Tolerance for Null Results." *Psychological Bulletin,* 1978, *86,* 638–641.

Rosenthal, R. *Meta-Analytic Procedures for Social Research.* Newbury Park, Calif.: Sage, 1984.

Rubin, D. B. "A New Perspective." In K. Wachter and M. Straf (eds.), *The Future of Meta-Analysis.* New York: Russell Sage Foundation, 1990.

Shadish, W. R. "Do Family and Marital Psychotherapies Change What People Do? A Meta-Analysis of Behavioral Outcomes." In T. D. Cook and others (eds.), *Meta-Analysis for Explanation: A Casebook.* New York: Russell Sage Foundation, 1992.

Shadish, W. R., Doherty, M., and Montgomery, L. M. "How Many Studies Are in the File Drawer? An Estimate from the Family/Marital Psychotherapy Literature." *Clinical Psychology Review,* 1989, *9,* 589–603.

Slavin, R. E. "Meta-Analysis in Education: How Has It Been Used?" *Educational Researcher,* 1984, *13*(8), 6–15, 24–27.

Slavin, R. E. "Best-Evidence Synthesis: An Alternative to Meta-Analytic and Traditional Reviews." *Educational Researcher,* 1986, 5–11.

Stigler, S. M. *The History of Statistics: The Measurement of Uncertainty Before 1900.* Cambridge, Mass.: Harvard University Press, 1986.

U.S. General Accounting Office. *Evaluation Synthesis.* Methods Paper 1. Washington, D.C.: U.S. General Accounting Office, 1983.

U.S. General Accounting Office. *WIC Evaluations Provide Some Favorable but No Conclusive Evidence on the Effects Expected for the Special Supplemental Program for Women, Infants, and Children.* GAO/PEMD-84-14. Washington, D.C.: U.S. General Accounting Office, January 1984.

U.S. General Accounting Office. *Housing Allowances: An Assessment of Program Participation and Effects.* Washington, D.C.: U.S. General Accounting Office, 1986a.

U.S. General Accounting Office. *Teenage Pregnancy: 500,000 Births a Year but Few Tested Programs.* GAO/PEMD-86-16BR. Washington, D.C.: U.S. General Accounting Office, January 1986b.

U.S. General Accounting Office. *Drinking-Age Laws: An Evaluation Synthesis of Their Impact on Highway Safety.* GAO/PEMD-87-10. Washington, D.C.: U.S. General Accounting Office, March 1987.

U.S. General Accounting Office. *Homeless Mentally Ill: Problems and Options in Estimating Numbers and Trends.* GAO/PEMD-88-24. Washington, D.C.: U.S. General Accounting Office, 1988.

U.S. General Accounting Office. *AIDS Forecasting: Undercount of Cases and Lack of Key Data Weakens Existing Estimates.* Washington, D.C.: U.S. General Accounting Office, June 1989.

U.S. General Accounting Office. *Prospective Evaluation Methods: The Prospective Evaluation Synthesis.* Transfer paper 10.1.10. Washington, D.C.: U.S. General Accounting Office, November 1990.

U.S. General Accounting Office. *Health Services: Available Research Shows That Capacity Is Only Weakly Related to Volume.* Washington, D.C.: U.S. General Accounting Office, January 1991.

U.S. General Accounting Office. *Early Intervention: Federal Investments Like WIC*

Can Produce Savings. GAO/HRD-92-18. Washington, D.C.: U.S. General Accounting Office, April 1992.

Wachter, K., and Straf, M. (eds.). *The Future of Meta-Analysis.* New York: Russell Sage Foundation, 1990.

Wanous, J. P., Sullivan, S. E., and Malinak, J. "The Role of Judgment Calls in Meta-Analysis." *Journal of Applied Psychology,* 1989, *74*(2), 259–264.

Part Two

Practical
Data Collection Procedures

Evaluation design is usually considered the glamorous part of program evaluation. Evaluators love to discuss and debate ways to link program activities to outcomes. Equally important, however, is collecting the data once the evaluation design has been selected. Even the best evaluation designs come to naught if accurate data cannot be obtained, or if data are not collected in a reasonably reliable and valid way.

The next seven chapters discuss approaches to data collection. Some of these approaches are well known, such as use of agency record data and surveys. Others are not so common, such as using trained observer ratings and role-playing. The chapters in this part cover (1) trained observer approaches, (2) systematic surveys, (3) the systematic use of expert judgment, (4) use of role-playing, (5) focus groups, (6) field interviewing, and (7) use of agency record data. *Most evaluations will need to utilize more than one, and possibly several, of these approaches.*

John M. Greiner, in Chapter Ten, provides detailed procedures for undertaking *trained observer* ratings. Such ratings can provide data on a variety of physical conditions. These procedures can be used to evaluate changes in street cleanliness, street "rideability," park and playground maintenance, housing conditions, the condition of schools and other buildings, and the maintenance quality of child care and institutional facilities, among other uses. Ratings before and after specific program actions can be taken to help determine the effectiveness of those actions. Less widely used in program evaluations have been trained observer ratings of client functioning, such as in assessing the rehabilitation of persons with physical and mental disabilities.

The chapter describes systematic procedures that can be used to achieve reasonable interrater and across-time reliability for use in program evaluations. Because many public agencies have staff members who already undertake some form of inspection, they may find these procedures particularly feasible.

Thomas I. Miller, in Chapter Eleven, discusses a better known procedure, undertaking *systematic surveys,* particularly of program clients. No book on data collection for program evaluation would be complete without examining survey procedures. The chapter discusses many of the key elements needed for quality surveys. Sample surveys have been used by agencies to track such conditions as employment, housing, and health conditions. Surveys have been used by evaluators for decades. Often they are the key data collection procedure used to evaluate human services programs. Surveys are the only way to obtain statistically reliable data from respondents on ratings of services they have received; they can be a major way to obtain factual information on changes in behavior and "status" of respondents, especially *after* customers have completed the service. Surveys can also provide demographic information on customers as well as their perceptions of *what needs to be improved* in the service and *how much the service contributed* to any improvements they identified. The targets of surveys might be clients of particular services, households, businesses, or other agencies or levels of government that are customers of a service.

Most of the procedures described in Chapter Eleven can be applied whether a sample of a population or the full population is surveyed. Surveys of a program's customers will be particularly feasible if the program keeps records of clients' names, addresses, and telephone numbers. Surveys are especially attractive when costs can be kept relatively low, such as when mail administration is feasible. Mail surveys will often provide sufficiently accurate information if multiple mailings and telephone reminders or interviews are used to achieve reasonable response rates. Telephone surveys are practical when relatively small samples can be used to obtain the needed information.

Harvey A. Averch, in Chapter Twelve, discusses the *systematic use of expert judgment,* a technique rarely thought of as a way to collect data for program evaluations. Usually expert judgment procedures, such as Delphi, are used to provide estimates about the future. However, in some types of programs such as research and planning, evaluators may need to fall back on the judgments of knowledgeable persons. Such procedures also can be applied to programs for which hard data cannot be obtained for certain outcomes. Some evaluators may scoff at the systematic use of expert judgment, but it may be the only way to get reasonable information on some aspects of service quality.

While individual experts can have all sorts of biases, the collective use of experts in a systematic way can sometimes be helpful for an evaluation, probably in more situations than evaluators currently recognize. This chapter addresses many of the issues that arise, including selection of the experts and how to collect and combine their ratings.

Margery Austin Turner and Wendy Zimmermann, in Chapter Thirteen, describe a procedure that has been gaining attention in recent years—

role-playing. This technique has been applied particularly to assess discrimination in housing and employment. In these cases, paired role-players, two or more individuals with different racial/ethnic or gender characteristics, but who are otherwise similar, apply for housing or jobs. The differences in the treatment each member of these pairs receives can provide powerful evidence of how well equal opportunity programs have — or have not — achieved fairness in consideration of applications.

Turner and Zimmermann also point out the many applications of the procedure where paired role-playing is not needed. One role-player can call or visit facilities sponsored by a public agency to test the quality of the information or service the role-player requests. This is a technique the Internal Revenue Service has used to evaluate the quality of its agents who provide tax information to the public. Single role-players can be used, for example, to assess the quality of responses to requests for information from government tourist offices, public assistance offices, or almost any office that directly serves customers. While such strategies can be, and have been, used to bring discrimination cases against individual firms, that is not the function here. Rather, we are concerned with the procedure's use to provide aggregate data on many cases to help evaluate the quality and success of public programs.

To provide reliable statistical data, the key concern is to use systematic, reliable procedures and on enough cases or situations to be reasonably representative of the population of interest. Evaluators may not always have sufficient resources to obtain statistically representative information; however, in such cases, the evaluators can use role-playing at the beginning of evaluations to identify issues that the evaluation should cover.

Debra L. Dean, in Chapter Fourteen, describes the use of *focus groups,* an increasingly popular information gathering procedure. This approach is not normally intended to collect actual evaluation statistics since the number of persons involved in the groups is intentionally kept quite small. Focus group information is not intended to be statistically representative of the full population. These groups are becoming frequently used in case study and other fieldwork evaluations to provide clues to how well a program is working. Respondents in such instances are often program personnel as well as clients.

Focus groups can be important to program evaluators at the *front end* of their evaluations to help identify customer concerns that should be included in the evaluation design — both outcome and process characteristics. In addition, the groups can assist evaluators *after* data are collected to help them interpret the data; this is done by asking focus group members to suggest reasons the findings are as they are. Focus groups usually represent a very low-cost procedure, thus adding to their attractiveness to evaluators. They also offer a way that the sponsors of the evaluation, and subsequently the users of the evaluation report, can gain assurance that the evaluation has considered the interests of the programs' customers.

Demetra Smith Nightingale and Shelli Balter Rossman, in Chapter Fifteen, describe *field data collection* issues and procedures, particularly those involving interviews with persons knowledgeable about program implementation, quality, or outcomes. In recent years, increasing numbers of evaluators are using such fieldwork to obtain qualitative and quantitative information on how programs are working. They often seek information on both successes and problems in implementing programs in order to provide feedback to agencies for improving their programs.

A major problem for evaluators is deciding what procedures they should use to make the information more systematic and therefore more valid and credible. The authors provide numerous suggestions for accomplishing this. Many large-scale, federally sponsored evaluations in recent years have involved such examinations. Other chapters in this handbook have discussed qualitative, implementation, and case study type evaluations. The fieldwork that Nightingale and Rossman discuss is particularly applicable to these types of evaluations.

Harry P. Hatry, in Chapter Sixteen, discusses the *collection of data from agency/archival records* — probably the most common source of information for an evaluation. Most, and possibly all, public program evaluations require data from agency records, if only to obtain counts of the number of customers or cases the program has served. Agency records can pose a considerable challenge to evaluators, however. The field of evaluation is littered with examples of missing and incomplete records, differences in definitions and in data collection procedures for desired data elements, difficulties in gaining access to records, and other problems. The author identifies and discusses such problems and provides a number of suggestions for alleviating them.

Agency records are the source on which public agencies sponsoring evaluations will most likely depend initially. Information from records is, in general, the cheapest, most readily available source of data. Unfortunately, existing agency records seldom provide adequate information on the outcomes of program activities, and one or more of the procedures described in Chapters Ten through Fifteen will also be needed.

Other Data Collection Considerations

This set of chapters does not cover all the data collection procedures that evaluators might use. For some public programs, mechanical or electronic recording devices are increasingly used to track program outcomes. Examples are the use of various instruments to assess air and water quality and noise levels. "Ride meters" are used by some transportation agencies to measure bumpiness of roads. If the readings from such equipment can be correlated with more end-oriented outcomes, they can be even more effective. In some instances, road meter readings of road roughness have been correlated with driving comfort and potential car damage, and air and water pollution levels have been correlated with levels of health hazards. Some of the measuring devices, unfortunately, can be quite expensive, such as those that test water for toxic pollutants and condition of fish tissue. In such instances, the evaluators may need to use smaller samples and test less frequently.

Cost is an important consideration in all data collection procedures. These chapters identify some of the less costly ways to acquire information. A common cost reduction scheme is to use sampling, and to have smaller samples and reduced precision. Evaluators in all cases should review their precision needs. Calling for more precision than necessary will add to the cost of the evaluation. For example, requiring 95 percent confidence levels is likely to be overkill for many evaluation applications. How often do decision makers, those using evaluation findings, have such certainty in their decisions? Why not 90 percent, or even lower levels?

Another key issue for data collection is *quality control*. This element should be given explicit attention when data collection is planned. Quality control should be built into the data collection process. This means such steps as:

- Training thoroughly all data collection personnel
- Attempting to triangulate field findings with confirmatory responses from more than one respondent and from multiple sources
- Pretesting data collection procedures before full use
- Checking questionnaire wording for ambiguity and biases

One special way to assure better data quality is for all members of the evaluation team to visit the program, at least one of its sites, possibly as part of a pretest. This on-site experience can give the evaluators a reality check and enable them to do a better job of planning data collection.

Finally, evaluators will need to make important decisions about the amount of data to be collected. Evaluators may be tempted to seek large amounts of information about a wide range of program and service quality characteristics. At some point, overcollecting will overload the collection resources and cause significant difficulties in analysis of the data. The evaluators, in their initial planning, should make sure that each data element they include has a specific purpose and is likely to provide useful evaluative information. Advocates for particular data elements should be required to justify each element's inclusion. Otherwise, the evaluation may dissipate the data collection efforts and produce more quantity than quality in data collection.

10

Use of Ratings by
Trained Observers

John M. Greiner

Evaluators often encounter situations in which the outcomes of interest involve qualitative phenomena, conditions, or behaviors that can be classified, counted, or rated on an ordinal scale (for instance, dirtier, bumpier, less responsive). In such circumstances, an accurate, systematic technique for directly assessing these conditions using one's eyes, ears, and other senses can serve as an important evaluative tool. Indeed, as Yogi Berra succinctly put it, "You can observe a lot just by watching" (Peter, 1977, p. 295).

Consider, for instance, the following potential program evaluation tasks:

- Compare the effectiveness of private contractors versus municipal forces in providing park maintenance services.
- Evaluate the relative effectiveness of alternate street cleaning programs and identify factors that influence the results.
- Evaluate the impact of a tax limitation initiative (such as Massachusetts's Proposition 2½) on the quality and equity of street maintenance service.
- Assess the accessibility, courtesy, and responsiveness of public agencies to routine in-person and telephone requests for service.
- Assess the physical condition of a city's housing stock or public facilities (for example, classrooms), and subsequently evaluate the effectiveness of policies and programs undertaken to address the needs identified.
- Evaluate the relative effectiveness of alternate mental health programs based on changes in observed client behavior.
- Assess the quality of the care provided by nursing homes.

This chapter draws heavily from discussions of trained observer techniques in two recent International City/County Management Association/Urban Institute publications: Hatry, Greiner, and Swanson, 1987; and Hatry and others, 1992.

In these and many other situations, a systematic technique for assigning accurate, reliable grades based on direct visual observations can be — and *has
been* — employed to support program evaluation efforts. This technique involves the use of *trained observers.*

This chapter reviews the development and use of trained observer ratings for program evaluation and related applications. The discussion begins with a general description of the trained observer approach and a review
of the specific ways in which trained observer ratings can be — and have
been — used. The potential advantages, disadvantages, and limitations of
trained observer ratings are examined next; these must be kept in mind as
you decide whether to utilize trained observers in any given application.
The next several sections focus on the major steps involved in designing and
implementing trained observer ratings: choosing the characteristics to be
rated, developing the rating scales and forms, selecting and training the raters,
and conducting the actual observations. A special section is devoted to quality
control procedures, which are critical to ensuring the validity and credibility of trained observer ratings. Considerations in analyzing and presenting
trained observer results are reviewed next, followed by a discussion of time,
cost, and staffing requirements, and some overall conclusions. The references at the end of this chapter include additional examples of the use of
trained observer ratings for program evaluation and other applications as
well as descriptions of the actual rating scales and procedures that have been
employed in assessing specific conditions.

The Nature and Application of Trained Observer Ratings

Trained observers are persons who make ratings of conditions (or events)
by comparing their perception of the condition to a prespecified rating scale.
While most trained observer ratings have been based on *visual* perceptions
of conditions, any of the senses can be used — touch, smell, hearing, even
taste. The rating scales should incorporate detailed written definitions and/or
photographic benchmarks that enable the observers to assign precise grades
to the conditions they see. The technique should include systematic procedures to ensure the accuracy and consistency of the ratings between raters
and over time. When properly used, trained observers can provide accurate,
reliable, quantitative measures of program outcomes for use in program
evaluation.

Most applications of trained observers have, up to now, focused on
assessing facility maintenance, such as the care and appearance of public
parks and beaches; the condition of recreation centers, schools, dwellings,
and other public — and private — facilities; the bumpiness (rideability or walkability) and safety of streets and sidewalks; the visibility of street signs and
pavement markings; street cleanliness and other aspects of neighborhood
appearance; and the condition of public transportation facilities. Trained
observers have also been used to evaluate the impacts of mental health

programs on client behavior (here, the observers are usually trained clinicians), the responsiveness of employees to citizen requests, and the quality of the care provided by nursing homes (see Exhibit 10.1).

Trained observer procedures can also provide a practical, systematic approach for tallying *specific* items or conditions associated with the impacts of a program. Examples include the number of safety hazards in parks or playgrounds, "abandoned" vehicles left on private property, or petty street

**Exhibit 10.1. The Use of Trained Observers
to Help Evaluate the Quality of Care in Nursing Homes.**

Federal law requires that all nursing homes be inspected annually in order to be certified to receive Medicare and Medicaid payments. Since 1990, these inspections have focused on outcomes—quality of care, patient quality of life, protection of patient rights, and the quality of dietary, nursing, pharmacy, and other support services. The inspections draw on a variety of data collection techniques: trained observer ratings of physical facilities, group activities, and a sample of residents (and their rooms); interviews of residents and staff; physical measurements; reviews of records; and various specialized procedures (such as checking the accuracy of a sample of medications as they are distributed and quizzing randomly selected staff concerning proper emergency procedures). These techniques are used to obtain information on a lengthy list of items that jointly characterize various aspects of the quality of nursing home services: quality of life, quality of care, and so forth.

Among the many trained observer ratings used to help assess "quality of life" are ratings of accommodation to resident needs, resident clothing and grooming, the cleanliness and orderliness of resident rooms, the comfortableness of sound and temperature levels in resident rooms, and the degree to which the resident's room provides a homelike environment. The evaluation of "quality of care" includes trained observer ratings of the amount eaten by residents, the degree to which the dining environment enhances resident independence and well-being, and potential safety hazards. Trained observers rate dietary services in terms of the timeliness, appearance, flavor, temperature, and nutritional balance of the meals served. And the physical environment is evaluated with the help of trained observer ratings of the degree of visual privacy, lighting, ventilation (including presence of odors), and numerous other characteristics. Both two-level (yes/no) and three-level (A/B/C) rating scales are employed. Definitions are provided in a comprehensive manual prepared by the federal Health Care Financing Administration (HCFA), which also supplies the detailed rating forms used by all inspectors.

HCFA contracts for the inspections with state health departments. The field work is undertaken by full-time, multidisciplinary teams of four to seven professionals—nurses, dieticians, social workers, pharmacists, sanitarians, and so forth. A typical certification inspection requires three to four days and results in a list of citations for the major problems identified. These can have serious consequences for the nursing home, including decertification.

Nursing home inspectors receive extensive training using materials prepared by HCFA (see Health Care Financing Administration, 1992). For instance, in Michigan new inspectors undergo four weeks of full-time training, followed by on-the-job training with a survey team under the guidance of a trainer (who is not a regular member of the team). It takes six months for an inspector to be fully qualified. HCFA also requires that all nursing home inspectors complete a one-week training course at HCFA's Baltimore headquarters during their first year on the job.

Quality control for these inspections is exercised by HCFA and the state health departments. For instance, in Michigan the quality of nursing home inspections is controlled through monthly inservice training of all staff, analysis of complaints, and observation of survey teams by trainers working with new inspectors. In addition, HCFA personnel completely resurvey a 5 percent random sample of inspected nursing homes in *each* state. These reinspections occur within two months of the state inspection. HCFA is also implementing joint nursing home inspections (independent, parallel surveys with both state and federal inspection teams on site at the same time) and requiring that all surveyors pass a standard test designed by HCFA.

---

crimes in a given neighborhood (an application that has been used in New York City's Times Square area—see Fund for the City of New York, n.d.).

Among the many other potential applications, trained observers can be used to rate buses, subways, parks, and libraries in terms of how crowded they are. Such observers can evaluate the effectiveness of noise ordinances; the ease of filing complaints at city hall; and the presence of hazards, odors, and vermin at a landfill. Trained observers can also be used to determine the incidence of potholes, stray animals, malfunctioning traffic signals, or diseased shade trees.

Table 10.1 lists several of the characteristics that have been rated with the help of trained observers as well as some of the places where the technique has been employed. The exhibit also provides selected references to more detailed information on the scales and procedures that have been used in connection with trained observer ratings of specific types of conditions. For descriptions of program evaluations involving trained observer ratings, see "Before and After" (1985); Fund for the City of New York (1983); Greiner (1984); Greiner and Peterson (1986); Riccio, Miller, and Litke (1986); Thomas (1980); and "A Ticket to Clean Streets" (1982).

The information produced by trained observer ratings can be used in connection with most of the evaluation designs discussed in this handbook. The ratings can serve as outcome measures (the dependent variables) for before versus after assessments, controlled experiments, or quasi-experiments involving comparison groups or interrupted time series. By providing a systematic inventory of *potential* service needs (for example, the condition of the housing stock, the number of poorly maintained classrooms), trained observer ratings can serve as the basis for assessing "percentage of unmet need"—a key indicator of effectiveness for many programs. The ratings can also be used to measure certain independent or explanatory variables—for instance, to initially classify clients of mental health programs by problem severity for evaluating the effectiveness of alternate service delivery options.

Potential Advantages, Disadvantages, and Limitations

Trained observer ratings offer a number of potential advantages in connection with program evaluation.

- They provide a relatively easy and often inexpensive way to quantify conditions—and program *outcomes*—that would otherwise be quite difficult to measure.
- Despite their inherent subjectivity, when done properly, trained observer ratings can achieve considerable objectivity and reliability; under such circumstances, they have been accorded a high degree of validity and credibility by researchers and decision makers.
- Trained observer results can, in addition, be readily understood by public administrators (and the public), especially when photographic rating scales

Table 10.1. Some Applications of Trained Observer Ratings.

Characteristic Rated	Jurisdiction(s) Rated	Rating Scales and Procedures[a]

Park Maintenance	Alexandria, Va.[b]
	Arlington County, Va.
	Boston, Mass.[b]
	Charlotte, N.C.
	Charlottesville, Va.[b]
	Greenville, S.C.
	Honolulu, Hawaii
	King County, Wash.
	New York City
	San Diego (city), Calif.
	Sunnyvale, Calif.
	6 Jurisdictions in Volusia
	  County, Florida[b]
	17 Jurisdictions in the State
	  of Massachusetts[b]
		Hatry and others, 1992
		City of Greenville, 1990
		Wilson, 1989
		TriData Corporation, 1986
		Fund for the City of New
		  York, 1978

Beach Maintenance	5 Jurisdictions in Volusia County, Florida[b]	The Urban Institute, 1983
Building Maintenance (Public Buildings)	Alexandria, Va.[b] Charlottesville, Va.[b] Dayton, Ohio New York City (schools) Sunnyvale, Calif.	Moore, 1988 TriData Corporation, 1986
Housing Stock/Public Housing	Albany, N.Y. Charlottesville, Va. Charlotte, N.C. Dallas, Texas Kansas City, Mo. State of Texas	Hatry, Morley, Barbour, and Pajunen, 1991 City of Kansas City, 1989

Street Cleanliness[c]	Alexandria, Va.[b]
	Boston, Mass.[b]
	Charlotte, N.C.
	Charlottesville, Va.[b]
	Nashville, Tenn.[b]
	New York City
	St. Petersburg, Fla.[b]
	Savannah, Ga.
	Sunnyvale, Calif.
	Washington, D.C.
	8 Jurisdictions in Volusia
	  County, Florida[b]
	17 Jurisdictions in the State
	  of Massachusetts[b]
		Hatry and others, 1992
		Thomas, 1980
		Blair and Schwartz, 1972

Abandoned Vehicles	Charlotte, N.C.[b] Nashville, Tenn.[b] Prince Georges County, Md. St. Petersburg, Fla.[b] Washington, D.C.	Hatry and others, 1992
Street Rideability/ Bumpiness[c]	Alexandria, Va.[b] Boston, Mass.[b] Charlottesville, Va.[b] Nashville, Tenn.[b] St. Petersburg, Fla.[b]	Hatry and others, 1992 TriData Corporation, 1986

Table 10.1. Some Applications of Trained Observer Ratings, Cont'd.

Characteristic Rated	Jurisdiction(s) Rated	Rating Scales and Procedures [a]
	8 Jurisdictions in Volusia County, Florida[b] 17 Jurisdictions in the State of Massachusetts[b]	
Sidewalk Walkability[c]	Alexandria, Va.[b] Charlottesville, Va.[b] Nashville, Tenn.[b] St. Petersburg, Fla.[b]	Hatry and others, 1992 TriData Corporation, 1986
Responsiveness to Citizen Requests	Kansas City, Mo. Saratoga, Calif.	Center for Excellence in Local Government, 1988 Herman and Peroff, 1981
Functioning of Social Service and Mental Health Clients	Denver, Colo. Jefferson County, Colo. State of Michigan State of Oklahoma State of West Virginia	Millar and Millar, 1981
Quality of Nursing Home Care	Nationwide (all nursing homes receiving Medicare or Medicaid payments)	Health Care Financing Administration, 1992
Subway Conditions	New York City	Institute for Public Transportation, 1980
Petty Street Crime	New York City	Fund for the City of New York, n.d.
Solid Waste Disposal	Nashville, Tenn. St. Petersburg, Fla.	Hatry and others, 1992

[a]These references provide detailed information on some of the scales and procedures that have been used to rate the given characteristic. Complete citations are provided in the references at the end of this chapter.

[b]This condition was rated as part of a multiservice trained observer assessment covering a variety of services and characteristics: street cleanliness; bumpiness of streets and sidewalks; condition of signs, stop lights, and pavement markings; park maintenance; and/or the condition of public buildings.

[c]Ratings of street cleanliness, street rideability, and/or sidewalk walkability have frequently been coupled with ratings of curb and gutter conditions, street and traffic sign visibility/condition, traffic light operability, shade tree condition, abandoned vehicles, and similar conditions that can be observed along a street.

are used. Hence, they can contribute to the acceptance and utilization of the evaluation results.

- Trained observer ratings tend to focus on conditions as experienced by a typical citizen or other user of a service or facility. Thus, they can complement technical assessments of program outcomes by professionals.

- In most cases, trained observer ratings can be made by ordinary citizens without the need for expensive "experts." For many applications, existing government staff, students, or citizen volunteers can be trained to be competent raters.

Despite the above advantages, trained observer ratings must be used with caution. A number of potential disadvantages and practical limitations need to be kept in mind when deciding whether—and how—to employ trained observers.

- Trained observer ratings are designed for assessing characteristics that can be readily and directly *sensed* or experienced by the rater—observed, felt, heard, smelled, or tasted. They are not suited for determining the less obvious underlying factors and technical details associated with a condition.

- Because they often depend on visual observations of conditions or behavior, trained observer ratings can be hampered—and in some cases precluded—by uncontrollable situations that limit observability: crowds, parked cars, snow, privacy requirements, and so forth. To avoid such problems, the observations may have to be scheduled at times that are inconvenient from the rater's standpoint (for instance, on evenings or holidays).

- Because the raters must observe conditions firsthand, some applications of trained observers can pose potential physical dangers. For instance, ratings of dangerous neighborhoods or isolated parks, or "windshield" ratings made while driving slowly on congested or high-speed roads can be hazardous to the observer.

- Many trained observer ratings involve nominal or ordinal scales that cannot be interpreted in the usual absolute quantitative sense. For instance, numbers are often used to distinguish between the various conditions that make up a nominal scale, despite the fact that there is no consistent, quantitative relationship between the conditions (for instance, 1 = "safe," 2 = "hazardous," and 3 = "safety unknown"). Ordinal scales involve the assignment of numbers to conditions that exhibit a qualitative ordering (for instance, cleanliness ratings of 1, 2, and 3 where 1 is "cleaner than" 2 and 2 is "cleaner than" 3). For many such scales, the numbers merely serve as labels and can be replaced by letters or other symbols with no loss of information. (For instance, the above rating levels could be designated A, B, and C.) In these situations, the nominal or ordinal scale can limit the applicability of certain familiar and convenient statistical measures and techniques (averages, standard deviations, regression analyses, and so forth), which are valid only when the "distance" between adjacent rating levels is a constant.

- Trained observer ratings are not usually suitable for assessing subtle changes or especially complex conditions. The primary "instruments" used in making trained observer measurements are the human senses, and the ratings are strongly constrained by the physiological limitations of human perceptions and mental processes. For instance, trained observer scales usually involve relatively few distinct gradations (typically three to five grades). The number of different levels that can be used depends on the observer's ability to perceive differences in the characteristics being rated and to remember the detailed definitions associated with all the levels.

- Without considerable care in their design and implementation, trained observer ratings can easily become subject to the problems that potentially threaten *any* inherently subjective assessment process—imprecision, poor repeatability, and lack of interrater comparability. An evaluator choosing to use trained observers must put the necessary effort into systematic design of the rating scales, careful validation, adequate training, and extensive quality control. One must avoid the temptation to use trained observers as a "quick and dirty" way to quantify outcomes.

- The credibility of the trained observer results may be suspect if the observer is also involved in providing the service being rated. This sets up a potential conflict of interest that can compromise the rater's objectivity. Even if the rater remains unbiased, the *external credibility* of the evaluation may be damaged in such a situation. Such considerations can limit the applicability of trained observer ratings in cases where program staff *must* be used as the raters (because of access or confidentiality restrictions, the need for special expertise, and so forth).

- Finally, there is a danger (present in any evaluation effort) that trained observer ratings will become intrusive—that the observations will alter the conditions or outcomes being measured and hence affect the evaluation results. For instance, the presence of the raters may focus the attention of service delivery personnel on addressing the specific items and/or conditions being measured.

Most of the foregoing concerns can be addressed through proper design and sensitive implementation of the rating procedures—by carefully selecting the characteristics to be graded, developing adequate rating scales, properly choosing and training the raters, ensuring adequate quality control, and properly analyzing the results. These considerations are reviewed in the sections that follow.

Selecting the Characteristics to Be Rated

The first step in implementing trained observer ratings is to identify the *specific* features and conditions that will be rated. In some cases, the appropriate characteristics will be obvious from the program being evaluated. For instance, if the outcome of interest is the number of abandoned vehicles, the cleanliness of a park, the bumpiness of a road, or the "aroma" of a landfill, the evaluator can develop straightforward trained observer ratings focusing on a single attribute.

In other cases, the evaluator will have to analyze the various program objectives, breaking the relevant constructs into elements (and results) that can be more readily observed and rated. For example, if the objective is to evaluate the effectiveness of a building maintenance program, the concept of "building maintenance" might first be broken down into distinct maintenance concerns: maintenance of rooms, restrooms, halls and corridors, staircases, elevators, building exterior, and building grounds. Each of these elements can then be subdivided into more narrowly defined maintenance issues and responsibilities. Thus, "room maintenance" involves the condition of the ceiling, walls, windows, doors, floors, lighting and other electrical fixtures, other utilities (heat, ventilation), and any special equipment or conditions. For each of the foregoing items, one can either define an overall "maintenance rating" based on an assessment of the feature *as a whole* (for instance, an overall "ceiling maintenance rating" of 1, 2, 3, or 4 based on various combinations of observable conditions), or one can further disaggregate the item into a set of potential "problems" whose *individual* ratings will jointly provide an assessment of the maintenance of the feature. (For ceilings, these potential problems might include cracks or bulges, missing or damaged tiles, stains or other painting needs, and dirt or dust.) In general, the trade-off is between having a few complex rating scales versus many relatively simple ratings.

For instance, Greenville, South Carolina, breaks "park maintenance" into ten maintenance elements: paths, walks, and parking areas; benches and picnic tables; shelters, restrooms, and water fountains; play areas; ball fields; basketball courts; tennis courts; grass and lawns; shrubs, trees, and plantings; and litter (Wilson, 1989). Each of these elements is further subdivided into specific *observable* maintenance problems, such as the existence of weeds, broken glass, or overturned/broken benches. The trained observer ratings then focus on assessing the presence and extent of each potential problem. Charlottesville, Virginia, uses a similar approach (see Exhibit 10.3 later in this chapter).

On the other hand, New York City's Department of Parks and Recreation has focused its park maintenance ratings directly on the *overall* condition of key aspects of its park facilities—benches, comfort stations, fences, playground equipment, ball fields, shrubs, and so forth. There is no effort to assess the presence of specific types of problems.

A number of sources can be helpful in identifying the most relevant attributes, conditions, and potential problems to look for. The evaluator should consult program and service delivery staff, top-level management, members of relevant advisory and advocacy groups, and actual users of the service in question concerning the results they expect and the potential problems of greatest importance to them in connection with the service or program. Field observations of a range of situations and facilities are especially helpful. Maintenance checklists, inspection forms, standard operating procedures, and published standards can also suggest key factors and conditions to monitor.

Evaluators should exercise care in choosing the final list of features and problems to be rated. The characteristics selected should be readily observed or sensed by a rater. Check also for completeness (do they address all key aspects of the construct or outcome in question?), the absence of overlaps or redundancy, and the clarity and directness of the presumed association between the characteristic to be observed and the construct of interest.

Another important issue is the degree of disaggregation—how far to go in breaking a complex concept into discrete components. The list of items to be rated should be limited: a lengthy list will dilute the impact of the results for any one item while increasing the stress on the rater and the potential for error. (On the other hand, a more detailed listing is likely to be especially helpful for operating personnel in identifying where problems exist and what needs to be done to remedy them.) Greenville's park rating procedure explicitly addresses forty-two different types of maintenance problems; New York City's focuses on seventeen general features but uses more complex rating scales. Note that if the ratings focus on the presence of specific problems, an open-ended "other" category can always be included to catch any problems or concerns not explicitly listed.

Developing the Rating Scales and Forms

The next step is to specify precisely the rating scales and the associated forms. Before developing a *new* rating scale, explore the feasibility of using existing, pretested scales such as those cited in Table 10.1. In addition to the cost saving, utilization of existing scales has the advantage of drawing on tested, validated ratings—many of them complete with photographic standards. Literature from the fields of survey research, observational methods, and psychometrics can also be helpful. See, for instance, Miller (1983), Cronbach (1960), and Edwards (1957).

Several guidelines should be followed when developing a new rating scale for trained observers. If possible, the evaluator should first observe numerous examples of the condition(s) of interest to record, and perhaps photograph, the full range of potential conditions. Special situations and potentially difficult distinctions should be noted so that procedures or conventions can be developed to deal with them clearly and consistently.

No more than four or five major rating levels should be established, although midpoint ratings are also usually allowed to indicate that the condition falls between the major rating levels. It is essential that the conditions constituting each major level be defined with sufficient clarity and detail that a trained observer using the definitions can make accurate ratings with a minimum of guesswork and a high degree of consistency. The definitions should cover the entire range of conditions likely to be encountered, and each level of the scale should correspond to a meaningful perceived distinction. It is often conceptually useful to initially anchor the ratings by characterizing each grade in general terms such as "very clean," "moderately clean," "dirty," and "very dirty." When a scale involves more than three major rating levels, it is especially important to supplement the verbal descriptions with reference photographs that clearly depict the conditions and distinctions associated with each level.

The form of the rating scale will depend in part on the level of disaggregation used. At one extreme (no disaggregation), the evaluator could employ a *single, composite multi-attribute scale* that simultaneously addresses all relevant aspects (and distinctions) regarding the given condition. At the other extreme (extensive disaggregation), the evaluator can use *many simple, independent, single-attribute rating scales* that jointly capture the important aspects of the condition—in effect, an elaborate checklist of key features, each addressing a distinct aspect of the condition or concept of interest (and each rated separately).

The "simpler" conditions—involving single problems or attributes—can usually be adequately characterized using two- or three-level scales (present/not present, or present/partly present/not present). On the other hand, the more complex, multi-attribute constructs usually require the development of more elaborate scales containing four or more grades, each anchored by extensive definitions and reference photographs. The added complexity is needed to capture in a few grades the many important combinations, distinctions, and interactions among the characteristics that jointly define the overall condition or quality being assessed.

To illustrate these options, consider first some simple two- and three-level scales that have been widely used in rating park and building maintenance. For each of several *specific* types of *potential* maintenance problems listed on the rating form (for ceilings, these might include cracks or bulges, missing or damaged tiles, and the need for repainting), the trained observer assesses the *presence and extent* of the problem using a scale such as the following:

> NP = No Problems
> LIM = Limited Problems
> WID = Widespread Problems

A problem is "limited" if it involves *one-third or less* of the feature rated. A problem is defined as "widespread" if it is extensive in scope or frequency—that is, if it involves *over one-third* of a given feature or facility. Detailed written definitions are provided to allow the raters to identify each type of potential maintenance problem. For instance, the need for repainting a ceiling can be defined as the presence of chipped or peeling paint, the existence of stains or graffiti, or the presence of bare, untreated surfaces.

The evaluator may wish to add a separate assessment to determine whether each of the problems identified constitutes a hazard, perhaps using a two-level scale (present or not present). "Hazards" can be defined as problems that are potentially dangerous to health or safety, *regardless* of their extent.

"Street cleanliness" illustrates a construct whose complex and potentially subtle distinctions justify a four-level scale with extensive written and photographic definitions for each grade. Table 10.2 provides an example

Table 10.2. Example of a Multi-Attribute Scale for Rating Street Cleanliness.

Rating	*Description*
1	Street completely clean or almost completely clean; up to two pieces of litter are permitted.
2	Street largely clean; a few pieces of litter observable, but only in the form of a few isolated discarded items. On a generally clean blockface that otherwise merits a rating of 1, a single accumulation of uncontained trash (not set out for collection) with a volume less than or equal to the volume of a grocery bag should be rated 2.
3	Lightly scattered litter along all or most of the street or one heavy pile of litter, but no accumulations of litter large enough to indicate dumping. On a generally clean blockface otherwise meriting a rating of 1, a single accumulation of litter with a volume larger than that of a grocery bag but smaller than a standard 30 gallon garbage can (and not set out for collection) should be rated 3.
4	Heavily littered street; litter accumulation in piles or heavy litter distributed down all or nearly all the blockface. On a generally clean blockface that would otherwise be rated 1 or 2, a single accumulation of litter with a volume greater than that of a standard 30 gallon garbage can (and not set out for collection) should be rated 4.

Intermediate ratings of 1.5, 2.5, and 3.5 can also be used when appropriate.

Source: Hatry and others, 1992, p. 266.

of a street cleanliness scale that has been used by several governments. Note that the written criteria in Table 10.2 specify the distinctions between the severity of combinations of conditions (scattered trash versus piles of trash) that help to jointly define and distinguish the various levels of cleanliness. Photographic "standards" illustrating the distinctions between each of the four major grades have been developed to assist with the ratings (see Exhibit 10.2).

New York City's Department of Parks and Recreation has used several multi-attribute, multilevel rating scales for assessing park and recreation facilities. For instance, the four-level scale shown in Table 10.3 has been used to rate rest rooms.

New York's Board of Education uses a combination of simple (two-level) scales and more complex multilevel scales for rating the condition of schools and playgrounds (Moore, 1988). Seven-level scales are used to rate the material integrity, surface quality, and cleanliness of classroom ceilings and walls. Two-level (yes/no) scales are used to assess certain specific types of problems (door appearance, door operation, damaged/inoperable lights, and the like). Individual pieces of playground equipment are graded using a four-level scale (severe, moderate, minor, no problems), with a separate assessment of hazards.

Each type of scale has its advantages and disadvantages. The more elaborate multilevel, multi-attribute scales can allow one to assess a given outcome relatively quickly (with only a single rating), while providing the additional precision possible by having several intermediate grades. The frequent use of photographic standards in connection with such scales also enhances the reliability of the ratings.

Exhibit 10.2.
Examples of Photographic Standards
for Rating Street Cleanliness.

Rating 1: Clean

Rating 2: Moderately clean

Rating 3: Moderately littered

Rating 4: Heavily littered

Table 10.3. Example of a Multi-Attribute Scale for Rating Restrooms.

Rating	Description
1	All fixtures (sinks, bowls, and urinals) are intact and operating. Floors, walls, and ceilings are free from cracks and holes.
2	Some fixtures may be slightly damaged (for instance, chipped sinks or bowls, and/or leaky faucets). Walls, floors, and ceilings may be slightly cracked but are essentially intact.
3	Interior deterioration is evident. One or two fixtures may be inoperable; lighting fixtures, mirrors, and/or partitions may be broken or missing. Significant number of cracks exist in floors, walls, and/or ceilings.
4	Interior deterioration is widespread. Three or more fixtures may by inoperable; lighting fixtures, mirrors, and/or partitions are broken or missing. Extensive cracks and/or holes are present in floors, walls, and/or ceilings.

Source: City of New York. "Detailed Condition Assessment." New York: Department of Parks and Recreation, City of New York, n.d.

On the other hand, such scales can be difficult (and costly) to develop and validate. Unlike simple problem-oriented scales with only two or three rating levels, the attributes, distinctions, and definitions that form the basis of multilevel scales tend to differ considerably from feature to feature: a completely new scale must be developed, tested, *and remembered* (by the person making the ratings) for each feature or condition rated. Furthermore, because the ratings produced in connection with these scales are highly aggregated, the individual magnitudes and effects of the various underlying attributes are not available for further analysis.

In contrast, two- and three-level single-attribute (problem-oriented) scales are fairly similar from one type of problem to another, requiring simpler judgments and fewer subtle distinctions. This makes it easier to assess a large number of diverse items — including unexpected problems. (The list of potential problems can be readily modified to reflect new issues or concerns.) Furthermore, since each problem is rated separately, it is easier to discern relatively fine distinctions between — and changes in — *overall* conditions.

On the other hand, some precision is sacrificed in relying on only two or three rating levels. Moreover, it is likely to take longer to assess a given overall outcome (for instance, the quality of the housing stock) if it is decomposed into ratings of numerous individual problems than if a few less disaggregated, "overall" rating scales are used.

Regardless of the number of rating levels utilized, one should consider anchoring the definition of one or two levels to conditions that trigger special actions by program staff. For instance, in Dallas, where trained observer procedures have been used to assess the condition of the housing stock in certain neighborhoods, the rating levels have been defined so that a grade of "3" is just sufficient to require action by a city building inspector. Toronto has used a ten-part street condition rating scale in which the lowest grades require no repair work, the highest rating requires complete reconstruction of the road, and the remaining grades correspond to various less extensive repairs.

As noted above, the accuracy and consistency of trained observer ratings can often be improved by providing the observers with photographs illustrating the distinctions between rating levels. In some cases, one can use existing reference photographs such as those given in Exhibit 10.2 and in several of the references at the end of this chapter. When a special set of reference photographs has to be developed, the following procedure can be used. This technique is based on Thurstone's "method of equal-appearing intervals," a general approach for developing an equal interval scale often called the "Q sort" technique (see Thurstone and Chave, 1929; Edwards, 1957; and Cronbach, 1960).

1. Take a large number of pictures (50 to 100) of each facility or condition of interest (for instance, litter or cracks in walls). The photographs should include examples of the entire spectrum of conditions that can be encountered. Close-ups should be used to provide adequate detail on small features.
2. The photographs for a given condition should be numbered and given to five to ten "judges" for review. Each judge is asked to sort the photographs for a given condition independently, placing them in separate piles representing significantly different gradations in the condition. Each pile should correspond to a distinct rating on the desired scale and should be characterized in a word or two (for instance, very clean, moderately clean, moderately littered, very littered).
3. The results should then be analyzed to determine how frequently each photograph was assigned to each category by each judge. Determine the photographs for which there is the most agreement between the judges concerning the rating category to which they belong. These should serve as the "standards" for the corresponding rating level. One can also use the sophisticated (yet simple) statistical techniques associated with the Q-sort method to assign each photograph to a rating category and to assess its value as a "standard" (see, for instance, Edwards, 1957).

If, in the opinion of the evaluator, the final set of photographs does not adequately cover — or distinguish between — the full range of conditions expected, additional photographs should be taken, and the above process should be repeated.

Photographs are especially helpful in connection with scales that involve four or more levels and/or complex, multi-attribute definitions of the ratings. In such cases, the distinctions between rating levels may be rather subtle (especially for ratings toward the middle of the scale), and rating accuracy and consistency can often be improved by providing the trained observers with reference photographs illustrating those distinctions. The need for photographic anchors tends to be less critical in connection with two- or three-level scales focusing on individual problems since the distinctions tend to be clearer.

A final issue in developing trained observer scales is how to aggregate individual ratings of several items into an overall assessment of a given feature or construct. One approach is to develop a combined distribution (or score) for the ratings of all relevant items. (Of course, this is practical only if the rating scales for the various items all have the same number of levels.) For the two- and three-level park maintenance scales discussed previously, this approach corresponds to determining the total number and percentage of "limited," "widespread," "no problem," and "hazard" ratings for all the potential problems examined in connection with a given feature or facility (see Exhibit 10.3 later in this chapter).

The latter procedure assumes that each rating has the same importance in determining the overall score. However, it may be appropriate to weight the various items differently when preparing the overall assessment. For instance, in preparing a combined assessment of overall housing conditions, the City Development Department of Kansas City, Missouri, multiplies each of eight ratings (for roofs, exterior wall surfaces, windows, and so forth) by prescribed weights before computing the overall score. The weights were developed from prior studies designed to determine the relative importance of each housing characteristic to overall conditions (Hatry, Morley, Barbour, and Pajunen, 1991, p. 170).

Alternatively, one can develop a set of rules to create an overall rating from a set of individual ratings. Table 10.4 illustrates a procedure that has been used by Alexandria, Virginia, and other jurisdictions to combine the ratings of park or building problems for a given feature or facility into a single overall rating.

Note that many jurisdictions prepare aggregate overall assessments by averaging the relevant (numerical) ratings. While this is convenient, the validity of such averages may be compromised by the nominal or ordinal nature of the relevant rating scales, as explained earlier in this chapter.

To facilitate the trained observer process (and subsequent aggregation of the ratings), a convenient form should be designed for recording the results. This form should indicate the date, time, and location of the ratings,

Table 10.4. A Procedure for Deriving an Overall Facility Rating from Ratings of Individual Problems.

Overall Rating	Ratings of Individual Problems
1	No problems
2	A few "limited" problems
3	Many "limited" problems or one "widespread" problem
4	More than one "widespread" problem

Note: Half-point ratings (1.5, 2.5, 3.5) can be used to indicate conditions that fall between the defined points.

the name of the rater(s), and perhaps the weather (since weather conditions may affect the observations). Space should be provided on the form for the rater to record any other characteristics and potential explanatory factors that could be helpful in analyzing the data.

If the rating process is based on identifying and rating specific problems, the most common types of anticipated problems (as well as those whose importance merits a special search effort) should be listed explicitly on the rating form. The form should also provide places for the rater to record and assess any other problems encountered.

Exhibit 10.3 is an example of a form for recording and aggregating problem-based trained observer ratings of park maintenance conditions. It is designed to lead the rater through each step of the rating process, from problem identification to the preparation of overall summary ratings for each aspect of park maintenance examined. The basic definitions of the rating levels are repeated on the form as a convenience to the rater.

While most trained observers have—up to now—used paper rating forms, the School Scorecard program operated by New York City's Board of Education uses small, hand-held computers for recording ratings of playgrounds and school buildings. The computers, which originally cost about $3,000 each, weigh four and one-half pounds and are about the size of a legal pad. Using a pen wired to the unit, the rater "writes" the necessary information—for example, the playground name, the number and type of equipment—on a form displayed on the screen. The computer then displays the appropriate rating forms, one after the other, for each maintenance element or piece of equipment associated with the given playground. Each form includes a list of potential problems and ratings tailored to the given item. The rater assesses each feature or potential problem using the appropriate scale (which is provided by the computer) and notes whether it represents a hazard. The computer prompts the rater to provide all the necessary information, checks the rater's entries for completeness and logical consistency, and tallies the results as appropriate. At the end of the day, each rater's entries are uploaded to School Scorecard's main computer system, where all the trained observer results are checked and compiled.

Other technologies can also be helpful in connection with trained observer ratings. For instance, videotapes can be used instead of photographs to define the rating scales, to train the observers, and to document the conditions being rated. Using a videocam, staff can quickly and inexpensively record key conditions, even *before* the rating scales are completely specified. This could be helpful when the evaluation gets off to a late start, when the conditions of interest are changing rapidly, or when one cannot be sure at the outset that a formal evaluation is going to be necessary. Videotapes can also serve as an inexpensive way to document the conditions encountered in order to protect against possible challenges to the ratings or to justify potentially controversial follow-up actions (for instance, when evaluating the performance of contractors). And videocameras that can also record sound have considerable potential in connection with trained observer assessments of human services clients (of course, any such recordings generally require the permission of the client).

The availability of videocams can also reduce the number of trained observers needed and the time necessary to complete the ratings. Conditions at widely diverse locations can be videotaped simultaneously by relatively untrained staff and subsequently rated by a *single* trained observer. Videotaped conditions can also be used by the rating supervisor for quality control. In some cases, an evaluator might be able to take advantage of existing videotape records. For instance, many state highway departments already periodically videotape every mile of state-maintained highway, a process known as "photologging." Moreover, the Virginia Department of Transportation has been using videotape records to evaluate the performance of street maintenance contractors.

Regardless of the technology used, it is essential that before one proceeds with the ratings, all rating scales, forms, and data collection procedures be carefully pretested by several persons to ensure that they produce consistent results. Special attention should be given to the middle rating categories, which are usually the most difficult to distinguish.

Selecting the Raters and Conducting the Ratings

Although nearly anyone can be a trained observer, the best raters will have good eyesight and concentration, will be observant and conscientious about detail, and will be skilled at reading maps. Since the ratings can be tedious, the observers should be able to sustain their motivation and concentration for long periods.

Persons from many backgrounds have successfully served as trained observers. To avoid the possibility (or appearance) of bias, at least one member of each trained observer team (and preferably, all members) should be "neutral"—that is, not involved in the program being assessed.

While trained observer ratings can (and sometimes must) be conducted by individuals, the use of teams is preferable. Two pairs of eyes to identify problems and two opinions on ambiguous rating decisions are better than one. Team members can share the workload, each rating different conditions. Teaming can also contribute to the safety of the raters, if that is of concern (for instance, if the observations are made from motor vehicles or in isolated parks). On the other hand, the use of teams may increase the total cost of the ratings. A balance must be struck between ensuring the quality of the ratings and limiting their cost.

If the number of ratings needed is small (or there is plenty of time), all ratings should probably be conducted by a *single* trained observer or team of observers to minimize interrater consistency problems. For faster ratings or for assessing a large number of facilities or events, several different raters or rating teams can be used.

Exhibit 10.3. A Form for Recording Trained Observer Ratings of Parks and Recreation Facilities.

Name of Park/Facility: _____
Location (Streets): _____ Neighborhood Area: _____
Type of Park: _____ Name: _____
Date: _____ Weather: _____ Time of Day: _____

Key:
"—" – No such facility/not applicable
NP – No Problem
Lim. – Limited
Wide. – Widespread
Haz. – Hazard

		STEP 1: Identification of Problem		STEP 2: Rating of Each Problem	STEP 3: Element Totals	STEP 4: Aspect Totals
Aspect	Element	Potential Problem	Notes and Comments on Problems Found			
Landscaping	Grass and Lawns	Grass unmowed, unkempt				
		Weeds present in grass, fences				
		Grass not trimmed			NP ____	
		Grass not properly edged			Lim. ____	
		Grass brown, unhealthy, worn			Wide. ____	
		Broken glass hazard			Haz. ____	
		Other				
	Shrubs, Trees, Plantings	Require trimming				NP ____
		Weeds present in planted areas			NP ____	Lim. ____
		Dead shrubs, trees, foliage			Lim. ____	Wide. ____
		Broken glass hazard			Wide. ____	Haz. ____
		Other			Haz. ____	
Cleanliness	Litter	Litter rating of 2.5 or worse	Overall litter rating: ____			

Playgrounds and Playing Fields	Item	NP	Lim.	Wide.	Haz.
Play Areas	Equipment broken, cracked, or loose				
	Equipment defaced				
	Equipment needs repainting or refinishing				
	Area infested with weeds				
	Broken glass hazard				
	Other	NP	Lim.	Wide.	Haz.
Playing Fields and Courts	Basketball/tennis court lines or surface in poor condition				
	Equipment broken or damaged	NP	Lim.	Wide.	Haz.
	Base paths rutted, muddy				
	Base paths, skinned areas poorly defined				
	Playing fields infested with weeds				
	Broken glass hazard				
	Other				

Rest Rooms	Item	NP	Lim.	Wide.	Haz.
Odors and Cleanliness	Objectionable odors				
	Toilets, basins, mirrors, etc., dirty or stained	NP	Lim.	Wide.	Haz.
	Walls dirty or stained				
	Floors dirty, stained, littered, or wet				
	Broken glass hazard				
	Other	NP	Lim.	Wide.	Haz.
Maintenance	Lack of toilet paper, towels, etc.				
	Broken/leaking/inoperable fixtures	NP	Lim.	Wide.	Haz.
	Need for repainting (due to graffiti, etc.)				
	Other				

Exhibit 10.3. A Form for Recording Trained Observer Ratings of Parks and Recreation Facilities, Cont'd.

Aspect	Element	STEP 1: Identification of Problem — Potential Problem	Notes and Comments on Problems Found	STEP 2:	STEP 3:	STEP 4:
Other Facilities	Paths, Walks, Parking Areas	Dirt/gravel paths rutted, over-grown, muddy, blocked, etc.			NP ___ Lim. ___ Wide. ___ Haz. ___	NP ___ Lim. ___ Wide. ___ Haz. ___
		Paved walks have holes, ruts, water, defects, etc.				
		Parking area pavement rated 2.5 or worse	Overall pavement rating: ___			
		Broken glass hazard				
		Other				
	Park Benches and Picnic Tables	Tables broken, overturned or damaged			NP ___ Lim. ___ Wide. ___ Haz. ___	
		Table surfaces dirty, littered, greasy, etc.				
		Benches broken, overturned or damaged				
		Benches need painting or refinishing				
		Broken glass hazard				
		Other				
	Structures and Other Facilities	Structures dirty or stained			NP ___ Lim. ___ Wide. ___ Haz. ___	
		Structures damaged or broken, parts missing				
		Need for repainting (due to graffiti, etc.)				
		Lights/electric services broken or hazardous				
		Broken glass hazard				
		Other				

Key: "_" – No such facility/not applicable
NP – No Problem
Lim. – Limited
Wide. – Widespread
Haz. – Hazard

Source: City of Charlottesville, Va., and TriData Corporation (Arlington, Va.).

The provision of proper training is critical to the reliability and — ultimately — the credibility of the trained observer procedure since the quality of the training will, to a great extent, determine rater accuracy and interrater consistency. While the actual time needed to train the raters will depend on the number and complexity of the characteristics rated (and the scales used), no more than two or three days of training will usually be necessary.

Each rater or rating team should receive copies of the written definitions for each scale, any photographic standards, and a training manual. After a general introduction, the trainees should accompany the trainer to several preselected sites. The trainer should demonstrate how various conditions or events are rated and discuss the considerations that come into play in each case. The trainees should be shown examples of the *full* spectrum of possible ratings — the very bad as well as the very good — to help ensure that they do not rate moderate conditions too severely.

Two tests should be administered. The first is a practice test: all trained observer teams should independently rate a preselected site or event just as if they were making an actual rating in the field. Any difficulties with the procedures or interrater differences in the ratings should be discussed. Additional field training should be provided as needed.

The raters should then be given a realistic qualifying test involving several preselected sites and/or conditions. The team pairings for this test should be those that will subsequently be used for the actual ratings. The teams should summarize their results at the end of the field test, using the appropriate forms and procedures. The trainer should check the rating forms and summaries prepared by each team to identify any errors (or bad habits). The ratings should then be compared rater by rater (or team by team) with those of the trainer or judge. Individual biases or errors should be identified and corrected, with supplemental instruction and fieldwork provided as necessary. The training should continue until the rater and the trainer are in exact agreement for at least 70 percent of the ratings and agree within half a rating level for 90 percent of the ratings.

If there are a large number of facilities or events to be rated, the evaluator may need to specify a sample (or sampling rules) before proceeding with the ratings. Standard sampling techniques can be used. For each grouping of interest (for instance, units participating in the program being evaluated, units *not* participating in the program), a sample of perhaps 100 units should be selected.

Ratings of street or housing conditions can be made from a sample of blockfaces. The individual blocks can be chosen randomly or — alternatively — one can lay out a random 100–150 block route through each neighborhood of interest. A sample of rooms for assessing conditions in buildings can be obtained by establishing a simple sampling rule (for instance, walk along every corridor and rate every third room or enclosed area).

To rate a park, the trained observer team should begin by systematically walking around the facility, taking extensive notes on the problems (if any) encountered. After covering the entire facility, the team should complete the rating form, referring to the notes they made and re-observing items where there is a disagreement. For assessing linearly distributed features such as street cleanliness or housing conditions, "windshield" ratings from a moving vehicle can be used. The rating team drives slowly along the street in question, recording the ratings on the appropriate forms or into a tape recorder. Regardless of the procedure employed, the raters should refer frequently to the photographs and written definitions of the various scales.

The raters should be provided with good maps or floor plans for the features of interest. While it can sometimes be efficient to have the raters assess several kinds of facilities or conditions at one time, the observers should not be overloaded with too many simultaneous ratings or accuracy will suffer.

Quality Control Procedures

Because of the inherently subjective nature of trained observer ratings, adequate quality control is *critical* to ensuring the validity and credibility of the results. Key features to monitor (and control) include interrater reliability, repeatability, and of course, accuracy with respect to the written and visual (photographic) rating "standards." In addition to the quality control checks built into the initial training (described above), the following procedures should be used:

- The supervisor of the trained observer effort should periodically rerate 5 percent to 10 percent of the facilities or events assessed by each individual or team. The percentage of agreement between each rater and the supervisor should be computed, and any discrepancies should be discussed. (The observers should be informed that a sample of their ratings will be checked.)

  Special emphasis should be given to rechecking those items that received the "worst" assessments since these determine many of the key effectiveness measures. Verification of several of the worst ratings will also indicate whether the observers are rating some problems too harshly. (There is often a tendency to become too severe in rating moderate problems, especially when most facilities are in good condition.) Some ratings toward the middle of the scale should also be checked since these tend to be the hardest for the raters to distinguish accurately.

- The rating forms should be turned in as they are completed and reviewed by the judge or rating supervisor for errors, omissions, and logical consistency. If the ratings are entered directly into a hand-held computer, the computer can perform logical checks as the ratings are recorded and can require that any errors or omissions be corrected before the ratings continue.

- If the ratings are conducted over a period of several months or years, the trained observers should be periodically retested by the judge or rating supervisor. This can be done by having the observers rate photographs, slides, or videotapes of specific conditions or events, or by having them all rate the same site(s). The retest results should be compared with those of the judge and, where appropriate, analyzed for interrater reliability.

- When extensive trained observer ratings are to be conducted on a continuing basis, it can be helpful to create special computer programs for analyzing the ratings and identifying potential discrepancies. New York City has developed a number of programs for analyzing the weekly and monthly ratings prepared in connection with "Project Scorecard" (street cleanliness) and "School Scorecard" (condition of schools and playgrounds) (see Fund for the City of New York, 1983; Moore, 1988). The software estimates the reliability of individual raters and of the rating process as a whole from a statistical analysis of periodic rater "cross-checks" (in which all trained observers rate the same series of slides, buildings, or blockfaces). The cross-check data are also used to analyze differences *between* raters and to determine whether there is sufficient interrater consistency. In addition, each rater's latest ratings are checked against his or her past assessments of the same block or facility to identify unexplainable trends that might suggest that the rater is drifting from the prescribed rating standards.

If *any* of the quality control procedures described above indicate errors, discrepancies, or interrater reliability levels that exceed the established tolerances, the relevant problems should immediately be discussed with the observer(s) in question, with remedial training provided as necessary.

Analyzing and Presenting the Results

A wide variety of performance indicators can be prepared from the information collected by trained observers. For instance, such indicators can address the *overall* characteristics of facilities and events (an example would be the average number of maintenance problems found in a given type of building). It is also possible to prepare performance indicators that focus on the effectiveness of specific activities or on the incidence of specific types of problems.

The problem-based park maintenance ratings described previously illustrate the range of indicator options available. These results can usually be expressed in several alternate forms — as an "average" rating (average park cleanliness); as a percentage of the facilities rated (the percentage of ball fields with widespread maintenance problems); as a percentage of all the individual observations made (the percentage of all maintenance ratings that were "unsatisfactory"); or as an extreme (the number or percentage of park ratings that exceeded a certain critical level, the "worst" parks, the most common problems).

For some indicators, the trained observer results for specific items or features will first have to be classified as "satisfactory" or "unsatisfactory." For instance, a number of governments have determined that, for their purposes, a cleanliness rating of 2.5 or more on the four-point scale described in Table 10.2 and Exhibit 10.2 should be considered "unsatisfactory." Similarly, using the problem-oriented park rating scale described above (and illustrated in Exhibit 10.3), one could define a park or playground as being in "unsatisfactory" condition if it contains, say, one or more "widespread" maintenance problems, or — alternatively — if more than one-third of all the major park maintenance elements examined (ball fields, play areas, grass and lawns, and so forth) exhibit at least some problems. As noted previously, Dallas *designed* its housing condition scale so that a rating of 3 or more corresponded to an unsatisfactory situation (that is, one potentially in violation of city housing codes).

Unless the intervals between the points of the rating scale are equal in some absolute sense, the use of *average* ratings is not strictly correct and can distort the results. Although averages constitute a popular way to summarize numerical trained observer ratings, it is safer methodologically to use percentages (for instance, the percentage of ratings that exceed a given level). Percentages also have the advantage of being able to highlight the presence of serious problems, results that might be lost in an average rating.

The ratings can often be usefully disaggregated on the basis of geographic, demographic, and operational factors. For instance, park maintenance ratings can be broken down using the following categories:

- Type of facility (minipark, neighborhood park, recreation center)
- Neighborhood area, ward, or councilmanic district
- Maintenance district or service area
- Demographic characteristics of the neighborhood or clientele served (for example, income, racial mix, education)

Such breakouts can also be used to assess the *equity* with which services are being provided, that is, to identify differences in service outcomes between various neighborhoods and socioeconomic groups. In addition, the data can be grouped to examine the effects of potential confounding factors — weather, the timing of the observations, seasonality, traffic levels, or specific raters.

As noted previously, one of the advantages of trained observer ratings is that the results can be easily understood by the average citizen. Appropriate displays of the data can further enhance the accessibility and utility of the information. Figure 10.1 illustrates one such display, utilizing classroom maintenance ratings from New York's School Scorecard project.

Time, Cost, and Staffing Requirements

The cost of a trained observer effort is usually relatively modest, especially if existing personnel or citizen volunteers are available to conduct the ratings.

Total expenditures will depend on the number and type of facilities or events rated, whether the evaluator develops new rating scales or adapts materials used by others, the type of scales employed (multilevel, multi-attribute scales with photographic anchors versus single-problem "checklist" scales), and the frequency with which the ratings are repeated. Preparation of new, photographically anchored multi-attribute rating scales can require four weeks or more, while a set of single-attribute, problem-oriented rating scales can usually be developed in one to two weeks. Training typically requires no more than two to three days.

Some relatively small out-of-pocket expenses are also likely to be necessary. These include printing and reproducing the reference photographs, copying the forms and training manuals, underwriting vehicle expenses, and—in some cases—providing box lunches for volunteer raters during training.

The actual observations usually proceed rather quickly. On the average, an experienced trained observer team can rate a park in about thirty minutes. Trained observer assessments of classrooms, offices, public housing units, and similar facilities usually require twenty to thirty minutes per room. Skilled teams simultaneously rating several types of street conditions (rideability, cleanliness, traffic signs and signals) have been able to grade as many as 500 blocks a day traversing continuous, prespecified routes.

Adequate time, staff, and resources must also be devoted to quality control. As emphasized above, 5 percent to 10 percent of the results should be rerated by a "judge" or supervisor. A day or two should also be set aside for analyzing the follow-up results and for any retraining needed. The development of computer software for statistical analyses of rater and inter-rater reliability is potentially expensive and time-consuming unless one can adapt packages already used by other organizations. Such software is likely to be justified only in connection with extensive, multiperiod trained observer efforts.

Conclusions

Trained observer ratings can serve as an important program evaluation tool for assessing differences in key service quality conditions over time or in response to alternate programs. While not yet widespread, the technique can play a major role in program monitoring and in-depth program evaluation. Indeed, trained observer ratings are merely a systematic version of the kinds of inspections already used in connection with many government services. While most applications of trained observers up to now have focused on facility maintenance, the technique can be applied to a wide variety of conditions and outcomes—from assessing how crowded a bus is or how many petty street crimes occur to observing the posttreatment behavior of mental health patients and the quality of the care provided by nursing homes.

Figure 10.1. Presenting Trained Observer Results: An Example.

Citywide Summary

Percent of Schools at Each Scale Point (965 Schools)

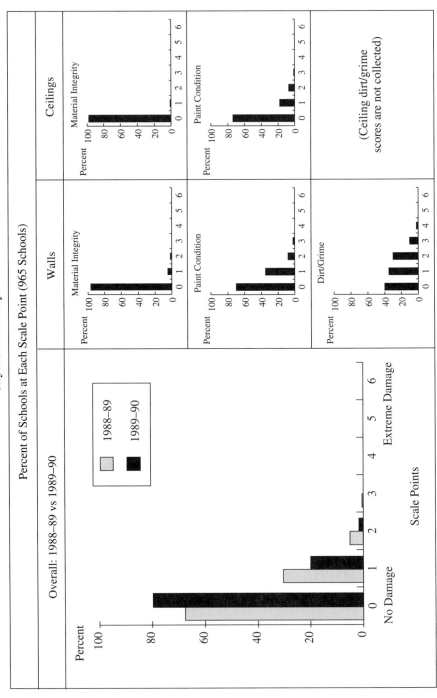

Figure 10.1. Presenting Trained Observer Results: An Example, Cont'd.

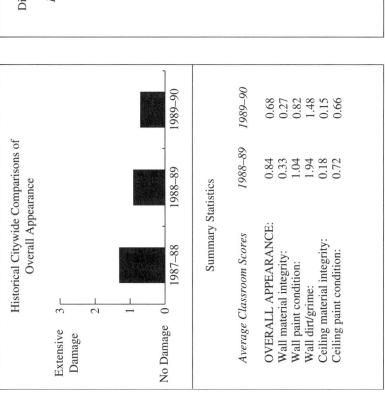

Historical Citywide Comparisons of Overall Appearance

Summary Statistics

Average Classroom Scores	1988–89	1989–90
OVERALL APPEARANCE:	0.84	0.68
Wall material integrity:	0.33	0.27
Wall paint condition:	1.04	0.82
Wall dirt/grime:	1.94	1.48
Ceiling material integrity:	0.18	0.15
Ceiling paint condition:	0.72	0.66

District Overall Appearance Rankings (Best to Worst)

District	Overall	District	Overall
5	0.37	27	0.67
13	0.43	Mn	0.67
26	0.43	3	0.67
31	0.45	29	0.71
25	0.48	17	0.71
16	0.48	1	0.72
75	0.48	8	0.75
7	0.50	14	0.78
2	0.50	19	0.78
SI	0.53	Bx	0.79
32	0.56	10	0.81
15	0.61	20	0.82
Qn	0.63	9	0.82
28	0.63	6	0.83
11	0.63	Bk	0.85
21	0.65	22	0.86
18	0.66	23	0.87
30	0.66	24	0.88
4	0.66		
12	0.67		

Source: T. Liebmann, "School Scorecard Report (Academic Year 1989–90)," School Scorecard Unit, New York City Board of Education (October 1990), p. 7.

With proper training and supervision, trained observer ratings exhibit a high degree of consistency between raters and over time. The resulting information can serve as the basis for accurate, reliable assessments of program outcomes and other key program characteristics. The technique offers a number of potential advantages. For instance, trained observer ratings tend to focus on conditions as experienced by citizens — the users of a program or facility. Such ratings can serve as a relatively inexpensive way to quantify conditions that would otherwise be difficult to measure. The ratings can usually be conducted by ordinary citizens, without the need for expensive "experts." And the approach can be readily understood by the public and by public administrators, which can help ensure the acceptance and utilization of the results.

These advantages must, however, be balanced against a number of potential disadvantages. For instance, trained observer ratings are usually practical only for assessing characteristics that can be readily and directly *sensed* or experienced by the rater. They are not usually suitable for rating complex or subtle conditions. The nominal or ordinal nature of many trained observer rating scales may preclude the use of averages and other familiar statistical measures and techniques. And considerable care must be exercised to ensure that the inherent subjectivity of the rating process does not impair the precision, repeatability, and interrater comparability of the results.

Most of the foregoing concerns can be addressed through careful design and implementation of the rating procedures — by appropriately selecting the characteristics to be graded, systematically developing the rating scales, carefully choosing and training the raters, ensuring adequate quality control, and properly analyzing the results. The importance of investing adequate time and resources on quality control cannot be overemphasized. The attention given to quality control, plus the care taken in developing and clearly documenting the various scales and procedures, elevates trained observer ratings from the status of "just watching" to a valid, systematic measurement technique capable of providing useful evaluative information for program managers, elected officials, and the general public.

References

"Before and After: Streets and Parks and the Returnable Container Law." *Public Papers of the Fund for the City of New York,* November 1985, *4* (entire issue 3).

Blair, L. H., and Schwartz, A. I. *How Clean Is Our City?* Washington, D.C.: The Urban Institute, 1972.

Center for Excellence in Local Government. "Achieving Excellence in Customer Service." Field Assessment Report for the City of Saratoga, California. Palo Alto, Calif.: Center for Excellence in Local Government, 1988.

City of Greenville. "City of Greenville Photographic Guide for the Evaluation of Park Maintenance." Greenville, S.C.: Office of Management and Budget, City of Greenville, 1990.

City of Kansas City. "Housing Conditions: Survey Results." Kansas City, Mo.: City Development Department, City of Kansas City, May 1989.

City of New York. "Detailed Condition Assessment." New York: Department of Parks and Recreation, City of New York, n.d.

Cronbach, L. J. *Essentials of Psychological Testing.* (2nd ed.) New York: Harper & Row, 1960.

Edwards, A. L. *Techniques of Attitude Scale Construction.* New York: Appleton-Century-Crofts, 1957.

Fund for the City of New York. "Development of Scorecard Monitoring System for the Department of Parks and Recreation." Final Report. New York: Fund for the City of New York, February 1978.

Fund for the City of New York. "Litter Survey Project." Progress Report. New York: Fund for the City of New York, August 1983.

Fund for the City of New York. *Police Patrol and Street Conditions.* New York: Fund for the City of New York, n.d.

Greiner, J. M. "The Impacts of Massachusetts' Proposition 2½ on the Delivery and Quality of Municipal Services." Washington, D.C.: The Urban Institute, September 1984.

Greiner, J. M., and Peterson, G. E. "Do Budget Reductions Stimulate Public Sector Productivity? Evidence from Proposition 2½ in Massachusetts." In G. E. Peterson and C. W. Lewis (eds.), *Reagan and the Cities.* Washington, D.C.: The Urban Institute, 1986.

Hatry, H. P., Greiner, J. M., and Swanson, M. *Monitoring the Quality of Local Government Services.* Management Information Service Report, *19*(2). Washington, D.C.: International City Management Association, February 1987.

Hatry, H. P., Morley, E., Barbour, G. P., Jr., and Pajunen, S. M. *Excellence in Managing: Practical Experiences from Community Development Agencies.* Washington, D.C.: The Urban Institute, 1991.

Hatry, H. P., and others. *How Effective Are Your Community Services? Procedures for Measuring Their Quality.* (2nd ed.) Washington, D.C.: The Urban Institute and the International City/County Management Association, 1992.

Health Care Financing Administration. *State Operations Manual: Provider Certification.* Transmittal 250. Baltimore, Md.: Health Care Financing Administration, U.S. Department of Health and Human Services, April 1992.

Herman, R. D., and Peroff, N. C. *Measuring City Agency Responsiveness: The Citizen-Surrogate Method.* Urban Data Service Reports, *13*(5). Washington, D.C.: International City Management Association, May 1981.

Institute for Public Transportation and the New York Public Interest Research Group. *Off the Track: Subway Service Derailed.* New York: Institute for Public Transportation and the New York Public Interest Research Group, 1980.

Liebmann, T. "School Scorecard Report (Academic Year 1989–90)." New York School Scorecard Unit, New York City Board of Education, October 1990.

Millar, R., and Millar, A. (eds.). *Developing Client Outcome Monitoring Systems:*

A Guide for State and Local Social Service Agencies. Washington, D.C.: The Urban Institute, 1981.

Miller, D. *Handbook of Research Design and Social Measurement.* (4th ed.) New York: Longman, 1983.

Moore, J. "School Scorecard Report (October, 1987–January, 1988)." New York: School Scorecard Unit, New York City Board of Education, March 1988.

Peter, L. J. *Peter's Quotations: Ideas for Our Time.* New York: Bantam Books, 1977.

Riccio, L. J., Miller, J., and Litke, A. "Polishing the Big Apple: How Management Science Has Helped Make New York Streets Cleaner." *Interfaces,* January–February 1986, *16*(1), 83–88.

Thomas, J. S. "Scorecard: Measuring Street Cleanliness." In F. O'R. Hayes and others, *Helping City Government Improve Productivity: An Evaluation of the Productivity Projects of the Fund for the City of New York.* Project report by Frederick O'R. Hayes Associates. New York: Fund for the City of New York, May 1980.

Thurstone, L. L., and Chave, E. J. *The Measurement of Attitude.* Chicago: University of Chicago Press, 1929.

"A Ticket to Clean Streets: Enforcing the Health and Administrative Code." *Public Papers of the Fund for the City of New York,* May 1982, *1* (entire issue 2).

TriData Corporation. "Rater's Manual for Capital Plant Assessment." (2nd ed.) Report for the Office of the City Manager — City of Charlottesville. Arlington, Va.: TriData Corporation, 1986.

The Urban Institute. "Guidelines for Trained Observer Ratings of Parks and Beaches." Washington, D.C.: The Urban Institute, October 1983.

Wilson, D. "The Use of Trained Observers to Evaluate Park Maintenance." Greenville, S.C.: Office of Management and Budget, City of Greenville, October 1989.

11

Designing and Conducting Surveys

Thomas I. Miller

Government administrators and elected officials love to claim that they possess a profound understanding of their public's needs, desires, and disaffection. Many of us suspect that their claim is more wish than wisdom. Day-to-day operations of government tend to be guided by an informal reading of public sentiment that is gleaned from citizen councils, the expert opinion of staff, friends of the managers, or wounded citizens whose complaints echo through city hall and fill the op-ed pages. Government officials seem to get closest to their constituents right after a snowstorm when the streets fail to get plowed fast enough, or when a military base is slated to be closed, or when a discount warehouse is planned for location adjacent to an established neighborhood.

Government administrators and elected officials are learning that storms of controversy provide meager evidence of the workaday values of the everyday people they govern. Surveys of the public, conducted following the basic precepts of survey design and analysis discussed in this article, are fast becoming the vehicle for genuine connection to the civic will. The results of a good citizen survey may represent the closest thing to the bottom line that officials of government — that nonprofit service-providing monopoly — can ever hope for. As Americans become ever more skeptical about receiving good value for the exploding costs of education, health care, personal safety, and other public services, the demand for accountability is erupting. Customer surveys, long a management tool in business, are becoming a first-line indicator of what is working and what is failing in government.

Surveys of the typical public, however, can give much more than evaluations of government service, though such evaluations arguably provide the most critical use to which surveys can be put. Answers to questions from a representative sample of community adults can show the changing demography of a jurisdiction — a shift toward lower-income residents, more single

271

fathers, more elderly people living alone (as in the federal government's Current Population Survey)—which can foreshadow shifts in service demand. A good survey can tell who uses certain government services and who doesn't, and why; and it can identify problems that could not be discovered using any other method (as in national crime victimization surveys). Surveys can tell how new programs might be viewed and what's not working with programs already in place. Surveys can even inform managers about how to inspire government personnel to provide better assistance to the public.

Many public administrators are shy of using this technology, being more comfortable with the traditional ways of keeping in touch with the public—and other ways can be effective in answering critical questions about the quality and direction of government. Administrative records, records about citizen complaints, and observers trained to scout out high-quality or shoddy government work can provide excellent foundations for judgments about government quality, efficiency, and general policy.

Surveys, however, have a number of important qualities: citizen surveys offer anonymity to respondents—these days the essential bodyguard to free speech when we are invited to speak truth to government; surveys structure answers to questions so that the point of view, characteristics, or use patterns of the governed can be summarized with little confusion; and good surveys, unlike any of the traditional methods of citizen input, provide citizen participation from a representative cross-section of the population—not just the most impassioned, the least busy, or the most vigorous.

In this chapter I describe the best ways to begin the survey enterprise, how to design the survey and to decide the best means of survey administration (mail, phone, in-person), how to construct the questionnaire, how to conduct the survey, and how to analyze and report the results.

Begin Before the Beginning

Good customer surveys are not just technically sound. The best surveys grow from well-conceived and well-articulated reasons for doing them. A survey done because a state legislator thought it was a good idea or one conducted because "we need some more information" is destined to prop up the short end of a conference table or gather dust on a shelf. The absolute first step for managers is to focus their attention on the reasons for doing the survey and the use to which the survey findings will be put.

Resist the temptation to hit the ground running by rushing to write questions or to hire some consultant to draft a questionnaire. Hitting the ground is simple. It's running that requires the warm-up. The author witnessed the crash of a poorly conceived survey about the arts in which questions were asked regarding residents' attendance at art events, their expenditures on art, their philanthropy toward art, and their own artistic endeavors. Although connected by "art," the questions were otherwise so unfocused and without apparent practical value that a recipient probably would not have been surprised to be asked whether he thought Elvis were still alive. Response was meager.

Be certain of the purposes of the survey. Write down what will be done differently with the results if they lean in one direction versus another. Identify the appropriate audiences. The arts survey was done to develop an arts master plan for a medium-sized community. No thought was given to ways other than a survey to gather information useful to the master plan — for example, on attendance, costs, expenditures, and philanthropic donations. Little distinction was made between the kinds of questions relevant to members of the public and those appropriate for private sector donors or the artists themselves.

Identify the political or personal will for doing the survey. Know what resources are available for conducting it. Make sure the real value of in-kind donations to the project are considered and be certain to calculate time as one of the most precious resources. The hapless arts survey mentioned above required the director of the Arts Council to spend two days photocopying and stuffing letters because $200 could not be found for a professional printer.

Before starting to write questions, determine whether the questionnaire to be developed will be most useful if it is conducted periodically rather than only one time. And think about the usefulness of comparative data so that the answers to questions you write will have richer meaning and greater utility.

Getting Started

Let us say that the task to be undertaken is to conduct a broad multipurpose citizen survey because a city council wants to get residents' opinions about policy options and service delivery and to get a sense of who lives in the community and who uses certain local services. Here are two guidelines that may be useful:

Convene a steering committee. Make certain that key stakeholders for survey results participate. This committee will give ideas that otherwise might never have been contemplated about the most appropriate topic areas for questions. And the participation of these key players will prevent carping about questionnaire construction and survey administration after the results come in.

Enlist the help of the top government officials. The agency manager, chief executive officer, or, for state and local governments, elected officials can be asked to lend their names by signing a letter introducing the survey or allowing workers to mention the officials' names in a phone call to increase residents' participation in the survey enterprise.

Designing the Survey

After the survey is designed, the next step is to decide who will be asked to respond to it. The most crucial decision in this phase concerns sampling, which is discussed below.

Sampling

With unlimited resources, sampling residents to participate in a survey would be no one's first choice. The reason we ask some but not all residents to answer our survey questions is that we don't have the resources to get everyone to participate. When every resident, or every user of a service, or all members of the target population answer questions, this is not a sample survey. Responses from everyone in the target population represent a census, defined in *Webster's Ninth New Collegiate Dictionary* as "complete enumeration of a population." Since a census is out of financial and time bounds for most needs, we must decide how to get *some* respondents to represent *all* respondents in the target population. This is what sampling is all about.

A sampling plan must give every resident in the community, state, or nation a known and independent chance to participate. This is the hallmark of what most laypeople refer to as a "scientific" survey. The opportunity for survey participation must not be biased. Interviewers who phone only their friends are unlikely to get a fair cross-section of the opinion no matter how wide a social net they cast. Interviewers who avoid administering an in-person questionnaire in low-income, high-crime areas likely will not get representative opinions about crime.

On the other hand, selecting every tenth person who walks into the mall between 9 and 10 A.M., 12 and 1 P.M., and 7 and 8 P.M. regardless of his or her size, ethnicity, surly demeanor, or high-brow clothing is likely to produce a better, fairer, more representative sample of that day's shoppers than allowing an interviewer to choose, haphazardly, whom and when to contact — no matter what the purpose of the survey. An approximation of random selection of survey participants — taking every *n*th person, choosing phone numbers in some random fashion — is the touchstone of good survey design.

Whom should respondents represent? All adult residents of the jurisdiction? If so, then sending the questionnaire in the utility bill probably won't do because some renters will be missed. Leaving the questionnaire at the city's recreation centers or publishing it in the paper likely won't get a sample of respondents whose demographic characteristics match the city's.

If the plan is to use results for designing an education campaign for the upcoming vote on the ballot amendment to raise state sales taxes for schools, draw every *n*th name from a list of active registered voters. If the question concerns emergency medical service, you might start with the complete list of people who called for or received that service during the last twelve months. Sample every *n*th person from that list. If vehicle occupancy along Main Street is what matters, then the target population is sampled (every *n*th car) from all cars along Main Street.

Ideal sampling requires a list of all possible participants who fit the target population. In the gray metal drawers of the real world, ideal lists don't exist. Consequently, a list of all possible participants must be developed or a method for selecting participants must be chosen that simulates a lottery in which residents are picked approximately at random.

For example, if ratings from last month's social service clients are sought and, in anticipation of the survey, the list of names and phone numbers of visitors has been collected, then a reasonable number of names can be chosen from the list by taking every tenth person. Start at some number between 1 and 10, chosen at random, and cycle through the list. (For example, choose the third person listed, then the thirteenth, twenty-third, thirty-third, and so on.)

If a sample of residents of the state is required, go through an analogous process using a commercial address listing service, one that includes the correct mailing address for every single-family home and apartment in the state. In this case, the computers of the address listing service will cycle through the entire list of thousands of dwelling units to select the relatively few households needed for the survey.

If a sample of service users are to be contacted at their homes, consider conducting the survey over the phone. You can use the phone book to select the sample—if an important twist is added. The phone book omits unlisted numbers (which, in some communities, includes over 20 percent of all phones), but residents with unlisted numbers should be covered in the survey, too. An adequate compromise is to cycle through the phone book (choosing numbers at every seventh column inch, for example) and then adding 1 to the phone number chosen. (If the ruler lands on 444–2639, dial 444-2640.) This so-called plus one dialing usually reflects the correct percentage of prefixes in the jurisdiction and gives everyone with a working phone a chance to be questioned.

More sophisticated variations on these simple random selection processes are possible. When the target population is first divided into meaningful groups and then a random sample is chosen from each group, this is called a stratified random sample. The stratified sample can increase the precision of estimate about communitywide opinion by decreasing sampling error. For example, in North Conrad, trash is hauled by private vendors, but in South Conrad, the city hauls the trash. Opinions about the quality of trash pickup may vary greatly depending on the area of town a person resides in.

If you want an estimate of the number of vehicles occupied by only one person on collector street ABC, select certain intersections for observation points. These intersections become clusters in which cars are sampled at random during the morning and evening rush hours (strata). This is a stratified random cluster sample. All such variations have implications for the precision of estimates about the target population. It is best to consult a survey research expert about the more complex survey designs (for example, Kish, 1965).

Targeting the Individual in the Household

Most surveys are conducted to get estimates of the opinions or circumstances of an entire community or an entire group of service recipients. When you can obtain the names of service recipients, it is possible to address the survey mailing to them or to ask for them directly on the phone or in person. But when a variety of information from community adults is sought, there won't be any names to start with. At best there will be a list of phone numbers or addresses. But phone numbers and addresses only permit a random sample of *households* when what is desired is a random, representative, sample of the *people* inside those households.

Achieving random sampling can be accomplished by mail (or by using a variation on the phone or in-person survey) with the following simple addition to the letter of invitation that accompanies the survey: "Please select the adult (anyone eighteen years or older) who most recently had his or her birthday. Please understand that year of birth plays no role in the choice." This will involve household members other than the most curious letter opener, the one with the most time to participate, the retired, or the elderly citizen.

Mail, Phone, or In-Person Interviews

In our collection of local government citizen surveys from around the country (Miller and Miller, 1991a), we found that the mailed survey was the most popular means of contacting residents (43 percent), followed by the phone survey (40 percent) and the personal interview (3 percent). About 6 percent used some combination of methods.

Deciding the best ways to survey the target population requires considerations of accuracy, speed, and cost. Although the need for low cost and quick reply can greatly influence the survey process, accuracy is the touchstone of survey sampling excellence. Accuracy refers to the extent to which respondents represent the population. A survey completed in twenty-four hours for free is worth nothing if its results cannot be generalized to the target population. Accuracy is affected by response rates, confidentiality, the type, order, and number of questions as well as coverage, or the ability of the survey to reach the target population.

Accuracy

The accuracy of a survey instrument can be affected by a number of different elements. The most important of these are discussed below.

Response Rates. City XYZ mailed a survey to residents and got a 25 percent response rate. The survey coordinator told city council members, "Twenty-five percent is pretty good for a mail survey. You can trust these results." The coordinator was wrong on two counts. Twenty-five percent is *not* a good response rate, even for a mailed survey on civic issues, and if the survey coordinator did nothing to test the accuracy of his sample of XYZ residents, the results should not be trusted, either.

These days, although there are noticeable differences in the response rates of excellent phone, mail, and in-person surveys, the differences tend to be small and the response rates of all three methods are low enough to require some investigation of or adjustment for those who do not respond. It is generally accepted that a well-conducted mail-out/mail-back survey can net a 45 percent–55 percent response rate. For phone surveys, response rates tend to fall between 60 percent and 75 percent while in-person interviews can net responses of around 85 percent. The difference in rates is, in itself, not enough to merit the choice of one method over another.

Nevertheless, response rates should be as high as possible since, with fewer respondents, larger differences are likely between the sample and the population it is supposed to represent. Response rates will tend to be better if administrators provide translators where one or two large minorities in a target population are unlikely to respond well to a questionnaire in English. Rates will increase if multiple attempts are made to contact hard-to-reach groups, if return postage is paid, when civic responsibilities are invoked by an inspiring cover letter, and when questions are clear, simply worded, and relatively few in number.

Confidentiality. An anonymous response is not the same as a confidential response. An anonymous response is given by a person whose answers cannot be traced to him or his household while a confidential response is made to someone who knows the identity (or location) of the respondent but promises not to divulge it. For a person wary of government's intentions, anonymity is the only absolute safeguard; confidentiality is a reasonable compromise.

Phone or in-person interviewers can promise only confidentiality of response, not anonymity. Once the respondent realizes that his location or name is known by the interviewer, his answers may be tainted. For example, imagine a respondent who, because of newspaper report and rumor, thinks that most of the local elected officials and all the top administrators are pro gay rights. The respondent believes in equal protection under local laws, but at the same time he has a strong personal dislike of homosexuals. When an interviewer calls or drops by, the resident may say that he approves of a proposed municipal antidiscrimination code to guarantee homosexuals equal rights in housing, but in fact, he or she may be feeling what is presumed to be community pressure to support the sexual preference code. Although influence of social pressure is greatest at in-person interviews, it operates by phone, too. (The November 1992 general election in Colorado proves the point. Tracking polls conducted by phone showed Amendment 2 — to omit homosexuals from equal rights protections — to be an overwhelming loss. In fact, voters passed it better than 56 percent to 44 percent.)

Mailed surveys that guarantee anonymity protect the respondent as much as is possible from feeling pressure to record the "right" things or from feeling angry about government intrusion. Nevertheless, some pressure and anger will linger even in the mailed survey, but absent from the mailed survey will be any threat that interviewer biases can influence answers given by residents. Such biases can occur in phone or in-person interviews.

Type of Question. The kinds of questions typically asked in a citizen survey lend themselves to all three methods of citizen contact. However, uncharacteristically complicated questions that may require visual aids, long answers, or substantial explanation and follow-up (probing) are best conducted during in-person interviews.

Most citizen surveys, especially those in which quality of services and quality of life are evaluated, rely on fewer and simpler questions. When the citizen survey includes policy questions, however, mailed questionnaires have advantages over the phone interview. The mailed questionnaire can incorporate diagrams or graphics to explain questions that would be difficult to convey (with today's technology) over the phone. Also, the mailed questionnaire lends itself better to lists wherein items must be put into priority—like choosing the three most important recreation facilities among a list of twenty (a very difficult task to accomplish over the phone). And the mailed questionnaire is simpler than phone interviews when questions call for repetitive responses—like rating each of twenty services on a scale of Excellent, Good, Fair, Poor.

Question Order. When question order is important, phone and in-person surveys are best. Perhaps most of the questionnaire is designed to evoke respondents' attitudes toward specific water conservation activities, but some of the questions relate to how respondents value water conservation in relation to other environmental concerns, like hazardous waste, air pollution, and groundwater contamination. Begin the phone interview without identifying its specific purpose (water conservation techniques); instead, give a more general reason for conducting the survey: "This survey is designed to find out what residents of Carlton think about several important issues facing the community today."

Question 1 may start, "I am going to name several environmental activities. Please tell me which one you feel has been most effective in your neighborhood. Which is the next most effective? The third most effective?" . . . "Abatement of water contamination, hazardous waste, air pollution, wildlife mismanagement, wetlands destruction, or the institution of water conservation?"

If this question appeared first on a mailed questionnaire, respondents might thumb through the entire instrument before returning to question one to give an answer. Were this violation of question order to occur, be assured that, alerted to the specific purpose of the study, more respondents would choose water conservation than if they had no chance to peek at the other questions (most of which focus on water conservation). Controlling question order occurs best by phone or in-person.

Coverage. Coverage refers to the ability of a particular survey contact method to reach the target population. For example, surveys of particular areas or neighborhoods of a community can be conducted best by in-person interviews or mailed questionnaires. Since phone numbers dialed at random rarely permit knowledge about residence location, phone surveys require screening questions to eliminate respondents outside the geographic areas of interest.

Mailed surveys often require from respondents good reading and writing skills, which may limit the surveys' coverage. To avoid compromising the ability to generalize results, you should consider an alternative. Populations with reading skills that are not good can be surveyed by phone or in-person; this way, which does not require the least educated to read, helps reduce their attrition, thus avoiding a possible skewing of the results.

Phone surveys, especially those using random-digit dialing have the advantage — like mailed questionnaires — of being able to reach all residents with access to phones, even those living in high-crime areas, dormitories, barracks, or in homes with unlisted numbers. Those without access to phones, however, typically are the poorest residents; mailed or in-person interviews will be required to ensure their participation. In-person interviews do not enjoy the same ease of access as phone surveys because interviewers may be reluctant to visit low-income areas, especially those with well-known crime problems.

Speed

No survey contact method is faster than the telephone. For a quick reading of sentiments about a ballot issue, a phone survey can be administered in a week or less (presuming the questionnaire itself is ready to go). However, the typical citizen survey requires no such rush and can be completed in a month's time by mail or in-person with the necessary follow-ups.

Cost

Unfortunately, with respect to cost, the in-person interview still is the costliest of survey contact methods. Getting interviewers into the field, returning when necessary to temporarily unoccupied residences, can be very expensive — so expensive, in fact, that this method of contact is rarely used for citizen surveys despite its other advantages over phone and mail.

Phone interviews can be expensive, too, roughly $15 to $20 per completed interview if all costs of design, administration, analysis, and reporting are included. By comparison, mailed questionnaires are a bargain. With adequate follow-up, mailed questionnaires can cost as little as $8 to $12 per completed survey (40 percent to 60 percent of the costs for a completed phone survey) including round trip postage, graphic layout of the survey instrument, photoreproduction of the survey and cover letters, survey and letter folding, envelope printing, envelope stuffing, editing and handling of the surveys once returned, and one reminder mailing with a second printing of the survey, data analysis, and reporting. And with mailed surveys, the cost per survey declines as the number of surveys goes up because with greater volume the cost per unit of photocopying and materials declines. Table 11.1 presents a summary of the relative strengths of each method for contacting respondents.

Table 11.1. Relative Strengths of Methods for Contacting Respondents.

Criteria	Mail	Phone	In-Person
Accuracy			
Response rate	45–55%	65–75%	75%+
Permits anonymity	High	Moderate	Low
Is free from interviewer bias	High	Moderate	Low
Handles various question types			
Long/complex	Low	Moderate	High
Visual aids	High	Low	High
Ensures question order	Low	High	High
Permits widest coverage			
Targets specific geographic areas	High	Low	High
Avoids education bias	Low	Moderate	High
Gives easy access to target population	High	High	Moderate
Speed of Administration	Month	Week	Month
Cost per Interview	$8–12	$15–20	>$20

Note: In this table, *high* means that this contact method satisfies the criterion best; *low* is worst compared to the other two methods.

Increasing Response Rates

A single mailing rarely produces an adequate response to a mailed survey. Generally, multiple mailings are needed — not only of a request for participation but of the questionnaire itself in case the prospective respondent has discarded the questionnaires sent earlier. Two mailings is a minimum. Three mailings is about all that can be expected within most survey budgets. Each mailing must include a self-addressed, stamped envelope to make returning the questionnaire easy.

Some press coverage planned for the initiation of the survey and two weeks later will help inform potential respondents that the survey is underway. When the research is complete, the results must receive adequate press coverage if the next survey research venture is to have credibility.

Because no single contact method is best, a combination is often the preferred approach. As long as sufficient planning occurs to avoid a rush, a mailed citizen survey with phone and in-person follow-up of nonrespondents often will provide the most accurate sample at the most reasonable price. As costs for in-person and phone follow-up generally are prohibitive, added to mailed questionnaires, we usually take a random sample of the addresses already sampled — that is, those who were sent a questionnaire but did not return it. That second sample is used for nonrespondent surveying to adjust results, if necessary. A phone directory that lists addresses in alphabetical order by street name is consulted. Where phone numbers for specific addresses can be obtained, phone calls are made. Where no phone number is listed, an interviewer is sent to the unit to drop off a questionnaire personally or to administer it in person.

Selecting Sample Size

It is not necessary to worry about sampling a minimum percentage of the target population. Surveys to predict winners in the presidential elections are based on less than one one-hundredth of 1 percent of the nation's voters. The minimum number to sample depends largely on how precise the estimates — of opinions, income, driving habits — need to be. That precision, in turn, depends on how variable opinions, income, or driving habits are in the jurisdiction.

Our estimate is almost certain to be inaccurate to some degree when a portion of residents or cars or households must reflect the opinions or circumstances of all residents or cars or households. If we wanted to estimate the height of all four-year-old girls in the United States, the average height of two four-year-old girls chosen at random would likely be pretty imprecise. The average height of a million girls, chosen at random, probably would be pretty close to the average height of the two million girls of that age living in the United States. This imprecision is called sampling error and it is intrinsic to the enterprise of selecting at random some cases to represent all cases.

A simple rule of thumb helps specify the sampling size. Generally, the maximum uncertainty due to sampling error — the margin of error, in journalistic terms — is expressed as a function of the absolute number of people sampled and the amount by which they differed in what is being measured. In opinion sampling, if everyone held the same opinion, one person only would reflect accurately the opinion of everyone. If opinions were split as much as possible (50 percent for the bond issue, 50 percent opposed), *then 100 residents chosen at random would give a margin of error — the 95 percent confidence interval in statistical terms — of ± 10 percent. With 400 people taken in a simple random sample, the margin of error drops by half to ± 5* percent. Even confidence intervals of 90 percent suffice in many cases (± 4 percent instead of 5 percent).

The precision required must be quantified. Will the Senate subcommittee be able to make an informed decision if the sample is 100 state residents of whom 56 percent favor the limited gambling initiative? The margin of error suggests that if all state adults were queried, somewhere between 46 percent and 66 percent of the population would favor the initiative. With 400 respondents, the 95 percent confidence interval ranges from 51 percent to 61 percent.

In another example, because of suspected contamination, it may be necessary to compare water quality as perceived by those residents living north of County Line Road to those living south of County Line Road. In that case, sample *no fewer than 100 in each area of concern.* And if the resources exist to sample 400 in each area, the results will be twice as precise in both sectors of the county.

Generally, for government surveys, 100 is a useful minimum number to accept *within each area or group for which estimates are required* — north and south; those living in single-family homes, apartments, or mobile homes; those driving on main arterials, collectors, side streets, or country roads. And if resources exist to sample 400 within each group, estimates could be twice as accurate.

Questionnaire Construction

The first precept of questionnaire design is that each question proposed should be judged against the purposes for which the survey is to be conducted and the uses for the information it will generate. Questions that are simply interesting should be deferred until money and time flow like water from faucets. Questions that ask all residents to evaluate services they seldom receive — like fire, emergency medical, or police services — will elicit a general impression about safety in the community but will give little evidence about how service recipients are treated by public safety personnel.

The second most important precept of questionnaire design is to steal widely. Three phone calls will net questions already asked by others that are relevant to your interests. The National Citizen Survey, a multipurpose questionnaire can be obtained free from the Center for Survey Comparisons, 3755 Sixteenth Street, Boulder, Colorado 80304; (303) 443-2200. Along with this generic instrument can come national norms of citizen evaluations of a variety of government services. Finally, many college extension services conduct surveys that professors will share. Other jurisdictions or archives in your own jurisdiction, no doubt, will reveal possible questions. Excellent references abound (Hatry and others, 1992; Miller and Miller, 1991a; Lavrakas, 1990; Fink and Kosecoff, 1985).

Excellent books have provided guidelines for writing survey questions (Sudman and Bradburn, 1982; Converse and Presser, 1976), but for the crafter of citizen surveys some general principles and specific examples will probably provide adequate foundation for building the survey instrument. The major principles, discussed below, address consistency, clarity, simplicity, security, and fairness.

Consistency

The beauty and the sorrow of open-ended questions become clear as we think about questions of consistency. Open-ended questions do not put words in the mouths of residents and they often seem so simple. But unless they are *very* simple — like "In what year were you born?" or "How many cans of Coca-Cola did you recycle today?" — they can be interpreted in many different ways. And compared to the answers to forced choice or close-ended questions, answers to open-ended questions can be nightmares to summarize. It is often best to pretest a questionnaire using many open-ended questions and then to offer as fixed options in the final survey the most common responses from the pretest.

Clarity

One of the deadliest threats to accuracy is questions that can be misinterpreted. The following section discusses the most common errors made in developing questions and how to avoid them.

    Vague Wording.
1.   "Do most people on your block feel that they have a lot in common with their neighbors, a little, or not much in common?"
2.   "Downtown Carlton should be more clearly defined. Agree__ Disagree__"
3.   "Has Carlton dealt effectively with blighted housing? Yes__ No__"

These questions all suffer the same shortcoming. They are vague. Who knows what most people on their block feel? By asking what the respondent feels, part of the vagueness to question 1 is removed. But what does it mean to have a lot in common with neighbors? Does this refer to material possessions, values, family status?

    No one can write a question that will be interpreted precisely the same way by every respondent, but special attention to possible misinterpretation can avoid many ambiguities that frequently appear in surveys. Common words with presumed meanings often are sinkholes for miscommunication. The words *income, frequently, transit, last year,* or *unemployed* are notoriously ambiguous. They should be replaced or modified with more precise terms; for example, in place of *frequently* use the number of times the activity may have occurred. *Income* becomes "total household income before taxes or deductions from all sources including gifts, welfare payments, interest, wages, tips, and personal income from private business or investments."

    Double-Barreled Questions. Survey questions can become muddled in other ways than by use of vague terms. The most common mistake in surveys is use of double-barreled questions. These are two or more questions masquerading as one. A few examples tell the whole story.

1.   "Do you feel the City of Carlton has been too tough, about right, or not tough enough in enforcing the city codes on such nuisances as animal control, weeds, messy yards, junk cars, and noise?
   Too Tough__ About Right__ Not Tough Enough__ Don't Know__"
2.   "I like the use of agricultural themes in Carlton's architecture, displays, and commercial art.
   Yes__ No__ Don't Know__"
3.   "Was the city employee courteous and helpful?
   Yes__ No__ Don't Know__"

Respondents may have competing opinions about the two or three options hidden in each question but they have a place to express only one opinion.

    Assumed Knowledge. Some survey questions confuse respondents because they assume knowledge or circumstances that may be untrue. For example, "By what means did you commute to work last week? auto, van, bus, bike, walk, other (circle all that apply)." What is the retired respondent to do? Or the student? It would be better to precede this question with a question like, "Did you commute to work or school last week?" Ask last week's commuters only the mode of travel they used.

Overlapping Response Categories. Imprecision of response options that are not mutually exclusive often makes citizen survey questions unclear. Respondents will answer questions that have overlapping categories, but there is a good chance that those with answers in the gray zone would give a different response to the same question if confronted with it a second time.

Any response category whose meaning is not distinguishable from other response categories can be considered an overlapping response. For example, how should a respondent interpret the following response options — Excellent, Very Good, Good, Poor, Bad? Not only is it virtually impossible to understand when a local service is poor but not bad, it is quite difficult for respondents to distinguish Excellent from Very Good.

Options indicating frequencies of behavior typically create distinctions without differences. Can respondents reliably distinguish among the first four options in Almost Always, Frequently, Usually, Sometimes, Rarely, Never? If at all possible, substitute frequency ranges for these ambiguous words — "On average, about how often did you put out newspapers for recycling from your home during the last twelve months . . . every week, one to three times per month, less than once a month but more than two times during the year, once or twice during the year, never?"

Age and income categories frequently suffer from imprecision portrayed in overlapping response options. For example, "How old are you? 18–25, 25–35, 35–45 . . . 65–75, 75 + ."

Simplicity

The simpler the questionnaire, the more likely it is to be understood and completed. To enhance simplicity, make the questions specific, short, and risk free, and place them in a context that will not influence answers. This is easier said than done.

Specificity. Specific questions give more reliable answers than general questions. "How are things these days? Very good, good, bad, or very bad." Such a question is so general that the same person may interpret it differently at different times. It is better if the interpretation is added by the questionnaire constructor. Try, "How do you rate your overall quality of life in Carlton?"

But sometimes the search for simplicity conflicts with the desire for specificity. For example, more reliable answers can be expected to a question like, "How often does traffic noise interfere with conversations in your home when windows are closed?" than a question worded, "How much of a problem, if any, is traffic noise in your neighborhood?" But the more specific question is longer. It is worthwhile to be mindful of trade-offs, but no pat formula exists for a trade-off between brevity and specificity.

Brevity. Long questions, especially in mailed questionnaires, are going to lose respondents. On complex questions, it is often impossible (and undesirable) to sacrifice understanding for brevity. Nevertheless, even complex questions must be succinct as they identify pros and cons of the issues. No complete description of all policy benefits or drawbacks is possible, but the key issues can be presented clearly and in a few sentences.

Should the number of questions grow so numerous that phone surveys exceed thirty minutes, in-person interviews exceed sixty minutes, and written questionnaires surpass ten pages, it may be wise either to reduce the number of questions or submit half the questions to a random half of the respondents and the other half of the questions to the remaining respondents. With only half the sample receiving certain questions, the precision of results will be reduced. Therefore, the number of respondents would have to be increased to regain the accuracy lost by dividing the questions among the original sample, or less precision would have to be tolerated.

Context Sensitivity. Don't create a hodgepodge by mixing questions that don't seem to go together. Respondents may be put off by what appears to be a disorganized questionnaire and their motivation to respond might flag. Notice how wary the following few questions might make a respondent feel.

Q 1. How do you rate street repair in your neighborhood?
Q 2. How do you rate your overall quality of life in Carlton?
Q 3. What was your total household income in 1990?
Q 4. Do you think that Carlton parks should receive more, less, or about the same budget as they do now?
Q 5. Are you aware of Carlton's Neighborhood Watch program?

Keep budget questions together. Ask all service evaluations in one section. If an agency wants to obtain citizen feedback on various policy issues, put policy questions toward the end, especially if they are moderately complex. End with demographic questions.

Finally, the context of a question can affect the answers. For example, questions asking respondents to identify whether they have purchased low-flow water fixtures are likely to affect any subsequent question intended to determine respondents' attitude toward water conservation in general. Or a set of questions about locations of potholes, auto damage due to unmaintained streets, and problems due to street sand or salt are likely to evoke a more negative evaluation of street repair that follows.

Security

Even the most innocuous questionnaire may intimidate respondents unused to the data collection exercise. It is best to put respondents at ease at the outset by asking questions that are not threatening, that are easy to answer, and that are interesting. For this reason, most demographic questions are relegated to the end of a questionnaire.

Many people would not want to continue the survey if the first question was "How old are you?" or "What is your annual income from all sources before taxes?" or "What is your ethnicity?" Such questions are easier to take after some trust is built (whether in-person, on the phone, or by mail) that there is a good reason for the survey and that the demographic questions will apply to that survey purpose.

In the process of going from general to specific (a process that survey researchers call funneling), respondents may be asked to give an overall evaluation of snow removal, and then to evaluate snow removal on major streets, snow removal on side streets. Then respondents may be asked to evaluate the speed of snow removal, the ability of sand trucks to cover the major streets quickly, and the safety of streets after sand trucks have passed.

Fairness

A survey will deliver useful evaluations of public services, quality of life, budget, and policy options only if the questions permit respondents the opportunity to give the full range of their opinions. A policy option can be presented in such a way that only a fool would be unaware of the "correct" response. If evaluations of city services are made on a scale from Great to Good, no one can give bad ratings.

Option Symmetry. Most cities ask residents to evaluate services on a stilted four point scale: Excellent, Good, Fair, or Poor (EGFP). While this is standard practice and it permits the full range of responses, EGFP provides more positive options (excellent, good, and fair) than negative options (poor); as a result, the number of respondents who do not give bad ratings probably is inflated compared to the number who would give bad ratings on a symmetrical scale (say, Very Good, Good, Bad, Very Bad). The positive response choice might make for great politics but it will produce lousy research.

The effect of biased response options can be appreciated better with several examples that are more obviously asymmetrical than EGFP. One gets the impression from reading these response options that city fathers and mothers don't really want to know (1) if they are doing a bad job or (2) how bad a job they are doing. One city, long in the business of citizen surveying, provides four baldly positive options and still cannot get itself to permit residents to register a bitter complaint in the only "negative" option remaining: "How satisfied are you with XYZ's snow removal? Extremely Satisfied, Very Satisfied, Satisfied, Slightly Satisfied, Not at All Satisfied."

Unbiased response options are symmetrical. Balanced responses have as many positive choices as negative. Examples include Very Good, Good, Bad, Very Bad; Very Satisfied, Satisfied, Dissatisfied, Very Dissatisfied

Strongly Agree, Agree, Disagree, Strongly Disagree; Too much, Too little, About right; Increase, Remain the Same, Decrease; Better than nearly all cities, Better than most cities, The same as most cities, Worse than most cities, Worse than nearly all cities.

Neutral middle categories are fine to add to symmetrical four point scales, too. For example, Neither good nor bad, Neither satisfied nor dissatisfied, Neither agree nor disagree, or No opinion.

Option Wording and Order. The wording of policy options can make a meaningful difference in how opinions are reported by city or county residents. Since most policy options are at least moderately complicated, it is essential that core aspects of the issue are communicated in the question succinctly and with equity to opponents and supporters. To do this fairly, help from advocates of all sides of the policy issue is required.

It generally is helpful to communicate a policy question by beginning with a short statement of background information, following with a summary of the pros and cons of the proposal, and ending with a request for opinion.

When the issues are weighty, it is helpful — but somewhat more expensive and complex — to alter the arguments so that the pro side is given first on a random half of the questionnaires and con is given first on the other random half. A separate analysis of results will tell if the order of argument swamped the importance of the issue itself.

Conducting the Survey

After the survey is completed, there is still preparation to do before you administer it. It needs to be reviewed by those who are knowledgeable; it needs a test administration to expose any ambiguities in the questions; assistants who will administer it must be trained. These steps and others are discussed below.

The Survey Steering Committee

Double check the survey questions and their layout with the survey steering committee before administering the survey. The committee will need to approve the questions, their "look" if administration is by mail, the avowed purpose of the survey as stated in a written or oral introduction, the timing of the survey and its anticipated completion, and any plan for the dissemination and use of results.

The committee members do not have to be methodological wizards; methods are the job of the survey researcher. Instead, members should represent geographic or policy areas to which the results will apply; an important part of their function is to represent points of view that conflict. Consensus on methods must be achieved before surveying begins.

Frequency of Surveys

Periodic surveys that evaluate government services have the advantage of providing solid evidence about residents' changing perceptions of government operation. However, a love of solid evidence is hard to sustain, especially when service evaluations tend not to change much from year to year. Though it lacks the thrill of steeply sloped graphs of economic cycles, the solid, barely moving trend of residents' perceptions is the steadfast foundation on which management decisions must be made and it requires the patience and investment given to the construction of any building foundation. Only when a noticeable deviation occurs from a fairly smooth trend line does the deviation, in itself, cry justifiably for attention.

In most communities where multipurpose surveys are done to evaluate services, the surveys are conducted no more frequently than once each year. More frequent surveying has the advantage of including changes that may be important from one season to the next. For example, surveys about crime or driving habits will change significantly from quarter to quarter in northern states where seasons affect such behaviors. Reports on changes each quarter may be more than many managers and citizen boards can digest, but an annual summary that includes data from each quarter will be more accurate than one reporting data gathered at only one time in the year. Also, it will escape the criticism that the results would be different if the survey were conducted in the fall instead of the spring, for example. Breaking the sample into four equal segments, then surveying one segment each quarter is estimated to increase costs by only 10 percent, compared to one annual administration (Hatry and others, 1992).

Pretest

Once the survey instrument is constructed and approved by the committee, test it on twenty people chosen at random. This sample need not be chosen with the rigor of a complete random sample but neither should respondents to the pretest be friends or co-workers exclusively. Administer the questionnaire just as planned for the full sample, then ask the pilot-test respondents simple questions about the clarity of the survey items and the simplicity of the format. In a recent pretesting we found that we had omitted one entire income range; also we learned that residents could not estimate the square footage of their property (so we asked them to estimate the number of cars that could be parked on their lawns).

Training

Whether the choice is to administer the survey by mail, phone, or in-person, survey assistants must be trained. They will conduct the interviews by phone or face to face, or they will open envelopes to place identifiers on questionnaires, code open-ended responses returned by mail, and ensure that all marks made by respondents will be legible to a data entry operator. All assistants will need to operate uniformly, asking questions in the same way and same order, with prompting only where specifically permitted and in a way that is clearly specified.

Open-ended responses, whether in mailed surveys or by phone, must be coded so that the code for "Air Quality"—say, the number 100—includes the same set of responses. For example, all coders must be aware that written responses such as "auto emissions," "smog," and "wood burning fireplaces" should be coded 100 for "Air Quality."

Training is part of quality control. Explain to assistants that a random sample of one in ten of their survey respondents (if by phone or in person) will be recontacted to verify a subset of survey responses. A supervisor should be kept on site in the field for in-person interviews or in the office when interviews are conducted by phone.

Trying Hard and Keeping Track

If surveys are conducted by phone or in person, it is essential that each number or address in the sample be tried on no fewer than three occasions at different times during the week to give residents a reasonable chance to participate. This is less a matter of fairness than a way to improve the sample's likelihood of providing opinions and characteristics that mimic the community as a whole. When only a single call is made to no avail on Wednesday night, the night worker or the young, active apartment dweller will probably be missed.

Be certain to keep track of the disposition of each attempted phone call. Record what happened each of the times a phone number was dialed—up to three times. Note whether the interview was completed, the line was busy, there was no answer, a business was reached instead of a residence, the potential respondent refused to participate, the answerer did not speak English, or the phone was disconnected. With such records a response rate and refusal rate can be calculated accurately.

Often a computer-assisted telephone interviewing (CATI) system simplifies accounting for call dispositions and skipping through complicated questions; it also avoids the need for separate data entry since interviewers type in results while they conduct the phone interviews. CATI systems flash precise question wording and prompt options onto a computer screen that is read by interviewers who record responses on the keyboard. Because the systems operate in computer networks, a supervisor can monitor survey progress. Generally CATI systems pay back only if several surveys are planned for their use.

Marked questionnaires on topics of civic interest should net a response rate over 50 percent with the following procedures: a postcard "warning" of the coming instrument, followed by two mailings if necessary, each with a complete copy of the questionnaire. Keep track separately of returns from the first and second mailings.

Reporting Results

Data Analysis

Simple analyses can be used for most government survey purposes. The following types are usually sufficient: percentages of respondents to each question option, average responses — age, income, years of residency — and the cross-classification of responses where the percentage is reported of items such as older versus younger residents who feel unsafe walking alone at night. Software that provides such tabulation is now readily available and inexpensive.

The most complicated analysis will be the one to get the total population estimates using demographic characteristics of the sample. Here the sample characteristics are first compared to known characteristics of the entire state, county, community, or other jurisdiction (perhaps drawn from census data); then results are weighted to correct for differences. This type of analysis is especially important if comparison of results for separate demographic categories of respondents (older versus younger; white versus other; better versus less educated) shows different opinions about the policies or programs evaluated.

Without a full survey of nonrespondents, results from groups underrepresented in the survey must be given more weight to reflect the proper balance in a representative sample. If half the target population are apartment dwellers but only a quarter of the survey's respondents live in apartments, then the 25 percent of survey respondents who are residents of apartments should be given twice their current weight. This adjustment is accomplished with weighting schemes permitted in data analysis software.

Report Writing and Presentation

In presenting the survey results, always construct an executive summary that gives an overview of methods and survey accuracy and highlights the main survey findings. Readers like bulleted lists. Meticulously document the survey methods, but display that section in an appendix. Augment tables of results with bar and pie charts. If the results are presented in person, have key findings in charts on slides or overheads (see Hendricks, Chapter Twenty-Three, this book). If audiences and the oversight committee expect conclusions and recommendations give them what the data support but no more.

Finally, many readers will need to confront the prospect of hiring a consultant. If stakes are particularly high, if the credibility of an outsider is especially valued, or if staff don't have the expertise or time, then a consultant is probably required.

Hiring a Consultant

Below are some basic guidelines for hiring a consultant:

1. What is the consultant's previous experience in survey research? Check references, noting how well the consultant has met deadlines.
2. How well does the consultant communicate results in writing? Get copies of recent reports. If they don't make sense to you, the consultant doesn't write well enough.
3. Will the consultant be willing to share the work with in-house staff? Find out how much the consultant has shared responsibility for the survey with staff and how well those staff felt the arrangement worked.
4. Do you think you might like to work with this consultant? Although you two are not getting married, you ought to feel, just a gut feel, that this person is reasonable, helpful, smart, cooperative, and maybe even a little excited about your project.

Will Better Service Necessarily Lead to Better Ratings by Residents?

What is a manager to do if $3 million of new library construction nets no change in citizen perception of library service? There is some evidence to suggest that there is no dollar-for-dollar relationship of expenditures to service ratings but that citizens can distinguish the best services from the worst (Miller and Miller, 1991b). Periodic collection of information from service recipients will get to the heart of the business that government is in; at the same time it will show when something is particularly awry in government. While surveys arguably provide the standard by which service delivery should be measured, other measures of service effectiveness are essential (Hatry and others, 1992).

Objective measures of effective service—in observer ratings or measures of output, for example—provide critical information to managers that augments the point of view of residents. The government may collect garbage three times a day and provide garbage cans on wheels and red carpets on which to roll them to the curb; but if the citizens don't like the garbage collection service, there is still a problem. Finding the substance of and the solution to that problem likely will require more contact with government clients—perhaps even more citizen surveying.

References

Converse, J. M., and Presser, S. *Survey Questions: Handcrafting the Standardized Questionnaire.* Newbury Park, Calif.: Sage, 1976.

Fink, A., and Kosecoff, J. *How to Conduct Surveys: A Step by Step Guide.* Newbury Park, Calif.: Sage, 1985.

Hatry, H. P., and others. *How Effective Are Your Community Services?* Washington, D.C.: The Urban Institute and International City/County Management Association, 1992.

Kish, L. *Survey Sampling.* New York: Wiley, 1965.

Lavrakas, P. J. Telephone Survey Methods: *Sampling, Selection and Supervision.* Newbury Park, Calif.: Sage, 1990.

Miller, T. I., and Miller, M. A. *Citizen Surveys: How to Do Them, How to Use Them, and What They Mean.* Washington, D.C.: International City/County Management Association, 1991a.

Miller, T. I., and Miller, M. A. "Standards of Excellence: U.S. Residents' Evaluations of Local Government Services." *Public Administration Review,* 1991b, *51*(6), 503–514.

Sudman, S., and Bradburn, N. M. *Asking Questions: A Practical Guide to Questionnaire Design.* San Francisco: Jossey-Bass, 1982.

12

The Systematic Use
of Expert Judgment

Harvey A. Averch

Although any public sector program may be evaluated by applying expert judgment, many standard texts argue that such evaluation is inferior to the more "scientific" kind. According to the texts, expert evaluations are more fragile and prone to error than other procedures (Rossi and Freeman, 1985, pp. 309–319). Compared to the massive literature on using experts in quantitative or qualitative forecasting or in estimating technological parameters, the reported literature on expert program evaluation is thin (Nevo, 1989; Geis, 1987; Weston, 1987).

The evaluation profession has its methodological roots in traditional social science where the use of experts is not common. Representatives of the mainline profession do not, in general, work in agencies where expert judgment may be appropriate or the only alternative—for example, in public or private research and development laboratories.

Yet evaluation by experts persists. For some types of programs and decisions, there may be no alternative way to evaluate; for some, there may be no more cost-effective way. If we believe that the information to be gained by evaluating should be proportional to the needs of decision makers and the available time, budget, and attention they have for evaluation, then conventional quantitative evaluations may be infeasible or inappropriate. If so, properly designed expert evaluations may be a cost-effective alternative. Expert evaluation is very common in assessing the results of science and technology programs and higher education programs. Indeed, it is the preferred method in these domains, although its validity and reliability remain relatively unresearched.

To help broaden the literature on this type of assessment, the chapter (1) identifies the kinds of programs appropriate for expert evaluation, (2) discusses the translation of expert judgment techniques from the estimation and forecasting domain to the evaluation domain, (3) describes the design and structure of some of the more prominent (and unconventional) procedures that may be used for evaluation, (4) lists some of the desired characteristics of experts and describes procedures for identifying and composing expert groups, (5) provides examples of the investments in money and time required for adequate expert evaluations, and (6) provides guidelines for selecting the most appropriate procedures from the alternatives available.

Evaluating Programs Under Input and Output Uncertainty

Decision makers and program evaluators should consider using expert evaluation when programs are subject to high uncertainty. Program uncertainty can be defined and identified by the following situation and conditions.

1. *Suppose that for* t *years some public agency has been operating a "program."*

2. *The agency cannot be certain about the effective quantity or quality of inputs it has bought during the* t *years, and there is no easy way to measure these.*
    Research and development agencies, for example, frequently cannot specify the real quantity and quality of scientific labor and capital they invest in or the factor proportions — the number of senior researchers, assistants, and instruments — that will lead to significant research output.

3. *The expected "benefits," "outputs," or "outcomes" of the program are highly uncertain or occur in the future.*
    Education is a case in point. Educators, at all levels, do not know with precision the quantities and qualities of teachers and physical plants that produce educated people. Although some educational outputs may be measured by standardized or criterion-referenced tests, the true educational program output is multidimensional. It can be known only in the very long run, and knowing it takes significant investment, such as tracking students over many years. We simply cannot know in the short run whether schools produce technically skilled, flexible workers capable of operating a complex modern economy, and good citizens capable of operating a competent democracy; indeed, it is difficult to know at all.

4. *The agency does not know with precision whether decision-relevant outcomes can be attributed to the inputs and the design of the program.*
    Suppose that, contrary to what economists usually assume, the relationship between inputs and outputs (the production function) is not technologically determined but instead twists and bends according to the mix of inputs purchased and the institutional arrangements in which they will be applied. In other words, the program design, the choice of inputs, and the outcomes interact strongly (Murnane and Nelson, 1984).

At time $t + 1$, a need arises from agency sponsors or managers to make a decision about the program. They may want information to improve performance—formative evaluation—or to learn whether the program should be continued, is worth the amount that has been invested in it—summative evaluation. Up to time t the program has been operating under input and output uncertainty as well as uncertainty about causal relationships; therefore, expert evaluation will likely be either the sole alternative or the most cost-effective alternative. Under such conditions, the job of the modern evaluator is to work collaboratively with decision makers or program operators to clarify the uncertainties and make the connections so as to improve management and performance. But working in this mode means the evaluator has become an expert adviser to the program.

Adapting Expert Judgment Techniques to Program Evaluation

With the decision that expert evaluation is the preferred mode, significant choice remains over the particular procedures to be used. Since procedures unique to evaluation purposes have not yet been developed, the methods to be used must be carefully adapted from standard processes such as parameter estimation and forecasting. For example, accuracy in estimation or forecasting is defined as the correspondence between an a priori expert judgment about a parameter and its real-world value or between a forecast and its realization. Accuracy in a priori estimation corresponds to validity in ex post program evaluation. In standard evaluations, validity is the correspondence between the actual program outcomes and the evaluation findings. However, expert evaluations are most appropriate when such a correspondence is difficult to establish. Thus validity of expert judgment in program evaluation means this: *a decision maker accepts some individual or collective expert judgment about a program and acts on its basis; as a result, social benefits are realized or social costs are avoided.* (In the language of benefit-cost analysis, social benefits would be additions to the tangible—and intangible—resources of a community or constituency that result from a program or project. Social costs would be the direct outlays to operate a program plus any indirect costs imposed on a community or constituency affected by the program.)

Similarly, reliability in estimation or forecasting ordinarily means the certainty with which an expert judgment reflects the true parameter and is not a result of random error. Reliability is necessary for validity in estimating the distribution of a parameter, but not sufficient. In an evaluation context, reliability means that *other experts looking at the same information would come to approximately the same judgments.* Some group judgment procedures, however, use initial nonreliability and conflict among experts to try to get valid and reliable estimates via formal or informal feedback.

Evaluators considering expert judgment need to be sensitive to trade-offs in validity, reliability, time required, information and operating costs, and clarity to prospective users. No procedure so far devised clearly dominates, nor are the more elaborate procedures necessarily more reliable or valid than less elaborate ones. The procedures described below are not exhaustive but only suggestive. Variants on each major procedure are easy to invent, depending on the particular trade-offs evaluators want to make. I have sorted the procedures according to whether the technical experts work inside or outside the evaluating organization, and if outside, according to the structure and mode of interaction among the experts.

Expert Evaluations from the Inside: Using Managers and Administrators

The experts who know a program the best are the people charged with managing it and the people who provide budget for it. They have access to the information the program creates and records in whatever standardized, routine reporting its parent agency requires; they also have immediate access to the views of working staff, constituents, and clients. If one wants to evaluate a public program subject to uncertainty as defined above, then a crude but rapid way to obtain information about performance is ask for the judgment of operating managers, higher-level administrators, and budgetary sponsors.

To obtain judgments from those closest to a program is essentially the most common kind of evaluation. All budget offices and legislative committees do this. Budget officers and committee staff have responsibility for tracking both the cost and the performance of programs in their domain. Operating managers and budgetary sponsors tell such evaluators a "story" about their program performance and cost over a budget cycle or a program lifetime, and the evaluators pose tough questions about performance and cost. Then they draw conclusions about whether the managers' claims are warranted. Depending on the credibility of the claims, the program receives rewards or punishments in the form of budget, staff, or other things the program values.

Knowledgeable inside evaluators are not under any illusions about managers' and administrators' incentives to find that the outcomes of the programs for which they are responsible are always both positive and intended. None are under any illusions about managers' and administrators' incentives to blame reported problems on shortages of funds, personnel, higher layers of bureaucracy, competitors, or adversaries. Public managers and administrators are well aware of the personal and programmatic costs of reporting problems or failures, and expert evaluators have to account for these costs in the stories they hear. However, when evaluators have some power over the managers or administrators or can specify the ways in which they present information, evaluators can, to a considerable extent, control incentives to deceive. And when they discover deception, they can impose penalties in budget or staff or remove decision-making authority, thus providing incentives for truth telling (Bendor, Taylor, and Van Gaalen, 1985).

Customarily, the stories program staff and administrators tell are checked by experts available in government or by outside witnesses. Evidence from clients and constituents is given heavy weight in budget and legislative agencies on both substantive and political grounds. By checking and collating multiple, simultaneous accounts of program performance, the evaluators assign a degree of credibility to the administrators' story. Assigning the appropriate degree of credibility requires good contextual information on the relations among program, clients, and constituents, but sophisticated evaluators will be sensitive to these.

Using Program Evaluation Staffs to Make Expert Judgments

Many agencies recognize a necessary, if limited, evaluation function and assign separate staff to carry it out, although that staff may not always be formally trained in standard evaluation techniques. Today, most federal and many state agencies contain evaluation bureaus designed to be semi-independent from program managers and to have no immediate stake in program outcomes. The job of these bureaus is to track programs and evaluate them objectively, that is, without the perspectives and biases of managers and operating staff. They carry out routine internal evaluations and display expertise on any performance questions that come up during ordinary bureaucratic transactions, including questions about interim or ultimate payoff raised by sponsors and constituents. When a rapid, low-cost, expert evaluation is needed, then the agency evaluation staff can be asked to provide it.

The recommendations produced by internal evaluators are frequently difficult to implement, but they may be less difficult to implement than those from outside experts. Here there is a trade-off in evaluation design. Internal recommendations may seem less threatening to an agency and, therefore, more acceptable. On the other hand, evaluation by prestigious, credible outside experts may give parent or oversight agencies an upper hand in forcing acceptance of recommendations that are unpleasant to the program being evaluated.

Collecting and Collating Information

Internal expert evaluators have access to the same routine reporting that program managers do, or they can obtain it. Like outside experts, they must rely on managers and operating staff for important tacit or unrecorded knowledge about the program, but they have easier and faster access than outside experts. Once program information has been collected, internal evaluators collate and compare their data and come to some overall view about program performance.

Checking for Validity and Reliability

Checks on validity and reliability may be "horizontal." The evaluators may ask for a reply to the draft evaluation from the program, or they may ask other people in the agency with technical knowledge to review the evaluation. Checks can also be "vertical." Superiors at different levels in the evaluation office hierarchy may review a draft evaluation for technical merit and organizational and political acceptability. Alternatively, internal expert evaluations may be turned over to outside peer reviewers in universities or contract research organizations.

Implementing Recommendations

Evaluation staffs, like external budget officials and legislators, have indirect power over a program's future, especially over future budget and staff. They can affect a program's internal reputation with its superiors and its external reputation with sponsors and clients—subject, of course, to the limited standing evaluation staffs have in addressing programs with heavy uncertainty. Thus, program incentives to gloss over evaluation results may be controlled.

An evaluation staff's power is, of course, coming through the hierarchical arrangements in the agency. Depending on political and administrative circumstance, agency heads may or may not be willing to coerce program staff into cooperating with internal evaluation staff. And agency heads may decide to control results from the evaluation office because the findings may not be consistent with the overall political and bureaucratic necessities for running the agency.

Using Outside Experts

For a variety of technical and political reasons, an agency may prefer to use outside experts to provide estimates of program outcomes. In this case, the agency supplies the experts with questions about a task, problem, or program; allows them to review available data; and then asks them to pool their knowledge and come to some collective judgment or recommendation. A single expert will not ordinarily be asked to make a formal systematic evaluation; the research literature suggests that collective judgments are more accurate than individual ones (Woudenberg, 1991). In any case, politically astute agencies know that it is much more difficult to attack collective judgments than individual judgments.

Selecting the Experts

Experts can be selected in many different ways. To get technical experts, an agency may use its past grant or contract experience, publications or citations in the field of interest, or recommendations from the members of a relevant "invisible college," the peers recognized by everyone in a given discipline or area. Technical experts may be mixed with political experts, or even program constituents and clients, to bring different perspectives to bear in the evaluation process.

Eliciting Systematic Judgments

Once the experts have been selected, many alternatives exist for eliciting judgments. Judgments can be made individually and aggregated, or they can be reached collectively. Since expert judgment is not commonly considered for ex post program evaluation, the discussion below concentrates on options that (1) have been used and documented, (2) could plausibly be adapted to evaluation purposes, and (3) have been partially tested for validity and reliability.

Unstructured, Direct Interaction (Informed Dialogue) Procedure

In an informed dialogue procedure, the agency brings a group of experts together for informed, face-to-face exchange of views. The agency's evaluation staff provides initial questions or terms of reference, collects pertinent information, and records the proceedings. The experts conduct face-to-face conversations resulting in agreements and disagreements. They may hold their conversations iteratively, in a series of meetings in which they try to achieve informal consensus. Reaching consensus via formal voting and polls is rare because it might reveal and record conflict. The idea is for the experts to talk long enough and intensely enough for everyone to arrive at roughly the same view.

During their meetings, the experts may obtain information from the program, sponsors, constituents, clients involved in the program, and even rivals of the program at hand. Side conversations and consultations outside formally scheduled meetings are generally permitted as they are not controllable anyway and they may help form the desired consensus.

Most evaluations of the outputs (information and education) of science and technology programs follow this informed dialogue format. Strategic behavior by the experts in promoting their own views and achieving their own private agendas through biased or self-interested evaluation of the outputs is, in principle, controlled by the norms of science and engineering practice, the so-called Mertonian norms. These norms include disinterestedness, organized skepticism, and willingness to share data and findings with the larger community working in the field (Merton, [1942] 1973). The Mertonian norms provide grounding for the conventional image of the way scientific research is done. They lead to "certifiable" knowledge in the conduct of research.

While highly common, the structured direct mode of expert judgment is one of the least formally researched. We do not really know whether the Mertonian norms prevail in expert scientific evaluations, nor do we know what conditions guarantee that they will prevail. The reported, finished consensus findings or recommendations rarely document the evolution of the experts' dialogue or the measures agency staff may have had to take to keep the dialogue on track and moving. In most cases, additional layers of technical, bureaucratic, and political review will be applied to a draft consensus report to check both substance and style.

Whether a consensus is valid and reliable is not well known. A good expert evaluation in science and technology fields is one that turns out to be useful to the sponsor. When scientific agencies like the National Science Foundation or the National Institutes of Health, or advisory organizations like the National Academy of Science use expert advice in evaluating programs, they assert that they have engaged the best experts and that standard scientific committee procedures are effective in eliciting program performance (Averch, 1993). Consequently, they imply that the judgments should be accepted and acted on. But we do not know whether self-interest and the ordinary afflictions of committee procedures, such as logrolling or dominance by strong personalities, are overcome by adherence to the norms for scientific disclosure. Indeed, fear that the norms could not apply to estimating and forecasting served as the impetus for inventing the structured, indirect forms of obtaining collective expert judgment. By controlling, channeling, and aggregating interactions, the inventors hoped that bias and self-interest would be controlled.

Structured, Indirect Interactions

Structured, indirect procedures — procedures that are *not* characteristically face-to-face — impose constraints on direct information flows and expert interchange to control common afflictions such as the pursuit of private agendas or "groupthink." The ideal format, if it could be designed and executed, would force rapid convergence to valid, reliable estimates, predictions, or problem solutions. However, no such ideal has yet emerged, although each procedure that has been tried has its own champions. As a limited sample of such procedures, in addition to the very well known and criticized Delphi procedure, we might list QCF (Quantitative Controlled Feedback) (Press, Ali, and Chung-Fang, 1979), NGT (Nominal Group Technique) (Delbecq, van de Ven, and Gustafson, 1975), devil's advocate (DA) and dialectical inquiry (DI) (Mason, 1969; Schwenk, 1990).

Delphi

The essence of the Delphi technique is structured, indirect, iterative, interaction among experts with centralized control, tabulation, and feedback of information and judgments. Dalkey and Helmer invented Delphi at the RAND Corporation in the 1960s to assist in solving complex systems problems for which there was little operating experience, such as the performance of complex new technologies or the emergence of new political-economic entities (Dalkey and Helmer, 1963). Traditionally, decision makers used Delphi to elicit estimates of unknown parameters in highly complex technological systems or to make forecasts of impacts deriving from complex, interactive social, environmental, or economic developments. Delphi has been adapted to decision making and policy-making (Rauch, 1979); nothing in its design prevents its use in ex post program evaluation. In the evaluation case, the collective judgment to be made is the current or expected worth of a given program or the comparative worth of alternative programs.

In Delphi, the experts do not have direct contact with each other. On each round or iteration, every expert submits his or her responses to a central "control" agent via memo, mail, or electronic medium. Control aggregates the information and recirculates the collective findings to the experts. The collective judgment on each round is presented statistically without any backup reasoning, although the experts may be asked to give the rationale for their judgment. Asking for reasons is more common in later iterations, especially if there is no convergence of opinions. No one knows who has contributed what judgment to the collective judgment. The expectation is that the experts will adjust and revise their estimates in succeeding rounds so as to reach agreement.

By aggregating and filtering the individual estimates or forecasts centrally and feeding them back on successive rounds, Delphi's inventors hoped that the collective estimate would converge, ideally to a valid estimate or forecast. By providing for controlled, structured dialogue and immediate feedback and interchange by participants, they hoped that biases would be reduced or eliminated. Of course, Delphi's inventors did not deal much with science advising or evaluation where the direct exchange of ideas is what is desired and the Mertonian norms work to control the biases.

In an evaluation context, the experts would be given a series of structured questions about a program or would be asked to make qualitative or quantitative estimates of performance. Then the standard procedures would be applied. Exhibit 12.1 specifies the steps in a Delphi procedure.

Exhibit 12.1. Steps in Delphi for Evaluation.

1. Develop the evaluation issues and questions that the experts will address.
2. Obtain data that the decision maker wants experts to examine and arrange any desired interviews with program staff. (The data can be agency records as defined in Hatry, Chapter Sixteen of this handbook, including previous evaluations, or interviews with people who hold relevant information about the program. The interviews could include focus groups as discussed in Dean, Chapter Fourteen, this volume.)
3. Design the instrument for addressing the issues and questions (for example, qualitative assessments, questions with numerical scales).
4. Select and contact the experts.
5. Administer the instrument, Round #1.
6. Collate, aggregate, and send the judgments from Round #1 back to the experts. This step is done by the person designated to be in control. (In estimation and forecasting, quartile and median responses are traditionally presented. These responses can also be included for a series of closed evaluation questions.)
7. Administer the instrument, Round #2.
8. Repeat Step 6.
9. Administer the instrument, Round #3.
10. Repeat Step 6.
11. Prepare final report on results. (Provide draft report to experts if appropriate.)

Woudenberg (1991) recently reviewed 102 published studies in which a Delphi technique was applied. Based on the weight of the reported evidence, he reports that it is no more accurate than other collective judgment procedures. Although Delphi does achieve consensus or convergence, Woudenberg concludes that it is achieved by the group pressure to conformity and not by coherent, rational processing of the common, ordered information received on successive rounds of estimation. In a comparison of Delphi with alternative expert procedures, Woudenberg finds that Delphi alternatives generally perform as well as Delphi and are frequently superior for the task selected (Woudenberg, 1991, p. 135).

Some Procedures with Built-In Conflict: Devil's Advocate and Dialectical Inquiry

In devil's advocate (DA) procedures, a recommended course of action or a plan is defined and presented by the experts to the user along with the assumptions and data that support it (Mason, 1969). Then the user assigns an advocate to carry out the most rigorous critique possible of the position on the table. The critique elicits the tacit assumptions in the recommendations or plans and forces the user to account for them in settling on particular actions or plans. The advocate, however, will offer no counter recommendation. In program evaluation using DA, a recommended position on the program would be offered by the experts along with supporting reasons and data, and the user or his agent would then critique it or hire someone to do it.

In dialectical inquiry (DI) procedures, a feasible, credible counter-recommendation is derived and presented along with its accompanying assumptions and data (Mason, 1969). The user then weights the recommendation and the counterrecommendation side by side. One of the two recommendations may be accepted. Alternatively, by systematic comparisons and contrasts, a third reasonable recommendation may be generated out of the dialectical inquiry with more strengths and fewer weaknesses. Exhibit 12.2 lays out the steps in the DI process as adapted to program evaluation.

Exhibit 12.2. Using Dialectical Inquiry in Evaluation.

1. Select and convene the experts along with the sponsor and users of the evaluation.
2. Designate a subset of experts to make an initial evaluation or assessment of the program. Suppose the initial evaluation is positive.
3. Designate another subset of experts to make *the best case possible* against the (positive) case made in Step 2.
4. The users or their designees conduct a structured debate between the two subsets of experts.
5. User selects the best argued case as presented in Steps 2 and 3 or creates a new synthesized evaluation. For example, in an educational program evaluation, the experts persuaded the user that results were positive on cognitive dimensions and negative on affective dimensions.

Both DA and DI procedures assume that open, direct conflict between experts will reveal tacitly held information and demonstrate clearly why experts disagree. Knowing the initial reasons for disagreement, will, it is hoped, eventually lead to a reliable and valid consensus.

Proponents of dialectical procedures argue that either one is superior to expert procedures without formal conflict—for example, Delphi. Standard Delphi results, by design, prevent the experts from articulating their assumptions and making them known to others. It follows that Delphi users may be unaware of critical assumptions (Mason, 1969).

Schwenk (1990) carried out a meta-analysis of the published empirical research on the validity and reliability of the three procedures. The meta-analysis is suggestive but not definitive for selecting among the procedures since almost all the reported tests of them involve undergraduate college students, not actual public decision makers.

Schwenk reports that DA procedures are superior to unstructured expert-based approaches in terms of predictive validity and quality of solutions with respect to the problems attacked. However, DI did not prove clearly superior to other structured approaches, at least when applied to ill-structured decision problems of the kind we would have in using DI as an evaluation procedure. Compared to each other, neither of the two conflict-based approaches was clearly superior.

In this chapter, programs with high uncertainty about inputs and outputs have been described as appropriate for evaluation by experts. Therefore, it follows that procedures that reveal assumptions will probably serve better than those that do not. However, no particular assumption-revealing procedure will dominate independent of the trade-offs discussed above.

Characteristics of Experts

Attention thus far has been on examples of expert procedures that can be adapted to program evaluation. Now we examine some of the traits and characteristics that we want the participating experts to have. The most important of these are coherence, reliability, and resolution (validity) (Chan, 1982).

A *coherent* expert is one who obeys the standard dictates of logic and probability. Such an expert does not assert that A and not-A exist simultaneously or that a conditional probability is higher than an unconditional one. For making forecasts, a *reliable* expert is one whose prior probabilities of events conform well to actual probabilities when they become known. Weather forecasting provides the standard example. When a weather forecaster predicts a 60 percent chance of rain and it does, in fact, rain 60 percent of the time, we say we have a reliable expert (a well-calibrated expert, in forecasting parlance). In other words, the forecaster is consistent with observed, real-world frequencies and so can be "trusted."

As noted, in program evaluation, reliability is defined by the expert's agreement with other experts. We want reliable, trustworthy experts because in many uncertain decision situations, such as judging the merit of a mental health program, there is no other way of checking for the absence of random error or the presence of bias than by comparing judgments across experts.

But reliability is not sufficient to make a good forecaster. A forecaster who was only reliable could simply keep delivering a standard forecast of 60 percent rain all the time. When a forecaster is also able to specify with precision what the actual probability of rain is on any given day, then we say the forecaster makes valid forecasts (has a high degree of *resolution*). Since we will incur costs in acting or not acting on particular weather forecasts, we want forecasters who can make reliable and valid forecasts. Similarly, we incur costs in using or not using an expert evaluation, so we want evaluators who we know will make reliable and valid judgments about program performance.

The very large literature on experts and on making judgments suggests that experts frequently do not possess all the properties we desire, especially in situations with high uncertainty. To the extent they do, they use certain strategies for enhancing their information and judgments (Shanteau, 1988), and these strategies suggest ways of formulating an appropriate evaluation process.

Experts, for example, rely on others in making their estimates. They obtain feedback and opinion from other experts. They use informal decision aids to avoid the biasing effects of heuristics: they break problems into small pieces; they examine prior decisions of other experts; they learn from each other. Whatever procedure for expert program evaluation one chooses, its design should assist the experts in implementing their personal strategies.

Identifying Experts and Composing the Group

Experts may be identified in a number of ways. Evaluation users generally find experts through direct or indirect reputational procedures. In the direct procedure, the user's staff identifies one or more experts by consulting with the program staff, clients, constituents, prominent academics, professional associations, or "invisible colleges." Experts initially identified may then be consulted about additional experts in a "snowball" process. In other words, the evaluator tries to assemble an unusually knowledgeable and respected cadre of experts, not a random sample of them. The danger of the standard snowball process is that it may reduce the breadth and variation required for a sound evaluation.

Using indirect procedures, one may find scientific and technical experts in a relatively objective way by counting their past publications and, more important, their citations. High publication and citation counts in peer-reviewed journals reflect the scientific utility that complementary and competing experts find in a person's work. Such counts can be a check on snowball procedures, since reputation, significant publications, and citations should all correlate. As computing costs continue to fall and the number of organized databases continues to rise, publications and citations can become a way of checking on the standard reputational procedures, at least for experts who publish in scientific or technical journals. There may be desired expert skills, of course, that leave no trace in any published record. For example, in evaluating a homelessness program, one might want a homeless person to be on an expert panel.

A major and unavoidable difficulty with constructing a cadre of experts in the standard way is that the experts cannot have entirely independent perspectives and information. They will usually know each other directly or know of each other, their professional styles, and their substantive output. The information they have will be partially redundant, so the actual amount of usable information per dollar invested in the evaluation process will have definite limits (Clemen and Winkler, 1985).

In a formative evaluation, if the evaluator could track program events with the advice and estimates a cadre gave at time $t + 1$, then the evaluator might be able to estimate the actual quantity and quality of information received. However, a group of experts called together to do an evaluation will generally offer judgment only once. The group will not usually be brought together again for updated evaluation. (In evaluating small research projects, experts sometimes provide *ex ante* estimates of quality and then examine the actual output through site visits or publication review.)

To maximize the amount of information from an evaluation for fixed evaluation outlays, the expert cadre should comprise more than technical, substantive experts. In addition to substantive experts, the group might include general purpose policy analysts, philosophers of evaluation, or stakeholders. This mix reduces the dependence among experts, widens the base of experience in the group, and allows important nontechnical questions to be raised. Furthermore, the diversity in perspectives may force the group to resolve arguments and clarify recommendations, although consensus may be more difficult to achieve. Such mixed groups of experts have been tried in evaluating energy and naval basic research with some success, as judged by sponsors and users (Kostoff, 1988). An evaluation by the Office of Naval Research (ONR) using such mixed groups is described below (Kostoff, 1988).

An Example of a Structured, Direct Expert Evaluation

The Office of Naval Research used an evaluation design invented in 1981 by the Department of Energy (1982). The office defines some of its programs as accelerated research initiatives (ARIs). These ARIs are designated as priority research areas for a period of five years. The output of the ARIs is supposed to accelerate scientific and technical progress in areas important to the Navy. In a 1988 evaluation, all the ARIs were classified into common scientific fields, and ONR convened mixed panels of experts to evaluate their progress in terms of information output. Each panel had experts with deep technical knowledge, experts with general cross-cutting knowledge, and naval officers and civilians from the operating branches. In other words, research users served on the panels.

Prior to the panel meeting, ONR's evaluation staff contacted other experts to help frame the issues. These panels met for one day to hear verbal presentations by the ARI operators, to provide written evaluations of each, and then to rank them. ONR next asked the panelists to fill out a written score sheet containing a number of factors considered important for the Navy's research and operating branches.

Having filled out their individual sheets, panelists discussed their individual rankings and gave each factor on their scoring sheet a consensus score. They then provided an overall score on the expected quality of each ARI. Once all the scores had been calculated, ONR was then able to apply routine statistical analyses to determine the relation of the overall score to the individual factors that were believed to be important *ex ante*. (This was a form of reliability check, since overall scores should be related to component scores on particular factors.)

The costs of evaluating the ARI output was substantial. Expert evaluation, by definition, is labor intensive. ONR out-of-pocket costs for expert panels ranged between $5,000 and $20,000 (Kostoff, 1988). These costs include salaries or consulting fees, travel time, and document preparation. However, ONR did not have to pay the full costs for all involved. If this had been required, given the large number of projects evaluated, the real costs would have been significantly greater.

On the other hand, for a "scientific" evaluation of programs like those run by ONR, even if one could be defined and even if it were technically feasible, the costs would also be very high. For example, a "traces" type of study might have been a feasible alternative here (Illinois Institute of Technology Research Institute, 1968). In such a study, investigators would sift the historical record, carry out interviews of researchers and users, and then induce the critical economic outcomes attributable to research; but for several hundred interconnected projects or programs the costs would also be very high and certainly not as timely. Cost, as noted earlier, is itself an item for trade-off; it must be balanced against the demands or needs of evaluation users, the time evaluators have available, the desired reliability, and so forth.

The Prospects for Expert Program Evaluation

Using the tacit and explicit knowledge of experts to make evaluations is not considered best practice in the evaluation profession compared to random experiments or statistical analysis of the relations between program inputs and outputs. However, for some programs, the use of experts in some form is the only feasible way to conduct an evaluation. For others, it can be a timely, cost-effective way.

Even though a large variety of procedures can be adapted for evaluation, few have been. Some comparisons have been made of alternative procedures for parameter estimation and forecasting but not for evaluation. From the perspective of cost-effective evaluation techniques, it would be nice to know how well an expert evaluation would correlate with one based on experimental or statistical methods. Perhaps the evaluation profession could mount an assessment of the two evaluation methods, including their relative decision utility.

Technical issues are unlikely to be decisive in program evaluations subject to uncertainty such as those in education, science, or health. Indeed, they are rarely decisive at all, since evaluations are part of a political and bureaucratic process. Programs with demonstrably valid, high-quality outcomes may not prosper and, conversely, those with demonstrably valid, low-quality outcomes may survive very well.

Assuming that some decision maker is interested in or impelled by requirements into doing expert evaluation, what form might be chosen? There are few people who are experienced in expert evaluations or who have participated in them. In my experience as a sometime evaluator of science and technology programs and as a decision maker who has used expert evaluations, procedures that force a wide range of participants to provide their reasoning and assumptions about a program turn out to be superior for decision making compared to narrow, prespecified, tightly centrally controlled procedures like Delphi.

Where uncertainties are high about inputs, outputs, and their relations, all the experts need to be made aware of them in relatively graphic ways rather than have uncertainties filtered somehow. Direct exposure to the biases of evaluators is probably a better way to correct for them than by preventing exposure through central filtering and aggregation. In other words, the unstructured, dialogue procedures carried out in science and technology program evaluation seem most appropriate. (The reader should note that science and technology program evaluation refers to outcomes, not to inputs, such as whether research output improves the performance of hardware systems. Proposals to conduct science and technology programs are, of course, *reviewed,* just as are proposed social programs.)

Having good and defensible reasons in arguing outcomes, positive or negative, may be more important than the actual outcomes. For the kinds of programs discussed here, the actual outcomes may never be available, or may be available only long after the decision is required. Decisions on whether to continue, stop, or modify a program demand defensible reasons since it is these reasons that will be examined closely by program advocates and opponents. Expert procedures characterized by participants with different skills and perspectives and intense dialogue among them almost by their nature will produce a broader range of defensible reasons.

References

Averch, H. A. "Criteria and Rules for Evaluating Competing R&D Megaprojects." *Science and Public Policy,* 1993, *20,* 105–113.

Bendor, J. S., Taylor, S., and Van Gaalen, R. "Bureaucratic Expertise Versus Legislative Authority." *American Political Science Review,* 1985, *79,* 755-769.

Chan, S. "Expert Judgments Made Under Uncertainty: Some Evidence." *Social Science Quarterly,* 1982, *63,* 428-444.

Clemen, R. T., and Winkler, R. L. "Limits for the Precision and Value of Information from Dependent Sources." *Operations Research,* 1985, *33,* 427-442.

Dalkey, N., and Helmer, O. "An Experimental Evaluation of the Delphi Method to the Use of Experts." *Management Science,* 1963, *9,* 458-467.

Delbecq, A. L., van de Ven, A. H., and Gustafson, D. H. *Group Techniques for Program Planning: A Guide to Nominal Group and Decision Processes.* Glenview, Ill.: Scott, Foresman, 1975.

Department of Energy. *An Assessment of the Basic Energy Sciences Program.* Report No. DOE/ER-0123. Washington, D.C.: Office of Energy Research, 1982.

Geis, G. L. "Formative Evaluation: Developmental Testing and Expert Review." *Performance and Instruction,* 1987, *26,* 1-8.

Illinois Institute of Technology Research Institute. *Technology in Retrospect and Critical Events in Science.* Chicago: Illinois Institute of Technology Research Institute, 1968.

Keeney, R. L., and von Winterfeldt, D. "On the Uses of Expert Judgment on Complex Technical Problems." *IEEE Transactions on Engineering Management,* 1989, *36,* 83-86.

Kostoff, R. (1988). "Evaluation of Proposed and Existing Accelerated Research Programs by the Office of Naval Research." *IEEE Transactions on Engineering Management,* 1988, *35,* 271-279.

Mason, R. O. "A Dialectical Approach to Strategic Planning." *Management Science,* 1969, *15,* B403-414.

Merton, R. K. "The Normative Structure of Science." In R. K. Merton. *The Sociology of Science: Theoretical and Empirical Investigations.* Chicago: University of Chicago, 1973. (Originally published 1942.)

Murnane, R. J., and Nelson, R. R. "Production and Innovation When Techniques Are Tacit." *Journal of Economic Behavior and Organization,* 1984, *5,* 353-373.

Nevo, D. "Expert Opinion in Program Evaluation." In R. F. Conner and M. Hendricks (eds.), *International Innovations in Evaluation Methodology.* San Francisco: Jossey-Bass, 1989.

Press, S. J., Ali, M. W., and Chung-Fang, E. Y. "An Empirical Study of a New Method for Forming Group Judgments: Qualitative Controlled Feedback." *Technological Forecasting and Social Change,* 1979, *15,* 171-189.

Rauch, W. "The Decision Delphi." *Technological Forecasting and Social Change,* 1979, *15,* 159-169.

Rossi, P. H., and Freeman, H. E. *Evaluation: A Systematic Approach.* Newbury Park, Calif.: Sage, 1985.

Schwenk, C. R. "Effects of Devil's Advocacy and Dialectical Inquiry on Decision Making." *Organizational Behavior and Decision Processes,* 1990, *47,* 161–176.

Shanteau, J. "Psychological Characteristics and Strategies of Expert Decision Makers." *Acta Psychologica,* 1988, *68,* 203–215.

Weston, C. "The Importance of Involving Experts and Learners in Formative Evaluation." *Canadian Journal of Educational Communication,* 1987, *16,* 45–58.

Woudenberg, F. "An Evaluation of Delphi." *Technological Forecasting and Social Change,* 1991, *40,* 131–150.

13

Acting for the Sake of Research: The Use of Role-Playing in Evaluation

Margery Austin Turner, Wendy Zimmermann

Overview

Every day government agencies interact with the public, providing information, processing applications, responding to complaints, and delivering services. How well are these interactions handled? Do people receive prompt responses from their government? Is the information provided to them accurate? Does everyone receive the benefits or services to which they are entitled? Are all individuals — men and women, minority and majority, young and old, literate and illiterate, handicapped and able — treated fairly? Although answering these questions is not a simple task, one way to address them is through the use of role-playing.

What Is Role-Playing?

Role-playing offers a methodology for directly assessing the overall quality of services provided to or treatment received by the public. In such an evaluation, individuals pose as job seekers, home buyers, benefit applicants, information seekers, or any other type of requestor in order to document service or treatment quality directly. Role-playing might be performed by single individuals to assess an agency's responses to requests for information or to complaints. Or role-playing might be performed by matched pairs (teams) of individuals to evaluate whether different groups of applicants receive equal treatment.

   Unlike most other research tools, role-playing allows evaluators to observe directly the treatment that people receive when they apply for services, ask for information, or complain about a problem. The methodology can be used to follow up on individual complaints of inadequate or inequitable service, to monitor the quality and evenness of service, to spot-check and provide feedback to service providers, or to evaluate treatment quality and equity comprehensively.

The simplest applications of role-playing do not require pairs of role-players but use any number of individuals to spot-check consistency or assess the quality of information or services provided to the public. While non-paired role-playing has not been applied as widely as paired role-playing, several such evaluations have been conducted. Evaluators in Kansas City, Missouri, and Saratoga, California, have employed role-playing to assess city employees' responses to requests for services and information (International City Management Association, 1981; Center for Excellence in Local Government, 1988). Similarly, the accuracy of information provided over the telephone by Internal Revenue Service (IRS) employees was evaluated by having individual role-players call with carefully scripted questions (U.S. General Accounting Office, 1989 and 1990). In applications such as these, evaluators can observe directly how public sector employees treat their clientele in known circumstances. Because many interactions between government workers and members of the public generally go unobserved, role-playing may provide the only feasible methodology for objectively assessing program performance.

A unique strength of paired role-playing, however, is in determining whether different groups of clients receive comparable treatment or services. In a paired role-playing evaluation, carefully matched teams are formed, with each team consisting of one member from each population group of interest — one man and one woman, for example, or one white person and one black, or one young person and one older individual. Both teammates apply for the same service or benefit, presenting themselves as equally eligible and equally in need. Pairs may also be formed in which the minority group role-player is slightly better qualified than the majority group role-player. Because both teammates are eligible for the same service or benefit, systematic differences in treatment across a significant number of cases provide convincing evidence of discrimination on the basis of race, sex, age, language, education, or any other attribute of concern to evaluators.

Paired role-playing has been used since the 1970s by private and public fair housing organizations to test for discrimination against minority home seekers by real estate and rental agents. Teams of blacks and whites (or Hispanics and Anglos) pose as home seekers with comparable family characteristics, housing needs, and resources. Teammates visit real estate and rental agents to inquire about the availability of houses and apartments, and about the terms and conditions of rent or sale. Agents who systematically treat comparable customers differently are, in effect, caught in the act of discriminating. Findings from such fair housing tests (or audits) have been admitted as evidence in state and federal courts, and have been used by local governments in determining the severity of discrimination in their communities (Fix and Struyk, 1993; Boggs, Sellers, and Bendick, 1993). In addition, the U.S. Department of Housing and Urban Development (HUD) has sponsored major audit studies to determine the incidence and severity of housing discrimination nationwide (Wienk and others, 1979; Turner, Struyk, and Yinger, 1991).

More recently, the matched role-playing methodology has been adapted to test for discrimination in hiring for entry-level jobs. Two exploratory studies — one focusing on the treatment of Hispanic men and the other on the treatment of black men — have established the applicability of matched role-playing beyond the housing context. In these studies, pairs of young men — minority and white — were matched on major characteristics relevant to the hiring decision; they then applied for entry-level positions advertised in the newspaper. Unfavorable treatment of minority applicants was recorded whenever they were unable to advance as far in the hiring process as their white Anglo counterparts (Cross, Kenney, Mell, and Zimmermann, 1990; Turner, Fix, and Struyk, 1991). The same basic methodology has also been used to determine whether car salesmen consistently quote women and blacks less attractive terms than males and whites and whether taxi drivers deny service to blacks who are trying to hail cabs on the street (Ayres, 1991; Ridley, Bayton, and Outtz, 1989). In almost any situation where one group of consumers may be treated less favorably than another, matched role-playing can be used to obtain direct evidence of any differences in treatment that actually occur.

The complexity and cost of implementing role-playing varies with the objectives and scope of analysis. In addition, role-playing raises significant ethical and legal concerns that warrant serious consideration. These range from the legality of using government employees as role-players to the ethical implications of deceiving employees and making false requests or applications. However, role-playing offers distinct advantages that make it a unique and convincing method for documenting the character and quality of service provided by government agencies and for determining whether systematic differences in treatment may be undermining program equity and effectiveness.

This chapter reviews key issues an analyst must address in designing an effective role-playing evaluation. Five major study design issues are discussed: selecting a sample for data collection and analysis, selecting and training role-players, conducting a role-playing evaluation, analyzing outcomes statistically, and identifying potential applications of role-playing.

Sampling

The first set of issues to address in designing a role-playing evaluation involves sampling. No evaluation, however ambitious, can record information about every transaction of interest; evaluators must select a sample of transactions for which role-playing will be conducted. Often, the validity of evaluation results hinges on the representativeness of this sample. In this section, we discuss three critical sampling issues:

- What is the universe of transactions?
- How big does the sample need to be?
- How should a sample be selected from the universe of transactions?

Regardless of the scope and objectives of an analysis, these three questions should be resolved before a role-playing evaluation gets under way.

Universe of Transactions

Every role-playing evaluation should be explicit about the universe of transactions or encounters to which its results apply. For example, if applications for permits or employment openings are accepted at five locations around the city, analysts need to decide in advance whether the results of their evaluation should be used to evaluate the treatment members of the public receive at one office, or whether results should assess treatment received regardless of the office visited. Evaluators might choose to send individual role-players to all five locations to assess differences among the offices or they might choose to target one office to analyze differences among staff members.

When paired role-playing was used to test for discrimination against minorities in employment, analysts initially hoped to analyze all entry-level hiring. To do so, however, would have required a sample representative of all entry-level job openings. In order to draw such a sample, every opening would have to have had a measurable chance of being selected for inclusion. In a simple random sample such as this one, every case in the universe should be identified so that it has an equal chance of being selected (see Newcomer, Chapter Seventeen of this volume).

Many entry-level jobs are advertised in newspapers; others are advertised with "Help Wanted" signs in the window, through employment agencies, or simply by word of mouth. Analysts concluded that it would be extremely difficult to identify all jobs advertised by word of mouth or with "Help Wanted" signs (Cross, Kenney, Mell, and Zimmermann, 1990). Therefore, the universe for analysis in the initial hiring discrimination studies was narrowed to openings advertised in the newspaper. Consequently, results from these studies reflect the incidence of discrimination in entry-level jobs that are advertised in the newspaper, not the incidence of discrimination in all entry-level hiring.

An alternative strategy, utilized by a group of fair employment advocates, targeted employment agencies. Role-players were sent to major employment agencies in a particular city, with repeat visits to agencies that showed evidence of possible discriminatory treatment. This sampling strategy did not yield definitive estimates of the incidence of discrimination in hiring, but it did yield very convincing evidence of discrimination by individual employment agencies (Boggs, Sellers, and Bendick, 1993). Thus, the scope and objectives of a role-playing evaluation, as well as the characteristics of transactions under investigation, need to be considered in defining the universe of transactions from which to draw a sample.

Sample Size

There is no single, easy answer to questions about required sample sizes. The answer depends on the purpose of the analysis, the desired degree of precision, and the extent to which comparisons will be made for subgroups within the sample. Small sample sizes—as few as ten or fifteen tests (each job that an individual or a matched team of role-players applies for is one test)—may be sufficient for complaint investigations or compliance monitoring but may yield ambiguous results if differences in treatment turn out to be small. Much larger sample sizes—250 tests or more—are required to support definitive measures of the incidence of discrimination, or if analysts wish to explore outcomes for different subgroups within the total sample.

Many local fair housing groups use paired role-playing to investigate actual complaints that real estate agents or landlords are discriminating against minorities, families with children, handicapped people, or other groups. The objective of these investigations is to determine whether there is support for a complaint or suspicion of discrimination, and to assemble evidence that may be used in court. Experienced fair housing groups typically send up to five or six pairs of role-players to a given agent or landlord. If several of these pairs experience differential treatment (or if differences in treatment are particularly flagrant for only one or two pairs), then there is good reason to pursue the matter legally, and the evidence from this small sample is likely to be very convincing in the courtroom (Boggs, Sellers, and Bendick, 1993).

However, when the objective of a role-playing evaluation is to yield definitive measures of the incidence of a particular problem, sample sizes must be substantially larger than five or six tests to provide statistically significant results. Most discussions of sampling error and statistical significance focus on the chance that what appears to be an important finding is in fact the result of random events or the chance that another sample from the same population would not support the same finding. This approach is sufficient for role-playing studies that do not compare the experiences of two or more matched teammates. For example, a role-playing study designed to determine whether a tourist information office or IRS help line is giving accurate information would need a sample large enough to minimize the chance of a false positive result—of incorrectly concluding that the public is being misinformed (see Newcomer, Chapter Seventeen of this volume). However, in a paired role-playing evaluation it may be equally important to guard against the opposite kind of error—against mistakenly concluding that there is no difference in treatment. In other words, the sample needs to be large enough to make it unlikely that evaluators observe a difference in treatment that does not really exist in the full population (a false positive or type I error), *and* to protect them from concluding that there is *no* difference in treatment when in fact a small but meaningful difference exists in the full population (a false negative or type II error).

To illustrate, in three recent studies of hiring discrimination, white Anglo applicants were favored over their minority teammates 12 percent to 33 percent of the time, as shown in Table 13.1 (Cross, Kenney, Mell, and Zimmermann, 1990; Turner, Fix, and Struyk, 1991; James and Del Castillo, 1992). The minority partner was less likely to be favored, but this result did occur — between 7 percent and 26 percent of the time. The first two studies summarized in Table 13.1, which were conducted by the Urban Institute, found large (and statistically significant) differences between the percentage of times the majority was favored and the percentage of times the minority was favored. This result strongly suggests that majority job applicants were considerably more likely to be favored than minority applicants. However, in the third study, conducted by the University of Colorado at Denver, the differences were relatively small; because of the small sample size in the Denver study, analysts concluded that outcomes favoring minority and majority job seekers essentially balanced each other out — that minorities were not subject to systematically unfavorable treatment. There is a risk in relying heavily on this result, however, because the small sample size leaves a high probability that the true differences in treatment may exist but go undetected.

In designing a full-scale evaluation in which statistically reliable results are an important objective, evaluators should obtain advice from a sampling expert. However, a rough rule of thumb is shown in Table 13.2, which provides estimates of the probability of detecting a difference in treatment of 5

**Table 13.1. Selected Results from
Hiring Discrimination Studies Using Paired Role-Players.**

	Percentage of Times Majority Teammate Favored	*Percentage of Times Minority Teammate Favored*	*Net Difference*	*Sample Size (numbers of pairs)*
Chicago — Hispanic/Anglo Study	33	8	25*	169
San Diego — Hispanic/Anglo Study (conducted summer 1989)	29	13	16*	191
Chicago — Black/White Study	17	8	9	197
Washington — Black/White Study (conducted summer 1990)	23	7	16*	241
Denver — Hispanic/Anglo Study	19	26	−7	140
Denver — Black/White Study (conducted summer 1990)	12	10	2	145

*indicates that the difference between the percentage of times the majority was favored and the percentage of times the minority was favored is statistically significant at a 95 percent or higher confidence level.

Sources: Cross, Kenney, Mell, and Zimmermann, 1990; Turner, Fix, and Struyk, 1991; James and Del Castillo, 1992.

percent to 20 percent, given sample sizes of 50 to 250. Table 13.2 shows that if there is a true difference of 10 percentage points between preference for the majority and preference for the minority, the chance of discovering this difference is only 40 percent with a sample size of 50, but rises to 93 percent with a sample size of 200. In other words, if whites are 10 percent more likely to be treated favorably than blacks, a sample size of 50 or 100 would probably be too small to detect this difference with statistical certainty.

Table 13.2. Probability of Discerning Differences between Pairs with Samples of Varying Size.[a]

| | | True Difference in Treatment Between Two Groups[b] (pecentage points) | | | |
		5	10	15	20
Sample Size[c] =	50	.171	.400	.671	.872
	100	.256	.630	.907	.990
	150	.333	.783	.977	.999
	200	.404	.877	.995	1.00
	250	.470	.932	.999	1.00

[a]This table sets the likelihood of a false positive (type I error) at 5 percent, and estimates the likelihood of a false negative (type II error) for different sample sizes and true differences. For these calculations, variance estimates are based on the Urban Institute's black-white employment discrimination study, conducted in Washington, D.C., and Chicago, Illinois.

[b]The first column, for example, assumes that the true difference between outcomes for whites and blacks is 5 percentage points. Entries in the column indicate the chance of discerning this difference, with statistical confidence of at least 95 percent, for various sample sizes.

[c]A sample size of 50 means that 50 *paired tests* were conducted. In a paired housing study, for example, each sample test is a visit by two teammates to a real estate office.

Selecting the Sample

Once the universe of transactions has been defined and a suitable sample size has been identified, a systematic procedure must be defined for selecting cases from the universe for inclusion in the sample. Sometimes the selection process will be straightforward, focusing on all transactions in a particular, narrowly defined category. If there have been complaints about a particular office or individual, evaluators may decide to conduct several role-playing visits targeted at that office or individual. In most circumstances, however, there will be good reasons to draw a random sample of locations, individuals, days, or times of day at which role-playing encounters will be conducted. As explained earlier, to ensure an unbiased, random sample, every case in the universe has to have a known probability of being selected for inclusion.

In the national housing discrimination study, random samples of advertisements for apartments and homes were selected from the classified sections of major newspapers. A three-step procedure was used to select the sample ads:

1. All the advertisements that qualified for selection were numbered sequentially.
2. A computer program was used to generate enough random numbers to produce the required sample size (for example, if a sample of 50 ads was needed from a total of 1,000, the computer generated 50 random numbers between 1 and 1,000).
3. The ads whose numbers corresponded to the random numbers generated by the computer were selected for inclusion in the sample.

This procedure ensured that ads at the end of the classified section were just as likely to be selected as ads at the beginning, and that there was no element of human choice in the decision to include or exclude an eligible advertisement from the sample.

Obviously, many other techniques can be designed to yield a reasonable probability sample. For example, evaluators could make an exhaustive list of all offices in which permit applications are accepted and select every third (or sixth, or tenth) office to produce the desired sample of offices to visit. Any systematic procedure that gives every case in the universe a measurable chance of inclusion should generate a defensible random sample; and such procedures should produce comparable results.

Selecting and Training Role-Players

One of the keys to conducting an effective role-playing evaluation lies in carefully selecting the role-players and ensuring they have the relevant characteristics. The results of any role-playing evaluation are based on the treatment or services received by individuals with known qualifications and characteristics. Therefore, evaluators will need to determine the major characteristics that are relevant to the study and decide which of those can be assigned (that is, fictitious) and which must be innate to the role-players. They will also need to determine what qualities they want in the individual role-players themselves to ensure that they do the job properly.

In evaluating whether two groups of individuals (black and whites or men and women, for example) are treated equally, evaluators will need to select pairs, or teams, of role-players. These individuals need to be matched on all characteristics relevant to the evaluation except for the one under examination (such as race, gender, or age). For nonpaired role-playing evaluations, in which role-players would individually assess, for example, the quality or consistency of services provided by a public agency, selection and training of role-players is still important but is considerably more straightforward.

Determine Key Characteristics for Role-Players

Role-players should be selected based on all characteristics that are relevant to the treatment or service provision being evaluated. For some evaluations this includes only objective characteristics, such as gender, age, or income, that are easily determined. However, it may also be necessary to select individuals according to intangible characteristics such as personality and demeanor, which are more difficult to define and involve more subjectivity in the selection process.

Clearly, the purpose of the study will determine the relevant characteristics. For example, a nonpaired evaluation of an agency that provides services to the elderly may require the role-players only to be elderly. However, in paired role-playing, matching the role-players presents a greater challenge. In the studies of housing discrimination where pairs of role-players had to appear to be equally qualified home buyers or renters, they were matched according to such criteria as their income, age, marital status, family size, types of job, assets and debts, and housing needs. For the employment discrimination studies the role-players were matched on age, education, work experience, skills, and physical build as well as on such intangible factors as articulateness, personality, and demeanor. Since employers may base their hiring decisions on how friendly or outgoing a person is, the role-players had to appear equally shy, gregarious, or aggressive.

Matching two individuals according to such characteristics as age, education, or physical appearance can be done in a straightforward and objective manner. However, in matching on such intangible traits as personality and articulateness, the process becomes much more subjective. For this reason, having more than one person interview the role-players and agree on the teams will help ensure well-matched pairs. Preferably, three or more people should interview each candidate and participate in the matching decisions. In the Urban Institute employment studies, members of the research team who varied in sex, gender, and race participated in the pairing decisions. This mix was to ensure agreement of the pairing among individuals with different perspectives. Evaluators may also want to consider using outside consultants to participate in the matching process.

While role-players can assume certain fictitious characteristics relevant to the evaluation, other attributes, such as sex or skin color, are innate and cannot be assigned or changed. Some evaluations may require role-players to have a certain physical appearance, level of articulateness, or unaccented speech, in which case role-players with those actual attributes have to be recruited. It may be appropriate, however, to alter other characteristics such as income, education, or address. Which characteristics can be altered also depends on the nature of the study. If, for example, role-players may be required to present documentation such as a driver's license or proof of income, the information that appears on that document obviously cannot be altered. In evaluations using pairs of role-players, certain characteristics can be altered for one of the role-players in a pair while others could be altered for both.

Role-players should also be selected on criteria that are not directly relevant to the evaluation but that may bear on outcomes. For example, if a government agency wants to evaluate whether women and men are treated differently when requesting information, they will want to ensure that both teammates appear as similar as possible in every respect except gender. Consequently, evaluators should control for such attributes as regional or foreign accents, extreme differences in height, and distinct differences in personality, such as aggressiveness or passiveness, even though these are not relevant to the subject of the evaluation. This way, if the person providing the information happens to discriminate against Southerners or particularly assertive people, the results of the study will not reflect a separate type of differential treatment from the one being evaluated.

Varying the Qualifications of the Role-Players

Another strategy for conducting a paired role-playing evaluation is to make the minority group role-player slightly *more* qualified than the majority group role-player with whom he or she is paired. The Fair Employment Council of Greater Washington conducted an employment discrimination study in which Latino job applicants were given better credentials than their Anglo counterparts. For example, Latinos could type sixty words per minute and Anglos only forty-five, or Latinos had managed a retail department while Anglos had worked as senior sales staff. In addition, where initial contact was by phone, Latinos always phoned first and Anglos second rather than alternating (Bendick, Jackson, Reinoso, and Hodges, 1992). Varying the qualifications of role-players can provide even stronger evidence of differential or discriminatory treatment if the less-qualified role-player is treated more favorably than the better-qualified role-player. If a public agency wants to determine whether black applicants for a job opening are treated the same as white applicants, evaluators might use a black role-player with slightly better qualifications — more experience, better grades — in conducting the evaluation. This weighting reduces the possibility that the white role-player could be chosen over the black for legitimate or unobservable reasons and could strengthen the credibility of a finding of discrimination.

The disadvantage of this type of matching is that if the differential treatment or discrimination is subtle, the evaluation may not reveal significant levels of difference. In other words, an employer might consistently prefer an equally qualified white applicant over a black applicant but might be swayed to hire a black applicant who is clearly better qualified. Since differential treatment of this kind might be more rare, a larger sample size would probably be needed to discern smaller incidences of differential treatment.

Recruitment and Selection of Role-Players

Recruiting individuals who will be dependable role-players and who are capable of role-playing and recording treatment is central to conducting a good evaluation. Aside from the characteristics described above relevant to the role being played, a number of characteristics are also desirable for the role-players themselves. Because the outcomes of an evaluation depend entirely on what the role-players observe and record, it is imperative that role-players be reliable and honest, and that they provide accurate information about their experiences. The role-players should also be objective about the issue in question, particularly if the study is potentially controversial or political, such as testing for race discrimination.

Other factors important for those participating in any type of role-playing evaluation are that they be organized, timely, detail-oriented, and motivated. Role-players should also be able to act, or portray someone different from themselves if the evaluation requires it. In addition to these traits, certain evaluations may have practical constraints. If the evaluation requires the role-players to travel around a city, visiting various agencies, for example, then the evaluation may require that role-players have cars and know the city or town well enough to be able to get around easily. If the role-players will be involved in detailed or complicated interactions, such as acquiring a business license, they may need to know a substantial amount about the issue in question. For certain issues role-players can be trained; for others it may be necessary to hire individuals who have substantive knowledge of the subject.

Government agencies may wish to use their own employees as role-players; some have done so. The General Accounting Office has used the role-playing methodology to evaluate the Internal Revenue Service's responses to questions about tax returns. Subsequently, the IRS began evaluating its own services, using employees as role-players (U.S. General Accounting Office, 1989, 1990). The Justice Department's Civil Rights Division recently initiated a fair housing testing program in which government employees pose as home seekers. Role-players who are employees may have the advantage of being knowledgeable about the service delivered or program in question and about how the system works. However, since confidentiality is key to a successful study, it is important that the role-players not be recognized by the persons with whom they are likely to interact. The legality and perceived acceptability of using government employees as role-players may vary by agency and by program. Analysts should therefore review the appropriateness of using employees for each evaluation.

In both of the Urban Institute employment discrimination studies students from nearby universities were recruited to act as role-players. Using students provided the benefits of relatively inexpensive labor and a pool of individuals who were interested in social science research and who were available during the summer on a full-time but short-term basis. In a citizen-surrogate study conducted in Kansas City, Missouri, students were also used as participant observers, or role-players. In this study, the students presented city agency employees with standardized questions and then recorded employees' responses (International City Management Association, 1981).

Conducting a Role-Playing Evaluation

Regardless of the type of evaluation — testing for discrimination, evaluating the timeliness of a telephone response, or analyzing the quality of a complicated service delivery — certain implementation issues are always relevant. These issues include developing a comprehensive data collection instrument, training the individuals who will be role-playing, managing the study, maintaining quality control, and keeping costs low.

Developing Data Collection Instruments

On completing a role-playing encounter (or one stage of a complex transaction), each role-player records the treatment he or she received. Subsequently, the experiences and outcomes reported by all the role-players can be objectively compared to assess treatment and determine whether systematic differences occurred. For paired role-playing evaluations, data collection instruments should be completed independently by each member of a pair, not jointly by a team of role-players. Differences in treatment are not directly observed or reported by the role-players. Instead, each individual simply reports on the treatment he or she received. Then, analysts use these data to make comparisons either between the experiences of two matched partners or among a group of role-players in a nonpaired evaluation.

To capture all relevant information about the transaction under evaluation the data collection instrument should, to the extent possible, be structured unambiguously, anticipate all possible outcomes (intermediate as well as final), and account for all important elements of treatment. In order to measure treatment or quality of service, as much information as possible should be quantifiable. While it is always a good idea to allow role-players to comment in narrative form, the amount of subjectivity and quality judgments that role-players make should be minimized.

A key factor in determining an instrument's format and complexity is the number of stages involved in the transaction. Many transactions may have only one stage. For example, an evaluation of how a local tourist office delivers information would involve a single interaction — a phone call, a walk-in visit, or perhaps a written request for information. Data collection for this type of study would involve reporting all relevant information related to this one encounter.

However, other transactions might be more complex and involve multiple stages, with numerous measures at each stage. The employment discrimination studies used a three-stage analysis — application, interview, and job offer. Figure 13.1 provides an overview of the entry-level hiring process and the types of treatment captured by the data collection instruments. Role-players reported whether they were able to successfully fill out an application for the job advertised, whether they obtained an interview, and whether they received a job offer. In these studies the data collection instruments also recorded the treatment a role-player received at each stage, including such information as how long they had to wait or what salary they were offered.

The survey instruments should be designed to capture all relevant information and anticipate all possible outcomes. If a study is evaluating treatment received by applicants for public benefits, the data collection instrument might capture not only whether a role-player was found to be eligible for assistance but also whether the appropriate questions were asked during the interview, and whether relevant documents were requested and reviewed. Because of the complexity of the job application process, the instrument used in the employment discrimination study was also designed to capture such treatment as the questions applicants were asked, the number of times they were interviewed, and the number of phone calls the role-players made to secure an interview or job offer.

Analysts may also want to measure qualitative aspects of the treatment role-players receive by asking them to record negative or positive remarks made to them about race, gender, or other attributes. These aspects of treatment are obviously difficult to quantify and are subject to the interpretation of the role-players. Urging the role-players to record comments of this type word for word is likely to increase accuracy. These comments are useful for adding texture and anecdotal detail to the more objective and quantitative results of the study.

Training Role-Players

In any role-playing evaluation, role-players should be systematically trained so that their behavior is consistent and the treatment they receive is recorded fully and objectively. Thus, training should include practice in playing the assigned role and in completing data collection instruments. When using the paired team methodology, another integral part of the training involves familiarizing role-players with their shared characteristics. In the housing discrimination study, for example, role-players had to be trained to remember all their assigned characteristics such as income, employment, and details of their financial situation. In addition, the pairs must be trained to approach the agents in the same manner, and express interest in the same type of housing.

Training role-players to act in a controlled manner—following the script—is key for making later assessments of the treatment they receive and for aggregating data. This uniformity is particularly important for paired role-playing. For example, in the employment discrimination studies it was assumed that employers may make hiring decisions based on the enthusiasm and personality of an applicant. Therefore, role-players were trained to ask employers similar questions and to behave similarly in the interview. Practice interviews were conducted in which each member of the team watched

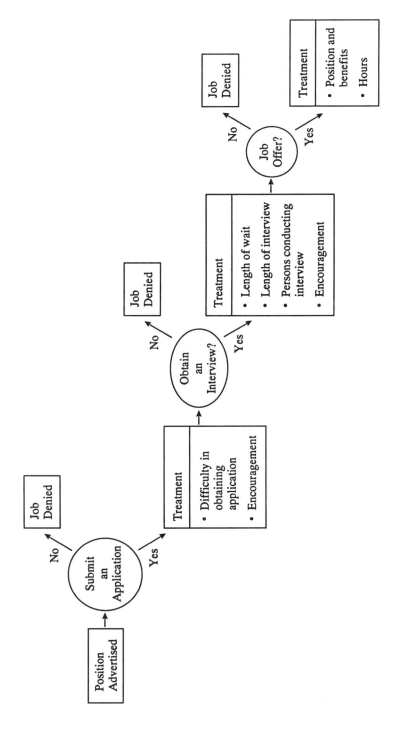

Figure 13.1. Flow Chart Showing Differential Outcomes and Differential Treatment in the Hiring Process.

the other so that he or she could imitate the teammate's responses and manner as well as practice those characteristics that had been assigned to both.

A more superficial but important element when role-players appear in person (rather than calling on the telephone) is physical appearance. For paired studies, role-players should be matched according to physical appearance and they should also dress similarly. To illustrate, in the car sales discrimination study, role-players who were sent to buy cars needed to project the same image. A well-dressed role-player might make a better and more serious impression on a care salesman than one who is poorly dressed (Ayres, 1991). This rule also applies to the role-players who participated in the housing and employment studies and is applicable, to some extent, to all evaluations in which the role-players make personal contact with the person or office being evaluated.

Also important to the training of role-players is coordination among players and accurate and timely reporting of treatment. For paired evaluations, the order in which teammates visit or call should alternate. For example, in both the employment and housing discrimination studies, half the time the minority testers called first; white Anglo testers called first the other half. If an evaluation requires role-players to respond to an advertisement, for example, it is important that both members of a team respond near the same time. In the employment discrimination studies role-players were required to phone an employer in response to an advertisement between ten and thirty minutes of one another. If the advertisement required going directly to the employer, they were required to visit between fifteen minutes and one hour of one another. Teammates also need to coordinate the number of phone calls made, to ensure that both display the same amount of interest in obtaining the job, house, or service.

Evaluators should also train role-players to record information accurately on the data collection instruments. This accuracy can be achieved by having them conduct practice tests or evaluations and practice filling out the instruments. Practicing the actual steps that role-players will have to take has proven invaluable in previous studies. In the employment discrimination studies, for example, the role-players remarked that the practice tests were the most valuable part of the training to them. If the role-players will be dealing with other types of forms, such as applications, they should practice filling out these forms. Such trial runs will also help them remember their assigned characteristics or biographies.

A key part of the training lies in emphasizing the confidential nature of the study as well as the importance of it. For any role-playing evaluation to succeed, the nature and timing of the study must remain secret. At the same time, role-players should understand the purpose and seriousness of the evaluation as well as the importance of their part in it.

Management and Quality Control

The importance of close supervision and careful management of a role-playing study cannot be underestimated. The validity of an evaluation's data depends critically on the reliability of information recorded by the role-players. Therefore, the methods used to ensure that role-players are honest and accurate in their recordkeeping may come under close scrutiny. There should be sufficient oversight of the role-players that a manager can follow the course of each individual interaction closely. The level of management needed depends on the number of sites, the number of role-players, and the nature of the study. If the role-playing is undertaken by telephone only, managers can simply listen to and observe the role-players. This type of supervision is more straightforward than that required for field work. In the employment discrimination studies, for example, one manager in each site supervised four to five teams, or eight to ten individuals. This level of supervision ensured that the manager was able to keep close track of every step involved in the interactions. If there are numerous sites (more than two or three, for example) an additional coordinator for all the sites may be needed.

Another way to maintain close supervision is to meet with each of the role-players daily or, if appropriate, require them to phone the office daily. In the employment discrimination studies, where close supervision and coordination were essential, the role-players were required to visit the office once a day and to call in at least twice a day. Managers should also review the data collection instruments on a regular basis to ensure that the role-players are filling them out as soon as they have finished a transaction when the information is fresh in their minds. Reviewing the instruments for completeness and accuracy also improves the quality of the data.

Throughout the history of role-playing evaluation, observers have had concerns about quality control, or, more specifically, about the possibility of role-players recording false information. As in all research that uses human subjects, this is a possibility. There are, however, ways to minimize the likelihood of its occurrence. One way is for role-players themselves to be audited. For instance, one of the phone numbers they are given to call could be a member of the evaluation team who would ensure that both members of the pair, or the nonpaired individuals, are completing the transaction completely and comparably. In addition, a number of the management techniques mentioned above serve to control the quality and validity of the data. Close supervision, checking the data collection instruments, and having the role-players make phone calls from the evaluation office all help the manager maintain control over the quality of the data collection. Evaluators may also consider making teammates "double-blind," where they do not know the outcomes of their partner's actions. The advantage of this approach is that the role-players will not be influenced in any way by the knowledge of what has happened to their partner. The disadvantage is that coordination becomes more difficult and must be handled entirely by a supervisor.

Cost Considerations

A number of decisions made in designing a role-playing evaluation affect its cost. The type of interaction being simulated obviously has an impact on how much it will cost. An evaluation that can be conducted entirely by mail or telephone would clearly require less labor and cost less than one in which role-players must travel around a city visiting numerous sites. Because those simpler types of evaluations require less time and labor per transaction and can probably be done from a single location, the costs would be considerably lower than the costs of a more complex evaluation. The employment discrimination studies, for example, involved more than one type of contact — telephone calls and in-person visits. The complexity of the study required one week of training, which also increased costs. Less complex evaluations, such as one that assessed the quality and accuracy of a written or telephone request for information from an agency, probably could be conducted with fewer role-players and less training.

Certain costs, however, will be constant across most evaluations. These include role-players' salaries (some studies have used unpaid volunteers), managers' salaries, office space, production of training materials and data collection instruments, and the costs of data analysis. Other possible expenses are telephone lines, postage, and travel expenses. Using government employees as role-players, if they do not use overtime, will help reduce costs for public agencies.

Another important issue in determining cost is sample size and the personnel time needed to conduct the evaluation. In the Hispanic-Anglo employment discrimination study, for example, eight pairs of role-players worked full-time for five weeks (plus one week of training), conducting a total of 360 tests. In the black-white study, ten pairs worked full-time for six weeks, finishing 476 tests. Each pair of role-players completed an average of ten tests per week, not including the last week of the study which was used to complete tests started in the previous weeks. In both studies role-players were paid a fixed amount for the weeks worked so that there was no financial incentive to fabricate data. Evaluators should also take into account the time it may take to initiate tests that ultimately cannot be included in the sample. The employment studies required initiating many more tests (50 percent to 100 percent more) than were ultimately included in order to achieve the desired sample size because role-players called and visited employers who had already filled the jobs or the role-players were unable to reach an employer to submit an application.

In a less labor-intensive and less complex evaluation, however, role-players working full-time may be able to complete many more than ten tests per week and, consequently, work for a shorter period of time. In addition, if the goals of the evaluation are to obtain a general assessment of how a program or office is operating, or to evaluate complaints received about a program activity, a large and statistically valid sample might not be needed and the purposes of the study could be achieved in a short time, with few tests, and at low costs. Thus, the cost of a study will vary widely depending on its goals, its complexity, the sample size, and how long it takes to conduct the evaluation.

Statistical Analysis of Paired Outcomes

Role-playing is an extremely powerful methodology because its results are intuitively clear and compelling to nontechnical audiences. The public can clearly understand findings that minors attempting to buy cigarettes were successful in three out of every five establishments they visited, or that information provided by a tourist bureau was accurate 85 percent of the time. Paired role-playing is particularly effective because its results directly document unfair differences in treatment. In the study of hiring discrimination against blacks, 20 percent of the time that young black men applied for entry-level jobs, they were unable to advance as far in the hiring process as *equally qualified* white applicants. This kind of result and the anecdotal evidence that can accompany it is extremely understandable and convincing to policymakers and to the general public.

Analysis of outcomes from a simple role-playing evaluation of program performance does not present any special statistical challenges. However, analyzing data from a paired role-playing evaluation requires considerable caution. This section focuses on three key issues to be addressed at the data analysis stage for a paired study focusing on differences in treatment. First, basic measures of differential treatment are discussed. Second, procedures for testing the statistical significance of these measures are introduced. And finally, the issue of random and systematic factors that contribute to the differences in treatment observed in a paired role-playing evaluation is discussed. All three of these issues apply specifically to analysis of paired outcomes. Analysis of results from a nonpaired role-playing study is much more straightforward and can be accomplished with more conventional measures and statistical tests.

Measuring Differences in Treatment

The key building block for analysis of data from a paired role-playing evaluation is a case-by-case determination of whether the two members of each team were treated the same or differently, and if there was a difference, which teammate was favored. In this analysis, the unit of observation is the team, and variables are constructed from the experience of the two teammates to measure relative outcomes.

To illustrate, in the studies of employment discrimination, analysts determined how far in the hiring process each applicant was able to progress. Specifically, was he able to submit an application? (stage 1), was he granted a formal interview? (stage 2), and did he receive a job offer? (stage 3). Then, outcomes for the two members of each team were brought together to determine whether one partner advanced farther than the other. A team was classified as majority favored (if the majority partner advanced to a higher stage than the minority partner), minority favored (if the minority partner advanced farther), or no difference (if they both reached the same stage). Finally, results were tabulated across teams, to report the share of cases in which the majority advanced farther than an equally qualified minority, and the share in which the minority advanced farther. Analysis can also be conducted using the individual teammates' experience as the unit of observation and comparing the overall outcomes for teammates of one type to the overall outcomes for teammates of the other type. For example, in the Hispanic-Anglo hiring discrimination study, analysts found that the Hispanic applicants received formal interviews 48 percent of the times they applied for entry-level jobs, compared to 64 percent for the white Anglo applicants.

Sometimes it is difficult to decide whether the two members of a team have really been treated differently or whether the differences are so negligible that they should be ignored. To illustrate, the housing discrimination study focused on the racial and ethnic composition of neighborhoods where minority and majority teammates were shown houses in order to determine whether minority home seekers were being steered away from predominantly white neighborhoods. For each teammate, analysts calculated the average percent black (or Hispanic) for neighborhoods where houses were shown. In other words, if a person was shown three houses—one in a neighborhood that was 10 percent black, one in a neighborhood that was 13 percent black, and one in a neighborhood that was 5 percent black—the average racial composition for houses shown to this partner was 9.3 percent black. Next, average neighborhood characteristics were compared for the two members of each team to determine whether the minority partner was shown houses in more predominantly black neighborhoods than the majority partner.

At this stage, a significance threshold was established to define a non-negligible difference in neighborhood composition. Analysts decided that small differences in average racial composition were not meaningful from a policy perspective and should not be counted as steering. If a minority partner was shown houses in neighborhoods averaging 3 percent black while his white partner was shown houses in neighborhoods averaging 2.5 percent black, it would be imprudent to classify this difference as a case of racial steering. In the housing discrimination study, analysts classified a team's experience as steering only if the difference in neighborhood racial composition exceeded a threshold of 5 percentage points. Thresholds were also defined for differences in average per capita income and differences in average house values.

Results like those outlined above represent the share of cases in which two comparable teammates received different treatment. In other words, they reflect the *incidence* of differential—or unequal—treatment. For many forms of treatment, this is the most logical measure. If the treatment you are concerned about is categorical, then teammates are either treated the same or one of them is favored over the other, with no degrees of difference. Examples of such categorical outcomes include the following:

- Did an applicant receive a job offer?
- Was an advertised apartment available for rent?
- Did a taxi driver stop to pick up the passenger?

Other outcomes, however, may vary in terms of degree:

- What hourly wage was the applicant offered?
- How many apartments were made available for consideration?
- How long did the passenger have to wait for a taxi?

The incidence of differential treatment can certainly be calculated for these *continuous* outcome measures, possibly using thresholds like those discussed in the racial steering example above. In addition, however, analysts can compute the *severity* of differential treatment for continuous outcome variables.

Severity measures reflect the magnitude of differences in outcomes between teammates. They are constructed by (1) calculating the average value of a given treatment measure across all teammates of each type and (2) comparing the averages for the two types of teammates. To illustrate, Table 13.3 presents several measures of the severity of discrimination in housing. On average, white homebuyers were told about 2.3 possible houses per visit to a real estate agent, compared to an average of 1.8 possible houses shown or recommended to their black counterparts. Thus, the severity of discrimination can be expressed as 0.5 houses on average per visit—or as 21 percent fewer houses for black homebuyers than for comparable whites.

In presenting measures of the differential outcomes it is important to recognize that the average outcome measures incorporate cases in which (1) no differences in treatment occurred, (2) one type of partner was favored, and (3) the other type of partner was favored. Thus, this type of severity measure reflects the *average* difference in treatment across all cases, including those in which no difference was recorded. This measure indicates how big an impact differential treatment has on overall outcomes, not how severe the differences are when they do occur. Alternatively, severity measures can be constructed for the subset of cases in which one teammate was favored over the other to reflect how severe differential treatment is when it does occur (Yinger, 1993).

Table 13.3. Measures of the Severity of
Discrimination in Housing from a Study Using Paired Role-Players.

	Difference[a]	*Percentage Difference*[b]
Black and White Homebuyers	0.476	20.8
Hispanic and Anglo Homebuyers	0.522	22.1
Black and White Renters	0.404	24.5
Hispanic and Anglo Renters	0.176	10.9

[a]Average number of houses shown or recommended to majority auditor minus average number shown or recommended to minority.
[b]Difference in houses shown or recommended as a percentage of the number shown or recommended to majority auditor.
Source: Turner, M., Struyk, R., and Yinger, J. *Housing Discrimination Study: Synthesis.* Washington, D.C.: U.S. Department of Housing and Urban Development, 1991.

Tests of Statistical Significance

In studies that are based on a probability sample of encounters and whose goal is to describe the total universe of such encounters, the next important analysis step is to test the statistical significance of incidence and severity measures. Suppose in a sample of one hundred cases, members of group A received more favorable treatment than their group B partners fifteen times, members of group B received more favorable treatment than their group A partners five times, and partners (A and B) were treated equally eighty times. Can the analyst reasonably conclude that group A is consistently favored over group B in the universe of all such transactions, or is there a real chance that this result is idiosyncratic — that another sample would have shown no such difference in treatment?

In more formal terms, one must test the null hypothesis that the incidence of preferential treatment for Group A ($I_a - 15$ percent in the example above) is actually zero. This hypothesis can be tested with a standard t statistic, which is calculated by dividing the incidence of preferential treatment by its standard error, and determining from a table of t statistics how likely it is that the resulting ratio could occur by chance. Analysts typically reject the null hypothesis if there is a 5 percent chance or less that the observed results could occur when there is no real difference for the populations as a whole. Sometimes, a more rigorous statistical standard is applied, requiring a 1 percent chance or less. In paired role-playing studies, there are actually three possible outcomes for any test. Specifically, the analyst actually needs to test (1) the hypothesis that the incidence of group A being favored (I_a) is zero, (2) the hypothesis that the incidence of group B being favored (I_b) is zero, and (3) the hypothesis that both are treated equally. Some researchers might also test that the difference between I_a and I_b is zero. In the example above, these would mean testing the hypothesis that 15 percent A-favored is significantly different from 5 percent B-favored.

Similar tests of statistical significance need to be conducted for measures of the severity of differential treatment. In this case, the appropriate measure is a difference-of-means test, which also produces a standard t statistic. Again, the observed difference in outcomes (D) is divided by its standard error, and a table of t statistics is used to determine whether the resulting ratio could reasonably have occurred by chance. If not, the analyst can reject the null hypothesis, that D is actually equal to zero in the population as a whole.

Systematic Versus Random Difference in Treatment

In addition to statistical significance tests, an analyst using the paired role-playing methodology must be aware of the distinction between systematic and random differences in treatment. Differential treatment of teammates can occur for both systematic and random reasons. To illustrate, suppose a landlord showed one apartment to a majority homebuyer but none to the minority partner, so that the case had been classified as "majority favored" for the outcome measure. This unfavorable treatment of the minority teammate might have occurred for systematic reasons: perhaps the landlord wants to keep minorities out of his building because he considers them poor tenants or because he fears that he will lose majority tenants if there are minorities in the building. On the other hand, the same unfavorable treatment may also have resulted from random factors. Perhaps the landlord received a call between the visits from the majority and minority teammates indicating that a tenant had been found for the apartment. Or perhaps the agent felt tired or ill at the time of the minority partner's visit. Any number of random events might result in differential treatment of two customers, differential treatment unrelated to race or ethnicity.

Simple measures of the incidence of differential treatment inevitably include some cases in which the majority role-player was favored because of discrimination and some in which he was favored for random reasons. In fact, the share of cases with "majority favored" outcomes may either over- or understate the true incidence of systematically unfavorable treatment of minorities, and (as yet) there is no foolproof mathematical or statistical procedure for disentangling the random and systematic components of these measures. Some analysts subtract the share of cases that are minority favored from the share that are majority favored to yield a net measure, which is intended to reflect the incidence of systematic discrimination (Wienk and others, 1979). Other analysts report the majority favored outcomes as a measure of the incidence of discrimination against the minority group and report the minority favored outcomes as a measure of the incidence of reverse discrimination. Both measures are displayed in Table 13.1.

Advanced statistical procedures can offer some insights into the relative importance of random and systematic differences in treatment in a paired role-playing evaluation. For example, multivariate regression or logistic analysis can be used to quantify the independent impacts of various observed factors on treatment outcomes and to estimate the residual role of random factors (Yinger, 1991). However, these procedures are technically complex and must be tailored to the circumstances of a particular data set.

Researchers continue to explore the issue of random and systematic contributions to observed differences in treatment, and to refine statistical and other procedures for disentangling the effects of random factors. In the meantime, however, simple measures of the incidence of differential treatment are straightforward and informative. It is reasonable to report that, for example, black job applicants receive less favorable treatment than comparable whites 20 percent of the time. Although not all of these cases of unfavorable treatment necessarily reflect systematic discrimination, they do reflect the incidence of unequal treatment. At the same time, it would make sense to report the incidence of white favored outcomes (7 percent), and the incidence of equal outcomes (73 percent). If the limitations of these simple measures are understood and the potential role of random factors is acknowledged, then complex statistical adjustments are not necessary.

Potential Applications of Role-Playing

The range of possibilities for using the role-playing technique in evaluations has not yet been fully explored. To date, paired role-playing has been used principally to test for racial and ethnic discrimination in housing and employment. However, role-playing can also be used to test for discrimination against other groups in other arenas. Nonpaired role-playing has been used, to a more limited extent, primarily to assess the quality of information and services provided by government employees.

While role-playing is an effective tool for many types of evaluations, it does have ethical, legal, and practical limitations that should be considered. These range from the legality of using government employees to the ethical implications of making false requests or applications. However, role-playing has distinct advantages that make it a unique and convincing method for evaluating programs and for measuring discrimination.

Innovative Applications for Role-Playing

Researchers have used the role-playing methodology to test for racial and ethnic discrimination in entry-level employment, housing rentals and purchases, car sales, and taxi service. The methodology has also been modified for application to mortgage financing and home insurance (Galster, 1993). Some banks have hired market research firms to use role-playing to uncover discriminatory behavior in their own offices ("Tracking Bias . . . ," 1992). For government agency purposes, the possibilities are wide ranging. Generally, the technique could be applied to many service delivery functions to evaluate equal treatment or quality of services. These may include information assistance, applications for benefits or licenses, or the functioning of a specific program.

The simplest applications of the methodology are for evaluations that do not use pairs or teams at all. A number of these types of evaluations have also been conducted. Health researchers in Minnesota and Massachusetts have used teenagers posing as would-be cigarette purchasers to determine whether restaurants, bars, stores, and hotels are locking vending machines and limiting sales to minors as required by law ("Smoking and Teens . . . ," 1992). Similarly, evaluators can analyze the quality of information given to the public on request generally (as opposed to whether two groups received different quality information) using the simple role-playing methodology, as was done in an assessment of city employees' responses to requests for services and information conducted in Saratoga, California (Center for Excellence in Local Government, 1988). For these types of applications, role-players can be trained in a group instead of in pairs so that all testers have the same relevant traits and knowledge, but sufficient differences to appear believable as ordinary citizens. Data collection and analysis can be based not on the differences within pairs but across the group of testers.

The role-playing methodology also lends itself to testing for discrimination on the basis of attributes other than race and ethnicity. The technique could be used to determine whether people with physical handicaps or low levels of education are treated equally well when requesting assistance or when receiving services. There may also be characteristics specific to a particular program or service that could be the subject of a role-playing evaluation. If an agency delivers services across a large geographic region, but it is easier for employees to deliver services to some areas than others, an evaluation could be conducted to determine whether employees are delivering services comparably to people from all regions. Or agencies that deliver a service from different offices or facilities can use role-playing to evaluate selected aspects of the quality of service at each such office or facility.

In addition to using pairs to test for differential treatment between two individuals, the role-playing methodology also lends itself to evaluations using testers in teams of three or possibly more. One strategy currently being explored is referred to as "sandwich testing" and requires the use of *three* matched teammates for each role-playing case (see Heckman, 1993). To illustrate, in an evaluation focused on the treatment of black job applicants, two teammates would be white and the third would be black. The order of their visits to the job site would be first a white, then the black, followed by the second white. If *both* whites are favored over the black, the evidence of systematic discrimination is very strong. If, on the other hand, the second white partner receives treatment comparable to the black, and only the first white partner is favored, then there is good reason to suspect that random factors have intervened. Sandwich testing has been used by local fair housing organizations in developing evidence in support of individual discrimination complaints, but it has not yet been used in scientific studies of discriminatory patterns.

To test for differences among more than two categories of clients, teams of three, or possibly more, could also be arranged. A team could include one white, one black, and one Hispanic role-player. This arrangement provides information on discrimination against members of two minority groups at once as well as the relative extent of discrimination against each group. This technique would provide a direct comparison of the levels of discrimination against, for example, blacks and Hispanics. However, using teams of three or more would add certain complications. Recruiting and forming these teams would take more time and effort than would forming pairs. Management and coordination would also be more complex, and for analysis purposes a slightly larger sample size might be needed. In some circumstances, three-way audits might also seriously increase the risks of disclosure, endangering the validity of the study as a whole. For example, three-way audits were considered in the most recent national study of housing discrimination, but there was great concern that agents in white neighborhoods would be "tipped off" by visits from both blacks and Hispanics in quick succession.

Potential Problems and Limitations

The role-playing methodology has significant limitations and poses some potential problems. Probably the major constraint on the use of this methodology is its cost. Because role-playing is labor intensive, cost considerations may severely limit sample sizes and the extent to which results can be generalized. In addition, there are some areas to which the methodology cannot be applied for practical reasons. To evaluate discrimination in hiring for jobs beyond entry-level openings would be extremely difficult because the qualifications of applicants are greater and matching pairs of role-players becomes more complicated as the relevant criteria expand. Personal references take on more importance at higher skill levels and verifying references and previous employment therefore poses a serious problem. Also difficult within the area of employment is evaluating promotions, where role-players could not be used at all. Placing role-players in jobs and ensuring that they conduct equivalent quality work over an extended period of time would be impractical and would raise a new set of ethical issues.

Particularly complex transactions, such as evaluating the driver's license application process where official documentation is required and tests must be taken, are more complicated to evaluate using the role-playing methodology. Similarly, an evaluation that would require role-players to have very specific traits or knowledge, such as obtaining a liquor license for a restaurant, would also be problematic to implement on a large scale. In order for the role-players to have the necessary traits, such as proof of restaurant ownership, the pool of potential role-players becomes very small and recruitment becomes more difficult. In addition, to obtain statistically significant results, sample size and cost issues make these types of evaluations impractical to do on a large scale.

Ethical and Legal Issues

A number of ethical and legal issues have been raised by the paired role-playing studies that should be considered in future evaluations. Some observers have criticized the methodology for deceiving or for entrapping the subjects of an evaluation. For one, Alan Greenspan, chairman of the board of governors of the Federal Reserve, has objected to the use of testing because it involves deception (see Edley, 1993). These observers are concerned about the implications of deceiving for purposes of research and about the privacy rights of the person or office being evaluated. Is it right to intrude on someone's business without that person's knowledge? Is that intrusion harmful because of the cost of interacting with role-players—even if the cost is only lost time? These are valid concerns. However, a convincing argument can be made that the benefits of role-playing far outweigh the drawbacks. Also, role-playing evaluations can be designed to involve as limited an intrusion as possible, taking up the minimum amount of time necessary.

In terms of privacy, most of the studies discussed here involve responding to offers (for homes, apartments, jobs, and services) that were publicly advertised and that are subject to laws or regulations barring discrimination. As for such studies constituting entrapment, there is no lure or incentive for people to act any differently from the way they would otherwise (Fix and Struyk, 1993).

Another issue is whether a government agency can use its own employees as role-players for an evaluation. While numerous studies cited in this chapter were conducted by public agencies, only one used its own employees as role-players. To avoid any possible conflict of interest, a public agency might choose to contract with an independent outside entity that would do the evaluation. Government audit agencies, however, have unique roles and therefore may not face the same problems as other public agencies. Because the legal issues involved vary according to the evaluation being conducted, each agency should independently examine the legality of conducting a role-playing evaluation as well as the legality of using their own employees as role-players.

Conclusion

Role-playing is a unique and innovative evaluation tool that has not yet been widely applied. Individuals can act as role-players in order to evaluate the quality of services or information provided by public agencies, giving evaluators direct observations on which to base their assessments. Similarly, the paired role-playing methodology allows analysts to directly observe differences in treatment between population groups. Other variations on the methodology are also possible, including using teams of three or more role-players. Because role-playing involves direct human observation, the results produced are particularly powerful. They also provide the power of narrative — role-players can give anecdotal evidence of their own individual experiences. For these reasons, this type of evaluation produces results in a form that is clear and convincing to the public and to policymakers and, at the same time, is useful to program evaluators.

References

Ayres, I. "Fair Driving: Gender and Race Discrimination in Retail Car Negotiations." *Harvard Law Review,* 1991, *104*(4), 817–872.

Bendick, M., Jr., Jackson, C., Reinoso, V. A., and Hodges, L. E. *Discrimination Against Latino Job Applicants: A Controlled Experiment.* Washington, D.C.: Fair Employment Council of Greater Washington, 1992.

Boggs, R., V.O., Sellers, J., and Bendick, M. "The Use of Testing in Civil Rights Enforcement." In M. Fix and R. Struyk (eds.), *Clear and Convincing Evidence: Testing for Discrimination in America.* Washington, D.C.: The Urban Institute Press, 1993.

Center for Excellence in Local Government. *Achieving Excellence in Customer Service: Field Assessment Report for the City of Saratoga, California.* Unpublished mimeograph. Saratoga, Calif.: 1988.

Cross, H., Kenney, G., Mell, J., and Zimmermann, W. *Employer Hiring Practices: Differential Treatment of Hispanic and Anglo Job Seekers.* Washington, D.C.: The Urban Institute Press, 1990.

Edley, C. "Implications of Empirical Studies on Race Discrimination." In M. Fix and R. Struyk (eds.), *Clear and Convincing Evidence: Testing for Discrimination in America.* Washington, D.C.: The Urban Institute Press, 1993.

Fix, M., and Struyk, R. J. "An Overview of Auditing for Discrimination." In M. Fix and R. Struyk (eds.), *Clear and Convincing Evidence: Testing for Discrimination in America.* Washington, D.C.: The Urban Institute Press, 1993.

Galster, G. "The Use of Testers in Investigating Mortgage Lending and Insurance Discrimination." In M. Fix and R. Struyk (eds.), *Clear and Convincing Evidence: Testing for Discrimination in America.* Washington, D.C.: The Urban Institute Press, 1993.

Heckman, J. "An Economic and Econometric Examination of the Audit Methodology." In M. Fix and R. Struyk (eds.), *Clear and Convincing Evidence: Testing for Discrimination in America.* Washington, D.C.: The Urban Institute Press, 1993.

International City Management Association. "Measuring City Agency Responsiveness: The Citizen-Surrogate Method. " *Urban Data Service Report,* 1981, *13*(5).

James, F., and Del Castillo, S. "We May Be Making Progress Toward Equal Access to Jobs: Evidence from Recent Audits." Unpublished manuscript, University of Colorado, Denver, 1992.

Ridley, S. E., Bayton, J. A., and Outtz, J. H. "Taxi Service in the District of Columbia: Is It Influenced by the Patron's Race and Destination?" Unpublished paper prepared for the Washington, D.C., Lawyers Committee for Civil Rights, 1989.

"Smoking and Teens: Strong Measures, like Banning Vending Machine Sales, Limit Minors' Access to Tobacco." *Washington Post,* Health News, Sept. 3, 1992, p. 7.

"Tracking Bias in Banks." *New York Times.* Feb. 16, 1992, p. 12.

Turner, M. A., Fix, M., and Struyk, R. J. *Opportunities Denied, Opportunities Diminished: Discrimination in Hiring.* Washington, D.C.: The Urban Institute Press, 1991.

Turner, M. A., Struyk, R. J., and Yinger, J. *Housing Discrimination Study: Synthesis.* Washington, D.C.: U.S. Department of Housing and Urban Development, 1991.

U.S. General Accounting Office. *Tax Administration: Accessibility, Timeliness, and Accuracy of IRS Telephone Assistance Programs.* GAO/GGD 89-30. Washington, D.C.: U.S. General Accounting Office, Feb. 2, 1989.

U.S. General Accounting Office. *Tax Administration: Monitoring the Accuracy and Administration of IRS' 1989 Test-Call Survey.* GAO/GGD 90-36. Washington, D.C.: General Accounting Office, Jan. 4, 1990.

Wienk, R., and others. *Housing Market Practices Survey.* Washington, D.C.: U.S. Department of Housing and Urban Development, 1979.

Yinger, J. *Housing Discrimination Study: Incidence and Severity of Unfavorable Treatment.* Washington, D.C.: U.S. Department of Housing and Urban Development, 1991.

Yinger, J. "The 1989 Housing Discrimination Study: Results and Implications." In M. Fix and R. Struyk (eds.), *Clear and Convincing Evidence: Testing for Discrimination in America.* Washington, D.C.: The Urban Institute Press, 1993.

14

How to Use
Focus Groups

Debra L. Dean

Efficient and effective provision of public services is a continuing concern in the public sector. Citizens are interested in obtaining public services that respond to their needs. Increasing interest in customer service and satisfaction provides public managers with an opportunity to reassess their own service provision efforts. Are public services meeting consumer needs and preferences? Are service purchasers — the taxpayers — satisfied with the quality and quantity of services provided. In short, how responsive are public services?

The profession of public administration sometimes regards responsiveness either as a function of elected officials or as a threat to professionalism. Many public managers assume that responsiveness flows through the electoral system. Voters elect officials to make laws and budgets for public service. It is assumed that decisions by *elected* officials are, by definition, responsive to the voters. In such circumstances, the administrator's job is to carry out the decisions of elected officials efficiently, professionally, and honestly.

Traditional methods of service provision are, however, giving way to demands for an increasingly responsive public sector. As noted by Osborne and Gaebler (1992, p. 15): "Today's environment demands institutions that are extremely flexible and adaptable. It demands institutions that deliver high-quality goods and services, squeezing ever more bang out of every buck. It demands institutions that are responsive to their customers, offering choices of nonstandard services; that lead by persuasion and incentives rather than commands; that give their employees a sense of meaning of control, even ownership. It demands institutions that empower citizens rather than simply serving them." Under such circumstances, it is increasingly important for public administrators to hear directly from consumers and taxpayers as well as their own employees. These types of exchange create a new feedback channel linking the public directly to public managers and employees.

Elections are better suited for making broad policy decisions than for tinkering with the details of service provision. The direct feedback channel allows public managers to make decisions informed by the preferences and experiences of service consumers, producers, and taxpayers. There are several ways to link public managers and the public. One of them is to adapt the techniques of market research to the public sector.

Public Sector "Market" Research

Many people equate marketing with sales and promotion of a product (Kotler, 1982, p. 5). This very restrictive view of marketing confines it to the private sector and fails to recognize the contributions it can make to the supply of responsive public services. One leading marketing scholar suggests that marketing can be seen as "a social process in which the material needs of a society are identified, expanded, and served by a set of institutions. . . . That view is appropriate for those interested in social values and public policy" (Kotler, 1982, p. 7). Kotler's observation suggests that market research techniques can be adapted to be useful to the public manager. This chapter examines one technique drawn from traditional market research that is now used in the public sector: focus groups. The intent here is to introduce focus groups to public managers by describing the focus group technique, providing examples, discussing the circumstances in which focus groups are useful, explaining how to conduct them, and listing some of the pitfalls a user of focus groups should avoid.

What Are Focus Groups?

A focus group is an informal, small-group discussion designed to obtain in-depth qualitative information. Individuals are specifically invited to participate in the discussion. Participants usually have something in common. Sometimes they will share demographic characteristics, such as income, or educational level. In other instances participants may all be users of a public service: they may all be served by the same postal route, or they may all be seeking building permits from a local government. Participants may also be employed by a single government agency, such as nurses at the county hospital or desk clerks at the state motor vehicle agency.

A focus group discussion is informal. Participants are encouraged to talk with each other about their experiences, preferences, needs, observations, or perceptions. The conversation is led by a moderator whose role is to foster interaction. The moderator makes sure that all participants are encouraged to contribute and that no individual dominates the conversation. The moderator manages the discussion to make sure it does not stray too far from the topic of interest. The moderator also follows up on participants' comments to obtain further details or to introduce new topics to the group.

The overall goal of any focus group is to reveal the participants' perceptions about the topics for discussion. Focus groups have the following characteristics:

- Each group is kept small to encourage interaction among the members.
- Each session usually last ninety minutes.
- The conversation focuses on a restricted number of topics. The actual number varies depending upon the objective of the session but is usually no more than three to five related subjects.
- The moderator has an agenda that outlines the major topics to be covered. These topics are usually narrowly defined to keep the conversation relevant.

Focus Groups and Surveys

Focus groups are a quite different data gathering mechanism from the random sample surveys with which many public managers are familiar. The two techniques require very dissimilar research designs and procedures, fulfill different needs, and produce different types of data. Focus groups are a form of qualitative research while surveys are usually quantitative. All the divisions that typically separate qualitative from quantitative research apply to the differences between focus groups and surveys.

One important difference between the two techniques is the size and selection of sample respondents. Surveys usually employ large, representative, randomly selected samples. Focus groups typically involve small, nonrandomly selected samples. Participants may not—indeed often do not—form a representative sample. Even if they were representative, the sample would be so small that its output would not be generalizable with any substantial degree of accuracy. Focus groups are not the appropriate technique for making inferences about a larger population. Rather, they offer a way to explore a topic in depth with a small group of participants drawn from an often narrowly defined target population.

Another difference between the techniques is the construction of questions. Surveys usually consist of a series of carefully constructed questions and precoded answers. Interviewers are instructed to read the question the same way each time to each respondent and not to deviate or explain the question to the respondent. Acceptable answers are defined in advance. Focus group discussions, by contrast, are far less structured than surveys. The conversation is allowed to develop naturally to provide an opportunity for new dimensions or insights to arise. Participants are encouraged to use their own words; they are not forced into selecting among predefined answers. This freedom provides an opportunity for the research to show not only what participants think about a topic but how they approach it and why they arrive at the conclusions they hold.

A third difference is how the results of the studies are handled. A survey researcher tabulates numerous responses to the same question. Thus a survey might ask: "Do you approve or disapprove of the way the president is handling his job?" and the results will be expressed in percentages approving and disapproving. In a focus group, the question might be: "What do you think about the president's performance so far?" The results will mention the full range of participant responses to this question: positive, negative, neutral, and mixed. It is usually safe to say that focus groups trade off the generalizability of a structured survey for an in-depth, detailed, open-ended exploration of an issue.

When Focus Groups Are Useful

Focus groups are more useful in some circumstances than others. It is important that an administrator know what kind of information he or she seeks before selecting the research technique to be used. Focus groups are most useful in the exploratory stages of research, or when an administrator wants to develop a deeper understanding of a program or service. Surveys are more useful when the need is to generalize structured results to a larger population.

Focus groups are very flexible. They can be used to hear from service consumers, purchasers (taxpayers) who may or may not actually consume a service, or from the providers of a service. The following hypothetical examples illustrate how focus groups can be utilized in the public sector.

Example 1: A local school district is spending $500,000 a year to keep six guidance counselors in each high school. District administrators want to know more about students' expectations of and experiences with their guidance counselors. This is a consumer-oriented focus group. Juniors and seniors from several high schools would be invited to a series of focus group discussion sessions. Questions such as the following might be asked:

> Have you been to see the guidance counselor at your school? Why or why not?
> Why did you go to see the guidance counselor?
> What happened?
> Did you find out what you wanted to know?
> How helpful was the guidance counselor?
> What was the most helpful thing the counselor told you?

Example 2: The state motor vehicle department is considering several designs for new automobile license plates. The previous plates were controversial and many citizens complained about them. The department wants to produce a plate that will be accepted by the public. A group of taxpayers is invited to a focus group session and shown the designs under consideration. The questions that might be asked of this group could include these:

How do you like the state's current license plates? Why
do you say that?
Here is one design under consideration. How do you like
it? Why do you say that?
Which of these designs do you like the best? Why?
Which design do you like the least? Why?
Which of the slogans do you prefer? Why?

Example 3: A federal agency is charged with implementing a new and complex antidiscrimination statute. Agency officials are concerned
about how already overburdened field workers will react to their
new responsibilities. Employees are invited to a focus group session about the new statute. Questions that might be asked of this
are these:

Are you aware of the new statute? What do you know about
it? What kinds of information do you need about this
statute to do your job effectively?
Do you foresee that enforcing the statute will require trade-
offs with other responsibilities? What are they? How
would you handle this?
Does it make sense in your office to assign a single field
employee to specialize in the new statute? Why or why
not? What other strategies might be employed to enforce the statute?

As these examples show, focus group discussions can be useful at all levels
of government and can be useful for obtaining feedback from consumers
of public services, taxpayers who may or may not be consumers, and from
public employees. Indeed, focus group discussions can be an integral part
of quality management initiatives which seek to improve public services both
from the perspective of the public and from the perspective of the service
providers.

Focus group discussions are useful in a wide variety of situations. As
mentioned previously, they are very helpful when the aim is to explore new
territory. They provide an excellent opportunity for issues to arise that have
not been anticipated by public managers. The discussion may engender suggestions or new ideas that will influence the design or distribution of services.
It may also provide managers with a view of how the public evaluates a service and what criteria and/or evidence they use to assess a public program.

Focus group discussions can be used to monitor a service already in
place. Are consumers satisfied or dissatisfied with services? Perhaps more
important to a manager, why or why not? What changes would the public
like to see? What problems are they experiencing in using the service? How
would they react to potential changes in the service?

Finally, focus group discussions are particularly useful when the manager has something concrete to show participants such as a new design for a license plate or a new brochure. For example, a new brochure may be slated for inclusion in tax bills. Administrators can find out in advance whether the information is presented in an understandable way. Do readers misconstrue parts of the information? What problems do they have with it? Does the new brochure provide the information that taxpayers want? What information should be included? Can certain points be left out as less relevant from the readers' point of view?

How to Conduct a Focus Group

Conducting a focus group is a multistep process. Attention should be given to all phases, but three steps stand out as critical to the success of a focus group research project: (1) selecting the participants, (2) writing the moderator's guide, and (3) communicating the client's needs to the moderator.

Participant Selection

Participant selection is a critical element in the process because the discussion will be substantially less fruitful if the people in the room do not come from the target population. Before conducting a focus group the sponsor must decide which group he or she wants information from. For example, questions about high school counseling services might be directed at several target groups: students who use the counselors, students who don't use the counselors, parents, teachers, even counselors themselves. Each of these groups represents a different target population. It may be useful to conduct focus groups with any or all of them. On the other hand, certain groups may be especially important. If a substantial number of minority students do not use guidance counseling services, the sponsor's highest priority may be to learn why. Under such circumstances, it might be wise to conduct focus groups with minority students who do not use the counselors.

Different target populations should not be invited to the same session, as they may inhibit each other's comments. The age, social status, job position, knowledge of participants, and other variables can have a major influence on the discussion. Participants can be expected to adjust what they say to the situation they are in. They may not, for example, be particularly candid in front of someone at a higher level in the organization. Similarly, care should be taken to select a moderator who will not bias the group simply by his or her demographic status. For example, when conducting a focus group with a racial minority, consideration should be given to having a moderator from the same minority group.

The definition of the target group should be as specific as possible. Subtle differences in the definition can have a major impact on who is actually invited to participate in the group. For example, recruiting a group whose members have annual *household* incomes of $50,000 or more will produce a different target group from recruiting participants who have annual *personal* incomes of at least $50,000. The second definition will tend to produce a set of participants with more disposable income than those who fit the first definition. Using the household income criterion, a participant would qualify if she and her husband each made $30,000 a year, while the same individual would not qualify under the personal income standard.

A careful and specific definition of the target group is important because focus group sample sizes are small and participants generally are not recruited by random sampling. Without the guidance of a tight definition, the members selected may be very unrepresentative of the desired target individuals. Narrow criteria will tend to homogenize the group on certain key dimensions, decreasing its variability and possibly improving its representativeness.

Criteria for recruiting do involve trade-offs. In general, the more narrow and specific the recruiting criteria, the smaller is the pool of people eligible for invitations to attend. Restrictions always increase the difficulty of finding and inviting potential recruits and also raise the cost of recruiting. Recruiting criteria must be narrow enough to ensure that members of the target group are invited while at the same time not restricting the pool to such an extent that costs are unreasonably high. The solution to this problem is to focus on the target group's most important characteristics. If the target group is the middle-class family, it may be necessary to invite only individuals with a specified household income. But it is not necessary to add the restriction that participants must be married, since middle-class families do include single-parent households. At the same time, it might be appropriate to screen out single individuals without minor children.

Focus group recruiting is done over the telephone but in other respects it is unlike survey interviewing. Random sampling techniques are not commonly used in recruiting. Participants are often recruited from membership lists, employee lists, or other databases. Recruiting is done with a screening questionnaire. The interviewer calls potential recruits and asks them a series of questions designed to determine whether they qualify for an invitation. Screening questionnaires, also called screeners, are written like any other survey but they are short and focused on whether the respondent meets the recruiting criteria. Respondents who do not meet the criteria are thanked for their time and the interview is concluded. Individuals who qualify are invited to the group and told where and when it will be held. Typically these are followed up with confirming letters that state the date, time, and location of the session and provide directions to the meeting place. The client is responsible for providing the recruiters with a screening questionnaire but moderators will sometimes supply them.

Focus group participants are usually compensated for their time and effort. The amount of money offered varies but it is usually higher for professionals or high-income participants and for participants in large cities. Note that focus group participation is voluntary. Required participation usually works poorly because involuntary participants often contribute only minimally to the discussion.

Incentive payments are made by cash or check at the conclusion of the focus group session. It is often inappropriate to offer public employees cash payments. Under such circumstances, other inducements may be appropriate and should be considered.

The Agenda

Another critical element in conducting a focus group is writing an agenda or moderator's guide. This guide outlines the major topics to be covered. The moderator refers to this agenda during the discussion to make sure that all important topics are discussed. The focus group moderator usually writes his or her own guide. The style of the agenda will vary among moderators. Some moderators prefer to work with a skeletal outline; others prefer a detailed guide with many follow-up questions.

Moderators' guides usually open with a general question that all participants can answer and will feel comfortable answering. The purpose of this question is to launch the discussion in a positive and supportive environment. If possible, initial questions should elicit useful information that will be used in the analysis. For sensitive topics, the initial questions may sacrifice analytical relevance in favor of initiating a comfortable conversation. Once a nonthreatening atmosphere is established, the discussion can be turned to topics of greater analytical interest.

Questions will become increasingly specific as the discussion proceeds. The focus group technique places great emphasis on informal and freewheeling conversation. Sometimes, in answering a general question, participants will bring up specific matters that are covered in the middle or end of the moderator's guide. If this happens, the moderator must decide on the spot whether to follow the conversation naturally or direct it according to the structure of the guide. Most moderators place a high premium on natural discussion and tend to allow the session to follow its own course, as long as it is relevant. In most circumstances, there is no need to control the sequence of the subjects. Indeed, the speed with which an issue arises can be of analytical interest because it is often an indicator of how important the subject is to the participants. The moderator should be told in advance if there is a need to control the conversational sequence.

Communication with the Moderator

Because the moderator is responsible for facilitating and guiding the conversation, it is obviously very important that he or she understand the needs of the sponsor. While this may seem obvious, it is sometimes forgotten. Moderators will produce better results if they understand what information their client needs. Equally important, moderators need to know what is unimportant to their clients. Because focus groups are unstructured unexpected comments may arise. A moderator who knows the client's needs will know when to follow up and when to ignore unexpected information.

In-House or Professional Research

One important question to answer at the beginning of the research process is whether to conduct the focus groups in house or use outside professional services. The primary advantage of conducting the groups in house is expense. Using employees to recruit participants will be less costly than paying professionals to do it. However, the decrease in out-of-pocket costs may well be offset by other considerations. Recruiters should be trained in interviewing techniques and in using the screening questionnaire. The quality of the discussion can be seriously compromised if participants do not come from the target groups. Outside professional organizations usually have the training and experience to handle recruiting. Inexperienced in-house efforts may appear to cost less but may in fact cost more in time, effort, and skewed results.

It is possible to use a staff member as a moderator. There are cost advantages to this course of action and an in-house moderator typically has more detailed inside knowledge than a professional brought in from outside. On the other hand, an in-house moderator typically has much less experience than a professional. An in-house moderator can also inadvertently bias the session by the way he or she responds to comments made by respondents. The temptation to react can be very strong, particularly if the moderator is directly involved in the program or service under discussion. A professional moderator will cost more, but this cost is usually offset by the moderator's greater experience and emotional distance from the topic.

Facilities

Focus group discussions are usually held in special facilities fitted for the purpose. The typical focus group session is held in a conference room equipped with a one-way mirror. The moderator and participants sit around the conference table. The observers sit in a small viewing room on the other side of the one-way mirror.

Focus group rooms are equipped with microphones; the discussion is audiotaped. The moderator should *always* tell the participants at the beginning of the session that it is being audiotaped. The tapes are not for any use other than research and analysis. They are never to be used for public service announcements or to be made public in any way. Participants are usually offered anonymity and this must be respected. It is good policy to destroy the tapes after the report is written.

Some focus groups are videotaped. Videotaping can be done with a fixed camera or with a camera and operator. Videotaping with a fixed camera usually adds little to the cost of a focus group session. A camera with an operator, however, will add significantly to the total cost. If the session is to be videotaped, participants should be told at the beginning of the session. As with audiotapes, videotapes must not be used for anything other than research purposes. Videotaping is done, but it is not standard practice. Since it adds costs to each session, videotaping should be considered carefully.

Schedules

Focus group research also requires a number of scheduling decisions. Most focus group sessions are conducted on Monday through Thursday evenings. Since such a large proportion of the population works during the day, most group discussions are held at night. Daytime focus groups cannot recruit most working people. If the target group is nonworking retirees or housewives not employed outside the home, daytime sessions are feasible.

As many as two sessions are conducted in a single evening, with one group meeting around 6 P.M. and another around 8 P.M. Friday evenings and weekends are usually not good times to schedule focus groups because participants cherish their formal nonworking hours.

The person scheduling the sessions must take into account competing activities. Group attendance can be affected by sporting events, holidays, and weather. The schedule should avoid holidays and evenings on which popular local or national sporting events occur.

Another scheduling consideration is the amount of lead time necessary to assemble a group and prepare a moderator's guide. Groups can sometimes be assembled with very little notice but doing so is more costly. If possible, the moderator and recruiters should be given at least three weeks advance notice — and more time is preferable.

Observing the Session

It is possible to observe a focus group while it is in session. Observing focus group discussions raises important ethical issues in both the private and the public sector. The ethical considerations are particularly important in the public sector because public programs can have such a substantial and long-term impact on individuals.

Participants should always be informed at the beginning of the group when observers are present behind the one-way mirror. In addition, observers should never discuss participants by name and should not make participants' comments public in any way. To do so is to violate the assurances of confidentiality that participants were given when being recruited for the group.

Remember that focus group participants must never be placed in a position that could compromise their legal status or violate their rights. For example, it would be unethical for a tax agency to gather a group of citizens and ask them if they cheated on their taxes last year. No research should ever be done if there is any question of violation of the participants' rights. This matter tends not to come up in the private sector when the focus group discussion is about cake mix, or mouthwash, or automobile polish. But it can a very important issue in the public sector. It should not be overlooked.

When observing a group is appropriate, observers should listen carefully to what the participants say as well as how they say it. Also, they should watch their body language and facial expressions. The number of people observing the group can vary from one to as many as ten. One major consideration is the number of people that can be accommodated in the viewing room. These rooms vary in size, but often accommodate no more than ten observers.

Observers should remember that even though they are divided from the group participants loud noises will carry through the one-way mirror. Laughter, exclamations, pounding, banging, and loud talk will all disrupt the session and remind participants they are being observed. All observers should be quiet and unobtrusive. Observers never approach participants after the session — either immediately or after a delay. Always remember that the goal of a focus group is to learn what the participants think; it is not to persuade them of anything.

Reports

Focus group reports are essentially debriefing summaries of the discussion sessions. Systematic techniques such as content analysis typically are not used. Instead, the moderator, often after talking extensively with the observers, writes a description of what transpired. Some focus group reports are very short and include only the highlights of the discussions. Others are far more detailed and provide lengthy quotations from participants. Transcriptions may also be made, although they tend to be expensive and lengthy.

Pitfalls of Focus Group Research

A public manager should be aware of several possible pitfalls surrounding focus groups. A major one is to select the focus group when this technique is inappropriate to your research needs. Focus group research is often much less expensive than random sample surveys, especially those with large sample sizes, and the promise of a greatly reduced cost can be very tempting. But cost should never drive the selection of a research technique. Focus group and survey research fulfill different needs. The focus group provides highly detailed information that usually cannot be reliably generalized to a larger population. Surveys are generalizable if the sample is chosen correctly, but the information they generate is usually less detailed and does not contain the same elements of informal spontaneity as can be produced in a focus group. The research technique chosen should depend upon your information needs, not your budget.

A second major pitfall in focus group research is inadequate communication between the sponsoring agency and the moderator. Because the moderator's job is to facilitate discussion, he or she must have as much information as possible about the sponsor's needs and concerns. This will allow the moderator to follow up on matters of interest to the sponsor. A moderator who does not know the agency's needs must fall back on his or her own knowledge and preferences—which can produce less than satisfactory results. Communication with the moderator throughout the process is essential.

At one time it was customary for the sponsor to send notes into the focus group during the session: to provide on-the-spot instructions or suggest additional questions. The moderator could read the notes and alter the discussion as necessary. Today the disruptive consequences of this practice are widely recognized and it is discouraged except under extreme circumstances. If the moderator fully understands the agency's needs, there will be no reason to interrupt the focus group with periodic instructions.

Finally, the manager must not allow him- or herself to become defensive if the participants criticize the program or services. Emotional involvement obscures the ability to observe carefully what is going on. Participants are not directing their comments at the observers, even if it seems as though they are. Maintain an emotional distance. You will get far more out of the discussion.

As a corollary, the manager must not blame the moderator if the participants do not like his or her product or service. It can be tempting to blame the moderator when the research does not turn out as anticipated. It may be painful to hear criticism from customers, but it is necessary to improve.

Conclusion

Focus group research is a tool for public managers interested in knowing more about the specific preferences and needs of consumers, taxpayers, and public employees. The technique is flexible and can produce a trove of new insights. Like any tool, however, focus groups can be misused. Public managers can gain a great deal from the technique, but they must also protect the rights of the participants.

References

Kotler, P. *Marketing for Nonprofit Organizations.* (2nd ed.) Englewood Cliffs, N.J.: Prentice-Hall, 1982.

Osborne, D., and Gaebler, T. *Reinventing Government: How the Entrepreneurial Spirit Is Transforming the Public Sector.* Reading, Mass.: Addison-Wesley, 1992.

15

Managing Field Data Collection from Start to Finish

Demetra Smith Nightingale,
Shelli Balter Rossman

In a variety of circumstances, evaluators need to obtain information about how local programs or agencies operate. One way to find out what is happening at the local level is to visit one or more sites and talk to a number of people. Federal and state officials and program managers routinely visit local programs (whether administered by federal, state, or local governments or private facilities providing services funded by government) to get a better sense of operational reality. Program evaluators conduct site visits to collect systematic information through surveys, participant observation, focus groups, or structured interviews with officials or staff. Federal and state officials with monitoring responsibilities visit local programs to review specific issues.

One method of data collection that has become very common among program evaluators is semistructured interviews with administrators, staff, and program customers, conducted to document various aspects of a program or agency. This type of fieldwork is frequently part of a process study, an implementation analysis, or an organizational assessment, and represents an attempt to systematically examine programs to avoid dependence on anecdotal information.

This chapter describes approaches to conducting fieldwork, focusing on multisite studies as part of formal evaluations as well as on less extensive efforts that are more appropriate for routine program monitoring and oversight. The chapter addresses the following:

- Objectives of fieldwork
- Design issues, including site selection, staffing, instrument development, and respondent selection
- Field visit protocol, including previsit training and preparation as well as on-site procedures
- Data maintenance and analysis

Objectives of Fieldwork

The details of fieldwork depend on the objectives of the data collection, which are based on the overall objectives of the study or project within which the fieldwork occurs. It is important to have an understanding of what the fieldwork is intended to achieve, how it fits into the overall conceptual framework of the project as a whole, and the categories of information it is expected to collect.

The objectives of the fieldwork determine both the focus (priorities) and the scope (intensity) of the data collection activity. At least two types of fieldwork are commonly conducted: program management and program evaluation.

Program Management Fieldwork Model

Federal, state, and local program managers routinely conduct monitoring reviews that involve field visits, reviews of records, interviews, and observations. The topics or issues reviewed depend on the needs of management (such as determining compliance with regulations or improving program performance). Analysis may be quantitative or qualitative, generally based on predetermined management standards or criteria. The fieldwork is usually conducted by managers or staff of public agencies. The results typically are presented in site reports, and may lead to recommendations for corrective action or performance improvement.

Program Evaluation Fieldwork Model

Evaluators typically collect information on predetermined topics. The classification of topics is based on the overall evaluation project and its objectives. Various data collection methods are used including interviews, surveys, focus groups, observation, statistical compilations, and record reviews. Standard social science principles (such as validity, reliability, and objectivity) provide a framework for developing the fieldwork plan. Generally the fieldwork and the evaluation are based on theoretical models and hypotheses. Both qualitative and quantitative analysis may be conducted. The fieldwork is usually conducted by individuals who have some academic or professional training in research or evaluation. Evaluators can either be staff of public agencies or researchers from outside research organizations or universities. The results of their work are presented in project reports and often are integrated into other components of the evaluation.

Each of these and other fieldwork models can potentially involve similar types of data collection methods, but each is based on somewhat different professional practices and experience. The important point is that the specific objectives of the fieldwork, in a sense, set boundaries or standards for the data collection effort. Although it is not essential that a study have a clearly defined fieldwork model, one usually exists even if it is unstated. The model heavily influences specific details about how the fieldwork is designed, the types of data collection instruments used, and the types of quality control and analytic methods employed. These issues are discussed in the sections that follow.

Thus, fieldwork is conducted for at least two purposes:

1. To describe what is happening at the particular level being examined (local program, local community, state agency, and so on)
2. To explain why the situations are as they are

The specific objectives of a fieldwork effort usually fall under one or both of these two general purposes. Before researchers design the details of the fieldwork (discussed in the next section), it is critical that they articulate clearly and specifically the evaluation questions and issues that relate to the fieldwork portion of the study. Some field studies have very specific objectives, even though the overall evaluation addresses broader issues. For example, in most large-scale program evaluations that estimate client impacts, a field data collection effort may investigate in detail other aspects of the program being evaluated such as organizational structure, intake procedures, and staff job satisfaction. Many program evaluations include process analysis or implementation analysis — components that involve fieldwork to document specific details of a program. Those qualitative descriptions may then be transformed into quantitative program descriptor variables and incorporated into statistical analyses of program impacts. In most evaluations, it is necessary to build the fieldwork design around the basic evaluation questions.

An institutional analysis of the national Work Incentive Program (WIN) for welfare recipients, for example, was designed to examine the organizational, managerial, and service delivery characteristics of high- and low-performing state and local programs to determine how to improve performance (Mitchell, Chadwin, and Nightingale, 1979). The study had two components: (1) quantitative analysis of program performance, and (2) more qualitative analysis of the programmatic features of high- and low-performing programs. The second component relied heavily on information obtained by teams of evaluators who conducted fieldwork in forty-three local communities. Exhibit 15.1 lists the range of evaluation issues and questions that were objectives of that fieldwork as well as examples from other studies.

Design Issues

Once the evaluation questions, objectives, and issues of interest are clear, the evaluators need to make a number of design decisions. These include selecting sites, deciding the types of data collection instruments to use, identifying respondents, and determining staff requirements. All these decisions depend greatly on cost constraints that may exist for the evaluation. Evalu-

Exhibit 15.1. Examples of Field Research Objectives.

Mitchell, J. J., Chadwin, M. L., and Nightingale, D. S. *An Institutional Analysis of the Work Incentive Program.* Washington, D.C.: The Urban Institute, 1979.

Evaluation Objective:	Identify organizational, managerial, and service delivery features that differentiate high-performing WIN programs from low-performing programs.
Fieldwork Objectives:	1. Describe the organization, management, and service delivery in high- and low-performing WIN programs.
	2. Identify environmental, bureaucratic, and political factors that influence the way local programs are structured and managed.

Burbridge, L. C., and Nightingale, D. S. *Local Coordination of Employment and Training Services to Welfare Recipients.* Washington, D.C.: The Urban Institute, 1989.

Evaluation Objective:	Document interagency and intra-agency coordination of services for welfare recipients and identify different models of coordination.
Fieldwork Objectives:	1. Describe the range of activities that involve coordination across units within an agency and between agencies.
	2. Identify which agencies are involved in coordination.
	3. Identify incentives and disincentives to coordination.

Holcomb, P., and Nightingale, D. S. *Evaluation of the Western Interstate Child Support Enforcement Clearinghouse.* Washington, D.C.: The Urban Institute, 1989.

Evaluation Objectives:	1. Estimate the impact of the clearinghouse in five demonstration states on child support collections and government savings.
	2. Examine and assess the implementation and operations of the clearinghouse.
	3. Estimate the cost-effectiveness of the clearinghouse.
Fieldwork Objectives:	1. Document how the clearinghouse was planned, implemented, and operated.
	2. Assess the feasibility of implementing and operating the automated clearinghouse by identifying problems encountered and solutions applied.
	3. Identify differences in the clearinghouse across the five demonstration sites and reasons for the differences.

---

ations addressing similar or even identical questions may have very different fieldwork designs reflecting different cost constraints.

Site Selection and Staffing

Two issues are particularly important in selecting sites for field studies: (1) the unit of analysis, and (2) the extent to which the findings are to be generalized to other sites. Final decisions on how many sites to include in the field study, however, depend heavily on the resources available and the staffing required. In most field studies, decisions about staffing and site selection are made simultaneously.

Unit of Analysis. One of the first issues that should be addressed before sites are selected for a field study is clarifying the unit(s) of analysis for the fieldwork portion of the evaluation. The unit, or level, of analysis will determine the types of sites that will be selected for the field data collection. The unit of analysis is usually obvious from the evaluation questions. For example, if the primary evaluation objective is to document and analyze school management and organization, the units of analysis are local schools and the fieldwork sites will be schools. If the evaluation objective is to document "exemplary" approaches to serving teenage mothers, the units of analysis and the study sites are local programs serving this population.

These are fairly straightforward examples. In the real-world setting of evaluation, though, the choice is usually more complicated. There are often multiple dimensions to evaluations that require different levels of analysis. For instance, if the evaluation objective is to determine how teenage mothers feel about their circumstances and the services available to them, these mothers are the units of analysis. But the evaluators must decide how — that is, from what source — to identify the mothers: schools, hospitals, local programs, welfare rolls, cities, states. These then also become units of analysis. The final analysis might focus on mothers served by local programs in general, or on each local program (with the mothers each of them serve), or on both these levels of analysis. Thus, if the evaluators want to be able to discuss individual programs in their analysis, they should consider this when selecting the sites where fieldwork is to be conducted — for example, a city, a neighborhood, or one or more institutions or programs serving the city or neighborhood.

Multiple levels of analysis are common in program organizational evaluations, that is, evaluations not just focusing on individuals. In a national evaluation of coordination between welfare programs and job training programs, for example, a number of units of analysis are possible: local communities (within which all job training and welfare programs would be examined), states (within which all job training and welfare programs would be examined), one or more specific job training programs (which could be examined at the state or local level), or one or more specific welfare programs (which could be examined at the state or local level) (Burbridge and Nightingale, 1989).

When there are several possible units of analysis, decisions about site selection are typically based on how the information acquired in the fieldwork will be used by the evaluators. If the purpose is to prepare case studies each of which can stand on its own, it is not necessary to select the same types of sites. An examination of coordination, for instance, could include one or more local communities as well as one or more states. However, if the purpose is more analytic, perhaps to examine factors that encourage or discourage coordination between two programs, then the evaluation should select sites that represent as broad a range as possible of the various types of programs and situations.

The unit of analysis for a fieldwork evaluation should be obvious based on the overall evaluation issues specified. Common units of analysis are local programs, local offices, individual local facilities (such as libraries and schools), cities, neighborhoods, institutions, and states.

Number of Sites. Once it is clear what units of analysis should be used, the evaluators should decide how many sites to include. If the fieldwork mainly or totally consists of on-site activity, then the number of sites that can be included is determined by resource constraints. There are four main factors that affect the resource levels required for fieldwork: travel distance, length of time on site, level of staff required, and number of staff required. The total cost of each of these factors will be governed by the intensity of data collection. If the field effort is exploratory, involving unstructured data collection activities such as discussions with key officials or staff in a program, then each site visit can probably be limited to a short period of time — one or two days — when one evaluator works alone. That person, however, should probably be fairly senior to ensure that the exploration is as comprehensive as possible. At the other extreme, an evaluation that involves collecting detailed descriptions of program operations by surveying or interviewing a number of staff in each site will require more days on site, probably more than one staff person, and a longer period of time.

A number of Urban Institute evaluations of welfare and employment and training programs have included an implementation, or process analysis component. Typically, the fieldwork design involves a team of two evaluators, with one fairly senior and the other either a mid-level evaluator or a research assistant. The two-person team is on site for three to five days (depending on the size of the site or city and the scope of the inquiry). Two-person teams are used because that arrangement has proven to be most efficient for collecting accurate data and for analyzing and interpreting the information. The evaluation team can discuss issues and share contextual insights that greatly enhance the overall quality of information.

Following are types of activities that a two-person team of evaluators can be expected to accomplish in one day:

- Each person can usually conduct four to five one-hour interviews with staff, administrators, or community officials.
- Depending on the evaluation, the team together can conduct two or three focus groups (which may last one to two hours each).
- Each evaluator can administer seven, forty-five-minute in-person questionnaires.
- The team can review hard copy case records; a typical welfare case record review takes between fifteen and forty-five minutes, depending on what information needs to be extracted from the files.

Formal evaluations generally involve using all these data collection methods on site, and often other types as well, such as participant observation and statistical data collection. That means the resources devoted to each site visit depend on the mix of activities to be conducted. Fieldwork in formal evaluations can become quite expensive. For example, on-site fieldwork data collection that involves collecting data on programs in ten cities, each in a different state, using a two-person team (one senior evaluator and one mid-level evaluator) on site for one week per city, would require about one hundred person days, at a cost of $50,000 to $100,000 for labor, travel, per diem, and expenses. There would be an additional 100 to 200 person days for previsit preparations and postvisit report writing.

Of course, there are lower-cost staffing configurations that may be fully satisfactory for evaluations; these consist of program reviews, survey administration, or collection of routine statistical data. As an example, one public official (such as a state program monitor or a program administrator, a federal inspector or monitor, or an evaluator) can visit a local program for just one day and collect a substantial amount of information. As discussed below, the on-site time can be spent efficiently by using carefully developed data collection instruments, scheduling activities in advance, and following field protocol established before the site visit.

Sample Selection. The sample of sites for fieldwork can be selected in a number of different ways. At one extreme, the sampling method can be random, using standard probability sampling techniques. This method would require identifying a universe of possible sites, clustering or stratifying the sites on the basis of some criteria, and then randomly selecting within the strata or clusters. At the other extreme, the site selection process can be purely purposive, with specific sites or specific types of sites chosen, such as small rural sites with high poverty populations, or award winning programs considered exemplary, or large programs in high-growth economic labor markets.

Site selection for most field studies usually falls somewhere between these extremes. Evaluators examining exemplary program models might choose sites based on some feature of the program that is of particular interest—the specific populations served, unique locations, innovative program models, special organizational structure—and choose randomly from among sites meeting those criteria.

In large part, the selection of sites depends on whether the findings from the field are intended to be representative of some larger group of programs or sites or whether they are to be used for stand-alone case studies. If the data and information from the field sites are to be generalized to a larger group of sites or programs, the sites selected should be as representative as possible of the population of sites from which the sample is drawn. If the site information is to be used primarily for descriptive case studies and is intended to be illustrative only, then purposive sampling is sufficient.

Even if evaluators choose sites purposively, the selection should still be based on clear guidelines and criteria; in many cases these resemble the types of criteria one might use to select sites by random stratification or clustering. Examples of selection criteria include level of program performance, rural versus urban location, level of client income, level of client ethnic concentrations, labor market condition, on-site environment, and geographic location of site.'

In some field studies, site selection might evolve through the evaluator's soliciting interest from local jurisdictions, programs, or agencies. One Urban Institute study was designed to develop and then evaluate a management-oriented performance improvement model in state WIN programs (Nightingale and Ferry, 1982). The study could include only two states, and the following conditions were used to select them:

- The state agency had to have a strong potential for improvement while not currently performing at full capacity.
- The program administrators at the state level had to express a deep commitment to improving their operations.
- State officials had to be willing to participate actively in developing and implementing improvement strategies by making key staff available for the duration of the two-year project.

In the selection process, the evaluators compiled information showing how well each candidate state met the three criteria. The information was collected by review of program performance reports and from conversations with key state administrators.

There are no hard and fast rules about how to select sites for fieldwork studies. Site selection evolves from the general evaluation objectives. The evaluator must decide whether sites should represent maximum variation or maximum similarity. Regardless of how scientific the site selection process is, evaluators must have preestablished selection criteria that can subsequently be used in reporting the implications of the findings. The selection of sites should be based on the objectives of the evaluation, but the final decisions must also reflect consideration of the staffing that will be required in the field and the cost of the effort at each site.

Types and Scope of Instruments

Except in the most exploratory type of fieldwork, field evaluators will need to use one or more data collection instruments. At a minimum, the evaluation will need a field data collection guide that includes instructions for obtaining information from interviews, observations, surveys, case reviews, and focus groups. Instruments may range from highly structured to very unstructured.

The structured types of data collection instruments are best known and include surveys, questionnaires, tests, and data coding sheets. The least structured evaluations may have no formal data collection instrument. Between are semistructured data collection instruments that consist of topical areas or subject categories along with questions that the interviewer may use as well as suggested wording for asking about key issues. This section examines the advantages and disadvantages of a more structured versus a less structured data collection approach.

Trade Offs Between Semistructured and Structured Instruments. Table 15.1 compares structured and semistructured instrumentation on a few important features. First, in terms of staffing, the interviewer needs to be fully knowledgeable about the subject and possess strong interviewing skills if he or she is to use an unstructured data gathering approach. Interviewers need to be totally aware of the topics covered and be able to probe respondents for more or different kinds of information on a particular issue. Interviewers should also be able to guide and control the interview without leading or biasing the respondent. A more structured instrument requires less skill to administer and does not allow interviewers much freedom for elaboration. The main strength of a structured instrument, however, is that data collected with one are easily coded for maintenance in a database, which means that analysis can be conducted efficiently.

Second, a semistructured interview guide allows flexibility in the collection of data. Interviewers who are very knowledgeable and well prepared can ask respondents to expand on particular issues to obtain more or different kinds of information, as appropriate. This type of interviewing is not easy, but a skilled evaluator can gain valuable insight and knowledge by identifying potentially useful leads and following them to pursue details and explanations. There are risks to allowing such flexibility, as some interviewers pursue too much tangential information and fail to fully address the topical issue of concern. Evaluators should be cautioned about this potential risk in their data collection training, discussed in the next section.

Finally, a semistructured interview guide provides a rich amount of detail and represents a reasonable compromise between an unstructured approach, appropriate for a researcher working independently, and a highly structured approach, such as a questionnaire, that usually does not permit the evaluator to pursue interesting or important issues that may arise during the course of the interview. Again, though, there is some risk. Unlike structured data collection instruments, which typically are designed to collect standardized data by using close-ended responses or coded categorical responses, semistructured instruments tend to produce large volumes of qualitative notes. Unless the interview guide is carefully developed to focus directly on the required information, the evaluators may be inundated with volumes of notes that are difficult and time-consuming to organize and analyze. (See Caudle, Chapter Four of this handbook, for more guidance on analyzing qualitative information.)

Development of Semistructured Instruments. Careful development of semistructured instruments can guard against some of the pitfalls noted above, namely, the risk that interviewers may not fully address the issues of primary concern because of their desire to pursue other, albeit related, avenues of

Table 15.1. Relative Strengths of
Semistructured and Structured Field Data Collection Instruments.

	Semistructured Instruments	Most Structured Instruments
Administration	Require more preparation and training of interviewers Require interviewer to be able to control, direct, and close interview Allow easier establishment of rapport between respondent and interviewer	Are easier to administer Require straightforward and very specific training of interviewers Provide a limit on the length of the interview session Can be administered in person, by phone, or in writing
Flexibility	Allow interviewer maximum flexibility in sequencing of questions and in probing Encourage respondents to speak conversationally Can allow interview to stray too far unless interviewer is properly trained	Discourage probing Allow for minimal expansion in responses
Quality of Data	Quality of data depends on quality of interviewer	Quality of data depends on quality of structured questions
Quantity of Data	Can lead to massive amounts of data unless interviewer directs and controls interviews well	Place limits on the amount of data collected per respondent
Reliability of Data	Reliability depends on quality of interviewer and verification of information across multiple respondents	Reliability depends on quality and clarity of questions in instrument
Comparability of Data	Comparability depends on how well team members agree on intent of each topic	Comparability depends on how well questions capture variations in terminology across programs and different types of respondents
Analysis of Data	Make it difficult for individuals not involved in interviewing to analyze data Require qualitative analysis first that may eventually be quantifiable Require time-consuming, intensive analysis Provide richer detail on descriptions and variations, allowing more potential for analysis	Allow more routine and faster analysis since responses are more readily quantifiable Limit analyses to specific questions and categories included in the instrument

inquiry; and the risk of producing vast amounts of qualitative notes that may become unwieldy.

The topics in the interview guide should reflect the questions and issues specified for the study. Exhibit 15.2 presents an outline of a semistructured interview guide used in the WIN Performance Improvement Project noted above.

When using semistructured interview guides, evaluators can either use one guide that includes all topics that will be addressed in the field, or they can prepare a different interview guide for each type of respondent. Evaluators could prepare one guide for supervisors and one for staff, or one for personnel in one agency and another for personnel in a different agency. Separate guides allow the evaluators to list specific questions that relate directly to a particular program or staff level, which reduces the amount of question modification the interviewer has to do. A general interview guide offers the advantage of streamlining the data collection process and ensures

Exhibit 15.2. Outline of Interview Guide
Used in Kentucky Performance Improvement Project.

A. Personal Information/Background
   1. Position, job responsibilities
   2. Job expertise
B. Organization
   1. Structure/staffing configuration
   2. Host agency
C. Management Functions
   1. Planning and budgeting
   2. Goals/mission
   3. Monitoring
   4. Reporting/management information systems
   5. Training and technical assistance
D. Management Style
   1. Communication
   2. Distribution of authority
   3. Interorganizational relationships
   4. Innovativeness
   5. Supervisory activities
   6. Interpersonal activities
E. Service Delivery System
   1. Client flow
   2. Caseload management
   3. Provision of services
   4. Job development/job placement
   5. Subsidized employment
   6. Handling noncooperative clients
   7. Serving volunteers
F. Perceptions/Attitudes
   1. Job satisfaction
   2. Perceptions of program effectiveness
   3. Perceptions of program priorities

Source: Nightingale, D. S., and Ferry, D. L. *Assessment of the Joint Federal-State Performance Improvement Projects in the Work Incentive Program.* Washington, D.C.: The Urban Institute, July 1982.

maximum flexibility in each interview since the interviewer will have all possible questions readily at hand. If in the process of an interview, the interviewer realizes that the respondent can address other issues, the interview can be modified easily.

If a general interview guide is used, it is helpful to prepare a respondent/question matrix that indicates which questions are to be asked of which respondent. Table 15.2 presents an example of a respondent matrix, which serves at least two purposes. First, the interviewer uses the matrix to prepare for each interview, and by reviewing the interview and notes once they are coded by topic, the field teams can ensure that all topics specified for particular respondent types were addressed. Second, the matrix can aid the evaluators in assembling and organizing the information for analysis.

Table 15.2. Example of a Portion of a Respondent/Question Matrix.

Respondent Category	*Subject Codes*						
	Organization	*Tasks*	*Goals*	*Conflict*	*Training*	*Jobs*	*Child Care*
Local ES office manager	X	X	X	X	X	X	X
Local ES-WIN supervisor	X	X	X	X	X	X	X
Local ES-WIN staff	X	X	X	X		X	
Local SAU-WIN supervisor	X	X	X	X	X		X
Local SAU-WIN staff	X	X	X	X			X
Local welfare IMU supervisor	X		X	X			X
Local welfare IMU staff	X		X	X			X

Source: Mitchell, J. J., Chadwin, M. L., and Nightingale, D. S. *Implementing Welfare-Employment Programs: An Institutional Analysis of the Work Incentive Program.* Washington, D.C.: The Urban Institute, 1979.

Respondent Selection. Interview guides and other data collection instruments should be developed in a way that allows straightforward identification of the types of individuals who will be interviewed in a site — recognizing that the type of person to be interviewed will also affect the content of the instrument. This means, for example, developing an interview guide that has topics delineated as clearly as possible without compromising the detail. As with site selection, respondent selection can be made either randomly or purposively. If the focus of the field evaluation is to document or describe activities of particular types of personnel, such as managers, police officers, fire fighters, social workers, or data processing clerks, then it is appropriate to select respondents randomly if all staff cannot be interviewed. More typically, though, it is often necessary to interview a number of different types of individuals, possibly even from different agencies. In this case, in advance of the field visit the evaluators should carefully identify the different types of respondents to be interviewed. To the extent possible, evaluators should interview more than one person in a particular category. In a program that includes one manager and three supervisors, each responsible for similar work units that consist of five staff each, evaluators should interview two or three of the supervisors and a number of staff. Interviewing multiple respondents will ensure that the information obtained is not biased because one person, rather than another, was selected for the evaluation.

The fieldwork will be most efficient if the site visit interviews are prepared for in advance. The specific persons who will be interviewed should be identified and notified ahead of time. If possible, interview appointments should be set up before evaluators arrive at the site. And, in developing the interview guide, evaluators should determine in advance which topics or questions will be addressed to each respondent.

Interview Guide. The actual interview guide itself can be produced in a number of different forms. Most typically, an interview guide is reproduced on sheets of paper that can either be bound into a booklet or simply stapled together. Then each interviewer can be given one of the guides to use in all interviews, recording responses in a separate notebook; alternatively, the interviewer could use one booklet for each interview, with responses from that interview written in designated spaces on the form.

In another approach that has been used in several Urban Institute evaluations, the interview guide is duplicated on index cards (3×5, 5×8, or even larger) rather than on paper. Each card lists one topic and all questions related to it. The cards can be coded to identify the type of respondent (or agency) for whom the topic and questions are relevant, and each can include a code that can later be used for organizing the information and responses. Exhibit 15.3 presents a sample card from an interview guide.

Experience has shown that the index card interview guide has a number of benefits. The same guide (set of cards) can be used a number of times without falling apart. This is no small benefit for multisite evaluations that might involve interviewing dozens of respondents in each site. In addition,

Exhibit 15.3. Example of One Topic in a Semistructured Interview Guide.

[Topic] 10. Child Care		*[Sites]* Salem, Seattle
		[Respondents] Welfare staff
[Interviewer Note]		[Ask of the highest ranking person in the office, and verify with other staff.]
[Subtopics]	A.	Which of the following child care *funding sources* are available for FIP/AFDC clients?
		Title XX funds?
		WIN funds?
		AFDC disregard funds?
	B.	Which *staff* are *responsible* for authorizing the expenditure of child care funds for a particular client?

Source: Nightingale, D. S., Holcomb, P., and O'Brien, C. T. *The Structure and Operation of the Washington State Family Independence Program.* Washington, D.C.: The Urban Institute, February 1990.

the cards can be organized or reshuffled in a number of ways to allow the interviewer to streamline each interview. This allows maximum flexibility in controlling each interview. Semistructured interviews may not follow the sequence of issues and questions in the guide; a skilled interviewer will do well to allow the respondent to continue a flow of thoughts, as long as issues that are in the guide are being addressed. As discussed below, the interviewer can politely guide the discussion to relevant issues that are of interest. Using a set of cards, the interviewer can unobtrusively review all cards if necessary without distracting the respondent by flipping through pages and paper sheets. This flexibility has proven to be quite valuable in allowing the respondent to continue to discuss issues as they arise, rather than saying, "We will return to that in a minute."

Field Visit Protocol

The successful completion of a fieldwork project requires careful attention to a number of procedural or logistical details before, during, and after the site visits. This section discusses the critical procedures that should be part of a field visit protocol in an evaluation that includes fieldwork. Field evaluators should be fully trained on these details. Procedures should be followed precisely to ensure that the information collected is of high quality, that different evaluators collect information in a comparable manner, that the fieldwork is minimally obtrusive, and that confidentiality is maintained to the maximum extent possible.

Previsit Preparations

The successful completion of the on-site portion of a field evaluation depends critically on careful preparation before the site visit actually occurs. Evaluators should not underestimate the importance of the previsit activities. Previsit preparations include a variety of activities, from setting up site-specific files of existing materials to handling logistical arrangements and recruiting and training field staff.

During the early stages of planning an evaluation, materials should be assembled from a variety of sources, such as government program files, site narratives, grant applications, existing databases, or prior field trips or evaluation files. Where feasible, these materials should be disaggregated into files associated with the designated field sites. A log of contacts (such as phone conversations with the contact person/site director) can also be included in each folder. For evaluations in which many documents are being collected from each site, attach a checklist of materials requested to the site's master folder. The materials should be checked off as they are received. Follow-up requests should be made and noted on the log, as needed.

Site Clearances. Initial contact with field sites should identify any constraints that might affect scheduling. For example, the evaluators may need to obtain clearances from higher levels in an agency or to ascertain whether other evaluations are underway in the same site. If entry clearances or interview authorizations are needed, the evaluator should clarify who is responsible for obtaining approvals (that is, the evaluator or the contact person), whose permission must be sought, and what information will be needed to facilitate the process. Scheduling must be sufficiently flexible to accommodate delays due to bureaucratic obstacles; nevertheless, planning should include actions that can be taken to minimize schedule slippage.

Scheduling Visits and Interviews. Several factors, including travel distance and level of staffing required, affect site selection. These should be considered during the site selection stage. Early communication with selected sites should identify (1) a central contact person who can serve as liaison to the evaluation, and (2) a tentative schedule or possible alternative schedules for the visit. This scheduling will permit advance planning of logistics, such as travel reservations and field staffing. Economies of scale in both travel savings and staffing often can be achieved when visits to geographically linked sites can be scheduled together.

Information packages should be assembled and given to the local contact person to provide background information about the evaluation. These should include

- An overview of the evaluation objectives, as well as the scope of each field visit
- Assurances that confidentiality procedures will be followed
- A sample schedule that the evaluation team would like to follow, indicating who the team wants to interview or meet with, for how long, and the times each day that the team members will be available

Either the field visit team or staff in the local agencies might schedule the interviews. The division of responsibility should be clearly established. During that discussion, the evaluators should review with the contact person the list of potential respondents, verifying that appropriate categories of respondents have been identified and getting suggestions regarding other persons who may have key information. Usually the initial interviews should be with the contact person/program director, then with program staff, and finally with outside or linkage agencies. However, the sequence may be of minor importance where the evaluation team is attempting to build up information for a later interview.

The evaluators will need to decide whether they will conduct individual or group interviews and determine the appropriate setting for conducting the interviews as part of the arrangements. If interview topics are sensitive or there is a need to ensure confidentiality, one-on-one rather than group interviews should be planned and private or semiprivate rooms should be secured for the sessions. Even when confidentiality is not an issue, reasonable efforts should be made to secure quiet, unobtrusive settings for interviewing to minimize distractions that can reduce the quality of responses.

Once the field visitation has been scheduled, personnel at the sites may be notified by phone or mail of the dates for the visit. Several days prior to the actual visit, telephone contact should be made with the contact person to confirm the plans, review the proposed agenda, and ensure the scheduling of interviews.

Defining Information Needs. If the evaluators intend to collect copies of records or documents while on site, they should discuss their needs in advance, encouraging site personnel to assemble the information before the visit. This is especially helpful if a large number of documents or files are needed or if the site has limited resources such as a small staff or limited access to duplicating equipment that might make it difficult for them to produce many copies in a short time.

Staffing Assignments. Decisions about the division of labor should be made as early as possible so that field staff know which sites they will cover and, within sites, which interviews they are responsible for conducting. Once field assignments are established, staff should review materials already collected in the site files such as organization charts, management information reports, and fiscal forms. At the same time, staff should review the checklist of requested documents, noting which materials still need to be collected either in advance or on site.

The issue of field staff safety bears special mention. Risks, both real and perceived, of working in low-income, high-crime, or inner city areas, can make it difficult to entice qualified individuals to staff certain projects. It is crucial to consider the kinds of actions that may be taken to ensure staff safety; following are some examples:

- Use two-person teams for interviews in high-risk areas, possibly including someone local who is familiar with the situation.
- Schedule interviews only in public locations, such as libraries, fast-food restaurants, or other well-lit high-traffic facilities.
- Train staff to take appropriate precautions (such as having a clear set of directions and a map, a sufficient quantity of gas); teach them the kinds of situations to avoid (such as parking and walking a long distance in unfamiliar territory).

Project Orientation. Unless the fieldwork is of very short duration or involves fewer than three field personnel, the team should prepare a document specifying procedures that field data collection staff are to follow. Such a document is useful both for previsit training of field personnel and as a reference in the field.

The documents should include the following:

- The overall objectives of the evaluation and the specific purpose(s) of the field visits
- Item-by-item instructions for administering instruments, including the definition of terms as used for the project

- Advice on how to gain respondent cooperation and, where necessary, procedures appropriate to obtaining informed consent
- Confidentiality requirements, including privacy, during interviews
- Procedures for conducting interviews
- Procedures for collecting other data, such as structured observations, questionnaire distribution or administration, or record audits
- Quality control procedures, including instructions on how to edit field notes
- Administrative requirements, such as accounting and reporting procedures for reimbursement of travel, per diem, and so on
- Recommendations for time management

Training. An important consideration for data collection is gaining respondent cooperation. The level of cooperation secured will be partially dependent on the interviewer's being able to listen to the respondent's concerns and to respond accordingly. Before going into the field or sending staff, the evaluators should consider the kinds of issues or resistance that may be raised by respondents. Training should incorporate answers to the anticipated questions and should include having team members practice appropriate responses and procedures to follow when confronted with unforeseen events that pose threats to data collection. Large evaluations videotape these mock interviews: replaying them provides immediate and forceful feedback to the interviewers.

Site Packets. Before the field trip, staff should review the planned on-site procedures to assess their need for field supplies and equipment, such as writing implements, notepads, and other office supplies that they should bring. We have found that two long (one hour) or three short interviews can be recorded in a field notebook. Staff should plan to take a few extra notebooks on each field visit to avoid running out.

If visits to several sites have been linked, or if staff anticipate collecting large amounts of bulky material, it may be desirable to bring along prepaid mailing labels/envelopes to send completed materials back to their home office. Since data, such as interview responses, may not be replaceable if lost, it is probably reasonable to use courier-type services. Although such deliveries cost more than regular mail, they have sophisticated tracking capabilities, which virtually guarantee that packages will not be lost.

On-Site Procedures

The field visit protocols developed before conducting site visits provide guidance and direction for the evaluators while they are in the field. This section discusses important on-site activities for which evaluators should be prepared.

Maintaining the Schedule/Interviewing Protocols. There will be times when scheduled respondents become unavailable. While it is not possible to guarantee a response rate in advance, with appropriate planning and effort (such as careful scheduling, following protocols for encouraging respondent cooperation, and having plans for refusal conversion), the team should be able to achieve a high interview completion rate. Professional demeanor and ability to conduct interviews without exhibiting judgment or excessive sympathy are particularly important.

If respondents are reluctant to cooperate, field staff should attempt to convert reticence into cooperation. A first step is to ascertain whether the respondent has unanswered questions or concerns that can be resolved, thus permitting the interview to proceed. For example, the timing may be poor, and rescheduling in person or by phone might resolve the impasse. If this approach does not succeed, it may be best to back off and allow another interviewer or evaluation supervisor to attempt the interview at a future time.

Depending on the circumstances, it may be possible to proceed without a specific interview, or it may be crucial to attempt a refusal conversion. Reassigning the interview to another staff member sometimes can have positive results. Perhaps the original staff member's demeanor, though acceptable to most people, bothered the respondent; maybe the respondent was having a bad day the first time, but will be in a more compliant mood later. It may be that recontacting the respondent flatters the individual into seeing his or her participation as crucial to the study's success.

If it is not specifically noted in the interview guide, the interviewer should plan exactly which individuals are going to be asked which questions in each site. The evaluators should ask for information from those individuals who are likely to be most knowledgeable about each particular item. It is desirable to verify the information by eliciting comparable information from multiple respondents. However, there are often constraints on both the interviewer and the interviewees that make it impractical to ask all questions of all respondents. Final decisions about which questions to ask which respondents should be made with care. Such decisions are usually made prior to field visits. To make sure coverage of subject matter, cross-verification, and designated interview length are satisfactory, a matrix of all interview guide items and all respondents can be created (See Table 15.2 for a portion of such a matrix.)

A pilot test, or pretest, should be conducted in at least one site. In most evaluations, the pilot site can also be part of the formal field evaluation since most of the same information will be collected.

Exhibit 15.4, an Urban Institute staff presentation, summarizes fifteen major field protocol guidelines. These have been found to help field evaluators conduct smoothly run interviews, yielding accurate information.

Other guidelines that can be used on site to ensure the accuracy of the information being obtained include the following:

• Individually or as a team, decide which questions will be asked of whom, with the purpose of ensuring that every question will be asked of at least

Exhibit 15.4. Field Protocol.

---

1. Interviewer should know the question backward and forward prior to making the field visit.
2. Interviewer should know the purpose of each question. Train interviewers properly as part of field visit preparation.
3. Be on time. Let respondent know if you are running late. Allow time for getting lost.
4. Establish a positive first impression. Be appreciative at the start of the respondent's knowledge and willingness to cooperate. Take time with the introduction (5–8 minutes, maximum).
5. Assure confidentiality and define what that includes, where needed.
6. Note-taking is important—record responses verbatim. Note interviewer's impressions, observations, or interpretations separately in brackets.
7. Ask respondent to pause, as needed, to permit complete recording of response.
8. Do not contradict respondent; probe his or her position.
9. Ask about references to legislation, acronyms, or persons that you are not clear about.
10. Record information as stated even if you dislike the respondent or disagree with the responses.
11. Remain alert throughout each interview. Interview time should probably be limited to about one-hour sessions.
12. Identify primary and secondary questions/issues, for consistency across interviews, in case some items must be omitted to stay within time limitations. Avoid asking too many questions; this should be addressed during instrument pretesting and field preparation.
13. Two-person field teams offer the advantage of division of labor. If this is feasible, one person can take responsibility for ensuring comprehensive coverage of interview items while the other takes responsibility for accurate and complete recording of responses.
14. Clean notes as soon as possible, preferably right after the interview but definitely that day.
15. Send thank-you letters.

Source: Holcomb, P. "Field Protocol." Staff presentation. Washington, D.C.: The Urban Institute, March 1993.

two potentially knowledgeable respondents. For example, on service delivery issues, the same items might be asked of both the program director and a line supervisor or the line supervisor and service delivery staff.

- Never assume that one respondent's response is totally accurate, even on what appear to be factual issues, such as when the program began.
- If something is unclear, do not assume the respondent's meaning and do not simply write the response down; take the initiative in clarifying responses until you *understand* what is being said.
- When different people are simultaneously conducting interviews, they should communicate frequently—daily, if possible—to compare experiences and to generate a common understanding of the overall picture.

When an interview is finished, the respondent may express interest in knowing what the evaluators are finding. Similarly, when all interviews are completed in a site, an administrator may want to discuss with the evaluators findings or conclusions they have drawn. Evaluators will naturally be thinking about preliminary findings before they leave the site but they should not attempt to draw conclusions or make recommendations while in the field. Later phases of the evaluation (after the site visits) should be devoted to analysis.

It is very tempting to provide immediate feedback to program directors, but evaluators should resist this temptation until all information collected in the field has been carefully organized, verified with other evaluators on the team, and analyzed. Thus, evaluators should be prepared to respond politely to such requests by explaining that they have accumulated a large amount of information and material that will have to be reviewed and analyzed before it can be reported. This response may make the evaluators slightly uncomfortable, but it is much more desirable than realizing later that they had given program officials partial or incorrect findings.

Collecting and Recording Information. Field evaluators should be given materials that help them explain the purpose and process of the study to their sources, as well as permit them to move efficiently through the planned interview. Interviewers should take time before each interview — five minutes should be sufficient — to review the questions to be asked, especially as they relate to a specific respondent and the types of information that person can be expected to provide.

Each interview should begin with a brief introduction to the project. (See Exhibit 15.5.) It is important that each respondent understand the project and the purpose of the interview. Explaining the project takes only one or two minutes but is one of the most important parts of the interview. In these first few minutes, the interviewer should establish an environment that places the respondent at ease.

Exhibit 15.5. Example: Introducing the Project to the Respondent.

INTRODUCTION/BACKGROUND

[Urban Institute's role in the evaluation: purpose of this set of interviews.]

We are researchers with the Urban Institute, a private non-profit policy research organization in Washington, D.C. We have been awarded a contract by the Legislative Budget Committee of Washington State to evaluate the state's Family Independence Program (FIP). This first wave of interviews focuses on early planning and implementation issues and problems associated with FIP. We are also interested in learning about the flow of clients through your system. We will be interviewing staff in local CSOs, ES offices, and JTPA offices in each of the ten study sites. We will be conducting subsequent interviews approximately every six months over the course of the next four years.

Source: Nightingale, D. S., Holcomb, P., and O'Brien, C. T. *The Structure and Operation of the Washington State Family Independence Program.* Washington, D.C.: The Urban Institute, February 1990.

Immediately after the introduction, the interviewer should address confidentiality. If the respondent's identity is going to be noted in a report, that must be explained. If all information is to be confidential, that needs to be explained. Confidential interviews are more likely than "public" interviews to produce rich detail — if the respondent understands the confidentiality pledge and if he or she believes that the interviewer will abide by the pledge. This is true even if the information being requested is not sensitive. (See Exhibit 15.6.)

Exhibit 15.6. Example: Statement of Confidentiality.

[Assure Confidentiality.]

> It is very important for us to learn how the Family Independence Program (or Opportunities Program) operates here, problems you may have identified, and suggestions for how a program like this should be run. As you know, FIP is a new . . . program and it is essential for us to document its implementation and on-going development. We need your cooperation to do this, since you are the people who know the most about welfare and employment and training programs and the problems that must be overcome. We are not employees of any state agency, nor are we auditors. We are under contract to the Legislative Budget Committee (LBC) to evaluate the FIP program. We will be submitting reports to the LBC, but in these reports there will be no way that anyone could identify what any particular individual told us. We pledge confidentiality—the sources of our interview information will not be divulged to anyone else here in this office, city, or state.

Source: Nightingale, D. S., Holcomb, P., and O'Brien, C. T. *The Structure and Operation of the Washington State Family Independence Program.* Washington, D.C.: The Urban Institute, February 1990.

The evaluation also should establish procedures for handling and storing the information collected, particularly if it is confidential. The procedures for maintaining confidentiality may range from not entering respondents' names into any databases that are constructed to devising systems of randomly generated identification numbers maintained in secured computer files.

After the introduction, it is helpful to "break the ice" with an initial question designed to get desired background information on the respondent and to ease into the interview. After this, the evaluator should move into the substance of the interview.

As the interview progresses, the interviewers should be alert to whether they are collecting the appropriate content and level of detail. Occasionally the interviewer may need to take more control, using body language to encourage or discourage the respondent's comments (for example, if something that is being said is of particular importance, sit forward or maybe nod the head to encourage continued discussion). If the respondent is drifting or giving more detail than is desired, the interviewer may have to redirect the respondent's focus. Similarly, when a respondent is providing information that is too sketchy, the interviewer should probe for more explicit details. If a card system is used, during the course of the interview, the evaluators flip through interview guide cards one card at a time, asking only the items appropriate to each respondent. Exhibit 15.3 earlier presented a sample card on which subject code (question or item number) and topic appear on the first line. On the next line relevant respondent categories are identified; these also can be coded. If an item requires special field staff handling, an Interviewer Note can be included (in Exhibit 15.3 the interviewer note is presented in brackets).

There are several ways to record the information from an interview: audio- or videotaping it or transcribing it into notebooks or directly onto interview forms. An alternative that has been used in a number of Urban

Institute studies involves recording responses into spiral-bound notebooks of index cards. Each response can be coded (repeating the question/item number used in the interview guide. Ideally, answers dealing with separate subjects are recorded on separate cards, but often during an interview, the respondent addresses more than one question of interest at a time. In that case, the response can be cross-coded for each question in the interview guide. The index card notebooks have perforations along the top of each card for easy removal from the binding if necessary. If the information is going to be reviewed and maintained manually rather than with a word processor, the cards can be separated and filed according to topic after the site visit for later analysis.

Daily Reviews. After the day's interviews are completed, interviewers should go back over the material they obtained to add subject codes, respondent codes, and site codes where needed. The material should be "cleaned" and clarified to be sure it is legible and meaningful to other members of the evaluation team. For example, only agreed-on abbreviations should be used.

Some evaluators may choose to dictate each day's interview notes into a tape recorder. The tapes can later be transcribed for analysis or preparation of site reports. The taping process also allows the evaluators an opportunity to review the day's information carefully.

If there is more than one evaluator at the site, the team should briefly review their respective findings and experiences to identify possible areas of inconsistency, issues that may have been missed totally (such as a question none of the respondents was able to answer because it was outside everyone's scope of responsibility), or areas that need further clarification or detail. The end-of-day debriefings afford valuable exchanges of information that can be helpful in later analysis. The team may want to tape record those sessions.

Data Maintenance and Analysis

Once qualitative data have been amassed, it can be used to generate several types of inferences, such as frequencies, trends, contingencies, and intensities, in addition to providing rich anecdotal evidence. Caudle, in Chapter Four of this volume, describes in detail qualitative data analysis methods. This section highlights a few of the more important data issues related to field evaluations.

Most important, the evaluators need to decide how to summarize systematically the large quantity of information collected. Analyzing qualitative data is roughly equivalent to performing analysis in which the documents under scrutiny are the records of interview responses. Such analysis involves organizing the data into a relevant set of content categories or topics and a set of response alternatives for each category.

Even when data sets are derived from semistructured, open-ended instruments, evaluators should identify preliminary categories and possible responses prior to data collection. This structure provides guidelines that help to orient data collection efforts. For example, anticipating certain themes and possible responses can help field staff determine whether interviews are achieving the evaluation objectives or whether evaluators need to probe further or refocus the respondent's attention. Usually preliminary categories or topics can be proposed during the fieldwork planning stage, based on the evaluation questions or hypotheses. Often the range of response alternatives also can be anticipated. However, these predetermined coding possibilities should be flexible as new themes may emerge during the data collection process, or anticipated topics or responses may never materialize.

One approach is to have field evaluators sort the data for each identified evaluation topic or category using the response alternatives postulated prior to actual data collection. In this approach, the coding scheme is finalized based on feedback from field staff who are asked to identify categories or response alternatives that do not fit the data. Adjustments can be made either by expanding or collapsing the initial choices of topics or responses. As staff sort the data they can flag any anecdotes or quotes that might enrich the final report.

A more rigorous approach is to divide the evaluation staff into two teams which independently review a sample of records. Based on this review, each team develops a set of content categories and response alternatives for each category. The teams convene as a single group to discuss and merge the categories and response selections. Once consensus is achieved, a sample of interviews should be split into subsamples of respondents. Each team receives one subsample which they code using the agreed-on scheme; then the teams exchange samples and repeat the categorization process. This approach tests both intracoder reliability (the degree of consistency with which a coder interprets similar responses) and intercoder reliability (the degree of consistency in interpretation among different coders).

If consistency in coding is unacceptably low, there are several options for improving reliability:

- Categories can be tightened and redefined to reduce the chances for miscoding.
- A post–data collection training session can be held to increase intercoder reliability by making coders more familiar with the categorization system.
- Instead of having staff code every item for a series of interviews, each staff member can be assigned responsibility for coding the same set of evaluation questions for all interviews, thus becoming the coding specialist for specific items, and thereby increasing intracoding reliability.

The approaches described above are for use when the data are manually sorted and coded. The proliferation of personal computers and specialized software packages has greatly facilitated this sorting process. There are content analysis programs that generate lists of unique words in one or more documents as well as the frequency of occurrence of each word, and search programs that permit exploration of whether and in what context certain key words are used. These and others have streamlined qualitative data analyses. While we are intrigued by these possibilities, we have not as yet tested their utility; therefore we are unable to suggest which approaches are useful or what limitations might be encountered in a variety of evaluation circumstances.

Conclusion

The fieldwork portion of evaluations provides an opportunity to collect rich detail that can augment other, more quantitative, data that are included in an evaluation. Too often, fieldwork is approached in an informal or haphazard manner that results in massive amounts of notes that cannot be easily analyzed. Evaluators should pay careful attention to developing fieldwork procedures, designing fieldwork data collection instruments, and preparing plans for managing and analyzing the information collected. Carefully implemented, fieldwork data collection can produce valid and credible information that cannot be obtained from other sources of data.

References

Burbridge, L. C., and Nightingale, D. S. *Local Coordination of Employment and Training Services to Welfare Recipients.* Washington, D.C.: The Urban Institute, 1989.

Holcomb, P. "Field Protocol." Staff presentation. Washington, D.C.: The Urban Institute, 1993.

Holcomb, P., and Nightingale, D. S. *Evaluation of the Western Interstate Child Support Enforcement Clearinghouse.* Washington, D.C.: The Urban Institute, 1989.

Mitchell, J. J., Chadwin, M. L., and Nightingale, D. S. *Implementing Welfare-Employment Programs: An Institutional Analysis of the Work Incentive Program.* Washington, D.C.: The Urban Institute, 1979.

Nightingale, D.S., and Ferry, D. *Assessment of the Joint Federal-State Performance Improvement Projects in the Work Incentive Program.* Washington, D.C.: The Urban Institute, 1982.

Nightingale, D. S., Holcomb, P., and O'Brien, C. T. *The Structure and Operation of the Washington State Family Independence Program.* Washington, D.C.: The Urban Institute, 1990.

16

Collecting Data
from Agency Records

Harry P. Hatry

The source of data most often used by evaluators is records kept by either the agency delivering the service being evaluated or by other agencies that have records relevant to the work of the program being evaluated. The term *agency records,* as used in this chapter, refers to data that are obtained from secondary sources, not from original data collection efforts such as survey information, interviews, and trained observer ratings. Examples of agency record data include information on client characteristics, quantity of work done, response times, information on the disposition of the work (such as number of clients successfully completing services), recidivism, and number and type of complaints.

It is tempting to evaluators to accept agency records at face value and not look critically at the information they contain. This chapter discusses some of the issues and problems that can arise with use of agency records and suggests ways to alleviate these difficulties. The chapter first identifies and discusses potential data collection problems and ways to alleviate them, then examines quality control issues and suggests steps for the *process* of record data collection.

The published literature contains little discussion of the issues and problems in collecting data from agency records. This is obviously not a favorite topic of evaluation authors. Among the few authors who address the topic, even if only briefly, are Babbie (1989), Kiecolt and Nathan (1985) (primarily for use of archived *survey* data), Krippendorff (1980), Nachmias and Nachmias (1987), Singleton, Straits, Straits, and McAllister (1988), and Webb, Campbell, Schwartz, and Sechrest (1966).

The following persons provided helpful suggestions for this chapter: Brenda Ashford, Caterina Gouvis, Adele Harrell, Blaine Liner, Elaine Morley, Lisa Newark, and Shelli Rossman, all of The Urban Institute.

Note that throughout this chapter, the word "client" is used in a general sense. Some programs, such as criminal justice programs, work on "cases." Other programs may have different terms for the subject of their work; for example, road maintenance programs focus on segments of roadways.

Potential Problems

Table 16.1 lists a number of problems that evaluators are likely to face when using agency record information. Each of these is discussed below.

Missing or Incomplete Data

In many if not most instances, information on some clients or work elements will be missing or incomplete. These gaps will affect the overall accuracy of the information. This applies whether the evaluators are attempting to obtain data on all clients/work elements or are drawing samples. If the proportion of missing or incomplete cases is substantial for a category of cases that are important to the evaluation, this problem will be a major evaluation concern.

The evaluator should first determine whether it will be feasible to obtain the missing or incomplete information. Often this will not be possible, such as when client data are sought for periods of time that are far in the past. In such cases, the evaluators should determine whether the number of missing cases will prevent them from answering questions important to the evaluation. If so, they may even have to terminate the entire evaluation.

Missing data have caused substantial evaluation problems, for example, in a number of state efforts to evaluate economic development programs. In some programs, lists of businesses assisted by the programs were not carefully kept. The evaluators needed the names of the businesses and their addresses in order to obtain business ratings of the services they had received. The evaluators had to ask program staff to put client lists together as well as they could, recognizing that these lists would be incomplete to an unknown extent.

The problem was even worse in a national evaluation of local programs bringing social services into schools to help reduce school dropouts. Many of the programs sampled did not have lists of clients served, data on the duration of their program, and extent of client participation in various program activities. The evaluators had to reconstruct this information from case files and staff memories.

The evaluators should consider treating missing information in a number of ways:

• They can leave out the data from tabulations. To calculate percentages, or averages, the evaluators would not count the missing data in either the numerators or denominators. For example, suppose the evaluators

Table 16.1. Potential Problems in Data Collection
from Agency Records and Possible Ways to Alleviate Them.

Problem	Possible Ways to Alleviate the Problem
1. Missing or Incomplete Data	• Go back to the records and related data sources (such as by interviewing program staff) to fill in as many gaps as possible. • Determine whether part or all of the evaluation needs to be modified or terminated. • Exclude missing data *or* provide a "best estimate" of the missing values.
2. Data Available Only in Overly Aggregated Form	• Where feasible, go back into the records to reconstruct the needed data. • Do new, original, data collection. • Drop the unavailable disaggregations from the evaluation.
3. Unknown, Different, or Changing Definitions of Data Elements	• Make feasible adjustments to make data more comparable. • Focus on percentage changes rather than absolute values. • Drop analysis of such data elements when the problem is insurmountable.
4. Data That Are Linked Across Time and Clients	• Be sure that the outcome data apply to the particular clients/work elements covered by the evaluation. • Track the clients/work elements between agencies/offices using such identifiers as social security numbers. • Look for variations in spellings, aliases, and so on.
5. Confidentiality and Privacy Considerations	• Secure needed permissions from persons about whom individual data are needed. • Avoid recording client names. Instead use code identifiers. • Secure any lists that link code identifiers to client names. Destroy these after the evaluation requirements are met. • Obtain data without identifiers from agency employees.

are calculating the proportion of events completed on time. They know there were one hundred cases. The records show that sixty were completed on time, twenty-five were not, and timeliness for the other fifteen cases could not be determined. The percentage of timely completion would be 60/85 or 71 percent. Alternatively, include the count of the missing data in the denominator of the percentages so that the denominator represents the total number of cases, even though the case records on some may be missing or incomplete. This, in the above example, would give a percentage of 60/100, or 60 percent. The second is the more conservative figure for the on-time percentage.

- Assign values to the missing data elements that are believed by the evaluators to best represent the population of interest, such as by using the mean of the available observations. For example, if data on earnings are missing for members of a particular ethnic group, the average earning of those in the ethnic group *for whom earning figures are available* might be substituted for the missing data. The overall average earnings for all ethnic groups would then include these estimates of earnings for the missing clients. In some instances, the evaluators may want to apply more sophisticated procedures involving the use of equations that attempt to predict the values of the missing data based on a number of other variables for which data are available. Each of these imputation methods, however, can result in biased estimates. For technical discussions of these options, see Little, Rubin, and Rubin (1987, 1990).

- Delete the incomplete cases but assign a new weight to each complete case to compensate for the deleted cases.

Which of the above options should be used will depend on the specific evaluation situation. Probably the best option is to analyze the data using all these approaches to determine whether important findings are sensitive to the problem.

Data Available only in Overly Aggregated Form

Sometimes the data are aggregated rather than ascribed to individual cases. This is a variation of the first problem. Frequently, evaluators want to provide disaggregations, or breakouts, of data. For example, evaluators might want to assess water quality for various segments of a body of water using agency record data on various water quality characteristics (such as dissolved oxygen, clarity, and chemical content). The data available in the records might not provide sufficient past data on each segment of interest. There may be little that evaluators can do in such instances. They can attempt to collect new data for such breakouts. This will be possible if the program is just beginning and the evaluator can build this data collection into the program's procedures. However, it is likely to be quite difficult, or impossible, to reconstruct past water quality data in the detail desired.

Similarly, if evaluators are attempting to use natural comparison groups (see Chapter Six on natural "experiments," this volume), the data needed for some breakouts may not be available for the comparison groups. The groups may be served by another agency or even another government jurisdiction that did not collect or record the information in the detail needed. In such cases, the evaluators will likely have to forego that breakout detail in their comparisons.

In some situations, the evaluators may be able to go back into the records to obtain the needed data. Public agencies often track complaints they receive but do not tabulate complaints or disaggregate them into needed categories, such as by type of complaint, location of complaint, or other characteristics that may be important to the evaluators. In this type of situation, the evaluators may be able to go back into individual case records and obtain the desired level of detail.

Before the design phase of an evaluation is completed, the evaluators should check the availability of data needed for their proposed evaluation plan and make any needed adjustments. It will be a fortunate evaluation team that is able to obtain record data on all the disaggregations they would like to make.

Unknown, Different, or Changing Definitions of Data Elements

Evaluators should ascertain how the major data elements they are collecting are defined and collected. This information is essential if they are to assess the accuracy and comparability of the data used. It is particularly important when the evaluators obtain information from different sites or different agencies, or collect data from several years during which data collection procedures might have changed.

A classic example of use of different definitions by different public agencies is that of school dropout rates. Comparisons of school dropout data across school districts and states can be fraught with pitfalls. Dropout rates have been calculated in many different ways by school systems. The rates may represent the ratio of the number of students graduating in a given year divided by the number of students entering at the beginning of that year. Or, they may represent the number graduating in a given year divided by the number who entered as freshmen four years earlier. Agencies may or may not take into account the number of students who transferred into or out of the school system. Agencies may count GED (General Educational Development) students in different ways, or handle differently the number of students who graduate earlier or later than their class. Some of these definitional issues are matters of judgment as to how the rate should be defined; in other cases they may involve logic errors. In any case, consistency and comparability across years and across school systems is needed when comparisons are being made.

A problem sometimes found in human service programs is that of *duplicated counts*. Some records of clients may count people each time they returned for service—in situations where the evaluators need unduplicated counts. This problem may require the evaluators to reconstruct counts from the data files or to make estimates of the amount of duplication, perhaps based on sampling the records.

Another typical example is cost information. Different agencies might include or exclude various cost elements, such as the salaries or upper level supervisors, the way indirect costs are handled (such as fringe benefits, rent, and supplies), depreciation of equipment, and capital costs. Currently, generally accepted standards of what to include in cost comparisons do not exist.

The following steps should help evaluators avoid or at least alleviate data definition problems:

- Identify the definitions and data collection procedures that have been used by the program and check for significant changes over the time period included in the evaluation. Evaluators should identify likely problems at the start of the evaluation.

- Where differences in definitions or data collection procedures are found, make appropriate adjustments, for example, by excluding those data elements for which data are not available in compatible definitions across comparison groups, or by examining the original information and identifying appropriate adjustments.

- Work with percentage changes rather than absolute values. Compare percentage changes from one year to the next among comparison groups (for example, percentage changes in the reported crime rates of various cities), even though the data that are being compared are based on somewhat different definitions and data collection procedures. This adjustment may provide roughly right comparisons as long as the definitions and procedures for each individual agency or office remained stable over the time period covered by the evaluation.

- Keep a record of data definition problems that have not been fully solved and estimate the impacts of these problems on the final evaluation findings.

Data That Are Linked Across Time and Clients

In some situations, the evaluators need to link data from different agencies or even different offices within the same agency, such as to track the impacts of a public program. These offices and agencies may use different identifiers, or they may track clients/work elements in different ways. Sometimes they do not use the same name for the same element. They may use social security numbers or other special client identifiers rather than names. Offices may use variations of clients' names. Some offices may identify clients by household and others by individual household member. All these circumstances present problems to the evaluation team.

The evaluators need, first, to identify the presence of such problems. Some may require special data collection efforts, close examination of names to identify name variations (for example, considering multiple identifiers such as age, addresses, and social security numbers to verify identities), and, perhaps, special computer runs to identify and link together the relevant data on the units of analysis for the evaluation.

Another problem can arise when evaluators want to learn what happened to each client (or each element of work) when the clients entered the program in one year and the results data are drawn from a later year. Evaluators must be sure that the results data are for the clients they are tracking. The problem is, perhaps, best explained by an example:

One state's department of human services developed a computerized tracking system to provide information on the success rates of its clients. The agency initially calculated the number of successful case closures in each year and the number of cases handled in the same year. It divided one by the other to estimate the percentage of cases successfully closed. But this was incorrect; the numerator and the denominator represent different cases. Instead, the system should be tracked cohorts of incoming clients—clients entering in a given year—over a specific duration of time to identify the percentage of clients who achieved specific outcomes after the specified time period. If the evaluators find that an agency's reports provide such misleading information, they, with the agency's help if possible, will likely need to examine individual records to obtain more valid percentages of clients with successful outcomes.

A similar problem, particularly for human service programs such as social and mental health services, is the timing of follow-ups to determine program outcomes. If samples of clients are drawn without consideration of how long a period has elapsed since service began or ended, and outcomes are not all measured for the same time interval, the measurements will yield data on clients whose length of program participation will likely have varied widely. To avoid these irregularities, evaluators should use a standard time period for obtaining outcome indicators such as "the percentage of clients starting service in 1993 who twelve months later showed significantly improved functioning." For such indicators, the evaluators will need a precise definition of "significantly improved functioning," and apply it to all clients being tracked.

Confidentiality and Privacy Considerations

Evaluators sometimes face obstacles in obtaining information from agency records because the data are confidential. This problem occurs often when human services, education, and criminal justice programs are being evaluated. It can also arise when evaluators seek any type of sensitive information such as a person's income.

Evaluators must protect the privacy of anyone about whom they obtain data, whether from records, surveys, or interviews. This protection can be provided in a variety of ways:

• Do not record a person's name. In some instances, it may be sufficient for the agency to provide numbers rather than names, to the evaluators. However, if the evaluators need to track the client, they should take precautions similar to those discussed below to protect client names.

• Number each client and carefully secure the list that cross-references the numbers to clients' names. Such lists should usually be destroyed after all the evaluation needs are met.

• Do not include in evaluation reports any information that might enable a reader to link a particular finding to an individual client. Sometimes the evaluators may want to cite a particular case. If so, they should obtain permission, preferably in writing, from those able to give such permission. A classic example of this problem occurred in an evaluation of state export activities in the Northeast. Because the chemical export market in Delaware is dominated by the DuPont Corporation, the U.S. Census Bureau does not release information on the amount of chemical exports in the state. If this information were made public, business competitors could readily identify DuPont's level of activity. The evaluators, therefore, had to forego using chemical export data on Delaware. Fortunately, however, such cases tend to be rare.

A major problem in evaluation can be the need to obtain permission to access individual records. Evaluators of a national school dropout prevention program needed permissions from local program staff, administrators of the school systems that had implemented the program, and the parents of sampled students to review agency record information on individual program clients such as grades, test scores, attendance records, and incidence of disciplinary action. Securing such permissions can be quite time-consuming and expensive. On the other hand, when the evaluators are employees of the agency whose program is being evaluated and the needed data come from the agency's own records, there is seldom a problem. When evaluators are from outside, agency employees can be asked to transcribe pertinent information for them without including individual identifiers. Such protected access can break an impasse, especially if the employees (or agency) can be paid for the time involved in collecting the needed data. Such data, however, cannot be linked to records from other agencies.

If an agency contracts with another organization to deliver the service being evaluated, the contractor may resist access to their records on individual clients. In such situations, the evaluators should attempt to obtain voluntary compliance by working with the contractor.

Quality Control

Data errors can occur at any point in record keeping. To help maintain data quality, evaluators should consider the following steps.

Data Checks for Reasonableness

The widespread use of computers and the availability of inexpensive software has greatly simplified the process of checking data for certain types of errors. Such procedures are particularly important when many different persons are involved in data collection or data entry and many data are involved. Information that comes to the evaluators in the form of computer tapes can have many inaccuracies, such as missing, inaccurate, or contradictory data due either to entry errors or errors in the original data collection. Evaluators will generally need to "clean the data," checking them for reasonableness before making computations, whether they are managed by computer or manually. Such checks could include the following:

• Assign ranges of possible values to each data element, and check to see if any of the data fall outside those ranges. For example, an entry of 110 for a person's age would be flagged either manually or by computer. Also, where applicable, make sure the computer, or manual data processors, can distinguish between such entries as the number "zero," "not applicable," and "don't know."

• Check consistency across data elements. With computers, elaborate checks can be made. For example, persons above certain ages are not normally employed in full-time positions. A computer could readily check for such problems. In an examination of drug testing programs, evaluators found clients in the database who had the same identification number and birthday but had a different race or sex. The evaluators went back to the original data source to correct what they found to be data entry errors.

• Look for missing data, flagging these instances so that decisions can be made about how to deal with them (as discussed earlier).

Staffing Considerations

Evaluators should ensure that the staff collecting the data are given sufficient instruction and training about what to look for. If different staff collect information on the same elements, they should be trained to collect comparable data and to identify differences that occur. They should be instructed to bring problems to the attention of the evaluation team for decisions on how to handle differences in data definitions.

One approach to alleviating data collection problems is to have data collectors specialize. One person can be assigned responsibility for gathering specific data elements from agency records at all sites. This option, however, may not always be feasible.

Other Suggestions for Obtaining Data from Agency Records

The quality of data can be enhanced by actions taken prior, during, and after the initial information has been obtained from the fieldwork. The following sections offer suggestions for quality assurance steps in each of these three phases.

Before Actual Field Data Collection Begins

1.   Make friends with those agency staff who originated the data. If evaluators are seeking data from people they do not know, making the acquaintance of the data originators can be very helpful in gaining assistance and information throughout the data gathering effort.

2.   Try to deal directly with the persons most familiar with the data records. If the evaluators need access to agency records, they should learn how the files are organized. They should ask those familiar with the records to identify possible problems, such as changes in definitions that have occurred over time, problems in getting the needed data, and likely reliability and validity problems. This effort gives evaluators a reality check on their data plans, helps them anticipate problems, and helps them assess what information they can most likely obtain.

3.   If evaluators ask an agency to provide data rather than requesting access to agency files, they should make the task as easy as possible for the agency staff by such steps as the following:

- Give the agency as much advance notice as possible.
- Put the request in writing and provide clear, full descriptions of the data needed.
- Tell the agency people why the data are needed but be flexible. The agency staff may be aware of problems with specific data items and be able to suggest suitable alternatives.

4.   Request samples of the data formats and definitions before you go into the field to gain a better perspective on what data are available.

5.   In some cases, it may be necessary and appropriate to compensate the agency for the extra time and effort required to generate the requested information. This might occur, for example, if (a) the information in the format and detail that the evaluators need requires major new computer runs on the agency's databases, or (b) the evaluators cannot gain direct access to data files or individuals but are willing to use data without individual identifiers if agency employees are willing to transcribe the data from the records.

In the Field

6.   Whether they are collecting completed agency reports or are extracting data from agency files, the evaluators should talk with the persons who are providing the data and who know something of its content. They should ask about data definitions, their limitations, and especially any problems in how the data have been obtained. Even if the evaluators believe they

have obtained such information before the start of field data collection, they should check again while in the field.

7.   The evaluators should learn the form and detail in which the data are available. Data collectors will need to determine whether to forego some of the information wanted, try to obtain data not currently in the desired form or detail, or accept the less-than-ideal data situation.

8.   For each item of data collected, the evaluators should identify the periods of time covered by that item. Frequently, items of data will apply to different time periods requiring the evaluator to make adjustments or at least to identify the discrepancies when they write their reports. For example, data for some elements may refer to calendar years, fiscal years, or school years.

9.   Similarly, for data elements intended to cover specific geographical areas, the evaluators should identify what geographical areas apply to each data element. Some outcome data, for example, might be reported by organizational-unit coverage (such as police precincts, fire districts, regional districts, and offices). Other outcome data might be reported by census tracts or by neighborhood. This diversity may or may not present problems for the evaluation. Also, the geographical boundaries may have changed over the time period covered by the evaluation. Evaluators need to know the extent of such problems so they can make decisions on ways to accommodate them.

After Initial Data Have Been Obtained

10.   Determine for each data element how missing or incomplete data should be handled. Decisions to drop a certain element or case or to make a specific adjustment should be reached, when possible, prior to data analysis.

11.   Check for illogical, inconsistent data. Where appropriate, ask the data source for the correct data.

12.   Send data back to originators for verification—in situations where the originators are likely to be able, and willing, to make such verification.

13.   Thank agency sources for their assistance. Let them know that their help has been valuable and appreciated.

14.   Document and provide appropriate caveats in the evaluation report. The evaluators should provide their best judgments on the effects of these data problems on the findings.

Some Final Comments

Agency records will be the source of much important data in many, if not most, evaluations. At the very least, evaluators are likely to need to identify the amount or type of work that is the subject of the evaluation (for example, the number of customers or work items). Inevitably, evaluators will find less than perfect data from agency records. Whether these data come from the agency in which the program is located, another agency in the same government, a contractor of the government, or another jurisdiction, the evaluators need to assure that they know the definitions and content of the various data elements being collected. The evaluators will need to ascertain that the data they use are sufficiently comparable for them to compare different groups or the same group across time.

Evaluators should be aware that obtaining data from agency records will present unexpected difficulties. The challenge is to make needed adjustments that do not compromise the overall quality of the evaluation.

References

Babbie, E. *The Practice of Social Research* (ch. 11). (5th ed.) Belmont, Calif.: Wadsworth, 1989.

Kiecolt, K. J., and Nathan, L. E. *Secondary Analysis of Survey Data.* Newbury Park, Calif.: Sage, 1985.

Krippendorff, K. *Content Analysis: An Introduction to Its Methodology.* Newbury Park, Calif.: Sage, 1980.

Little, R., Rubin, J. A., and Rubin, D. B. *Statistical Analysis with Missing Data.* New York: Wiley, 1987.

Little, R., Rubin, J. A., and Rubin, D. B. "The Analysis of Social Science Data with Missing Values." In J. Fox and J. S. Long (eds.), *Modern Methods of Data Analysis.* Newbury Park, Calif.: Sage, 1990.

Nachmias, D., and Nachmias, C. *Research Methods in the Social Sciences* (ch. 13). (3rd ed.) New York: St. Martin's Press, 1987.

Singleton, R., Jr., Straits, B. C., Straits, M. M., and McAllister, R. J. *Approaches for Social Research* (ch. 12). New York: Oxford University Press, 1988.

Webb, E., Campbell, D. T., Schwartz, R. D., and Sechrest, L. *Unobtrusive Measures: Nonreactive Research in the Social Sciences* (ch. 3 and 4). Chicago: Rand McNally, 1966.

Part Three

Practical
Data Analysis

The time to think about how data will be analyzed and reported is early in the evaluation planning. Conceptualizing what the audience for an evaluation will desire in terms of analytical sophistication and precision can help evaluators select among the many techniques available. Mapping out what the end product should look like provides some of the structure needed to guide planning of analysis procedures.

Constraints on evaluators' choices among analytical options go beyond what their clients will expect in reports, however. Time and resources will affect the type of data collected, and thus the sorts of analytical techniques that can be used. In many cases, evaluators must rely on data that others have collected, or on the format that others prefer for further collection efforts. Evaluators' skills in effectively applying and reporting analytical techniques may also limit the possibilities for analysis of evaluation data.

The chapters in Part Three present techniques for analyzing data collected in evaluation efforts. The three chapters cover (1) selection, application, and reporting of inferential statistics; (2) the application and interpretation of regression analysis; and (3) the use of benefit-cost techniques in program evaluation.

The three authors describe analytical techniques in nontechnical terms to clarify the relative advantages and disadvantages of the various options. In each chapter the author describes the purpose of the techniques and the types of evaluation questions that are most amenable to application of each; the assumptions or requirements of the data and the data collection methods that must be met to utilize each analytical technique effectively; the sorts of information that should be provided in reports about application of each technique; and the possible limitations that may accompany application of the techniques.

Kathryn E. Newcomer, in Chapter Seventeen, describes a variety of statistical techniques available to evaluators. She identifies the most important issues that evaluators should address when applying statistical techniques to strengthen the conclusions drawn from the findings. Basic distinctions among statistical techniques are described; procedures are outlined for drawing samples and applying statistical tools; criteria are provided for evaluators to use in choosing among the data analysis techniques available; and guidance is given on reporting statistics appropriately and clearly. Illustrations of the application of chi-square, t test, and multiple regression are provided.

Charles S. Reichardt and Carol A. Bormann, in Chapter Eighteen, provide additional information about the application of regression analysis. They demonstrate how regression analysis may be applied in four evaluation scenarios: the randomized experiment, the regression-discontinuity design, the nonequivalent comparison group design, and the interrupted time series design. Reichardt and Bormann's discussion of data requirements and optimal reporting supplements the information provided by Rog, Marcantonio and Cook, and Dennis in their descriptions of these designs in Chapters Six, Seven, and Eight.

James Edwin Kee, in Chapter Nineteen, offers guidance on the application of benefit-cost techniques in program evaluation. Opportunities to apply the various benefit-cost options are outlined along with the issues evaluators must address should they select one of these techniques. Kee provides guidance to evaluators as he describes cost-effectiveness analysis and its capabilities, differentiates among the various types of benefits and costs that should be arrayed in any benefit-cost analysis, offers suggestions on the valuation of benefits, identifies common problems surrounding the measurement of costs, and provides guidance on presenting benefit-cost information to decision makers.

Authors of each chapter carefully delineate the issues evaluators should address as they select and report the results of analyses. They discuss factors affecting such decisions and the potential threats to the validity of results provided in evaluation reports. Replicability with the assurance of consistent results is the hallmark of valid and appropriate data analysis.

17

Using
Statistics Appropriately

Kathryn E. Newcomer

Statistics may be used in a variety of ways to support program evaluation endeavors. When quantitative data are collected and systematically arrayed to depict program inputs, outputs, or outcomes, the numbers (statistics) should accurately portray the phenomena measured. The accuracy of conclusions supported by statistics is affected by a number of decisions made throughout data collection efforts and evaluation planning.

This chapter identifies factors that affect the validity of statistics and offers guidance to evaluators on selecting and interpreting statistics. Other chapters in this volume have referred to statistical decisions, such as determining an adequate sample size and selecting an appropriate measure of a program effect. This chapter offers more background for such decision making and illustrates some of the most frequently used statistical techniques. First, some basic distinctions among statistical techniques are described. Second, procedures are outlined for testing statistical hypotheses and establishing decision rules. Third, criteria are offered for evaluators to consider when selecting statistics. Finally, guidance is provided on reporting statistics appropriately and clearly.

Descriptive and Inferential Statistics

When any phenomena are counted, the numbers can be tabulated according to a variety of procedures. If the resulting statistics, such as averages, are used to describe a group of items, the figures presented are called *descriptive statistics*.

In many situations the population of program recipients, or even service providers, is so large that to survey the entire population would be too costly. Instead, a sample is drawn from the population with the hopes of generalizing the quantitative results to the population. To ensure that the statistics can be generalized with confidence, the manner in which the sample is drawn is of critical importance. If a group of units are selected in a systematic fashion such that the probability for each unit to be selected from the larger population is known, the group can be referred to as a *probability sample*. When statistics are computed from the sample with the intention of generalizing from the sample to the population from which the sample was drawn, the statistics are referred to as *inferential statistics*.

Generalizing from Samples

The accuracy of inferences drawn from a sample to a population is critically affected by the sampling procedures used. Four principles should guide evaluators when they select samples.

- *The population of interest must be reasonably known and identifiable.* This criterion presents a challenge for evaluators when records are not comprehensive. Therefore, evaluators should make efforts to ascertain whether the reason that records are not inclusive may be indicative of any bias.

- *A sampling technique should be used in which the probability for selecting any unit in the population can be calculated (probability sampling).* Evaluators should use a sampling technique such as using random numbers to select units (random sampling), perhaps using the tables of random numbers in textbooks or in statistical software, or selecting every *n*th unit in the population (systematic sampling). When there are specific subgroups within the population of particular interest, the evaluators may divide the population into such subgroups and apply probability sampling techniques within each of the subgroups—an approach called *stratified sampling*.

- *A sample should be drawn that is of appropriate size relative to the size of the population to which generalization is desired.* Basic statistics textbooks and software provide formulas that can be applied to identify appropriate sample sizes as long as the evaluators can specify how much confidence they wish to have in the results and the amount of error they are willing to accept.

- *Even though probability sampling is applied, evaluators should examine a sample to ensure that it is truly representative of the population to which the evaluators hope to generalize* on variables of critical interest, such as demographic characteristics like gender and race. Probability sampling can help rule out chance variation that may conceal true relationships or impede accurate identification of program effects, but it cannot guarantee that the sample contains certain units or people in the same proportion as they exist in the population of interest.

When the data collection strategies make the use of probability sampling techniques impossible, as when evaluators do not have access to the full population, using statistics for inferential purposes become a problem. In such cases, statistics should not be generalized from the sample to the population; evaluators should take even greater care to test the representativeness of the sample and to identify sources of bias that render the sample unlike the population from which it was drawn. The statistics might then be used for inferential purposes with explicit recognition that the statistical inferences are not as valid as the numerical representation of confidence indicates.

Statistical techniques have been developed to test whether the numbers generated from a sample can be generalized to the population from which it was drawn, given the particular sample size and the variation within the sample. Such techniques generate statistics that estimate the *statistical significance,* or generalizability, of the data. The chi-square and the *t* test are the two statistics most frequently used to address the question of generalizability of the data. (Applications of each of these statistics appear in Appendices 17.A and 17.B.)

Estimating the Strength of Relationships

Other statistical techniques have been developed to assess the strength of relationships between or among variables of interest, as displayed in Table 17.1. For example, Pearson's correlation coefficient (r) is often used to assess the strength of the relationship between two continuous variables. Other coefficients, such as lambda, have been developed for use when variables have been measured in a nominal fashion and any numbers assigned do not have a numerical meaning and cannot be ordered or added.

Coefficients have also been developed for variables measured on ordinal scales (that is, where the numbers assigned to the characteristic of interest have an implicit order even though the distance between the values is not equal, such as Likert attitudinal scales). Gamma is the most frequently used statistic to convey the level of covariation between ordinal variables.

Some statistical techniques have been designed to discern the relationships among three or more variables. These techniques provide statistics that indicate how strongly any set of the variables analyzed covary. In regression, for example, the *R-square* statistic conveys the strength of the relationship between the predicted and actual values of the dependent variable.

Table 17.1. Estimating the Strength of Relationships.

How are the variables measured?	An appropriate coefficient	Range
Nominal	Lambda	−1 to +1
Ordinal	Gamma	−1 to +1
Interval	Pearson's r	−1 to +1
Interval	With bivariate regression: r-square	0 – 100%
Interval	With multiple regression: R-square	0 – 100%

Since *R-square* ranges from zero to 100 percent, the description it provides of the strength of the predictive relationship is quite vivid for audiences.

Statistical Hypothesis Testing

To apply inferential statistics a systematic procedure called statistical hypothesis testing should be used. First, a statistical hypothesis identifying the relationship between any two variables of interest must be specified. For example, to test a statistical hypothesis that there is no relationship between two variables, a *null hypothesis* is stated. The null hypothesis in program evaluation is that the program has no effect in achieving the intended outcome. For example, *access to home health aides does not affect medical costs for emergency care* might be a null hypothesis for an evaluation of a home health aid program.

When the null hypothesis is not rejected, the sample data do not permit a conclusion that the program is effective. Appendix 17.A illustrates application of the chi-square test of statistical significance in which the null hypothesis is not rejected, with an appropriate interpretation of such results.

When data are drawn to test the null hypothesis of no effect, if the program truly has no effect and the data support this, there is no problem. Similarly, if the program has the intended effect and the test data demonstrate this, again there is no problem.

Problems arise when there is a discrepancy between the true situation and the test results; in this case an erroneous conclusion can be drawn. If the true situation is that the program does *not* have the desired effect but the statistics calculated suggest that it does, an error called a false positive, or type I error is committed. If the true situation is that the program *does* have the desired effect but the test data suggest that it does not, a false negative or type II error is committed.

It is difficult to protect against both types of errors, so the costs of committing each should be considered and greatest attention paid to avoiding the more costly one. In some cases a false positive may be more costly to the public than a false negative. For example, when evaluators conclude a false positive, that a very costly teenage pregnancy prevention program is effective when it really is not, the result may be that future funding is wasted on an ineffective program. On the other hand, a false negative conclusion that an effective airline regulation is not working may mean that the regulation is not reauthorized. In any case, aspects of the evaluation design that may make either a false positive or a false negative more likely should be carefully considered. Table 17.2 identifies design features that may make an evaluation vulnerable to either a false positive or a false negative finding. Evaluators should weigh the consequences of committing both false positive and false negative errors, and then identify ways in which they might minimize the more costly error.

Any measurement precautions that help protect the evaluator from committing a false negative increase the *statistical power* of the test—the

**Table 17.2. Evaluation Design Features
Likely to Generate False Positives or False Negatives.**

Design Feature	Raises Likelihood of False Positives	Raises Likelihood of False Negatives
1. Threats to Validity:		
a. The sample is made up of volunteers	*	
b. The same questions are used on a pretest and on a posttest	*	
c. Experimental mortality—only the more motivated group members remain in the program to be measured	*	
d. "Hawthorne effect"—the program participants are aware they are being measured and change their behavior in the desired direction	*	
e. The program is new and program staff or participants are more motivated than they might be later in the life of the program	*	
f. Control group tries to compensate for their failure to receive treatment		*
g. Staff fears harm to control group and tries to compensate		*
h. Measurement procedures are unreliable		*
2. Other Design Characteristics:		
a. Sample size too small		*
b. Time period for measurement too short		*
c. "Control" group receives "treatment" from other sources		*
d. Program not fully implemented		*

capability of a statistical test to accurately detect effects or differences between groups. Once the relative costs of committing a false positive and a false negative are considered, evaluators can develop a decision rule that reflects the level of confidence they wish to have in their decision to generalize from their sample to the population. Since the probabilities of committing a false positive and a false negative are inversely related, the more evaluators protect against one type of error, the more vulnerable the test will be to the opposite error.

Selecting a Statistical Confidence Level. The specified decision rule states how confident the evaluator wishes to be that a false position will not occur. This decision rule provides the *confidence level* for the test.

The confidence level reflects the amount of evidence evaluators want to have to ensure that they are correct in concluding that the program does produce the observed effect. In the physical and social sciences a 95 percent confidence level is conventionally used as a decision rule for testing statistical hypotheses. The null hypothesis to be tested is that the treatment does not have the intended effect. If the findings are sufficiently deviant from what the probability tables predict if the null is true, the null hypothesis is rejected. This decision allows one to generalize the findings for the sample to the population from which it was drawn with the confidence that, over the long run, a test of this type should result in a false positive error only five times out of one hundred.

For many, if not most, public program purposes, 95 percent may be excessive. Conclusions for which evaluators are 80 percent or 90 percent confident may be quite adequate and reduce the size of the sample needed, thereby reducing costs. When the costs to the public of committing a false negative are high — for example, judging an effective program to be ineffective because of obtaining data from a very small sample — it may be appropriate to go beyond convention and use even an 80 percent confidence level. While such a figure indicates that the risks of committing a false positive are greater than typically accepted, this lower confidence level helps hedge against making a false negative error and dooming a program because the data do not seem to indicate that the program is effective.

Conducting a test that achieves significance at the 95 percent confidence level is typically interpreted in either of the following ways:

- One would obtain findings like this only five times out of one hundred samples if the null hypothesis (of no effect) were really true.
- One can be 95 percent confident that the sample findings were not simply the result of random variation.

When the null hypothesis is rejected (using the 95 percent decision rule), it is appropriate to state that the sample data are "statistically significant at a confidence level of 95 percent." Concluding that quantitative data are "statistically significant" tells the audience that, following conventional statistical hypothesis testing procedures, the data appear to be representative of the population from which the sample was drawn. However, generalizability can be subject to many other threats such as a selection bias due to the evaluator's not being able to obtain data on some of those in the sample (for example, their refusal to complete surveys), or those in the sample being volunteers. Even if the numbers demonstrate that the findings are "statistically significant at the 95 percent confidence level," other problems with the representativeness of the sample may render the generalization inappropriate.

Practical Significance

The terms *significance* or *statistical significance* are conventionally reserved for the judgment that sample data results can be generalized to the population from which the sample was drawn. A separate judgment should be made regarding the magnitude of the effect that is being measured. In fact, the presentation and terminology used should clarify that two separate judgments are made — the first being whether the sample data can be generalized, and the second being an evaluation of the size of the effect: slight, moderate, strong. Judgments about the size of the effect reflect what the evaluators view as the practical importance of the measured effect. For example, if a new mathematical curriculum in a high school appears to raise students' achievement scores 1 percent, even if the large sample drawn indicates that the effect is "statistically significant," the size of the impact of the curriculum may seem inconsequential.

There are no standards available for evaluators to use when interpreting the magnitude of the size of the observed effect (or observed relationship between two or more measures). For example, most statistics measuring the magnitude of relationships between measures range from 0 to 1, or −1 to +1, and the closer to 1 (or −1) a number falls, the stronger the relationship. There are no conventionally accepted rules to indicate what number is high enough to call "high." The best way to evaluate such numbers is to compare them to appropriate referents such as comparable figures for previous years, for other administrative units, or for comparable programs. Appropriate and meaningful comparisons are absolutely essential to lend credibility to measures of magnitude.

Using a Confidence Interval to Convey Results. When the magnitude of a program effect is given, the results should be reported as a *confidence interval* — that is, the sample statistic should be stated with a margin of error such as plus or minus 2 percent. Reporting an effect without such a margin of error is not appropriate for it incorrectly implies too much precision in the measures. Program effects should be given as falling within a range. For example, one might report that "among clients still receiving welfare benefits, the figure was five to ten percentage points lower for those who had completed the job training program than for the clients who did not complete the training." Appendix 17.B explains the calculation of a *t* value, which allows evaluators to present the findings as a confidence interval.

Reporting of both statistical significance and the size of program effects should be clear. Both findings should be reported and interpreted for the audience. For example, a difference between treatment and control groups may be minuscule, yet be statistically significant at a specified confidence level. On the other hand, a difference may be impressive in magnitude but not statistically significant, usually because of small sample sizes. Will policymakers care if a new program raises third graders' reading scores by .2 percent? Probably not; it is too small a gain if the program is at all costly.

Selecting Appropriate Statistics

Evaluators should use several criteria to ensure selecting the most appropriate statistics in a particular situation. Exhibit 17.1 displays three categories of criteria that evaluators should use in deciding which statistical technique will be most appropriate: question-related, measurement-related, and audience-related criteria. The substantive questions identified to guide an evaluation, the data collection decisions made about how to measure the phenomena of interest, and the type of audience the evaluator is addressing all affect selection of statistical techniques.

Exhibit 17.1. Criteria for Selecting Appropriate Data Analysis Techniques.

A. *Question-Related Criteria*
    1. Is generalization from sample to population desired?
    2. Is the causal relationship between an alleged "cause" and alleged "effect" of interest? Is it an impact question?
    3. Does the question (or statutory/regulatory document) contain quantitative criteria to which results can be compared?

B. *Measurement-Related Criteria*
    1. At what level of measurement were the variables measured: nominal (for example, gender); ordinal (for example, attitudes measured with Likert-type scales); or interval (for example, income)?
    2. Were multiple indicators used to measure key variables?
    3. What are the sample sizes?
    4. How many observations were recorded for the respondents: one, two, or more (time series)?
    5. Are the samples independent or related? That is, was the sample measured at two or more points in time (related)?
    6. What is the distribution of each of the variables of interest, such as bimodal, normal?
    7. How much precision was incorporated in the measures?
    8. Are there outliers affecting calculation of statistics, that is, extremely high or low values that skew the mean and other statistics?

C. *Audience-Related Criteria*
    1. Will the audience understand sophisticated analytical techniques such as multiple regressions?
    2. Will graphic presentations of data (such as bar charts) be more appropriate than tables filled with numbers?
    3. How much precision does the audience want in numerical estimates?
    4. Will the audience be satisfied with graphs depicting trends or desire more sophisticated analyses such as regressions?
    5. Will the audience understand the difference between statistical significance and the practical importance of numerical findings?

As described earlier, sample data are usually selected with the intention of generalizing results to the population from which the sample units were drawn. Statistics that test generalizability include chi-square and t. Which of these statistics is selected depends on how the variables were measured. Chi-square can be used no matter how variables are measured, but the t test requires that the dependent variable (typically the program effect) be measured at the interval level—for example, unemployment rate.

No matter which analytical technique is selected, both the statistic used to assess statistical significance and the magnitude of an effect or strength of the relationships analyzed should be reported. Table 17.3 displays questions evaluators may ask and statistical techniques frequently used to address them.

Selecting a Technique to Estimate Program Impact

When evaluators address impact questions and wish to estimate or predict an impact by measuring the relationship between the alleged cause—the

Table 17.3. Selecting Statistical Techniques.

Purpose of the Analysis	How the Variables Are Measured	Appropriate Technique	Appropriate Test for Statistical Significance	Appropriate Measure of Magnitude
To compare a sample distribution to a population distribution	Nominal/Ordinal	Frequency counts	Chi-square	NA*
	Interval	Means/medians Standard deviations/ Interquartile range	Chi-square	NA
To analyze a relationship between two variables	Nominal/Ordinal	Contingency tables	Chi-square	Percentage difference
	Interval	Contingency tables/test of differences of means	Chi-square or t	Difference in means
To reduce data through identifying factors that explain variation in a set of measures	Nominal/Ordinal	NA	NA	NA
	Interval	Factor analysis	t	Pearson's correlations
To sort units into similar clusters or groupings	Nominal/Ordinal	NA	NA	NA
	Interval	Cluster or discriminant analysis	t	Equivalent of R-square
To predict or estimate program impact	Nominal/Ordinal	Loglinear regression	t and F	R-square,
	Interval	Regression	t and F	beta weights
To describe or predict a trend in a series of data collected over time	Nominal/Ordinal	Regression	t and F	R-square, beta weights
	Interval	Regression	t and F	same as above

Note: *NA = not applicable.

program—and the alleged effect, other statistical procedures are applicable. The manner in which the variables were measured limits the number of statistics available to evaluators. The most fundamental constraint is whether the variables were measured at the nominal, ordinal, or interval level of measurement. With *nominal measures,* frequency distributions and contingency tables that array frequency counts are the most often used techniques for analyzing data. In fact, if any of the variables of interest are nominal, contingency tables are the best option. Table 17.4 presents a model contingency table.

Table 17.4. A Model Contingency Table.

		Motorcycle Accident-Related Fatalities *by Status of Helmet Laws in Thirty-Six States in 1991*	
		State Has Law Requiring *Motorcyle Rider to Wear Helmet* *N = 14*	*State Does Not Have* *Helmet Law* *N = 22*

Motorcycle accident-related
  fatality rates per 1,000
  population			

Fewer than 10		57%	28%
10–25		21%	27%
Over 25		21%	45%
	Total	99%*	100%

*Total does not add up to 100% due to rounding.

With *ordinal measures,* contingency tables and frequency distributions are still the most likely choice for analysis. Some researchers prefer to treat ordinal measures as if they are equivalent to interval measures, and they choose analytical techniques typically reserved for interval measures such as regression. However, unless an ordinal scale contains at least five values, it is probably best to treat the scale as a nominal measure. Even if the scale contains five or more values, it is best first to examine the observed frequencies and then determine whether the range in the actual responses is sufficient for the scale to be treated as an interval measure. For example, if the vast majority of clients rated services 4 or 5 on a five-point scale, the measure should not be treated as if it were interval when a statistical technique is selected.

With *interval measures* evaluators have the widest range of alternatives. When evaluators wish to explain an effect (what analysts call a *dependent variable*) with other variables, regression is often used.

Applying Regression

Regression is an analytical technique often used to predict values for a *criterion,* or *dependent variable,* of interest based on historical trends in that criterion or on other factors that are assumed to influence it. The model underlying simple regression is a straight line that represents the average change in the criterion across time or in the other factors assumed to influence it (called *predictors*). We could fit a regression model to summarize the trend in infant mortality rates over time, or we could generate a regression model that relates age of the mother and availability of the Women-Infant-Children (WIC) nutrition program benefits to infant mortality rates to assess the effectiveness of past expenditures.

Simple regressions model only linear relationships, but variations permit more complex relationships to be modeled, such as curvilinear relationships in which the criterion of interest may rise over a period of time, then level off or even fall. For example, in some training or counseling programs there may be a ceiling effect. Improvement in outcome criteria may progress only to a certain level at which additional training or counseling may even be counterproductive. Some programs designed to affect behavior may also be influenced by natural phenomena, such as local governmental programs to reduce water usage; there may be seasonal variation in the criterion for programs like this. Additional predictors can be incorporated into a regression that will produce a curve rather than a straight line, and that will represent change in factors that influence change in the criterion of interest.

Regression is frequently used in connection with policy or program evaluations to produce estimates of changes in behaviors that policies or programs produce. For example, historical data on teenage pregnancy rates or recidivism among parolees might be used to estimate the impact of programs implemented to affect these behaviors. Regression might also be used in needs assessments connected with the development of new programs, such as estimating the proportion of homeless persons in need of mental health care in order to gauge the resources needed in a new program.

A statistical formula is used to identify the best fitting regression line, or curve, that is closest to the observed data. That is, the statistical technique finds the line or curve that minimizes the sum of the squared differences between each observed value and the value predicted by the line.

Since regression is most often used to generate predicted values, or estimates, the statistics of most pertinence calculated with the regression analysis are the measures that indicate how well the mathematical model that is generated fits the data. The measure of fit that is most often reported is called the *coefficient of determination,* also known as the R-square. This coefficient is a ratio that ranges from zero to 100 percent and corresponds to how much of the variation in the criterion of interest can be predicted by the selected predictors. The higher the coefficient, the better the fit and the higher the predictive power of the regression model. For example, an R-square value of 90 percent indicates that 90 percent of the variation in the criterion can be explained by the predictors selected for the analysis.

The impact that each predictor has on changes in the criterion variable can also be depicted with the *unstandardized regression coefficients,* or *slopes,* that are generated with a regression. A slope signifies how much change will occur in the criterion variable for a one-unit change in each predictor; it can be any positive or negative number. For example, each additional pregnancy in a family dependent on public assistance programs might translate into an additional $4,500 in federal expenditures per family per year.

The relative impact that each predictor has on the criterion can be assessed through comparing the magnitude of the *standardized regression coefficients,* or *beta weights,* that are provided with a regression analysis. Here the regression coefficients are transformed to common units (numbers of standard deviations) to facilitate comparisons across variables that are measured in different metrics, such as years of schooling versus scores on aptitude exams. Unlike unstandardized regression coefficients, the beta weights range from -1 to $+1$, give the relative importance of one predictor in relation to the others, and compare the strength of different predictors. A predictor with a beta weight of .8 can be said to have twice as strong an impact on the criterion as another predictor that has a beta weight of .4.

The statistical significance of regression results can be tested using the conventional t statistic to assess the significance of each predictor. If a variable turns out to be statistically significant using the t statistic, the correct interpretation is that there is a generalizable relationship between that variable and the predicted variable. A predictor could be statistically significant, yet the magnitude of the relationship with the criterion could be so low that the predictive power of the regression is weak.

A test for statistical significance of the entire regression model also can be used. The F test of the R-square can assess the significance of the entire model. The F statistic is very similar to the t statistic, and is interpreted in much the same manner. If any of the individual predictors is statistically significant, the F will be. If the F is significant but none of the predictors show significance, there are problems with high intercorrelations among the predictors that should be investigated.

The R-square is critical for interpreting any regression. If the R-square value is low, say below 25 percent, then the predictive power of the model is weak and little confidence should be put into the statistics generated from the regression. Caution should be exercised when regressions predicting program effects yield a low R-square value, for the ability to predict effects may be too low to be of practical importance.

When predictions are generated from regression models, confidence intervals should be placed around the estimates to indicate how precise they are. That is, an estimate should be given in a band with a lower and upper estimate. The size of the band reflects the standard error, or sampling error, estimated by the regression model. The better the derived equation fits the observed data, the higher will be the value of R-square and the smaller the band around the estimates. Conversely, the weaker the predictive power of the regression, the lower the R-square value, and the larger the band around the estimates.

When the criterion of interest is measured at the nominal level, a form of regression called loglinear regression may be used. The criterion is treated as the presence or nonpresence of an attribute, such as a success or failure, and the slopes of the predictors can be interpreted as probabilities of increasing or decreasing the occurrence of the "success." An application of regression to a program evaluation scenario appears in Appendix 17.C. A model table illustrating how to report regression appropriately is provided along with a model interpretation.

Selecting Techniques to Sort Measures or Units

When multiple indicators have been used to measure a phenomenon of interest, such as a program effect, there are two basic approaches to reducing the data to a smaller number of factors. Evaluators can either aggregate measures that are prespecified to capture the effects (or variables) of interest, or they can use analytical techniques to identify patterns in the measures that indicate, post hoc, that there are observable patterns in the measures.

When criteria for measuring a program effect, or quality of services, for example, are set for evaluators, the measures used can simply be aggregated. A summary index can be used that weights different measures and then sums the total.

When evaluators are unsure of what basic factors best express the criterion of interest, they can use analytical techniques that sort through the indicators to identify covariation that might permit the creation of indices. Factor analysis is the technique most frequently used for such data reduction purposes.

The logic supporting factor analysis is that there are underlying factors that explain the observed variation in the indicators. The correlations among the indicators are examined to identify patterns suggesting independent groups of covarying measures that might actually be reflecting more fundamental factors. An evaluation of air controllers' responses to new regulations might start with a set of forty-five indicators but with factor analysis reduce these to five basic concerns.

Sometimes evaluators may wish to sort units such as delivery sites into groups to identify characteristics of high or low performers. If the criterion on which the units are evaluated as low and high is known beforehand, discriminant analysis can be used to identify the other characteristics of the units that will best predict which units will score high on the criterion measure. Discriminant analysis is similar to regression in that it identifies linear combinations (models) of other variables that best predict the groupings — of high and low performers, for example. To illustrate, suppose evaluators of Veterans Benefits offices were trying to identify key characteristics of the offices scoring highest on a measure of efficiency. Discriminant analysis might allow them to use fifteen different indicators describing the offices to identify characteristics most likely to predict high scores on efficiency.

When the criterion on which units are to be segregated is not known beforehand, cluster analysis can be used to identify like groupings. Cluster analysis is similar to factor analysis in that the correlations among the variables are examined to identify highly correlated clusters of variables that differentiate among the units. Characteristics of programs such as the level of administrative work load and other contextual characteristics might be used to identify clusters. An evaluator of an interjurisdictional program, such as legal services to the poor, might be interested in identifying clusters of offices that appear to operate under many of the same constraints. In this case, cluster analysis might be applied to identify characteristics that seem to differentiate most consistently across the offices.

Other Factors Affecting Selection of Statistical Techniques

In addition to considering how statistics will be used in an evaluation, evaluators must consider other criteria when selecting a statistical technique. Sample size, for instance, may have a dramatic effect on an analysis; a small sample may render findings "insignificant" or ungeneralizable, thus precluding any further analysis.

When sample size is very small, certain methods lose their statistical power. Many statisticians have argued that the most frequently used test of statistical significance, chi-square, should not be employed unless the expected frequency of each cell in a contingency table is at least five. However, other statisticians have shown that the test is robust (acceptable) even when this rule is broken (Camillia and Hopkins, 1978; Bradley, Bradley, McGrath, and Cutcomb, 1978). In any case, most statistical software provides a Yates correction or Fishers Exact Test in place of chi-square results when the expected frequency rule is broken.

In addition to the actual size of a sample, the number of observations recorded for the units of interest is also pertinent to decision making regarding statistical techniques. For example, when two or more observations are taken on the same units, change over time may be analyzed, and the notion of related samples is introduced, leading to the selection of statistics created just for such situations. When many observations are available on a specific phenomenon, such as traffic fatalities over a series of years or infant mortality rates for specific jurisdictions over a period of years, time series techniques employing regression may be applied.

Before employing any statistical technique, evaluators should examine the distribution of the units along each of the variables or measures. Such basic frequency analysis will indicate how much the units vary on each of the variables. For example, if race is of interest in an analysis of the impact of a management training course on managers, and only two of fifty-six training participants are minority group members, it will be impossible to use race as a variable in any analysis. If age of program participant is of interest in an evaluation, but a sample contains only fifteen- and sixteen-year-olds, the low variation on age rules out many analytical techniques. When a variable is measured at the interval level but the sample range is very narrow, the techniques available are limited to those appropriate for ordinal variables.

Similarly, if measurement was intended to be expressed in intervals but responses indicate that respondents could not make such fine differentiation, then techniques requiring interval measures are again ruled out. For example, survey questions asking researchers to report the percentage of their time devoted to research, administration, and teaching are intended to yield interval measures given in percentages. However, if almost all respondents respond "about half" or "about one-third" to these questions, this level of precision suggests that these variables should be analyzed as ordinal, not interval, measures.

The question of how to handle outliers frequently arises. Basic statistics such as the mean and standard deviation can be skewed by extreme values (outliers). It may be tempting to report statistics without the inflating effect of units that vary wildly from most other units. One option is to select statistics that are not affected by outliers, such as a median, in place of a mean, and an *interquartile range* (the interval capturing the middle 50 percent of the scores) in place of a standard deviation. When applying more sophisticated techniques, such as regression, a good option is to conduct and report analyses both with and without outliers.

Evaluators should ascertain whether highly sophisticated techniques with numerical statistics will be accessible and desirable for their clients. Anticipating clients' preferences may automatically disqualify some techniques. Evaluators should use a statistician to help make decisions about specific statistical techniques. The most frequently used statistical software, SPSS, SAS, and MINITABS, are quite user friendly and well documented, but they do not obviate the need for consulting a statistician.

Reporting Statistics Appropriately

Clarity is essential when statistical results are reported. The level of detail provided is again contingent on clients' expectations and preferences. Exhibit 17.2 offers a number of suggestions for reporting statistical analyses.

The degree to which the tables and graphs providing statistical results are user friendly is also quite important. To assist readers, consolidation of numerous analyses is helpful. Unfamiliar abbreviations, acronyms, and software jargon are often confusing to readers. Complete information about how variables were measured should accompany reports, with sufficient information to allow the reader to ascertain whether the analysts knew what the evaluators were doing.

A good reality test of completeness is for the evaluators to examine the statistics reported and the explanatory information provided and ask themselves whether an analyst outside the project could write a report on the data provided without needing any additional data. Replicability is a hallmark for any analysis.

Exhibit 17.2. Tips for Presenting Data Analyses.

A. Identify Contents of All Tables and Figures Clearly
   1. Use the title to identify variables or measures used.
   2. Label all variables or measures with adequate detail.
   3. Provide exact wording of questions on table/figure.
   4. Identify program components and program results (alleged causes and alleged effects).
B. Indicate Use of Decision Rules in Analysis
   1. State whether missing or inapplicable responses are included in the analysis.
   2. If values of variables were collapsed, such as low and high, state where cutoffs were made.
   3. If the term *average* or *midpoint* is used, state whether this means mean or median.
C. Consolidate Analyses Whenever Possible
   1. Present only the percentage reporting yes for questions to which the possible responses are *yes* or *no*.
   2. Present in one table percentages for a series of substantively related questions.
   3. Collapse responses to contrast *agrees* versus *disagrees,* or similar options, omitting *unsure* responses if appropriate.
D. Do Not Abbreviate
   1. Do not present shortened titles or labels used during data processing in tables and figures.
   2. Do not use acronyms.
   3. Do not use statistical symbols to represent statistics.
E. Provide Basic Information About Measurement of Variables
   1. Give the minimum and maximum value for each variable used.
   2. Give the sample size (or number of respondents reporting) for each variable displayed in the table/figure.
   3. Provide complete information about the scale or measurement mechanism used; for example, "scale ran from 1 (meaning Not at All Relevant) to 5 (meaning Completely Relevant).
F. Present Appropriate Percentages
   1. Provide percentages, not raw figures.
   2. Clearly identify base from which percentages were calculated.
   3. Calculate percentages on the appropriate base; for example, 85 percent of the treatment group scored high on the criterion, *not* 32 percent of those scoring high were in the treatment group.
G. Present Information on Statistical Significance Clearly
   1. Present the confidence level used in each table, such as 90 percent or 95 percent.
   2. Be consistent in reporting confidence levels across all tables in a report.
   3. Show the reader which statistics were significant through use of asterisks with clear legends.
   4. Do not simply present raw values of statistics, such as chi-square or standard errors, and expect readers to calculate statistical significance.
H. Present Information on the Magnitude of Relationships Clearly
   1. Distinguish between statistics showing the statistical significance of relationships and statistics measuring the strength of relationships or the magnitude of effects.
   2. Present the confidence interval or error band around measures of strength or magnitude in a user-friendly manner, such as "program participants' scores were from 20 percent to 24 percent higher than those of the comparison group."
   3. Comment on the importance of the magnitude of the relationship or effect as well as noting whether it was statistically significant.
I. Use Graphics to Present Analytical Findings Clearly
   1. Use zero as the starting point for axes in graphs.
   2. Use appropriate scales so that figures will not be unduly distorted.
   3. Use colors whenever possible to present more than one line on the graph.
   4. Label lines on graph, not in a legend.
   5. Do not use more than four different patterns or colors to represent groups if at all possible.

The last step in completing a thorough analysis of quantitative data is to report any threats to the statistical validity of the information provided. Common weaknesses are use of too-small samples and application of techniques without meeting all assumptions or criteria appropriate for their use. The challenge for the evaluator is to provide a user-friendly explanation of all decisions made and a critical assessment of the statistical accuracy that the tests can reasonably be expected to provide.

Reporting Statistical Results to High-Level Public Officials

The advice offered here for reporting statistical results applies in most situations. However, reports for high-level officials, such as mayors and legislators, present a special case. Typically these clients are not concerned with technical issues such as statistical confidence and confidence intervals. In fact, they may not want to hear evaluators' findings diluted by statements specifying that the numbers may (or may not) fall within a range.

The unique challenge to evaluators reporting directly to the highest-level decision makers is to convey the tentative nature of statistical results accurately without excessive hedging. Certainty is simply not part of a statistician's vocabulary; statistical inference offers best estimates, not specific answers.

When high-level decision makers request specific answers, evaluators should attempt to prepare their audience to receive less than certain data. Detail about confidence levels need not be offered in a briefing or an executive summary as long as it is provided somewhere in a written report. Confidence intervals are actually not too exotic, since politicians are accustomed to hearing their popularity polls reported as percentages plus or minus a margin of error. An estimate with a range of uncertainty (plus or minus 10 percentage points, for example) may be acceptable.

A distinction between statistical and practical importance may be too much to provide to high-level decision makers. Instead, only those findings that are of practical importance should be presented. Whether it is statistically significant or not, a small change in an effectiveness or efficiency measure should probably be omitted from a report.

For a high-level audience, graphic presentations showing trends typically will be preferable to tables filled with numbers. For example, a time trend will be more impressive than a set of regression coefficients.

Conclusion

Planning for statistical analyses begins when the planning for any evaluation effort starts. Opportunities and decisions regarding which techniques may be appropriate and which statistics should be reported are affected by decisions made early in evaluation planning. As evaluators make decisions about how to analyze data they must have in mind the sort of reporting format (highly quantitative? rich in detail?) that their clients will want in an analytical report. In addition to clients' expectations, the questions that are addressed, the measurement decisions made, and the need to depend on samples to generalize quantitative results to larger populations all shape evaluators' decision making regarding statistics. Statistics never speak for themselves, but evaluators must take great care to ensure that they speak with statistics accurately and clearly.

Appendix 17.A

An Application of the Chi-Square Statistic

The Problem. Evaluators have collected data from two independent samples of participants in a substance abuse counseling program for teens and young adults, ages 12 to 21. Thirty participants were randomly assigned to a control group. They were receiving the individual counseling that had constituted the normal service provided to all participants in the program. Another thirty participants were randomly assigned to participate in group counseling sessions in addition to individual counseling. The evaluators want to know whether they can generalize the findings from these two samples to the population of participants in this program. In particular, they are interested in learning whether the group therapy provides an additional benefit to the participants in the individual counseling program. For a criterion variable, the evaluators have asked the parents and guardians of the participants to evaluate the participants' ability to cope with everyday responsibilities after they have received the treatments for three months. A nominal scale was used to record the parents' evaluations, where 1 indicated No Discernible Improvement, and 2 indicated Some Improvement. The evaluators feel that a sample of sixty young people is not very large and they fear that too stringent a test might lead them to conclude that the group therapy has no added benefit, when in fact it does. They want to protect against drawing such a false negative conclusion, so they set their confidence level at 90 percent.

The Data: Ability to Cope with Everyday Responsibilities by Type of Counseling.

	Participants in Drug Abuse Treatment Receiving	
	Individual Counseling Only (N = 30)	Group Therapy with Individual Counseling (N = 30)
Assessed improvement at 3 months:		
No discernible change	60%	57%
Some improvement	40%	43%

The Solution. A chi-square test of statistical significance can be calculated for these data. The chi-square tests the null hypothesis that there is no difference in success across the two groups. Calculation of chi-square first involved computing what would have been the expected frequencies in the table if the null hypothesis were true, then comparing these expected frequencies with the observed frequencies. A chi-square distribution can be consulted to identify the value of chi-square that would be needed to reject the null hypothesis and allow 90 percent confidence in this conclusion. To use a chi-square table one must figure the degrees of freedom; for chi-square this number is calculated as (the number of rows in the table − 1) multiplied by (the number of columns in the table − 1). For the problem at hand, the degrees of freedom is (2 − 1), or 1. For a 90 percent confidence level and 2 degrees of freedom a chi-square table indicates 2.07 as the number that must be exceeded in order for the null hypothesis — that there is no generalizable difference between the success rates for the two groups — to be rejected. Thus the decision rule for this problem follows: If the calculated chi-square exceeds 2.07, the null hypothesis of no difference in the success rates of the two treatments will be rejected.

Below are the steps in testing the hypothesis of no effect for this problem:

Step 1. We compute chi-square (no doubt using a computer). Chi-square is the sum of the squared difference between the expected frequency and the observed frequency divided by the expected frequency for each cell.

Step 2. We compare the computed chi-square for this table to the decision rule we set earlier. In this case our computed chi-square of .24 is less than 2.07, so we cannot reject the null hypothesis of no difference between the two treatments.

Step 3. To convey our finding in an appropriate manner we would use wording such as the following: "Based on our sample of sixty participants in the two treatments there was no significant difference between the two treatments in terms of the criterion measure we have selected in this test." Note that we do not conclude that the group counseling did not have any effect, only that we cannot generalize any effect based on the sample in this particular instance. Had we drawn a much larger sample, we would have been able to reject the null hypothesis and conclude that there was a difference, even assuming the same observed relative frequencies. In fact, 40 percent of those receiving individual counseling showed improvement compared to 43 percent of those who received group therapy in addition to the individual counseling. This 3 percent difference is interesting and might lead us to conduct another test with a larger sample size.

Appendix 17.B

An Application of the t-Test Procedure

The Problem. A consulting firm conducted a hiring audit to observe whether employers treat foreign-sounding job applicants differently from the way they treat non–foreign-sounding job applicants. The evaluators wanted to test whether employers would be more likely to ask foreign-sounding applicants to show documents to verify their citizenship than they would be to ask non–foreign-sounding applicants for such information. Sixteen pairs of applicants were matched on educational level, work experience, and oral communication skills. One of each pair spoke with a foreign accent; the other had no accent.

The evaluators are aware that a total sample of thirty-two is quite small, but they are also aware that the issue they are testing is very controversial. They feel that the conventional confidence level of 95 percent, one that is used as the standard by the U.S. General Accounting Office, will be most acceptable to their audience. They decide to take the more conservative option of testing for observed differences in either direction rather than testing only for the probability of a bias *against* the foreign-sounding group. In this case *conservative* means that it will be more difficult to draw a conclusion of differential treatment incorrectly (thus making a false positive) than if they had chosen to test only for bias in one direction.

The Data: Proportion of Applicants with and without Foreign Accents Asked to Supply Documentation.

	Group 1 *Non–Foreign-Sounding*	*Group 2* *Foreign-Sounding*
Sample size	16	16
Proportion asked to supply documentation:	37.5%	75.0%

The Solution. The *t* test of statistical significance can be calculated for these data. This technique tests the null hypothesis that there is no difference between the proportion of foreign-sounding applicants who were asked to show documentation to verify citizenship and the proportion of non–foreign-sounding applicants who were asked to show such documentation. A *t* distribution can be used to identify the value that the *t* statistic should exceed to support the conclusion that the observed difference in the two sample proportions is large enough to generalize to the population from which the job applicants were drawn. In other words, if the null hypothesis is rejected for this sample, the evaluators may generalize the difference they observed to the larger population using an appropriate vehicle, such as a confidence interval placed around the observed value, to convey their best estimate of the differential treatment one might expect in the population to which they wish to generalize.

In consulting a table showing the t distribution, one first must calculate the degree of freedom for this problem, which is computed as the size of the sample in group one minus one plus the size of the sample in group two minus one. In this example the degrees of freedom = $(16 - 1) + (16 - 1)$, or 30. As the evaluators wish to test for a significant difference in either direction and they have chosen a 95 percent decision rule, the value that the observed t must exceed to demonstrate statistical significance is 2.042. Thus the decision rule for this problem is the following: If the calculated t statistic exceeds 2.042, the null hypothesis—there is no difference between the two groups in the proportion of job applicants asked to supply documents to verify their citizenship—will be rejected.

Steps in conducting the t test for this problem:

Step 1. We calculate t (no doubt using a computer). Here t equals the difference of the means for the two groups divided by the standard error of that difference.

Step 2. We compare the computed t statistic to the decision rule we set earlier. In this case the t statistic equals 2.23: the difference between the groups $(.375 - .750)$ divided by the joint standard error $(.168)$. In this case the observed t statistic is 2.23 which exceeds the criterion level specified in the decision rule of 2.042; thus, the null hypothesis can be rejected.

Step 3. To convey our finding appropriately we can start by stating: Based on our sample of sixteen pairs of matched job applicants, there is a statistically significant difference in the proportion of foreign-sounding and non–foreign-sounding applicants being asked by employers to provide documentation verifying citizenship. Since we rejected the null hypothesis of no difference, the next question to be addressed is this: How big is the difference between the groups? To address this question we may use the standard formula for a confidence interval to place around the observed difference between the proportions reported for the two groups. The observed difference is 37.5 percent. The interval to be placed around this value is the joint standard error multiplied by the t value for a 95 percent confidence level for this problem. Thus the interval will be $(.168) \times (2.042)$, or .343.

We can then conclude that based on this sample of sixteen pairs of matched job applicants, using a 95 percent confidence level, the proportion of foreign-sounding applicants asked to supply documentation to verify their citizenship is somewhere between 3.2 percent and 71.8 percent higher than the proportion of non–foreign-sounding applicants asked to supply such documentation. This interval is quite large, undercutting our confidence in specifying very precisely how differently the two groups appear to be treated, but this result is appropriate since our sample is quite small relative to the number of potential job applicants in whom we are interested.

In this example our findings are statistically significant, indicating that, at least based on the numbers, they are generalizable to the broader population and the magnitude of the observed difference in treatment is large enough for us to suggest that differential treatment did occur. However, there are other questions that evaluators should ask about the findings. For example, how comfortable do we feel that the sample truly represents all employers? Should we limit our findings to the sorts of employers actually represented in the sample—by geographic and industry-specific characteristics, for example? How do we know that personal characteristics of the applicants other than their accents did not affect the employers' attitudes toward them? With such a small sample, we would definitely want to be cautious in presenting our findings.

Appendix 17.C

Application of Regression

The Problem. A new counseling program offers assistance to parents who are receiving their children back after they had been placed in foster care. Evaluators are evaluating the percentage of children who reenter foster care within twelve months. The program has been implemented in thirty-four of eighty-one reporting sites in California, so the percentage of reentries in jurisdictions where the service is provided can be compared to jurisdictions where the service is not yet provided. The evaluators recognize that there are other factors that affect whether a child will reenter foster care, and they have measured some of these to be included in the regression model. The predictors of reentry in the regression model include the following:

X1 = Parent Counseling Program (if present, X1 = 1; if not present X1 = zero)

X2 = Extent of Child's Behavior/Mental Health Problems (measured as a scale of 1 to 10 where 10 indicates the most severe mental health problems)

X3 = Child's School/Learning Aptitude (measured on a scale of 1 to 10 where 10 indicates high aptitude)

X4 = Age of Child at Entry into Foster Care

X5 = Length of Stay in Foster Care (in months)

X6 = Reason for Entry into Foster Care (measured on a scale of 1 to 10 where Abuse is 10)

The Data. Multiple Regression Results Predicting Reentry into Foster Care for Children in Eighty-One Sites in California.

Goodness of Fit of Regression: R-square = 67%
Confidence Band Around Estimates: +/− 4.5%
Regression Coefficients:

Predictor	Standardized Coefficient	Unstandardized Coefficient	Level of Significance
Parent Counseling	−.62	−3.7	S.S.* at 95%
Child's Behavior/Mental Health	.48	2.3	S.S. at 95%
Child's School/Learning Aptitude	−.35	−1.4	S.S. at 95%
Age of Child at Entry	.71	3.8	S.S. at 95%
Length of Stay	−.21	−.8	Not S.S. at 95%
Reason for Entry	.82	2.9	S.S. at 95% level

*S.S. = statistically significant

Interpretation. The relatively high R-square is of critical importance in interpreting the output of the regression in the foster care reentry example. The reported R-square tells us that 67 percent of the variation in the percentage of children released to their parents who reentered foster care within twelve months after release can be explained by the six predictors. Slightly over two-thirds of the variation can be explained by the six predictors, and that is fairly impressive. There are still other factors that would predict reentry, since the R-square value is not 100 percent.

The confidence band that would be placed around any estimates we would make is fairly small—plus or minus 4.5 percent. The small band reflects the rather good fit of the data to the regression model, as is reflected in the high R-square value.

Turning to the standardized regression coefficients, we see that five of the six are statistically significant by the decision rule we have set of a 95 percent confidence level. Only the length of stay in foster care is not statistically significant. A comparison of the coefficients reveals that the three strongest predictors are reason for entry into foster care, age of the child, and the parental counseling program, in that order. The sign and magnitude of the coefficient suggest that the parental counseling program does have the intended effect of decreasing the proportion of children who reenter the foster care system after being returned to their parents. However, the reason for original entry into foster care and the age of the child are stronger predictors of reentry than the availability of the parental counseling program.

In this example it would probably not be very helpful to compare the unstandardized regression coefficients. Three of the six predictors are ordinal scales, and interpretation of their effects would not be straightforward. The program being evaluated is coded as either present or not—a fairly simplistic assumption—that makes interpretation of the unstandardized coefficient for that variable comparable to a t test of differences between the two conditions while controlling for the other predictors. In this case, having the counseling program available appears to reduce the percentage of the children reentering foster care by 3.7 percentage points (plus or minus .3).

Evaluators interpreting the output of this regression would be able to conclude that the program has the intended effect and that the model explaining reentry appears to be quite strong. The high R-square value is quite encouraging, and the percentage point reduction in reentry rates linked to introduction of the program appears reasonably strong. Contextual information is still needed to interpret the magnitude of the effect. For example, evaluators would need to know what existing rates were during the years preceding institution of the program, what policy objectives were for reduction of reentry rates (if any exist), and perhaps reentry rates for other western states with similar programs, to place the findings in a more meaningful context.

References

Bradley, D. R., Bradley, T. D., McGrath, S. G., and Cutcomb, S. D. "Type I Error Rate of the Chi-Square Test of Independence in R × C Tables That Have Small Expected Frequencies." *Psychological Bulletin*, 1978, *85*(6), 1290–1297.

Camillia, G., and Hopkins, K. D. "Applicability of Chi-Square to 2 × 2 Contingency Tables with Small Expected Cell Frequencies." *Psychological Bulletin*, 1978, *85*(1), 163–167.

Further Reading

Textbooks

Anderson, A.J.B. *Interpreting Data*. London: Chapman and Hall, 1989.

Bohrnstedt, G. W., and Knoke, D. *Statistics for Social Data Analysis*. Itasca, Ill.: Peacock, 1982.

Cohen, S. S. *Practical Statistics*. London: Edward Arnold, 1988.

Foreman, E. K. *Survey Sampling Principles*. Vol. 120: *Statistics: Textbooks and Monographs*. D. B. Owen and others (eds.). New York: Dekker, 1991.

Godfrey, M. G., Roebuck, E. M., and Sherlock, A. J. *Concise Statistics*. London: Edward Arnold, 1988.

Goodman, L. A. *Analyzing Qualitative/Categorical Data* J. Magidson, ed.). Lanham, Md.: University Press of America, 1978.

Groninger, L. D. *Beginning Statistics Within a Research Context*. New York: HarperCollins, 1990.

Healey, J. *Statistics: A Tool for Social Research*. (2nd ed.) Belmont, Calif.: Wadsworth, 1990.

Hedderson, J. *SPSS/PC + Made Simple*. Belmont, Calif.: Wadsworth, 1990.

Jaccard, J. *Statistics for the Behavioral Sciences*. Belmont, Calif.: Wadsworth, 1983.

Loether, H. J., and McTavish, D. G. *Descriptive and Inferential Statistics: An Introduction*. (4th ed.) Old Tappen, N.J.: Allyn & Bacon, 1992.

Meier, K. J., and Brudney, J. L. *Applied Statistics for Public Administration*. (2nd ed.) Boston: Duxbury Press, 1987.

Renner, T. *Statistics Unraveled: A Practical Guide to Using Data in Decision Making*. Washington, D.C.: International City Management Association, 1988.

Runyon, R. P., and Haber, A. *Fundamentals of Behavioral Statistics*. (7th ed.) New York: McGraw-Hill, 1991.

Sharp, V. F. *Statistics for the Social Sciences*. Boston: Little, Brown, 1979.

Siegel, S. *Nonparametric Statistics for the Behavioral Sciences*. (Rev. ed.) New York: McGraw-Hill, 1988.

Walsh, A. *Statistics for the Social Sciences: With Computer Applications*. New York: HarperCollins, 1990.

Welch, S., and Comer, J. *Quantitative Methods for Public Administration*. (2nd ed.) Chicago: Dorsey, 1988.

Special Topics

Achen, C. H. *Interpreting and Using Regression*. Sage University Paper series on Quantitative Applications in the Social Sciences, series no. 07-029. Newbury Park, Calif.: Sage, 1982.

Asher, H. B. *Causal Modeling*. Sage University Paper series on Quantitative Applications in the Social Sciences, series no. 07-003. Newbury Park, Calif.: Sage, 1976.

Berry, W. D., and Feldman, S. *Multiple Regression in Practice*. Sage University Paper series on Quantitative Applications in the Social Sciences, series no. 07-050. Newbury Park, Calif.: Sage, 1985.

Cohen, J. *Statistical Power Analysis for the Behavioral Sciences*. New York: Academic Press, 1977.

Converse, J. M., and Presser, S. *Survey Questions: Handcrafting the Standardized Questionnaire*. Sage University series on Quantitative Applications in the Social Sciences, series no. 07-063. Newbury Park, Calif.: Sage, 1986.

Edwards, W., and Newman, J. R. *Multiattribute Evaluation*. Sage University Paper series on Quantitative Applications in the Social Sciences, series no. 07-026. Newbury Park, Calif.: Sage, 1982.

Hartwig, F., and Dearing, B. E. *Exploratory Data Analysis*. Sage University Paper series on Quantitative Applications in the Social Sciences, series no. 07-016. Newbury Park, Calif.: Sage, 1979.

Henkel, R. E. *Tests of Significance*. Sage University Paper series on Quantitative Applications in the Social Sciences, series no. 07-004. Newbury Park, Calif.: Sage, 1976.

Hildebrand, D. K., Laing, J. D., and Rosenthal, H. *Analysis of Ordinal Data*. Sage University Paper series on Quantitative Applications in the Social Sciences, series no. 07-008. Newbury Park, Calif.: Sage, 1977.

Klecka, W. R. *Discriminant Analysis*. Sage University Paper series on Quantitative Applications in the Social Sciences, series no. 07-019. Newbury Park, Calif.: Sage, 1980.

Levine, M. S. *Canonical Analysis and Factor Comparison*. Sage University Paper series on Quantitative Applications in the Social Sciences, series no. 07-006. Newbury Park, Calif.: Sage, 1977.

Lewis-Beck, M. S. *Applied Regression: An Introduction*. Sage University Paper series on Quantitative Applications in the Social Sciences, series no. 07-022. Newbury Park, Calif.: Sage, 1980.

Lodge, M. *Magnitude Scaling: Quantitative Measurement of Opinions*. Sage University Paper series on Quantitative Applications in the Social Sciences, series no. 07-025. Newbury Park, Calif.: Sage, 1981.

McDowall, D., McCleary, R., Meidinger, E. E., and Hay, R. A., Jr. *Interrupted Time Series Analysis*. Sage University Paper series on Quantitative Applications in the Social Sciences, series no. 07-021. Newbury Park, Calif.: Sage, 1980.

Ostrom, C. W., Jr. *Time Series Analysis: Regression Techniques*. Sage University Paper series on Quantitative Applications in the Social Sciences, series no. 07-009. Newbury Park, Calif.: Sage, 1978.

Reynolds, H. T. *Analysis of Nominal Data.* Sage University Paper series on Quantitative Applications in the Social Sciences, series no. 07-007. Newbury Park, Calif.: Sage, 1977.

Schrodt, P. A. *Microcomputer Methods for Social Scientists.* Sage University Paper series on Quantitative Applications in the Social Sciences, series no. 07-040. Newbury Park, Calif.: Sage, 1984.

Wildt, A. R., and Ahtola, O. T. *Analysis of Covariance.* Sage University Paper series on Quantitative Applications in the Social Sciences, series no. 07-012. Newbury Park, Calif.: Sage, 1978.

Statistical Software

Minitab, Inc. *Minitab Reference Manual for DOS, Release 8.* State College, Pa.: Minitab, 1991.

Norusis, M. J. *SPSS/PC + Studentware.* Chicago: SPSS, 1988.

Norusis, M. J., and SPSS, Inc. *SPSS/PC + 4.0 Base Manual.* Chicago: SPSS, 1990.

Norusis, M. J., and SPSS, Inc. *SPSS/PC + 4.0 Statistics.* Chicago: SPSS, 1990.

SAS Institute, Inc. *SAS User's Guide: Basics, Version 5 Edition.* Cary, N.C.: SAS Institute, 1985.

SAS Institute, Inc. *SAS User's Guide: Statistics, Version 5 Edition.* Cary, N.C.: SAS Institute, 1985.

Schaefer, R. L., and Farber, E. *The Student Edition of Minitab Release 8.* Reading, Mass.: Addison-Wesley Publishing Company, 1992.

18

Using Regression Models to Estimate Program Effects

Charles S. Reichardt, Carol A. Bormann

Earlier chapters have described four research designs that are widely used for estimating program effects: the randomized experiment, the regression-discontinuity design, the nonequivalent comparison group design, and the interrupted time series design. This chapter explains how to analyze data from each of these four designs, using simple but effective statistical techniques that fall under the rubric of regression analysis.

The first section describes the purpose of statistical analysis. The four sections that follow explain how to analyze data from each of the four research designs. The purpose of the presentation is not to make you a statistical expert but rather to give you a sense of the logic behind the statistical analyses.

The Tasks of Statistical Analysis

The purpose of the four designs is to estimate the effects of a program or treatment. For example, an evaluation of the first year of "Sesame Street" estimated the effects of the television series on preschool children's learning and readiness for school (Ball and Bogatz, 1970). To estimate the effects of "Sesame Street," or of any other program, three tasks must be accomplished.

The Statistical Significance of a Treatment Effect

The first task is to show that the treatment effect is statistically significant. An introduction to statistical significance testing is given earlier in this volume in Chapter Seventeen by Newcomer. However, it is useful to review briefly the meaning of statistical significance tests.

Preparation of this chapter was supported, in part, by Grant U01-AA08778 from the National Institute on Alcohol Abuse and Alcoholism. The authors thank the editors of the volume for their helpful comments.

Perhaps the purpose of a statistical significance test can best be understood in the context of a randomized experiment. In the simplest of such experiments, individuals are randomly assigned to two treatment groups: an experimental group that receives the program being evaluated and a control or comparison group that does not receive the program being evaluated. If the program has an effect, the two groups will perform differently on an appropriate outcome measure. The problem is that even if the program being evaluated has no effect, the performance of the two groups on the relevant outcome measure will not be identical. One group would perform better on average than the other group simply because of chance differences introduced by the random assignment.

Therefore, the question facing the researcher is not whether there is *any* difference in performance between the two groups on the outcome measure, but whether the difference in performance is larger than would be expected by chance. This is the question that is answered by using a statistical significance test. If the results of the test are *statistically significant,* it means the observed difference is too large to be reasonably attributed to chance differences and therefore is indicative of a treatment effect.

Imagine a randomized experiment with five individuals assigned to each of two groups. The hypothetical data from this experiment are presented in Table 18.1. The first column in the table gives each individual's outcome score. The second column indicates whether the individual is in the experimental or comparison group. With these data, a statistical significance test can be performed using a t test. The results of such a test are a t value, degrees of freedom (df), and an obtained p value. By convention, the 5 percent *level of statistical significance* is used. This means that if the obtained p value is less than or equal to .05, the results are judged to be statistically significant; otherwise, they are not. For the data in Table 18.1, the results are $t = 3.60$, df $= 8$, $p = .007$. Because $p < .05$, one would conclude that the mean difference between the scores in the experimental and comparison conditions was statistically significant, and therefore, larger than could reasonably be expected by chance. In other words, the mean difference between the groups provides evidence in favor of a treatment effect.

Table 18.1. Data from a Hypothetical Randomized Experiment.

Outcome Score	Group
20	Experimental
24	Experimental
27	Experimental
18	Experimental
23	Experimental
16	Comparison
19	Comparison
10	Comparison
15	Comparison
11	Comparison

It is possible for a mean difference between treatment groups to be statistically *in*significant, even though a treatment effect is present, simply because the treatment effect is small relative to the background noise of chance differences. The *power* of a statistical significance test is a measure of the test's ability to detect small treatment effects when they are present. One way to increase the power of a statistical significance test is to increase the size of the sample (that is, the number of individuals included in the randomized experiment). Power also can be increased by adding covariates to the analysis, as described below. Wise researchers verify that the power of their statistical test is adequate given the size of the treatment effect that is likely to arise. Kraemer and Theimann (1987) provide computational procedures for calculating by hand the power of simple statistical significance tests and Borenstein and Cohen (1988) provide a program for calculating power using a computer (also see Cohen, 1977; Lipsey, 1990).

The Size of a Treatment Effect

The results of a statistical significance test reveal whether an estimated treatment effect is larger than reasonably could be expected by chance. But the results of a statistical significance test do not reveal how *large* the treatment effect is. The second task of statistical analysis is to estimate the size of the treatment effect. Without this information, one cannot judge whether the effect is of practical importance and whether the treatment is worth the extra cost and effort required to implement it. To make informed decisions, policymakers need to know the size of treatment effects.

Unfortunately, the size of a treatment effect can never be known exactly. In a randomized experiment, for example, the mean difference between the outcome scores in the experimental and comparison groups is an estimate of the average effect of the treatment. However, this mean difference in outcome scores will not be exactly equal to the average effect of the treatment. The mean difference also will reflect the effects of differences between the groups that were inevitably introduced by the vagaries of random assignment. Because the size of these chance differences cannot be known exactly, neither can the size of the treatment effect. The best that can be done is to estimate the size of the treatment effect within a margin of error for a given level of confidence. The margin of error takes account of the effects of chance differences.

The margin of error depends on the level of confidence that one desires to have in the results. Conventional practice is to use the 95 percent level of confidence when calculating the margin of error. Once the level of confidence is chosen, the treatment effect estimate and the margin of error are packaged together in what is called a *confidence interval*.

For example, an estimate of the average treatment effect for the data in Table 18.1 is equal to the mean difference between the groups on the outcome variable, which is 8.20. The 95 percent margin of error for this estimate can be easily calculated using a computer program and is equal to 5.26. So a 95 percent confidence interval is equal to 8.20 $\pm$ 5.26. This means that we can be 95 percent confident that the average treatment effect in the population from which the sample was drawn is between 2.94 and 13.46, assuming there are no other threats to validity in the study.

It is important to include the confidence interval when reporting the size of a treatment effect to keep readers from being misled. For example, there is a substantial difference between estimating the average effect of a program as 10 plus or minus 5 with 95 percent confidence, and estimating the average effect of a program as 10 plus or minus 50 with 95 percent confidence. In the first case, the effect of the program is almost certainly positive, while in the second there is a good possibility that the program's effect is negative. Presenting the estimate of the program's effect as 10 without reporting a margin of error would fail to convey the appropriate degree of uncertainty about the estimate (Reichardt and Gollob, 1987).

The size of the margin of error for a given level of confidence is called the *precision* of the estimate of the treatment effect. For a given level of confidence, one would like the margin of error to be as small as possible, just as one would like the power of a statistical test to be as high as possible. Like power, precision can be increased by increasing the sample size or by adding covariates, as described later.

Discovering and Removing Biases

The estimate of an effect can be biased by a variety of threats to validity. It is important to recognize these potential sources of error and to try to remove their biasing effects. A recurring theme in the present chapter will be the value of drawing pictures of the data both to get a feel for the information they contain and to spot potential sources of bias.

Although most of what follows concerns statistical analysis, the reader should keep in mind that fancy statistical procedures may not be the most efficient means of reducing or removing biases. For this purpose, thoughtfulness in data collection often is superior to sophistication in statistics. Glass (1988) provides an illustration of this principle based on the data in Figure 18.1. This figure shows the enrollment in Denver public schools from 1928 to 1975. As marked by the arrow, court-ordered desegregation began in 1969. The research question of interest is how much of the decline in enrollment following 1969 was due to the court mandate and subsequent "white flight." No degree of statistical machination could answer this question satisfactorily using the data in the figure. However, the question could be answered well with a few thoughtfully chosen refinements in data collection. As Glass (1988, p. 460) explains, this question

> could be resolved fairly conclusively by breaking down and plotting in several alternative ways the total enrollment series in Figure [18.1]. Breaking the enrollment data down by grade might cast a little light on things. If it's really white flight that

is causing the decline, one might expect a larger decline at the elementary grades than at the secondary grades, particularly grades 11 and 12 where parents would likely decide to stick it out for the short run. If enrollment data existed separately for different ethnic groups, these time series would provide a revealing test. If they showed roughly equal declines across all ethnic groups, the "white flight" hypothesis would suffer a major setback. Data on enrollment that could be separated by individual school, neighborhood, or census tract would be exceptionally valuable. These various units could be ranked prior to looking at the data on their susceptibility to white flight. Such a ranking could be based on variables like "pre-1969 ethnic mixture," or "mobility of families based on percentage of housing values mortgaged or amount of disposable income." If the large enrollment declines fell in the highly susceptible regions, the pattern would constitute some degree of support for the white flight hypothesis.

As you conduct statistical analyses, ask yourself the following questions. Is the effect statistically significant? How large is the effect? How might the estimate of the effect be biased and how can these biases be removed?

Randomized Experiment

In a randomized experiment, individuals are assigned to treatment conditions at random. After the different treatments are administered, the indi-

Figure 18.1. Enrollment in Denver Public Schools.

Note: The arrow marks the beginning of court-ordered desegregation.
Source: Glass, 1988. Copyright 1988 by the American Educational Research Association. Reprinted by permission of the publisher.

viduals are assessed on an outcome variable. The difference between the mean of the outcome scores in the different treatment groups is an estimate of the average effect of the different treatments. A test of the statistical significance of the estimate and a confidence interval for the size of the effect can be calculated as described above. Detailed discussion of randomized experiments is provided earlier in this volume in Chapter Eight by Dennis.

In interpreting the results of a randomized experiment, it is useful to draw a picture of the distribution of the outcome scores for each treatment group separately and to examine these pictures to get a sense of how the scores differ. One thing to look for is a difference between the treatment groups in the variability of the scores. This is evidence that the effect of the treatment varies across different individuals, a topic discussed further below. In addition, standard statistical significance tests and confidence intervals assume that the variability is roughly equal in the two groups. If the variability of the outcome scores appears dramatically unequal across the groups *and* if the sample sizes in the groups are dramatically different, alternative statistical procedures (for example, an unpooled-variance t test) might be appropriate. A statistical consultant can help with these determinations.

It is also useful to examine the pictures of the data to learn whether the distributions are symmetric or skewed. A positive skew means that many scores are piled up at the low end of the distribution, with scores trailing off at the high end so there are some high scores that are quite far removed from the rest of the pack. Income and net worth, for example, are usually positively skewed since most incomes pile up at the low end but a few people have quite high incomes. Negative skew is the opposite; most of the scores pile up at the high end with scores trailing off at the low end.

When a distribution of scores is skewed, the mean can be a poor way to characterize the center of the scores and so perhaps should not be used for estimating a treatment effect. The mean also can be a poor way to characterize the center of a distribution if there are a few very extreme scores (outliers), especially if the sample size is small. If the mean is suspect for either reason, calculate the median (that is, the score at the 50th percentile) because it usually is more representative of the center when a distribution is skewed or has outliers. Then see whether the difference between the medians tells the same story as the difference between the means. Also try repeating the analysis using the means but with the outliers removed. If the difference between the medians is dramatically different from the difference between the means or if the results change with the outliers removed, you may want to use alternative methods for calculating statistical significance tests and confidence intervals. Possible alternatives might be nonparametric procedures or procedures using trimmed distributions. See a statistical consultant for assistance.

Including Pretests in the Study

In contrast to the outcome (or posttest) measure that is collected after the different treatments are administered, a pretest measure is collected before the treatments are administered. Pretest measures need not be included in a randomized experiment, but there can be substantial advantages to including them.

Checking Random Assignment. In field studies, the random assignment of individuals to treatment conditions is often corrupted (Boruch and Wothke, 1985; Braucht and Reichardt, 1993; Conner, 1977). If random assignment was successfully implemented, the distributions of pretest scores should be similar across the treatment groups. However, if random assignment was corrupted, the distributions might be quite different. Therefore, pretest scores can be used to check the integrity of the random assignment procedure. If random assignment appears to have been compromised, it might be necessary to use the analysis strategies described in the section on the nonequivalent comparison group design.

Coping with Differential Attrition. Some of the participants in the study might drop out before the outcome measure is collected. Such attrition is a potential source of bias in the study, especially if the rate of attrition differs across the treatment groups. In particular, bias is introduced if individuals who would score high (or low) on the outcome measure tend to drop out from one treatment group more (or less) than from the other treatment group. Pretest measures are necessary to try to correct for this bias.

Understanding the nature of any differential attrition requires comparing, across the treatment conditions, the pretest scores of individuals who dropped out of the study with the pretest scores of the individuals who did not drop out. Taking account of differential attrition requires making adjustments in the outcome scores based on differences between the groups on the pretest scores. The methods for making these adjustments are the same as the methods for analyzing data from the nonequivalent comparison group design, which is described below. The best course of action is to try to avoid attrition as much as possible.

Increasing Power and Precision. Including one or more pretest measures in a statistical analysis as covariates can increase the power or the precision of the results. One such analysis is called an analysis of covariance. In regression terminology, you regress the outcome measure onto both the pretest measure and a variable representing treatment-group membership. Alternatively, pretests could be used as blocking variables rather than covariates, but this is a bit more complicated and will not be considered here (see Reichardt, 1979). In either case, you might want to ask a statistical consultant for assistance with the analysis.

The increase in power and precision that can be obtained by including a pretest in the analysis as a covariate depends on the correlation between the pretest and the outcome measure. The higher the correlation, the greater the power and precision. For example, adding a pretest that correlates .5 with the outcome measure increases power and precision as much as increasing the sample size by 33 percent. Adding a pretest correlated .75 with the outcome measure increases power and precision as much as increasing the sample size by 128 percent. Since collecting data on a pretest often is less expensive than increasing the sample size, it is worthwhile to spend some time contemplating the types of pretest measures that are likely to be highly correlated with the outcome. Often a pretest that is operationally identical to the posttest is the best choice.

Assessing Treatment-Effect Interactions. In addition to estimating the average effect of the treatment, it is also valuable to study treatment-effect interactions, which means studying how the size of the treatment effect varies across different types of individuals. The meaning of a treatment-effect interaction can perhaps best be understood graphically.

Figure 18.2 presents a scatterplot of the results of a hypothetical randomized experiment. Outcome scores vary along the vertical axis while

Figure 18.2. Data from a Hypothetical Randomized Experiment
with a Positive Treatment Effect and No Treatment-Effect Interaction.

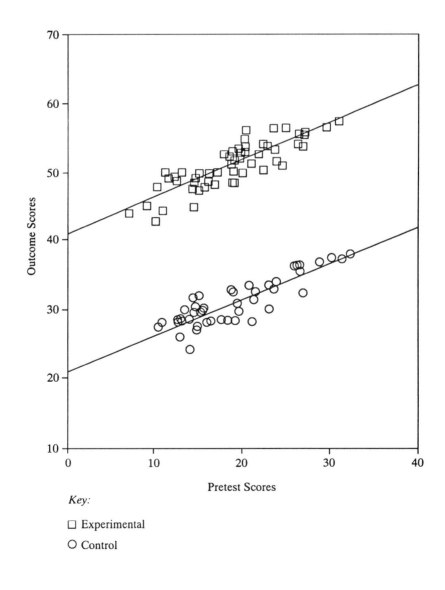

Key:

☐ Experimental

○ Control

pretest scores vary along the horizontal axis. The scores for individuals in the experimental group are denoted by squares. The scores for individuals in the control group are denoted by circles. The regression line for the regression of the outcome scores on the pretest scores is drawn in the figure for each group separately. The upward slope of the regression lines means that individuals who were high on the pretest also tend to be high on the posttest or outcome, and vice versa.

Notice that the mean of the squares and circles along the horizontal (pretest) dimension are close to equal (that is, the groups are not displaced horizontally). This shows that individuals were randomly assigned to the treatment groups. Also notice that the squares are higher than the circles on the vertical (outcome) dimension (that is, the regression lines are displaced vertically). This reflects the effect of the treatment. The squares are about twenty points higher on the outcome variable than the circles, revealing an average treatment effect of about twenty points. The 95 percent confidence interval for the average treatment effect in the plotted data runs from 19.7 to 21.1. Notice that the regression line in the experimental group is also about twenty points higher than the regression line in the control group. When the pretest is added to the analysis as a covariate, the treatment effect is literally estimated as the vertical displacement between the regression lines, rather than as the difference between the outcome means in the two groups, as would be the case without the pretest.

Also notice that the treatment effect is the same regardless of the individual's pretest score. For example, the treatment effect is about twenty points both for individuals with relatively high pretest scores (say 30) and for individuals with relatively low pretest scores (say 12). This effect is readily apparent from the observation that the regression lines are parallel, indicating that the effect of the treatment does *not* interact with the pretest scores.

Now consider Figure 18.3. The squares are higher than the circles and the regression line for the experimental group is displaced above the regression line for the control group, both of which reflect the average effect of the treatment. But the size of the treatment effect varies with the individual's pretest score. Individuals with high pretest scores (say 30) have a treatment effect of about fifty points (the 95 percent confidence interval runs from 46.6 to 51.5), while individuals with low pretest scores (say 12) have a treatment effect of about twenty points (the 95 percent confidence interval runs from 19.6 to 23.1). This result shows that the effect of the treatment interacts with the pretest and is readily apparent from the observation that the regression lines are not parallel.

In Figure 18.4, the interaction between pretest and treatment is even more extreme. The effect of the treatment is positive in the population on average and for individuals with high pretest scores, but the treatment effect is negative for individuals with low pretest scores.

The implication is that the data analyst needs to pay attention to both the average and the interactive effects of the treatment if appropriate policy implications are to be drawn. For example, although a novel teaching method

Figure 18.3. Data from a Hypothetical
Randomized Experiment with a Treatment-Effect Interaction.

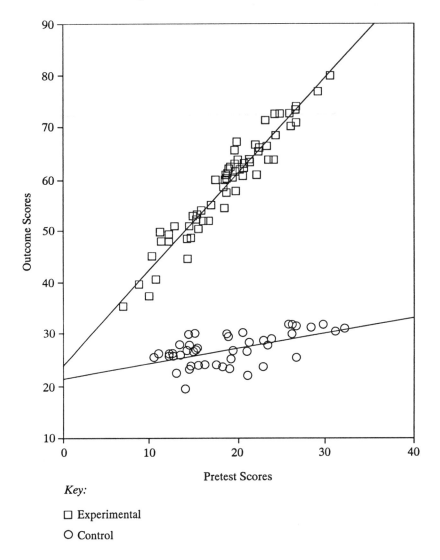

Key:

☐ Experimental

○ Control

might be superior to the old teaching method on average, the old method might nonetheless be superior for low-ability students. In this case, it would be better to tailor the teaching method to the type of student rather than to apply the new teaching method blindly to all students.

Outliers and Curvilinearity

When pretest measures are included in the analysis, it is important to plot the data, as in Figures 18.2 through 18.4, and to examine both the plots and the fit of the regression lines. Look for interactions so they can be taken

Figure 18.4. Data from a Hypothetical
Randomized Experiment with a Crossover Treatment-Effect Interaction.

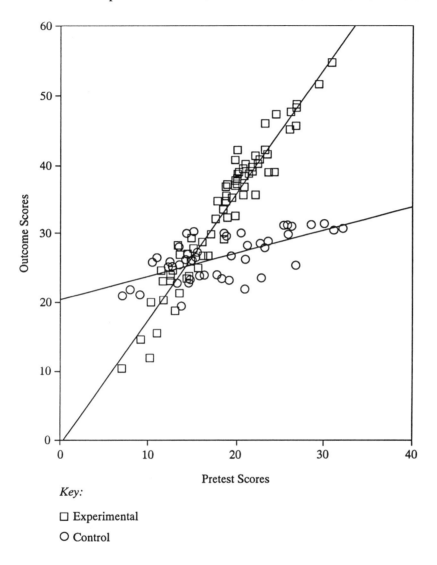

Key:

□ Experimental
O Control

into account in the analysis. Also look for outliers and evidence of curvilinear-ity. *Curvilinearity* means that the regression "lines" that best fit the data are curved rather than straight. An outlier can make it appear as if either an average effect or an interaction is present when it is not. If outliers are present, try removing them and repeating the analysis to see how much difference the outliers make. Curvilinearity that is not recognized can hide an interac-tion or lower the power and precision of the analysis. Curvilinearity can be taken into account either by transforming the data or by polynomial regres-sion. More details are given in any standard regression text (for example, Hamilton, 1992; Draper and Smith, 1981), or see a statistical consultant.

An Example

In a simple randomized experiment described in Ryan, Joiner, and Ryan (1985), ninety-two students in an introductory statistics class recorded their pulse, height, weight, gender, how much they smoked, and how much they typically exercised. Each student then flipped a coin to determine his or her treatment assignment. Heads meant they were to run in place for a minute; tails meant they were to rest quietly. A minute later, the students took their pulse again. The resulting data are distributed with the Minitab computer software program and available in Ryan, Joiner, and Ryan (1985).

An examination of the data revealed an error requiring that one student's data (in row 54) be omitted from the analysis. For the remaining data, plots of the distributions of the pretest pulse data in the two treatment groups looked reasonably similar. However, there were statistically significant differences between the treatment groups on height ($t = 2.5$, df $= 89$, $p = .01$) and weight ($t = 2.29$, df $= 89$, $p = .03$), and there were significantly fewer women in the experimental group ($N = 10$) than in the control group ($N = 24$) according to a chi-square goodness-of-fit test ($\chi^2 = 5.76$, df $= 1$, $p = .02$). The corresponding sample sizes for the men were 24 and 32, respectively, and this difference was not statistically significant. It appears that the random assignment might have been somewhat compromised by women who chose not to run in place even though their coin showed heads.

The mean of the pulse rates at posttest was 72.3 in the control group and 91.9 in the experimental group. This mean difference of 19.6 beats per minute was statistically significant ($t = 6.48$, df $= 89$, $p < .001$, 95% confidence interval $= 13.5$ to 25.5). Adding the pretest pulse as a covariate in an analysis of covariance reduces the width of the confidence interval for the size of the effect by 29 percent (treatment effect estimate $= 19.15$; 95% confidence interval $= 14.89$ to 23.41). Based on either analysis, it is clear that running in place significantly raised the pulse in this population of individuals. A plot of the posttest pulse versus the pretest pulse for each group is given in Figure 18.5. This plot suggests that there is no interaction between the treatment and the pretest pulse ($t = .92$, df $= 87$, $p = .36$).

However, there is a statistically significant interaction between the treatment and weight ($t = 3.74$, df $= 87$, $p = .0003$). This interaction is revealed in the plot of the posttest pulse versus weight for each group in Figure 18.6. The interaction means that the treatment has a smaller effect for heavier individuals than for lighter individuals. In particular, for each pound increase in weight, the effect of the treatment on posttest pulse is reduced on average by .44 beats per minute (95% confidence interval $= .21$ to $.67$).

This interaction is probably due to a confounding between weight and gender. As further examination of the data reveals, the interaction arises because running in place has less effect on men (treatment effect estimate $= 12.9$) than women (treatment effect estimate $= 34.4$), and men tend to weigh

Figure 18.5. Data from the Pulse Study (Ryan, Joiner, and Ryan, 1985)
Showing a Positive Treatment Effect and
No Interaction Between the Treatment and the Pretest Pulse Rate.

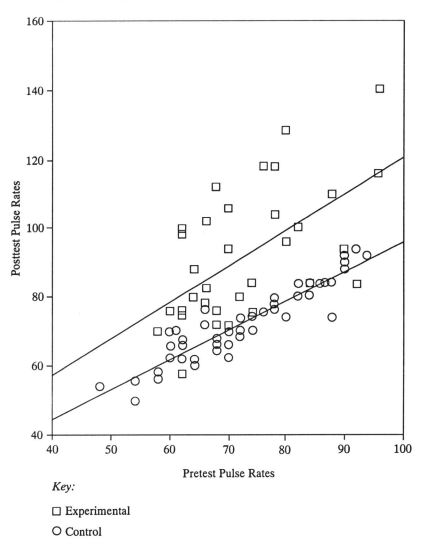

Key:

□ Experimental

○ Control

more than women. In addition, the interaction between treatment and weight is not statistically significant when the data for each gender are analyzed separately. Thus the plot in Figure 18.6 could easily be misleading if one were not careful to examine the data in greater depth. In addition, if extrapolated beyond the reasonable range of the data, the regression lines in Figure 18.6 would suggest that running in place actually slows the pulse in very heavy individuals. The moral is that you need to keep your wits about you when analyzing data.

Figure 18.6. Data from the Pulse Study (Ryan, Joiner, and Ryan, 1985)
Showing an Interaction Between the Treatment and Weight.

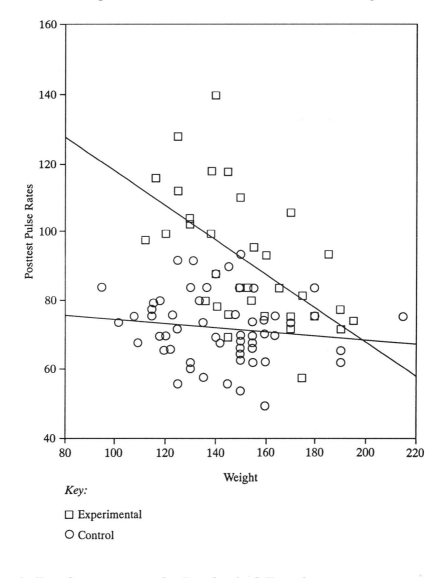

Key:

□ Experimental

O Control

Concluding Comments on the Randomized Experiment

Although randomized experiments can be biased, especially by differential attrition, they are a potentially powerful tool for estimating treatment effects. When well implemented, a randomized experiment can produce results that are more credible and precise than the results from any other design. Evaluators implementing a randomized experiment in a field setting will find it useful to collect pretest measures that are highly correlated with the outcome measure so as to increase the precision of the estimate of the treatment effect. It is also useful to collect pretest measures to assess (1) the integrity of the random-assignment process, (2) differential attrition, and (3) treatment-effect interactions.

Regression-Discontinuity Design

In the regression-discontinuity design, individuals are assigned to treatment conditions based on their scores on a quantitative pretest measure. Specifically, a cutoff score on the pretest is specified and individuals with pretest scores above the cutoff are assigned to one treatment condition while individuals with pretest scores below the cutoff are assigned to the other treatment condition. After individuals are assigned to treatment conditions, the different treatments are administered, and each individual is assessed on an outcome measure. Detailed discussion of the regression-discontinuity design is provided by Marcantonio and Cook in Chapter Seven of this book.

To estimate the average effect of the treatment, a separate regression line is fitted to the data on each side of the cutoff score. The vertical displacement between the two regression lines at the cutoff point is an estimate of the effect of the treatment for individuals near the cutoff point. For example, consider Figures 18.7 and 18.8. Both figures contain scatterplots of the outcome scores versus the pretest scores. The vertical line denotes the cutoff point on the pretest. The squares denote the scores of individuals who receive the treatment (individuals in the experimental group). These individuals all had scores on the pretest that fell below the cutoff. The circles denote the scores of individuals who do not receive the treatment (individuals in the control group). These individuals all had scores on the pretest that fell above the cutoff. Separate regression lines have been fitted to the data in each group and are plotted in the figures.

In Figure 18.7, there is no treatment effect. As a result, the two regression lines fall on top of one another, indicating that there is no vertical displacement or break between the lines at the cutoff point. In Figure 18.8, there is a positive treatment effect. As a result, the regression line for the experimental group is displaced above the regression line for the control group. The vertical displacement between the two lines is the estimate of the size of the treatment effect at the cutoff point.

Curvilinear Regression Lines

The regression lines must be properly fitted to the data in both the experimental and control conditions; otherwise a bias in the estimate of the treatment effect can occur. In particular, a bias can occur if the true relationship between outcome and pretest is curvilinear in one or both treatment groups but a straight regression line is fitted to the data.

The biasing effect of curvilinearity is demonstrated in Figure 18.9. In this figure, there is no scatter in the data around the true (curvilinear) regression line, meaning that the outcome scores can be perfectly predicted

Figure 18.7. Data from a Hypothetical
Regression-Discontinuity Design Where the Treatment Has No Effect.

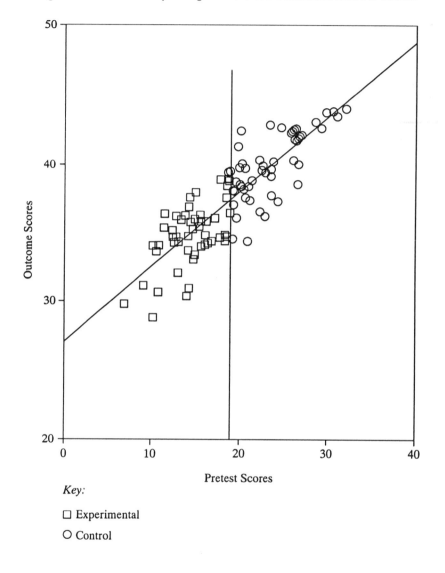

from the pretest scores. This is unrealistic, but to include scatter might make the main point of the example less clear. Also notice that the true relationship between the pretest and outcome scores is curvilinear. Since there is no break in the data at the cutoff point, there is no treatment effect. However, if linear regression lines were fitted to the data as shown in the figure, there would be a break between the lines at the cutoff point. This means that an analysis of the data using linear regression lines would find a treatment effect when in fact there is none. Only if the curvilinearity in the data were properly modeled would the analysis reach the correct conclusion about the absence of a treatment effect.

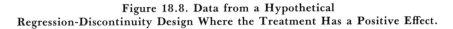

Figure 18.8. Data from a Hypothetical
Regression-Discontinuity Design Where the Treatment Has a Positive Effect.

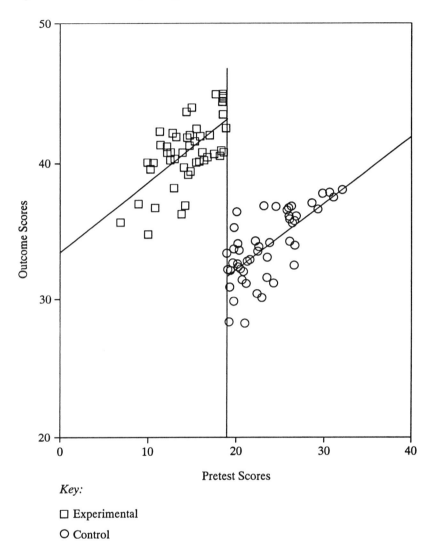

To determine the shape of the true relationship between the outcome and pretest, it helps to plot the data. If the data have a lot of scatter around the true regression lines (unlike the plot in Figure 18.9), sometimes the shape of the relationship can be more easily discerned by adding a *median trace*. A median trace is created by dividing the scatterplot into vertical columns (either of equal width or of equal numbers of data points) and calculating the median of the outcome scores within each column. These medians are then plotted on top of the scatterplot. Often a median trace reveals the nature of the relationship more clearly than the scatterplot of the original data alone.

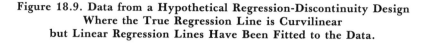

Figure 18.9. Data from a Hypothetical Regression-Discontinuity Design
Where the True Regression Line is Curvilinear
but Linear Regression Lines Have Been Fitted to the Data.

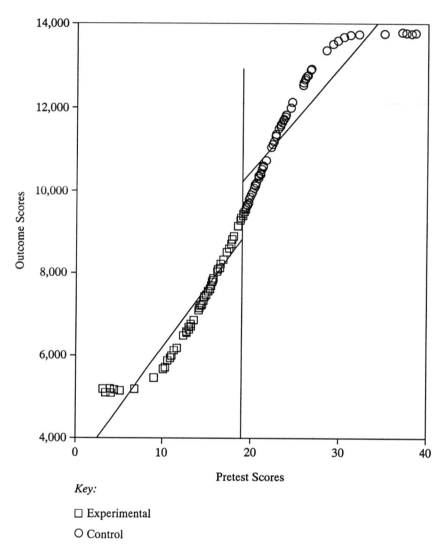

Key:

□ Experimental

○ Control

An example of a median trace is presented in Figures 18.10 and 18.11 (Moore and McCabe, 1989). In the early 1970s, American men were subject to a military draft conducted by lottery. Priority numbers were supposed to be assigned at random according to the day of birth. Controversy arose over the randomness of the assignment of priority numbers in 1970. Figure 18.10 plots the draft priority number on the vertical axis and the day of birth on the horizontal axis. A quick look at this plot suggests that no relationship exists between the two variables, as would be the case if the lottery were random. However, the median trace plotted by month in Figure

Figure 18.10. Plot of the Selective Service
Draft Priority Numbers Versus Day of Birth for 1970.

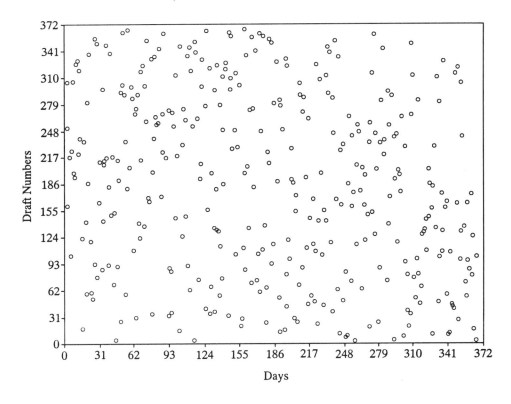

18.11 shows a clear downward slope, which reveals the true relationship that exists in the data (men born later in the year tend to have lower priority numbers) and provides confirming evidence of the faulty randomization procedure.

Another technique for assessing the shape of a regression line is to smooth the data in the scatterplot using a moving average (or moving median). A moving average of length five, for example, is generated by taking the average of the outcome scores for the individuals with the lowest five pretest scores. This average is plotted on the scatterplot above the third lowest pretest scores. The lowest pretest score is then dropped and the average of the outcome scores for the individuals with the five next lowest pretest scores is calculated and plotted above the fourth lowest pretest score, and so on. A moving average can also be calculated for other lengths to determine which one is the most revealing.

If curvilinearity is detected, curvilinear rather than straight regression lines need to be fitted. This change can be accomplished by transforming

**Figure 18.11. A Plot of the Selective Service Draft
Priority Numbers Versus Day of Birth for 1970 with a Median Trace by Month.**

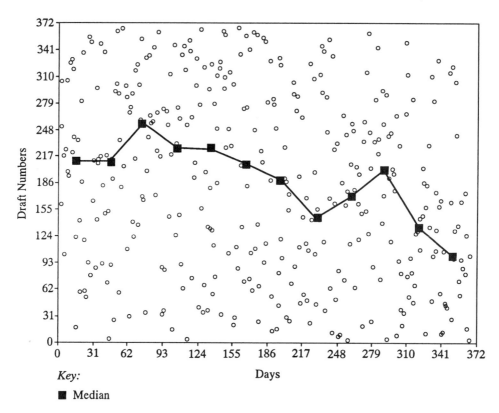

Key:
■ Median

Source: From INTRODUCTION TO THE PRACTICE OF STATISTICS by David Moore and George McCabe. Copyright © 1989 by W. H. Freeman and Co. Reprinted by permission. Data from Feinberg, 1971.

the data or by using polynomial regression. In either case, a statistical consultant might prove helpful. Usually the fitting process involves a good bit of trial and error. After each trial, it is recommended that the residuals from the regression analysis be plotted against the pretest scores. The residuals are the discrepancies between the data points and the regression line. Plotting them often can help reveal where the regression line fails to fit the data.

Treatment-Effect Interactions

It is possible that the effect of the treatment is different for individuals with different scores on the pretest. In other words, there may be a treatment-effect interaction with the pretest. An example is given in Figure 18.12. In this figure there is a large displacement between the regression lines at the cutoff point revealing that the treatment has a positive effect for individuals near the cutoff point. The size of the treatment effect varies, however, de-

pending on the individual's pretest score. If both regression lines are extrapolated onto the other side of the cutoff point, as is done in the figure, the
treatment effect for individuals with low pretest scores is shown to be much
larger than the treatment effect for individuals with high pretest scores.

There is a potential problem here: drawing the conclusion that the
treatment effect differs for individuals with different pretest scores requires
extrapolating the regression lines as described above, and the further the
lines are extrapolated, the greater is the chance for error. The possibility
for an increase in error arises because the regression lines are being extrapolated into regions in which there are no data. The regression line for the

**Figure 18.12. Data from a Hypothetical
Regression-Discontinuity Design with a Treatment-Effect Interaction.**

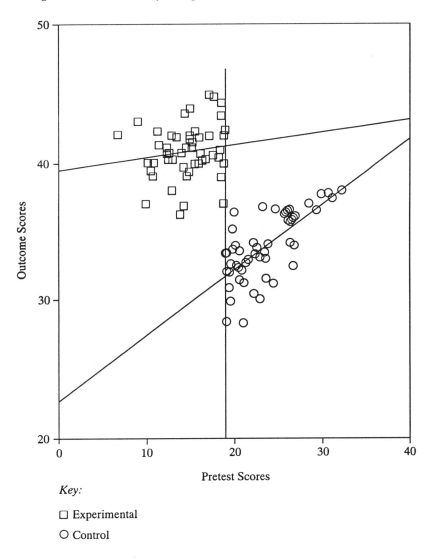

Key:

□ Experimental

○ Control

experimental group is being extrapolated onto the other side of the cutoff point where none of the individuals received the treatment. The converse holds for the regression line in the control group. Researchers should place more confidence in the estimate of the treatment effect at the cutoff point than at any other point on the pretest because the estimate at this point involves the least amount of extrapolation and therefore is the most credible and precise.

Nonetheless, it is important that an interaction between the treatment and the pretest be taken into account when fitting the regression lines. To ignore an interaction when one is present (that is, fitting parallel regression lines when the lines are not parallel) can bias the estimate of the treatment even at the cutoff point. Therefore, regression lines must be fitted to take account of an interaction if one is present, but conclusions about the effect of the treatment for individuals with pretest scores other than at the cutoff should be drawn with caution.

Other Sources of Bias

Any source of discontinuity in the regression of the outcome on the pretest scores that is not due to the treatment is a potential source of bias. A bias could be introduced if more individuals in one group drop out of the study than do individuals in the other group. For such reasons it is important to assess the nature and degree of any differential attrition.

A bias also can be introduced if the assignment to treatment conditions is not based on the cutoff score as is assumed. For example, a bias could be introduced if individuals with pretest scores on the "wrong" side of the cutoff are able to alter or lie about their pretest scores so as to be admitted to the treatment group. Evidence that this has occurred might be obtained by plotting the distribution of the pretest scores and looking for gaps or dips in the distribution near the cutoff score. Such manipulation of cutoff scores was alleged to have occurred in a civil service examination for engineering positions in Chicago in 1966 (Freedman, Pisani, Purves, and Adhikari, 1991, p. 51). There were fifteen job openings and 223 applications. A plot of the distribution of the examination scores is given in Figure 18.13. The substantial gap between the highest fifteen scores and the rest of the scores in the distribution suggests that some were altered.

An Example

The study, described earlier, of the effect on subjects' pulse rate of running in place was a randomized experiment. However, this study could be turned into a regression-discontinuity design simply by deleting data based on a cutoff score. Suppose that individuals had been assigned to treatment conditions using a cutoff score based on their initial pulse rate. In particular, suppose that all individuals with a pretest pulse rate higher than 70 had been

Figure 18.13. The Distribution of Scores
on a Civil-Service Examination in Chicago in 1966.

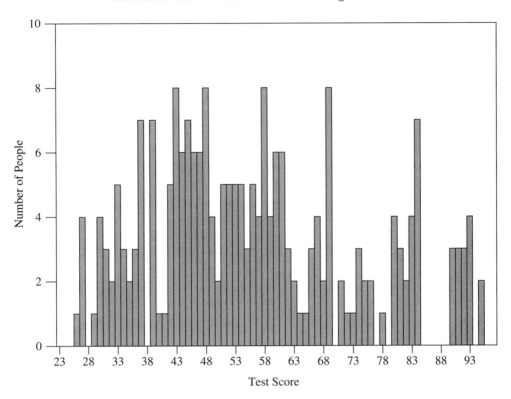

Source: Freedman, Pisani, Purves, and Adhikari, 1991, p. 51. Reprinted by permission of W. W. Norton and Company.

assigned to the experimental condition; as a result, the data from individuals in the experimental condition who had a pretest pulse of *70 or below* will be ignored. Conversely, suppose that all individuals with a pretest pulse rate of 70 or below were assigned to the control condition; in this case, the data from individuals in the control condition who had a pretest pulse *above 70* will be ignored. This assignment produces the data in Figure 18.14 which, for all intents and purposes, is a regression-discontinuity design.

With these data, the effect of the treatment can be estimated by the discrepancy between the regression lines at the cutoff point. This estimate is 20.72 (95% confidence interval = 7.4 to 34.0), which is statistically significant ($t = 3.16$, df = 38, $p = .003$). The result agrees well with the results produced when the data from the study were analyzed as a randomized experiment. Note, however, that the estimate of the treatment effect from the regression-discontinuity design is less precise—that is, the confidence interval is wider—than the estimate from the randomized experiment, partly because of the loss of data.

Figure 18.14. Data from the Pulse Study (Ryan, Joiner, and Ryan, 1985)
in the Form of a Regression-Discontinuity Design.

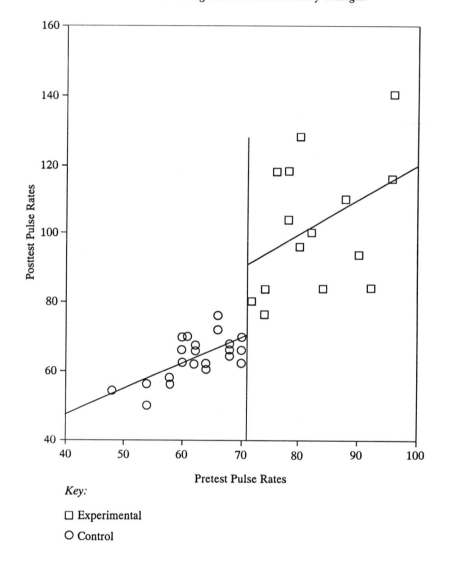

Key:

□ Experimental

○ Control

Concluding Comments on the Regression-Discontinuity Design

The regression-discontinuity design is particularly well suited for studying
treatments that are assigned on the basis of need or merit. In these cases,
a quantitative assessment of need or merit can be used as the pretest. As
a result, the design can sometimes be implemented when the random assignment of individuals to treatment conditions is not possible.

Nonetheless, the randomized experiment has at least three advantages
compared to the regression-discontinuity design. First, the randomized experiment can accommodate some misfitting of the regression model and still

produce a reasonable estimate of the effectiveness of the treatment. This is much less true for the regression-discontinuity design. For example, if the relationship between the pretest and the outcome is curvilinear and this curvilinearity is not correctly modeled, the estimate of the treatment effect at the cutoff point in the regression-discontinuity design can be biased. However, in the randomized experiment, incorrectly modeling curvilinearity can reduce precision and power, but it will not bias the estimate of the average effect of the treatment.

Second, while it is more important that the correct regression model be fitted in the regression-discontinuity design than in the randomized experiment (for the reason just noted), doing so is usually more difficult because data are missing compared to a randomized experiment. A regression-discontinuity design is essentially a randomized experiment with missing data. A comparison of Figures 18.2 and 18.8 shows that the data either above or below the cutoff point are missing for each treatment group in the regression-discontinuity design, unlike the data for the randomized experiment. Because of these missing data, it is far more difficult to be confident about correctly modeling both curvilinearity and treatment-effect interactions in the regression-discontinuity design than in the randomized experiment.

Third, even if the correct regression model is fitted to the data, the estimate of the treatment effect in the regression-discontinuity design will be less precise (and the statistical significance test will be less powerful) than the estimate of the treatment effect in the randomized experiment. Even under ideal conditions, more than two-and-a-half times as many subjects are required in the regression-discontinuity design to have the same degree of precision and power as in the randomized experiment (Goldberger, 1972).

Nonequivalent Comparison Group Design

Unlike the randomized experiment, in the nonequivalent comparison group design, individuals are not assigned to treatment conditions at random. Nor are individuals assigned to treatment conditions according to a cutoff score on a pretest, as in the regression-discontinuity design. Rather, in the nonequivalent comparison group design, individuals are assigned to the treatment conditions in some other, nonrandom fashion. They might self-select themselves into treatment conditions, or researchers might assign the treatments to preexisting groups, such as schools, that were formed previously in a nonrandom fashion. As a result, the nonequivalent comparison group design is often used to study the effects of a disability, or the effects of treatments to which random assignment would be unethical, such as the results of dropping out of school. Further discussion of the nonequivalent comparison group design is provided in Chapter Six of this volume by Rog.

Without random assignment to conditions, the individuals in the different treatment groups can, and usually will, differ in substantial ways. These differences are called *selection differences* and can masquerade as a treatment effect. Even in the absence of a true treatment effect, the outcome scores in the treatment groups are likely to differ substantially because of initial selection differences. As a result, selection differences are a threat to validity and must be taken into account when data from a nonequivalent comparison group design are analyzed.

The two simplest and most commonly used statistical procedures for taking account of selection differences are analysis of covariance and gain-score analysis. Both procedures use the pretest scores to control the biasing effects of selection differences. Which, if either, procedure is appropriate depends on the circumstances.

Analysis of Covariance

Suppose the two treatment groups differ on the pretest because individuals who have high scores on the pretest tend to be in one group more than the other. Further, suppose that individuals with high scores on the pretest tend to have high scores on the outcome or posttest. Because of these initial selection differences, the groups will differ on the posttest even in the absence of a treatment effect.

Analysis of covariance takes account of the effects of the selection differences by statistically matching individuals on their pretest scores before drawing comparisons between the groups on the outcome scores. In particular, analysis of covariance estimates the average effect of the treatment as the mean difference in outcome scores between individuals from the two treatment groups who are statistically matched on their pretest scores.

This procedure serves to remove selection differences as measured by the pretest. Nonetheless, there are two potential inadequacies in this approach. First, if there are selection differences between the groups that are not measured by the pretest but that influence the posttest, these will not be controlled for by the analysis of covariance and therefore, will still bias the estimate of the treatment effect. The more highly correlated the pretest is with the posttest, the less room there is for selection differences that are not measured by the pretest and that influence the posttest. Therefore, the best pretests to use for removing selection differences are generally those that are highly correlated with the posttest. This usually means using a pretest that is operationally identical to the posttest (Campbell and Boruch, 1975; Cronbach, 1982, points out this will not always be true, however). In addition, the analyst can use more than one pretest in the analysis of covariance. In this case, the analysis of covariance will match on all the pretests that are included in the analysis before drawing comparisons of the outcome scores. But no matter how many variables are included in the analysis, in most instances a reasonable suspicion will remain that not all the sources of selection differences have been taken into account. If the suspicion is correct, the analysis will remain biased by selection differences.

Second, selection differences will not be properly controlled for if any of the pretests that are included in the analysis are measured with error. Unfortunately, measurement error is ubiquitous in the social sciences. However, procedures have been devised for taking account of measurement error in the pretests (or covariates) in the analysis of covariance. If there is only a single covariate in the regression analysis, all that is required is an estimate of the reliability of the covariate (Campbell and Boruch, 1975; Reichardt, 1979). If multiple pretests are included in the analysis, the most widely used correction procedure requires multiple measures of each covariate and performs the analysis using a structural equation modeling program such as LISREL (Jöreskog and Sörbom, 1988) or EQS (Bentler, 1989). In either case, assistance from a statistical consultant may be required.

Gain-Score Analysis

Gain-score analysis requires that the pretest be operationally identical to the outcome or posttest variable. In this case, the pretest can be subtracted from the posttest to create a gain score for each individual. The average effect of the treatment is then estimated as the mean difference in gain scores between the treatment groups.

To understand how gain-score analysis takes account of selection differences, consider Figures 18.15 and 18.16. In both these figures, the mean pretest and posttest scores for the experimental and control groups are plotted. Gain-score analysis assumes that if there is no effect of the treatment on average, the line connecting the pretest mean to the posttest mean in the experimental group will be parallel to the line connecting the pretest mean to the posttest mean in the control group, as in Figure 18.15. In other words, gain-score analysis assumes the treatment has no effect on average if the average gain from pretest to posttest in the experimental group is the same as the average gain from pretest to posttest in the control group.

A treatment effect is present on average only if these two lines are not parallel, as in Figure 18.16. In this case, the average effect of the treatment is what accounts for the difference in the slopes of the two lines. In other words, the treatment effect is the average gain from pretest to posttest in the experimental group minus the average gain from pretest to posttest in the control group.

In both figures, selection differences account for the mean difference between the groups on the pretest. Gain-score analysis assumes that in the absence of a treatment effect, the size of these selection differences will remain the same at the time of the posttest. If, in the absence of a treatment effect, the groups would remain as far apart at the time of the posttest as they were at the time of the pretest, gain-score analysis provides an unbiased estimate of the average treatment effect. On the other hand, if in the absence of a treatment effect the groups would either grow farther apart (for example, the rich getting richer and the poor getting poorer) or come closer together (for example, due to regression toward the mean), gain-score analysis will be biased.

Figure 18.15. Pretest and Posttest Means
Showing No Treatment Effect in a Gain-Score Analysis.

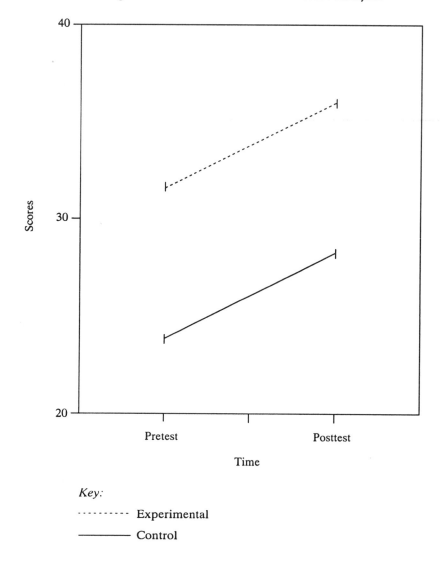

Additional pretest variables can be added to the gain-score analysis as covariates so as to adjust for any initial selection differences on these variables via statistical matching and to assess treatment-effect interactions. However, if the pretest that was used to create the gain score is added as a covariate, the result is the same as would be obtained by using analysis of covariance rather than gain-score analysis.

An Example

The study of the effect of running in place on pulse rate described previously was a randomized experiment. However, we can create a nonequivalent

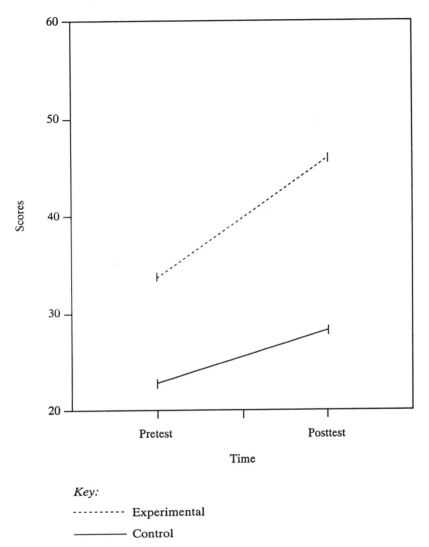

**Figure 18.16. Pretest and Posttest Means
Showing a Positive Treatment Effect in a Gain-Score Analysis.**

comparison group design by imagining that data are available only for the women who were in the experimental group and only for the men who were in the control group. The plot of the pretest pulse rate versus the posttest pulse rate for these individuals is presented in Figure 18.17. These data represent a nonequivalent comparison group design, as evidenced by the horizontal displacement between the pretest scores in the two groups showing that there is an initial difference between the groups on the pretest pulse rate.

A gain-score analysis of the data in Figure 18.17 produces an estimate of the treatment effect of 33.6 (95% confidence interval = 29.20 to 38.00). The estimate of the treatment effect from the analysis of covariance

Figure 18.17. Data from the Pulse Study (Ryan, Joiner, and Ryan, 1985)
in the Form of a Nonequivalent-Comparison-Group Design.

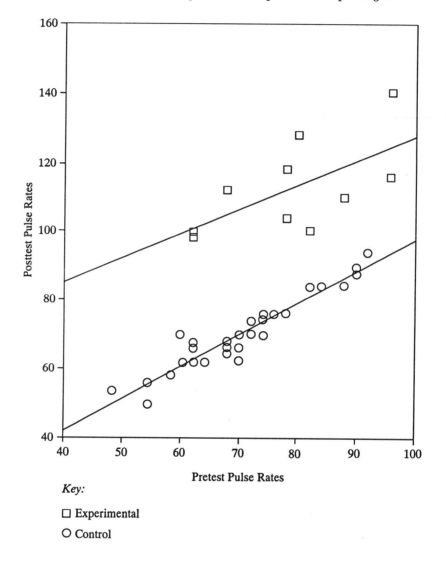

Key:

□ Experimental

○ Control

with the pretest pulse rate as the covariate is 34.86 (95% confidence interval = 30.34 to 39.37). The estimates from these two analyses are similar
because the correlation between the pretest pulse rate and the posttest pulse
rate under resting conditions was 0.92, which is very high. The results from
the gain-score analysis and the analysis of covariance will not always be so
similar.

These estimates of the treatment effect from the analysis of the data
as a nonequivalent comparison group design are not very close to the estimate of the average effect of the treatment as derived from the randomized
experiment (which was about 19). But the estimates from the nonequivalent

comparison group design are close to the estimate of the effect for women alone as derived from the randomized experiment (which was 34.4). This is probably what should be expected given the way in which this nonequivalent comparison group design was created (with only women in the experimental group and only men in the control group). Seldom will the nature of selection difference be so well known, however. In most practical circumstances, it will usually be more difficult to make sense of the results from nonequivalent comparison group designs.

Concluding Comments on the Nonequivalent Comparison Group Design

Other statistical models for taking account of selection differences (besides the analysis of covariance and gain-score analysis) are available. Many of these procedures, such as selection modeling and modeling propensity scores (see Rindskopf, 1986), are relatively complex statistically and probably require the help of a statistical consultant. Unfortunately, just as with the analysis of covariance and gain-score analysis, there is no guarantee that any of these statistical procedures will adequately account for selection differences. The problem is that properly implementing any of these methods requires information about the nature of selection differences that is usually not available. The reason is that assignment to treatments was not random as in a randomized experiment or was not determined by a known pretest as in the regression-discontinuity design.

Uncertainty about how properly to control for selection differences is the great weakness of the nonequivalent comparison group design. The only resolution for this uncertainty is to use a range of assumptions about the nature of the selection differences and thereby produce a range of estimates of the size of the treatment effect; even then caution must be used in interpreting results (Reichardt and Gollob, 1987). In other words, while researchers can report that a range of estimates derived from a variety of statistical analyses is their best guess about the size of the treatment effect, they should forthrightly acknowledge that this best guess could be far wrong. Otherwise researchers run the risk of misleading their audience.

Usually the best way to deal with initial selection differences is to try to make them as small as possible when the study is being designed and implemented. One way to do this is to forsake the nonequivalent comparison group design in favor of the randomized experiment.

Interrupted Time Series Design

In the interrupted time series design, measurements are made repeatedly at regular intervals before the treatment is introduced, the treatment is then introduced, and measurements are again repeated at regular intervals (for a total of K time points). Further discussion of the interrupted time series design is provided by Marcantonio and Cook in Chapter Seven of this handbook.

The term *unit* is used here to refer to the entity about which data are collected. The interrupted time series design can be implemented with a single unit ($N = 1$) or with multiple units ($N > 1$); in either case the units can be either individuals or groups of individuals. In one instance, Blose and Holder (1987) used the interrupted time series design to assess the effects of the liberalization of drinking laws in North Carolina. In this study, N was equal to one, and the unit was a community because data on traffic fatalities were collected at the level of the community. In contrast, Smith, Gabriel, Schoot, and Padia (1976) used the interrupted time series design to assess the effects of the Outward Bound program on participants' self-confidence using approximately $N = 200$ individuals as the units. The time series of these data are plotted in Figure 18.18. The vertical line just past week 15 indicates the point at which the individuals participated in the Outward Bound program. The scores plotted at each time point are average responses across a random sample of the two hundred participants.

Figure 18.18. Mean Levels of Self-Confidence
Before and After Participation in an Outward Bound Program.

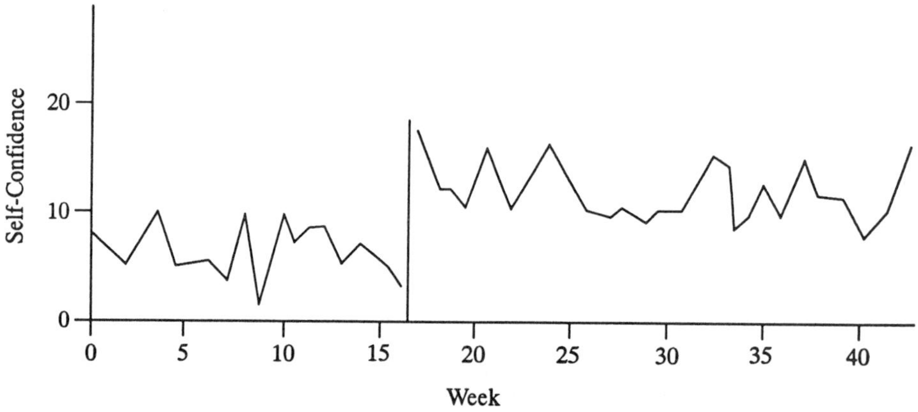

Sources: Smith, Gabriel, Schoot, and Padia, 1976. Copyright 1976 by Sage Publications. Reprinted by permission of Sage Publications, Inc. Also Glass, 1988. Copyright 1988 by the American Educational Research Association. Reprinted by permission of the publisher.

To estimate the effect of the treatment, the first step is to model the trend in the data collected before the treatment was introduced. This trend is then projected forward in time and compared to the trend in the data collected after the treatment was introduced. The difference between the projected and actual trends is the estimate of the treatment effect. In Figure 18.18, for example, the trend in the self-confidence data before participation in Outward Bound is lower than the trend in the data after participation. As a result, it appears as if Outward Bound has a positive effect on self-confidence in the population of individuals in the study.

As Marcantonio and Cook emphasize in Chapter Seven of this handbook, the interrupted time series design is very similar to the regression-discontinuity design. The only difference is that in the regression-discontinuity design, assignment to treatment conditions is determined by a cutoff score on a pretest measure; in the interrupted time series design, the assignment to treatment condition is determined by a cutoff score based on chronological time. This distinction has an important implication that will be described below, but for the most part, the logic for the analysis of data from the interrupted time series design is similar to the logic for the analysis of data from the regression-discontinuity design.

Just as in the regression-discontinuity design, whether the estimate of the treatment effect is unbiased in the interrupted time series design depends on whether the trends in the data, both before and after the treatment is introduced, have been accurately modeled. To achieve this accuracy, the researcher must correctly model any curvilinearity. Curvilinearity can be modeled by either transforming the data or using polynomial regression. In time series analysis, a data transformation called first-order differencing can be used to remove linear trends, second-order differencing can be used to remove quadratic trends, and so on (Box and Jenkins, 1970; McCleary and Hay, 1980). A statistical consultant can be helpful here. Correctly modeling the trends in the data also means that treatment-effect interactions must be properly taken into account. In the context of the interrupted time series design, a treatment-effect interaction means that the treatment effect changes over time.

Just as in the regression-discontinuity design, smoothing the data (using either a median trace or a moving average as described above) can make it easier for the analyst to recognize both curvilinear trends and treatment-effect interactions. As an illustration, Figure 18.19 is a time series plot of shipments of oil to service stations in France (Hogarth, 1980). By looking at these data, can you describe the nature of the effect of the Arab oil embargo toward the end of 1973 and the effect of increases in the price of oil toward the beginning of 1976? The time series in Figure 18.20 is the same data after smoothing (see Makridakis and Wheelwright, 1978) and reveals the nature of these effects much more clearly. Notice how the effect of the oil embargo in 1973 is quite abrupt while the effect of price increases in 1976 is more gradual.

The one important distinction between the regression-discontinuity design and the interrupted time series design arises because of possible autocorrelation of data. Different from outcome data in the regression-discontinuity design, the outcome data in the interrupted time series design are likely to be correlated among themselves. That is, the observation at time 1 in the time series is likely to be correlated with the observation at time 2, which is likely to be correlated with the observation at time 3, and so

Figure 18.19. Time Series Plot of Shipments of Oil to Service Stations in France.

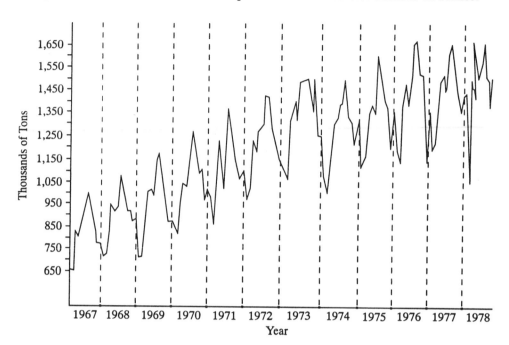

Source: From R. Hogarth, *Judgement and Choice.* Copyright 1980 by John Wiley & Sons. Original figure supplied by S. Makridakis and B. Majani. Reprinted by permission of John Wiley & Sons, Ltd., and Spyros Makridakis.

on. Such autocorrelation produces no bias in the estimate of the size of the treatment effect using standard regression procedures, but it does bias statistical significance tests and confidence intervals that are created by standard regression procedures. This bias occurs because standard regression procedures assume that there is no autocorrelation among the data points. To control for the effects of autocorrelation among the outcome scores, the regression analysis must be modified. Three different approaches for this are described below. Which one is most appropriate depends on the circumstances. In any case, seeking help from a statistical consultant is probably advisable.

ARIMA Modeling

The autoregressive, integrated, moving average (ARIMA) modeling approach assumes that the degree of autocorrelation in the observations is constant over time. ARIMA modeling uses the data to estimate the degree of autocorrelation and then adjusts the regression analysis accordingly (Box and Jenkins, 1970; McCain and McCleary, 1979; McCleary and Hay, 1980). One potential advantage is that ARIMA modeling can be used with $N = 1$. One potential drawback is that the number of time points (K) must usually

Figure 18.20. Time Series Plot of Shipments of Oil to Service Stations in France After Data Smoothing.

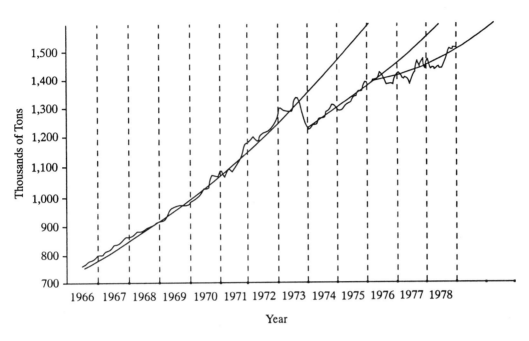

Thousands of Tons

1,500 —

1,400 —

1,300 —

1,200 —

1,100 —

1,000 —

900 —

800 —

700 —

1966 1967 1968 1969 1970 1971 1972 1973 1974 1975 1976 1977 1978

Year

Source: From R. Hogarth, *Judgement and Choice.* Copyright 1980 by John Wiley & Sons. Original figure supplied by S. Makridakis and B. Majani. Reprinted by permission of John Wiley & Sons, Ltd., and Spyros Makridakis.

be relatively large. Some statisticians suggest that the number of repeated observations (K) must be at least fifty, but the minimum size of K depends on the variability in the data: If there is relatively little variation (which is more likely when the unit is a group of individuals such as a community or state than when the unit is an individual) the minimum value for K might be substantially smaller.

If N is greater than 1, ARIMA modeling could be applied to the data from each unit separately, or the data at each time point could be aggregated across the units (as in the Outward Bound study) and ARIMA modeling applied to the aggregated data. The first approach would allow the researcher to assess individual differences in the effectiveness of the treatment while the second might allow K to be smaller. Unfortunately, many software packages either do not offer ARIMA modeling or do not provide the options for using ARIMA modeling to estimate the effects of treatments. The BMDP program is one that allows both (Dixon, 1985).

Multivariate Analysis of Variance

The multivariate analysis of variance (MANOVA) approach allows the autocorrelations among observations to have any constant or nonconstant pattern over time (Swaminathan and Algina, 1977). The MANOVA approach uses the data to estimate the autocorrelations at each time point and then adjusts the regression analysis accordingly. By relaxing the assumption made by ARIMA that the degree of autocorrelation is constant over time, MANOVA gains the advantage that K can be quite small. The disadvantage is that by relaxing this assumption, N must be substantially larger than K. The MANOVA analysis fits a common (aggregate) trend to the data from all N units and estimates the average effect of the treatment across all N units.

Hierarchical Linear Modeling

The hierarchical linear modeling (HLM) approach requires that N be substantially greater than 1 but, unlike the MANOVA approach, does not require that N be greater than K or even that observations be collected at the same time points on the different units (Bryk and Raudenbush, 1987, 1992). The HLM approach fits regression models at two different levels. At the first level, HLM fits a regression model and estimates the effects of the treatment for each unit individually. At the second level, HLM fits a regression model to the estimates of the treatment effects from the first level allowing for the inclusion of additional covariates. The model at the second level provides an estimate of the average treatment effect and estimates of interactions of the treatment with any of the covariates that are included. By using two hierarchical levels of analysis, the HLM approach circumvents the need to model the nature of the autocorrelation among the observations.

Concluding Comments on the Interrupted Time Series Design

The interrupted time series design can be biased by "history" or other threats to validity (see Chapter Seven of this volume). One way to remove these biases is by adding a "control" time series of observations that is susceptible to the same biases as the experimental series but is not given the treatment. The data from the control series can be analyzed just like the data from the experimental series. The treatment effect is then estimated as the difference between the discontinuity in the experimental series at the point of the intervention and the discontinuity in the control series at the same time point.

One advantage of the interrupted time series design, compared to the other three designs described in this chapter, is that the interrupted time series design allows the researcher to study the time course of the treatment effect. For example, the researcher can assess whether the treatment effect occurs abruptly or is delayed, and whether it increases, decreases, or remains the same over time. The models for studying the time course of the treatment have been especially well developed within the ARIMA modeling approach (Box and Tiao, 1975).

Conclusions

When estimating the effects of treatments using any of the four designs described above, we recommend the following practices.

Draw pictures of the data. Pictures can help you decide which statistical analyses are appropriate and can help you interpret the results of statistical analyses.

Watch for improper fits in the statistical analysis such as a linear regression line being fitted to curvilinear data. Fitting the wrong model can bias the estimates of treatment effects.

Assess treatment-effect interactions. Treatment-effect interactions reveal how a treatment effect varies either across individuals or time. Understanding how the effect of a treatment varies is as important, if not more so, than estimating the average effect of the treatment.

Ask yourself if there are any hidden biases in the statistical analyses. For example, it is usually impossible to determine from the data alone whether the analysis of covariance properly takes account of selection differences in the nonequivalent comparison group design. You also have to understand the logic of what the analysis of covariance does and, using your (imperfect) substantive knowledge of the study, decide whether that logic fits the circumstances.

Report the degree of uncertainty forthrightly in the results. Biases cannot all be removed with complete certainty. As a result, there will always be uncertainty about the size of treatment effects. Researchers should make sure that readers are not misled into believing that the results are more certain than is warranted. Proper presentation of results includes using both confidence intervals and multiple analyses when you are not sure which single analysis is correct.

References

Ball, S., and Bogatz, G. A. *The First Year of "Sesame Street": An Evaluation.* Princeton, N.J.: Educational Testing Service, 1970.

Bentler, P. M. *EQS Structural Equations Program Manual.* Los Angeles: BMDP Statistical Software, 1989.

Blose, J. O., and Holder, H. D. "Liquor-by-the-Drink and Alcohol-Related Traffic Crashes: A Natural Experiment Using Time-Series Analysis." *Journal of Studies on Alcohol,* 1987, *48,* 52–60.

Borenstein, M., and Cohen, J. *Statistical Power Analysis: A Computer Program.* Hillsdale, N.J.: Erlbaum, 1988.

Boruch, R. F., and Wothke, W. "Seven Kinds of Randomization Plans for Designing Field Experiments." In R. F. Boruch and W. Wothke (eds.), *Randomization and Field Experimentation.* New Directions for Program Evaluation, no. 28. San Francisco: Jossey-Bass, 1985.

Box, G.E.P., and Jenkins, G. M. *Time-Series Analysis: Forecasting and Control.* San Francisco: Holden-Day, 1970.

Box, G.E.P., and Tiao, G. C. "Intervention Analysis with Application to Economic and Environmental Problems." *Journal of the American Statistical Association,* 1975, *70,* 70–92.

Braucht, G. N., and Reichardt, C. S. "A Computerized Approach to Trickle-Process, Random Assignment." *Evaluation Review,* 1993, *17,* 79–90.

Bryk, A. S., and Raudenbush, S. W. "Application of Hierarchical Linear Models to Assessing Change." *Psychological Bulletin,* 1987, *101,* 147–158.

Bryk, A. S., and Raudenbush, S. W. *Hierarchical Linear Models: Applications and Data Analysis Methods.* Newbury Park, Calif.: Sage, 1992.

Campbell, D. T., and Boruch, R. F. "Making the Case for Randomized Assignment to Treatments by Considering the Alternatives: Six Ways in Which Quasi-Experimental Evaluations in Compensatory Education Tend to Underestimate Effects." In C. A. Bennett and A. A. Lumsdaine (eds.), *Evaluation and Experiment: Some Critical Issues in Assessing Social Programs.* New York: Academic Press, 1975.

Cohen, J. *Statistical Power Analysis for the Behavioral Sciences.* (Rev. ed.) New York: Academic Press, 1977.

Conner, R. F. "Selecting a Control Group: An Analysis of the Randomization Process in Twelve Social Reform Programs." *Evaluation Quarterly,* 1977, *1,* 195–243.

Cronbach, L. J. *Designing Evaluations of Educational and Social Programs.* San Francisco: Jossey-Bass, 1982.

Dixon, W. J. *BMDP Statistical Software.* Berkeley: University of California Press, 1985.

Draper, N. R., and Smith, H. *Applied Regression Analysis.* New York: Wiley, 1981.

Feinberg, S. E. "Randomization and Social Affairs: The 1970 Draft Lottery." *Science,* 1971, *171,* 255–261.

Freedman, D., Pisani, R., Purves, R., and Adhikari, A. *Statistics.* (2nd ed.) New York: Norton, 1991.

Glass, G. V. "Quasi-Experiments: The Case of Interrupted Time Series." In R. M. Jaeger (ed.), *Complementary Methods for Research in Education.* Washington, D.C.: American Educational Research Association, 1988.

Goldberger, A. S. *Selection Bias in Evaluating Treatment Effects: Some Formal Illustrations.* Discussion Paper 123-72, Madison, University of Wisconsin, Institute for Research on Poverty, 1972.

Hamilton, L. C. *Regression with Graphics: A Second Course in Applied Statistics.* Pacific Grove, Calif.: Brooks/Cole, 1992.

Hogarth, R. *Judgement and Choice.* New York: Wiley, 1980.

Jöreskog, K. G., and Sörbom, D. *LISREL 7: A Guide to the Program and Applications.* Chicago: SPSS, 1988.

Kraemer, H. C., and Thiemann, S. *How Many Subjects? Statistical Power Analysis in Research.* Newbury Park, Calif.: Sage, 1987.

Lipsey, M. W. *Design Sensitivity: Statistical Power for Experimental Research.* Newbury Park, Calif.: Sage, 1990.

McCain, L. J., and McCleary, R. "The Statistical Analysis of Simple Interrupted Time-Series Quasi-Experiments." In T. D. Cook and D. T. Campbell, *Quasi-Experimentation: Design and Analysis Issues for Field Settings.* Chicago: Rand McNally, 1979.

McCleary, R., and Hay, R. A., Jr. *Applied Time Series Analysis for the Social Sciences.* Newbury Park, Calif.: Sage, 1980.

Makridakis, S., and Wheelwright, S. C. *Interactive Forecasting: Univariate and Multivariate Methods.* (2nd ed.) San Francisco: Holden-Day, 1978.

Moore, D. S., and McCabe, G. P. *Introduction to the Practice of Statistics.* New York: Freeman, 1989.

Reichardt, C. S. "The Statistical Analysis of Data from Nonequivalent Group Designs." In T. D. Cook and D. T. Campbell, *Quasi-Experimentation: Design and Analysis Issues for Field Settings.* Chicago: Rand McNally, 1979.

Reichardt, C. S., and Gollob, H. F. "Taking Uncertainty into Account When Estimating Effects." In M. M. Mark and R. L. Shotland (eds.), *Multiple Methods for Program Evaluation.* New Directions for Program Evaluation, no. 35. San Francisco: Jossey-Bass, 1987.

Rindskopf, D. "New Developments in Selection Modeling for Quasi-Experimentation." In W.M.K. Trochim (ed.), *Advances in Quasi-Experimental Design and Analysis.* New Directions for Program Evaluation, no. 31. San Francisco: Jossey-Bass, 1986.

Ryan, B. F., Joiner, B. L., and Ryan, T. A., Jr. *Minitab Handbook.* (2nd ed.) Boston: Duxbury, 1985.

Smith, M. L., Gabriel, R., Schoot, J., and Padia, W. L. "Evaluation of the Effects of Outward Bound." In G. V. Glass (ed.), *Evaluation Studies Review Annual: Volume 1.* Newbury Park, Calif.: Sage, 1976.

Swaminathan, H., and Algina, J. "Analysis of quasi-experimental time-series designs." *Journal of Multivariate Behavioral Research,* 1977, *12,* 111–131.

19

Benefit–Cost Analysis
in Program Evaluation

James Edwin Kee

Benefit-cost or cost-benefit analysis is a useful quantitative tool of the program evaluator. It can be used in evaluations of existing programs to assess their overall success or failure, to help determine whether the program should be continued or modified, and to assess the probable results of proposed program changes.

At its most useful, benefit-cost analysis can identify and provide information on the full costs of programs and weigh those against the dollar value of the program benefits. The evaluator can then calculate the net benefits (or costs) of the program; examine the ratio of benefits to costs; determine the rate of return on the original investment; and compare the program's benefits and costs with those of other programs or proposed alternatives.

In five sections, this chapter examines the uses and limits of benefit-cost analysis in program evaluation. The first section compares benefit-cost analysis with an alternative economic tool — cost-effectiveness analysis — that is sometimes more useful for the program evaluator. It also compares the use of benefit-cost analysis in the public and private sectors and provides a simple illustration of a benefit-cost analysis. The second section provides a framework for benefit-cost analysis that will assist the evaluator in identifying and considering a full range of benefits and costs — direct and indirect, tangible and intangible. The third section examines the most challenging problem in benefit-cost analysis — the valuation of benefits — and provides several examples to assist the evaluator in meeting this challenge. The fourth section looks at the problems associated with measuring costs and some techniques often used by evaluators. The final section examines alternative methods an evaluator might use in presenting benefit-cost information to the decision maker.

Benefit-Cost and Cost-Effectiveness Analyses

Benefit-cost analysis is an applied branch of economics that attempts to assess service programs by determining whether total societal welfare has increased (in the aggregate more people have been made better off) because of the project or program. Benefit-cost analysis is a set of practical, systematic procedures program evaluators can use in identifying and placing dollar values on all the costs and benefits of a program. At its heart are three rather simple-sounding steps:

1. Determine the benefits of a proposed or existing program and place a dollar value on those benefits.
2. Calculate the total costs of the program.
3. Compare the benefits and the costs.

These simple steps, however, pose a real challenge to the program evaluator. Even when benefits can be calculated in unit terms, such as a certain number of lives saved, placing a dollar value on each unit is often quite difficult. For many intangibles (national security, wilderness values, quality of life, environmental purity) determining both the unit of analysis and its dollar value can prove problematic.

Nevertheless, even when the evaluator cannot capture all the benefits and costs in quantitative terms, the benefit-cost procedure can uncover important issues in analyzing a program's success or failure. It may sometimes lead to an implicit valuation of some intangibles that may have been hidden in rhetoric. For example, if the costs of Program X exceed the "hard" benefits (that is, those that are quantifiable in dollar terms) by an amount y, the intangibles must be worth at least y to the public and their decision makers or the program should be reconsidered.

Cost-Effectiveness Analysis

The major costing alternative to benefit-cost analysis is cost-effectiveness analysis, which relates the cost of a given alternative to specific measures of program objectives. A cost-effectiveness analysis could compare costs to units of program objectives—for example, dollar per life saved on various highway safety programs.

Cost-effectiveness analysis is often the first step in a benefit-cost analysis; it is especially useful when an evaluator cannot place a dollar value on program benefits but the program's objectives are clear and either singular or sufficiently related so that the relationship between the objectives is evident. For example, if the goal of certain education programs is to prevent high school dropouts, alternative programs can be compared by analyzing the costs per dropout prevented or per increase in percentage of students graduating.

The major advantage of cost-effectiveness analysis is that it frees the evaluator from having to express all benefits in monetary terms. Program outcomes can be addressed according to their multiple attributes. For education programs, for example, student learning can be assessed in terms of improved test scores, physical education programs can be assessed in terms of improvements in various physical skills of the participants, and programs to increase college placement can be assessed in terms of numbers of students placed in various colleges (Levin, 1983). In none of these cases does the evaluator have to weigh the costs against a dollar value of benefits. The evaluator simply presents the results to the decision maker who then decides whether the various outcomes are worth the dollar cost. This often is a very effective—and inexpensive—method of providing comparative program cost data to decision makers.

Government programs, however, frequently generate more than one type of cost and benefit. A weapons system might have both offensive and defensive uses; an education program might target more than one population group in the school system. The mix of benefits may depend on how the program is designed and implemented. When conducting a cost-effectiveness analysis comparing programs with multiple objectives, the evaluator may need to place weights on the relative benefits to assist the decision maker in his or her comparisons.

Musgrave and Musgrave (1989) provide an illustration using expenditures on education. Expenditures on elementary education might contribute more to literacy than outlays on higher education; however, expenditures on higher education might contribute more to advancing technology than a similar amount spent on elementary education.

Suppose a $3 billion expenditure on elementary education produces a twelve-unit gain in literacy and a three-unit gain in technology, whereas a $3 billion expenditure on higher education produces only a three-unit gain in literacy but a fifteen-unit gain in technology. Units might be a function of percentage increases in the literacy rate or new patents. Can the evaluator compare the two programs? If the units are valued equally—1 percent increase in literacy equaling a 1 percent increase in patents—the clear winner is the higher education expenditure. If, however, because of distributional reasons (literacy programs would help disadvantaged people) or other value judgments, a literacy unit is given a 50 percent greater value than a technology unit, the evaluator might conclude that the elementary education program is preferable. Ultimately, the key issue here is the valuation of the units for both programs. An evaluator can help the decision maker by comparing the costs to various units of output and by indicating any explicit or implicit valuation.

There are two major disadvantages of cost-effectiveness analysis compared to benefit-cost analysis. First, in considering programs with multiple benefits, unless the evaluator assigns weights to each benefit to obtain a common denominator for comparison purposes, the comparison often becomes highly subjective. Yet assigning weights often becomes at least as problematic as assigning dollar values to each benefit. Second, a cost-effectiveness analysis does not produce a "bottom line" number, with benefits exceeding costs or costs exceeding benefits. Thus, if a program costs $1 million and produces ten units of outcome x, twelve units of outcome y, and twenty units of outcome z, how is the evaluator to make a judgment concerning the cost-effectiveness of the program? The question for the decision maker is whether the outcomes produced are worth the $1 million expenditure. Thus, where it is possible to value the outcomes in monetary terms, that valuation is more likely to be of assistance to a decision maker than simply listing the program outcomes and comparing those outcomes to total costs.

A Private Sector Analogy

In many respects, benefit-cost analysis of government programs is similar to financial analysis conducted in the private sector as existing and potential investment opportunities are considered. Government and its taxpayers are investing funds to achieve certain societal benefits, just as a firm is investing its funds to achieve certain profit objectives.

When a private firm analyzes existing projects it must answer two questions. First, should the firm have done the project at all — that is, is the project producing a satisfactory net return to the firm? Second, what other options are there for the use of the firm's resources? Public agencies and their evaluators must ask similar questions. First, is the program a success — that is, has it improved societal welfare? Second, should the program be continued when weighed against alternative uses for the government's funds?

For most private sector projects, benefits and costs do not occur simultaneously. The firm must engage in research and development of a proposed project, develop a marketing strategy, provide funds for capital investment, and hire and train labor before it begins production of the product. It then attempts to price the product to maximize the firm's profit and net return on its investment.

For government programs there are also start-up costs, such as expenditures on studies or consultants, and capital costs. There may be costs associated with advertising the program and developing the constituency for it, and there are the continuing costs of operating it. Most government programs are not priced (at least not to maximize profits), thus benefits are broader than any monetary return to the government — even though revenue may be important from a budgetary perspective.

In assessing the success or failure of the project, the private firm must also consider that it had alternative uses for the funds spent on the project — alternative projects or even passive investment in U.S. Treasury notes or bonds — and thus expects a certain return on its investment.

A government also has alternative uses for its tax dollars or borrowing capacity. It could return the money to its citizens in the form of tax reductions and thus allow more spending in the private sector. If it must bond for the project, those funds are unavailable for alternative investment choices.

Thus, both private and public entities are concerned with the *opportunity cost* to them of continuing the program or project instead of shifting resources now devoted to the program or project to an alternative. Opportunity cost is defined as the foregone alternative for those resources.

Benefit-Cost Illustration

Table 19.1 illustrates benefit-cost calculations of a project's benefits and costs. The illustration is a five-year project, which required $2 million in research and development funds and a $12 million capital investment. The table illustrates a straight-line five-year depreciation (or spreading out) of the capital costs at $2 million a year (assuming a $2 million salvage value at the end of five years), with operations and maintenance costs and the beginning of benefits in year two.

At the end of the five-year period the agency has spent $23 million and reaped total benefits of $24 million for a five-year net benefit (benefits less costs) of $1 million. From the agency's perspective, was the project a success? Because of the heavy research and development costs at the front end of the project, the agency lost money during the first two years of the project and did not begin to turn a profit (see the benefits exceeding the costs) until the third year.

Table 19.1. Illustration of Benefit-Cost Analysis
(in thousands of dollars).

	Costs				
Year	Research and Development	Capital	Operations and Maintenance	Total	Total Benefits
1	$1,500	$2,000	$0	$3,500	$0
2	$500	$2,000	$2,000	$4,500	$3,500
3	$0	$2,000	$2,500	$4,500	$5,500
4	$0	$2,000	$3,000	$5,000	$6,500
5	$0	$2,000	$3,500	$5,500	$8,500
Totals	$2,000	$10,000	$11,000	$23,000	$24,000

Year	Benefits-Costs	Present Value, Benefits-Costs (at 10%)
1	($3,500)	($3,500)
2	($1,000)	($909)
3	$1,000	$826
4	$1,500	$1,127
5	$3,000	$2,049
Totals	$1,000	($407)

Net Present Value @ 10% ($407)
Net Present Value @ 5% $219

The agency or the government financing the agency also had alternative investment opportunities for its funds. When it lost $3.5 million in the first year of the project, it lost the opportunity to use those funds elsewhere. The $3.5 million loss in year one is more costly than the same amount in later years because of this lost opportunity cost or loss of potential gain. In order to incorporate the concept of opportunity cost, benefit-cost analysis employs *present value analysis* which converts all costs and benefits to their present value at the beginning of the project, in year 1. (Many benefit-cost examples start with a year 0 and this will affect the formula for determining net present value of a project. However, for public sector program evaluations a year 0 makes little sense.)

The opportunity costs to the agency are expressed as the real rate of return — r — available to the agency at the beginning of the project. The benefits (B) less costs (C) in year two can be expressed as $B - C/(1 + r)$; year three as $B - C/(1 + r)(1 + r)$ or $B - C(1 + r)^2$; year four as $B - C/(1 + r)^3$; and year five as $B - C/(1 + r)^4$. Thus the $1 million loss in year two in the illustration has a "present (year one) value" of only $909,000, assuming a 10 percent real rate of return (or interest rate) for the agency, because the $1 million could have been generating a return during the year before it was lost. Similarly, the year three profit of $1 million has a "present (year one) value" of only $826,000.

For the five-year period, the net benefits less costs of the project can be calculated using the following formula:

$$NPV = B^{y1} - C^{y1} + \frac{B^{y2} - C^{y2}}{1 + r} + \frac{B^{y3} - C^{y3}}{(1 + r)^2} \ldots \frac{B^{yx} - C^{yx}}{(1 + r)^{x-1}}$$

Using the formula, either year by year, or using a present value function in a calculator or spreadsheet yields a net costs-over-benefits figure of $407,000 using a 10 percent interest rate. Thus, instead of a five-year net benefit of $1 million when present value was not calculated, the agency actually lost $409,000 on the project.

Present value analysis is often extremely sensitive to the choice of the appropriate interest rate (usually referred to as the *discount rate*) for the agency. If instead of 10 percent, the agency's opportunity costs were reflected by a 5 percent interest rate, then the net present value yields a positive net benefit of $219,000.

An alternative approach is to determine the *return on investment (ROI)* on the project. The ROI is the discount rate that would make the present value of the project equal to zero. In the illustration, the ROI is approximately 7 percent on the project. The government agency can then assess the success or failure of the project based on whether it considers a 7 percent rate of return satisfactory given other opportunities the agency might have had in year one.

Continuing or Not Continuing the Project. Should the agency continue the project in the illustration? By year five the project is yielding total benefits of $8.5 million and net benefits of $3 million on expenditures of $5.5 million. Certain costs incurred by the agency are now *sunk costs*—that is, funds that have already been spent and resources used. They have no relevance for decisions about whether to continue the project. They have achieved (or not achieved) benefits. Thus the funds previously spent on research and development and on capital costs are not considered by the agency in deciding whether to continue the project.

The agency is concerned only with its current and future costs and expected continued benefits. Will it need to spend additional dollars to modify the program? Will it need to upgrade its facilities and equipment? What is the salvage value of current capital involved in the project or its opportunity costs for alternative uses, if any? Is there still a need or demand for the agency's product or has it become obsolete? Thus the project's continuation faces an evaluation that is different from the retrospective analysis of the project's net benefits.

Table 19.2 illustrates a decision-making framework for the continuation of the project from Table 19.1. Assume that an additional $500,000 must be spent in year 6 to develop enhancements for the agency product to allow it to continue to meet citizen needs and demands. Further, assume that the facilities and equipment have a salvage value of $2 million and can be used for another five years with some increase in maintenance. Finally,

Table 19.2. Illustration of Benefit-Cost Analysis (in thousands of dollars).

	Costs				
Year	Research and Development	Capital	Operations and Maintenance	Total	Total Benefits
6	$500	$400	$4,500	$5,400	$9,000
7	$0	$400	$5,000	$5,400	$8,500
8	$0	$400	$6,000	$6,400	$8,500
9	$0	$400	$7,500	$7,900	$8,000
10	$0	$400	$8,000	$8,400	$7,500
Totals	$500	$2,000	$31,000	$33,500	$41,500

Year	Benefits-Costs	Present Value, Benefits-Costs (at 10%)
6	$3,600	$3,600
7	$3,100	$2,818
8	$2,100	$1,736
9	$100	$75
10	($900)	($615)
Totals	$8,000	7,614

Net Present Value @ 10% $7,614
Net Present Value @ 5% $7,803

assume that while there is still a demand for the agency's product, that demand is likely to decrease over the next few years.

From year 6 to year 10 the agency is projected to spend $33.5 million and achieve total benefits of $41.5 million, a net benefit of $8 million, with a net present value in excess of $7 million. The project which might have achieved only a marginal return of 7 percent during its first five years, now projects a significant return in years six, seven, and eight, while not turning negative until the final year of the project. Unless the agency has a very appealing alternative, the analysis is likely to lead to a continued production of this product.

Total Versus Marginal Benefits and Costs. The benefit-cost illustration reveals an important, and often missed, distinction for the program evaluator—the difference between total and marginal benefits and costs. In assessing the overall profitability of the project, an agency will consider the total costs involved in getting the project started through its operation's cycle. But at any point in time, when an agency is deciding whether to continue or discontinue a project or program, it will consider only its marginal costs and benefits.

Marginal cost is defined as the incremental (additional) cost of producing one more unit of output. *Marginal benefit* is the incremental benefit generated by that one unit of output. While in practice analysis is not done on single incremental units in determining whether to continue production of a product or program, the evaluator attempts to analyze the program at the margin: What are the benefits that the program is now generating versus its costs?

Thus in the illustration above, in year 6 an agency may decide to enhance its program line by spending another $500,000 on research and development because it anticipates marginal benefits of $9 million against marginal costs (including the $500,000) of $5 million along with the continued use of the existing capital facilities.

Public-Private Sector Similarities and Differences. The above benefit-cost illustration is equally applicable to the private or public sectors. Both a public agency and a private firm are concerned with costs and benefits and their timing. Both must consider alternative uses for their funds, including their opportunity cost. Both must consider a range of cost considerations: one-time costs, recurring costs, land, labor, and capital.

There are, however, two key differences:

- *Distributional considerations:* While a private firm needs to know its customers for marketing purposes, it is unconcerned with whom it sells its product to, just so there is a market to buy the product. A public agency must be concerned with who benefits as well as the amount of benefit because government programs are often designed to redistribute resources from high-income taxpayers to low-income groups in our society.

- *Spillovers:* Private firms are unconcerned with costs that might be incurred by third parties (those not buying the product). For example, if a local community has built a new road to a plant or if effluent from the plant pollutes a downstream locality or places strains on the government's wastewater treatment plant, these spillover costs (*or externalities*) are not taken into account by a private firm when it analyzes its profit margin. The firm will "internalize" these costs only if government taxes, regulates, or otherwise holds the firm accountable.

Regardless of government action, however, these spillovers must be considered by government in any program evaluation. Public agencies must be concerned with their programs' distributional consequences and potential spillover effects, both positive and negative, because they are concerned with the broader societal notion of welfare and not just profit (or revenue) for the government.

Framework for Analysis

Exhibit 19.1 provides a framework for conducting a benefit-cost analysis of a program. This framework is applicable both for the analyst who is examining a proposed program and for the program evaluator who is analyzing an existing program.

In conducting a benefit-cost analysis as part of a program evaluation, the first step is to identify all the known benefits and costs of the program, to the government, to the program clients or beneficiaries, and to others not directly involved in the program. There are several distinct categories of benefits and costs: real versus transfers; direct and indirect; tangible and intangible. Each of these categories is explained and examples given to assist the evaluator.

For each benefit or cost, it is important to state its *nature* clearly, to show how it is being *measured,* and to list any *assumptions* made in the calculations of the dollars involved. The statement of the assumptions is particularly critical because the dollar values often hinge on an evaluator's assumptions. Those assumptions need to be made explicit to the decision maker and also be subjected to a *sensitivity analysis* to determine the extent to which they control the outcome of the analysis.

One advantage that the evaluator has in examining an existing program is that the benefits and costs should be clearer than they were at the time the program was proposed. The number of beneficiaries should be known, and historical cost data will provide details that would earlier only have been estimated.

Real Benefits and Costs Versus Transfers

Real benefits and costs represent net gains or losses to society whereas transfers merely alter the distribution of resources within society. Musgrave refers

Exhibit 19.1. Benefit/Cost Framework.

Benefit	Indicator: Nature of Benefits	Measure	Dollar Value	Assumptions
Real Direct Tangible Intangible Indirect Tangible Intangible				

Cost	Indicator: Nature of Cost	Measure	Dollar Value	Assumptions
Real Direct Tangible Intangible Indirect Tangible Intangible				
Transfers				

to such transfers as pecuniary gains or losses (Musgrave and Musgrave, 1989). Real benefits include dollars saved and dollars earned, lives saved and lives enriched, increased earnings and decreased costs to taxpayers, and time saved and enhanced quality of life. In contrast, some societal gains are directly offset by other losses. For example, a local tax abatement program for the elderly will provide a tax-saving benefit to some but a cost of equal amount to others (higher taxes or lower services).

Transfers also occur as a result of a change in relative prices of various goods and services as the economy adjusts to the provision of certain public goods and services. For example, in evaluating a water project for agricultural purposes, the real costs would include various factors of production, such as wages paid to labor, concrete, pipe and other materials. Real benefits might include increased agricultural yield from the land. Transfers might include the relative increase of farm wages or the profits of farm implement manufacturers as compared to other wage earners or firms. With transfers, the gain to one person or group is offset by a loss to another individual or group.

Transfers are often important to policymakers. Many government programs involve the subsidizing of one group by another in the society and thus should be clearly identified where possible. But from an overall societal perspective, transfers do not increase total welfare; they merely redistribute welfare within society.

Chain-Reaction Problem. A common error often made in benefit-cost analysis is to make the project or program appear successful by counting secondary benefits that arise from it while ignoring secondary costs. For example, if a government builds a road, the primary benefits are the reduction in transportation costs (time spent and fuel consumed) for individuals and businesses. Profits of adjacent restaurants, motels, and gas stations may also have risen as a result of increased traffic, leading in turn to increased profits in the local food, bed-linen, and gasoline-production businesses. Economist Harvey Rosen (1992) calls this the "chain-reaction game"; if enough secondary effects are added to the benefit side, "eventually a positive present value can be obtained for practically any project" (p. 258).

Rosen notes that this process ignores the likely losses from building the road. Profits of train operators may decrease as some of their customers turn to cars for transportation, and increased auto use may push up the price of gasoline, increasing costs to many gasoline consumers. At the very least, secondary costs must be counted as well as secondary gains. In many cases, these "transfers" often cancel one another, with the gains to some equalling the losses to others.

Direct and Indirect Benefits and Costs

Direct benefits and costs are closely related to the primary objective(s) of the project. Indirect or secondary benefits and costs are by-products, multipliers, spillovers, or investment effects of the project or program.

Direct costs include the expense of personnel, facilities, equipment and material, and project administration. Indirect costs are unintended costs that occur as a result of a government action. The dam built for agricultural purposes, cited above, may have flooded an area used by hikers, hunters, or fishermen, who have lost the value of this recreational area.

Although many transfers do counterbalance one another, there are frequently indirect benefits of government programs that are indeed significant and should be counted. An often-cited example of indirect benefits is space exploration, which has spun off numerous technologies that have benefited other industries.

In another example, a government job training program may have the chief purpose of placing marginal workers into well-paying jobs, but an indirect benefit might be the reduction (a cost savings) in welfare payments made by government to former recipients who now have become taxpayers. However, the loss of welfare benefits is a cost to the welfare recipient. The "societal" gain is only the increase in total earnings of the former welfare recipient.

The Question of Tax Revenue as a Benefit. Is the revenue realized by the government in increased taxes also a benefit? Or can it be used to offset government costs? If the program is designed to be self-sufficient, as is the case with many government authorities or quasi-public agencies, then the revenues returned to the government in the form of user fees and taxes are important for the analysis.

Most government programs are not designed to produce a monetary return to government itself, but to its citizens. There are two issues here. One is a double-counting problem: you cannot claim both total gains in wages and profits *and* taxes to the government; taxes are a subset of the wages and profits; the second is a transfer question: many economists argue that taxes are simply a transfer from the taxpayer to the government; they make the taxpayer worse off and other government beneficiaries better off.

The latter question relates to the important distributional questions inherent in benefit-cost analysis. The benefits and costs of agency programs almost always occur to different groups. An irrigation project may benefit farmers by providing low-cost water, leading to higher farm profits. However, if the full costs of the project are not recaptured in user fees from the farmer, the general taxpayer has subsidized the benefits to the farmer. This situation may be desirable from a public policy standpoint, but the extent of the subsidy should be clear to the policymaker.

Tangible and Intangible Benefits and Costs

Tangible benefits and costs are those you can readily convert to dollars or express in equivalent dollar proxies. Intangible benefits and costs are those for which you cannot or choose not to assign an explicit price, such as the value of wilderness or an increased sense of community. The process of assigning values to costs and benefits and various methods of approaching the intangibles are discussed in a later section; this, however, is perhaps the greatest weakness in benefit-cost analysis. Placing a dollar value on many intangible benefits is especially difficult.

Determining the Geographic Scope of the Analysis

While the focus of an analysis may be within a certain jurisdiction, such as a state, there may be benefits or costs that spill over to neighboring jurisdictions. The question for the evaluator is whether to consider only those benefits and costs that accrue to the population within the jurisdiction for which the evaluator is doing the analysis.

One method of dealing with these spillovers or externalities is through transfer pricing, or estimation of the value of the subsidy or cost prevention measure, if deemed important for the analysis. If in the agricultural water project illustration, water salinity increases downstream (a condition that might be caused by water evaporation in a reservoir used for irrigation purposes), downstream areas might be compensated for the increased salinity or the evaluator might estimate the cost of installing a desalination process in the reservoir before the water is released to flow downward.

There is a tendency for evaluators of existing projects to ignore spillover costs and benefits if these are not costed in some fashion; but ignoring them can be unwise, as these spillovers often have political consequences. By attempting to measure their benefits or costs you gain insight into the total effects of the project. At the very least, external benefits and costs should be acknowledged even if not fully accounted for or priced.

For example, if 1,000 persons from a neighboring jurisdiction use the county mass transit system, paying a daily fare of $3.00 per round trip, one benefit to the county government is the user fee revenue generated by the out-of-county riders. However, the benefit to those riders might well exceed $3.00, when the value of their time saved, reduced gasoline usage, and automobile (and personal) wear and tear are calculated. To the extent that total benefits to the out-of-county riders exceed the $3.00, politicians might be able to argue for a subsidy from the neighboring jurisdiction to support the county's transit system. This argument would be particularly cogent if the transit system was not self-supporting (as few are) and required a subsidy from in-county taxpayers. Thus, unless the neighboring county contributed to the transit system, in-county taxpayers would also be subsidizing out-of-county riders.

Water Project Illustration. Table 19.3 provides a simple illustration of the benefits and costs of an agricultural water project — a dam and reservoir — using the categories in the suggested framework of analysis. Analysis of a specific project, however, will be much more complex, involving many more costs and benefits than are listed in the illustration. In addition to the information on the nature of the benefits and costs provided in Table 19.3, using the outline presented in Exhibit 19.1, the evaluator would indicate how the benefit or cost is being measured, key assumptions relative to the measurement, and the estimated dollar value (where appropriate).

The placement of certain benefits and costs in one category or the other (direct versus indirect or tangible versus intangible) is somewhat arbitrary and involves the judgment of the evaluator. The category into which each benefit or cost is placed is not so important as ensuring that all benefits and costs are considered. Some of these are obvious; others might be determined by examining original project justification material and by discussing the project with those affected by it. Because many of the benefits and costs are

Table 19.3. Benefits and Costs of a Dam and Reservoir for Agricultural Purposes.

Real Benefits	Nature of the Benefit/Cost
Direct:	
Tangible	Increased farm output
	New supply of water
Intangible	Maintaining family farms
Indirect:	
Tangible	Reduced soil erosion
Intangible	Preservation of rural society
Real Costs	
Direct:	
Tangible	Construction material, labor, operations and maintenance
	Direct program supervision from agency
Intangible	Loss of recreational value of land or river
Indirect:	
Tangible	Administrative overhead of government
	Diversion of water and its effects on downstream users and wildlife
	Increased salinity of water released downstream
Intangible	Loss of wilderness area
Transfers:	Relative improvement of profit for farm equipment industry
	General taxpayers may be subsidizing the farmers

difficult to measure, it is important to indicate any significant assumption that affects the analysis. For example, in measuring "increased farm output" in Table 19.3, the evaluator should indicate whether the valuation is based on gross output value, or some net value, such as increased farm profits. In addition, the evaluator should indicate whether the output increase is due to greater yield from current agricultural land or whether it results from placing more land into production. The following sections explore the issues and problems of measuring and valuing benefits and costs.

Measuring Benefits

After all possible benefits and costs are identified, the next step is to measure them. From a private firm's perspective, their computation is straightforward. The benefits are the revenues received; the costs are the firm's payments for its factors of production (land, labor, and capital); net benefits (or costs) are the difference between the two. Both are measured by market prices.

The evaluation problem is much more difficult for government programs because benefits and costs of these may not be reflected or easily measured in market prices. Also, cost issues pose some problems, but measuring program benefits is generally more difficult than determining costs. The more complex the program objectives (such as those for Urban Renewal), the more difficult will be the benefit analysis because it often involves multiple goals aimed at different beneficiary groups (business interests, the poor, the middle class, and so on).

There are numerous potential sources of data for analysis of program benefits:

1. Existing records and statistics kept by the agency, legislative committees, or agency watchdogs—such as the U.S. General Accounting Office
2. Feedback from the program's clients, either the general population or the subset of the population the program is serving, obtained through a questionnaire or focus group
3. Ratings by trained observers
4. Experience of other governments or private or nonprofit organizations
5. Special data gathering

Evaluation design and data collection procedures are discussed more fully in previous chapters in this volume; however, a caveat is in order: data collection is not cost free. While the evaluator wants to have as much information as possible on both benefits and costs, he or she must weigh the value of the increased accuracy gained from the accumulation of new data against the costs associated with the data collection. Thus the first order of priority for the evaluator is to assimilate *existing* data to determine whether it is sufficient for the analysis. The more costly the project or program, the more the evaluator may want to supplement existing data with new data collected by the evaluator through questionnaires, experiments, surveys, or other research evaluation techniques.

Valuing the Benefits

Most economists argue that despite their imperfections, market prices are the best valuation of a benefit. Therefore the evaluator should use a *market value* when one is available, or a surrogate such as *willingness to pay*. For most government programs the recipients are not paying for the benefits received; therefore, the evaluator must make an alternative assessment of value. For example, the value of a "free" outdoor swimming pool might be the amount people are willing to pay for a similar swimming experience in a private or nonprofit pool.

Cost Savings as a Benefit. *Cost avoidance* or cost savings are also benefits. Thus an anticrime program might measure dollars saved from avoided burglaries. An antiflood program might measure dollars saved from avoiding flood damage. A health program might measure avoided costs such as medical care expenditures and loss of productivity. To determine the amount of cost avoidance, the evaluator would have to look at historical data and trends before and after implementation of the government program and estimate the effect of the program on other government spending and the general public.

For example, if a new dam built for flood control purposes prevented a loss of $10 million from flooding that periodically occurred in the community, the $10 million is a cost savings. The annual benefit to the community would be expressed as $10 million times the risk that such a flood would occur in any given year. If on average the community was flooded every ten years, than the yearly benefit would be $1 million ($10 million times 1/10).

Similarly, if the financial loss to burglaries was increasing at a rate of 10 percent a year in a community and a new "neighborhood watch" program decreased the loss increase rate to just 2 percent a year, the evaluator might conclude, all other factors remaining the same, that the program had saved the community an 8-percent-a-year increase in losses. While it is true that "all other factors" seldom remain exactly the same, the evaluator needs to assess whether other significant events or changes in the community might also have affected the burglary rate.

Often the government expenditure can be justified solely on the savings to the government itself. Thus a prenatal health care program for low-income women might have reduced the incidence of low-weight births by one-half. The savings to the federal-state Medicaid program alone might exceed the costs of the prenatal program. However, it is not always easy for the evaluator to conclude that expenditures in Program X led to a decrease in Program Y. There may be other factors — unrelated to Program X — that also contributed to the decrease in Program Y.

Time Saved as a Benefit. *Time saved* is a tangible benefit. However, measurement of its value is more subjective. Each person may value his or her time differently. A common method of estimating the value of time is by using the economists' theory of work-leisure trade off. When people have control over the hours they are working, they will work (including overtime) until their subjective value of leisure is equal to the income they would gain from one more hour of work — their after-tax wage rate.

Using the after-tax wage rate is not without problems. Many people cannot choose their hours of work, and not all uses away from the job are equally valuable. For example, to avoid spending time in rush hour traffic, persons who dislike driving might be willing to pay at a rate exceeding their wages. On the other hand, persons who use the road for non–rush hour, pleasure driving, might not care about the opportunity cost of their time. Thus the value of a person's time will vary with when the saved time occurs and with the particular circumstances.

An alternate valuation of time is to look at willingness to pay for faster transportation. If commuting by train is more expensive but quicker than commuting by bus, we can infer how much travelers are willing to pay to reduce their commuting time and therefore their valuation of their time. In another example, if people pay to use a new toll road at a cost of $1 and save fifteen minutes in travel time, we can infer that the value of time saved to them is at least $4/hour. The average benefit may be higher: some commuters may be willing to pay more than $1 to save fifteen minutes. On the basis of several such studies, a reasonable estimate of the effective value of traveling time is about 60 percent of the before-tax wage rate (Rosen, 1992, citing Small, 1983). The average nonagricultural wage is generally used as the wage-rate measurement, leading to a value of time at $6 to $7 an hour.

Valuing Lives. Saving lives, or *lives saved,* is clearly a real, tangible benefit — an inestimatable value to the person whose life was saved — and the justification for many government health and safety programs. Our religious and cultural values suggest that life is priceless, and numerous examples (such as the child who fell into the well hole in Texas) show that people have expended an enormous amount of time and money to save just one life. But considering life to be priceless poses a problem for the evaluator. Kenneth A. Small (cited in Rosen, 1992, p. 255) notes that if the value of life is infinite, any project that leads to even a single life being saved has an infinitely high present value. This position, however, leaves no sensible way to determine the admissibility of projects. If *every* road in the United States were a divided four-lane highway, traffic fatalities would undoubtedly decrease. Does it follow, then, that four-laning every road in the country would be a good project?

Similarly, we could save many lives if we reduced the speed limit nationwide to twenty-five miles an hour. What is the cost here? It is the lost time involved for movement of people and goods. Since we have chosen not to impose such a slow speed limit, does this mean that we do not value lives saved as much as the cost of time? Implicitly yes, so lives do not have an infinite value. The question for the evaluator is how to value a life.

Economists have developed two methods to value a human life. The first, which is often used in civil court cases, estimates the individual's lost earnings for his or her remaining life. The problem is that this would cause us to value a young college graduate on the verge of a career more highly than a senior citizen who has retired or who has few work years remaining. A second approach looks at people's acceptance of higher-risk jobs and their related higher salaries as payment for a higher probability of death. Thus, it is possible to impute a value of life based on a willingness to forego the higher salary. The problem with this approach is the uncertainty surrounding the job risk and whether people have a knowledge of the death probability versus the salary rewards. In addition, people differ widely in the extent of their risk aversion.

Do these dilemmas mean that the evaluator's task is hopeless? Certainly if the chief benefit of a government program is to save lives, a benefit-cost analysis will be extremely sensitive to the evaluator's choice of a dollar figure per life saved. In such a case, it is not clear that a benefit-cost analysis is superior to a cost-effectiveness analysis, which would simply calculate the cost of the program per life saved without making a judgment on the value of life. But what if the program also has other objectives, such as preventing serious injuries or property damages? One approach is to relate total program costs to several measures of effectiveness, some of which might be quantified in dollar terms (property damages prevented) while others would be quantified in nondollar terms (so many lives saved or serious injuries prevented). While this approach does not produce one bottom-line figure, it does provide the decision maker with all the relevant information about the program.

Looking at the problem in a slightly different way, the National Highway Traffic Safety Administration (Office of Regulatory Analysis, 1990) has converted injuries prevented to "equivalent" fatalities prevented based on "willingness to pay" (determined by a study of what individuals typically pay for small increases in their safety) and the cost that the rest of society bears when an individual is killed or injured. Their values per injury ranged from $4,000 to $1.5 million (1986 dollars) depending on the severity of injury, with an average value of about $100,000. Assuming a fatality cost of $2 million they determined that 20 injuries were "equivalent" to one fatality, and have analyzed programs (such as passive restraint requirements) on a cost per "equivalent" life saved.

Even with this approach, the National Highway Traffic Safety Administration needed to use a figure ($2 million) for loss of life in order to convert injuries to equivalent fatalities. While placing a value on life may seem insensitive, in a world of scarce resources we may have no choice. One method is to determine the value of life required for the analysis to indicate a positive net benefit and simply leave to the decision makers the question of whether that amount is appropriate. In any case, where lives saved are a major component of the benefit equation, the specific assumptions on the valuation of a life must be made clear and a sensitivity analysis conducted to determine how sensitive the final benefit-cost results are to the choice of valuation.

In estimating how many lives were saved or injuries avoided, evaluators typically use before and after studies to determine the effectiveness of certain government programs or health and safety requirements. This often is a major evaluation problem, however, as program outcomes may be affected by other concurrent factors (such as use of alcohol and drugs or willingness to use seat belts).

Increased Productivity or Wages. *Increased productivity* is a common benefit goal of many government investment programs, either capital investments, such as roads, bridges, water projects, and other infrastructure developments, and human capital investments, such as education and job training. Typically these benefits might be measured in increased profits or lifetime earnings.

An evaluation of an education program designed to decrease the rate of high school dropouts could compare unemployment rates and earnings of such dropouts with high school graduates (using data from the U.S. Department of Labor's Bureau of Labor Statistics). There are two distinct benefits of finishing high school. The first is to the individual, measured by increased lifetime earnings less transfer payments the individual would have received from government (unemployment compensation or welfare payments), minus the increased taxes the individual now must pay to the government. The second benefit is to society, measured by decreased transfer payments made to the individual and by the increased taxes he or she pays. The Job Corps illustration at the end of the chapter provides one approach to presenting this type of information.

Economic development projects are often justified on the grounds that they create new jobs. Furthermore, some jobs are viewed more favorably than others. "Export" jobs (those that produce goods and services that extend beyond the jurisdiction) are thought to create additional jobs within a community. Economists use *multipliers* to determine total new job creations and the choice of an appropriate multiplier is often subject to debate — it clearly is a key assumption that must be identified for the decision maker. If the new jobs reduce the level of unemployment in a jurisdiction they certainly produce measurable benefits both for those previously unemployed and for the government (increased taxes and decreased transfer payments). However, if the new jobs create an in-migration of families, the net benefits to the jurisdiction are not as clear. New families create costs to the community in terms of increased service demands even as they bring new revenues. Evaluators often fail to consider those community costs sufficiently.

In many cases an evaluator is looking at programs that have already incurred costs but may have a benefit stream, such as increased lifetime wages, that extend beyond the timeframe for the program. It is important to convert that future stream of benefits into present value.

The Value of Recreational Benefits. *Recreational values* are typically based on the concept of "willingness to pay." The evaluator first must determine the number of people who have visited a particular recreational area and then attempt to value each "user day" of recreation. Several techniques are used.

One approach is to ask recreational users what they would be willing to pay to use a particular recreational area (park or wilderness). The problem with this technique is that respondents may answer "strategically." If they think they may have to pay to use a favorite park in the future, they may give a figure lower than the true value to them. On the other hand, if they think the response may influence continued provision of the recreation, they may place a value higher than the true value. In many cases, statements of "willingness" have differed from actual behavior.

A second technique is to actually cost out what users pay to travel to the recreation area — plane fares, rentals, gasoline, travel time, and so on. This works best for recreational sites, such as national parks, that draw visitors from a wide area.

Finally, evaluators sometimes look at similar recreational experiences in the private sector. The value of public swimming pools or tennis courts might be assessed at rates similar to the costs to users of similar private facilities in the area.

In addition to the value to users, recreational areas may have some indirect benefits that should be valued. The availability of urban recreation may reduce the incidence of juvenile delinquency and the cost of the local criminal justice system. Major recreational areas may draw out-of-state visitors who increase local profits in hotels, restaurants, and related establishments. There also may be some indirect costs, including road congestion and increased recreational injuries.

Option or existence value is an offshoot of the "willingness to pay" concept for certain types of recreation. Even if a person does not intend to visit a wilderness area, for example, that person may desire to preserve some wilderness areas in the country in order to maintain the option for himself or others of visiting them at some time in the future, or a person may simply value knowing that wilderness areas exist. Putting a price tag on these values is difficult although surveys have attempted to ascertain the value to individuals.

Land Values. *Increased land values* may be a benefit depending on the geographic scope of the analysis. The larger the scope, the more likely it is that a transfer of wealth rather than a net increase in value is occurring. Thus, if a government investment decision increases the value of one parcel of land by making it more accessible (a highway interchange is built adjacent to the parcel), the effect is to make other parcels of land relatively less valuable, assuming the interchange has not increased the total demand for land in the jurisdiction. A new community park may increase the value of the residences near the park relative to those residences farther away from it, but it is unlikely to have an overall impact on the demand for housing in the community.

Alternatives to Market Prices. Because evaluators are not always satisfied with market price or "willingness to pay" as the only basis for benefit evaluation, they have developed a variety of attempts to frame value in alternative ways. In examining a Louisiana coastal wetlands program, researchers determined that its market value was about $500 an acre, based on willingness to pay. But when researchers asked individuals what they would be willing to pay for the *services* provided for the wetlands, its value turned out to be much higher. Depending upon how the future value of the acreage was calculated, commercial fishing added between $317 and $846 per acre; trapping, $151–$401; recreation, $46–$181; and storm protection, $1,915–$7,549. In addition, some argued that the wetlands is a large solar energy receptor that supports the production of economically valuable products such as fish and wildlife. This energy can be converted to a value of a similar amount of energy from fossil fuels. When these values were combined (and there may be some double counting), researchers gave their best estimate of the economic value of Louisiana wetlands as between $2,500 and $17,000 for each acre depending on the discount rate assumed (Constanza and Wainger, 1990).

The wetlands example indicates the wide range of estimates of value that could be attached to certain program benefits. These broad estimates are particularly likely when there is no comparable private sector market for the benefit, when the benefit has some intangible qualities, or when the nature of the benefit can be viewed from a number of different perspectives.

Table 19.4 provides a summary of benefits often found in government programs, some approaches to their measurement, and issues and assumptions with which the evaluator must be concerned.

Measuring Costs

Costs are commonly believed to be somewhat easier to measure than benefits. This is true if all the costs are contained within the agency operating the program. Unfortunately, the real world is seldom so cooperative. For example, most government programs require supervision and general administrative overhead, and many impose costs on the private sector. Thus program costs to other agencies and third parties must be measured as well as the costs to the agency managing the program. Costs include indirect expenses to other governmental agencies (including overhead agencies like finance and purchasing), and costs imposed on private individuals and firms (such as the cost of complying with regulations).

   Direct costs, such as for personnel, material, and equipment, are often relatively easy to account for and are contained in agency budget and financial documents. Indirect costs, however, are more difficult to assess. The evaluator also has to decide how to deal with certain capital and intangible costs. Cost allocation issues have received significant attention in financial and accounting journals; however, there are many areas where there is not universal agreement on the best approach. Several approaches are discussed below.

Cost Categories

In examining various types of program costs, both direct and indirect, the following categories will assist the evaluator:

1.   *One-time, fixed, or up-front costs:* planning, research and development (R&D), pilot projects, computer software, and others
2.   *Ongoing investment costs:* land, buildings and facilities, equipment and vehicles, initial workforce training
3.   *Recurring costs:* operations and maintenance; personnel salaries, wages and fringe benefits; materials and supplies; overhead costs
4.   *Compliance costs:* time required for citizens to fill out forms; cost to business of new health and safety or EPA regulation
5.   *Mitigation measures:* to prevent a cost to government or to others; for example, pollution control equipment or relocation costs for affected persons or animals

Valuing Indirect Costs

Many consulting firms and other profit and nonprofit agencies, such as colleges and universities, employ a standard indirect cost allocation figure on

Table 19.4. Approaches to Measuring Benefits.

Benefits	Approaches to Measurement	Key Issues and Assumptions
Lives Saved	1. Estimate individual lost earnings. 2. Choose arbitrary value ($1 million) and test sensitivity of analysis to figure. 3. View as an "intangible" and weigh with other information.	• Are individuals valued equally, or are the young and productive more valuable than the old and less productive? • Where principal benefit is lives saved, cost-effectiveness analysis may be the superior analytical approach.
Time Saved	1. Multiply after-tax hourly wages by hours saved. 2. Collect indications of users' willingness to pay tolls to save time.	• Individuals value time differently. • Not all individuals could convert time saved into increased earnings. • Some individuals would pay more than others to save time.
Costs Saved or Avoided	1. Analyze costs before and after program action and measure differences. These include costs saved by individuals as well as government.	• Other nonprogram factors may influence costs. • Costs saved to some may be costs borne by others and thus may simply be a transfer rather than a net gain for society.
Increased Output	1. Measure increase units times unit value based where possible on "willingness to pay." 2. Use private sector market price where available or price of similar private good or service.	• Be aware of *co-production* and *multicausation* problems. • Public output may not have a similar private sector value. • Survey data may not lead to accurate pricing.
Increased Productivity	1. Measure increased output or profits to firms. 2. Measure increase in lifetime earnings for individuals.	• Increased taxes collected by government are a transfer from individuals and firms and while important, cannot be double counted with the broader benefit.
Increased Jobs	1. Measure gain in lifetime earning for residents of jurisdiction. 2. Measure gain to jurisdiction from increased revenues as a result of in-migration of jobs.	• Increased taxes paid by residents are a transfer; increased taxes paid by new workers as a result of in-migration must also be offset with the costs of providing services to the new families.
Increased Recreation	1. Multiply number of recreational user days times willingness to pay. 2. Measure travel costs of visitors of national parks to gauge value. 3. Spillover benefits may include cost savings (reduced crime or health costs) and increases in local economy.	• User fees charged may be an insufficient indication of value, especially if fees are kept low to encourage greater use of facilities. • Similar private sector recreational facilities may offer possible indication of willingness to pay. • Recreational facilities often must be disaggregated to determine values (open spaces versus specific facilities).

top of their direct costs—often computed at 30 percent to 60 percent of the total direct costs or a subset of direct costs, such as personnel expenditures. State and local governments also use an indirect cost allocation figure in determining reimbursement for certain federal grants-in-aid programs. These percentages are based on total administrative overhead costs compared with all other expenditures (or all personnel expenditures) from all other programs.

The major controversy with such indirect cost allocations is whether a specific program really adds marginal cost to the overhead agencies. That is, does the program cause increased administrative burdens on the central administrative staff? A state government will have an office for the governor and attorney general, a legislature, and certain overhead agencies (finance, personnel, purchasing) regardless of whether a particular program exists; but additional programs do cause additional workload on those agencies, which may require an increase in their personnel and other needs. The application of the appropriate overhead rate is a significant judgment call for the evaluator; the analysis might be highly sensitive to the choice made.

Costs to the Private Sector. Government often shifts program costs to the private sector, especially in regulatory activity. When the Environmental Protection Agency (EPA) mandates the installation of scrubbers on electric utilities or the purchase of higher-cost low-sulfur coal in order to reduce acid rain (as legislated in the 1991 Clean Air Act), the program expenses are not just the regulatory agencies' costs of enforcing the new requirements. The costs to the electric utilities, which will likely be passed forward to the consumers of the utilities' power, must also be considered.

Sometimes costs to the private sector are easy to identify, such as the increased expense of manufacturing an automobile that has a passive restraint system. At other times, regulations impose additional reporting requirements, causing an increase in clerical staff for business or a loss of time to individuals who must wade through the additional bureaucratic regulations and procedures. These costs should be identified and valued. Time lost should be valued just as time saved was valued on the benefit side of the analysis.

Valuing the Use of Capital. The cost of capital assets should be spread out over their expected useful life. There are many standard depreciation schedules for buildings and other capital equipment. For government programs an estimate needs to be made of the asset's useful life considering physical deterioration, potential for obsolescence, salvage value at the end of the program, and other factors. Normally, the asset (minus its final salvage value) is depreciated equally for each year of its life (straight-line depreciation); however, there may be factors that suggest a more rapid depreciation during the project's early life. The market value of the asset is not a useful guide for depreciation unless the agency expects to use the asset for a limited time period.

Land poses a particular problem because, unlike other capital facilities and equipment, it is not consumed; however, it has alternative uses.

Land used for one activity cannot be used for another; however, it can be sold to raise funds for other activities. Its value for a particular program is its opportunity cost to the government—normally expressed as the market value of the land times the prevailing rate of interest for government investments (for example, the long-term U.S. Treasury bill rate). In addition, if the land was taken out of the private sector, the government is foregoing revenue from private sector landowners in the form of property taxes. While some economists consider all taxes to be transfers, an evaluator might conclude that this lost revenue represented part of the cost of the program operations.

Sometimes a program will use land or other capital assets already owned by government. This use, however, is not free. The use of the capital assets in Program X, results in an *opportunity cost* for using them in Program X rather than in Program Y or for another government purpose. An alternative costing approach to the one suggested earlier for land (market value times interest rate) is to determine the assets' fair market rental value. Many governments have established auxiliary enterprise functions to recover the costs of certain types of capital goods, such as computers or office facilities, through rental charges.

Valuing the Damage Effects of Government Programs. Unfortunately, government actions do not have only beneficial effects; some impact the environment adversely, and others have unintended consequences on certain populations. A new dam may flood a wildlife habitat, or an urban renewal program may displace low-income housing.

Often governments try to mitigate adverse consequences of their actions and the compensation costs are considered in the analysis. However, even if the government has not taken actions to mitigate damages to others, those damages should be counted. If it is impossible to calculate the dollar value of the damage (such as certain environmental consequences), one method of evaluating the damage is to calculate what it would have cost the government to mitigate the damage had it chosen to do so. For example, if a government action eliminates a feeding ground for certain wildlife, the evaluator might calculate the value of that loss by determining what it would have cost the government to provide an equivalent habitat.

Other Cost Issues. *Sunk costs* are defined as investments previously made in a program or project—such as original research and development costs—compared to ongoing costs. In evaluating the total benefits and costs of a program, the evaluator will consider all previous costs. However, when recommending future action on a program or project, sunk costs should be ignored as they have no impact on the marginal costs and benefits of continuing the project or program.

Interest costs are sometimes counted as a program or project cost if the program was financed through debt. The interest cost would be included if the program or project was designed to be self-sufficient with revenues paying for total costs (as with a specific recreational facility or a water or sewer project). From a budgetary perspective, interest payments are clearly a cost. Some economists argue, however, that interest payments simply reflect the government's time payment for money and that different governments' needs to borrow vary greatly. Therefore, if the evaluator is doing a comparison of programs across jurisdictions, the inclusion of interest payments, while representing a real cost to the jurisdictions that are borrowing, may give a faulty comparison of program efficiency.

Analysis of Benefits-Costs

Once the evaluator has determined the range of benefits and costs and placed dollar values on them (or chosen not to in the case of certain intangibles), the next step is to present the information in a usable format for the decision maker. There are three possible approaches, all of which might be used:

1. A *retrospective* analysis that looks at historical data on benefits and costs and converts them into a net present value for the program
2. A *snapshot* analysis that looks at current year benefits and costs
3. A *prospective* analysis that projects future benefits and costs of the program based on the retrospective analysis

Importance of Converting Stream of Benefits and Costs to Present Value

Program evaluation almost always requires the analyst to compare benefits and costs that occurred in different time periods. For example, a program designed to prevent students from dropping out of high school may require substantial expenditures during the targeted students' high school years but yield benefits many years into the future. The program's costs are almost all up front and include expenditures for additional teachers, counselors, and materials as well as lost earnings of the students who stay in school. Long-term benefits include increased productivity of the student in future years (higher wages) and cost avoidance by government (reduced welfare and criminal justice expenditures). But a million dollar cost in year 1 is more costly than a million dollar benefit in year 20. Government has lost the value of the million dollars for those twenty years.

Economists convert the stream of benefits and costs of a project or program to equivalent dollars through the use of present value analysis. The *net present value* of a program is expressed as the sum of benefits (B) minus costs (C) in year 1 plus $B-C/1 + r$ in year 2 (where r = the government's discount rate), plus $B-C/(1 + r) (1 + r)$ in year 3, and so on, using the formula expressed in the benefit-cost illustration in this chapter.

Choice of an appropriate discount rate for government is subject to considerable debate. Many economists argue for the use of a before- or after-tax private sector interest rate based on the theory that government expenditures require taxation or borrowing that takes money out of the private sector, and therefore government should be held to a similar investment standard. Others argue that government exists to operate programs the private sector will not; therefore, a low *social discount rate,* 2 percent to 3 percent, is the appropriate standard. Still others suggest using the rate at which government can borrow funds (such as long-term Treasury bill rates for long-term projects) as the best measure of a government's opportunity costs.

It is important for the evaluator to recognize that conducting a present value analysis is not the same as adjusting for inflation. But a decision to use current (nominal) or constant (adjusted for inflation) dollars does affect the choice of an appropriate discount rate. If benefits and costs are not discounted for inflation, the choice of a discount rate should reflect the full market rate, that is, a real rate of return plus inflation. However, if the stream of benefits and costs is adjusted for inflation and expressed in constant dollars, the selected discount rate should be a real rate of return (such as a private sector rate — or government rate — minus inflation). Regardless of the decision to express results in nominal or constant dollars, the valuation of benefits and costs must be consistent with the discount rate.

During the Reagan-Bush administrations, the U.S. Office of Management and Budget (OMB) mandated the use of a 10 percent discount rate for federal government programs. This rate was chosen during the early 1980s when inflation was high; it is unduly excessive in a low inflation economy. OMB also required agencies to deflate the stream of future benefits and costs, reducing them by the current inflation rate. OMB's requirement that agencies use an "inflated" discount rate and a deflated stream of benefits and costs doubly penalizes agency projects that have high up-front costs and long-term benefits. Recently, under President Clinton, OMB has adjusted its discount rate policy, requiring agencies to use prevailing Treasury bill rates.

Because there is no universal agreement as to the appropriate discount rate, evaluators are urged to use a range of discount rates and determine whether the results of the analysis are sensitive to the choice of discount rate. If so, then this issue must be drawn to the attention of the decision maker.

Presenting the Results

The *net present value* of benefits minus costs or costs minus benefits is the most traditional format for government agencies to use in presenting the results of the program evaluation; however, a benefit-cost ratio is sometimes used when comparing similar programs. The *benefit-cost ratio* is determined by dividing total present value of benefits by total present value of costs. If benefits equal $20 million and cost $10 million, the program is said to have a benefit-cost ratio of 2 to 1 or 2.0. Unlike those in the private sector, government evaluators usually do not conduct a *return on investment (ROI)* analysis; however, that also can be computed. It is the appropriate discount rate to yield total present value benefits equal to costs.

There are three critical issues in presenting the results of a benefit-cost analysis. First is the perspective of the evaluator. Second is the use of a *sensitivity analysis* to determine how certain key assumptions might affect the outcome of the analysis. Third is how nonquantifiable costs and benefits are handled in the analysis.

The "Appropriate" Perspective. Benefits and costs are often in the eye of the beholder. A cost to one person or government agency may appear to be a benefit to another. For example, if the federal government provides a low-cost loan to a state government for public infrastructure purposes, the costs of the loan may differ depending on whether the program is being evaluated from the perspective of the federal or the state government. To the federal government, the cost is the opportunity cost of the funds (borrowed at long-term Treasury rates) less the repayments made by the state government. The state government, however, would be concerned only with its outlays, not the opportunity cost to the federal government. From the taxpayers' perspective, the general federal taxpayer is subsidizing a particular group of taxpayers in the state benefiting from the program.

Similarly, federal regulations to reduce air pollution will provide a large and diffuse benefit to the general taxpayer/citizen while the costs will be borne initially by the industries being regulated and ultimately by some group of individuals — the consumers of the firm's products in terms of higher prices, shareholders in terms of less profits, or workers in terms of lower wages. Who bears the ultimate cost of the regulation depends on a complicated reading of supply and demand issues — for the firm's product, for capital, and for labor.

The evaluator might approach the evaluation task from a number of perspectives. The broadest perspective would be societal in which costs and benefits are considered no matter where they fall. A less universal perspective would be from a particular jurisdiction, focusing on its benefits and costs (a local or statewide perspective) while ignoring spillover benefits and costs to neighboring jurisdictions. A third perspective would concentrate on the government's own cash flow or budgetary impact — how much the program is going to cost and how much new revenue it will bring in. Finally, a benefit-cost analysis could be conducted from the perspective of a group of taxpayers or clients on whom the program has an impact.

Which of these perspectives is appropriate depends on the purpose of the evaluation. If the evaluation is being conducted to determine whether a proposed government expenditure will pay for itself in terms of increased revenue, the appropriate perspective would be a budgetary or cash flow perspective. However, in most cases government agency programs are designed to yield societal benefits, not just a revenue return to government. Therefore, the broader perspective is usually more appropriate.

Sensitivity Analysis. It is important for the program evaluator to test the sensitivity of the analysis to particular assumptions. What is the probability that those assumptions will occur? The advantage of LOTUS 123 and other computer-run spreadsheets is that they now allow the evaluator to examine a range of alternative assumptions and determine how they impact the analysis.

For example, an analysis of a highway safety program to prevent drunk driving will make certain assumptions about the number of lives saved and injuries prevented by the program. How confident is the evaluator of those numbers? If there were other nonprogrammatic factors that influenced the results (such as safer cars), how are those considered in the assumptions? Is $2 million the correct value to use for a life saved? What if a higher, or lower, figure were used? Where key assumptions are critical to the results of the analysis, they should be clearly identified for the decision maker.

Intangibles. No matter how creative the evaluator, there will be some benefits and costs that defy quantification. Even if you can value the cost of an injury, that dollar figure will not fully capture the pain and suffering involved, and financial savings from burglaries prevented does not fully capture the sense of security that comes with crime prevention. These are often important components of the benefit-cost equation and they should be identified and explained as clearly as possible. There is a tendency to relegate these issues to an afterthought or footnote. The danger with this approach is that benefits and costs that are easily identified and valued tend to drive the evaluation.

The best method for introducing issues surrounding intangible benefits and costs is to relate them to the dollar results. For example, if the analysis reveals net costs over benefits of $2 million but also reveals certain environmental benefits that could not be converted to dollars, it is easy to highlight the question of whether the environmental benefits over the period studied were worth the $2 million cost. If there were intangible costs as well as benefits, the benefits would have to be worth $2 million plus the intangible costs for the program to be considered a success. By juxtaposing dollars against intangibles, the evaluator asks the decision maker to weigh the intangibles against the known costs (or costs over dollar value of benefits).

An Illustration — The Job Corps. Table 19.5 provides an example of a benefit-cost analysis of the Job Corps program prepared for the U.S. Employment and Training Administration (Mathematica Policy Research, 1982). The analysis considered total social benefits and costs and further divided those into the perspective of the non-corpsmember (federal taxpayer) and the corpsmember. Recognizing that benefits of job training programs accrue long after program costs, the evaluators interviewed and monitored over a fifty-four-month period a sample of corpsmembers and non-corpsmember youth from a similar background. They concluded that overall the Job Corps was achieving the program objectives: increasing employment and earnings, improving future labor-market opportunities, reducing dependence on welfare, and reducing criminality.

Overall, the evaluators found that social benefits exceeded costs by over $2,300 in 1977 dollars or by 46 percent of costs (that is, the benefit-

Table 19.5. Estimated Net Present Values per
Corpsmember Under the Benchmark Assumptions (1977 Dollars).

	Perspective [a]		
	Social	Non-Corpsmember	Corpsmember
Benefits			
1. Output Produced by Corpsmembers			
• In-program output	$ 757	$ 673	$ 83
• Increased postprogram employment output	3,276	0	3,276
• Increased postprogram tax payments	0	596	−596
2. Reduced Dependence on Transfer Programs			
• Reduced public transfers	0	791	−791
• Reduced administrative cost	172	172	0
• Increased utility from reduced welfare dependence	+	+	+
3. Reduced Criminal Activity			
• Reduced criminal justice system costs	1,253	1,253	0
• Reduced personal injury and property damage	1,366	1,366	0
• Reduced stolen property	300	462	−162
• Reduced psychological costs	+	+	+
4. Reduced Drug/Alcohol Abuse			
• Reduced drug/alcohol treatment costs	31	31	0
• Increased utility from reduced drug/alcohol dependence	+	+	+
5. Reduced Utilization of Alternative Services			
• Reduced costs of training and education programs other than Job Corps	244	244	0
• Reduced training allowances	0	33	−33
6. Other Benefits			
• Increased utility from redistribution	+	+	+
• Increased utility from improved well-being of corpsmembers	+	+	+
Total Benefits	$7,399	$5,621	$1,777
Costs			
1. Program Operating Expenditures			
• Center operating expenditures, excluding transfers to corpsmembers	$2,796	$2,796	$ 0
• Transfers to corpsmembers	0	1,208	−1,208
• Central administrative costs	1,347	1,347	0
2. Opportunity Cost of Corpsmember Labor During the Program			
• Foregone output	881	0	881
• Foregone tax payments	0	153	−153

[a]In addition to the value to society as a whole, the estimates are calculated from the non-corpsmember and corpsmember perspectives in order to indicate redistributional effects. In this way, corpsmembers are treated like nontaxpayers (except for their own taxes) to simplify the exposition, and the non-corpsmember category encompasses everyone in society other than corps-members.

Table 19.5. Estimated Net Present Values per
Corpsmember Under the Benchmark Assumptions (1977 Dollars), Cont'd.

	Perspective		
	Social	Non-Corpsmember	Corpsmember
3. Unbudgeted Expenditures Other Than Corpsmember Labor			
• Resource costs	46	46	0
• Transfers to corpsmembers	0	185	−185
Total Costs	$5,070	$5,735	−$665
Net Present Value (Benefits minus Costs)	$2,327	−$115	$2,442
Benefit-Cost Ratio [b]	1.46	0.98	1.99

[b]The numerators for the benefit-cost ratios include all the benefits listed in this table as either positive benefits or negative costs, and the denominator includes all the costs listed in this table as either positive costs or negative benefits.
Source: Mathematica Policy Research, 1982.

cost ratio was 1.46). Naturally, the bulk of the benefits accrued to corpsmembers in terms of increased employment output and net benefits to corpsmembers exceeded $2,400. A majority of the costs were borne by non-corpsmembers (the federal taxpayer), but that group also received considerable benefits in terms of increased tax payments by corpsmembers, reduced welfare, reduced criminal justice costs, and less personal and property damage. Costs exceeded benefits for non-corpsmembers by only $115. The evaluators also listed certain intangibles, simply indicating their positive value without attempting to assign them a value (reduced psychological costs, improved well-being of corpsmembers). Had the total social costs exceeded benefits, these intangible benefits might have been more crucial to the analysis.

I find two faults with the data in the table. First, although the benefits and costs were expressed in a present value (1977 dollars), the choice of a discount rate is not made explicit in the table or presented in the summary information provided to the decision maker. Since the evaluators are dealing with a future increased earnings stream of the corpsmembers, the choice of a higher (or lower) discount rate might significantly affect the analysis. Second, while summary data indicate that alternative benefit-cost calculations were made for a wide range of assumptions and a "sensitivity analysis . . . confirms that [the] Job Corps is an economically efficient program" (Mathematica Policy Research, 1982, p. vii), there is no summary of the key factors that influenced the outcome of the analysis. The evaluators do note the importance of corpsmembers displacing other workers in the labor markets, but they make no attempt to calculate this cost to non-corpsmembers. If such displacement was substantial, it obviously would have a negative cost impact on the analysis.

Particular Problems in a Benefit-Cost Analysis. A number of additional challenging problems confront the program evaluator conducting a benefit-cost analysis. Two of these, equity issues and multiple causation problems, are discussed below.

Equity Concerns. While distributional issues may not be important in private sector financial analysis, they are important in examining benefits and costs of government programs. Of concern to policymakers is not just the total benefits and costs but also who benefits and who pays. These threads are not always easy to untangle, but when there are strong distributional consequences to the program, the issues should be noted. One method of doing so was the approach used by the Job Corps evaluators in Table 19.5—breaking down total costs by specific sets of beneficiaries: the corpsmembers and all others (the non-corpsmembers). Most programs target specific beneficiary groups with the general taxpayers bearing the cost burden.

Some researchers have suggested that benefits and costs should be weighted. For example, the evaluator could weight a benefit or cost to a low-income family at twice the value of a similar benefit and cost to a middle-income family and three times as much as a similar benefit to an upper-income family. The issue here is deciding on the appropriate weights. This determination must be a subjective judgment, and it may be one on which the evaluator and the policymakers do not agree.

Multiple Causation Problems. Perhaps the most difficult issue for evaluators is identifying and quantifying benefits that are influenced by factors outside the government program, including *multiple-causation* and *co-production* issues. For example, a government program to prevent low-weight births will set up screening programs, provide nutritional information to pregnant women, and perhaps even provide food stamps or vouchers. If the incidents of low-weight births decline, can the analyst conclude that the program was the cause of the decline? These types of programs are heavily influenced by how the client group responds (the co-production issue). There may be other influences on pregnant women that also affect their behavior (the multiple-causation issue). Without a controlled experiment it is hard to know which influence had the greatest effect. There may be other programs aimed at the issue, operated by different agencies or levels of government or nonprofit organizations. How can the evaluator determine which of the programs had the desired effect or calculate the amount of the effect for each of the programs?

There are no easy answers to this problem. Government seldom conducts controlled studies of its programs, the Job Corps evaluation in the illustration above being an exception. The evaluator can compare program effects in areas where there are no other programs or attempt to get the clients to reveal which program had the desired impact. The evaluator will need to be resourceful to identify relevant comparisons.

Conclusion

Benefit-cost analysis and cost-effectiveness analysis are not panaceas that will provide decision makers with "the answer." However, if evaluators provide an accurate framework of benefits and costs—attempting to identify them, measure them, and value them—they can give decision makers a wealth of information on which to base better decisions.

The biggest danger in such analysis is the "black box" syndrome. Instead of laying out the relevant issues, assumptions, and concerns, the evaluator may be tempted to hide the messiness of the analysis from the decision maker, presenting a concise answer as to net benefits or costs, or cost-effectiveness. A Scotsman once proclaimed that the "devil is in the detail"; however, it is the detail, the assumptions and the sensitivity of the analysis to particular assumptions, that may be of most use to the decision maker in judging the value and usefulness of the evaluator's work.

One way to highlight information for decision makers is to use a table that identifies key assumptions and the effect of marginal changes in the assumptions on the analysis. Table 19.6 is a simple illustration of this approach. A baseline analysis is presented for a proposed highway bypass designed to save area commuters time. Key assumptions on valuation of benefits would include the number of commuters being served by the bypass, the amount of time saved, and the valuation of that time. In addition, the choice of an appropriate discount rate may be critical as costs are predominantly upfront (the construction of the bypass) whereas the benefits accrue over a long period of time. In the illustration, clearly the choice of a discount rate and the valuation of the commuters' time saved have the greatest effect on the analysis; these would be key issues for decision makers.

In Chapter Twenty-two of this handbook, Sonnichsen indicates that decision makers often have neither the time nor the desire to plow through a detailed evaluation such as a benefit-cost analysis. They are looking for "the answer." It is the evaluators' task to provide information in such a way that the policymakers can focus on the key questions and assumptions and their relationship to a range of possible answers.

Table 19.6. Presentation of Benefit-Cost Results
(Simple Transportation Example).

Baseline Analysis:	*20 year benefits-costs:*
Key Assumptions:	
• 10,000 commuters save 15 min/day	$14 million
• Time valued at $7 hour	
• Real discount rate of 3 percent	
Effect of Changes in Key Assumptions on Baseline Analysis:	
• 1,000 commuters served greater or less than baseline	+/– $2 million
• Time valued at $1 more or less than baseline	+/– $3.5 million
• Commuter savings 1 minute more or less than baseline	+/– $1.4 million
• Discount rate 1 percent higher or lower than baseline	+/– $12.5 million

References

Constanza, R., and Wainger, L. "Putting a Price on Swampland." *Washington Post,* September 2, 1990, p. B3.

Levin, H. M. *Cost-Effectiveness, a Primer.* New Perspectives in Evaluation, vol. 4. Newbury Park, Calif.: Sage, 1983.

Mathematica Policy Research. "Evaluation of the Economic Impact of the Job Corps Program." Third follow-up report. Washington, D.C.: Office of Policy Evaluation and Research, Employment and Training Administration, U.S. Department of Labor, September 1982.

Musgrave, R., and Musgrave, P. *Public Finance in Theory and Practice.* New York: McGraw-Hill, 1989.

Office of Regulatory Analysis. *Final Regulatory Impact Analysis, Extension of the Automatic Restraint Requirements of FMVSS 208 to Trucks, Buses, and Multipurpose Vehicle Weight Rating of 8,500 Pounds or Less and an Unloaded Vehicle Weight of 5,500 Pounds or Less.* Washington, D.C.: Office of Regulatory Analysis, National Highway Traffic Safety Administration, November 1990.

Rosen, H. S. *Public Finance.* (3rd ed.) Homewood, Ill.: Irwin, 1992.

Part Four_____

Planning and Managing Evaluation for Maximum Effectiveness

_____

Program evaluation involves many challenges beyond the issues that arise in evaluation design, data collection, and data analysis. Evaluators should make all reasonable efforts to (1) gain and hold the interest, confidence, and support of policymakers, managers, and other intended users of evaluation information; (2) maintain the cooperation of program managers, staff, clients, and others who provide needed evaluation data; (3) present evaluations clearly; and (4) stimulate the actions needed to improve public programs and communicate their value to policymakers and the public.

The five chapters in this part of the handbook describe methods for planning and managing evaluation programs and projects as well as ways to present evaluation results and get those results used. These chapters discuss

- Management of evaluation units
- Management of individual evaluation projects
- Evaluators as change agents
- Effective reporting of evaluation results
- Maximizing the use of evaluation findings

Evaluation planning and management are still more art than science. Those in charge of evaluation programs and projects face difficult challenges in producing credible findings and in getting their findings used by policymakers, managers, and other stakeholders. Since procedures for these areas are far less formalized than are the procedures for research design, data collection, and data analysis, it is not surprising that differences appear among the authors of these chapters. Some chapter authors see the planning and management of individual evaluation projects as technical; others see these activities as highly political. In these less than fully charted waters, there is helpful guidance in both positions.

Eleanor Chelimsky, in Chapter Twenty, discusses planning for the success of a program evaluation unit. The chapter suggests how the evaluation manager can integrate program evaluation into policy formulation and program implementation. Chelimsky proposes ways that managers of evaluation units can establish and maintain the legitimacy of evaluation with their agency's top managers and with the unit's customers, analyze the information needs of the unit's principal customers, implement evaluation work that satisfies those information needs that can be met within the time and resources available, and establish and maintain the unit's credibility. The performance of each task is illustrated with experience from a major evaluation unit in the U.S. General Accounting Office.

James B. Bell, in Chapter Twenty-one, discusses the leadership and management of evaluation projects to produce information that policymakers and program managers will use to enhance program performance. The chapter shows how evaluation project managers can gain and maintain agreement with sponsors clarifying the evaluation mandate, staff and organize their projects, make productive assignments to evaluation staff, monitor the progress of individual assignments and of the project as a whole, ensure the quality of the evaluation products, and ensure that evaluation products are used to improve program performance.

Richard C. Sonnichsen, in Chapter Twenty-two, discusses how evaluators can develop roles as credible change agents within their organizations. The chapter suggests how evaluators can develop recommendations for organizational change, present their findings and recommendations effectively, and achieve implementation of recommended changes. Sonnichsen illustrates his suggestions with examples from the work of the Federal Bureau of Investigation's office of planning, evaluation, and audits.

Michael Hendricks, in Chapter Twenty-three, shows how evaluators can develop useful recommendations and present their results effectively. The chapter offers suggestions on developing effective evaluation reports including briefings, interim reports, draft reports, and other vehicles by which evaluators can convey and facilitate the use of their findings. Hendricks also discusses the use of graphics, videotapes, and computerized slide presentations to present evaluation findings.

Reginald Carter, in Chapter Twenty-four, explores ways in which evaluators can maximize the use of findings from outcome monitoring systems and from evaluation studies. He proposes that evaluators can increase the use of monitoring and evaluation results by involving program managers and staff in defining performance criteria, producing timely information, developing realistic recommendations that focus on program improvement, facilitating multiple uses of evaluation data, sharing evaluation results with broad audiences, reminding decision makers of findings and recommendations, and assisting in implementing recommended changes.

In the final chapter, the editors discuss quality control of the evaluation process, selection and training of evaluators, ethics and standards for evaluation work, and incentives for the conduct and use of program evaluation. They then discuss trends in program evaluation and conclude with suggestions for minimizing evaluation costs and documenting evaluation results.

20

Making Evaluation Units Effective

Eleanor Chelimsky

Planning to conduct individual program evaluations and planning organizationally for their collective production and use are two different things. The first involves the well-known process of determining, for a given policy question, the methods appropriate for answering it. This includes crafting the study design, establishing comparisons, developing the measures on which data will be collected, investigating the potential data sources, and describing the analytical techniques to be used. Such a planning process usually follows traditional research pathways and focuses on the *technical* (that is, the methodological and statistical) aspects of providing evidence on a point of policy.

Planning for the success of a program evaluation *unit,* however—one that is typically lodged within a larger organization—involves excursions into lesser-known terrain and constitutes an essentially *political* activity that is only partly technical in nature. It is the second kind of planning that is the subject of this chapter. Like all planning, it has a goal: *to make a difference in the quality of public policy and public programs by informing the decisions of policymakers through the findings of program evaluations.* Although this goal is both irreproachable and familiar, it is also quite vague. Planners need more specific objectives to ground it in reality. Three objectives seem appropriate:

1. To integrate the unit—to the degree possible—with the larger organization housing it
2. To produce strong studies that are recognized for their quality and that meet the information needs of the evaluation unit's customers

The views and opinions expressed by the author are her own and should not be construed to be the policy or position of the General Accounting Office.

3. To achieve measurable use of individual study findings somewhere within the government policy or program process

This governmental process, as defined here, includes policy or program formulation, execution, and assessment. The reason is that evaluation findings, depending upon their character, can be used not only to refine the delivery and measurement of existing services and to improve their effectiveness and outreach but also to shape the development of new initiatives and to determine future directions for a policy or program.

These three objectives are tied to the planning goal by the recognition that an evaluation unit is not likely to improve the quality of public policy or programs in the particular areas of its concern unless it is somewhat secure in its agency backing; produces methodologically sound, policy-targeted work that is respected by its customers; and achieves use of its recommendations at the relevant points in the policy or program process.

What kinds of activities, then, flow from this goal and these objectives? How does a planner specifically go about making an evaluation unit a success? Clearly, there may be many variations in different situations, but four tasks must be performed successfully if the unit is to survive and have an effect. The tasks, which constitute the organizing framework of this chapter, are the following:

1. Establishing and maintaining the legitimacy of policy and program evaluation with the larger organization's top managers *and* with the unit's chief customers (who may or may not be identical)
2. Analyzing the information needs of the unit's principal evaluation user
3. Understanding the mission, structure (both formal and informal), and culture of the larger organization
4. Establishing credibility; that is, selecting staff, choosing topics, and determining the methodological approaches that should be emphasized to produce the strongest possible user-oriented studies

These tasks are not mutually exclusive; they all work together to achieve the three objectives. For the unit to be integrated, there must be acceptance in the larger organization of the utility of evaluation (task 1). But acceptance will be more easily achieved if evaluations are of high quality (task 4), if customers are pleased with them and want more (tasks 1, 2, and 4), and if unit planners understand how evaluation can best fit within the larger organization's culture (task 3).

The first task, then, is to convince both the larger organization's officials and the unit's chief customers, on a continuing basis, that evaluation is worth doing and that its findings will be useful to them. Achieving this goal is not always easy, but it is crucial, given that a strong customer constituency and real support from the larger organization's top management are prerequisites for finding the resources needed to do the evaluations in the first place.

Establishing Legitimacy

Logically, it would seem that program evaluation should not be hard to justify to customers and organizational top managers. After all, among partisans of effective government and especially those who understand social science research and its capabilities, the need for program evaluation has been accepted for over twenty-five years. The reasons typically given today for this need are the same ones put forward in the 1960s when evaluation was just starting, and again in the 1980s when budget cuts were causing evaluation units to be dismantled throughout the federal government. One observer, decrying the cuts, noted that it is social science research that "produces the methods of measurement and analysis and the concepts that make measurements possible in social, economic and health problems. When society's leaders plan to change the economy, they need also to know the effects of their changes. We know that innovations—social, medical and technological— often fail and that they therefore need evaluation. Social science research provides both the tools and the data for such evaluations. More constructively, it also provides the research to improve the success rates of future innovations" (Mosteller, 1981, p. 5).

One problem impeding the use of social science research is that not all top managers and policymakers in government or in the private sector understand *how* evaluation can improve public programs. Second, for those who do understand, it is not always clear that evaluation will help them personally. On the contrary, evaluation is seen by many managers—especially officials in government agencies—as a potential source of embarrassment. Evaluations are, in fact, often discouraged by decision makers, their results anticipated with apprehension, and their findings largely unused because of things like hierarchical bureaucratic relationships (such as "pleasing one's boss"), internal agency conflicts (jurisdictional arguments about who has the right to do what) or just the everyday competition for resources (Chelimsky, 1977). These reactions to evaluation are not exclusively American, as shown by a British view of the "bureaucratic infighting" that had to be dealt with by London's Central Policy Review Staff (Blackstone and Plowden, 1988, pp. 36 and 40–52).

Evaluations can interrupt agency routines and hurt individual decision makers' careers simply by examining outcomes (rather than process) and by making their findings public. Since assessing outcomes involves determining whether a program or policy works, negative findings are a real possibility, and when an evaluation report has been made public, its information can no longer be limited to the private use of a decision maker. Instead, it may provide persons other than that decision maker with information that could adversely affect him or her. In sum, in the minds of many managers and policymakers, evaluation—at least in the near term—represents both a threat to their progress and support for their competitors.

An important distinction to be made here is between internal and external evaluation units. The organizational considerations just discussed relate mostly to *internal* evaluation: the kinds of difficulties confronting an evaluation unit that must assess the larger organization's policies or programs. Although an external evaluation unit may have many of the same problems, it may not have them all. For example, an external evaluation unit does not risk embarrassing other decision makers within the larger organization by evaluating their programs, but it does have the additional burden of having to fit a unit of social scientists into the organization's culture and specific personnel framework. Although this situation may not be especially arduous for all evaluation units, it is an important problem for program evaluation units set up in budget offices, inspector general offices, or state legislative offices. The particular difficulty here is that doing things differently from the rest of an organization can exact a considerable toll in staff frustration, isolation, arguments over the meaning of terms and real battles over who does the "right" work (USGAO/PEMD-90-18, 1990).

Even when top managers or policymakers are well disposed toward program evaluation, the technical nature of reports may cause difficulty for them in understanding which are the most important findings of an evaluation or how to apply those findings to new policies and programs. When customers are outside the organization — legislative decision makers, for example — they also may not see how evaluations can be of benefit to them or how to interpret and use the lessons learned.

Such situations point to the need for an "evaluation broker" and the utility of having the head of an evaluation unit play such a role. The job of an evaluation broker is "to prepare and present information in usable form to the policymaker," to assure "the transmission of social knowledge from the point of origin to the point of use in the policy process" (Sundquist, 1978, p. 127). Important strategies the unit head can use to persuade top managers of the value of evaluation are clarifying the contribution a proposed evaluation can make to policy or program management and explaining why that would be important; bringing new findings to the attention of policymakers in language that allows their significance to be understood; and explaining how findings should be interpreted and applied and what areas of uncertainty they incorporate.

The kinds of activities that help in establishing legitimacy can be illustrated by recent experience at the U.S. General Accounting Office (GAO). GAO is a legislative agency whose main function is auditing and whose personnel are primarily auditors conducting financial or "performance" audits. Social scientists make up only about 10 percent of the agency's professional staff (U.S. General Accounting Office, 1990, vol. 1). For GAO, the major customer has always been the Congress. However, for resources, for political and administrative support, and for general policy direction, any unit within GAO must rely on the agency's top management. This separation of sponsor and user means that *both* of them need to be convinced of an evaluation's potential utility.

The top managers of GAO decided in 1979 to form an evaluation unit because they were persuaded that the agency needed to innovate in matters of method and to develop an improved capability for handling the increasingly complex policy questions coming from Congress. The new unit, called the Institute for Program Evaluation (IPE), began its work in June 1980. In 1984, the unit's name was changed to the Program Evaluation and Methodology Division (PEMD).

Convincing the agency's top management of the importance of program evaluation, then, was no problem for the evaluation unit. However, establishing the credibility of evaluation *below* the very highest levels of management needed to be accomplished. Even though resources and support for an evaluation unit are typically determined by top management, over the longer term the utility of evaluation must be demonstrated to the satisfaction of almost every management level in the larger organization if the unit is to survive.

The reason *generalized* support is essential is that any unit is at its most vulnerable in its first years:

> The possibility that a new bureau will be destroyed by its enemies is a real one. Its functional rivals are other agencies whose social functions are competitive with those of the bureau itself. . . . Its allocational rivals are other agencies which compete with it for resources, regardless of their functional relationships with it. . . . If the new bureau has strong functional rivals, or if it is designed to regulate or inhibit the activities of powerful social agents, then it will be severely opposed from the start. These antagonists often seek to capture the new bureau's functions themselves, or suppress them altogether. Hence they try to block it from establishing a strong external power base. The bureau may have to fight strongly during its infancy to avoid being disbanded or swallowed by some larger existing bureau [Downs, 1967, p. 10].

The evaluation unit at GAO, then, was not in the best of all possible bureaucratic positions, being subjected to both functional and allocational competition. Also clear was that support coming rapidly enough to help the unit survive its first years could come only from customers who would recognize the value *to them* of the evaluation services provided by the unit. The question was how to develop an effective external constituency for the unit in time to ward off what seemed a likely early demise. External sources of support for a new unit are usually weak and dispersed, if they exist at all, and identifying and developing them takes time. The challenge, then, was to work fast and well, maximizing priority work efforts with the Congress and GAO's top management while trying to hold steady—or at least not worsen—the unit's situation within the agency.

This strategy had as its aim both to buy the unit enough time to demonstrate what evaluation could do, and at the same time, given a few strong, well-received studies, allow it *also* to begin acquiring needed credibility within the agency.

Persuading legislative staff and members of Congress that evaluation could be useful to them turned out to be a fairly straightforward matter. Although in 1980–1981, there didn't seem to be much enthusiasm on Capitol Hill for evaluation research, the horizontal structure of legislative bodies was a help: different opinions prevail in different committees, and there is no agency head to enforce "political correctness" in vertical fashion. Thus, it was not difficult to find a few committees that were interested in seeing what evaluation could do for them; two of them, in fact, called the unit with requests for particular studies — one on chemical warfare and the other on the AFDC program. This was enough to get started.

The early evaluation studies produced at GAO generated genuine interest in the Congress (see, for example, U.S. General Accounting Office, GAO/IPE-81-1, 1981; GAO/IPE-82-2, 1982; GAO/IPE-83-6, 1983; GAO/PEMD-84-4, 1984; GAO/PEMD-84-6, 1984). Phone calls from committee staff began coming regularly, asking what the evaluation unit could do, how soon it could produce work, and what its staff capabilities were. By the end of 1982, some real congressional support for evaluation, in general, seemed to be emerging. In part, this was the result of the unit's efforts to persuade: for example, maintaining continuous dialogues with customers on progress and decisions, orienting the ongoing work toward customers' information needs, producing work that stood up under scrutiny. But also important, the *unit* had worked to learn how the Congress operated, to grasp the role that evaluation (or information generally) could play in those operations, and to develop evaluative products that took both of these points into account.

Analyzing Customer Information Needs

In some cases, when sponsors and users of evaluations are identical — for example, when an agency head asks an evaluation unit within the agency for information that he or she will use on the effectiveness of a program — and when the unit's staff themselves do the evaluation, knowledge of customer information needs and modes of operation may be acquired without much effort. With continuing daily relationships, such knowledge accumulates almost by osmosis. But even so, staff trained in social science methods may not be the most astute observers of the political relationships that critically influence the relevance and usefulness of an evaluation.

Sometimes, however, sponsors and users are *not* identical. Evaluators may be separated from and even unfamiliar with their customers, or the milieus may be politically distinct — for example, evaluation staff from some faraway office in the Department of Defense (DOD) conducting an evaluation whose chief user is the Secretary of Defense, or executive branch agency evaluators conducting a study for a congressional committee. Then it is always critical to analyze the customer's environment carefully if an evaluation unit is to succeed.

This is necessary for several reasons. Evaluators, whether they are analysts, researchers, or scientists, are separated from policymakers by different goals and different tolerances of uncertainty. The evaluator's "rationality" (or assumptions about what is "true") may be seen as lacking in "pragmatism" by a policymaker, while the policymaker's use of compromise to achieve a political end may conflict with the analyst's understanding of "what the data show." Evaluators believe in systematic approaches to solving problems and tend to define uncertainty quite carefully; policymakers tend to believe that the best solution is the one presented with the most convincing arguments or backed up by the most prestigious authority (Beranek, 1979).

These differences in goals, methods, and concepts of evidence naturally bring in their wake differences in priorities and strategies. As a result, evaluators may see the need for research everywhere and policymakers may not see it anywhere. The priorities of legislative policymakers, for example, are in the following order with respect to a particular issue: "First, legislators consider the effect on constituents (how do they feel about it?); second, they consider legislative feasibility (is there a consensus to do something about it?); and only in the last place do they consider substantive information (what do we know about it?)" (Voss, 1979, p. 3). Somewhere within the legislator's *last* priority lies the evaluator's *top* priority. Also, one should expect emotional issues (that is, constituent issues) to dominate legislative agendas, and timeframes for legislative action to be geared to time in office rather than to the amount of time needed to solve a problem.

What are the implications of such major differences between policymakers and evaluators? First, it is extremely important for evaluators to understand the political environment within which evaluation findings will or will not be used. Second, policymakers may be as unfamiliar with evaluation methods and the best ways of using study findings as evaluators typically are of the policy and political context of their own work.

In planning for GAO's evaluation unit, then, to get some understanding of this congressional milieu that is so critical to the unit's success, unit staff made a thorough study of the literature on congressional politics, procedures, "folkways," and use of information. They conducted a number of interviews with members of Congress and committee staff; and they queried managers throughout GAO with regard to their prior experience in performing audits for the Congress. The effort was made not just to understand the congressional milieu but also, as a way of shaping unit priorities, to determine the most important legislative information needs that could be satisfied using the methods of program evaluation. (For example, investigative questions involving narrow or personal accountability issues and general management concerns did not seem especially appropriate as focuses for a program evaluation unit.)

This research showed six important ways in which evaluators can respond usefully to the needs of legislative policymakers and their staff. First, answer evaluative questions, of course, but also, get the information to the legislative user *rapidly* enough to fit the time constraints of the congressional negotiation or decision process. Second, sift through the quantities of *existing* evaluative information to synthesize, analyze, and present succinctly that which is clearly relevant to the question at hand. Third, refine, where possible, the formulation of that question-at-hand so as to be sure of the feasibility of obtaining the information sought and the appropriateness of that information to the legislative need. Fourth, identify major gaps in available information for future attention by evaluators and policymakers. Fifth, assess plans for new programs or policies and review evaluation reports for old ones. Sixth, help legislative staff to develop evaluative questions about program effectiveness and efficiency needed in the oversight of executive agencies.

With these guidelines an evaluation unit can establish a strategy for working with its customers that includes the following four elements identified by the GAO unit's research:

1. *Always negotiate the issues to evaluate in terms of the information need.* The GAO unit begins every request for a study by a meeting with the congressional sponsors to better understand and operationalize their policy question. This ensures, first, that an issue is in fact researchable; second, that it can be answered, given time and resources available, with the needed degree of conclusiveness; and third, that the congressional users understand exactly what they will be getting and agree to its likely usefulness. The idea here is not to begin a two-year job if the information need does not require it, or when only six months are available.

2. *Provide frequent briefings and maintain continuing communications on progress.* Agreement on the evaluation design is really just a first step. Even with an appropriate study design, many things can go wrong during the execution of an evaluation that may interfere with its timeliness (for example, the principal investigator leaves or gets sick) or conclusiveness (for example, the data counted on are unavailable or unusable). Thus, the second element of the strategy is to brief the customer frequently, to ensure, first, that he or she knows what is happening in the evaluation, what problems are being encountered, and what changes may be necessary to the final product agreed on earlier; and second, that the *evaluators* know how the customer's information needs may be changing over time. In this way an effort can be broadened, altered, or cut back, depending on the circumstances, in timely fashion.

3. *Develop and test a mix of evaluative tools.* To confront the tension between the customer's need for rapid provision of evaluative information and

the reality that designing and executing strong evaluations can take a long time, it is important to include, as an integral part of the strategy, the development, adaptation, and testing of new methods that can combine soundness with at least relative speed.

This strategy helps to achieve more relevance and timeliness in the evaluation product; little if any reduction in evaluative quality; a gradually increasing understanding of the evaluative process by the customer; more satisfaction on the part of that customer; and as a result, improved use of evaluative findings. (Examples of tools developed by the GAO evaluation unit have been the evaluation synthesis [Methodology Transfer Papers, GAO/PEMD-10.1.2], case study evaluations [Methodology Transfer Papers, GAO/PEMD-10.1.9], the prospective evaluation synthesis [Methodology Transfer Papers, GAO/PEMD 10.1.10], and the cross-design synthesis [U.S. General Accounting Office, GAO/PEMD-92-18, 1992]).

4. *Obtain feedback.* Finally, to ensure that customer information needs are not changing and that work products, productivity, and responsiveness are continuing to meet customer needs, it is of the greatest importance to hear *directly* from those customers. Ask which performance areas need bolstering, what could have been improved, and whether, overall, they are satisfied with the work product.

In many cases, this step of the strategy may not seem necessary because of the availability of other measures of success (appreciation at hearings, letters of thanks, and so forth). However, it is important to remember that all aspects of work may not be equally resplendent and finding out which ones need to be improved can only be accomplished through direct, personal, and confidential communication with the users of an evaluation.

How do these imperatives for a customer strategy coincide with what a larger agency may expect of its evaluation unit? After all, a unit housed within a larger organization must always consider the expectations of that organization in planning and executing any customer strategy. But since those expectations may not be explicit and since organizational rejection can imperil any new unit, unit planners have a serious need to analyze what is and is not acceptable within the larger organizational environment. The next section deals with this issue.

Understanding the Larger Organization

Although a customer strategy elaborated by an evaluation unit can be planned independently from that of the larger organization (based on differing expectations for the unit), the less the execution of that strategy hinders or conflicts with the larger organization's mission, structural apparatus, and culture, the more it will be facilitated.

For an evaluation unit in a centralized agency, such as the Office of

Management and Budget (OMB), the need to understand missions, structure, and culture will involve several levels. Unit personnel must understand the agencies of the executive branch generally: how their individual missions relate to those of OMB, and whether or to what degree agency decision making is structured to take evaluation findings into account. Also, the unit must understand its larger organization (OMB) and the relationship of the social science culture to the "budgeteer" culture within that agency's environment.

In the case of GAO, the mission of the agency—to serve the Congress via independent, objective studies—was identical with that of the evaluation unit, except that in the other units of GAO the studies were typically audits; in the new unit they would be evaluations. Because of this difference, the goals and priorities of the studies were also very different. Other units used accounting methods and focused largely on the costs of programs and the potential for savings; the evaluation unit used social science methods and focused on measuring the effectiveness of programs or policies and the potential for improved outcomes (Chelimsky, 1985).

The commonality of mission across GAO units thus masked major disparities in methods, products, and staff. It was true that the evaluation unit at GAO was not expected to conduct audits but rather to do evaluations and other methodologically complex studies. The scope of these studies, however, would span the same topical areas in which the rest of GAO worked, and since the evaluation unit had only co-equal rather than primary jurisdiction in *any* area, a number of conflict areas could be foretold: (1) competition from other divisions over the work the evaluation unit would do; (2) uncertainty among congressional customers unfamiliar with the differences between evaluations and audits as to when one or the other would be appropriate; and (3) the potential for hostility from individual units within GAO if and when the evaluation unit should receive an important assignment in that unit's "area."

This organizational context pointed to the need for an explicit effort at differentiation on the part of the evaluation unit's planners. The unit's priorities would be set in methodological rather than substantive terms, and its topics would be selected in such a way as to minimize overlap within GAO. An effort would *also* be made to demonstrate how the quality of the unit's studies would enhance the larger agency's prestige generally and increase its reputation for both objectivity and methodological expertise in particular.

These considerations signified at least one essential change in the customer strategy discussed above: the unit would need to avoid requests from the Congress involving studies that could be construed as audits. Instead, it would pass these to the relevant auditing unit—of course, with the agreement of the requesting committee.

Initially, a priority for the new office was to try to train auditors in social science methods, pursue targeted collaborative efforts with other units, or critique the work of those units, all of these being tasks that GAO top management had originally felt might hasten the adoption of evaluation techniques at GAO. After a year of experience, however, it became clear that these efforts tended to produce misunderstanding and irritation rather than learning for at least three reasons. First, it was not clear to people at GAO that there *were* differences (along with commonalities) between an audit and a program evaluation. Second, prior auditor training in methods, particularly in establishing cause-and-effect relationships and internal or external validity, conflicted dramatically with social science methods in those and other areas. Finally, another unit at GAO, whose work was entirely devoted to the development of training courses for GAO, objected to the evaluation unit's involvement in training.

Therefore, a more promising, less confrontational path was taken, one that would involve an indirect effort to produce reports that could generate congressional enthusiasm, and as a by-product, demonstrate to GAO's auditors the potential benefits of using social science tools. The evaluation unit did, however, decide to continue developing "methodology transfer papers" — introductory monographs designed to build an awareness within GAO of study design, statistical sampling, and so forth — as a relatively low-key, useful form of dissemination within GAO (see Methodology Transfer Papers, GAO 10.1.2 and following).

Finally, to better understand the culture the unit was expected to influence, unit evaluators examined the auditing methods used at GAO and adopted some of them (notably, various quality control procedures) that could be employed in combination with the peer review that is typical in the social sciences but little used at GAO except in the evaluation unit. The purpose here was to minimize, to the degree possible, *unnecessary* differences in the work procedures between the other divisions of GAO and the new unit.

In the broader sense, however, trying to harmonize the social science and accounting cultures is not easy: differences in training, in mindset, in method, and in vocabulary are all very great. On the other hand, a strategy of indirect pressure, based on customer demand, *did* pay off in increasing the unit's credibility. Additionally helpful were top management's efforts to create an interdisciplinary climate at GAO, as shown by the inclusion of social scientists in some audit teams (U.S. General Accounting Office, 1990, vol. 1).

The results, then, of analyzing both the information needs of the evaluation unit's chief customer and the cultural and organizational aspects of the larger agency tended to reinforce sharply the importance of strong, well-documented evaluation studies that can (1) convince customers that evaluations may not only be sound and useful but also timely, (2) maintain the interest and reward the faith of the organization's top managers, and (3) demonstrate to other types of auditors or analysts that evaluation is in fact both feasible and rewarding to perform. Producing such strong studies, in turn, puts an emphasis on the unit's ability to recruit expert staff, to choose topics very carefully (at least at first), and to use and develop a wide array of customer-oriented methodological approaches — in short, to set policies for the unit that will promote the growth of its reputation for expertise.

Establishing Credibility

In any evaluation unit, the kinds of staff who need to be recruited will be determined by the topical coverage required by the customer's information needs, the menu of methodological approaches needed to fill them, and the effort to differentiate the unit from its functional and allocational rivals. To have credibility, an evaluation unit needs to demonstrate expertise in all the topical areas of customer interest. For example, the GAO evaluation unit must be knowledgeable not only in the social programs on which evaluation has traditionally focused but also in program areas such as the environment, defense, or agriculture, in which evaluations have been less plentiful. Timeliness is also a major issue as are usefulness, clarity of expression in reporting, and grace in communicating with customers and agency staff.

Criteria for staff selection in an evaluation unit, then, may include skills in evaluation methods, both quantitative and qualitative; knowledge of specific areas of public policy; writing ability; and the ability to deal well with people. GAO's top management allocated about 115 positions to the evaluation unit, 96 of which were for professional staff. Instead of accountants, public administrators, or MBAs, the unit recruited social scientists and operations researchers with an occasional "hard" scientist (that is, typically, a chemist, physicist, mathematician, or engineer) to work in areas like defense or the environment. Disciplines were and remain varied in the unit, and evaluation teams are deliberately interdisciplinary. More than 90 percent of the unit's researchers have advanced degrees, with about 65 percent holding doctorates.

It turned out to be quite difficult to find evaluators already trained in program evaluation methods who also had in-depth knowledge of topical areas like the environment or agriculture. Some analysts had worked on defense or transportation programs, but for the most part, they had not. The topical areas best represented among program evaluators even today seem to be education, public assistance, health and mental health, drug abuse, and criminal justice issues.

A useful strategy may be to (1) recruit staff with training in quantitative and/or qualitative methods who have strong substantive knowledge of a particular topic area, (2) expose them to program evaluation methods, and (3) team them with people who are expert in methodology but perhaps not in the particular topic area.

At first, the effort to select expert staff and get them to come to GAO was quite arduous. It involved developing a national network including well-known scholars and professors in all the areas relevant to work of the Program Evaluation and Methodology Division as well as officials and managers in other organizations. It also required devoting a great deal of time to interviewing and detailed reference checking. But as the work of PEMD became better known and the source-network expanded in size, many candidates began to apply for each available position and, as a group, they appeared to be better trained, more experienced, and increasingly talented as time passed.

Every evaluation unit must choose its personnel based on its own analysis of what its sponsors and users need and what types of evaluation it wants to emphasize. Whatever the mix of staff, it is important to find people who are as interested in seeing their work be useful as they are in producing and getting credit for it.

GAO's experience lends credence to several notions about evaluator staff. First, it seems easier for people with evaluation training to master a new substantive area than it is for people with substantive knowledge to learn the methods of evaluation. Second, certain evaluators are interested in social program or policy evaluation exclusively; efforts to attract some of them to other areas, such as environmental or defense evaluation, for example, may not be successful. Third, two types of people appear to adapt successfully within an evaluation unit: those with basically methodological interests who want to apply particular approaches to programs in many different areas, and those who want to delve deeply into a particular topic and stay there. Clusters of experts of both types currently work together in GAO's evaluation office, allowing the development of a body of program evaluation work in a fairly sizable number of topical areas, such as defense, health care delivery and technology, education, public assistance, the environment, transportation, agriculture, and immigration.

In choosing topics for a new unit to evaluate, it is important (1) to maximize the likelihood of at least a few early, resounding successes; (2) to ensure that technical content is combined with obvious policy relevance; and (3) to show that evaluations can be responsive to customer requests involving short timeframes. Thus, a first portfolio of evaluation studies might feature a number of small evaluations in traditional areas that involve low risk and can demonstrate the feasibility of conducting evaluations; one or two more ambitious evaluations of program effectiveness that can be expected to make a splash; and the development of procedures that provide greater timeliness in responding to customer requests such as evaluation synthesis, a variant of meta-analysis. Overall, the first portfolio should probably emphasize caution over innovation, since any major failure in the first two to three years could be devastating to the effort to establish a reputation. As was done by GAO's evaluation unit, an independent, permanent advisory group might be established to counsel the unit on the appropriateness of its planned work.

An initial focus of GAO's evaluation unit was on retrospective evaluation, largely because this was traditional, prudent, and most similar to auditing. Almost from the beginning, however, it was clear the unit would have to develop or adapt prospective methods as well, if customers' information needs were to be met. In effect, congressional committees often ask policy questions that look forward, not back, such as these: What changes, if any, can we expect if we implement this proposed program? Does its design make sense? Is it powerful enough to bring about the effects people say it will have? Does the problem addressed by the program warrant the likely cost? The approach taken by GAO's evaluation unit, therefore, has been to use a variety of techniques and methods: case studies, evaluability assessments, surveys, and process and impact evaluations as well as meta-analysis and forecasting. Increasingly, it has become necessary to employ multiple methods in the same study, both to shore up weaknesses in individual methods used alone and to deal with customer questions. Congressional customers are typically less interested in what happened in the past than in why it did, and how the lessons learned from an evaluation might apply to a new program. So a quasi-experimental design using time series analysis, for example, is typically backed up not only by a comprehensive literature review but also by an explanatory process evaluation or set of case studies and an analysis of policy implications.

Very important to the strategy for producing sound evaluations has been continuing advice from eminent people in the field at important points in the studies: advice on evaluation design, data sources and data analysis, appropriateness of emphasis, methodological clarity in the presentation of findings and so on. A Visiting Scholar program has also been established in GAO's evaluation unit. This program allows a different evaluator each year to spend two days a month in the evaluation unit to critique ongoing studies and to follow some of them from initiation to final draft.

Finally, sound studies must not only *be* sound, they must also *appear* sound — that is, they must be credible — if they are to be useful to their customers. Important to such credibility is, of course, establishing the objectivity of the evaluation and writing a report that is not difficult to read. In this regard, GAO's evaluation unit learned that candor about methodological weaknesses and clarity of expression are extremely precious qualities. Indeed, perhaps the best guarantee of integrity in an evaluation is the honesty with which it is presented, honesty about *what* has been learned and *how* it was learned. For example, evaluators need to discuss the design features of their study and say not only what was done, but why some desirable things could not be done; make clear exactly what data were collected, from whom, and how; present their response rates and say what was done about non-responders; and account for their data analysis and explain the general strengths and weaknesses of their study. This kind of candor is not a barrier to the use of an evaluation. On the contrary, it avoids misuse of the findings, it demonstrates the objectivity and competence of the evaluators, it may even disarm some of its critics, and it recognizes the reality that all methods have limitations.

Clarity of expression for readability, in this context, means the absence of evaluation jargon. Although terms-of-art cannot always be successfully eliminated, making sure that the report can be understood easily by decision makers is an important opportunity to increase the credibility, the readership, and eventually, the policy use of the study.

Summary

In planning for an effective evaluation unit, it is important to understand the political environments of both the unit's main customer and the larger organization in which it is embedded. The requirements generated by both these analyses are the best bases for determining the characteristics of the evaluation unit that will allow it to survive and succeed. Maintaining the confidence of top management, recruiting high-quality staff, selecting the "right" topics to evaluate, and producing strong studies are also important aspects of planning. Again, they need to be done within the context of a specific customer and a specific organization.

The head of the evaluation unit becomes a kind of evaluation "broker," moving up and back between users and the unit, top management and the unit, and functional or allocational rivals and the unit. He or she must keep a sharp eye out for changing customer needs and organization climates and be ready to adjust unit policies accordingly; also, he or she should get plenty of advice, be liberal with quid pro quos, and be ready to compromise on occasion. However, compromises can never go so far that they waste evaluation unit resources, endanger the credibility of the work, or improve civility at the expense of quality outcomes.

Organizing and running an effective evaluation unit may not be an activity for everyone. My own guess is that the odds are about six to five against success: just good enough, really, to keep the game going. However, the importance of that game is considerable, especially today when it has become almost as hard to diagnose a problem as it used to be to agree on solutions. Evaluation is the only tool that can tell us, based on empirical evidence, what our problem is and what actions we can take that are likely to resolve it, whether it is in our health care systems, our international competitiveness, our technology transfer, or our urban schools.

Recent years have brought increasing knowledge, practice, acceptance, and use of evaluation both in the United States and abroad, in executive and legislative branches, at national as well as state levels of government. What is needed now is for legislative and central agency policymakers to elicit stronger evaluations from executive agencies and use them in oversight or management; and for individual agency heads to make room for evaluation units in their midst, allow them to target the important problems facing their agencies, and ensure that their findings are heard and used, where appropriate, in agency decision making.

References

Beranek, W., Jr. *Choosing and Using Scientific Advice in the State Legislature.* Indianapolis, Ind.: Holcomb Research Institute, June 1979.

Blackstone, T., and Plowden, W. *Inside the Think Tank: Advising the Cabinet 1971–1983.* London: Heinemann, 1988.

Chelimsky, E. *Analysis of a Symposium on the Use of Evaluation by Federal Agencies.* Vol. 2. McLean, Va.: MITRE Corporation, July 1977.

Chelimsky, E. "Comparing and Contrasting Auditing and Evaluation." *Evaluation Review,* 1985, *9*(4), 483–503.

Downs, A. *Inside Bureaucracy.* Boston: Rand, 1967.

Methodology Transfer Papers. *The Evaluation Synthesis.* GAO/PEMD-10.1.2. Washington, D.C.: U.S. General Accounting Office, n.d.

Methodology Transfer Papers. *Content Analysis: A Methodology for Structuring and Analyzing Written Material.* GAO/PEMD-10.1.3. Washington, D.C.: U.S. General Accounting Office, n.d.

Methodology Transfer Papers. *Designing Evaluations.* GAO/PEMD-10.1.4. Washington, D.C.: U.S. General Accounting Office, n.d.

Methodology Transfer Papers. *Using Structured Interviewing Techniques.* GAO/PEMD-10.1.5. Washington, D.C.: U.S. General Accounting Office, n.d.

Methodology Transfer Papers. *Using Statistical Sampling.* GAO/PEMD-10.1.6. Washington, D.C.: U.S. General Accounting Office, n.d.

Methodology Transfer Papers. *Developing and Using Questionnaires.* GAO/PEMD-10.1.7. Washington, D.C.: U.S. General Accounting Office, n.d.

Methodology Transfer Papers. *Case Study Evaluations.* GAO/PEMD-10.1.9. Washington, D.C.: U.S. General Accounting Office, n.d.

Methodology Transfer Papers. *Prospective Evaluation Methods: The Prospective Evaluation Synthesis.* GAO/PEMD-10.1.10. Washington, D.C.: U.S. General Accounting Office, n.d.

Methodology Transfer Papers. *Quantitative Data Analysis: An Introduction.* GAO/PEMD-10.1.11. Washington, D.C.: U.S. General Accounting Office, n.d.

Mosteller, F. "Taking Science Out of Social Science." *Science,* 1981, *212*(4492), 5.

Sundquist, J. L. "Research Brokerage: The Weak Link." In L. Lynn (ed.), *Knowledge and Policy: The Uncertain Connection.* Washington, D.C.: National Research Council, National Academy of Sciences, 1978, pp. 126–144.

U.S. General Accounting Office. *Disparities Still Exist in Who Gets Special Education.* GAO/IPE-81-1. Washington, D.C.: U.S. General Accounting Office, 1981.

U.S. General Accounting Office. *CETA Programs for Disadvantaged Adults.* GAO/IPE-82-2. Washington, D.C.: U.S. General Accounting Office, 1982.

U.S. General Accounting Office. *Chemical Warfare: Many Unanswered Questions.* GAO/IPE-83-6. Washington, D.C.: U.S. General Accounting Office, 1983.

U.S. General Accounting Office. *WIC Evaluations.* GAO/PEMD-84-4. Washington, D.C.: U.S. General Accounting Office, 1984.

U.S. General Accounting Office. *An Evaluation of the 1981 AFDC Changes.* GAO/PEMD-84-6. Washington, D.C.: U.S. General Accounting Office, 1984.

U.S. General Accounting Office. *Diversifying and Expanding Technical Skills at GAO.* GAO/PEMD-90-18, vol. 1, 14–15; GAO/PEMD-90-18S, vol. 2, 22–48; 31–39. Washington, D.C.: U.S. General Accounting Office, April 1990.

U.S. General Accounting Office. *Cross Design Synthesis: A New Strategy for Medical Effectiveness Research.* GAO/PEMD-92-18. Washington, D.C.: U.S. General Accounting Office, 1992.

Voss, G. "The Integration and Use of Research Within the Federal System." Unpublished paper presented at the Operations Research Society of America/Institute of Management Sciences conference, Hawaii, June 14, 1979.

21

Managing Evaluation Projects
Step by Step

James B. Bell

The theory and methods of public program evaluation meet the reality of policy-making and program management and operations through the conduct of individual evaluation projects. Uncertainty about current performance and narrow political interest challenge an evaluator to maintain focus and political neutrality while undertaking the difficult, technical task of carrying out an evaluation. As Eleanor Chelimsky noted in Chapter Twenty of this book, managers and policymakers often view evaluation initially as an unknown that can block their own progress while providing support for their competitors.

Against a backdrop of demanding technical requirements and a dynamic political environment, the goal of program evaluation project management is to develop, with available resources and time, valid and useful information products that achieve the intended purpose of the project. Typically, such an evaluation supplies information on program performance and policy, and management decision makers are expected to use this information to enhance the program performance. Secondary aims of evaluation project management are development of evaluation staff and education of the project sponsor and other clients about program evaluation.

This chapter uses several definitions that are clarified here. *Evaluation project management* is a process of considerations, decisions, and activities engaged in by the leadership of an evaluation project to facilitate its conduct. The evaluation managers must transform the mandate, resources, and schedule for a project into valued evaluation products and outcomes. Generally, evaluation management is led by a *project director* who is directly accountable to the project sponsor for successful completion of the evaluation.

The *evaluation staff* or *evaluators* are the individuals who conduct the evaluation, that is, those whose work is facilitated by evaluation leadership. At times, the evaluation staff includes the project director and other senior evaluators who usually have major roles in carrying out an evaluation as well as responsibilities for project management.

The evaluation mandate is the direction on the analytic purpose and intended use of evaluation findings given to evaluation management by the project sponsor. The *sponsor* is the organization paying for the evaluation. Usually the *client* also is the sponsor, but sometimes a *client* organization other than the sponsor is identified and is expected to use the evaluation products. Besides the sponsor and direct client(s), there are generally multiple audiences who hold a stake in the substance of an evaluation — groups whose vying interests further complicate the evaluation environment. Finally, the *program* is the evaluation subject and encompasses the environment, policies, practices, resources, activities, organizations, and individuals being evaluated.

At its core, program evaluation is a human discovery process. One of the most important challenges of day-to-day project management is to create an atmosphere that fosters insight and creativity among project staff and other evaluation participants. Simultaneously, there must be sufficient focus and discipline to accomplish the evaluation mandate on schedule with available resources. Because evaluation takes place in a complex and unpredictable environment, project management is more art than science; no generic prescription for successful management exists. Instead, the advice in this chapter focuses on five areas that are essential to effective project management: (1) clarifying the evaluation mandate, (2) staffing and organizing for success, (3) making assignments productive, (4) monitoring interim progress, and (5) ensuring product quality and usefulness.

The aims in each of these areas of emphasis are presented in Table 21.1. The aims are ideals that are not likely to be fully achieved in the context of an individual evaluation. They emphasize the state that should be sought in each area of project management. Considered together, they encourage evaluation management to be dynamically responsive to the mandate for each evaluation by finding opportunities to assure and enhance the value of the sponsor's evaluation investment throughout the course of the project.

This advice on evaluation management is not novel. Nonetheless, to achieve these aims in an evaluation project is very difficult. Constraints, such as inadequate or inappropriate evaluation staff or an individual representing the sponsor organization who is difficult to work with, tend to overwhelm efforts to pursue optimal management of evaluation resources and activities. By examining the specified areas of evaluation management and providing practical suggestions on ways to accomplish the aims listed in Table 21.1, this chapter is intended to aid evaluation project managers. In addition, each area of evaluation management is also addressed from a different perspective in one or more of the other chapters in Part Four of the handbook. For example, there are discussions of staffing considerations in chapters by Chelimsky and Sonnichsen that complement the advice on staffing presented here.

Table 21.1. Evaluation Management Areas and Aims.

Area of Evaluation Management	Aim
Clarifying the Evaluation Mandate	Complete agreement between sponsor and evaluation management about the purpose, scope, resources, method, workplan, and schedule.
Staffing and Organizing for Results	Demonstration by staff, through past efforts, of the mix of qualifications needed to conduct the evaluation. Staff are organized into a structure that maximizes each member's contribution and ensures control of evaluation expenditures and schedule.
Making Assignments Productive	Assignments that are product oriented, well defined, and agreed on by evaluation managers and the staff who will undertake the effort. The sum of all assignments equals completion of all evaluation products. Each assignment is appropriate to the capabilites of the individuals/groups undertaking it.
Monitoring Interim Progress	Project monitoring information that accurately portrays and links technical progress on evaluation products, expenditures, and schedule status; a monitoring process that contributes to and sustains project momentum.
Ensuring Product Quality and Usefulness	Evaluation products given high ratings for usefulness. The evaluation products are used by policy and program management decision makers to accomplish the purpose of the evaluation.

Evaluation projects differ greatly in purpose, scope, size, method, and complexity. They also differ according to the nature of the program or organization being evaluated, the type of sponsor, and the affiliation, working style, and qualifications of staff conducting the evaluation. The differences in characteristics presented by each evaluation set unique bounds for management of that project. For example, there are managerially significant distinctions between evaluations conducted by in-house staff and those conducted by outside organizations. An in-house project may be constrained by the depth and range of the capabilities of in-house evaluation staff. Outside evaluators may possess better technical capability but less working knowledge of the subject program. They may be insensitive to existing political relationships in and around the program.

Besides the organizational relationship between the sponsor and evaluator, there are other characteristics of an evaluation project that influence evaluation management. A program's prior history of evaluation is significant. Must new measures be developed and tested or will evaluators use existing well-accepted tools? How were prior evaluations viewed by this sponsor and other stakeholders? Managing the first evaluation of a program presents more challenges than an evaluation that replicates well-established and accepted protocols. In the latter, management seeks high-quality execution without expecting to develop new methodology in the process. In contrast, methodology development usually is the dominant activity in first-time evaluations. These evaluations are more difficult to manage because the activities are less amenable to routinization. Finally, the scale of the evaluation and the amount of professional staff effort greatly affect evaluation management, logistics, and operations.

The five sections that follow provide a discussion of each of the areas of evaluation management that are the focus of the chapter. In each section, practical suggestions are offered for realizing the aims in that area of project management. A concluding section summarizes the chapter's advice.

Clarifying the Evaluation Mandate

Imagine a meeting in which the project sponsors present their review of the draft final report for the evaluation. The report does not match the expectations of the sponsor. There is no time to adjust the evaluation. The deficiencies identified in the report cannot be corrected by altering the way the evaluation results are presented. The problem stems from unresolved differences between evaluation management and the sponsor about the interpretation of the evaluation mandate.

The evaluation director and staff who had this experience did not fully comprehend the necessity of establishing and maintaining complete agreement with the sponsor (and the client if different from the sponsor) about the evaluation mandate. Evaluators should not misread the sponsor's tacit acceptance of the original project plan and interim progress reports. Evaluation management cannot assume that a fundamental difference about the mandate will surface through these pro forma activities. While there may be a solid agreement at the start of the evaluation, either the sponsor or the evaluation management may change their expectations during the project period. If so, this shift must be discussed and a revised agreement forged.

Gaining Initial Agreement

Depending on the depth and complexity of the evaluation and of the differences between sponsor and evaluators about the evaluation mandate, clarification of the expectations of both sides concerning the evaluation results should be formalized orally or in writing. When a written clarification is needed, it should be created in the least expensive manner possible. For example, evaluation management may document key points about the mandate in a memorandum for the record, with a copy forwarded for review by the evaluation sponsor.

When clarifying the evaluation mandate, the evaluation user, purpose, scope, design and method, resources, schedule, and other technical requirements must be elicited from the sponsor and others who originally shape an evaluation. This is done by the evaluation management — those most directly responsible for success of the evaluation. The same understanding of the evaluation mandate must be shared by those funding and those managing the evaluation.

As the evaluation management and the sponsor gain and maintain agreement about the evaluation mandate, their shared understanding establishes a framework for considering next steps in project management. Failure to agree on the scope and primary purpose of the evaluation or to resolve potentially troublesome issues of approach, schedule, or budget are common problems that cause evaluations to falter. For example, the sponsor may wish to avoid placing a data collection burden on certain individuals or groups or may want to develop findings based on a regionally representative stratified sample. Evaluation management must be aware of such preferences at the start of the evaluation, or resources and time may be wasted.

Many evaluations are justified on the basis of serving multiple purposes; this goal, however, may impede clarification of the mandate. The separate purposes for an evaluation range from identifying ways to improve program organizational performance to developing new evaluation methodology. When multiple purposes exist, evaluation management should discuss with the sponsor the relative importance of the different purposes. Inevitably there are resource trade-offs; optimal achievement of the most important purpose may be jeopardized if multiple purposes are pursued.

Sometimes there is a single purpose for an evaluation, but there are differences about the implication of that purpose for the scope of measurement. In a common example, the sole purpose is to identify ways to improve program performance, but there are two or more views about the implications of "ways to improve program performance." Under one view of the evaluation scope, program operations (process) is a peripheral focus of measurement—the program is to be treated as a "black box" in an analysis of the outcomes of individual participants. Program operations are subject to little or no independent investigation during the evaluation. A contrasting interpretation of the scope of this evaluation sees the program operations as a measurable process. Program performance might be improved if program operation is examined, According to this view, a major focus of the evaluation is the inner workings of the program.

Continuing this example, the evaluators must work with the sponsor to resolve whether the focus of analysis will be solely on participant outcomes or will also include the program operations. Evaluation management might suggest how this difference can be resolved by reconciling the two interpretations to shape an optimally feasible and useful evaluation mandate. The scope of the evaluation can be defined to encompass program operations and participant outcomes. If so, the agreed-on purpose is clarified: to find ways to improve participant outcomes by investigating the relationship between participant outcomes and program operations.

Checking the Mandate During the Evaluation

Both the sponsor and evaluation management may, with good reason, change their interpretation of the mandate during the course of the evaluation. This change must be disclosed to the other party, and agreement should be reached on any shift in the evaluation mandate. The sponsor may respond to a changed agenda for decision making during the course of the evaluation: a new legislative proposal or an executive initiative may cause the sponsors to shift their views of the preferred measurements taken during the evaluation. Often sponsors fail to communicate effectively with evaluation management when their expectations for the evaluation change.

Evaluation management can defend against unknown shifts in the evaluation mandate by involving the sponsors in discussions of the evaluation mandate throughout the project period. They can accomplish this involvement by integrating checks on the mandate into routine evaluation activities such as the sponsor's review of an evaluation data collection and analysis plan. By describing to the sponsor the data that will be collected, evaluation management creates an opportunity for discussing possible shifts in the sponsor's expectations for the evaluation. Regardless of whether changes are identified, the project record should note that the sponsor has rechecked the mandate.

The sponsor's review of the evaluation data collection and analysis plan must be structured to draw attention to how the evaluators have operationalized the evaluation mandate. Table 21.2 is from an evaluation sponsored by the National Institutes of Health (NIH). It shows how evaluators translated the evaluation mandate into action by presenting the data sources and indicators for three evaluation questions under Topic A: Effects on Research. This evaluation is designed to address several topic areas and evaluation questions through a combination of survey research and analysis of secondary data such as that provided by the grantees as part of their annual progress reports. Most of the indicators for the questions in Table 21.2 are generated through a Clinical Investigator Survey (CIS) that will be mailed to a representative sample of NIH-sponsored investigators involved in "patient-interaction research." Indicators to address these questions also are generated through IMPAC, the U.S. Public Health Services' automated extramural grants information system operated by NIH.

Finally, sometimes a shift in the evaluation's mandate is so great that a separate and distinct effort to renegotiate the project purpose, budget, and schedule is required. A change in program leadership, for example, might precipitate such major renegotiations.

Staffing and Organizing for Results

Imagine that the evaluation project director is chairing a staff meeting. The agenda is planning for a major project activity, a series of in-depth qualita-

Table 21.2. Linking Evaluation Questions, Data Sources, and Indicators.

Topic A: Effects on Research		
Question	*Data Source*	*Indicator*
A1. Is research productivity qualitatively or quantitatively different at General Clinical Research Center (GCRC) and non-GCRC research institutions?	• Clinical Investigator Survey (CIS), Section B, Research Outcomes	• number of follow-on Public Health Service (PHS) research grant awards • follow-on PHS research grant numbers • follow-on PHS research grant relatedness • number of follow-on PHS research grant applications • follow-on PHS research grant application intent • non-PHS follow-on award source • number of related journal atricles • related journal article listing • other dissemination activities
	• IMPAC (the computer-based information system of the extramural programs of NIH/PHS)	• total dollars awarded • total dollars awarded human subjects research • total dollars awarded per activity • total dollars awarded per administering organization
A2. Do certain classes of research appear to need GCRC support more than other classes?	• CIS, Section A: Research Characteristics	• number of patients • number of volunteers • patient/volunteer characteristics • maximum invasiveness level • clinical research characteristics • use of control group • type of research resources • number of inpatient days • number of outpatient visits • non-human subject research materials • use of GCRC Center • type of Center resource
A3. Are there differences in the characteristics of research investigators who use GCRCs?	• CIS, Section C: Clinical Research Resources	• percent time (spent) on clinical research • percent time (spent) on basic research

Source: Data Collections and Procedures: Evaluation of the NIH General Clinical Research Centers (GCRC) Program, James Bell Associates, February 1991. (unpublished)

tive case studies. Case study execution requires intimate knowledge of the characteristics of the subject program and its environment and context. A keen understanding of the nuances of administering in-depth case studies is needed. The project director realizes that the level of knowledge and skill of the staff members with case study responsibilities does not meet the requirements of the project. What happened? Why is the project on the verge of a crisis? There was a misjudgment about staffing. Even if the problem can be corrected, the evaluation will fall behind schedule and waste resources because individuals with the wrong qualifications were selected for the evaluation.

With a clarified evaluation mandate, the next area essential to evaluation management is staffing and organization. Who will conduct evaluation activities? How will they be organized to carry out their project responsibilities? A simple answer is that the project staff should embody the qualifications needed to conduct the planned evaluation activities on schedule in a high-quality and effective manner. The staff should be available and motivated. If the evaluation has more than three staff members, they should be organized into teams with well-defined roles. The number of teams, team size, and the scope of team responsibility should be consistent with the number of project staff, the evaluation purpose, and the expected products and general workplan of the evaluation.

In short, evaluation staff who possess the appropriate qualifications are needed. They should work under an organizational structure that facilitates full use of their capabilities. In many evaluations, individuals from the sponsor and subject program or outside experts also are part of the evaluation project organization. The effective involvement of internal or external advisory groups can enhance evaluation performance.

Selecting Appropriate Staff

The range of qualifications available among candidate evaluation staff varies depending on project circumstances. An evaluation assigned to an in-house evaluation unit usually presents staffing choices that are defined by the evaluation qualifications and competing duties of the staff of that unit. If the same project becomes an external evaluation, the pool of potential evaluators expands and the process of selecting individuals is altered. Regardless, the same general approach to project staffing should apply.

As a first step, a staffing matrix should aid decisions about staffing. Typically, the substantive and methodological qualifications needed to conduct the project are arrayed in rows in the matrix and the identities of candidate staff members are listed in the columns. The cells of the matrix are then marked for individual(s) whose qualifications demonstrated in past similar or related evaluations match those needed to conduct the tasks and activities required for this evaluation. Table 21.3 is the staffing matrix for

Table 21.3. Staff Qualifications Matrix.

Qualification Requirements	Staff Member Qualifications						
	A	B	C	D	E	F	G
Substantive							
National Center for Research Resources (NCRR) biomedical research resources and services programs	X	X				X	X
National Institutes of Health (NIH) and national biomedical research programs and institutions	X	X	X	X	X	X	X
The relationships among biomedical research, new drug/device/procedure, regulation, clinical practice standards, health care finance/delivery and inpatient and outpatient hospitals and services	X	X	X	X	X	X	
Methodological							
Evaluation design for complex programs in biomedical research environment	X	X			X		
Primary and secondary data collection including interviews, surveys, and extracting data from hardcopy and electronic records	X	X		X	X	X	X
Data analysis including use of quantitative and qualitative methods	X	X	X	X	X	X	X
Formulating and reporting plausible and workable recommendations for program redesign	X	X	X	X	X	X	

Source: Adapted from the *Technical Proposal to Conduct an Evaluation of NIH General Clinical Research Centers Program,* James Bell Associates, April 1990. (unpublished)

the multidisciplinary NIH evaluation discussed above. The qualifications on the left reveal the nature of the evaluation and provide a starting point for staffing decisions: What substantive and methodological qualifications are needed for this evaluation, and who among those individuals available for this project has demonstrated these capabilities?

Substantive qualifications are the knowledge, skills, and experience that demonstrate familiarity with the program and subject area. They indicate whether enough basic understanding of the program and environment is present in professional staff to provide a foundation for executing the evaluation. The ideal substantive qualifications encompass knowledge of all pertinent aspects of the subject area within and around the scope of the evaluation.

In the NIH evaluation cited above, staff needed to understand quickly both the requirements in the federal program guidelines and the operations of the decentralized clinical research centers funded by NIH. Knowledge was also needed about the philosophical and historical underpinnings of NIH-sponsored clinical research, and of the biomedical and behavioral research environments. Prior experience working with laboratory and clinical investigators and research administrators in grantee institutions was also advantageous.

In judging substantive qualifications, managers should make allowances for the transfer of substantive knowledge across subject areas. For example, a current initiative in many social programs is "services integration," or the coordination of services from different organizations. Knowledge gained about services integration in one program should apply in evaluations of other social programs with services integration objectives. Similarly, common functions and processes are present in most social programs. Administration and management, financing, client intake, case management, and management information systems are functions found in many social programs. Knowledge in these functional areas is transferrable across programs.

Although not an initially appealing alternative, successful evaluations can be conducted by evaluation staff with a low level of substantive knowledge. This is possible if the project allows for an evaluation learning period; evaluators can be among the fastest learners.

Without staff who have training and experience in data collection and analysis methods, the evaluation will flounder. Assessment of needed methodological qualifications may reflect the requirements of each stage of a project — evaluation design and instrument development, data collection, data analysis and interpretation, and report writing. It is useful also to consider distinctions among quantitative social science methods such as survey research, statistical and mathematical modeling, and qualitative research. Distinguishing staff candidates who have capabilities in quantitative and qualitative methods is helpful. Typically, an evaluator possesses one or the other of these methodological capabilities, but not both.

In addition to substantive and methodological qualifications, strong interpersonal relations and communication capabilities are essential to successful evaluations. Many evaluations suffer because staff lack the interpersonal skills needed to facilitate evaluation activities. Individual staff members should have interpersonal skills and experiences appropriate to their roles in the project.

Because they are less likely to be formally documented, these personal qualifications are also less likely to be codified in a staffing matrix. For example, some individuals who appear to have solid substantive qualifications may be too doctrinaire or zealous. They may have rigid preconceptions of program strengths and weaknesses, or may be otherwise ill suited to conducting an independent evaluation. Neutrality and objectivity are necessary so that the evaluation can be fair and incisive in assessing the knowledge gained through data collection and analysis activities. The critical importance of interpersonal and communications skills is emphasized throughout Part Four of the handbook.

Finally, in staffing decisions the *level* and not just the *type* of training, knowledge, and experience required is crucial. There should be a mix of senior and junior staff that is appropriate to the problem-solving challenge of the project. For example, a pioneering analysis of a previously unevaluated program or policy requires a greater share of effort by senior staff. In contrast, in a project that is a replication of an earlier study, junior professional and support staff may play a larger role. The senior professionals will retain technical leadership and other overarching responsibilities, but their share of total project labor should decline in an evaluation where the detailed technical approach has been tested.

Organizing for Results

Organizing evaluation staff into teams or groups with mutually exclusive but complementary project responsibilities is central to effective project management. The use of teams and especially the exchange of information among them suggests a nonhierarchical, collegial structure that still allows the narrower focus needed to accomplish project tasks and responsibilities. The number and size of teams is dictated by the number of staff involved in the evaluation. A team has at least two members, but an individual may serve on more than one team. There should also be a synthesis group if there are technical teams.

Technical teams can be defined by their functions in the evaluation process such as data collection or analysis. They may also be differentiated by method, subject matter, or another organizing concept suited to that evaluation. Effective team configurations reflect a workable division of responsibilities among staff considering the types of effort needed to carry out the evaluation and the qualifications of individuals on the staff. When evaluation teams are organized by method, for example, one team may carry out the quantitative research while another team performs qualitative research. While each team conducts all stages of applying the method for which they are responsible there is also a constant exchange of information between the teams. In fact, there should be project staff who bridge methods by participating on both teams.

In addition, as shown in Figure 21.1, it is advisable to form a synthesis group to shepherd the efforts of the technical teams. A synthesis team is suggested for all evaluations involving more than one technical team. Working closely with the evaluations director, the synthesis group plays a key role in project management. It is involved in most aspects of planning evaluation assignments, monitoring technical progress, and interpreting and integrating products and results from completed evaluation activities. Thus, in the synthesis group the evaluation parts are brought together and shaped through internal peer review into the information products that will present the evaluation results. Building on the example depicted in Figure 21.1, in the synthesis group the qualitative team leaders will review and approve plans for quantitative analyses for relevance and importance.

For many projects, an internal work group and an external advisory group are also advantageous (see Figure 21.1). A client/sponsor work group helps to promote an exchange of information among the project staff and key

Figure 21.1. Organization of an Evaluation Project.

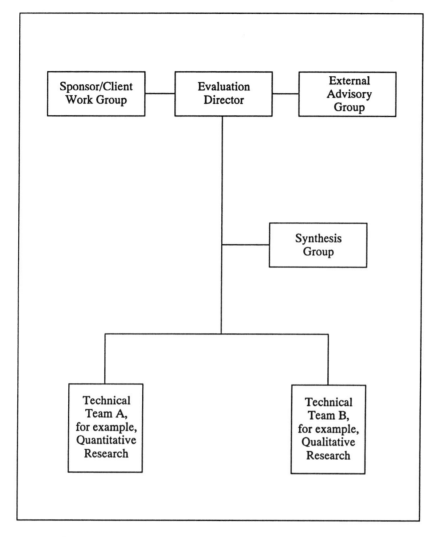

Source: Adapted from the Technical Proposal *To Conduct an Evaluation of NIH Implementa-tion of Section 491 of the Public Health Service Act, Mandating a Program of Protection for Research Subjects,* James Bell Associates, August 1991. (unpublished)

individuals representing the sponsor or subject program. Program policy-makers and managers should be involved if they have expected to use evalu-ation findings to improve program performance. These work groups primarily facilitate active involvement of evaluation sponsors and users in planning and reviewing evaluation progress. Work group members may also be first reviewers of draft products developed by the core evaluation staff. An inter-nal work group also is an effective mechanism for gaining access to program staff or data sources and resolving project issues, such as dissimilar views of the evaluation mandate.

An external advisory panel is composed of experts on the evaluation subject or methodology who are independent outsiders to the evaluation. Their effort usually is applied to project quality assurance. External advisory group composition should reflect the evaluation purpose. For instance, top methodologists should oversee decisions on evaluation design if rigorous methodology is emphasized in the evaluation mandate. Their role is to assure that evaluation design and execution meet applicable standards.

Making Assignments Productive

Imagine that three-quarters of the project schedule and budget have been spent but that only one-half of the evaluation work has been done. The evaluation staff has put forth good effort, but one reason for the slow and more expensive pace is the way evaluation activities were initially conceived and assigned. Ambiguous, uncoordinated assignments sap project resources and undercut the knowledge contribution possible through an evaluation.

In evaluation projects in which the results and experiences of one activity are integrally related to many other activities, a very careful and coherent procedure for making assignments is needed to achieve optimal "relatedness" among activities and a productive evaluation overall. Evaluation management must ensure that each staff member has at all times a clear and well-defined assignment governing his or her efforts on the evaluation. In combination, the results of the individual assignments must equal the intended evaluation products.

Size, schedule, and other evaluation characteristics influence the mechanism through which project assignments are made. In large evaluations, assignments usually occur at multiple echelons, with the number of organizational levels dependent on the number of participating staff and the level of staff effort in a typical month. A national program evaluation with seven to ten professional staff members, for example, may have three echelons. The project director makes assignments to team leaders; the team leaders make assignments to small groups within their teams. These groups then fashion assignments for individuals in the group. The role of an echelon more than one level above the individual or group receiving an assignment varies among projects. The tighter the project budget and schedule, the greater the need for the top echelon to agree on the details of the assignments at all echelons.

Effort spent gaining well-conceived and agreed-on assignments should not strain the evaluation resources and schedule. A project must maintain momentum by integrating the effort required for planning and initiating assignments into daily, weekly, and monthly activities. Only a very small share of total project labor and a moderate share of total evaluation management effort should be devoted solely to assignment making.

Shaping Individual Assignments

To shape assignments for individual staff members, evaluation management should first determine the set of interim products needed for the next period of the evaluation. This set of needed products then must be parceled into mutually exclusive assignments. Each staff member should know his or her boundaries and the boundaries of the most nearly related assignments of other staff members. The instructions or guidelines for the assignments should be ordered rationally for each staff member, with considerable attention given to the preconditions and interrelationships among individual steps in carrying out the assignment.

The product, resources, completion date, and other provisions of an assignment also should match the capabilities of the individuals receiving the assignment. Evaluation management should keep the scope and requirements of each assignment within or very near the capabilities actually demonstrated on other evaluations by the individual(s) receiving the assignment. Sometimes junior professionals, for example, underestimate the complexity of an activity and enthusiastically seek assignments that they are too inexperienced to complete.

In making assignments, evaluation management should encourage open discussions between those who will oversee the assignment and those who will carry it out. The result should be agreed-on assignments. The person conducting an assignment should believe he or she can deliver the product stipulated in the assignment. It also is advisable to establish ground rules about reporting unanticipated problems in carrying out evaluation assignments, discussed in the section on monitoring interim progress. When a staff member has trouble with an assignment, project resources are wasted unless management knows and adjusts quickly.

Evaluation management also should encourage staff development by including some new challenges in individual assignments. Each evaluation staff member needs the opportunity to grow professionally without being overwhelmed by the new challenges. Evaluation management should know the next level of challenge suitable for each staff member, including the managers themselves.

Formalizing Assignments

When making an assignment, evaluation management should formalize an agreement about the assignment with the affected evaluation staff member(s). Assignments should be codified in an oral or written agreement in which the level of detail is roughly consistent with the amount of resources to be employed for the assignment, its relative importance, and the certainty that the assigned individual(s) will accomplish the desired product on schedule and within budget. The agreement should concentrate on specifying the expected product, the major milestones in product development, the resources set aside for the assignment, and the expected completion date.

While the provisions of an assignment agreement are important, examples that illustrate the expected product of the assignment are invaluable. They facilitate clear dialogue and decisions about executing an assignment and show how the work was or might be carried out. The best illustrative materials are products of assignments from similar studies, such as a spreadsheet used to track survey follow-up or a sample analysis output report. If actual examples are not available, sketches and outlines expressing the content of the assigned product should be substituted.

The flow chart in Figure 21.2 is a schematic representation of the placement process for child abuse and neglect cases. The flow chart was used to guide the effort of evaluators assigned to develop a written description of foster care placement avoidance programs in five localities. The flow chart emphasizes the common core elements of case placement operations: the points where the evaluators' descriptions should focus. Describing each local placement avoidance program using a common definition of core elements sets the stage for identifying meaningful differences in operations among the five programs.

The form of the assignment agreements will vary, depending on the management style of those making the assignment. The use of written agreements has the advantage of creating a record and reference source for the future. Oral agreements are suitable when the purpose and scope of the assignment are very clear to all parties and the assignment is routine for that staff member or group. Such agreements are also suitable when a history of effective unwritten agreements exists for a similar assignment to the same individual or group. However, when evaluation management has any doubt about assignment completion, it is better to have written notes documenting key aspects of the assignment. Initiating a project activity based solely on word of mouth and attempting to recall an assignment from memory can create unnecessary confusion and uncertainty.

Finally, the written terms of an assignment agreement can be used again in other evaluations, but there must be safeguards against inappropriate use of the assignment language in a later project. Once an assignment has been documented, there may be a tendency to reuse the language just because it is already written without regard for how it should be tailored for its use in a current evaluation.

Monitoring Interim Progress

Imagine that despite monitoring reports indicating timely progress, evaluation management discovers that data collection will not be completed until well after the planned completion date. Evaluation management realizes that interim monitoring has not been penetrating enough to detect the true extent of technical progress. Was the most common progress monitoring error committed: Did management mistakenly accept the appearance of originally planned levels of effort and expenditures as commensurate levels of technical progress?

Interim monitoring should accurately assess the status of an evaluation at a specific point in time. In addition to the technical progress on evaluation products, the monitoring reports should inform evaluation management about the calendar time and labor spent and remaining for each product.

Figure 21.2. Flow Chart to Guide Descriptions of How Local Child Welfare Programs Work.

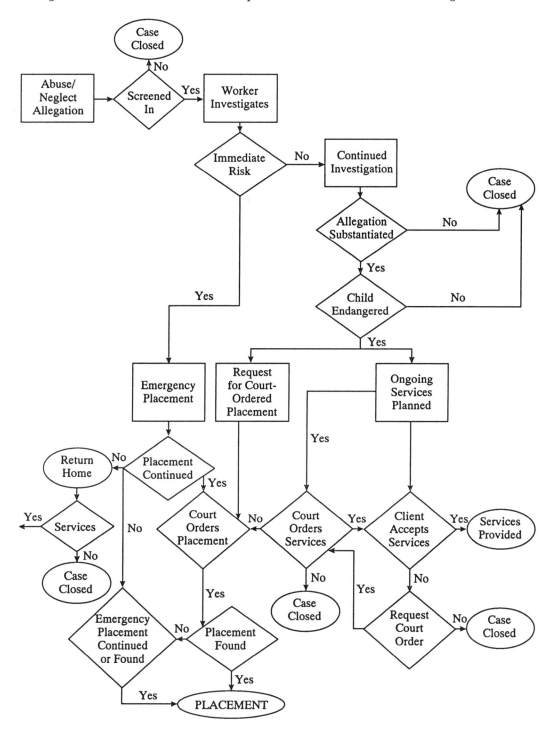

Source: Adapted from the Technical Proposal *To Conduct an Evaluation of NIH Implementation of Section 491 of the Public Health Service Act, Mandating a Program of Protection for Research Subjects,* James Bell Associates, August 1991. (unpublished)

Systematic monitoring also should provide incentives for staff to accomplish evaluation products. Interim progress monitoring should be a constructive endeavor, one that encourages creativity and recognition of evaluation opportunities and problems. In short, the monitoring process should help evaluation management and staff to complete a high-quality, useful evaluation on budget and schedule. It also should identify opportunities to enhance the value of the evaluation product(s). The following suggestions should help readers avoid common monitoring problems by focusing on well-specified product milestones, well-timed monitoring reports, and effective use of monitoring information.

Well-Specified Milestones

Evaluation assignments should have progress milestones for each evaluation product covered by the assignment. The milestones should be part of a description of the monitoring process for that assignment. When errors of omission or commission made during assignment lead to poorly specified product milestones, interim monitoring may be ineffective in pinpointing the true status of evaluation product completion. In other words, if the milestone events for completing an evaluation product are wrong, it is likely that the product will be incomplete, delayed, or flawed.

In a common situation, the completion of a cross-agency data collection protocol is specified as the next to last milestone in creating data collection plans. Presuming that creation of a cross-agency data collection protocol is feasible, the last milestone is a brief, low-intensity period of initial data acquisition during which individual agencies try to transfer the data stipulated in the cross-agency protocol. Such a trial often reveals that a separate milestone is needed to complete agency-specific data collection protocols because of the unique characteristics of local data systems. It simply is not possible to use a generic data collection protocol without carefully tailoring it to each agency's circumstances.

Well-Timed Monitoring

Interim progress monitoring absorbs evaluation resources. Too much monitoring can cause unwarranted loss of resources, but too little monitoring may permit the squandering of project resources on unproductive efforts. Progress monitoring is appropriate when the forward momentum of the project is maintained or enhanced through monitoring. Effort should not be distracted from productive project activity for monitoring purposes, nor should evaluation resources be wasted on unproductive efforts because monitoring did not detect a difficulty.

To establish the monitoring schedule, start with the intended completion dates for major products, such as completion of a literature review or a data collection and analysis plan, and move backward. Monitoring milestones for each major product should be defined by considering the steps in product development. Consider the time and effort needed previously to accomplish each step. Sometimes a step may involve a small amount of labor but require substantial calendar time. An example of a calendar-sensitive activity is acquisition of data from a government agency. However, any activity requiring support and effort outside the span of control of evaluation management should be more carefully considered in setting a monitoring schedule.

A monitoring approach based solely on elapsed time should be avoided, e.g., monthly progress markers unrelated to product completion. Such an approach complicates efforts to establish coherent staff assignments because monitoring by elapsed time disregards the natural development cycle for evaluation products. For some assignments, this will create opportunities for an inexperienced staff member to flounder for lengthy periods because the time between monitoring reports is too long. For other assignments, progress will be reported prematurely, or no progress will be reported, just because the monitoring date has arrived before a natural point of closure has been reached in developing the evaluation product. Both occurrences may lead to missed opportunities for evaluation management to digest interim findings and redirect the project effort accordingly. These are foregone chances to optimize the evaluation investment.

Ineffective Use of Monitoring

Well-defined interim milestones and well-timed monitoring do not guarantee effective use of progress monitoring information. The managers who conduct the monitoring must be able to interpret monitoring information and respond appropriately. They must be able to engage in constructive discussions with those whose work is being monitored and know how to revise subsequent assignments in response to monitoring findings.

It is not enough for senior management to establish a workable monitoring process. In a larger evaluation, it is especially important that the mid- and lower-level management staff be able to apply those tools. They must be able to interpret monitoring data and to adjust staff assignments accordingly. A common failing of evaluation monitoring is that the project director and senior project management assume that their monitoring approach will translate automatically into effective monitoring by lower echelon evaluation management staff. They should appreciate the need to orient and train these staff, and understand the level of monitoring involvement required of senior evaluation management staff. When there is uncertainty about the quality of monitoring, senior management staff should heighten their own participation at all levels of the project. Since carrying out an evaluation is a dynamic activity, it is unlikely that a monitoring plan can be used without adaptation during the life of the project.

There are many other ways interim progress monitoring can derail.

Milestones may be well defined but the indicators of milestone achievement flawed (an irony for an evaluation project). A common mistake, for example, is acceptance that an assignment is completed because of the existence of a draft document. Without a careful review of the document, managers cannot establish that the assignment is complete.

Ensuring Product Quality and Usefulness

Imagine that it is six months after an evaluation was completed. The project director is inquiring about the response to program recommendations included in the final report. These alternatives were well received initially by the evaluation sponsor, but no action to implement program changes has occurred. Through further inquiry, the evaluation director learns that the program staff were unable to plan implementation of the recommendations. They were uncertain about how to conceptualize change in their operating system without harming performance. They also were reluctant to accept certain crucial findings contained in the report that established the rationale for the suggested alternatives. In short, although methodology experts had attested to the competence of the evaluation, key people who had to act on the evaluation did not accept its credibility or could not implement the recommendations easily. How should evaluation management ensure that those who must act on the recommendations perceive them as valuable and useful?

While methodology and technical execution — meeting the standards of the pertinent social science discipline — are central to evaluation quality, they are not sufficient standards if program policy and management decision makers are expected to act on the evaluation findings and recommendations. These groups will want to see convincing evidence that the evaluators understand the subject program; that the evaluation is based on appropriate data; that recommendations are clear about why and how to modify the program; and what is likely to happen if the recommended changes are made.

When an evaluation offers ill-founded recommendations, these often demonstrate that the evaluators did not understand the program's purpose and operations. For example, evaluation management may not comprehend that operational objectives for a program are set at the local level. If so, the evaluators may mistake the lack of strong national objectives as a sign of a weak program performance and recommend formulation of clearer national objectives. In such a case, if evaluation management had used appropriate quality assurance steps such as checking carefully with program staff at both the national and local levels early in developing the evaluation, the findings and recommendations might not have been so divorced from the program reality.

The quest for high-quality, useful evaluation products should permeate all facets of evaluation management — from clarifying the evaluation mandate to the final polishing of the last deliverable report. Report outlines, preliminary briefings, and draft reports are useful for gaining agreement about the contents and style of written documents. As described below, these practices help to shape evaluation reports so they can be used by sponsors and program staff.

A Four-Step Process for Written Reports

Usually the written reports developed in an evaluation are the main tangible evidence that an evaluation has occurred. The reports must convey the essence of an evaluation in informative and understandable terms. What practical steps can evaluation management take to assure that project reports meet this requirement?

An effective approach is to develop written reports in four steps, with involvement in each step by the sponsor, subject program staff, and, if warranted, outside experts. This approach is predicated on establishing agreement about the content of the report(s) through outlines and briefings before extensive effort is spent writing the report text.

The first step is to establish an outline for each project report that explains its purpose, the titles and intended contents of the chapters and sections, and the planned length and style of the document. Agreement on this outline should be accomplished very early in the project, or as part of the original clarification of the evaluation mandate. In fact, one way to codify the technical aspect of the mandate, such as the evaluation, purpose, and scope, is to develop a detailed outline of the planned evaluation report(s).

Each report outline should be referenced as a source of guidance often in the early preparation stages and throughout data collection and analysis. The possible need to modify the outline of a report should be part of the dialogue among evaluation management and evaluation staff as well as sponsor and subject program representatives.

At the earliest possible point in the project, the second step in report development should begin. A briefing package should be constructed following the outline. It should cover the key points to the contained in each chapter and section of the report. The objective is to summarize the essence of the report before it is actually written. In a briefing format using exhibits and other short forms of written communication, such as "bullet" lists, the content of the forthcoming report(s) can be discussed without the time required in developing high-quality narrative text. With the project results presented as early as possible in preliminary form, the evaluation staff and sponsor can identify strengths and weaknesses while time and resources are still available for making corrections.

The first two steps of report development are comparatively inexpensive, designed to convey report contents without incurring the cost of writing fully developed documents. The third step is normally one of the most expensive evaluation activities because it involves producing a full-scale draft report. While this report should be complete and readable, the emphasis should be on technical content. Editing and polishing the document should not be done until the technical contents of the final report are reviewed and confirmed.

The draft final report should be subjected to intensive review by the sponsor, subject program staff, and any outside experts included in the project as advisers. However, dissemination of the draft report should be carefully controlled; the evaluation management should limit reviewers to those who are familiar with the project and understand that the draft report is not a final product.

The final step in report development is polishing the written document to ensure effective communication of the evaluation results to the intended evaluation audience. Since this phase can absorb resources that might have been more usefully spent in other project activities, it is wise to avoid overpolishing. Some reports have very limited audiences that do not require the same level of editing needed for a high-profile document distributed to the public.

At one extreme, this final step in evaluation may involve restructuring and rewriting the draft report to enhance its power to communicate. This is done without altering the essential meaning of the technical evaluation information contained in the accepted draft report. It requires a combination of well-developed technical knowledge of the evaluation and sound writing skills. At the other extreme, polishing a proof, editing to enhance grammar, spelling, and punctuation, and to correct other mistakes that may appear in text or exhibits.

Conclusion

This chapter provides advice on the management of program evaluation projects beginning with the goal of evaluation management: optimal achievement of the mandate for each evaluation through the responsive, effective application of resources available for the evaluation. To achieve this goal, evaluation management must focus on five areas:

1. Clarifying the Evaluation Mandate
2. Staffing and Organizing for Results
3. Making Productive Assignments
4. Monitoring Interim Progress
5. Ensuring Product Quality and Usefulness

Though attention to these five areas will not guarantee a well-managed evaluation, it should help to avert many of the most common causes of ineffectively managed evaluations. Even so, evaluation management must also be alert to other problems that may compromise achievement of the evaluation mandate. Lapses in general work planning, recordkeeping, or data collection and analysis supervision, for example, may also affect the way an evaluation turns out.

Another, more specific level of evaluation management advice contains practical suggestions for realizing the aims in each area of evaluation management. There are tips on ways to conduct selected evaluation management activities such as an efficient method of rechecking the evaluation mandate with the evaluation sponsor during the course of the project. This verification can be accomplished by integrating the rechecking into normal evaluation activities, such as the review of the data collection and analysis plan.

Exhibit 21.1 summarizes the practical suggestions for the five areas of evaluation management discussed in this chapter. The sixteen suggestions listed in the exhibit should be addressed by evaluation project management regardless of the size of an evaluation.

The cost of evaluation management activities should be accepted as an integral and necessary part of the cost of conducting an evaluation. Wherever possible, evaluation management costs should be contained by imaginatively integrating evaluation management and technical evaluation activities. In a well-managed project there is a seamless connection between evaluation management and the technical conduct of the evaluation.

Exhibit 21.1. Practical Suggestions for Evaluation Management.

Clarifying the Evaluation Mandate
1. Gain agreement on the evaluation mandate before or very early in the evaluation.
2. Check this agreement periodically during contacts with evaluation clients and sponsors.
3. Minimize the cost of maintaining agreement by integrating checks on the mandate with technical evaluation activities, such as client review of a draft data collection and analysis protocol.
4. Beware of tacit agreements.

Staffing and Organizing for Results
5. Use a staffing matrix and observations about interpersonal communication skills to facilitate initial selection of staff members.
6. Organize evaluation staff members into teams based on project tasks, evaluation methodology, or subject matter responsibilities.
7. In evaluations with two or more teams, form a synthesis group to foster coherent effort across the technical teams.

Making Assignments Productive
8. Be very clear about each assignment's product, outcome, or end point as well as resources and expected completion date.
9. If possible, use well-chosen examples from similar projects to illustrate expected products.
10. Formalize assignment agreements.

Monitoring Interim Progress
11. Don't confuse expected activity and expenditure levels with commensurate technical progress.
12. Time monitoring episodes to complement and not impede product development.
13. Ensure that project management staff are effective monitors.

Assuring Product Quality and Usefulness
14. Involve the sponsor, program, and other representatives of the evaluation audience in a four-step report development process.
15. Start early in the project with an outline, and then use a briefing to gain agreement about the content of the report.
16. Solidify the agreement on report content through follow-up briefings on draft products; reserve polishing and editing resources until the technical content is finalized.

The cost of evaluation management must be appropriate. Small-scale evaluations cannot afford the burden of overly rigorous evaluation management activities, such as extensive written documentation of the evaluation mandate or staff assignments. More difficult evaluations will require higher levels of evaluation management. If the sponsor is inconsistent about the evaluation mandate, more attention will be needed in this area. Similarly, if there are concerns that evaluation staff are not optimally qualified, more attention must be paid to whether the proper expertise is being applied to each important evaluation assignment.

The goal of evaluation management and the aims in each management area apply even in very small-scale evaluations. Suggestions must be adapted depending on the type, size, duration, and other distinguishing characteristics of the evaluation project. A small project conducted in fewer than thirty days by a single evaluator would not involve use of a staff qualifications matrix, for example. Nevertheless, a solo evaluator needs to carry out a careful review of his or her personal qualifications for the evaluation at hand. It is necessary to gauge the presence of shortcomings in substantive, methodological, or interpersonal qualifications, even if only one person is conducting the evaluation. In a one-person evaluation, qualification deficits can be compensated for through the use of publications and the help of others who have the needed expertise. Discussions with the client can be structured to fill gaps in the evaluator's substantive knowledge of the policy or program being evaluated.

In sum, effective management can dramatically influence the level of contribution made by an evaluation. If the aim of the evaluation remains in focus and appropriate staff and other evaluation resources are applied to well-defined activities consistent with those aims, the possibility that the evaluation will generate valuable knowledge and spark improvements in policies and programs should increase. Put simply, a valid and useful evaluation depends as much on effective management as on elegant study design.

Further Reading

Alkin, M. C., Daillak, R., and White, P. *Using Evaluations: Does Evaluation Make a Difference?* Newbury Park, Calif.: Sage, 1979.

Carlson, R. H., and Crane, A. B. "Planning and Managing Useful Evaluations." In J. S. Wholey, K. E. Newcomer, and Associates, *Improving Government Performance.* San Francisco: Jossey-Bass, 1989.

Chelimsky, E. "Old Patterns and New Directions in Program Evaluation." In E. Chelimsky (ed.), *Program Evaluation: Patterns and Directions.* Washington, D.C.: American Society for Public Administration, 1985.

Chelimsky, E. "The Politics of Program Evaluation." In H. S. Bloom and R. J. Lights (eds.), *Evaluation Practice in Review.* New Directions for Program Evaluation, no. 34. San Francisco: Jossey-Bass, 1987.

Downs, A. *Inside Bureaucracy.* Santa Monica, Calif.: Rand Corporation, 1967.

Drucker, P. F. *Management: Tasks, Responsibilities, Practices.* New York: HarperCollins, 1983.

Goldenberg, E. N. "The Three Faces of Evaluation." *Journal of Policy Analyses and Management,* 1983, *2*(4), 515–525.

Guba, E. G., and Lincoln, Y. S. "The Countenances of Fourth-General Evaluation: Description, Judgment, and Negotiation." Paper presented at the joint meeting of the Evaluation Network, Evaluation Research Society, and the Canadian Evaluation Association, Toronto, Canada, October 1985.

Patton, M. Q. *Creative Evaluation.* Newbury Park, Calif.: Sage, 1981.

Patton, M. Q. *Utilization-Focused Evaluation.* (2nd ed.) Newbury Park, Calif.: Sage, 1986.

Peters, T. J., and Waterman, R. H. *In Search of Excellence.* New York: HarperCollins, 1982.

Rossi, P. H. "Standards for Evaluation Practice." *New Directions for Program Evaluation,* no. 15. San Francisco: Jossey-Bass, 1982.

Rossi, P. H., and Freeman, H. E. *Evaluation: A Systematic Approach.* Newbury Park, Calif.: Sage, 1989.

Schmidt, R. E., Scanlon, J. W., and Bell, J. B. *Evaluability Assessment: Making Public Programs Work Better,* pp. 4–5. Human Services Monograph Series, v. 14. Washington, D.C.: Project Share, 1979.

Sonnichsen, R. C. "Communicating Excellence in the FBI." In J. S. Wholey (ed.), *Organizational Excellence.* Lexington, Mass.: Lexington Books, 1987.

Wholey, J. S. *Evaluation: Promise and Performance.* Washington, D.C.: The Urban Institute, 1979.

Wholey, J. S. *Organizational Excellence: Stimulating Quality and Communicating Value.* Lexington, Mass.: Heath, 1987.

22

Evaluators as Change Agents

Richard C. Sonnichsen

Evaluation-generated information enjoys no preferential treatment in organizations and often competes with other data available to decision makers. One way for evaluators to increase the likelihood that evaluation data will compete successfully in this environment, and achieve the goal of having an impact on an organization, is to develop and structure their evaluation activities to complement a change-oriented approach to the evaluation process.

One of the most effective means for evaluators to achieve change in organizations is by writing recommendations to accompany evaluation reports. Recommendations, based on evaluation findings, can serve as a vehicle to insert evaluation data into the administrative apparatus of the organization, thus ensuring visibility and scrutiny of the evaluation report. Recommendations for change are an integral part of the evaluation — not an afterthought to conclusion of data collection and analysis. Good recommendations will take into consideration the internal and external organizational environment and any restraints that might inhibit their full implementation.

Optimally, evaluators and program administrators together will frame recommendations by developing agreement on recommended courses of action for program improvement. Good recommendations are timely, realistic, directed to the proper person or entity, comprehensible, specific, and easily translated into action. Change-oriented evaluators will conduct follow-up procedures to ensure full implementation of approved recommendations.

Recommendations should be viewed by evaluators as an important component in the evaluation process, functioning as the link between evaluation findings and the organization. Without recommendations, evaluation findings can easily succumb to bureaucratic resistance and organizational inertia, thus precluding internal debate on the findings as well as positive impact on the organization.

This chapter describes the prerequisites for organizational change, the benefits that accrue to evaluators who view themselves as change agents, the skills needed by evaluators to influence organizational policies, and the organizational environment in which evaluators work. The advocacy approach to evaluation, whereby evaluators actively participate in the organizational decision-making process, will be presented as essential for evaluators seeking to have a positive influence on organization programs.

This chapter also discusses how to convert evaluation findings to organization actions through the effective development, framing, writing, and placement of recommendations. Effective methods for presenting findings are described along with advice on how to integrate the entire evaluation process, from solicitation of evaluation topics to the dissemination of evaluation reports, into the organization's administrative apparatus.

This chapter offers evaluators a prescription for success through the use of recommendations as an important device for effecting change and increasing the implementation of evaluation results. The suggestions offered are based on a review of the literature, the author's study of internal evaluation offices in several federal agencies (Sonnichsen, 1991), and the author's ten years of experience directing an internal evaluation office in the Federal Bureau of Investigation (FBI).

Understanding Organizational Decision Making

One of the initial steps for evaluators who wish to promote program evaluation as a valued tool in the decision-making process is to carefully examine the institution's decision-making apparatus, that is, how decisions are made and data are gathered and assimilated in support of the process. Once decision procedures are understood, the evaluation approach can be structured to complement the decision-making process.

In conceptualizing evaluation, many evaluators have the somewhat naive expectation that unbiased, scientific research should appeal to decision makers who will then incorporate such findings in their deliberations and decision making about important matters. Some evaluators labor under the delusion that elegant methodologies, eloquent reports, and scientific neutrality are sufficient qualities to ensure that evaluation results will be used. The ubiquitous lament in the evaluation literature over the lack of use of evaluation reports, coupled with the argument by Weiss (1988) that even enlightenment may be considered a form of evaluation utilization, should serve as visible reminders that the evaluation process does not always lead to better decisions. Evaluation, like other organizational functions, competes for attention in the organizational arena along with a host of other special interests, political realities, and resource constraints.

Evaluation has failed to become a mainstream event in many organizations and often tends to operate at the periphery of the decision-making process. The evaluation literature is replete with examples of the failure of much of the evaluation effort to produce positive results—that is, be used by the organization to improve programs. The judgmental nature of evaluation may be partially responsible for evaluation nonuse. Therefore an extra burden is placed on evaluators, who must not only conduct evaluations but also market the benefits of program evaluation as a value-added organizational exercise.

Modern organizations today are complex structures with diverse work forces in which numerous entities compete for resources, power, and the ability to influence policies and operations. In organizations where this competition is encountered, decision making is not always a rational, linear event, and evaluators have no automatic guarantee that their findings will be incorporated into organizational decision-making processes. They cannot be sure that evaluation results will even be discussed in organization debates about operations and administrative policies and procedures. Evaluators should realize that they enjoy no preferred position over other organizational mechanisms for the accumulation and distribution of information but must create a demand for their product.

Utilization of evaluation results in organizations is the subject of an ongoing debate in the evaluation community. Different views of utilization may best be illustrated by the positions of Patton (1988) and Weiss (1988). Patton, a leading advocate of a pragmatic, user-oriented approach to evaluation, claims that utilization-oriented evaluators are frequently successful in getting their results used. Weiss, on the other hand, sees less immediate "instrumental" utilization occurring and adds "enlightenment," or the influence of evaluation results at some future point in time, as one criterion for judging evaluation utilization.

The imperative for evaluators, therefore, is to recognize the arena in which evaluation operates, understand organizational dynamics, tailor their procedures and techniques to market the evaluation process effectively, and become one of the voices in the organization. Successful evaluation efforts can then be measured by the impact the evaluation process has on major organizational policies.

Using Evaluation to Promote Organizational Change

Organizational change is a complex process, dependent on a multitude of conditions, realities, and individual personalities. Change in organizations requires a confluence of ideas, timing, support of top management, an organizational tolerance for risk, and individuals prepared to confront uncertainty in order to examine alternative ways to conduct organization business. Evaluators can seldom control all the factors necessary for positive organizational change. However, they do have the power to prepare themselves to take advantage of opportunities for change when organizational opportunities are present and recognized. The goal of change-oriented evaluators should be to influence the organization by producing independent, un-biased, empirical evidence of the operations and performance of organizational entities. To effect positive change in organizations through evaluation, evaluators should develop a comprehensive knowledge of the organization, including its culture, its programs and their context; they must demonstrate a commitment to the use of evaluation as one of the tools available to produce change.

Understanding the organizational environment and the decision-making process is vital because decisions are the precipitating vehicles for introducing change in organizations. For program evaluators to participate in the deliberation process in organizations, they must understand that this entry into the change process will require them to transfer their research findings from evaluation reports to the pragmatic organizational arena where decisions are made.

Attributes for Successful Evaluators

Evaluators wishing to effect positive organizational change must develop themselves to operate effectively in the organization environment. In addition to a philosophical orientation to the evaluation process as a change mechanism, evaluators should develop the attributes that will facilitate their acceptance as change agents by the organization. This section describes five attributes that can be developed by evaluators to help promote the successful use of evaluation as a vehicle for change in organizations.

The primary attribute for evaluators who wish to influence policy in organizations is the belief that they can indeed cause change and affect organizational decisions. Kiefer and Stroh (1984) refer to organizations where people understand that they have the capacity to create the future of the organization and determine their own destiny as *metanoic* organizations. Individuals in this type of organization believe that they are responsible for the quality of both their personal lives and the organization, and that collectively they can shape their own destiny.

A second desirable attribute for evaluators is the ability to think critically. Evaluators must develop the capacity to review and ponder organizational activities and question basic organizational assumptions. They must see critical thinking not as a pessimistic judgmental process but as a cognitive activity seeking fresh approaches to problems. Brookfield (1987) suggests that critical thinkers have the ability to challenge assumptions and explore alternatives to existing ways of doing things. He believes that "reflective skepticism," the challenging of entrenched beliefs, behaviors, and structures, will lead to productive engagements with problems.

Third on the list of attributes for change-agent evaluators is credibility. A recent study of evaluation activities at the federal level found that evaluator credibility was cited as the single most important component determining the success of internal evaluation offices (Sonnichsen, 1991). The credibility of an evaluation staff is an aggregate of several factors, with the sum total being greater than any single element. Perceptions of the evaluation staff held by the members of the organization is affected by the personal reputation of the evaluation staff director, the skills and experience of the individual evaluators, the historical reputation for independence of the evaluation office, and the quality of the evaluations it produces.

Credibility is a fragile mosaic of components subject to continual reaffirmation. Any perception of evaluator bias or a lack of confidence by organizational actors in the evaluation product can quickly damage the credibility of the evaluation staff. Without a perception within the organization that evaluators are credible, the evaluation process has a diminished chance for success.

Fourth on the list of attributes for evaluators wishing to influence organizations, and closely related to credibility, is objectivity. Evaluators hoping to influence organizational policy and activities must continually assert their objectivity through their behavior in the organization when collecting data, issuing reports, and writing recommendations. Any hint that bias has affected findings or recommendations in an evaluation significantly erodes the ability of evaluators to influence the organization.

The fifth attribute is a complete understanding of the organization's administrative apparatus and knowledge of how decisions are made. As important as the first four attributes are, they will be inconsequential if the evaluators do not possess this one. Elegant methodology and eloquent report writing are insufficient for successful evaluation if information obtained during evaluation efforts fails to gain the attention of the decision maker at the appropriate time. It is critically important for evaluators to recognize the importance of timing and appropriate methods of presenting evaluation results. Recognition of the need for timely information helps ensure that evaluation findings and recommendations will be considered throughout the organization. Whether to use written reports, oral briefings, or memoranda to disseminate evaluation results will be dependent on the urgency of the need for the data and the desires of the client.

The Craft of Evaluation

The essence of evaluation, and its potential benefit to organizations, is its capacity for an unemotional, unbiased, data-driven examination of organizational policies, administration, and operations. Evaluation is fundamentally an information-producing process designed to increase the quality of organizational decisions. Its value to the organization derives from the credibility of the information produced and the ability of the evaluators to link the evaluation findings with the organizational decision-making process, thereby influencing organization activities through recommendations for positive change.

The goal of evaluation is to use data to improve the performance of programs and, by extrapolation, organizations and government agencies.

In order for this condition to occur, evaluators need to market their product, or optimally, create a demand for their work, their findings, and reports. This is the area where evaluation ceases to be a technical skill and becomes a craft. Why should anyone want to read an evaluation report or review the findings of an evaluation? The burden on evaluators is to create an expectation that an organization member can derive some benefit by becoming familiar with the results of evaluations. This section will discuss practical approaches to writing reports and publicizing the results of evaluations within organizations.

Writing and Disseminating Evaluation Reports

One finding in a recent study of internal federal evaluation offices (Sonnichsen, 1991) was that evaluation has a greater impact on an organization when evaluation procedures are routinized in the organization and understood by the employees. Writing and widely disseminating reports at the completion of evaluations helps build the image of evaluation as an integral component in the administration and management of an organization. At the completion of each of its evaluations, the FBI evaluation office disseminates two copies of a written report to all fifty-six FBI field offices and each headquarters division. This practice not only publicizes all evaluation results but also maintains the awareness of FBI managers and executives that evaluation is used to aid the decision-making process.

Each report has a short (three to ten pages) executive summary that encapsulates the entire report and is written for the busy executive who may not have time to read the complete document. An attempt is made to keep the report within thirty to fifty pages; each one is bound in a distinctive red cover designed to separate these reports from other FBI communications. Evaluators should take every opportunity to disseminate their evaluation reports. Reports are tangible evidence that an evaluation was conducted; they help reinforce and maintain the evaluation enterprise in an organization.

Solicitation of Evaluation Topics

Applying the technique of evaluation to an organization's most important issues and problems contributes to the creation of an evaluation ethic in an organization. Evaluators should strive to apply their skills and energies to issues that are important to the organization. To ensure that the FBI evaluation staff maintains its visibility in the organization and does not become enmeshed in mundane issues, the views of each of fifty-six special agents in charge of FBI field offices and the eleven assistant directors assigned to FBI headquarters in Washington, D.C., are solicited annually.

Using a frequency count as a prioritizing mechanism, the final list of topics is submitted to the director for approval and constitutes the annual work plan for the evaluation staff. The inclusion of all organization constituencies in the selection of potential evaluations and the dissemination of the results of all evaluations helps generate interest in, and ownership of, the activities of the evaluation staff, and helps perpetuate the use of evaluation in the management of an organization. In the FBI this annual list of planned evaluations is supplemented with requests from the director and program managers, a five-year review of all major investigative programs, and self-initiated studies.

Presentation of Evaluation Findings

One common reason that evaluators often fail to produce positive changes in organizations may be their inability to introduce their reports successfully into the organizational decision-making process. Evaluation reports that are unread obviously cannot have an impact on organizational policies. No evaluation can affect an organization unless the information it produced reaches appropriate decision makers prior to their deliberations. Many evaluation reports simply do not affect organizations because evaluators do not understand the mechanisms for converting the findings of an evaluation into a format that is compatible with the routine organizational decision-making procedure. Effective conversion and transmission of evaluation data to the organization is organization specific and may occur through oral briefings, written reports, formal and informal meetings, casual conversations, or direct contacts with interested stakeholders and the organizational executives involved in decision making. Even within organizations different clients may exhibit preferences for one approach over another.

Whenever possible, evaluators should brief senior agency executives in addition to giving them evaluation reports. An oral briefing of thirty minutes or less is an excellent way to precipitate discussion and generate debate on evaluation findings. Well-organized presentations of empirical data at meetings of major agency actors reduces the impact of parochial, emotionally charged arguments. Forcing public discussions about evaluation findings clarifies the issues and facilitates the decision-making process. FBI evaluators strive to be included on the agendas of meetings when senior officials meet to discuss evaluation results.

The FBI evaluation staff routinely use an overhead projector for briefings, an approach that has advantages for both the evaluator and the audience. The overhead transparency focuses the attention of the audience on the topic being discussed while allowing the briefer to recall the details of the evaluation without extensive referral to notes. The use of transparencies also permits a fluid return to previously discussed items of interest without any loss of continuity in the briefing.

Converting Evaluation Findings to Organizational Action

A complete understanding of the organization's decision-making apparatus is essential for evaluators who want to contribute to organizational change.

Organizations develop idiosyncratic processes for decision making that grow from an accretion of rules and procedures plus the personalities of incumbent managers. Authority levels vary with the magnitude of the decision, with major organizational decisions made by senior management. Evaluators can contribute to the decision-making debate only if evaluation results come to the attention of the decision makers in a format congruent with other data available and at the appropriate time.

Use of Decision Memoranda

To convert evaluation findings to organization action, evaluators should report their results the same way other material is made available to management for decision making. One of the primary vehicles for action in many organizations is a decision memorandum suggesting a course of action and directed to a manager with sufficient authority to implement the recommendation. Recommendations serve as a vehicle for moving ideas from the conceptual stage to the policy-making arena where they are debated and approved or disapproved. Without recommendations, an evaluation report can be ignored or fall victim to bureaucratic inertia, and thus fail to have any impact on the organization. Recommendations link the evaluation process with the organization. They are tangible evidence that an evaluation was conducted and they keep the evaluation results alive by requiring executive action.

In the Federal Bureau of Investigation all evaluation recommendations are submitted by memoranda to the director for approval. After approval, implementation of the recommendations becomes the responsibility of the appropriate manager. The FBI evaluation staff issues recommendations with all its reports to ensure action on evaluation findings. Absent a recommendation for action, good ideas and changes advocated by evaluators rarely are implemented. A recommendation is difficult to ignore; it demands that the organization act and that something be done. The change model of evaluation assumes that the essential ingredient for effecting change is a commitment to making recommendations at the completion of evaluations and conducting follow-up at some reasonable point after approval and implementation to learn the status of the recommended action.

Advocacy Role for Evaluators

Traditionally, evaluators have viewed their work as terminating with the issuance of a report. For evaluators wishing to effect organizational change, however, this approach is inappropriate. Typically, information furnished to senior managers reflects the opinions and positions of various constituencies in the organization, each with their own viewpoint and agenda. In this environment, an evaluation report without an advocate may not receive adequate representation during deliberations about organization activities and policies. Action-oriented evaluators can correct this potential deficiency by participating in the organization decision-making process and advocating the findings and recommendations found in the report.

Advocacy evaluation, which blends independent, scientific evaluation practices with an evaluator change-agent perspective, is one approach to creating change in organizations through evaluation (Sonnichsen, 1988). Advocacy evaluation is defined as the active involvement of both evaluators and their supervisors in the organizational process of discussion, approval, and implementation of recommendations. Evaluators should promote the recommendations only after the completion of an independent, objective, defensible evaluation of a program or policy. Approaching evaluation from an advocacy perspective requires that the evaluators are objective and knowledgeable observers of programs and can offer senior management unbiased views of the workings of organizational programs. Advocacy evaluation is appropriate for evaluators striving to be viewed as influential players in the organizational culture.

Issuing recommendations and actively participating in the organizational debate over their approval and implementation reinforces the influence of evaluators in organizations and helps develop evaluation as an important component in an organizational structure.

Developing Effective Recommendations

Once evaluators are accepted by the organization as contributors to change and understand the change-oriented approach to the evaluation process, they should consider how best to frame their recommendations. Recommendations should not be afterthoughts of evaluation efforts, but deliberate, empirically based suggestions for organizational action.

Conceptual Elements of Recommendations

Recommendations are both normative and future oriented. Recommendations are normative statements about how things should be. They are grounded in but depart from the evaluation report, which describes what is. Conceptually, recommendations are judgments by evaluators, based on the findings of the report, about changes in program activities that are likely to bring about some desired future condition. Shedding the retrospective role of evaluation, the recommendation writer looks forward, proposing activities that are expected to improve program effectiveness.

Writing Good Recommendations

The actual writing of the recommendation is a critical component of the evaluation process if the evaluation effort is to influence the organization and contribute to change. The ultimate purpose of the recommendation is to convert evaluation findings into action statements that are directed to alternative ways of conducting organizational business.

Recommendations are an opportunity for evaluators to transform their efforts at data collection and analysis into a prescription for organizational improvement. They present opportunities to influence organizations and in some cases to effect dramatic changes, as evidenced in the following two examples. Hendricks and Handley (1990) report that recommendations by the Inspector General of the U.S. Department of Health and Human Services showed how to enroll 13,500 more children into Head Start Centers at no additional cost. In 1975, the FBI, acting on evaluator recommendations, made a paradigmatic shift in the philosophical approach to conducting criminal investigations, focusing on the *quality* of investigations and eliminating the emphasis on the *quantity* of statistical results produced (Sonnichsen, 1987). The FBI evaluation staff makes recommendations an integral part of every evaluation and routinely effects significant organizational improvements (Sonnichsen, 1991).

Qualities of Well-Written Recommendations

A well-written recommendation has five basic qualities; it should be timely, realistic, directed to the appropriate person or entity, comprehensible, and specific. Incorporating these characteristics into recommendations helps ensure their implementation.

Of the five qualities of well-written recommendations, timeliness has supremacy over the others. If evaluators do not produce their findings when management needs them, the evaluation may become inconsequential. An elegant, methodologically sound evaluation has little value if the decision has already been made. From the beginning of an evaluation, evaluators must be acutely aware of any time requirements affecting the results and recommendations.

In writing recommendations, evaluators must consider the organizational environment, weighing resource and budget constraints, political pressures, and organizational conditions that might affect implementation. If recommendations are impossible to implement, the program manager has easy justification for ignoring them.

Recommendations must be specifically directed not only to a manager with the authority to accept them but also to an individual who will be responsible for implementing the suggested changes. Failure to designate someone to oversee implementation allows the inertia of organizations to smother the recommendations.

Recommendations should be simple and very specific. They must be understood by all those affected. They should be organized into specific tasks. Each recommendation should encompass only one idea. If there is a division of responsibility for implementing the recommendation, this should be spelled out in detail, especially if it involves crossing organizational structures.

The actual number of recommendations varies with the situation. Evaluations of complex administrative procedures may require extensive detailed recommendations. The FBI evaluation staff once recommended fifty-six changes in an administrative area that involved complex information retrieval. More often, they recommend four to eight programmatic changes.

Linking Recommendations with Findings

Successful recommendations, although judgments by the evaluators on ideas for program improvement, should be linked to the evaluation findings and grounded in the empirical evidence presented in the evaluation report. The experience of the evaluators and their observations formed during the evaluation are essential ingredients used to frame the recommendations. Equally important, however, is a solid nexus between the recommendations and the evaluation findings. Without this explicit linkage, the potential for management approval and implementation of the recommendations diminishes.

Conditions Where Options Are Appropriate

Recommendations are not the only tool available to evaluators wishing to change organizations. Under some circumstances, it may be appropriate to offer options instead of recommendations (Wholey, 1986). Options allow evaluators to present alternative scenarios for decision makers when dealing with complex issues. Options would be appropriate in the following circumstances: (1) there is no preponderance of evidence elevating one course of action over another; (2) the client for the evaluation is more comfortable with options and has requested them; or (3) a political decision has to be reached and the stakeholders want to debate each potential alternative. When writing options, it is desirable to enumerate in detail the consequences of choosing each one; both the positive and negative outcomes likely to result from selecting a particular course of action should be given.

Options are particularly germane when the goal of the evaluators is to engender ownership of proposed change in the affected organization entities. In 1992, the FBI evaluation office was asked to review the bureau's organizational structure and decision-making process with the goal of improving organization efficiency. Due to the magnitude of the undertaking and the probability that radical changes might be appropriate, an advisory panel was established to review the evaluators' findings. Evaluators presented the advisory panel with options for organization change and improvement that surfaced during data collection.

Framing and Placement of Recommendations

Framing recommendations for evaluation reports is a deliberate, evolutionary process that occurs throughout the evaluation, culminating with evaluator interpretation of the findings based on knowledge gained while conducting the evaluation. Recommendations are solutions to problems. As such, they are developed throughout the course of the evaluation while the evaluator examines a program and discusses problems and potential solutions with interested stakeholders, program participants, and key administrators. Unfortunately, most evaluators concentrate the vast majority of their time and energies on the findings and very little time on writing the recommendations. This division of labor is reversed for the program managers who are much more concerned with the recommendations than the report itself (Patton, 1989).

A significant dichotomy can exist between evaluation findings and recommendations. The differences are both philosophical and physical. Philosophically, evaluators should view the evaluation findings as an accurate description of the conditions they encountered and not subject to change once finalized. Reports contain descriptive and empirical data based on observations, statements by persons interviewed, and the review and analysis of qualitative and quantitative data. Recommendations, on the other hand, are crafted by the evaluators, sometimes with the assistance of program personnel, and are subject to their judgments and interpretation of the data.

Physically, recommendations need not be contained within the final evaluation report but may be presented in a separate memorandum or letter accompanying the report. It is not uncommon to alter or change recommendations based on funding or human resource constraints. The report itself, however, should rarely be modified; an exception would occur if inaccuracies were detected. Separating the recommendations from the evaluation findings maintains the integrity of the report while allowing necessary and productive debate over the recommended solutions to program problems.

Using the recommendation process to promote organizational change demonstrates that evaluations address complex issues which, in turn, require complex solutions. Recommendations, therefore, may be subject to the polemics that often surround complicated problems. However, the organizational debates that surround the approval and implementation of recommendations should not detract from the factual information contained in the report.

Recommendations can be thought of as the engine of the evaluation report. Difficult to ignore, recommendations function as the springboard to organizational debate over the merits of the evaluation and its findings. They move the evaluation throughout an organization, through the approval process and administrative apparatus of the organization. This journey generates review and debate and gives internal publicity to the evaluation findings.

Following Up Implementation of Recommendations

Many times, program managers will have limited incentives to implement approved recommendations, especially when they disagree with them or when implementation would require substantial change to their operations. For this reason, it is good evaluation practice to develop procedures to follow up on the implementation of recommendations. Appropriate follow-up obviously is dependent on the scope and complexity of the initial recommendations. In any event, a timeframe for follow-up should be established when recommendations are formulated, putting responsible entities on notice that a formal inquiry will be forthcoming to determine implementation status. Initial follow-up is often set for six months after the decision is made to accept a recommendation. This period allows the program manager adequate time to review the approved recommendations and begin implementation. If, in the judgment of the evaluators, implementation has failed to produce satisfactory results, they have the option of discussing implementation problems with program personnel and arriving at a satisfactory resolution or advising the original approving authority. Evaluators should understand the importance of following up on recommendations. If change is to be effected, this important step in the evaluation process must occur.

Relationship Between Evaluators and Program Administrators

When evaluators learn they cannot successfully operate in isolation from the realities of the organization, they have begun the first step toward successful recommendation writing. Writing recommendations requires that evaluators be cognizant of the prevailing conditions which may have effects on the recommendations. When evaluators fail to recognize important internal and external circumstances that affect programs and recommended changes, their shortcoming may have negative consequences and prevent the timely implementation of positive changes in a program.

Critical elements of the evaluation environment are the reactions of the program manager (ranging from hostile to cooperative) and the perceived size of the impact of evaluation recommendations on current and future program decisions (Patton, 1989; Sonnichsen, 1990). Knowledge of program conditions can be gained through open exchanges with the program manager throughout the evaluation. The recommendation process is not an isolated endeavor. Optimally it should constitute an engagement between evaluators, key program administrators, and staffs working jointly to develop problem-solving activities that will improve the program. Failure by evaluators to develop a cooperative relationship with program administrators may jeopardize the full implementation of recommendations. Evaluators should establish this relationship with program staff at the outset of an evaluation, not at the conclusion when recommendations are being formulated.

The ultimate goals of the recommendation writer are approval and implementation of the recommended changes and program improvement. Considerable progress toward this goal can be enhanced by engaging key policymakers and program personnel in the recommendation writing process. Consulting program personnel and other affected parties not only improves the quality of the recommendations but increases the potential for their successful implementation. Although the evaluator brings a fresh, objective view of programs and problems, program personnel are more intimately familiar with the details of a program and with the impediments that may constrain recommended changes. Additionally, program personnel are ultimately responsible for implementation; when they participate in formulating recommendations, they build a sense of ownership that often leads them to facilitate the implementation process.

During an evaluation of FBI training of new special agents, a lack of communication between evaluators and the training academy management team precipitated an emotional rejection of the draft recommendations. Underlying the training academy response was a belief that their educational expertise was ignored during the development of the recommendations. Special care must be exercised by evaluators when evaluating highly specialized or technical programs where program personnel are considered experts in their field. Failure to involve these personnel in recommendation development almost certainly dooms any chance that the recommendations will be acceptable.

Conversely, collaboration with program personnel during the framing of recommendations increases the potential for successful implementation. Hendricks and Handley (1990) report that evaluators in the U.S. Department of Health and Human Services, who were studying physician licensure and discipline, met regularly with officials in the agency responsible for these issues. Through this collaboration, the two groups reached consensus on key recommendations and the secretary accepted them all.

Although consensus among evaluators and program personnel on program improvements is seldom attainable, it is nevertheless worth attempting. Evaluators should therefore maintain empathy with program personnel during the recommendation writing phase of an evaluation. After all, it is the program personnel who are most knowledgeable about the intricacies of the program and who will ultimately be charged with the responsibility for implementing approved recommendations.

Conclusion

Much of evaluation practice is about change, the examination of programs and organizational operations, and the exploration of alternatives for improving organizational performance. However, unless the evaluation findings reach the attention of the appropriate decision makers, the efforts of evaluators may become inconsequential and their goal of influencing the organization substantially diminished.

The utilization of evaluation results in the decision-making process should not be a haphazard event but a routine occurrence. For this to happen, evaluators must view themselves as change agents, take steps to recognize the organizational deliberative process, and develop evaluation procedures congruent with that process. Evaluators wishing to influence organizations should learn to view evaluation as a change mechanism and develop attributes that will enhance their acceptance in organizations.

Once evaluators are familiar with the organizational environment and decision-making process, and have gained acceptance in the organization, they still need to convert the evaluation findings to organizational actions. One effective method to accomplish this is by writing recommendations to accompany evaluation reports. Recommendations contained in a decision memorandum force organizational officials to deal with the issues raised by the evaluation. Evaluators should develop the necessary expertise in developing and writing recommendations and presenting evaluation findings to organizational decision makers. This important step, at the conclusion of evaluations, will ensure debate on evaluation results and increase the likelihood that evaluation findings will be used in the organizational deliberation process and influence the organization in a positive manner.

Recommendations are an appropriate device to translate the findings of evaluations into organizational action. Recommendations, properly conceived and given exposure in decision-making memoranda, link the evaluation process with the decision-making process and help ensure that evaluation findings are debated in the organizational decision-making arena. Evaluators, functioning as change agents and using the techniques discussed in this chapter, have an opportunity to employ their skills in service to organizations, influencing and effecting positive change in organizational policy and operations.

References

Brookfield, S. D. *Developing Critical Thinkers: Challenging Adults to Explore Alternative Ways of Thinking and Acting.* San Francisco: Jossey-Bass, 1987.

Hendricks, M., and Handley, E. A. "Improving the Recommendations from Evaluation Studies." *Evaluation and Program Planning,* 1990, *13,* 109–117.

Kiefer, C. F., and Stroh, P. "A New Paradigm for Developing Organizations." In J. D. Adams (ed.), *Transforming Work.* Alexandria, Va.: Miles River Press, 1984.

Patton, M. Q. "The Evaluator's Responsibility for Utilization." *Evaluation Practice,* 1988, *9*(2), 5–24.

Patton, M. Q. Evaluation seminar, Wintergreen, Va., 1989.

Sonnichsen, R. C. "Communicating Excellence in the FBI." In J. S. Wholey (ed.), *Organizational Excellence.* Lexington, Mass.: Lexington Books, 1987.

Sonnichsen, R. C. "Advocacy Evaluation: A Model for Internal Evaluation Offices." *Evaluation and Program Planning,* 1988, *11,* 141–148.

Sonnichsen, R. C. "Organizational Learning and the Environment of Evaluation." In C. Bellavita (ed.), *How Public Organizations Work.* New York: Praeger, 1990.

Sonnichsen, R. C. "Characteristics of High Impact Internal Evaluation Offices." Unpublished doctoral dissertation, Department of Public Administration, University of Southern California, 1991.

Weiss, C. H. "If Program Decisions Hinged Only on Information: A Response to Patton." *Evaluation Practice,* 1988, *9*(3), 15–28.

Wholey, J. S. "Options, Not Recommendations." Paper presented at the American Evaluation Association Meeting, Kansas City, October 1986.

23

Making a Splash: Reporting Evaluation Results Effectively

Michael Hendricks

If a tree falls in the forest and no one hears it, does it make a sound? If an evaluation report falls on someone's desk and no one reads it, does it make a splash? None whatsoever, yet we evaluators still rely far too often on long tomes filled with jargon to "report" our evaluation results.

When I first joined the U.S. Department of Health, Education and Welfare (HEW) almost twenty years ago, my new office had just received an excruciatingly dense, three-volume evaluation of nursing homes. It took me several days of intense study to understand the findings, and there would be no briefings for the important officials. Anyone could have predicted (correctly, as it turned out) that this evaluation would attract nothing but dust. We can, and must, do better.

The only reason for doing evaluations is to make that splash, to have that impact, to change situations in a desired direction (Hendricks, 1991). Some call this "speaking truth to power," but what good is speaking truth if power isn't listening? Unless we find more effective ways to help our audiences listen, all our good works are likely to go for naught. How we report our results is often the difference between creating a tiny ripple or making a proper splash.

This chapter offers several specific ideas for improving our reporting. But first let us consider six overall principles that should guide all our efforts. Keeping these principles in mind from the beginning of an evaluation will almost always help:

- Remember that the burden for effectively reporting our results is on us, the evaluators, not on our audiences.
- Be aggressive. Instead of waiting for audiences to request information, actively look for chances to report results. Report regularly and frequently, appear in person if at all possible, and target multiple reports and briefings to specific audiences and/or issues.

- As Thoreau would say, "Simplify, simplify." Our audiences are usually busy and their interest is pulled in different directions, so pare ruthlessly to determine the key points. If the core message creates interest, quickly follow up with more details.
- Study the audience. Learn about their backgrounds, interests, concerns, plans, pet peeves, and so on. Even something as simple as including examples from the home states or regions of audience members can make reporting much more effective.
- Focus on actions. Audiences are rarely interested in general information; they usually want guidance that will help them decide what to do next.
- Report in many different ways. Rather than using only one reporting technique or another, produce several written products, give personal briefings, develop a screenshow presentation, produce a videotape, and so on—all with powerful graphics and helpful recommendations.

These principles should suggest at least two different ways in which we can improve our reporting. First, we can *improve our final reports.* Final reports are often necessary, but long, intimidating ones accomplish little. Second, we can *develop new, more effective techniques for reporting* our results. New ways to present written products, personal briefings, action recommendations, graphics, and other techniques are being developed all the time. As evaluators, we must test these, refine them, and adapt those that will help us deliver our message.

Reporting via Final Reports

Conventional wisdom notwithstanding, a final report is often *not* essential for making a splash or for influencing a situation. In fact, putting our evaluation findings on paper is sometimes counterproductive. For one briefing for the Secretary of the U.S. Department of Health and Human Services (DHHS), for example, only six people were invited, there was nothing in writing, and the briefing officially "never occurred." In this instance, the topic was so controversial that the only way to deliver the results without distortion was to agree to do so off the record and with no final report.

More typically, though, final reports *are* important, and to make a splash, these final reports must be as action oriented as possible. But what makes an evaluation report action oriented?

Table 23.1 lists a number of characteristics of an evaluation report along five dimensions: (1) structure, (2) style, (3) content, (4) perspective, and (5) resolution. For some of these characteristics, traditional and action-oriented reports look very much alike. For most characteristics, however, the two types are strikingly different. As evaluators, we need to keep these important differences in mind when we plan and write our reports (see Hendricks, 1985).

Table 23.1. How to Write an Action-Oriented Evaluation Report.

Aspects of the Evaluation Report	Type of Evaluation Report	
	Traditional	Action Oriented
Structure		
Number of reports	1	More than 1
Scope	Comprehensive	Focused
Length	Long	Short
Order of findings	Inductive	Deductive
Executive summary	Sometimes	Always
Table of contents	Yes	Sometimes
Appendices	Yes	No
Style		
Tone	Detached	Involved
Person	Third	First or second
Voice	Passive	Active
Language	Dry: jargon, technical language	Rich: anecdotes, examples, photos
Tense	Past	Present
Sentence length	Medium/Long	Short
Content		
Background	Detailed	Brief
Hypotheses	Yes	No
Methodology	Detailed	Brief
Analyses	All details	Overall approach
Findings	All	Selected
Graphics, figures	Some	Many
Perspective		
Point of view	Neutral	Audience's
Ideal author	Outsider	Insider
Resolution		
Length of study	Medium/Slow	Fast
Conclusions	Yes	Yes
Interpretations	Sometimes	Yes
Recommendations	Sometimes	Yes
Suggested follow-up	No	Yes
How disseminated	Publicly	Privately first

Action-oriented reports are often *structured* as a series of short reports (fifteen to twenty pages maximum) rather than one all-inclusive document, with each report carefully focused on a particular issue or targeted toward a particular audience. Within DHHS, for example, the inspector general recently produced two separate reports on resident abuse in nursing homes. The first report, targeted for one audience and recommending specific actions, dealt solely with *understanding and preventing abuse*. The second report, for a different audience and recommending different actions, dealt with a different aspect of the problem: *resolving physical abuse complaints*. Each report contained an executive summary and a table of contents, and each presented the most important items first, regardless of the original study design.

Appendices were not included, but additional information was provided separately on request.

The *style* of an action-oriented report is involved and active, not detached and passive as in traditional reports. This immediacy is achieved by speaking in the first or second person, by using shorter sentences and present tense, and by including true-to-life anecdotes, direct quotes, personal incidents, short case studies, metaphors, analogies, illustrations, examples, and especially photographs when possible and cost effective.

Regarding *content,* an action-oriented report spends very little time describing a study's background and methodology or presenting its hypotheses or detailed analyses. The findings themselves—especially graphic displays of the findings—form the bulk of such a report. These findings are presented from the audience's own *inside perspective,* not that of a neutral outsider.

Almost invariably, an action-oriented report is most concerned about its *resolution,* or what will happen next. To make a splash, a report is delivered as quickly as possible, with clear conclusions, distinct interpretations, and specific recommendations. Equally important, the report often contains detailed suggestions for implementing and following up on these recommendations. Finally, an action-oriented report is often first disseminated privately, not publicly, in order to let key audiences consider their next steps without outside pressures.

Reporting via Other Written Products

Following these suggestions will improve our final reports, but are there other written products we can use to report our findings? The answer is "Yes," and often these other products can be just as effective as a final report—and sometimes even more so.

Draft Reports

Draft reports can be especially valuable precisely because they are still subject to change. You may include in a draft report information that you may or may not intend to include in a final report, usually to raise sensitive issues that have not received enough attention. As an example, a colleague and I once evaluated a county's senior citizen lunch program. At that time, the federal government was pressuring local programs to increase the level of participants' voluntary contributions. However, this particular county was already collecting an *above*-average contribution from persons with *below*-average incomes. So we recommended in our draft report that the county lower (not raise) the suggested contribution for senior-citizen lunches. As you can imagine, we generated a lively discussion about this issue (Hendricks and Hatry, 1985).

Other Documents

Other documents can include internal memoranda, interim progress reports, talking papers, question-and-answer statements, written responses to other documents, chapters in edited books, press releases, op-ed items in newspapers, conference proceedings, texts of speeches, brochures, policy papers, written testimony, association newsletters, and articles in professional journals. Each of these products targets a specific audience, and each can be used productively.

Index Cards

One very creative written product is a three-by-five index card. While I worked for the DHHS Inspector General (IG), helping to manage his national evaluations, he would regularly have one-on-one private lunches with the secretary and other top agency officials. Naturally we wanted him to discuss our evaluations at these lunches, but it was unrealistic to expect him to carry along a progress report. We began providing him a single three-by-five index card for each of the evaluations that might be relevant for his luncheon partner. Because these cards were convenient, the IG usually looked at them on the way to lunch, and he often found ways to interject our information into the discussion. As a result, top DHHS officials discussed our evaluations routinely, not just on special occasions.

Reporting via Personal Briefings

Final reports and other written products are often effective, but personal briefings are often even *more* effective. By now I have witnessed or delivered well over one hundred briefings for officials at all levels of government — city, county, state, national, and international — and in private and nonprofit agencies. From those experiences, I can attest that the payoff from a well-done briefing is almost always very high (see Hendricks, 1982; Office of Inspector General, 1990).

True, briefings do have disadvantages. A poor presenter can undermine the message, the material to be presented must be selected very carefully, briefings can be hard to schedule quickly given everyone's busy schedules, and external events can diminish their impact. One ill-fated briefing was interrupted three times by phone calls from the White House, and another briefing had to be stopped when the audience was more intent on a sudden snowstorm paralyzing the Washington area than on the presenter. On both these occasions the impact of the briefing was admittedly minimal.

The strong advantages of personal briefings, however, more than offset these risks. A briefing brings together the key actors for a much-needed opportunity to discuss the issues, and their discussion almost always creates a certain momentum for action. Most important, though, briefings have the advantage of fitting with the way managers normally operate. Mintzberg (1973) has documented that managers rarely sit and read documents for long stretches of time, so why should we expect them to change their management style for us? Instead, we evaluators need to tailor our communications to fit our audience's style, and personal briefings fit their style very nicely.

Exhibit 23.1 summarizes the steps in presenting an effective briefing: (1) prepare materials, (2) set the stage, and (3) deliver the briefing. Notice that two of these three steps are completed before the briefing begins. The key to an effective briefing is in the preparation; what occurs *before* the briefing is at least as important as what occurs *during* it.

Exhibit 23.1. How to Present an Effective Briefing.

Step 1: Prepare the Briefing Materials
- Select information to include in the briefing
- Prepare six to ten briefing charts
- Prepare a handout for each member of the audience

Step 2: Set the Stage for the Briefing
- Determine the presenter, assistant, and liaison
- Invite a small, select audience
- Practice, practice, practice!
- Establish and distribute a written agenda
- Make all miscellaneous arrangements

Step 3: Deliver the Briefing
- Explain the purpose of the briefing
- Grab attention immediately
- Encourage interaction at any time
- Provide a balanced briefing
- Ask for a response from those being evaluated
- Facilitate a lively discussion

Step 1: Prepare Materials

The first step to an effective briefing is to prepare the various materials to be used. We must first select our key results (study background, findings, conclusions, and recommendations) and then prepare some visual aids for presenting this information. These visual aids are very important, and no briefing should occur without them.

Different people prefer different media, including flip charts, blackboards, slides, overhead transparencies, and computer screens. My personal favorite is a set of six to ten large briefing charts mounted on lightweight foamboard (Hendricks, 1984b). This mounting makes the charts sturdy yet lightweight and flexible for moving during the briefing. In addition, these charts should be

- *Large,* at least thirty by forty inches, and with large print. One briefing failed miserably the moment the presenter placed his stationery-sized charts on a table at least thirty feet long. Effective briefing charts should be easily read from a full forty feet away.

- *Concise,* with only a few words on each chart and on each line of each chart. Effective charts summarize information rather than repeat the text of the final report.

- *Informative* independently, so that the charts by themselves convey a great deal of information. One useful way to check the informativeness of briefing charts is to have someone read the charts without knowing any other information. If she learns the message simply by reading the charts, they will be effective.

- *High quality,* in order to reflect the high quality of your evaluation. Primary colors are often helpful (provided they are not too expensive), and it is essential to use neat lettering and to check for spelling. More than one presenter has been embarrassed by misspelling a word on a chart.

- *Helpful to the presenter* during the briefing. Briefings are important moments, and presenters are sometimes nervous. If the charts are designed to guide the presenter smoothly through the briefing, she will feel more relaxed. One effective trick is to include, in light pencil, extra comments the presenter wants to add over and above the words printed on the charts. These crib notes are not visible from the audience, but they help the presenter to remember important points. Be careful, though, not to make these notes too light or too small. One of the best stand-up comedy acts I have ever seen was a hapless presenter who kept leaning over and squinting at his charts after every few sentences; his audience was quickly rolling in the aisles!

In addition to the visual aids, and every bit as important, is an individual handout for each member of the audience. These handouts should contain exact duplicates of the briefing charts plus any additional items that might be discussed during the briefing (background legislation, study methodology, detailed tables or figures, and so on). The handouts are valuable in providing a tangible product to take away from the briefing and in helping audience members to a better understanding of the results. Not everyone in the room may have a clear view of the briefing charts, for example, or some may have poor hearing.

Step 2: Set the Stage

The second step to an effective briefing is to set the stage. First, determine who will deliver the briefing. One presenter is best because audiences seem to lose their focus when the presenter changes in mid briefing. Choose this presenter carefully, even though the choice may not win you friends.

I was once involved in informing a dedicated and talented evaluator that he could not personally present the results of his very interesting evaluation to the secretary of DHHS. This evaluator was the deputy director of his regional office, and since his boss had been away on a temporary assignment during the entire study, he himself had designed, implemented, analyzed, and written the evaluation report. The results were his in every sense, and now he had the chance to speak truth to power.

There was only one problem. Power in this case was a brand-new secretary who had never before been briefed by our office. It was naturally very important that this first briefing go as well as possible, and the evaluator was a less-than-inspiring presenter. Against all humane instincts, my superior and I had to recall the office director (who *was* an especially dynamic presenter) from his leave in order to present the briefing. The evaluator has probably never forgiven us, but I know he understands the importance of presenting the best possible briefing.

The presenter should have an assistant handy with ready access to all the important evaluation documents and analyses. There may be times when a detailed question arises, and the presenter does not want to stop the briefing while he looks for the answer. Having the assistant find this information allows the flow of the briefing to continue.

A high-level liaison should also sit with the presenter and assistant, in order to introduce the briefing, elaborate on findings when necessary, and defend the presenter from hostile questions or remarks. Because the presenter is almost always lower ranking than the audience, such a liaison is often necessary to counterbalance any attempts by audience members to discredit or intimidate the presenter.

Next, invite a small, select audience of no more than fifteen to twenty people. Larger audiences are possible, but such a session becomes more a presentation than a briefing since the intense discussion necessary for a briefing is difficult with many persons.

Third, and perhaps most important of all, practice the briefing at least three times: first with a friendly audience, next with a more neutral one, and finally with an audience primed to be as skeptical and challenging as possible. Time each practice to ensure that the presentation stays within the allocated period. This practice is invaluable for anticipating likely questions and for fine tuning the briefing.

Next, establish a written agenda of the briefing and distribute it to all members of the audience at least two days in advance. This agenda might specify an introduction by the liaison, the presentation itself, a short response from staff of the program that has been evaluated, and a long general discussion. Including the response from the program staff is an especially effective way to allow all issues to be presented for discussion.

Finally, make those detailed, miscellaneous arrangements that may appear to be trivial but can be crucial for an effective briefing. These include providing to those who will attend advance materials (the written agenda plus a list of attendees, summary of the briefing, and perhaps a full copy of the report); arranging the chairs in the best configuration for comfortable discussion; and focusing the lighting, first on the presenter and then on the discussants.

Step 3: Deliver the Briefing

The final step to an effective briefing is actually to deliver the briefing. The liaison can begin by explaining the background of the issue(s) and the purpose of this particular briefing and by introducing the presenter and assistant. It is then important that the presenter take absolutely no more than one-third of the total time for the presentation.

Since members of the audience probably have many different issues on their minds, it is critical to grab their attention immediately. One clever presenter dropped a very heavy, 212-page computer printout on the table and announced "These, Mr. Secretary, are your reimbursement codes for medical oxygen!" Another scattered an armload of illegal drugs and exclaimed "All these drugs were confiscated from within one mile of this building!"

Others have used photographs, slides, or videotapes. One especially poignant briefing began with a three-minute, homemade videotape of an elderly woman sitting on the steps of her boarding home and talking of the horrors of living there. From the moment the tape began, the audience was focused intently on the plight of this resident and others like her.

After the opening, a presenter should be informative yet understandable (no jargon unless everyone understands it), true to life (quotes, examples, and anecdotes that help to animate results), professional (neat dress and demeanor), and balanced (attempting to be *fair,* not the impossible-to-achieve *objective*). An important part of being balanced is admitting when we do *not* know the answer to a question. When this occurs, the presenter should not try to bluff but should promise to follow up and provide the answer as soon as possible. If a presenter bluffs and gets caught, he loses all credibility.

The presenter should also interact with members of the audience so they begin to feel part of a discussion. This means explicitly asking the audience to interrupt with questions at any time, not using a microphone, script, lectern, or pointer to create a barrier between the presenter and the audience, and responding positively when audience members do interrupt.

After the presentation (twenty minutes in a sixty-minute briefing), it is wise to schedule a five-minute response from the manager whose program is being discussed. This strategy has several advantages: (a) it gives the audience a more comprehensive briefing, (b) it helps to start the general discussion, and (c) not least important, it shows that the presenter is trying to be as balanced as possible. Following this response, the liaison should invite the audience to discuss the issues for the remaining time, giving special emphasis to the recommendations for action.

Reporting via Action Recommendations

Recommendations for action are often the most important way we evaluators report our results, and through our recommendations we have the potential to improve programs dramatically. At DHHS, recommendations from one evaluation showed how to enroll 13,500 more children into Head Start centers at no additional cost (Office of Inspector General, 1984). In Delaware, recommendations from another evaluation convinced the state to redesign completely its job training program for welfare recipients (Trutko and others, 1986). In both instances, evaluation recommendations obviously made a big splash.

Despite this potential, though, we evaluators have generally paid woefully little attention to how we might improve the recommendations from our evaluations (Hendricks, 1984a; Patton, 1988). There are several possible reasons for this neglect, but the most important reason may be the completely mistaken belief that offering effective recommendations is a straightforward and simple process that flows naturally from the conclusions of an evaluation. Nothing could be further from the truth. Here, then, are twelve practical suggestions for more effectively developing, presenting, and following-up on our recommendations (for more detailed advice, see Hendricks and Handley, 1990; Hendricks and Papagiannis, 1990).

Suggestion 1: Allocate Sufficient Time and Resources to Developing Recommendations

We evaluators commonly err by devoting far too little time to developing possible recommendations, discussing them with key people, revising them as needed, and discussing them again. Too often we view recommendations as an add-on step that we address at the last minute. As one evaluator remarked, "Our readers devote only 5 percent of their attention to our findings and 95 percent of their attention to our recommendations. Yet I think we spend 95 percent of our time on study findings and only 5 percent of it on developing recommendations."

Developing effective recommendations is more a process than an action, and, like all processes, it requires time to be done well. Time must be set aside for thinking about recommendations at the beginning of an evaluation and at every point during it. One effective technique is to use color-coded index cards to record ideas from the first days of an evaluation. On white cards, record possible findings (which may or may not be confirmed later), and on yellow cards, jot down possible recommendations that you want to consider further. Reviewing these yellow cards each day forces one to think about possible recommendations throughout the evaluation.

Cynthia Roberts-Gray uses another technique. She and her colleagues specify, again at the very beginning of an evaluation, which recommendations will be offered if the evaluation yields certain findings, and which other recommendations will be offered if the evaluation yields different findings. Then everyone sits back and waits for the data to determine the recommendations (Roberts-Gray, Buller, and Sparkman, 1987).

Suggestion 2: Consider All Aspects of the Issue Fair Game

We evaluators should feel free to make recommendations about any issue for which credible information is available. I once ignored this rule, much to my regret. At the time, my colleagues and I were advising DHHS evaluators on what actions to recommend to the secretary in order to encourage more private physicians to participate in the Medicaid program. Although most physicians reported that low reimbursement rates were the main barrier, we assumed (incorrectly, as it turned out) that recommending higher reimbursement rates was simply untenable given the severe budget cuts then occurring. We advised the evaluators to focus their recommendations on ways to alleviate other physician complaints.

You can imagine our surprise and deep embarrassment when, after the first recommendations were presented, the secretary asked spontaneously whether the evaluators had any recommendations for changing the reimbursement rates! Fortunately, the evaluators had drafted some possible new reimbursement rates for just such a situation, and a productive discussion ensued.

This painful lesson was useful when another colleague and I later evaluated a county's Special Supplemental Food Program for Women, Infants, and Children (WIC). Because we took pains to address all aspects of the issue — eligible and needy populations, certification, nutrition education, food assistance, outreach, and office automation — county officials could find recommendations on whichever aspects they wished to focus (Hendricks and Roth, 1986). And their interests were not necessarily those we might have predicted in advance.

Suggestion 3: Draw Possible Recommendations from a Wide Variety of Sources

Good recommendations can come from anywhere, and we evaluators should cast a wide net when looking for ideas. I once helped to evaluate Operation Care and Share, a national food assistance program sponsored by the White House's Office of Private Sector Initiatives and thirty-three private firms. As we developed our recommendations, we drew ideas from reporting forms completed by local projects, discussions with national sponsoring organizations, telephone interviews with key community leaders, and our own judgment (Aid Association for Lutherans, 1986). Each source contributed useful, and often unique, possibilities.

Suggestion 4: Work Closely with Agency Personnel
Throughout the Process

It is important to work closely with agency personnel as we develop our recommendations. In a study of factors affecting the acceptance of recommendations (Oman and Chitwood, 1984), close collaboration between the evaluator and agency personnel was a primary factor associated with a higher-than-average level of acceptance. "It is a basic tenet in the art of management that analyses and policies that are generated from within an organization are likely to be better received than those that are imposed from on high" (Leman and Nelson, 1981, p. 105).

There are several advantages to having evaluators and agency personnel collaborate on recommendations. Collaboration provides an experienced sounding board, it refines the agency personnel's own solutions to problems, and it allows agency personnel to object to recommendations and to help find acceptable modifications. "Meeting with agency personnel can help with more than just the substance. Sometimes syntax is critical. You can find the right word — versus 'red flag' ones — when you've met with them and have more knowledge" (M. R. Yessian, interview with E. Handley, November 1986).

DHHS evaluators studying physician licensure and discipline met repeatedly with officials in the agencies responsible for these issues. As a result, the two groups reached consensus on several key recommendations for the secretary, and they also agreed to present a new recommendation suggested by the agency. Perhaps not coincidentally, the secretary accepted every recommendation.

However, we evaluators also run certain risks when we work closely with program officials and program staff. The major risk is of becoming overly involved with their perspective and losing our own objectivity. If this loss of independence occurs, we might be tempted to protect our good relations by sidestepping controversial issues, equivocating on negative findings, or being less than candid.

Another risk is that we may come to value consensus so highly that we agree to present only those recommendations that have been approved by lower-level personnel. If so, controversial recommendations may not rise through the system and the chances of achieving major change may be diminished.

A final risk of close collaboration is that officials might become so intrigued by a tentative recommendation that we are considering that they make changes prematurely, even before our evaluation is complete and our recommendation certain. This situation could be disastrous since the weaknesses of the recommendation might not yet be known. So we must convince officials *not* to act on any of our early ideas until the evaluation is complete and the recommendations can be presented in final form.

Suggestion 5: Consider the Larger Context
Within Which the Recommendations Must Fit

Policies and programs do not exist in a vacuum, and neither do our recommendations. Sometimes the rational solution is not the best solution (Bozeman and Massey, 1982), so we need a solid understanding of the larger context in order to offer effective recommendations. "Unless the sociological, political, and organizational contexts are explicitly taken into account in developing policy recommendations, the recommendations probably will not be sufficiently implemented to achieve the desired results" (Majchrzak, 1984, p. 75).

I once helped to design an approach by which the Indonesian Ministry of Education and Culture could assess progress on its five-year plan for education (Hendricks, 1986). Our approach provided information about (1) the planning process, (2) programs across the ministry, and (3) specific programs. Because we knew that the ministry's immediate task was to draft the next five-year plan, we recommended that it concentrate its efforts on the first two activities and postpone its evaluations of specific programs. If we had not considered the larger context, we might have unwisely recommended that the ministry disperse its efforts among all three activities at once.

Suggestion 6: Generally Offer Only
Realistic Recommendations

We evaluators should almost always recommend actions which can be controlled by the program manager and which are likely to succeed (Palumbo and Nachmias, 1983; Stanfield and Smith, 1984). I say "almost always," because sometimes we may need to offer a recommendation with little or no chance of being accepted, especially if we feel an ethical responsibility.

Earlier I described an evaluation of a county's senior citizen lunch program and my colleague's and my decision to recommend that the county should *lower* (not raise, as it probably hoped) the suggested contribution for lunch. Even though our recommendation had very little chance of being accepted, we felt a professional obligation to make our recommendation, and we believe the county respected us for doing so.

Suggestion 7: Decide Carefully Whether to Be
General or Specific

How general or how specific should our recommendations be? Do we recommend that "situation X should be corrected," or should our recommendation specify that "in order to correct situation X, this person, working with these other people, should take these steps in this particular order by these dates"? Sometimes very general recommendations are better since they allow officials to decide for themselves which specific steps they will take. Evaluators once recommended that DHHS change the federal payment rate to states for child support enforcement activities. These evaluators were very careful *not* to recommend a specific new rate or even how a new rate should be determined; they simply recommended that DHHS correct some obvious inequities. The secretary and other top officials agreed, and the responsible agency developed new rates that were accepted and implemented.

Sometimes, though, very specific recommendations are better. Unless specifics are outlined, it may not be clear what needs to be done, when the action is needed, or who needs to take action. "Merely saying that something should be done—without saying how—is an abdication of responsibility" (Majchrzak, 1984, p. 75). Also, we evaluators sometimes lose credibility when we have no specific actions to recommend, especially when our evaluation reveals problems that have been noted by others in the past.

Unfortunately, there are no blanket rules for deciding between general and specific recommendations. Even within the same evaluation, some recommendations might need to be general and others more specific. In the Operation Care and Share evaluation mentioned earlier, we recommended some very specific changes (for example, "mail materials in August"). However, we were not comfortable recommending detailed ways in which the autonomous national partners should interact with each other, so our recommendations in this area were more general.

Suggestion 8: Think Twice Before Recommending Fundamental Changes

We evaluators may sometimes need to recommend fundamental changes in a program or policy. Earlier I cited evaluations recommending that Head Start enroll children differently and that Delaware completely redesign its job training program for welfare recipients. These recommendations were accepted, and fundamental changes were made, all with good results.

However, evaluations such as these tend to be the exceptions to the rule. It is generally more appropriate to recommend incremental improvements within an existing framework—building on current activities and suggesting gradual changes (Murphy, 1980). Agency personnel tend to resist fundamental changes and such changes are often politically less palatable than incremental improvements; also, recommending fundamental changes comes very close to redesigning a program. And that is a difficult task requiring a sophisticated set of skills that evaluators may not always possess (Sadler, 1984).

Suggestion 9: Show the Future Implications of Recommendations

Simply recommending that certain actions be taken is rarely sufficient. Officials will usually want a fuller understanding of the implications of their action. Wise evaluators anticipate this need and provide, whenever possible, best estimates (or perhaps a range of estimates) of both the costs and consequences of the recommendations. Because our recommendations often interact with each other, we should also try to estimate the costs and consequences of likely combinations of recommendations (House and McLeod, 1977).

Suggestion 10: Make Recommendations Easy to Understand

All communications should be easy to understand, but this is doubly important for recommendations. How can officials approve changes if they cannot understand what they are being asked to approve? Busy officials often rush from issue to issue during the day, and recommendations that are easy to understand help them to grasp more quickly what is needed (see Larsen, 1985).

First, we can categorize our recommendations in some meaningful way (Patton, 1982). In the Indonesian project mentioned earlier, we categorized recommendations into "those for assessing the planning process" versus "those for assessing across the ministry." This distinction allowed the audience to focus on those recommendations relevant to their immediate concern. Other ways to categorize recommendations might include major versus minor; short term versus long term; firm versus tentative; or administrative versus regulatory versus legislative.

Second, we can place our recommendations carefully within our reports. My preference is to integrate my recommendations directly into the text — alongside the relevant findings — to help officials understand what is recommended and why. At the same time, though, these recommendations must be carefully distinguished from findings, with no confusion where one stops and the other starts. The format presented in Exhibit 23.2 is one I use to accomplish both these objectives.

Suggestion 11: Stay Involved After Recommendations Have Been Accepted

Our role as evaluators includes more than simply gathering, analyzing, and presenting data. Our role also includes helping to implement and monitor

Exhibit 23.2. Effective Format for Presenting Recommendations.

DEA has negotiated with the Board of Education an excellent main contract which provides better-than-average service at lower-than-average cost (see Table 4, page 13).

Recommendation: DEA should continue to contract with the Board of Education for the bulk of its meals.

the recommendations that are accepted. "The policy game is not a relay with the analyst running the first (analytical) lap and then turning the baton over to the politician to run the last (political) lap while the analyst watches passively (if painfully) from the sidelines. If the analyst drops out after the first lap, he will discover that his recommendations are gradually modified, compromised, and discarded so that the final, adopted policy hardly resembles his proposal" (Behn, 1981).

One way we can stay involved is by reminding key people about our recommendations and about the actions they require. Human nature being what it is, agency personnel sometimes need to be reminded that a problem does exist, that action does need to be taken, and that officials have agreed to certain changes.

We can also stay involved by developing implementation plans after our recommendations have been accepted or by planning an implementation strategy in advance. Our willingness to help plan an implementation can sometimes encourage officials to accept our recommendations in the first place. Showing the steps that would be needed in implementing a recommendation can usually help overcome resistance to accepting that recommendation.

In other circumstances, we evaluators may become even more involved, even helping with the implementation itself. One recommendation from the Operation Care and Share evaluation mentioned earlier was to improve the program's monitoring system. After the program's steering committee accepted this recommendation, they asked us to revise the form for gathering standardized information from local projects. We did this, and the new reporting form was accepted in toto and became an integral part of the next year's monitoring system.

Suggestion 12: If a Recommendation Is Not Accepted Look for Other Opportunities to Recommend It Again

We evaluators often become discouraged when our recommendations are not accepted the first time they are presented; but it is naive to expect that all our recommendations will be accepted or that they will all be implemented immediately. Furthermore, as an "invited intruder" (Baum, 1982), evaluators often threaten the officials' role. Accepting outside ideas from us may be seen as an admission that they cannot solve the problems within their domain.

For these reasons, we should not expect to have every recommendation accepted. But we should keep offering those recommendations we believe are warranted. Events change, officials move to other positions, new information is obtained, we gain more credibility — all of which can lead to a more receptive environment for exactly the same recommendations.

Reporting via Graphics

"A picture is worth a thousand words." How often we hear this old saying, and how true it is. Defined as the simultaneous presentation of words, numbers, and images, graphics are often our most effective technique for reporting our results, for four main reasons: (1) they allow a large amount of data to be displayed and absorbed quickly, (2) they reveal patterns that are not always apparent in the text or even in a table, (3) they allow easier comparisons among sets of data, and (4) they often have a powerful impact on our audiences (see Tufte, 1983; 1990).

A badly designed or badly constructed graphic, however, may need 1,000 words just to explain it, so we need to be especially careful when we use this type of presentation aid. Exhibit 23.3 is a summary of how to present effective graphics.

Exhibit 23.3. How to Present Effective Graphics.

Step 1: Write a message sentence.
Step 2: Decide what type of comparison this message implies.
Step 3: Experiment with several different graphics to show this comparison.
Step 4: Select the graphic that conveys the message best.
Step 5: Actually construct the graphic.
Step 6: Pilot-test the graphic and revise if necessary.
Step 7: Insert the final graphic into the report or briefing.

Step 1: Write a Message Sentence

Our first step, and one of the most critical, is to state our message clearly. What exactly do we want to say? More important, what exactly do we want our audience to learn? If we cannot state our message clearly and concisely, we cannot even begin to design our graphic. Conversely, once we determine our message, it is usually easy to design an effective graphic.

We can best state our message by writing it as a sentence: "Performance improved steadily until the 1987 legislative changes" or "Most complaints come from first-time beneficiaries" or "Oklahoma is the best-performing state." Having developed this compact message, it would be a waste not to use it, so we can keep it as the title of our graphic (rather than a dull title such as "Performance Over Time" or "Sources of Complaints").

Step 2: Decide What Type of Comparison This Message Implies

Most messages will imply a graphic that shows one of four comparisons: (1) comparing *different parts of a whole* shows the different proportions of the total taken by each component, (2) comparing *different units* shows the relative rankings of separate but comparable entities, (3) comparing *different points in time* shows longitudinal trends, and (4) comparing *two different variables* shows the correlation between the variables (see Zelazny, 1991).

For example, the message "Performance improved steadily until the 1987 legislative changes" implies that we have compared different points in time; "Most complaints come from first-time beneficiaries" implies that we have compared different parts of a whole; and "Oklahoma is the best-performing state" implies that we have compared different units.

Step 3: Experiment with Several Different Graphics to Show This Comparison

Now that we have determined the type of comparison our graphic must show, we realize that there are several different ways to display each type of comparison. Before choosing one of these graphics for our report or briefing, we should first sketch as many options as possible, as shown in Figures 23.1 through 23.4.

• To compare different parts of a whole, we can use various types of pie charts (intact or with one or more slices exploded or omitted for emphasis), 100 percent column charts (the same filling as in a pie chart, but re-baked into a rectangular pan), or sliding bar charts (see Figure 23.1).

Figure 23.1. How to Compare Different Parts of a Whole.

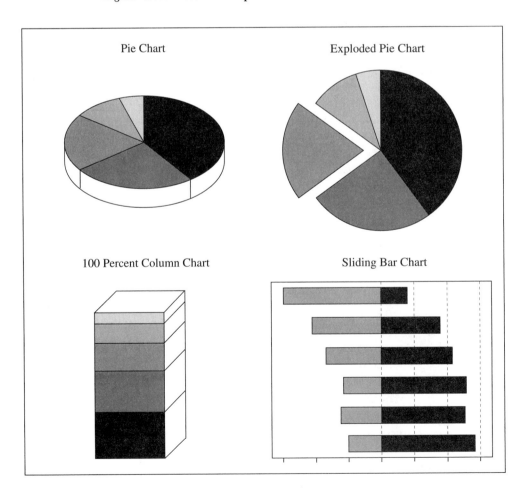

• To compare different units, we can use various types of horizontal (not vertical) bar charts (individual, segmented, clustered, deviation, or range), histograms (for frequency distributions), maps, or the very clever concept of small multiples a la *Consumer Reports* (see Figure 23.2).

Figure 23.2. How to Compare Different Units.

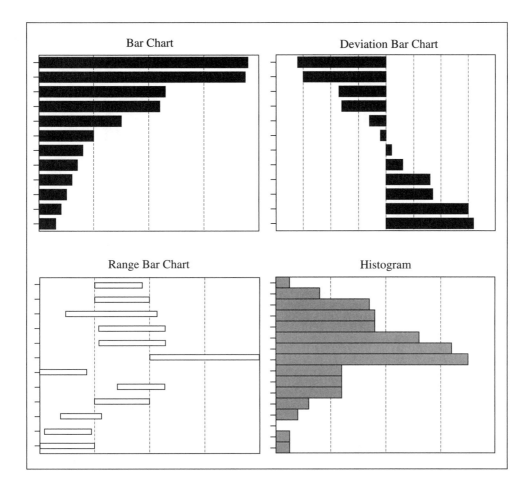

• To compare different points in time, we can use various types of line charts (single, multiple), mountain charts, vertical bar (column) charts, pictographs (also called space-time continuums), or historical timelines (see Figure 23.3).

• To compare two different variables, we can use scatterplots (also called scattergrams) or paired-bar charts. Because the relationships in scatterplots can be difficult to detect visually, it is usually wise to fit both the trend line and the best-fitting curve to the data points (see Figure 23.4).

Figure 23.3. How to Compare Different Points in Time.

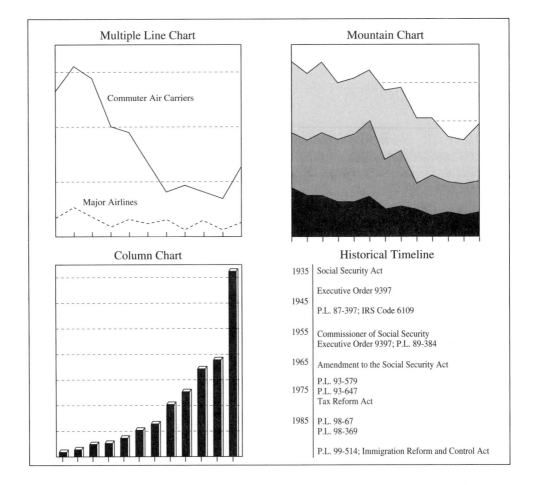

Step 4: Select the Graphic
That Conveys the Message Best

Given these many different ways to report each message, which graphic is best? Unfortunately, there is no simple formula for choosing, but it can help to ask the following:

- Which graphic is most *accurate?* Which one best conveys our message and nothing but our message?
- Which graphic is *simplest?* Which one conveys the greatest number of ideas in the shortest time with the least ink in the smallest space?
- Which graphic is *clearest?* Which one emphasizes the data to let us easily and readily see the message?
- Which graphic is most *attractive?* Which one most pleasantly reflects an artistic element?

Figure 23.4. How to Compare Two Different Variables.

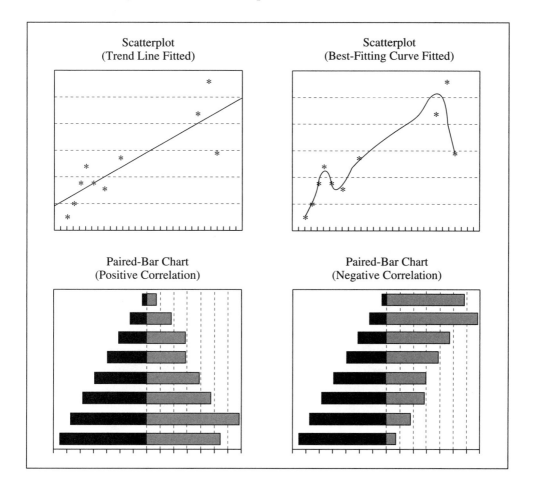

If we cannot choose between two equally good graphics at this point, this is not a problem. We can simply construct both graphics and decide between the two after pilot testing each one on outside viewers (see Step 6).

Step 5: Actually Construct the Graphic

Once we select the best type of graphic for our message (scatterplot versus paired-bar chart, for example), we must actually construct it. Today there are several computer software programs available, including Applause II, CA-Cricket Presents, Charisma, Harvard Graphics, Lotus Freelance, Lotus Graphwriter II, Lotus Spreadsheet (version 2.3 or higher), Microsoft Chart, Microsoft PowerPoint, Pixie, and Quattro Pro. In addition, DrawPerfect has the advantage of being compatible with the popular WordPerfect word processing program (see Office of Inspector General, 1990).

Regardless of the program used, constructing an effective graphic is not simple; it requires a blend of substantive, statistical, and artistic sensitivities. At a minimum we must know the basics of a good graphic: title, axes, data points, tick marks and grid lines, footnotes, labels, borders, scales and scale lines, plotting symbols, data regions, reference lines, data labels, markers, scale breaks, and so on (Cleveland, 1985).

Step 6: Pilot Test the Graphic and Revise If Necessary

Once we construct our graphic, does it convey our message as well as we hope? The only way to find out is to show it to a group unfamiliar with our results—if possible, to people very much like the officials who will be the audiences for our reports and briefings.

    In general, it is better to pilot test with copies of the graphic than with the originals. While originals undoubtedly look better, in reality almost everyone will receive a copy, so the copies are what must be effective. A good strategy is to show a copy *without* the message title and simply ask "What does this graphic say to you?" Then show a copy *with* the message title and ask "Is this the message you saw?"

    More frequently than we might imagine, the answer will be "No," and for any of several common reasons. Our scales may be inconsistent or partially broken, our raw data may be unadjusted or uncorrected, three-dimensional graphs may seriously distort our message (a common frustration for readers of *USA Today,* the *Washington Post,* and now even the U.S. General Accounting Office), we may have filled our graphic with "chartjunk," and so on. If so, we must revise our graphic and pilot test it again on a new audience.

Step 7: Insert the Final Graphic into the Report or Briefing

The best way to think of a graphic is as a *visual paragraph*—certainly with a format different from a written paragraph but still just another paragraph in our report. Like other paragraphs, each graphic should present a clear message, have each of its parts support this message, and be internally coherent. Also, as with all other paragraphs, the graphic should fit into the report or briefing at the appropriate place.

    The best place is immediately after the graphic's message is first mentioned in the text or during the briefing. When a person reads or hears "As Figure x shows . . . ," she wants to see Figure x then, not two paragraphs later or on the next page. Achieving this placement means that written reports may have some blank spaces at the end of some pages. This is not ideal, but it is better than forcing the reader to stop reading the message in order to search for the graphic.

Graphics for Written Reports vs. Briefings

One final, very important point is that graphics that are appropriate and useful in a written report are not always appropriate and useful in a personal briefing. In fact, these same graphics can sometimes hinder a briefing. A graphic in a written report is analogous to a magazine advertisement; a viewer can study each graphic as long as necessary and even return time and again to check the details. But a graphic used in a briefing is more like a billboard by the highway; a viewer has only one, fleeting chance to grasp the message as it flashes by.

One expert recommends that briefings use graphics twice as simple and four times as bold as those we use in our reports. Briefings are usually not the time for graphics requiring careful, detailed study. We should simplify the graphics for a briefing and refer the audience to more detailed graphics if they want additional information.

Reporting via Other Techniques

Videotapes

Videotapes are becoming increasingly popular for reporting evaluation results, especially as they become cheaper and easier to use. Even fairly sophisticated editing equipment, which was prohibitively expensive only a few years ago, is now easily affordable by organizations and even individuals. And almost every office has equipment for broadcasting a videotape on one or several television sets.

There are two basic ways to use videotape. One is to videotape local conditions, persons, operations, and outcomes and to play this footage so audiences can have a closer feel of local-level reality. Earlier I mentioned a briefing that opened with a very moving videotape of an elderly woman on the steps of the boarding home. A videotape could as easily show outdated agricultural processing techniques, women receiving instructions in oral rehydration therapy, industrial wastes polluting a river, or many other activities.

A second way to use videotape for reporting evaluation results is to videotape an entire briefing and allow audience members to view it at their leisure. This strategy, which is an especially popular way to lobby Congress these days, is risky because audiences may never watch the briefing. And if they do, they cannot have the general discussion that is so important for building consensus and generating momentum for action. However, for busy officials who cannot congregate soon for an in-person briefing, such an electronic briefing might be an acceptable alternative at times.

Computerized Presentations

A similar but less portable technique is a computerized slide show or a slide presentation designed to be displayed automatically on a personal computer screen. The individual slides are created beforehand (using the ScreenShow capability of Harvard Graphics, for example) and are stored in sequence in the software. Alternating text charts with visual graphics is an especially effective way to present a strong message in both words and illustrations. At a command, the slide show begins with the first slide and continues through the presentation.

The evaluation office at the U.S. Food and Drug Administration regularly uses computerized reporting, and some of their presentations are quite impressive. They select from multiple options for how long an individual slide is displayed, how it is erased, how bars grow and lines run before the audience's eyes, and they even allow the audience to determine which parts of the briefing they would like to emphasize or delete. While these presentations suffer from many of the same disadvantages as do videotapes, they can be very effective in certain circumstances and with certain audiences.

Conclusion

The many suggestions of this chapter can perhaps best be summarized into four fundamental principles for effectively reporting evaluation results. First, we must *adopt the proper attitude*. We must acknowledge that reporting our findings is an integral and critical step in the evaluation process (not an added burden after our "real" tasks are completed), admit that it is *our* responsibility (not our audiences') to ensure that our results are conveyed effectively, and to become much more aggressive about our "marketing" efforts. With this proper attitude, we will continue to develop effective new reporting methods; without it, we will continue to miss opportunities already available to us.

Second, we must *celebrate variety*. This chapter alone highlights several different reporting techniques — written products, personal briefings, action recommendations, graphics, videotapes, and computerized presentations — and other possibilities no doubt exist. Furthermore, we have seen great variety within each technique; written products, for example, could involve draft and final reports, memos, press releases, op-ed articles, newsletter items, written testimony, or even index cards. Rather than view this variety as an intimidating, paralyzing array of possibilities, we must applaud the diversity of techniques available and try to master as many as possible. Relying on only one method for reporting our results is simply not good enough any more.

Third, though, we must also *tailor our reporting very carefully,* and in two ways. First we must choose our reporting techniques to suit our audiences. If one audience prefers reading, then we must prepare effective written products. If another audience prefers face-to-face discussions, then personal briefings would be more appropriate. Simply because our reporting toolbox is full does not mean we use each tool for every job; every good worker knows when to use her hammer and when her screwdriver.

In addition, we must also tailor how we use the tool(s) we decide to use. We have seen that each written report has its own structure, style, content, perspective, and resolution. How to write this specific report? We have also seen that the same results can often be graphed in different ways. Which graphic to present? These are important decisions that must flow not from old habits but from a conscious, deliberate, case-by-case strategy for conveying our results most effectively.

Fourth, we must *stay focused on the bottom line.* In reality, top-quality reporting is not our most important goal. Our most important goal is for our audiences to understand our results, to see their many implications, to realize what actions are needed, to grasp the best ways to accomplish those actions, to take action, and to follow up on the impacts of those actions. In other words, we must never forget that our results are merely one input into a process of change. Offering straightforward conclusions, sensible recommendations that flow directly and obviously from those conclusions, and practical implementation plans are some of the ways we can help effect those changes.

If we follow these four fundamental principles and adopt some of the specific suggestions offered in this chapter, I believe we will be pleasantly surprised to find that many audiences will be receptive, even eager, to hear our message. Whether we rise to this challenge will determine whether our results create only a tiny ripple or the proper splash they deserve.

References

Aid Association for Lutherans. *A Short-Term Evaluation of 1985 Operation Care and Share.* Appleton, Wis.: Aid Association for Lutherans, 1986.

Baum, H. S. "The Advisor as Invited Intruder." *Public Administration Review,* Nov./Dec. 1982, 546–551.

Behn, R. D. "Policy Analysis and Policy Politics." *Policy Analysis,* 1981, 199–226.

Bozeman, B., and Massey, J. "Investing in Policy Evaluation: Some Guidelines for Skeptical Public Managers." *Public Administration Review,* 1982, *42,* 264–269.

Cleveland, W. S. *The Elements of Graphing Data.* Belmont, Calif.: Wadsworth, 1985.

Hendricks, M. "Oral Policy Briefings." In N. L. Smith (ed.), *Communication Strategies in Evaluation.* Newbury Park, Calif.: Sage, 1982.

Hendricks, M. "Finis." *Evaluation News,* 1984a, *5,* 94–96.

Hendricks, M. "Preparing and Using Briefing Charts." *Evaluation News,* 1984b, *5*(3), 78–80.

Hendricks, M. "Convey Meaning Through Evaluation Reports: Thoughts on Editing and Writing Reports." Paper presented at annual meeting of American Educational Research Association, Chicago, April 1985.

Hendricks, M. *An Approach to Evaluating Repelita IV.* Washington, D.C.: MH Associates, 1986.

Hendricks, M. "Making a Splash: How Evaluators Can Be Better Communicators." *Development Communication Report,* 1991, *72*(1), 1, 10–11.

Hendricks, M., and Handley, E. A. "Improving the Recommendations from Evaluation Studies." *Evaluation and Program Planning,* 1990, *13,* 109–117.

Hendricks, M., and Hatry, H. P. *An Evaluation of the Montgomery County Senior Nutrition Program.* Washington, D.C.: MH Associates, 1985.

Hendricks, M., and Papagiannis, M. "Do's and Dont's for Offering Effective Recommendations." *Evaluation Practice,* 1990, *11*(2), 121–125.

Hendricks, M., and Roth, J. *An Evaluation of the Montgomery County Health Department's Special Supplemental Food Program for Women, Infants, and Children (WIC).* Washington, D.C.: MH Associates, 1986.

House, P. W., and McLeod, J. *Large-Scale Models for Policy Evaluation.* New York: Wiley, 1977.

Larsen, J. K. "Effect of Time on Information Utilization." *Knowledge,* 1985, *7,* 143–159.

Leman, C. K., and Nelson, R. H. "Ten Commandments for Policy Economists." *Journal of Policy Analysis and Management,* 1981, *1,* 97–117.

Majchrzak, A. *Methods for Policy Research.* Newbury Park, Calif.: Sage, 1984.

Mintzberg, H. *The Nature of Managerial Work.* New York: HarperCollins, 1973.

Murphy, J. T. *Getting the Facts: A Fieldwork Guide for Evaluators and Policy Analysts.* Santa Monica, Calif.: Goodyear, 1980.

Office of Inspector General. *Program Inspection of Head Start Enrollment and Attendance.* Washington, D.C.: U.S. Department of Health and Human Services, 1984.

Office of Inspector General. *Technical Assistance Guides for Conducting Program Evaluations and Inspections.* Washington, D.C.: U.S. Department of Health and Human Services, 1990.

Oman, R. C., and Chitwood, S. R. "Management Evaluation Studies: Factors Affecting the Acceptance of Recommendations." *Evaluation Review,* 1984, *8,* 283–305.

Palumbo, D. J., and Nachmias, D. "The Preconditions for Successful Evaluation: Is There an Ideal Paradigm?" *Policy Sciences,* 1983, *16,* 67–79.

Patton, M. Q. *Practical Evaluation.* Newbury Park, Calif.: Sage, 1982.

Patton, M. Q. "The Future and Evaluation." *Evaluation Practice,* 1988, *9*(4), 90–93.

Roberts-Gray, C., Buller, A., and Sparkman, A. "Linking Data with Action: Procedures for Developing Recommendations." *Evaluation Review,* 1987, *11,* 678–684.

Sadler, D. R. "Evaluation and the Logic of Recommendations." *Evaluation Review,* 1984, *8,* 261–268.

Stanfield, J., and Smith, N. "Management Consulting and Evaluation." *Evaluation and Program Planning,* 1984, *7,* 87–93.

Trutko, J., and others. *Gaining Ground: Public Assistance Program Redesign in Delaware.* Arlington, Va.: James Bell Associates, 1986.

Tufte, E. R. *The Visual Display of Quantitative Information.* Cheshire, Conn.: Graphics Press, 1983.

Tufte, E. R. *Envisioning Information.* Cheshire, Conn.: Graphics Press, 1990.

Zelazny, G. *Say It with Charts.* Homewood, Ill.: Dow Jones-Irwin, 1991.

24

Maximizing the Use
of Evaluation Results

Reginald Carter

Evaluations are conducted primarily to provide decision makers with informed options for improving programs. Once an evaluation is completed there are ways to increase the likelihood that the results will ultimately be used to improve the program. This chapter provides examples of how evaluations are used and focuses on ways to maximize their use. The chapter is divided into two parts: how to use findings from (1) ad hoc evaluation studies and (2) client outcome monitoring systems.

A number of writers have identified important factors impacting the use of evaluation findings: the extent of stakeholder involvement (Patton, 1986), prioritization of studies (Muscatello, 1988; Wholey, 1983), organization characteristics, political circumstances, and evaluation techniques (Weiss, 1972, 1977; Caplan, 1977; Alkin, Daillak, and White, 1979; Rothman, 1980). This chapter supplements earlier research with practical guidelines for evaluators and managers interested in increasing the usefulness of evaluation results. The first section focuses on ad hoc evaluations, with five recommendations for improving the use of evaluation results. The second section concentrates on how performance monitoring data can be most effectively utilized to improve programs.

Ad Hoc Evaluations

In some cases the evaluation question is clear, commitment to using information is strong, and the study results provide the basis for an acceptable recommendation that is immediately implemented. These cases are rare. Most evaluations do not have an immediate, concrete, and observable effect on specific decisions and program practices. Patton reviewed the use by key participants (project officers, decision makers, evaluators) of findings from twenty national health program evaluations (Patton, 1986). He concluded that evaluation studies often have important impacts on programs, but these tend to be modest. However, "none of the impacts described was the type in which new findings from an evaluation led directly and immediately to the making of major, concrete program decisions. The more typical impact was one in which the evaluation findings provided additional pieces of information in the difficult puzzle of program action, permitting some reduction in the uncertainty within which any federal decision maker inevitably operates" (Patton, 1986, p. 34).

In addition, evaluation results are often absorbed quickly into an organization's culture. Immediately, old assumptions are no longer valid and a new definition of program reality is substituted as a result of the study. The new definition, however, seldom changes the operation of the program significantly. Rarely does *any* event significantly change the operations of a program.

Although most evaluations have modest impacts, there are five ways to increase the use of evaluation results: (1) develop realistic recommendations that focus on program improvement, (2) explore multiple uses of study data, (3) constantly remind decision makers of findings and recommendations, (4) share findings and recommendations with broad audiences, and (5) assign evaluation staff to assist in implementing recommendations.

Develop Realistic Recommendations
That Focus on Program Improvement

Decision makers want to improve programs. They appreciate focused evaluations that provide realistic options based on a systematic and independent assessment of programs. Too often evaluation staff focus on the methodology used to create the findings and devote only limited time and resources to developing realistic recommendations flowing from the findings. To maximize the adoption of recommended changes, evaluators need to change this distribution of resources so there is much more emphasis on the early identification and development of acceptable program improvements.

One way to obtain a preview of likely evaluation results is to complete a thorough analysis of the first 10 percent of the findings. Often this preliminary assessment will provide a valid basis for developing a set of potential recommendations for program changes. The preliminary recommendations should then be reviewed informally by as many of the stakeholders as possible, to obtain their perspectives on potential practical final recommendations. This approach was a routine practice at the Michigan Department of Social Services, Evaluation Division (1974–1984). In the majority of evaluations, this analysis of the first 10 percent of findings was highly predictive of the major results across 100 percent of the data collected. Chapter Twenty-two has further suggestions on how to develop effective recommendations.

Explore Multiple Uses of Study Data

Evaluators often limit the use of evaluation data to the questions of hypotheses under investigation. The information collected may, and usually does, have meaning and use to others in the organization for purposes well beyond the intent of the original evaluation study. Backup data should be available in summary tables at the end of the report for use by different audiences for different reasons. Customized data tables and analyses should be available to members of the organization to answer a wide range of other questions. Agencies who use such data for testing their own hypotheses greatly appreciate the information although it was collected for a different reason. The act of sharing the data creates goodwill and maximizes the use of the evaluation effort.

Some of the most widely used databases developed by the Michigan Department of Social Services were simple demographic program profiles of clients broken down by county. These simple databases were used to describe the program being evaluated (such as adult home help, day care). The demographic information included types of clients, number of clients, geographic distribution, growth rate over time, and expenditures. They were used extensively by program management, fiscal agency analysts, budget analysts within the organization, and client advocacy groups as the factual basis for resolution of many policy issues totally unrelated to the original evaluation questions. In short, the data were used extensively beyond the original evaluation questions because they were valid, available, complete, and widely accepted by other stakeholders. These various audiences had their own evaluation and policy concerns, and they wanted a valid, current database with which to test their own hypotheses and to support their own positions.

The recommendations may not be the most significant product of an evaluation study. The availability of the database can enable an unexpected use by a wide variety of users. Organizations can benefit from the distribution of databases for secondary use by a number of audiences. Sometimes evaluation recommendations are not accepted, but other changes are introduced because of the information provided by the study. These unintended changes can be very important.

A good example of unintended program changes from evaluation studies is the Staff-Caseload Studies of the Michigan Department of Social Services in 1980 (Carter, 1985). The intent of the four caseload studies was to develop valid caseload-to-staff ratios. This original intent was not achieved. However, the four evaluations showed no relationship between policy requirements and client outcomes, and this result helped lead to a streamlining project that reduced the number of program requirement manual pages by 56 percent (from 1,902 to 847 pages). Removed from the manual were requirements with no legal basis or proven relationship to program outcomes. The reduction in ineffective program requirements was positively accepted by first-line workers and supervisors.

Constantly Remind Decision Makers of Findings and Recommendations

Each organization has a unique history and culture. Each time an evaluation study is completed, there is an opportunity to alter the culture by changing perceptions held by the agency's members. When the evaluation report is initially released, there is focused scrutiny of the data, methodology, and recommendations. If the study results are widely accepted and the recommendations are implemented, then the study's *imprint* can be significant. This imprint can be reinforced with frequent reminders to the organization's members to pay attention to the study results. Evaluators and managers should

- Write agency newsletter articles describing the findings, the recommendations, and the successful implementation of changes in order to educate the members of the organization
- Prepare presentations for the agency director to ensure that the findings are being incorporated into the director's thinking and public statements
- Make recommendations for similar changes in other program areas so the organization's members begin to think beyond the one-time implications of a single evaluation
- Remind other managers of the evaluation results during critical executive committee meetings or in informal settings

In short, work through whatever formal and informal channels of communication are available to educate and remind agency members of the use of evaluation studies. When new agency managers join the organization, evaluators should brief them on prior agency evaluation findings still felt to be timely and send them copies of the studies. This action introduces them to the evaluation history of the agency.

Share Findings and Recommendations with Broad Audiences

Traditionally a formal evaluation report is prepared with a set of recommendations as to how the results should be interpreted and used to alter or reinforce current program operations. Stakeholders vary in their interest in the methodology and statistics used to arrive at the recommended changes. Most are primarily interested in how the program should change as a result of the new information provided by the study. Most will disagree with the methodology only when they also disagree with the recommended changes.

The evaluation findings and recommendations should be presented in a concise, factual executive summary with a technical appendix or report available for a complete understanding of the methodology and statistics used. Evaluators should identify the limitations of the design and findings, but highlight the recommended options available to the decision makers. Stakeholders are generally limited to those involved in particular program deci-

sions (such as agency director, program staff, fiscal or policy oversight organizations, advocate groups, legislators). These stakeholders need to be
defined and the recommendations presented to them.

The agency, when appropriate, should share the evaluation results
with a much broader audience than the immediately affected stakeholders.
Ways to accomplish this are suggested in Table 24.1: providing interviews
with the media, briefing oversight organizations, and sharing evaluations
with universities and with those in other agencies.

Table 24.1. Sharing Results with Broad Audiences.

Audiences	Suggested Strategy
General Public	Agency staff should have interviews with local newspapers, radio and TV news shows, and talk shows to promote broad distribution of the findings to the general public. By portraying management as interested in systematically assessing programs and as committed to developing the most effective intervention possible, the staff can enhance the image of the organization.
Oversight Organizations	Agency staff should schedule regular briefings for oversight organizations to share evaluation results with them and to answer their questions once the study findings are available. This openness to sharing information can reduce skepticism by oversight agencies and client advocacy groups.
University	Evaluators should regularly make a list of completed studies available to local universities and other academic groups and offer them copies of the studies and information describing how the results were used to improve the organization.
Other Professional Staff	Evaluators should share the evaluation results with other agencies in other states. Evaluators and managers should publish the results in professional journals specializing in evaluation or program areas. It is often helpful for both program and evaluation staff jointly to write and present findings from evaluation projects at professional meetings.

Source: Mobray, 1988.

Assign Evaluation Staff to Assist in Implementing Recommendations

Evaluation staff generally do not have experience in program management,
and this limits their ability to propose practical recommendations to improve
programs. In addition, program staff are often skeptical of advocates for
change who have not operated a program. Evaluation staff can gain valuable program experience and future credibility by being assigned to assist
program staff in implementing recommendations from evaluation findings.

Implementation of these five recommendations should enhance the
use of ad hoc evaluations. The impact of ad hoc studies is often restricted
to a relatively short period of time during which the results are initially
released. Evaluators and managers need to be acutely aware of this time

limitation and seek maximum effective exposure and discussion of the evaluation findings and recommendations. Evaluation reports, like all other reports, need to be presented in a clear, concise, and interesting fashion in order to be read and understood by decision makers. Hendricks (Chapter Twenty-three of this volume) presents a very helpful set of recommendations on how best to present evaluation findings.

Ongoing Performance (Outcome) Monitoring

One of the most important factors constraining the use of ad hoc evaluation studies is the limited opportunity that exists for the findings and recommendations to improve the organization. The findings receive greatest attention in the short period when the study's results are being released and assessed. Very soon afterward the results become dated and less acceptable as reflecting current practice.

One way to provide continuous evaluation data is to design a strategy for ongoing collection of client outcome information. With such data the organization might regularly develop ways to improve the program by assessing current outcome impact (Carter, 1983). This approach lacks the explanatory power of a formal evaluation design, but it provides increased opportunities to improve program policy and practice by stimulating routine review of factors impacting program performance. Affholter (in Chapter Five of this volume) shows how evaluators can design and implement outcome monitoring approaches.

Public organizations need to institutionalize the collection of outcome information so it is regularly assessed and released in management reports. Examples of outcome monitoring systems include the following:

- The Maxey Boys Training School in Michigan has been collecting information annually on the "graduates" of this delinquency training school six and twelve months after release. Data gathered includes police arrests and work, school, or training status. This client-specific information is reported quarterly to workers at the school (Residential Care Division, 1992).

- Pressley Ridge Schools privately operate seven programs located in four states and serving emotionally and/or socially disturbed youth. Funding for these programs includes both private and public sources. Five of the programs annually conduct follow-up surveys one to two years after youth leave the program. The programs include foster care, an alternative school and partial hospitalization program, a therapeutic wilderness camp, and a residential treatment center. The process of collecting the outcome information is described by Fabry, Hawkins, and Luster (forthcoming).

- The Florida Department of Health and Rehabilitative Services has prepared an annual report to the legislature on the outcomes of all child welfare programs since 1985 (see Affholter, Chapter Five of this volume). Beginning in 1992, the department was required to report outcomes across all programs.

•   The Minnesota Trade Office (MTO) of the Minnesota Department of Trade and Economic Development provides assistance to over three hundred small to medium-sized corporations interested in exporting their products. In 1989, the office began to measure the satisfaction level of the companies using their services, which included publications, seminars, workshops, trade shows, overseas trade office services, library services, and trade leads. In addition, the office defined a set of positive quantitative outcomes: exporting to a new country, increasing export sales, increasing export-related employment, and initiating pre-export activities. Customers were first asked if they had achieved a desired outcome after they received MTO services. If they had, they were asked the extent to which they credited the MTO with helping them achieve the outcomes (Quillan and Jarvis, 1991).

Pressley Ridge Schools illustrate ways in which outcome monitoring can be used effectively by local agencies. The executive director has been collecting client specific outcome information since 1986. Some of the uses have included the following:

•   Orienting new Board members to the impact of Pressley Ridge programs by sharing brief status reports on specific graduates contacted through outcome follow-up processes.
•   Providing outcome data demonstrating the effectiveness of current programming to the staff, clients, and families to assure them that the interventions have a known success rate.
•   Using outcome information as a marketing technique to demonstrate the success of Pressley Ridge Schools' programs. Outcome information, especially in new markets in which competitors do not have comparable data, provides an important advantage in attracting new purchasers of services.
•   Using outcome information to identify program weaknesses and subsequently modifying the program to improve effectiveness. One program added a drug awareness training element because of the high incidence of drug use reported for discharged youth.

Other uses for program outcome data that have been suggested by Hatry and others (1992) are to demonstrate accountability, support resource allocation requests, justify budget requests, bolster employee motivation, support performance contracting, implement quality control checks on efficiency measurement, enhance management control, improve communication between citizens and local government officials, and improve services to customers.

    The major advantage of outcome monitoring information is that it creates many routine opportunities to influence changes in a program because the information is obtained regularly. This situation is very different from the one-time release of evaluation study results. The factors impacting the utilization of ongoing outcome monitoring can be substantially different from one-time evaluation findings.

Some of the elements that will encourage greater utilization of outcome monitoring data are (a) providing timely performance data, (b) providing the data in sufficient detail that the responsible manager can identify the performance for his or her area of responsibility, (c) ensuring that program staff actively participate in selecting the outcome measures and the data collection process, (d) increasing confidence in the validity of the data, (e) demonstrating the usefulness of outcome data, (f) repeating the measurements on a regular basis, (g) mandating outcome reporting, and (h) developing appropriate information systems to track clients over time.

Timely Data

Outcome data should be released as soon as possible after the follow-up period has ended. Pressley Ridge Schools collect outcome information annually on "graduates" who completed treatment one to two years earlier. Ideally, the outcome reports should be released more frequently; Maxey Boys Training School in Michigan released outcome reports every six months.

Detailed Breakouts

Each outcome indicator should be disaggregated by such important program characteristics as work units, geographic location, client and worker demographics, and caseload of workers. Such breakouts should provide program managers with enough relevant information that they can begin to understand some of the factors potentially influencing different outcome levels. Year-to-year comparisons of outcome data should be limited to similar work units so that the major focus is on improvements within the work units.

Worker Participation

Program staff should be encouraged to participate actively in both the selection of the outcome measures and the process by which the outcome information is collected. Their ownership of the data elements will enhance the likelihood that they will perceive the findings as an accurate reflection of their performance. Once articulated, outcome measures can help all workers to keep focused on better ways to improve their performance.

Perception that Data Are Valid

In order to have credibility, the outcome data need to be perceived as reasonably accurate by the program staff and top management. Data validity can be assured in a variety of ways as reflected in Table 24.2: checking the

Table 24.2. Ways to Assure Data Validity.

Strategies	
Check Accuracy	Agency staff should routinely check the correctness of the outcome information reported. This can be accomplished through conducting systematic checks on a random sample of cases. Known "skeptics" should be confronted with validity information to refute claims that the data are invalid. Certain members of the organization, especially analysts and first-line workers, are likely to be aware of what information is accurate, and which data elements within the system are suspect. A small advisory group comprising first-line workers, computer analysts, and evaluators should annually check the validity of data, the appropriateness of policy instuctions on how to collect and record data, and the timeliness in training of first-line workers.
Publish Results of Validity Check	The results of the validity checks should be widely publicized so workers and managers know that the accuracy and completeness of specific data fields are being monitored. It is not uncommon to find that only 50 percent of required data is actually documented in case records. This finding suggests that frequently data are either never captured by workers or never placed in the client record.
Cross-Check Outcomes	Agencies should cross-check outcome measures whenever possible. Pressley Ridge Schools employs teachers during the summer to collect outcome information on recent "graduates." They attempt to interview several independent sources of outcome information. When they receive two believable sources providing the same answer they note the data as "verified." This checking helps to maintain data validity. Most outcome data used in their analysis are verified.
Obtain High Response Rate	Agencies should be able to collect outcome information on 60 percent to 80 percent of the clients completing a program. This is a realistic goal attained by several small agencies collecting outcome information. With large client populations a random sample is often used because of the cost involved in collecting outcome data. The longer the follow-up period, the lower the response level. However, Pressley Ridge Schools were able to locate 92 percent of the 1987–88 cohort (in the summer of 1989), 88 percent in the summer of 1990, 81 percent in the summer of 1991, and 78 percent in the summer of 1992.
Ensure High Face Validity	Outcome measures should have high face validity. They should be obvious results such as high job retention for employment and training programs, low re-arrest rates for delinquency invervention, low re-abuse rates for abuse and neglect treatment programs, and increased employment levels for economic development projects. Such objective measures are preferable to subjective indicators like client satisfaction surveys. A suggested list of outcome measures with face validity across a wide variety of programs can be found in Carter (1988) and Hatry and Fountain (1990).

accuracy of outcome data, publishing the results of validity checks, cross-checking outcome data, obtaining high response rates, and ensuring that outcome measures have high face validity.

Demonstrate the Usefulness of the Outcome Data

Outcome information needs to be used visibly once it becomes available to an organization. For example, since 1986 the state of Florida has collected outcome information on services for children and has used the data to (1) monitor the effectiveness of contracted services, (2) restructure programs, (3) improve service coordination, (4) target program monitoring efforts, and (5) improve the accuracy of the data presented in widely circulated outcome reports.

There are several ways to maximize the use and usefulness of outcome data:

• Encourage and train managers to seek information as to which program characteristics are impacting or explaining changes in the outcomes. Use by managers will also increase program staff interest in the outcome data.

• Similarly, encourage program managers to provide explanatory information along with the performance reports they provide to higher levels, particularly when the reported outcomes differ significantly from expected outcome levels.

• Publicize the outcomes for work units internally to create constructive competition between work groups directed at improving outcome results. Comparisons should include both changes in outcomes within a work group over time and a comparison of absolute outcome levels. To provide fair comparison, the comparisons should include work groups that have approximately the same workload difficulty (such as similar types of clients).

• Require program managers to estimate the impact of their budget requests on subsequent outcome levels. These estimations should lead not only to better resource allocation decisions but also to stronger justification for budget requests. Legislative oversight committees are often impressed positively with any systematic attempt to measure the results of programs. The collection of outcome data demonstrates the program's commitment to good management practices and thus provides another reason for refunding the program. That is, program managers should justify their budget proposals on the basis of the outcomes anticipated if the proposed level of resources is provided.

• Encourage program managers to use outcome information in their speeches, daily discussions, meetings, and press interviews. However, these presentations should also be clear about the limitations of the outcome data so that outcome findings are not misrepresented as reflection of a cause/effect relationship between the program and the outcome level. Such misrepresentation is a pitfall that the media and persons with opposing viewpoints will likely exploit.

Repeat the Measurements

Outcome measurements should be collected at least quarterly. A major advantage of continuous data reporting is that measurements are repeated enough that (1) changes over time and time trends can be identified and (2) the agency gains more confidence in the data because of the consistency of the findings. The first time any new program performance data are released to agency staff there is skepticism about the information because of its uniqueness or other methodological factors involved with the data collection process. If the findings are repeated consistently over several periods, the results begin to be perceived as having reliability and will gain increasing acceptance by agency staff.

The results of ad hoc evaluations, on the other hand, are often viewed as reflecting the unique characteristics of the evaluation design and are not accepted as a basis for making program changes. The one-time nature of ad hoc evaluations severely limits its potential impact. Moreover, a one-time study quickly becomes forgotten by many of the members of the organization unless they were personally involved with the collection of data or experienced a negative or positive impact from the results of the evaluation. In short, the results of ongoing monitoring are more likely to be utilized because they are continuously being exposed to both old and new audiences each time they are released.

A major advantage of ongoing reporting, as contrasted to one-time studies, is the development of a historic database. The data allow managers to assess systematically the results of program innovations over time. The collection of comparable data from year to year enables managers to know whether their current program is able to remain effective even as client characteristics change.

Mandating Outcome Reporting

There is a trend in federal as well as local government to require agencies to collect outcome information. For example, Florida has recently mandated outcome reporting for all services within the Department of Health and Rehabilitative Services. In 1993, Minnesota passed performance measurement legislation requiring all state agencies to develop outcome measures for their programs and to report these findings annually to the governor, legislature, legislative auditor, and other oversight agencies. On a smaller scale, Milwaukee County several years ago passed a law mandating the collection of client satisfaction information from social services department clients using purchase of services such as day care.

Program outcome reporting should be required as part of budget submissions so budget requests can be justified in terms of the outcomes expected for the resources sought. Traditionally, budget requests have been based on factors such as caseload estimates or inflation cost increases. In Sunnyvale, California, the city council determines budgets for each of its programs on the basis of expected outcomes (Osborne and Gaebler, 1992, pp. 142–145).

Mandating the collection of outcome data is effective if sufficient resources are available to produce the outcome information. Such a requirement has the advantage of being much more routinized, and thus, not subject to the varying priorities of individual agency managers. In addition, mandated requirements have a higher status in the eyes of the agency staff than optional or voluntary activities. However, its disadvantage is that it may be seen as undesirable by operating agencies, who then give only lip service to its implementation.

Develop Appropriate Information Systems

Some outcome information has unique characteristics that require adaptations in order to track clients over time, especially after they leave the program. This applies whether the clients are in public health, social service, mental health, employment and training, corrections, or economic development programs. Maxey Boys Training School and Pressley Ridge Schools have had small enough populations each year (500) that all information on the clients can be stored manually or on a small personal computer. Florida has used a variety of approaches based on the available databases: the computer mainframe for client information, personal computers, manual reporting systems, contractor-provider reports, and specialized evaluation studies.

Most human service agencies have reporting systems designed to provide monthly counts of the types of clients served and the services received. These reporting systems are generally not designed to track specific individuals over time, across programs, or after clients leave the system. Outcome monitoring, thus, may require modification of current program data collection systems.

Conclusion

This chapter describes a number of ways to increase the use and usefulness of both ad hoc evaluations and performance monitoring systems. Table 24.3 summarizes the chapter's key suggestions.

Fabry, Hawkins, and Luster (forthcoming) have outlined some of the important limitations of outcome monitoring systems. The main shortcoming is that the outcome data cannot identify specific program changes needed to increase effectiveness. However, once a consistent outcome pattern has been identified, a more thorough ad hoc evaluation study may be able to identify the key causal variables affecting the outcomes. In short, outcome monitoring results can be an initial filtering mechanism for identifying useful ad hoc evaluations.

These two approaches to asessing the performance of programs can be effectively used in tandem to reinforce the value of each. In most agencies it is too costly to conduct evaluation studies annually across all programs. However, outcome monitoring data disaggregated by potentially important causal factors can help define a larger investment in a highly focused evaluation effort. Both types of information can be extremely helpful in responding to the increasing interest in agencies, justifying their use of public and private funds.

Table 24.3. Ways to Increase Use of Evaluation and Outcome Monitoring.

Ad Hoc Evaluations

1. Develop realistic recommendations that focus on program improvement.
2. Explore multiple uses of study data.
3. Constantly remind decision makers of findings and recommendations.
4. Share findings and recommendations with broad audiences.
5. Assign evaluation staff to assist in implementing recommendations.

Ongoing Performance (Outcome) Monitoring

6. Timely reports should be provided.
7. Reports should include detailed breakouts by program, client, and worker characteristics.
8. Program staff should actively participate in defining outcome measures and in the data collection process.
9. Outcome data should have high face validity.
10. The use of outcome information should be demonstrated.
11. Outcome measurements should be repeated on a a regular basis.
12. Performance monitoring can be mandated to ensure the collection of data over time and different political administrations.
13. Outcome information systems may need to be modified to reflect the unique needs of tracking clients over time.

References

Alkin, M., Daillak, R., and White, P. *Using Evaluations: Does Evaluation Make a Difference?* Newbury Park, Calif.: Sage, 1979.

Caplan, N. "A Minimal Set of Conditions Necessary for the Utilization of Social Science Knowledge in Policy Formulation at the National Level." In C. Weiss (ed.), *Using Social Research in Public Policy Making.* Lexington, Mass.: Lexington Books, 1977.

Carter, R. *The Accountable Agency.* Newbury Park, Calif.: Sage, 1983.

Carter, R. "The Analyst Corner: Streamlining Policy." *New England Journal of Human Services,* 1985, *4,* 29–30.

Carter, R. "Success Measures for Public Administrators." *New England Journal of Human Services,* 1988, *1,* 29–34.

Fabry, B., Hawkins, R., and Luster, C. "Monitoring Outcomes of Services to Severely Disturbed Children and Youths: An Economical Follow-Up Procedure for Mental Health and Child Care Agencies." *Journal of Mental Health Administration* (forthcoming).

Hatry, H., and Fountain, J. R. (eds.). *Service Efforts and Accomplishments Reporting: Its Time Has Come.* Norwalk, Conn.: Governmental Accounting Standards Board, 1990.

Hatry, H., and others. *How Effective Are Your Community Services?* (2nd ed.) Washington, D.C.: The Urban Institute, 1992.

Mobray, C. "Getting the System to Respond to Evaluation Findings." In J. A. McLaughlin, L. J. Weber, R. W. Covert, and R. B. Ingle (eds.), *Evaluation Utilization.* San Francisco: Jossey-Bass, 1988.

Muscatello, D. "Developing an Agenda That Works: The Right Choice at the Right Time." In J. A. McLaughlin, L. J. Weber, R. W. Covert, and R. B. Ingle (eds.), *Evaluation Utilization.* San Francisco: Jossey-Bass, 1988.

Osborne, D., and Gaebler, T. *Reinventing Government.* Reading, Mass.: Addison-Wesley, 1992.

Patton, M. Q. *Utilization-Focused Evaluation.* (2nd ed.) Newbury Park, Calif.: Sage, 1986.

Quillan, D., and Jarvis, J. "But, how good? Grading Minnesota's Export Program." *The Entrepreneurial Economy Review,* 1991, *10*(3), 25–30.

Residential Care Division, Office of Children and Youth Services. *Annual Report 1990.* Lansing: Michigan Department of Social Services, 1992.

Rothman, J. *Using Research in Organizations: A Guide to Successful Application.* Newbury Park, Calif.: Sage, 1980.

Weiss, C. H. "Utilization of Evaluation: Toward Comparative Study." In C. H. Weiss (ed.), *Evaluating Action Programs: Readings in Social Action and Education.* Boston: Allyn & Bacon, 1972.

Weiss, C. H. "Introduction." In C. H. Weiss (ed.), *Using Social Research in Public Policy Making.* Lexington, Mass.: Lexington Books, 1977.

Wholey, J. S. *Evaluation and Effective Public Management.* Boston: Little, Brown, 1983.

25

Conclusion: Improving Evaluation Activities and Results

Harry P. Hatry, Kathryn E. Newcomer,
Joseph S. Wholey

Many opportunities exist for managers to use evaluation to improve program design and program performance. This handbook presents a variety of approaches for evaluating program performance and getting evaluation results used. In this final chapter, we discuss important related topics: (1) quality control of the evaluation process, (2) selection and training of evaluation personnel, (3) standards and ethics in evaluation work, and (4) incentives for the conduct and use of program evaluation. We then discuss trends in program evaluation and present some concluding observations.

Quality Control of the Evaluation Process

A major purpose of program evaluation is to examine the quality of public services. Evaluators should be concerned with the quality of the evaluation work as well, both in individual evaluations and across evaluations. Earlier handbook chapters suggest a number of quality control steps to take in managing evaluation activities; for example, checking for missing data and checking for consistency in the definitions of data items when data are collected from different offices or different years.

Here, we are concerned with quality control of the entire evaluation process. Evaluation offices should implement such quality control processes as the following:

• Provide for peer review of both evaluation designs and draft evaluation reports. The peer review might be undertaken by evaluators in the agency, evaluators in another part of government, or experts from universities or consulting firms. These peer reviews should include people familiar with the type of program being evaluated; many evaluation problems can occur because evaluators lack knowledge of the program.

•   Give staff in the agencies and programs that have been evaluated the opportunity to respond to draft evaluation findings. This step is valuable both politically and as a quality control step. The feedback can identify important problems in the evaluation itself. In an evaluation of drug programs in Dade County, Florida, for example, after reviewing the draft report the agencies whose programs were evaluated noted that an important group of client records had been overlooked by the evaluators. This required the evaluation team to reopen its data collection and analysis activities and rework its findings.

•   Provide for periodic outside peer reviews of the evaluation office, as the U.S. General Accounting Office has done (see Chelimsky, Chapter Twenty of this volume). Such reviews should identify any patterns of weakness in evaluation design, data collection procedures, or report presentations and suggest steps to increase the usefulness of the evaluation findings. Reviewers should also identify alternative approaches not currently being used by the evaluation office. Any office tends to slip into standard modes of operation. Outside critics may be in the best position to identify the need for changes.

•   Regularly review the work of evaluation contractors. Provide oversight of evaluation contractors' work while it is under way, including review of evaluation designs and draft evaluation reports (see Bell, Chapter Twenty-one of this volume). After the final report has been submitted, the quality and timeliness of the contractor's performance should be assessed, taking into consideration the time and resources that were available.

Evaluator Selection and Training

Getting skilled, trained evaluators is an important prerequisite for quality evaluations (Chelimsky, Chapter Twenty, and Sonnichsen, Chapter Twenty-two of this volume). Though there is room for diversity in the backgrounds and knowledge of evaluators, some prerequisites apply to all evaluation teams. Evaluators should become knowledgeable about the organizational context of any program they assess, for example. Knowledge of the mission and legislative mandate for a program is necessary, though not sufficient, to guarantee a fair reading on program performance. Evaluators should be aware of the many evaluation strategies available and how they may be matched most effectively to evaluation questions.

Evaluators need a variety of skills to be effective. They should be good analysts. They should be gifted at listening. Evaluators should also possess marketing skills. They must communicate the value of evaluation to policymakers and managers who may not appreciate the benefits to be derived from systematic evaluation efforts.

An evaluation usually requires a team rather than a single individual.

The evaluation team needs knowledge of organizational contexts, legislative mandates, evaluation designs, data collection and analysis methods, and the ability to listen and to communicate evaluation findings and recommendations, both orally and in writing. All the needed knowledge and skills, however, need not reside in a single individual. An evaluation team can also use outside members for services such as survey research, data processing, and editing.

Educational background is likely to be of only limited usefulness in selecting evaluation personnel. Good grades in evaluation-related courses will likely increase the probability that candidates know what they are doing, at least with regard to the technical aspects of evaluation work; but some individuals with such training do not adapt well to operating environments in which resource constraints preclude elaborate designs such as controlled experiments. The authors have worked with many fine evaluators whose backgrounds may seem quite surprising, such as history majors. Program evaluators most need logical, systematic approaches to their work; such abilities can be found in people with many different backgrounds. Examples of past evaluation work should be sought to help determine the skill levels of candidates for evaluation positions.

Agencies should provide periodic training opportunities for both experienced and newer evaluation staff. Such training should not be limited only to detailed technical matters such as advanced statistical techniques but should also include such topics as questionnaire design and the effective presentation of evaluation results.

Standards and Ethics

Evaluation is still an emerging profession, characterized by a diversity of approaches. Diversity in perspectives can be fruitful, and interdisciplinary evaluation teams can be especially productive. The existence of such diversity highlights both the difficulty of, and the need for, development and widespread adoption of standards for evaluation practice.

Certain norms should guide all evaluators' work, regardless of their discipline. In planning their work, for example, evaluators should ensure that evaluation criteria are relevant and that evaluation findings will be available in time for important policy and management decisions. Within available resource constraints, evaluators should ensure that their data are valid and that their conclusions are valid. Evaluators should ensure adequate training for data collectors, pretests of data collection schemes, ongoing quality control testing of data collection, and security of the resulting data. The bases for decisions about what, when, and how to measure should be clear to evaluation clients.

Standards exist for certain segments of the evaluation profession (see Davis, 1990). U.S. General Accounting Office "Yellow Book" standards guide the work of its auditors and evaluators as well as those in agency offices of inspectors general, for example (Comptroller General, 1988). In 1982 the

Evaluation Research Society promulgated general standards for evaluation work (Rossi, 1982). In 1992, its successor, the American Evaluation Association, began efforts to develop a new set of standards for evaluation practice. The Joint Committee has published a set of standards for evaluation of education programs (Joint Committee on Standards for Educational Evaluation, 1994).

One of the most difficult dilemmas for evaluators is ensuring that the benefits of evaluation exceed its costs. Evaluators may be asked to expend resources on evaluation projects that they believe are unlikely to yield useful data. Evaluators and auditors may be asked to answer evaluation questions that they consider unanswerable given realistic time and resource constraints or the realities of program design. Under such conditions, evaluators should consider segmenting the problem: conducting small pilot studies designed to clarify what is knowable in the short term, what additional information is likely to be useful, and what it would cost to get and use additional information.

If evaluation findings are likely to influence public support for the program or have other political repercussions, evaluators may face pressures to slant their findings in one direction or another. They may receive more or less subtle cues from their superiors indicating that such slanting is desired. These situations are always difficult. An evaluator who faces such pressures and is unable to resolve them may be forced to move elsewhere. One possible solution is for the evaluator to indicate the assumptions that would lead to a particular conclusion—and then show in a "sensitivity analysis" how different assumptions would lead to different conclusions. Another option the evaluator can take in extreme circumstances is "whistleblowing": reporting to the agency's inspector general that such pressures have been exerted. If the pressures are subtle, however, whistleblowers may find themselves in untenable situations later on.

Information obtained in evaluations should not violate program participants' anonymity, confidentiality, or privacy rights. If the evaluators want to quote or refer to particular individuals, they should usually obtain the written permission of the people to be referenced. For some evaluations, the evaluators will be required by a federal agency to obtain "informed consent" prior to obtaining records on or conducting interviews with individuals. The Education Commission of the States defines such informed consent as follows: "a person must voluntarily give his or her consent before information about that person can be released to someone else, and consent must be based on a full understanding of what information will be exchanged, with whom it will be shared, and how it will be used" (Education Commission of the States, 1991, p. 2). The commission's report on information sharing is a good source for a comprehensive discussion of the meaning of confidentiality.

Obtaining informed consent forms can become quite cumbersome and time-consuming. Evaluators should determine in advance what requirements apply to a particular evaluation.

Evaluators may need to consider alternatives such as requesting data without any personal identifiers or requesting group data only. Both these options, however, preclude linking data on the same individuals from different sources.

A major concern arises if courts subpoena evaluators' records and these include data permitting identification of individuals who have been guaranteed confidentiality. This possibility poses a legal question that evaluators should refer to their own legal advisers. Evaluators should not automatically provide such subpoenaed information before determining their legal rights. In some but not all cases, the confidentiality of the responses is protected under law.

Incentives for Undertaking Program Evaluation and Using Evaluation Findings

For evaluation to be useful in improving program performance, evaluation findings and recommendations must be used by legislators, executives, and managers. Evaluators can provide information that may guide decisions to improve performance, but political and bureaucratic will must be present for change to occur.

Evaluation is often threatening to the administrators whose programs are being evaluated. Evaluations may provide ammunition for those who want to reduce program expenditures or dramatically change the program's direction. Many so-called summative evaluations performed by the federal government fall into this category. We believe, however, that a major purpose of most program evaluations should be to provide information that helps program managers and staff to improve their programs. This more constructive approach should be emphasized by agencies — public and private — and by evaluators themselves. To get the most out of evaluation, those at higher levels should create incentives for — and remove disincentives to — performance-oriented management and management-oriented evaluation. Here we suggest some incentives for constructive use of program evaluation:

- Regardless of who sponsors the evaluation, evaluators should seek input from program managers and staff on evaluation objectives and criteria. Where appropriate, evaluators should include the program manager and key program staff on the evaluation team, or as reviewers of the evaluation design and draft reports. Program managers should be kept aware of the progress of evaluations and be given the opportunity to review evaluation findings before they are made public.

- The legislative body, chief executive, or agency head might mandate periodic program evaluations, or at least the regular monitoring and reporting of program outcomes. For example, the Florida Legislature has mandated an extensive amount of performance monitoring, with initial emphasis on the Department of Health and Rehabilitative Services (see Affholter, Chapter Five of this volume). Many states have moved to require regular reporting of a variety of indicators of school district and individual school performance. Among others, the state of Oregon has embarked on an ambitious effort to establish statewide goals and agency objectives, set program and budget priorities, and measure performance (Oregon Progress Board, 1992).

- The legislative body, chief executive, or agency head could ask program managers to set target levels of performance in terms of key service quality and outcome indicators at the beginning of the year—and to report progress in achieving those targets quarterly and at the end of the year. This step is most applicable in situations where regular outcome monitoring is used rather than ad hoc program evaluations.

- To the extent feasible, the chief executive or agency head should take steps to build achievement of program results into performance appraisal systems for managers and supervisors. (We do *not* recommend that government agencies jump quickly into linking pay to program results, however. Once money is brought into the picture, the chances of hurting morale and being counterproductive escalate tremendously.) If achievement of organizational objectives is included in performance appraisals, both those appraised and those doing the appraising should recognize that factors outside the managers' control may affect program results. The managers appraised may have been the beneficiaries of windfalls, or the victims of "pratfalls" due to external factors. (For example, the outcomes of job training programs can be affected by changes in the local economy that are beyond the control of the program manager.) Such problems can be alleviated if performance targets are adjusted to reflect the influence of factors beyond the control of program managers, such as client characteristics and local economic conditions.

- The chief executive or agency head could develop performance contracts with program managers and with contractors to deliver specific results—both outputs and outcomes. The United Kingdom, New Zealand, and the state of Florida have been experimenting with such performance contracting.

- To encourage managers and staff to identify opportunities to improve efficiency and effectiveness, legislators or executives could permit agencies to retain a share (say 50 percent) of any savings they achieve from improved service delivery that results in lower costs. The agency should be given considerable flexibility in the use of such funds. The savings probably should be provided only for a limited amount of time, such as one or two years, even though the improvement lasts for many years.

- Legislators or chief executives could give agencies and programs the option of either continuing to be under strict personnel controls and restrictions on line item/object class transfers or being held accountable for program results with substantial added flexibility regarding personnel and financial management. Such efforts are being tried in New Zealand; pilot projects along similar lines are authorized under the Government Performance and Results Act (U.S. Congress, 1993).

Most of these items are steps that program managers and evaluators cannot take by themselves. They must be taken by higher-level officials in governing bodies of private organizations or in the executive and legislative branches of government.

Trends in Program Evaluation

The environments in which managers and evaluators work have become more challenging as taxpayers and legislators grow more insistent on economy, efficiency, and return on investment. Audit organizations are being asked to explore questions of program effectiveness. The demand for evaluation has grown, partly in response to the antigovernment sentiment and taxpayer revolts of the past two decades.

Throughout the world—in Australia, New Zealand, and the United Kingdom, for example, and in many local and state governments and federal agencies in the United States—efforts are underway to stimulate better public management, improved government performance, more highly valued public services, and renewed public confidence in government. These efforts ("strategic management," "market-driven management," "total quality management," "results-oriented management," and "value for money" approaches) all focus on results, agreement on appropriate performance indicators, timely information on performance, and delegation of authority in return for accountability for outcomes (see U.S. Office of Personnel Management, 1991; Osborne and Gaebler, 1992; Wholey and Hatry, 1992; U.S. Congress, 1993). Legislators at all levels of government have become interested in the use of markets and quasi-market forces to allocate public resources. In both public and private organizations innovative delivery strategies are viewed as opportunities to stimulate better performance and to put resources where they will produce the most bang for the buck.

Markets for information on program results have expanded as legislators and executive branch policymakers have requested feedback on program results. In response to Job Training Partnership Act (JTPA) requirements, for example, the U.S. Department of Labor has worked with state and local program officials to develop a system for monitoring JTPA program performance (Uhalde, 1991). The JTPA performance monitoring system sets performance targets in terms of agreed-on performance indicators such as employment rate at follow-up (approximately thirteen weeks after the completion of program services) and weekly earnings at follow-up. The performance of each local service delivery area is measured each year using either telephone surveys of trainees or payroll records maintained in state employment security agencies. Each area's results are compared with performance targets that are adjusted to reflect the influence of client characteristics and local economic conditions. States use the JTPA performance monitoring system and state-developed incentive systems to reward high performance by local service delivery areas (Barnow, 1992). The Government Performance and Results Act of 1993 requires agencies to measure program performance annually.

The expanding market for information on program performance has also been evident in changes thrust on the auditing profession. Legislative bodies as well as government executives have called on auditors to report on program results as part of the increasing use of performance audits — quite a stretch from the financially focused audits of the past (Davis, 1990).

Many of the trends in evaluation practice that began in the 1980s are likely to continue through the 1990s and on into the next century. Below, we identify a number of these trends.

First, in recent years, the focus of more evaluation efforts has been on those intended to help programs improve themselves. This trend is likely to continue, with even more emphasis on evaluations assessing the extent to which the program was actually implemented as planned and examining problems in service delivery.

Second, legislative branch organizations will increase their reviews of program outcomes through various versions of program evaluation. They will increasingly include "program results" auditing as part of their audit and program review functions. Legislative branch evaluations will likely be of mixed quality, especially if executive branch agencies lack data on results and legislative branch evaluations are forced to rely on post hoc evaluation designs. Many of these audits and program reviews will encourage executive branch agencies to undertake regular monitoring of program quality and outcomes in terms of agreed-on performance indicators. Legislative branch evaluations will likely increase their use of surveys to obtain information on service quality and client satisfaction.

Third, the use of regular, at least annual, monitoring of program quality and results will continue to expand at all levels of government and in the private nonprofit sector (see Affholter, Chapter Five of this volume). Regular feedback of performance information can create intangible incentives for higher performance. A number of public and private organizations are now producing "report cards" monitoring the quality of health care, including patient satisfaction with health care, for example. Some pioneering local governments, such as those in Charlotte, Dayton, New York City, Savannah, and Sunnyvale, have been monitoring the quality and outcomes of their services for many years (Wholey and Hatry, 1992). A number of states have established monitoring systems to assess performance in elementary and secondary schools; the desire for such data is likely to continue. At the federal level, the Government Performance and Results Act of 1993 will create a framework for ongoing monitoring of the quality and value of government services. The Act requires strategic planning, goal setting, performance monitoring in terms of agreed-on performance indicators, and annual reporting of program performance to the Congress and the public and provides opportunities to implement pilot projects that will test the value of increased management flexibility (U.S. Congress, 1993). Legislative demands for performance monitoring and evaluation are likely to keep evaluators busy for years to come.

Fourth, as performance monitoring expands, we expect to see increased use of "benchmarking," leading to development of "standards" and comparisons across public and private agencies. The up side of this is that we should see more case studies of high performers, and generalizations from those case studies to identify, document, and disseminate promising program approaches ("best practices"). The process through which Peters and Waterman (1982) identified the essence of "excellence" in the private sector offers a useful model. The authors first used a monitoring system that compared the performance of different firms. They identified firms that were performing especially well given the conditions they faced in their own industries. Peters and Waterman then conducted case studies of these "high performers" and identified eight principles that characterized outstanding performance. A similar process could be implemented in any program area: "in search of excellence in maternal and child health" or "in search of excellence in employment and training programs," for example. Using a combination of performance monitoring, case studies, and syntheses across case studies, evaluators could identify the characteristics of those programs or projects that are achieving the best (or most improved) performance. (A natural extension would be the implementation of pilot projects testing new program strategies; these pilot projects could be designed to facilitate evaluation.) The resulting information could then be used in training and technical assistance to disseminate the service delivery strategies that appear most successful.

A down side to interagency comparisons is the difficulty in assuring that the agencies are truly comparable, possibly resulting in unfair comparisons for some agencies.

Fifth, as a result of increasing emphasis on performance monitoring as well as legislative branch interests, expanded use of client feedback procedures is likely over the next decade. Bolstered by enhanced technological capabilities, the use of telephone and mail surveys of samples of program customers is likely to continue to grow (see Miller, Chapter Eleven of this volume). The ease of computer-assisted telephone surveying and data entry is likely to increase the use of these techniques. Customer feedback procedures will often raise validity problems, however; some public agencies may rely on nonrepresentative samples or accept overly high nonresponse rates in attempting to draw inferences about their clientele.

Sixth, trained observers, bolstered by the use of photography and videotaping (perhaps even holographic devices), are likely to be used increasingly to track the physical condition of roads, parks, buildings, public housing, and neighborhoods (see Greiner, Chapter Ten of this volume). It is likely that such procedures will also be applied more frequently to assess contractor performance. Photographs and videotape recordings can be used to obtain more accurate observer ratings. The challenge of assuring the validity and reliability of this mode of data collection must still be faced, however.

Seventh, data entry and analysis are almost certain to become much faster and less expensive for evaluators. Technology is already available that permits direct scanning of responses from handwritten self-administered questionnaires or field entry of trained observer ratings. The decreasing costs of the technology will make such capabilities more accessible. Evaluators will benefit greatly from this change; they will find it more feasible to use open-ended questions since computers can facilitate analyses. Data processing will continue to become faster and more flexible. As public managers increasingly have computers available, they will be able to obtain client feedback and other information about program performance more quickly.

Eighth, advances in computer technology will also allow easier production of attractive, multicolored reports. The accessibility of such tools will enhance the capability of evaluators and program managers to draw attention to their data. A danger here is that overdone visuals may confuse readers or deflect questions about the accuracy and validity of the evaluation findings. (For recommendations on presentations, see Hendricks, Chapter Twenty-three, this volume.)

Ninth, there will be greater opportunities for controlled experiments that randomly assign larger units of analysis (offices, districts, or counties, for example) to alternative service delivery approaches. Such experiments are easier to implement than those requiring random assignment of individuals. They involve much smaller samples and therefore require the use of nonparametric statistics to assess the relative effectiveness of alternative services (see Siegel and Castellan, 1988). We expect to see somewhat expanded use of such controlled experiments in coming years, perhaps using matched-pair designs in which the agency identifies pairs of offices or districts with similar characteristics and randomly assigns one member of each pair to each of two service delivery approaches.

Tenth, we expect to see somewhat greater use of the regression-discontinuity design, where (1) services are rationed based on some index of need or merit and (2) that index is reliably related to the outcomes that would occur in the absence of services (see Marcantonio and Cook, Chapter Seven of this volume). Unlike controlled experiments, which can be disruptive to normal program operations, the regression-discontinuity design will often be more practical in public and nonprofit organizations.

Eleventh, the rise in demand for program results for oversight purposes will undoubtedly increase the attention to performance assessment in schools of public policy and administration, other professional schools, and government management training programs. Managers will be under heightened pressure to undertake and report program performance measurements on a regular basis, and the market for training managers in such endeavors will undoubtedly respond. As a result, government management training programs will increasingly contain modules on performance measurement and more rigorous program evaluation procedures: what performance measurement and evaluation entail and how the resulting information can be used to help improve programs.

Finally, public bodies will find it more and more attractive to attempt to link financial rewards to program performance. This trend will increase interest in and support for performance monitoring and other forms of program evaluation. However, such incentive systems will be very difficult to implement in ways that are fair both to program staff and to the public. The problem of the influence of external factors will continue to plague practitioners. When possible, managers and evaluators should make statistical adjustments in performance measures or performance targets to account for the influence of those outside forces.

Final Thoughts

At the beginning of this handbook, we suggested two primary reasons for evaluation activities: to achieve greater accountability in the use of public or donated funds, and to help agency officials to improve their programs. We believe that the latter purpose should usually be the primary one. In the long run, improving services should be the main rationale for allocating resources to evaluation activities, whether for ad hoc, in-depth evaluations, or for regular, ongoing monitoring of program results.

Given the trend toward increased monitoring and evaluation of government and private sector performance, the challenge for evaluators will be to respond to these new opportunities and ensure that evaluation leads to more effective programs. Because most government and nonprofit agencies operate under severe financial constraints, evaluation funds will always be vulnerable. Thus, it is vital that evaluators demonstrate beneficial results from their work. *We suggest that evaluators monitor and report on the results of their activities.* Evaluators should document the financial and nonfinancial costs of evaluation work, evaluation activities undertaken, actions taken in response to these evaluations, and obstacles encountered in assessing program performance and getting evaluation results used. Evaluators should document the impacts that their evaluations have and develop case studies of evaluations that have been used to add value to government programs.

Evaluators should devise practices that are as low cost as possible, both to reduce their vulnerability to budget cuts and to get the most product from limited resources. Throughout this handbook we have attempted to identify low-cost evaluation options. Evaluators should consider such approaches as the following:

- Using less powerful research evaluation designs
- Using smaller sample sizes
- Resisting the temptation to seek unnecessarily large amounts of information
- Using mail and telephone surveys rather than in-person interviews (with follow-ups to increase response rates), if necessary accepting lower response rates than ideally desired
- Avoiding excessive precision in sampling and statistical analysis (For example, 95 percent confidence levels may be too costly; such precision is not really needed in many program evaluation efforts.)

Program evaluation, whether low cost or high cost, is by no means a panacea. It does not substitute for quality implementation of programs. It is not likely to provide definitive information. What evaluation can do is provide reasonably reliable, reasonably valid information about the merits and results of particular programs operating in particular circumstances. Necessary compromises will inevitably mean that the users of the information will be less than fully certain of the validity of the evaluation findings. In a world full of uncertainties and hazards, however, it is better to be roughly right than to remain ignorant because a "conclusive" evaluation was unaffordable.

References

Barnow, B. S. "The Effects of Performance Standards on State and Local Programs: Lessons for the JOBS Program." In C. F. Manski and I. Garfinkel (eds.), *Evaluation of Welfare Training Programs.* Cambridge, Mass.: Harvard University Press, 1992.

Comptroller General of the United States. *Government Auditing Standards.* Washington, D.C.: U.S. Government Printing Office, 1988.

Davis, D. F. "Do You Want a Performance Audit or an Evaluation?" *Public Administration Review,* 1990, *50*(1), 35–41.

Education Commission of the States. "Confidentiality and Collaboration: Information Sharing in Interagency Efforts." Washington, D.C.: Education Commission of the States, January 1991.

Joint Committee on Standards for Educational Evaluation. *The Program Evaluation Standards.* (2nd ed.) Newbury Park, Calif.: Sage, 1994.

Oregon Progress Board. "Oregon Benchmarks: Standards for Measuring Statewide Progress and Government Performance." Salem: Oregon Progress Board, December 1992.

Osborne, D., and Gaebler, T. *Reinventing Government.* Reading, Mass.: Addison-Wesley, 1992.

Peters, T. J., and Waterman, R. H. *In Search of Excellence.* New York: HarperCollins, 1982.

Rossi, P. H. (ed.). *Standards for Evaluation Practice.* New Directions for Program Evaluation, no. 15. San Francisco: Jossey-Bass, 1982.

Siegel, S., and Castellan, N. J., Jr. *Nonparametric Statistics for the Behavioral Sciences.* (2nd ed.) New York: McGraw-Hill, 1988.

Uhalde, R. J. "Performance Measurement in Federal Job Training and Education Programs." Paper prepared by the Division of Performance Management and Evaluation, Employment and Training Administration, U.S. Department of Labor, 1991.

U.S. Congress, Senate, Committee on Governmental Affairs. "Government Performance and Results Act of 1993." 103rd Cong., 1st sess., report no. 103-58, June 16, 1993.

U.S. Office of Personnel Management. *Federal Total Quality Management Handbook.* Washington, D.C.: U.S. Government Printing Office, 1991.

Wholey, J. S., and Hatry, H. P. "The Case for Performance Monitoring." *Public Administration Review,* 1992, *52*(6), 604–610.

Name Index

A

Abrami, P. C., 208, 211, 212, 227
Achen, C. H., 415
Adhikari, A., 438, 439n, 454
Affholter, D. P., 13, 20, 96, 581, 582, 594–595, 597
Agar, M. H., 70, 94
Agranoff, R., 84, 94
Ahtola, O. T., 416
Algina, J., 452, 455
Ali, M. W., 300, 308
Alkin, M. C., 532, 576, 588
Anderson, A.J.B., 414
Anderson, J., 155n, 175, 190
Appenzeller, G. W., 96, 106, 116
Asher, H. B., 415
Ashery, R. S., 155, 159, 186
Ashford, B., 374n
Averch, H. A., 49, 234, 293, 300, 307
Ayres, I., 312, 324, 335

B

Babbie, E., 70, 71, 72, 74, 78, 84, 88, 94, 374, 385
Ball, S., 134, 152, 417, 453
Bangert-Drowns, R. L., 199, 227
Baranowski, T., 41, 68
Barbour, G. P., Jr., 243, 255, 269
Barker, L. B., 155n
Barnow, B. S., 597, 601
Bartlett, S., 160, 188, 193
Basch, C. E., 42, 61, 65–66
Baum, H. S., 564, 573
Bayton, J. A., 312, 336
Beaman, A. L., 201, 202, 207, 227
Becker, B. J., 204, 218, 227
Behn, R. D., 564, 573
Bell, J. B., 17, 30, 38, 490, 510, 533, 591

Bell, R. M., 178, 181, 188
Bendick, M., Jr., 311, 313, 314, 319, 335
Bendor, J. S., 296, 308
Bentler, P. M., 181, 186, 443, 453
Beranek, W., Jr., 499, 508
Berk, R. A., 120, 132, 150, 152, 155, 158, 159, 162, 164, 180, 186, 191
Berman, P., 61, 66
Berra, Y., 239
Berry, W. D., 415
Bertrand, J. T., 178, 186
Bickman, L., 125, 129, 132
Blackstone, T., 495, 508
Blair, L. H., 243, 268
Blalock, H. M., 181, 186
Bloom, H. S., 181, 186
Blose, J. O., 448, 453
Bogatz, G. A., 134, 152, 417, 453
Boggs, R., 311, 313, 314, 335
Bohlig, E. M., 177, 188, 193
Bohrstedt, G. W., 414
Bonito, A. J., 176, 177, 181, 182, 187, 188, 193
Borenstein, M., 419, 453
Bormann, C. A., 121, 179, 388, 417
Boruch, R. F., 155, 156, 158, 162, 172, 173, 186–187, 190, 199, 227, 423, 442, 443, 453, 454
Box, G.E.P., 449, 450, 452, 454
Bozeman, B., 561, 573
Bradburn, N. M., 282, 292
Bradley, D. R., 402, 414
Bradley, T. D., 402, 414
Braucht, G. N., 423, 454
Brekke, J. S., 180, 187
Brink, S. G., 58, 66
Brizius, J. A., 96, 99, 105, 117
Brookfield, S. D., 537, 548
Brown, E. D., 162, 179–180, 190
Brudney, J. L., 414

Bryant, F. B., 218, 227
Bryk, A. S., 203, 227, 452, 454
Buller, A., 559, 574
Burbridge, L. C., 353, 354, 373
Bush, G.H.W., 481

C

Calista, D. J., 61, 62, 67
Camillia, G., 402, 414
Campbell, D. T., 120, 122, 123, 126, 132, 133, 134, 138–139, 143, 144, 147n, 149, 150, 151, 152, 153–154, 155, 158, 159, 170, 177, 178, 181, 187, 220, 228, 374, 385, 442, 443, 454
Campbell, M. D., 96, 99, 105, 117
Caplan, N., 576, 588
Caplan, R. D., 181, 191
Cappelleri, J., 174–175, 191
Carey, R. G., 70, 74, 94
Carlson, R. H., 532
Carter, R. K., 96, 110, 117, 128, 490, 576, 578, 581, 584, 588
Castellan, N. J., Jr., 179, 191, 599, 601
Catalano, R. F., 181, 189
Caudle, S. L., 13, 21, 64, 69, 358
Cavanaugh, E. R., 175, 190
Cecil, J. S., 162, 186
Chadwin, M. L., 352, 353, 361n, 373
Chafee, J., 212, 213
Chalmers, I., 216, 219, 220, 221, 226, 227
Chalmers, T. C., 211, 221, 222, 227–228
Chan, S., 303, 308
Chase, G., 104, 109, 114, 117
Chave, E. J., 253, 270
Chelimsky, E., 226, 228, 490, 493, 495, 502, 508, 510, 511, 532, 591
Chen, T. T., 50, 51, 66
Chitwood, S. R., 560, 574
Chung-Fang, E. Y., 300, 308
Clark, N., 41, 61
Clayton, A. C., 188–189, 196
Clemen, R. T., 305, 308
Cleveland, W. S., 570, 573
Clinton, W. J., 481
Cohen, J., 59, 66, 155, 160, 161, 166, 187, 415, 419, 453, 454
Cohen, P. A., 208, 211, 212, 227
Cohen, S. S., 414
Comer, J., 414
Conner, R. F., 423, 454
Constanza, R., 475, 488
Converse, J. M., 282, 291, 415
Cook, T. D., 13, 20, 120, 121, 123, 126, 132, 133, 134, 143, 147n, 149, 152–153, 155, 157, 170, 177, 178, 179, 181, 187, 199, 200, 204, 208, 209, 212, 215, 218, 220, 221, 223, 228, 388, 431, 448, 449, 599

Cook, T. J., 42, 66, 180, 181, 187
Cooper, H. M., 204, 207, 209, 212, 215, 216, 221, 223, 228
Cordray, D. S., 14, 45, 121, 132, 158, 186, 198, 199, 202, 205, 210, 211, 213, 214, 215, 217, 219, 220, 222, 224, 225, 226, 227, 228, 229
Cox, W. M., 175, 178, 189
Crane, A. B., 532
Cronbach, L. J., 96, 117, 178, 187, 248, 253, 269, 442, 454
Cross, H., 312, 313, 315, 336
Curtin, T. R., 173, 187
Cutcomb, S. D., 402, 414
Cutter, G., 41, 68

D

Daillak, R., 532, 576, 588
Dalkey, N., 300, 308
d'Apollonia, S., 208, 211, 212, 227
Davis, D. F., 4, 10, 592, 597, 601
Davis, T.R.V., 141, 142n, 153
Dean, D. L., 49, 127, 235, 301, 338
Dearing, B. E., 415
Delbecq, A. L., 300, 308
Del Castillo, S., 315, 336
Dennis, L. E., 176, 187
Dennis, M. L., 14, 20, 121, 133, 155, 156, 158, 159, 162, 163, 164, 173, 176, 177, 178, 180, 181, 182, 186, 187–188, 193, 194n, 388, 422
Detsky, A. S., 155, 188
Devine, E. C., 204, 228
Devine, W. R., 176, 191
Dickersin, K., 217, 228
Dixon, W. J., 451, 454
Dobson, L. D., 42, 66
Doherty, M., 217, 230
Downs, A., 497, 508, 532
Draper, N. R., 427, 454
Drucker, P. F., 533
Durlak, J. A., 200, 202, 228

E

Edin, K., 151, 153
Edley, C., 334, 336
Edwards, A. L., 248, 253, 254, 269
Edwards, W., 415
Efron, B., 181, 188
Einhorn, H. I., 201, 228
Ellickson, P. L., 178, 181, 188
Elmore, R. F., 62, 66
Emshoff, J., 47, 66
Erven, J. M., 143, 153
Eveland, J. D., 61, 65

F

Fabry, B., 581, 587, 588
Fairbank, J. A., 163, 176, 177, 181, 182, 187, 188, 193
Fairweather, G. W., 155, 162, 188
Farber, E., 416
Farquhar, J. W., 144, 153
Farrington, D. P., 155, 188
Feinberg, S. E., 454
Feldman, D., 181, 188
Feldman, S., 415
Ferry, D., 357, 360n, 373
Fetterman, D. M., 185, 188
Fielding, J. L., 71, 91, 92, 94
Fielding, N. G., 71, 91, 92, 94
Fine, M., 70, 71, 89, 92, 94
Fink, A., 282, 291
Fischer, R. L., 14, 45, 198, 213, 215
Fisher, R. A., 155, 158, 160, 172, 188, 193
Fisk, D. M., 5, 10
Fiske, D. W., 178, 187
Fitz-Gibbon, C. T., 41, 66, 96, 100, 105, 117
Fix, M., 311, 312, 315, 335, 336
Fleischer, M., 61, 68
Flynn, P. M., 164, 188–189, 196
Foreman, E. K., 414
Fountain, J. R., 101, 110, 117, 584, 588
Freedman, B., 159, 189
Freedman, D., 438, 439n, 454
Freeman, H. E., 41, 42, 53, 56, 67, 96, 118, 121–122, 123, 132, 293, 308, 533
Fuller, R. K., 164, 189, 195

G

Gabriel, R., 448, 455
Gaebler, T., 338, 349, 586, 589, 596, 601
Galster, G., 332, 336
Geis, G. L., 293, 308
Gilbert, F. S., 175, 189
Glass, G. V., 133, 138–139, 154, 158, 165, 171n, 200, 203, 223–224, 228–229, 420–421, 448n, 454
Glenn, J., 100
Godfrey, M. G., 414
Godwin, L. B., 155n
Goldberger, A. S., 441, 454
Goldenberg, E. N., 533
Goldkamp, J. S., 162, 189
Goldschmidt, P., 204, 229
Gollob, H. F., 420, 447, 455
Gomez, H., 155, 186–187
Goodman, L. A., 414
Goodman, R. M., 62, 66
Gossett, W. S., 191, 192–193
Gottfredson, M. R., 162, 189
Gottlieb, N. H., 58, 66

Gouvis, C., 374n
Greene, J. C., 92, 94
Greenspan, A., 334
Greer, K. C., 173, 186
Greiner, J. M., 233, 239, 242, 269, 599
Griffith, J., 45, 58, 67
Groninger, L. D., 414
Gruder, C., 199, 228
Guba, E. G., 70, 71, 79, 85, 91, 92, 93, 94, 533
Gueron, J. M., 215, 229
Gummersson, E., 73, 94
Gunter, M. J., 87, 88, 89, 90, 91, 94–95
Gustafson, D. H., 300, 308
Guzzo, R. A., 200, 229

H

Haber, A., 414
Hall, G. E., 47, 57, 66, 67
Hall, S. M., 155, 189
Hamilton, L. C., 427, 454
Handley, E. A., 543, 547, 548, 558, 560, 574
Harrell, A., 374n
Hartwig, F., 415
Hatry, H. P., 1, 5, 10, 96–97, 101, 110, 117, 118, 236, 239n, 243, 244, 250n, 255, 269, 282, 288, 291, 292, 301, 374, 552, 574, 582, 584, 588, 590, 596, 597, 602
Hawkins, J. D., 181, 189
Hawkins, R., 581, 587, 588
Hay, R. A., Jr., 415, 449, 450, 455
Healey, J., 414
Heckman, J., 333, 336
Hedderson, J., 414
Hedges, L. V., 198, 203, 204, 207, 223, 224, 228, 229
Hedrick, T. E., 129, 132
Helmer, O., 300, 308
Helms, J., 205, 210
Hendricks, M., 290, 490, 543, 547, 548, 549, 550, 552, 553, 554, 558, 559, 561, 573–574, 581, 599
Henkel, R. E., 415
Hennigan, K. M., 139, 141, 143, 153
Herman, R. D., 244, 269
Hildebrand, D. K., 415
Hodges, L. E., 319, 335
Hogarth, R. M., 201, 228, 449, 450n, 451n, 454
Holcomb, P., 353, 362n, 368n, 369n, 370n, 373
Holder, H. D., 448, 453
Hopkins, K. D., 402, 414
Horst, P., 15, 17, 38
House, P. W., 563, 574
Howard, K. I., 163, 175, 178, 189, 195
Hubbard, R. L., 175, 190

Huberman, A. M., 64, 67, 69, 73, 76, 79, 81, 86, 87, 88, 90, 91, 92, 94
Hunter, C. P., 54, 66
Hunter, J. E., 203, 204, 223, 229

J

Jaccard, J., 414
Jackson, C., 319, 335
Jackson, S. E., 200, 229
James, F., 315, 336
Jarvis, J., 582, 589
Jencks, C., 151, 153
Jenkins, G. M., 449, 450, 454
Joiner, B. L., 428, 429, 430, 440, 446, 455
Jones, P., 183, 189
Jöreskog, K. G., 443, 454
Judd, C. M., 41, 50, 59, 66

K

Katzell, R. A., 200, 229
Kay, P., 17, 38, 50, 67
Kaye, E., 30, 38
Kee, J. E., 388, 456
Keeney, R. L., 308
Kenney, G., 312, 313, 315, 336
Kidder, L. H., 70, 71, 89, 92, 94
Kiecolt, K. J., 143, 153, 374, 385
Kiefer, C. F., 537, 548
King, J. A., 41, 66
Kirk, J., 92, 94
Kish, L., 275, 292
Klecka, W. R., 415
Knoke, D., 414
Kosedoff, J., 282, 291
Kostoff, R., 305, 306, 308
Kotler, P., 339, 349
Kraemer, H. C., 161, 166, 169, 171n, 189, 419, 454
Krause, M. S., 178, 189
Krippendorff, K., 78, 93, 94, 374, 385
Kulka, R. A., 189, 194

L

Laing, J. D., 415
Lamas, G. A., 155, 189
Larsen, J. K., 563, 574
Lavrakas, P. J., 282, 292
Lehman, A. F., 210, 214, 217, 219, 224, 229
Leighton, G., 160, 189, 192
Leithwood, K. A., 47, 66
Leman, C. K., 560, 574
Levenson-Gingass, P., 58, 66
Levin, H. M., 458, 488
Levine, M. S., 415
Leviton, L. C., 200, 228

Lewin, K., 51, 66
Lewis-Beck, M. S., 415
Liebmann, T., 267n, 269
Light, R. J., 53, 66, 202, 204, 226, 229
Lincoln, Y. S., 70, 71, 79, 85, 91, 92, 94, 533
Liner, B., 374n
Lipsey, M. W., 42, 51, 53, 63, 67, 68, 155, 160, 161, 166, 189-190, 200, 202, 204, 215, 218, 219, 223, 226, 228, 229, 419, 455
Litke, A., 242, 270
Little, R., 377, 385
Lodge, M., 415
Loether, H. J., 414
Lofland, J., 69, 70, 88-89, 93, 94
Lofland, L. H., 69, 70, 88-89, 93, 94
Lohr, B. W., 147-148, 150, 153
Loucks, S. F., 47, 57, 66, 67
Luborsky, L., 161, 190
Luft, H. S., 150, 153
Luster, C., 581, 587, 588
Luthans, F., 141, 142n, 153

M

McAllister, R. J., 374, 385
McAuliffe, W. E., 155, 159, 186
McCabe, G. P., 434, 435n, 436n, 455
McCain, L. J., 450, 455
McCleary, R., 143, 153, 415, 449, 450, 455
MacDonald, E. D., 155n
McDonald, R. M., 63, 67
McDowall, D., 415
McGaw, B., 223-224, 229
McGrath, S. G., 402, 414
McKinlay, P. D., 160, 189, 192
McLeod, J., 563, 574
McSweeny, A. J., 135, 136n, 153
McTavish, D. G., 414
Majchrzak, A., 561, 562, 574
Makridakis, S., 449, 450n, 451n, 455
Malinak, J., 200, 208, 211, 231
Marcantonio, R. J., 13, 20, 121, 133, 157, 179, 388, 431, 448, 449, 599
Martinson, R. M., 161, 190
Mason, R. O., 300, 302, 303, 308
Massey, J., 561, 573
Matt, G. E., 200, 229
Maxwell, P. J., 175, 189
Maynard-Moody, S., 62, 67
Meidinger, E. E., 415
Meier, K. J., 414
Meinert, C. L., 217, 228
Mell, J., 312, 313, 315, 336
Merton, R. K., 299, 301, 308
Miles, M. B., 64, 67, 69, 73, 76, 79, 81, 86, 87, 88, 90, 91, 92, 94
Millar, A., 244, 269-270
Millar, R., 244, 269-270

Miller, D. C., 74, 94, 248, 270
Miller, J., 242, 270
Miller, M. A., 276, 282, 291, 292
Miller, M. L., 92, 94
Miller, T. I., 127, 234, 271, 276, 282, 291, 292, 598
Min, Y., 217, 228
Mintzberg, H., 554, 574
Mitchell, J. J., 352, 353, 361n, 373
Mobray, C., 580n, 588
Mohr, L. B., 122, 132
Montgomery, D. A., 47, 66
Montgomery, L. M., 217, 230
Moore, D. S., 434, 435n, 436n, 455
Moore, J., 243, 250, 263, 270
Morley, E., 243, 255, 269, 374n
Morris, L. L., 41, 66
Mosteller, F., 495, 508
Mullen, P. D., 204, 229
Murnane, R. J., 294, 308
Murphy, J. T., 562, 574
Muscatello, D., 576, 589
Musgrave, P., 458, 465, 488
Musgrave, R., 458, 465, 488

N

Nachmias, C., 374, 385
Nachmias, D., 374, 385, 561, 574
Nathan, L. E., 143, 153, 374, 385
Nay, J. N., 15, 17, 20, 38, 50, 67
Nelson, R. H., 560, 574
Nelson, R. R., 294, 308
Nevo, D., 293, 308
Newark, L., 374n
Newcomer, K. E., 1, 313, 314, 388, 389, 417, 590
Newlove, B. W., 57, 67
Newman, J. R., 415
Nienstedt, B. C., 143, 153
Nightingale, D. S., 49, 236, 350, 352, 353, 354, 357, 360n, 361n, 362n, 369n, 370n, 373
Norusis, M. J., 416
Nurius, P. S., 200, 229

O

O'Brien, C. T., 362n, 369n, 370n, 373
Ohlin, L. E., 155, 188
Oliverio, A., 180, 190
Olkin, I., 198, 203, 204, 223, 224, 229
Oman, R. C., 560, 574
Onion, M. L., 176, 187
Orlinsky, D. E., 178, 189
Orwin, R. G., 199, 202, 216–217, 221–222, 228, 229
Osborne, D., 338, 349, 586, 589, 596, 601

Ostrom, C. W., Jr., 415–416
Outtz, J. H., 312, 336

P

Padia, W. L., 448, 455
Pajunen, S. M., 243, 255, 269
Palumbo, D. J., 61, 62, 67, 180, 190, 561, 574
Papagiannis, M., 558, 574
Passamani, E., 159, 190
Patton, M. Q., 5, 10, 42, 67, 69, 70, 72, 76, 79, 86, 91, 93, 94, 96, 118, 533, 536, 545, 546, 548, 558, 563, 574, 576–577, 589
Pedhazur, E. J., 167, 190
Pentz, M. A., 51, 56, 60, 67
Peracchio, L., 134, 153
Peroff, N. C., 244, 269
Peter, L. J., 239, 270
Peters, T. J., 106, 107, 118, 533, 598, 601
Peterson, G. E., 242, 269
Pfaffenberger, B., 78, 94
Pillemer, D. B., 202, 204, 229
Pisani, R., 438, 439n, 454
Plowden, W., 495, 508
Poole, W. K., 180, 181, 187
Popper, K. R., 90, 94
Portnoy, B., 61, 65
Posavec, E. J., 70, 74, 94
Press, S. J., 300, 308
Presser, S., 282, 291, 415
Pressman, J. L., 62, 67
Price, R. H., 181, 191
Probstfield, J., 181–182, 191
Purcell, A. T., 175, 190
Purves, R., 438, 439n, 454

Q

Quarton, R. J., 150, 154
Quillan, D., 582, 589

R

Rabinowitz, O., 131, 132
Rachal, J. V., 155n, 163, 176, 177, 181, 182, 187–188, 193
Radin, B. A., 84, 94
Ramirez, G., 204, 229
Rauch, W., 301, 308
Raudenbush, S. W., 203, 227, 452, 454
Rauma, D., 150, 152
Ray, M. L., 92, 95
Reagan, R., 481
Redner, R., 179, 180, 190
Reichardt, C. S., 121, 174–175, 179, 191, 388, 417, 420, 423, 443, 447, 454, 455
Reinoso, V. A., 319, 335
Renner, B., 173, 190

Renner, T., 414
Reveal, E. C., 104, 109, 114, 117
Reynolds, H. T., 416
Rezmovic, E. L., 56, 67-68, 180, 190
Ricci, E. M., 87, 88, 89, 90, 91, 94-95
Riccio, L. J., 242, 270
Ridley, S. E., 312, 336
Riecken, H. W., 155, 156, 158, 159, 164, 190
Rimer, B. K., 50, 67
Rindskopf, D., 447, 455
Ringwalt, C. L., 173, 187
Roberts-Gray, C., 61, 62, 67, 558-559, 574
Roebuck, E. M., 414
Rog, D. J., 13, 18, 20, 38, 119, 125, 129, 132, 152, 388, 441
Rohman, L. W., 162, 190
Rosen, H. S., 466, 472, 488
Rosenbaum, D., 173, 187
Rosenthal, H., 415
Rosenthal, R., 216-217, 222, 229-230
Ross, H. L., 133, 138-139, 144, 153-154
Rossi, P. H., 41, 42, 53, 56, 67, 96, 118, 121-122, 123, 132, 293, 308, 533, 593, 601
Rossman, S. B., 49, 236, 350, 374n
Roth, J., 559, 574
Roth, W., 100
Rothman, J., 576, 589
Rubin, D. B., 149, 154, 214, 230, 377, 385
Rubin, J. A., 377, 385
Runyon, R. P., 414
Rutman, L., 17, 38
Ryan, B. F., 428, 429, 430, 440, 446, 455
Ryan, T. A., Jr., 428, 429, 430, 440, 446, 455

S

Sadler, D. R., 562, 575
Saunders, S. M., 175, 178, 189
Scanlon, J. W., 15, 17, 38, 533
Schaefer, R. L., 416
Scheirer, M. A., 13, 21, 40, 45, 56, 58, 61, 62, 63, 67-68, 119
Schmidt, F. L., 203, 204, 223, 229
Schmidt, R. E., 17, 38, 533
Schoot, J., 448, 455
Schrodt, P. A., 416
Schwartz, A. I., 243, 268
Schwartz, R. D., 374, 385
Schwenk, C. R., 300, 303, 308-309
Scott, A. G., 179, 190
Scriven, M., 48, 68
Seaver, W. B., 150, 154
Sechrest, L., 42, 47, 51, 68, 155, 162, 173, 179-180, 190, 374, 385
Sellers, J., 311, 313, 314, 335
Sensenbrenner, J., 96, 118
Shadish, W. R., 204, 217, 219, 230
Shanteau, J., 304, 309
Sharp, V. F., 414

Sherlock, A. J., 414
Sherman, L. W., 162, 180, 186, 191
Siegel, S., 179, 191, 414, 599, 601
Silverman, M., 87, 88, 89, 90, 91, 94-95
Silverman, W. A., 172, 191, 195-196
Simon, H. A., 176, 191
Singer, B., 161, 190
Singleton, R., Jr., 374, 385
Slavin, R. E., 202, 203, 219, 224, 230
Small, K. A., 472
Smith, H., 427, 454
Smith, J. D., 23, 29, 38-39
Smith, M. F., 50, 68
Smith, M. L., 223-224, 229, 448, 455
Smith, N., 561, 575
Sobell, L. C., 175, 191
Sonnefeld, L. J., 202, 228
Sonnichsen, R. C., 487, 490, 511, 533, 534, 535, 537, 539, 542, 543, 546, 548, 591
Sörbom, D., 443, 454
Sparkman, A., 559, 574
Stanfield, J., 561, 575
Stanley, J. C., 120, 122, 123, 132, 178, 187
Stanley, T. D., 175, 191
Steckler, A. B., 62, 66
Stigler, S. M., 200, 230
Straf, M., 220, 231
Straits, B. C., 374, 385
Straits, M. M., 374, 385
Straw, R. S., 155n
Stroh, P., 537, 548
Strosberg, M. A., 17, 39
Struyk, R. J., 311, 312, 315, 329n, 335, 336
Sudman, S., 282, 292
Sullivan, S. E., 200, 208, 211, 231
Sundquist, J. L., 496, 508
Swaminathan, H., 452, 455
Swanson, M., 239n, 269

T

Taylor, S., 296, 308
Tesch, R., 70, 80, 95
Theisen, A. C., 155n
Thiemann, S., 161, 166, 169, 171n, 189, 419, 454
Thomas, J. S., 242, 243, 270
Thoreau, H. D., 550
Thurstone, L. L., 253, 270
Taio, G. C., 452, 454
Tipple, C., 115, 118
Tornatzky, L. G., 61, 68, 155, 162, 188
Trochim, W.M.K., 150, 151, 154, 174-175, 191
Trutko, J., 558, 575
Tufte, E. R., 111, 118, 565, 575
Turner, M. A., 49, 234-235, 310, 312, 315, 329n, 336
Tyroler, H. A., 181-182, 191

U

Uhalde, R. J., 596, 602

V

van de Ven, A. H., 300, 308
Van Gaalen, R., 296, 308
Van Maanen, J., 70, 95
Van Sant, J., 87, 90, 95
Vinokur, A. D., 181, 191
Viscusi, W. K., 133, 154
von Winterfeldt, D., 308
Voss, G., 499, 509

W

Wachter, K., 220, 231
Wainger, L., 475, 488
Wallace, L. W., 163, 191
Walsh, A., 414
Wanous, J. P., 200, 208, 211, 231
Waterman, R. H., 107, 118, 533, 598, 601
Watson, K. F., 159, 191
Weatherley, R., 63, 68
Webb, E., 374, 385
Weiss, C. H., 122, 132, 535, 536, 548, 576, 589
Welch, S., 414
Wells, E. A., 181, 189
Weston, C., 293, 309
Wheelwright, S. C., 449, 450n, 451n, 455
White, P., 532, 576, 588
White, S. O., 162, 179–180, 190
Whiteley, R. C., 106, 118
Whitmore, E., 92, 95
Wholey, J. S., 1, 12, 15, 16, 17, 18, 23, 27n, 29, 38, 39, 50, 68, 96–97, 106, 118, 180, 191, 533, 544, 548, 576, 589, 590, 596, 597, 602
Wholey, M. S., 27n, 29, 39
Wienk, R., 312, 331, 337
Wildavsky, A. B., 62, 67
Wilde, O., 116
Wildt, A. R., 416
Wilson, D., 243, 247, 270
Wilson, J. Q., 155, 188
Wilson, O., 143
Windsor, R. A., 41, 68
Winer, B. J., 167, 172, 191
Winkler, R. L., 305, 308
Winnie, R. E., 5, 10
Wittes, J., 181–182, 191
Wolcott, H. F., 76, 82, 91, 93, 95
Wortman, C. B., 131, 132
Wortman, P. M., 199, 218, 227
Wothke, W., 423, 453
Woudenberg, F., 298, 302, 309
Wright, P., 62, 67

Y

Yeaton, W. H., 47, 68, 200, 229
Yessian, M. R., 560
Yin, R. K., 64, 68, 72, 73, 76, 83, 90, 91, 92, 95
Yinger, J., 312, 329, 331, 336, 337
Yusaf, S., 181–182, 191

Z

Zelazny, G., 565, 575
Zimmerman, W., 49, 234–235, 310, 312, 313, 315, 336

Subject Index

A

Accountability, and outcome monitoring, 99–101

Accuracy: in expert judgments, 295; of surveys, 276–279, 280

Action recommendations, reporting with, 558–564

Activity or participation log, for process evaluation, 55

Ad hoc evaluations, utilization of, 576–581

Administrators: and change agents, 546–547; expert judgment by, 296–297

Agency records: aggregated data in, 376, 377–378; approaches for, 374–385; background on, 374–375; concept of, 374; conclusion on, 385; data elements in, 376, 378–379; linked data in, 376, 379–380; missing data in, 375–377; permissions to use, 381; problems with, 375–381; for process evaluation, 55; quality control for, 381–382; for quasi-experiments, 143, 148–149, 152; and staff, 382, 383; suggestions for, 382–384

Aggregation: in agency records, 376, 377–378; of expert judgments, 301; of trained observer ratings, 255–256, 258–260

Aid Association for Lutherans, 559, 573

AIDS Forecasting study, 218–219, 224, 226

AIDS study, power analysis in, 167–169

Albany, New York, trained observers in, 243

Alcohol and Drug Abuse Services Administration (ADASA), 196

Alcohol, drug, and mental health (ADM) disorders, synthesis of studies on, 214, 217, 219, 224

Alexandria, Virginia, trained observers in, 243, 244, 255

American Evaluation Association, 593

Analysis of covariance: for nonequivalent comparison group design, 442–443; for randomized experiments, 423

Applicability. *See* Generalization

Archival data, for quasi-experiments, 143, 148–149, 152. *See also* Agency records

Arlington County, Virginia, trained observers in, 243

Assessment. *See* Evaluability assessment; Quality assessment

Assignments: formalizing, 523–525; management of, 522–524; for randomized field experiments, 172–175

Association of Government Accountants, 4

Attrition: differential, 423, 438; and randomized field experiments, 163–164, 175–176, 182–183, 195

Audits: and evaluation units, 502–503; external, for qualitative evaluation, 92; of outcome monitoring, 115, 116; of role-playing, 325; trends for, 597; use of, 4

Australia: audits in, 4; computing tool from, 81; performance in, 596

Automated information systems, for outcome monitoring, 107–108

Autoregressive, integrated, moving average (ARIMA), in interrupted time series design, 450–451, 452

B

Barbados, randomized field experiments in, 156, 178

Benchmarking trends, 598

Benefit-cost analysis: approaches for, 456–488; background on, 456; concept of, 457; conclusion on, 486–487; and cost-effectiveness analysis, 457–459; data analysis for, 480–486; data sources for, 470; direct and indirect, 466–467, 476, 478–480; examples of, 460–464, 468–469, 483–485; frame-

611

work for, 464–469; geographic scope of, 467–469; issues for, 485–486; marginal or total, 463; measuring benefits for, 469–477; measuring costs for, 476, 478–480; and multiple causation, 486; perspective for, 482; in private sector, 459–460, 463–464, 478; reporting, 481–486, 487; standards for, 593; steps in, 457; tangible and intangible, 467, 483; and transfers, 464–466; valuing benefits for, 470–477

Benefit-cost ratio, 481

Benefits: concept of, 11; measuring, 469–477

Bernard's dilemma, 181–182

Bias, discovering and removing, 420–421

Biomedical Data Processing (BMDP), 181, 451

Boston, trained observers in, 243

Briefing, personal: delivery of, 557; graphics for, 571; materials for, 554–555; reporting with, 553–557; staging of, 555–557

Buffalo, New York, methadone study in, 193–194

C

Camden, New Jersey, methadone study in, 193–194

Canada: audits in, 4; trained observers in, 253

Capital, valuing use of, 478–479

Case studies: for process evaluation, 55, 64; for qualitative evaluation, 71, 83–84, 92

Causal models, for process evaluation, 59

Center for Excellence in Local Government, 244, 268, 311, 332, 336

Center for Survey Comparisons, 282

Central Policy Review Staff, 495

Chain reactions, of benefits and costs, 466

Chains of events, and process evaluation, 42–44, 52, 53, 64

Change agents: approaches for, 534–548; attributes of, 537–538; background on, 534–535; conclusion on, 547–548; and decision making, 535–537, 540–541; and organizational action, 540–542; program administrators and, 546–547; recommendations by, 534, 542–546; reporting by, 539, 540–541

Charlotte, North Carolina: monitoring in, 597; trained observers in, 243

Charlottesville, Virginia: trained observers in, 243, 244, 247, 260n

Chi-square, applying, 391, 392, 407–408

Chicago: crime reporting in, 143; cutoff scores in, 438–439; role-playing in, 315, 316n

Chief Financial Officers Act of 1990 (P.L. 101-576), 4, 100

Child day care, and outcome monitoring, 112

China, randomized field experiments in, 156

Cincinnati Bell Telephone, directory assistance study at, 135–137, 144

Civil Rights Division, 320

Clarity, in questionnaires, 283–284

Clean Air Act of 1991, 478

Clinical Investigator Survey (CIS), 515–516

Cluster analysis, for data reduction, 402

Coding: for fieldwork, 372; integrity of, and synthesis, 221–223; for qualitative evaluation, 79–80, 88

Coherence, of expert judgments, 303

Colombia, randomized field experiments in, 156

Colorado, Amendment 2 in, 277

Colorado at Denver, University of, role-playing study at, 315

Community-based experiments. See Randomized field experiments

Components. See Program components

Comprehensive Employment and Training Act of 1973 (CETA), 214

Comptroller General of the United States, 20, 38, 593, 601

Computers: for benefit-cost analysis, 483; for graphics, 569–570; for qualitative evaluation coding, 80–81; for reporting, 560–570, 572; for telephone surveys, 289; for trained observers, 256; trends for, 599

Conclusion drawing: in outcome monitoring, 115–116; for qualitative evaluation, 93

Confidence building, and outcome monitoring, 104

Confidence interval: in reporting, 395, 400; and size of treatment effect, 419–420

Confidence level, statistical, 393–394

Confidentiality: of agency records, 376, 380–381; in fieldwork, 369–370; and role-playing, 320, 324; standards for, 593–594; and surveys, 277

Congressional Budget Office, 4

Congressional Research Service, 4

Connecticut, antispeeding law in, 144

Consistency, in questionnaires, 282. See also Reliability

Consultants: for role-playing, 318; statistical, 422, 423, 427, 436, 443, 447, 449, 450; for surveys, 290–291

Contact summary form, for qualitative evaluation, 81–82

Content analysis, of interviews, 78–80

Contingency table model, 398

Continuous quality improvement, and outcome monitoring, 101, 102

Convenience sampling strategy, 86

Cost avoidance, as benefit, 470–471, 477

Cost-benefit analysis. See Benefit-cost analysis

Cost-effectiveness analysis, and benefit-cost analysis, 457–459

Costs: categories of, 476; concept of, 11; in data collection, 237; and evaluability assessment, 33, 37; of expert judgments, 306; of fieldwork, 356; indirect, 476, 478–480; of management, 531–532; measuring, 476, 478–480; to private sector, 478; in qualitative evaluation, 73–74; of role-playing, 325–326, 334; of surveys, 279–280; of trained observers, 264–265

Coverage, for surveys, 278–279

Credibility: of change agents, 537–538; of evaluation unit, 504–507

Crime, and television, 139–141, 143

Crisis intervention services, outcome monitoring for, 101–102, 103, 108

Critical effect size: concept of, 158; in randomized field experiments, 166, 169–171

Current Population Survey, 272

Curvilinearity: in interrupted time series design, 449; in randomized experiments, 426–427; in regression-discontinuity design, 431–436

Cutoff trial, for randomized field experiments, 174

D

Dade County, Florida, quality control in, 591

Dallas, trained observers in, 243, 253, 264

Damaging effects, valuing, 479

Data: autocorrelation of, 449–450; multiple uses of, 578; usefulness of, 584–585

Data analysis: approaches for, 387–488; with benefit-cost analysis, 456–488; comprehensive, 77–78; for fieldwork, 371–373; on implementation, 57–58, 64–65; issues in, 8; overview of, 9–10, 387–388; preparation for, 76; in process evaluation, 57–58, 64–65; with regression models, 417–455; of role-playing, 327–331; with statistics, 389–416; for surveys, 290; in synthesis, 209–210, 223–225

Data collection: with agency records, 374–385; approaches to, 233–385; with expert judgment, 293–309; with fieldwork, 350–373; with focus groups, 338–349; on implementation, 54–57, 64–65; issues in, 8, 236–237; overview of, 9, 233–237; in process evaluation, 48–49, 54–57, 64–65; for qualitative evaluation, 74–77, 90; rigor of, 90; with role-playing, 310–337; structuring, 76–77, 215–216; with surveys, 271–292; in synthesis, 208–209, 215–218; with trained observers, 239–270; winnowing results of, 217–218

Data evaluation, in synthesis, 209, 218–223

Data reduction: need for, 76; techniques for, 401–402

Dayton, Ohio: monitoring in, 597; trained observers in, 243

D.C. Initiative, 164, 173, 196–197

Debriefings, for qualitative evaluation, 88, 91

Decision making: and change agents, 535–537, 540–541; and recommendations, 579

Delaware: export data in, 381; job training in, 558, 562

Delphi technique, for expert judgments, 300–302

Denver: desegregation in, 420–421; role-playing in, 315; trained observers in, 244

Devil's advocate (DA), 302–303

Dialectical inquiry (DI), 302–303

Disaggregation: for synthesis, 224; of trained observer ratings, 248, 249, 264

Discontinuity. See Regression-discontinuity design

Discount rate, in benefit-cost analysis, 461, 480–481

Discriminant analysis, for data reduction, 401

Distributional issues, of benefits and costs, 463, 486

Disulfiram Experiment, 164, 195

Document abstract, for qualitative evaluation, 81–82

Document examination, for qualitative evaluation, 74–75

Documentation: in evaluability assessment, 32, 36; for qualitative evaluation, 91–92; in reporting, 553

Documents. See Agency records

Drug Abuse Resistance Education (DARE), 173

Duke University Press, National Collegiate Software of, 81

DuPont Corporation, 381

E

Education: accountability in, 100; and process evaluations, 5

Education Commission of the States, 593, 601

Effect, concept of, 157–158

Effect size: concept of, 158; formula for, 165; in syntheses, 202–203, 204, 223–224

Effectiveness, in randomized field experiments, 179

Employment discrimination, and paired role-playing, 312–316, 318–329, 334

Environmental Protection Agency (EPA), 478

EQS, 181, 443

Equipment use, for process evaluation, 49, 55

Ethical issues: for focus groups, 347–348; and natural experiments, 131; for program evaluation, 592–594; of randomization, 133–134; in randomized field experiments, 174, 196; in role-playing, 312, 334–335

ETHNO, 81

Ethnography: for process evaluation, 49; and randomized field experiments, 185

Evaluability assessment: and alternative evaluation designs, 22, 25, 32, 35–36; approaches for, 15–39; appropriateness of, 17; background on, 15–17; concept of, 12, 16–17; conclusion on, 37–38; and cost reductions, 33, 37; criteria for, 16; documenting decisions in, 32, 36; and evaluation priorities, 22–23, 25, 28–29, 36; examples of, 23–31; and interrupted time series, 143; issues in, 15–16, 31–37; and manager's support, 31–33; and natural experiments, 128–129; planning phase for, 17; for process evaluation, 49–50; process of, 18–23, 50; and program design changes, 21–22, 29, 32, 35; and program intent, 18–20, 24, 26–27, 32, 33–34; and program reality, 20–21, 25, 32, 33, 35; successive iterations in, 32, 36–37; suggestions for, 32–33; user involvement in, 18, 23

Evaluation broker rule, 496, 507

Evaluation design: approaches for, 11–231; concept of, 11; and evaluability assessment, 22, 25, 32, 35–36; issues in, 6–8; for natural experiments, 119–132; for outcome monitoring, 96–118; overview of, 9, 11–14; for process evaluation, 40–68; qualitative, 69–95; for quasi-experiments, 133–154; for randomized field experiments, 155–197; selecting, 7–8; for synthesis, 198–231

Evaluation Research Society, 593

Evaluation synthesis, methods in, 201, 204–205, 206

Evaluation units: approaches for, 493–509; background on, 493–494; credibility of, 504–507; and customer information needs, 498–501, 506; goals and objectives for, 493–494, 503; guidelines for, 500–501, 505; legitimacy for, 495–498; organizational context for, 501–504; staff selection for, 504–505; summary on, 507; tasks for, 494

Evaluators: advocacy role for, 541–542; attributes of, 537–538; as change agents, 534–548; craft of, 538–540; preparation of, 73; priorities of, 22–23, 25, 28–29, 36; program administrators and, 546–547; selection and training of, 591–592, 599–600; and site effects, 89; skills of, 72–73; team selection for, 88

Evidence weighting, for qualitative data, 90

Experience-Based Career Education (EBCE), 47

Experiment, strength of true, 120–121. *See also* Natural experiments; Quasi-experiments;

Randomized experiments; Randomized field experiments

Expert judgment: adapting, 295–296; approaches for, 293–309; appropriateness of, 294–295; background on, 293–294; characteristics for, 303–304; costs of, 306; example of, 305–306; and implementation, 298; issues for, 306–307; by managers and administrators, 296–297; by outside experts, 298; for process evaluation, 49; by program staffs, 297–298; selecting experts for, 298, 304–305; structured and direct, 305–306; structured and indirect, 300–303; systematic eliciting of, 299–303; unstructured and direct, 299–300

Explanatory meta-analysis, as synthesis, 201, 204, 206

F

Factor analysis, for data reduction, 401

Fair Employment Council of Greater Washington, 319

Fairness, in questionnaires, 286–287

Family preservation programs: evaluability assessment for, 29–31; and outcome monitoring, 113, 114

Feasibility studies. *See* Evaluability assessment

Federal Bureau of Investigation (FBI), evaluators as change agents at, 535, 539–541, 543, 544, 547

Federal Communications Commission (FCC), 139–140

Federal Judicial Center, 158, 162, 188

Feedback, for qualitative evaluation, 91

Field notes, for qualitative evaluation, 77–78, 81–82, 92

Fieldwork: approaches for, 350–373; background on, 350; collecting and recording methods for, 369–371; conclusion on, 373; costs of, 356; data analysis for, 371–373; designing, 352–363; instruments for, 357–363; interviews for, 359–361, 362–363, 366–369; number of sites for, 355–356; objectives of, 351–352; on-site stage of, 366–371; orientation stage of, 365–366; previsit stage of, 363–366; protocol for, 363–371; respondent selection for, 361–362; sampling for, 356–357; scheduling, 364–365, 366–369; site clearances for, 363–364; site selection for, 353–357; staffing for, 355, 365; training for, 366. *See also* Randomized field experiments

Florida: outcome monitoring in, 100–104, 106, 108–110, 112, 114–116, 584–585, 587; performance in, 595

Florida Department of Health and Rehabilitative Services, 100, 115, 116, 117, 581–582, 586, 594

Fluoride mouth-rinse program, 45–45

Focus groups: agenda for, 345; approaches for, 338–349; appropriateness of, 341–343; background on, 338–339; characteristics of, 340; compensation for, 344–345; concept of, 339–340; conclusion on, 349; conducting, 343–348; examples of, 341–342; facilities for, 346–347; as in-house or professional, 346; and market research, 339; moderator for, 345–346, 349; observing, 347–348; participant selection for, 343–345; pitfalls of, 348–349; for process evaluation, 49; recruiting for, 344; reports of, 348; scheduling, 347; surveys compared with, 340–341

Formative evaluation: expert judgment for, 305; in process evaluation, 48–49

France: audits in, 4; and oil embargo, 449–451

Frequency analysis, applying, 402–403

Fund for the City of New York, 242, 243, 244, 263, 269

G

Gain-score analysis, for nonequivalent comparison group design, 443–445

General Clinical Research Center (GCRC), 516

Generalization: of qualitative data, 85; for randomized field experiments, 163–164; and sampling, 390–391; in synthesis, 225

Genesis House, 196

Government Performance and Results Act of 1993, 4, 5, 100, 596, 597–598

Governmental Accounting Standards Board (GASB), 4, 101, 110

Governor's Task Force on Mental Retardation (Tennessee), 29

Graphics: for comparisons, 566–568; computers for, 569–570; guidelines for, 568–569; for outcome monitoring, 111; placement of, 570; for qualitative evaluation, 82–83; reporting with, 564–571

Greenville, South Carolina, trained observers in, 243, 247, 248, 268

Groups. See Focus groups

H

Head Start, 5, 543, 558, 562

Health Care Financing Administration (HCFA), 241, 244, 269

Health education program, 58

Hierarchical linear modeling (HLM), in interrupted time series design, 452

History: in interrupted time series, 137; as threat to validity, 120, 124, 128

Hong Kong, randomized field experiments in, 156

Honolulu, trained observers in, 243

Housing discrimination, and paired role-playing, 311–312, 314, 316–318, 320, 322, 324, 328–331

Human services program monitoring, 107–108

HYPERQUAL, 81

Hypothesis testing, statistical, 392–394. See also Rival explanations

I

Illinois Institute of Technology Research Institute, 306, 308

Implementation: approaches to measuring, 52–60; data analysis on, 57–58, 64–65; data collection on, 54–57, 64–65; and expert judgment, 298; macro approach to, 61–62; management for, 528–530; micro approach to, 62–63; participants and activities in, 53–54; process and outcome data on, 58–60; of quality control, 590–591; of randomized field experiments, 159–160, 170–177, 179–181; of recommendations, 545–546, 563–564, 580–581; standard measure of, 57; types of analysis for, 61–64; and utilization, 53; variability of, 60–65

Inclusion rules, for synthesis, 218–220

India, randomized field experiments in, 156

Indirect unobtrusive measures, for process evaluation, 55

Indonesian Ministry of Education and Culture, 561, 563

Information systems: appropriate, 587; automated, 107–108; and customer needs, 498–501, 506; for implementation data, 56–57

Informed dialogue, 299–300

Institute for Behavioral Resources (IBR), 196

Institute for Public Transportation, 244, 269

Intensive Crisis Counseling Program (ICCP), 101–102, 103, 108

Interagency Council on Homelessness, 214

Interest costs, valuing, 479–480

Internal Revenue Service (IRS), 235, 311, 314, 320

Internal validity, of qualitative data, 85

International City Management Association, 239n, 311, 320, 336

Interquartile range, 403

Interrupted time series design: advantage of, 452; approaches for, 135–144; ARIMA in, 450–451, 452; comparison series added to,

137–139; concept of, 134; conclusion on, 452; extended, 144; hierarchical linear modeling in, 452; issues for, 142–144; multiple interventions for, 140–142; multivariate analysis of variance in, 451–452; regression models for, 447–452; simple, 135–137; single group reversal for, 141; switching replications for, 139–141, 144

Interval measures, 398

Interviews: coding, 80; in evaluability assessment, 19, 21; field debriefings on, 88; for fieldwork, 359–361, 362–363, 366–369; by phone or in person, 276–282; for process evaluation, 49, 55, 64; for qualitative evaluation, 75, 78–80, 88–89; strategies for, 88–89

Iterations, successive, for evaluability assessment, 32, 36–37

J

James Bell Associates, 30, 31, 38, 516n, 518n, 521n, 525n

Jefferson County, Colorado, trained observers in, 244

Job Corps, 483–485, 486

Job Training Partnership Act (JTPA), 106, 596–597

Judgment calls, in synthesis, 210–211, 212, 214, 215, 220, 222, 224. *See also* Expert judgment

K

Kansas City, Missouri: City Development Department of, 255, 269; role-playing in, 311, 320; trained observers in, 243, 244, 255, 269

Kentucky, Performance Improvement Project in, 360

King County, Washington, trained observers in, 243

Koba Associates, 196

L

Lanarkshire Milk Experiment, 160, 192–193

Land values, as benefit, 475

LaTrobe University, ACRI at, 81

Level of Use (LoU) scale, 57

LISREL, 443

Literature review, as synthesis, 200–202

Lives saved, as benefit, 472–473, 477

Louisiana, wetlands program in, 475

M

Mail surveys. *See* Surveys

Management information system (MIS), for implementation data, 56–57

Management of projects: approaches for, 510–533; areas and aims of, 511–512; and assignments, 172–175, 522–524; background on, 510–513; and clarifying evaluation mandate, 513–516; concepts in, 510–511; conclusion on, 530–532; constraints on, 511–513; and evaluability assessment, 31–33; and expert judgment, 296–297; goal of, 510; for implementation, 528–530; and initial agreement, 513–514; and interim monitoring, 515–516, 524, 526–528; and organizing teams and work groups, 520–522; of role-playing, 324–325; and staffing, 515, 517–520; suggestions for, 531–532

Mandate for evaluation: clarifying, 513–516; soliciting, 539–540

Market prices, valuing alternatives to, 475–476

Market research, and focus groups, 339

Massachusetts: role-playing in, 332; trained observers in, 243, 244

Mathematica Policy Research, 483, 485, 488

Maxey Boys Training School, 581, 583, 587

Measurement error, and analysis of covariance, 443

Median trace: in interrupted time-series design, 449; in regression-discontinuity design, 433–435

Medicaid: and benefit-cost analysis, 471; and evaluability assessment, 29; and quasi-experiments, 147–150; recommendations, 559; and synthesis, 205; and trained observers, 241, 244

Medicare, 148, 241, 244

Message or forms analysis, for process evaluation, 49

Meta-analysis, as synthesis, 201–204, 206

Methadone-Enhanced Treatment (MET) Study, 162, 163, 165, 176, 179, 180, 182, 193–194

Methodology Transfer Papers, 501, 503, 508

Michigan, trained observers in, 241, 244

Michigan Department of Social Services, 577, 578, 581, 583

Midwestern Prevention Project (MPP), and process evaluation, 51, 56, 59–60

Milwaukee County, monitoring in, 586

Minitab, Inc., 416

Minneapolis Domestic Violence Experiment, 162

Minnesota: audits in, 4; monitoring in, 582, 586; role-playing in, 332

Minnesota Department of Trade and Economic Development, 582

Monitoring: continuous, 585–586; fieldwork for, 351; focus groups for, 342; forms of, 97–99; ineffective, 527–528; interim, 515–516, 524, 526–528; mandated, 586–587;

of randomized field experiments, 159, 176–177; timing of, 526–527, 583; trends for, 597–598, 600; utilization of, 581–587. *See also* Outcome monitoring

Multipliers, for benefits and costs, 474

Multivariate analysis of variance (MANOVA), in interrupted time series design, 451–452

N

Narrative review, as synthesis, 200–202

Nashville, trained observers in, 243, 244

National Academy of Public Administration, 97, 117

National Academy of Science, 300

National Association of Local Government Auditors, 4

National Center for Research Resources (NCRR), 518

National Citizen Survey, 282

National Highway Traffic Safety Administration, 473

National Institute of Mental Health (NIMH), 219

National Institute on Alcohol Abuse and Alcoholism (NIAAA), 219, 417n

National Institute on Drug Abuse (NIDA), 155n, 196

National Institutes of Health (NIH), 300, 515–516, 518

National Science Foundation, 300

National Vietnam Veterans Readjustment Study, 195

Natural experiments: approaches for, 119–132; appropriateness of, 128–132; concept of, 13, 119, 121–122; conclusion on, 132; and constraints, 131–132; designing, 122–128; issues for, 119–122; nonequivalent group designs for, 125–127; patched-up designs for, 122, 127–128; posttest only design for, 126–127; pretest-posttest designs for, 123–126; and program stage, 130; reflexive control designs for, 123–124

Nebraska Prehearing Conference Program, 162

Negative case analysis, for qualitative data, 90

Netherlands, randomized field experiments in, 156

Neutrality, of qualitative data, 85

New Orleans, methadone study in, 193–194

New York City: Board of Education in, 250, 256, 267n; Department of Parks and Recreation in, 274, 250, 254n, 269; outcome monitoring in, 106, 109, 597; Project Scorecard in, 263; School Scorecard in, 256, 263, 264, 267n; trained observers in, 242, 243, 244, 247, 248, 250, 254n, 256, 263, 264, 267n, 269

New York Public Interest Research Group, 269

New Zealand, performance in, 595, 596

Nicaragua, randomized field experiments in, 156

Nominal measures, 398

Noncompliance, and randomized field experiments, 180–181, 182–183

Nonequivalent comparison group design: analysis of covariance for, 442–443; conclusion on, 447; example of, 444–447; gain-score analysis for, 443–445; for natural experiments, 125–127; regression models for, 441–447

North Carolina: audits in, 4; drinking laws in, 448

North Carolina Department of Community Colleges, 100, 118

NUDIST, 80, 81

Null hypothesis concept, 392

Nursing homes, trained observers for, 241

O

Observations: number of, and statistics, 402; for process evaluation, 49, 55, 64; for qualitative evaluation, 70, 74. *See also* Trained observers

Office for Treatment Improvement (OTI), 196

Office of Inspector General, 553, 558, 569, 574

Office of Naval Research (ONR), 305–306

Office of Private Sector Initiatives, 559

Office of Regulatory Analysis, 473, 488

Office of Technology Assessment, 4

Oklahoma, trained observers in, 244

Operation Care and Shield, 559, 562, 564

Opportunity cost, in benefit-cost analysis, 461, 479

Options, appropriateness of, 544

Ordinal measures concept, 398

Oregon: audits in, 4; community-level correctional services in, 62

Oregon Progress Board, 595, 601

Organizational records. *See* Agency records

Outcome data, on implementation, 58–60

Outcome monitoring: approaches for, 96–118; background on, 96–97; benefits of, 99–104; concept of, 13, 97–99; examples of, 98, 99, 101–102, 103–104; expectations unrealistic for, 111–113; focus clarity for, 113–114; indicators for, 105–106; and irrelevance, 114–115; issues for, 105–111; number of measures for, 106–107; performance measures for, 107–110; pitfalls in, 111–116; reporting results of, 110–111. *See also* Monitoring

Outliers, handling, 403, 422, 426–427

Outward Bound, 448–449, 451

Oxford Database on Perinatal Trials, 216, 219

Oxygen Experiment, 172, 195–196

P

Paired role-playing. *See* Role-playing
Parks and recreation facilities, rating form for, 258–260
Patched-up designs, for natural experiments, 122, 127–128
Performance appraisal, and evaluation incentives, 595
Performance indicators, in evaluability assessment, 19, 20, 28
Personal briefing. *See* Briefing, personal
Peru, randomized field experiments in, 156
Philadelphia Bail Guidelines Experiment, 162
Photographs, for trained observers, 251–254
Pittsburgh, methadone study in, 179, 193–194
Planning, by evaluation units, 493–509
Policy groups, for evaluability assessment, 18
Policymaking, and evaluation units, 493–507
Posttest only design, for natural experiments, 126–127
Power, statistical: concept of, 157; increasing, 419, 423–424; and randomized field experiments, 164–166; simplified analysis of, 166–169
Precision, increasing, 420, 423–424
Prenatal program, evaluability assessment of, 23–29
Present value analysis, of benefits and costs, 461, 480–481
Pressley Ridge Schools, 581, 582, 583, 584, 587
Pretest: in nonequivalent comparison group design, 442–443; in randomized experiments, 422–426; in regression-discontinuity design, 436–438; for surveys, 288
Pretest-posttest designs, for natural experiments, 123–126
Prince Georges County, Maryland, trained observers in, 243
Problem formulation, in synthesis, 208, 211–215
Process evaluation: approaches for, 40–68; background on, 40–44; and chains of events, 42–44, 52, 53, 64; concept of, 3, 13, 40; conclusion on, 65; and implementation variability, 60–65; for measuring implementation, 52–60; need for, 41–42; and program components, 44–52
Procter & Gamble, and outcome monitoring, 107
Productivity increase, as benefit, 473–474, 477
Program: aggregated and targeted types of, 41; concept of, 3, 41; stage of, and natural experiment, 130
Program components: applying process evaluation to, 44–52; criteria for, 47; describing, 45–48; and organizational culture, 62

Program design change: and evaluability assessment, 21–22, 29, 32, 35; process evaluation for, 60–65
Program design models, in evaluability assessment, 19–20
Program evaluation: agenda criterion for, 5–6; approaches for practical, 1–10; assessing feasibility and usefulness of, 15–39; background on, 1–2, 3–5; concept of, 3; conclusions on, 590–603; data analysis for, 387–488; data collection for, 233–385; environment for, 4; evaluation design in, 11–231; fieldwork for, 351–352; goal of, 2; incentives for, 594–596; meeting needs for, 5–9; and outcome monitoring, 98, 103; standards and ethics for, 592–594, 598; suggestions for, 600–601; as threat, 495–496; trends in, 596–600; utilization of, 489–602
Program intentions: and evaluability assessment, 18–20, 24, 26–27, 32, 33–34; and process evaluation, 44–52; specifying, 48–52
Program reality: and evaluability assessment, 20–21, 25, 32, 33, 35; and process evaluation, 52–60
Prospective evaluation synthesis (PES), methods for, 201, 205–206, 207, 213, 218
P.L. 101-576, 4, 100
Publication bias, in synthesis, 216–217
Purposeful sampling strategy, 86–87

Q

Qualitative evaluation: approaches for, 69–95; assumptions in, 69; and conceptual beliefs, 70–71; conclusion on, 93; costs in, 73–74; data collection and analysis for, 74–84; drawing and verifying conclusions for, 84–93; evaluator skills for, 72–73; flexible design of, 71–72; investigative process for, 69–70; issues in, 84–85; overreliance in, 87, 90; points in using, 70–74; and randomized field experiments, 185; suggestions for, 85–93
Qualitative Research Management, 81
Quality assessment: for randomized field experiments, 177–179; for synthesis, 220–221
Quality control: for agency records, 381–382; in data collection, 237; for implementation, 590–591; and management, 528–530; of role-playing, 325; for trained observers, 262–263
QUALOG, 80, 81
QUALPRO, 81
Quasi-experiments: approaches for, 133–154; background on, 133–135; concept of, 134; conclusion on, 151–152; design of, 121; in-

terrupted time series design as, 135–144; regression-discontinuity design as, 144–151

Questionnaires: constructing, for surveys, 282–287; for process evaluation, 55, 64; screening, for focus groups, 344

Questions, type and order of, 278

R

R-square (coefficient of determination), applying, 399, 400, 412–413

RAND Corporation, 300

Random (probability) sampling strategy, 87

Randomization: and internal validity, 120–121; and quasi-experiments, 133–134

Randomized experiments: advantages of, 440–441; conclusion on, 430–431; curvilinearity in, 426–427; example of, 428–430; pretests in, 422–426; regression models for, 421–431; significance in, 418–419; size of treatment effect in, 419; treatment-effect interactions in, 424–426

Randomized field experiments: analyzing, 177–183; approaches for, 155–197; appropriateness of, 158–159; assignments for, 172–175; attrition in, 163–164, 175–176, 182–183, 195; background on, 155–161; concepts in, 156–158; conclusion on, 183–185; design implications of, 162–163; design sensitivity for, 169–171, 196–197; designing, 161–170; effectiveness in, 179; examples of, 192–197; experimental contrast in, 161–162; implementation of, 159–160, 170–177, 179–181; issues for, 160–161, 183–184; multiple measures for, 178; and noncompliance, 180–181, 182–183; quality assessment for, 177–179; staff cooperation for, 170–172, 195–196; subgroups in, 181–182; suggestions for, 184–185; trends for, 599. *See also* Fieldwork

Rating scales: developing, 248–257; problem-oriented, 253, 256, 258–260

Recidivism, and outcome monitoring, 103–104

Recommendations: for action, 558–564; in ad hoc evaluation, 577; and agency personnel, 560; for change, 534; and decision making, 579; developing, 542–544, 558–559; disseminating, 579–580; framing and placement of, 544–545; implementation of, 545–546, 563–564, 580–581; organizational context for, 561; qualities of, 543–544

Records. *See* Agency records

Recreational values, as benefit, 474–475, 477

Reflexive control designs, for natural experiments, 123–124

Regression-discontinuity design: approaches for, 144–151; concept of, 134; conclusion on, 440–441; curvilinearity in, 431–436; examples of, 144–150, 438–440; for Medicaid, 147–150; for randomized field experiments, 174; regression model for, 431–441; and selection bias, 150–151; strength of, 147; treatment-effect interactions in, 436–438; trends for, 599

Regression to the mean, in interrupted time series, 136, 144

Regression model: applying, 398–405, 412–413; approaches for, 417–455; conclusions on, 453; for interrupted time series design, 447–452; for nonequivalent comparison group design, 441–447; in process evaluation, 59–60; for randomized experiments, 421–431; for regression-discontinuity design, 431–441; and statistical tasks, 417–421

Reliability: of expert judgments, 295, 297–298, 303–304, 306; of implementation data, 56; for qualitative data, 85

Replicate syntheses, issues of, 208, 210–211

Replication: for qualitative evaluation, 91; switching, for interrupted time series design, 139–141, 144

Reporting: with action recommendations, 558–564; approaches for, 549–575; background on, 549–550; of benefit-cost analysis, 481–486, 487; with briefings, 553–557; by change agents, 539, 540–541; characteristics of, 551–552; computers for, 560–570, 572; conclusion on, 572–573; confidence interval in, 395, 400; with documents, 553; draft, 552; final, 550–552; of focus groups, 348; with graphics, 564–571; with index cards, 553; and mandated monitoring, 586–587; of outcome monitoring, 110–111; principles for, 549–550, 572–573; of statistics, 403–405, 453; steps for written, 529–530; on surveys, 290; in synthesis, 210, 225–226; of trained observer ratings, 263–264, 266–267; with videotapes, 571

Research Triangle Institute (RTI), 196

Residential Care Division, 581, 589

Resources: and natural experiments, 129–130; and outcome monitoring, 103

Response rates: for surveys, 276–277, 280

Responsiveness, and focus groups, 338

Restrooms, rating scale for, 254

Return on investment (ROI), in benefit-cost analysis, 461, 481

Rival explanations: and natural experiments, 121, 130–131; for qualitative data, 90–91

Role-playing: applications of, 332–335; approaches for, 310–337; characteristics for, 317–319; concept of, 310–312; conclusion on, 335; conducting, 321–326; costs of, 325–326, 334; data analysis of, 327–331; ethical issues in, 312, 334–335; instruments for, 321–322; limitations of, 334; management of, 324–325; measures in, 327–329; qualification variation in, 319; quality control of, 325; recruitment for, 319–320; sample selection for, 316–317; sampling for, 312–317; sandwich testing in, 333; selecting players for, 317–320; and statistical significance tests, 330; and systematic or random differences, 330–331; training for, 322, 324; universe of transactions for, 313–314

Russell Sage Foundation, 198n, 204, 207, 213

S

St. Petersburg, trained observers in, 243, 244

Sample size: for randomized field experiments, 164–166; for role-playing, 314–316; and statistics, 402; for surveys, 281–282

Sampling: for fieldwork, 356–357; for outcome monitoring, 109; for qualitative evaluation, 86–87; for role-playing, 312–317; and statistics, 390–391; stratified random, 275; for surveys, 274–275; targeted individuals for, 275–276

San Diego: role-playing in, 315; trained observers in, 243

Saratoga, California: role-playing in, 311, 332; trained observers in, 244

SAS Institute, 416

Savannah, monitoring in, 597

Scandinavia, audits in, 4

Security, and questionnaires, 285–286

Selection differences: in nonequivalent comparison group design, 441–442, 443, 447; and regression-discontinuity design, 150–151; as threat to validity, 120, 124, 127–128

Sensitivity analysis: for benefits and costs, 464, 482–483; and standards, 593; in synthesis, 224–225

Significance: in agenda for evaluation, 6; concept of, 157; and role-playing, 330; statistical, 394–395, 417–419

Simplicity in questionnaires, 284–285

Site visits. See Fieldwork

Slopes (unstandardized regression coefficients), applying, 399–400

Social policy experiments. See Randomized field experiments

Southern Methodist University, Department of Sociology at, 81

Special Supplemental Food Program. See Women, Infants, and Children (WIC)

Spillovers, in benefit-cost analysis, 464, 466, 468, 482

Spousal Assault Replication Project, 183

SPSS, 416

Staff: and agency records, 382, 383; for evaluation unit, 504–505; expert judgment by, 297–298; for fieldwork, 355, 365; qualifications matrix for, 517–520; and randomized field experiments, 170–172, 195–196; and recommendations, 560

Staff-Caseload Studies, 578

Standardized regression coefficients (beta weights), applying, 400

Statistics: approaches for, 389–416; appropriate, 395–398; conclusion on, 405–406; and confidence level, 393–394; descriptive and inferential, 389–395; examples of, 407–413; for hypothesis testing, 392–394; for program impact, 396, 398; purpose of, 417–421; and regression applications, 398–405; reporting of, 403–405, 453; and sampling, 390–391; selecting, 401–403; significance in, 394–395, 417–419; for strength of relationships, 391–392

Strategic information resources management, qualitative evaluation of, 71–72, 73, 74–75, 78, 79, 80, 82, 83, 84

Street cleanliness, rating scales for, 250, 251–252

Sunk costs, in benefit-cost analysis, 462, 479

Sunnyvale, California: monitoring in, 586, 597; trained observers in, 243

Suppression effects, and outcome monitoring, 103–104

Surveys: advantages of, 272; approaches for, 271–292; background on, 271–272; conducting, 287–289; consultant for, 290–291; cost of, 279–280; data analysis for, 290; designing, 273–276; focus groups compared with, 340–341; frequency of, 288; guidelines for, 273; interviews for, 276–282; pretesting, 288; questionnaire construction for, 282–287; reasons for, 272–273; reporting on, 290; sample size for, 281–282; sampling for, 274–275; speed of, 279, 280; steering committee for, 273, 287; training for, 288–289; trends for, 598; trying and tracking for, 289

Sweden, randomized field experiments in, 156

Synthesis: approaches for, 198–231; background on, 198–199; conducting, 207–227; constraints on, 214–215; cross-design, 225; data analysis and interpretation in, 209–210, 223–225; data collection in, 208–209, 215–218; data evaluation in, 209, 218–223; generalization in, 225; inclusion rules for, 218–220; investigator-initiated, 211–212; issues in, 207–208; judgment calls in, 210–212, 214–215, 220, 222, 224; methods for, 199–207; policy-driven, 212–213, 217,

219; policy-oriented, 213–214, 217; problem formulation in, 208, 211–215; publication bias in, 216–217; replicate, 208, 210–211; reporting in, 210, 225–226; steps in, 208–210; summary on, 226–227; types of, 200–204; unique features in, 206–207

Syracuse University, School of Computer and Information Science at, 81

T

t test: applying, 391, 395, 400, 409–411; in randomized experiment, 418, 422

Taiwan, randomized field experiments in, 156

Target groups, for focus groups, 343–344

Taxes, and benefits and costs, 467

Teams: for fieldwork, 355; and project management, 520; selection and training of, 591–592; of trained observers, 257, 261

Telephones: computers for surveys by, 289; plus one dialing of, 275. *See also* Surveys

Television, and crime, 139–141, 143

Tennessee, prenatal program in, 23–29, 34, 35, 38

Tennessee Department of Public Health, 23

Texas: audits in, 4; trained observers in, 243

Text Analysis Package (TAP), 81

TEXTBASE ALPHA, 81

THE ETHNOGRAPHER, 81

Theory, used in process evaluation, 50–52

Time saved, as benefit, 471–472, 477

Time series. *See* Interrupted time series design

Timing: in agenda for evaluation, 6; of monitoring, 526–527, 583; of recommendations, 543

Toronto, trained observers in, 253

Total Quality Management (TQM): and assessments, 5; and outcome monitoring, 96, 106

Toward Improving the Outcome of Pregnancy (TIOP), 23–29

Trained observers: advantages of, 242, 244; applications for, 240–244; approaches for, 239–270; background on, 239–240; concept of, 240; conclusions on, 265, 268; costs of, 264–265; and data analysis, 263–264; limitations of, 245–246; quality control for, 262–263; and rated characteristics, 246–248; rating scales and forms for, 248–257; reporting by, 263–264, 266–267; selecting, 257, 261–262; training of, 261; trends for, 598–599

Training: for evaluators, 591–592, 599–600; for fieldwork, 366; for observers, 261; for role-playing, 322, 324; for surveys, 288–289

Training and Employment Program (TEP), 182

Treatment-effect interactions: in interrupted time series design, 449; in randomized experiments, 424–426; in regression-discontinuity design, 436–438; size of, 419–420

Triangulation, for qualitative data, 89–90

TriData Corporation, 243, 244, 260*n*, 270

Type I (false positive) and Type II (false negative) errors: and hypothesis testing, 392–393; and process evaluation, 42; and randomized field experiments, 157, 160, 170; and role-playing, 314–315, 316*n*

Type III error, 42

U

Uniform Crime Reports, 143

Unit of analysis, for fieldwork, 354–355

United Kingdom: breathalyzer study in, 137–139, 143, 144; educational accountability in, 100; evaluation units in, 495; performance in, 595, 596; randomized field experiments in, 156, 192–193

U.S. Bureau of the Census, 381

U.S. Congress: and GAO, 496, 497–498, 499, 502; and performance, 4, 100–101, 596, 598, 602

U.S. Department of Energy, 305, 308

U.S. Department of Health and Human Services (DHHS): and change agents, 543, 547; and evaluability assessment, 30; reporting at, 550, 551, 553, 556, 558–560, 562

U.S. Department of Health, Education, and Welfare (HEW), 549

U.S. Department of Housing and Urban Development (HUD), 311–312

U.S. Department of Justice, 320

U.S. Department of Labor, 106, 596; Bureau of Labor Statistics of, 473

U.S. Employment and Training Administration, 483

U.S. Food and Drug Administration, 572

U.S. General Accounting Office (GAO): and congressional needs, 4, 7; evaluation unit at, 493*n*, 496–506, 508–509, 591; and graphics, 570; Institute for Program Evaluation (IPE) of, 497, 498; and outcome monitoring, 96, 100–101, 106, 110, 118; Program Evaluation and Methodology Division (PEMD) of, 496, 497, 498, 501, 504–505; and qualitative evaluation, 86, 95; and role-playing, 311, 320, 336–337; standards of, 592–593; and syntheses, 198, 205, 206, 207, 208, 210, 211, 212–213, 217, 218–219, 220, 221, 224, 225, 226, 230–231; Visiting Scholars at, 506

U.S. Office of Management and Budget (OMB), 4, 10, 100, 481, 501–502

U.S. Office of Personnel Management, 596, 602

U.S. Public Health Service, IMPAC of, 515-516

U.S. Senate Governmental Affairs Committee, 100

Unobtrusive measures, for process evaluation, 55

Urban Institute: and agency records, 374n; and fieldwork, 355, 357, 362, 367, 370-371; and outcome monitoring, 110; and role-playing, 315, 316n, 318, 320; and trained observers, 239n, 243, 270

Utilization: of ad hoc evaluation, 576-581; in agenda for evaluation, 5-6; approaches for, 489-602; change agents for, 534-548; conclusion on, 587-588; and evaluability assessment, 18, 23; and evaluation units, 493-509; issues in, 8-9; management for, 510-533; maximizing, 576-589; of monitoring, 581-587; overview of, 10, 489-491; reporting for, 549-575

V

Validity: assuring, 584; of expert judgments, 295, 297-298, 304; of implementation data, 56; of qualitative data, 85; in randomized field experiments, 159-160, 177, 178; threats to, 120, 123-124, 220, 393, 420-421

Variability of scores, in randomized experiments, 422

Veterans Administration (VA), and disulfiram study, 195

Videotapes: reporting with, 571; for trained observers, 256-257

Virginia: audits in, 4; trained observers in, 257

Virginia Department of Transportation, 257

Volusia County, Florida, trained observers in, 243, 244

W

Washington, D.C.: drug abuse study in, 196-197; role-playing in, 315, 316n; trained observers in, 243

West Virginia, trained observers in, 244

Whistleblowing, 593

Women, Infants, and Children (WIC), Special Supplemental Food Program for: recommendations on, 559; and synthesis, 205, 207, 210, 212, 217, 226

Work Incentive Program (WIN), 352-353, 357, 360